Toyota Kluger & Highlander

Automotive Repair Manual

**by Geoff Wilson
and John H Haynes**

Member of the Guild of Motoring Writers

Models covered:

Toyota Kluger & Highlander - 2003 – 2014
Two-wheel-drive and all-wheel-drive models

Haynes Australia Pty Limited
haynes.com

Acknowledgements

Wiring diagrams provided exclusively for Haynes Solution Builders.

© **Haynes Australia Pty Limited 2015**

ABN 59 618 618 992
With permission from J.H. Haynes & Co. Ltd.

A book in the Haynes Automotive Repair Manual Series

ISBN-13: 978-1-62092-191-3

ISBN-10: 1-62092-191-X

While every attempt is made to ensure that the information in this man-ual is correct, no liability can be accepted by the authors or publishers for loss, damage or injury caused by any errors in, or omissions from, the information given.

Contents

Haynes mechanic, author and photographer

About this manual

Its purpose

The purpose of this manual is to help you get the best value from your vehicle. It can do so in several ways. It can help you decide what work must be done, even if you choose to have it done by a dealer service department or a repair shop; it provides information and procedures for routine maintenance and servicing; and it offers diagnostic and repair procedures to follow when trouble occurs.

We hope you use the manual to tackle the work yourself. For many simpler jobs, doing it yourself may be quicker than arranging an appointment to get the vehicle into a shop and making the trips to leave it and pick it up. More importantly, a lot of money can be saved by avoiding the expense the shop must pass on to you to cover its labour and overhead costs. An added benefit is the sense of satisfaction and accomplishment that you feel after doing the job yourself.

Using the manual

The manual is divided into Chapters. Each Chapter is divided into numbered Sections, which are headed in bold type between horizontal lines. Each Section consists of consecutively numbered paragraphs.

At the beginning of each numbered Section you will be referred to any illustrations which apply to the procedures in that Section. The reference numbers used in illustration captions pinpoint the pertinent Section and the Step within that Section. That is, illustration 3.2 means the illustration refers to Section 3 and Step (or paragraph) 2 within that Section.

Procedures, once described in the text, are not normally repeated. When it's necessary to refer to another Chapter, the reference will be given as Chapter and Section number. Cross references given without use of the word "Chapter" apply to Sections and/or paragraphs in the same Chapter. For example, "see Section 8" means in the same Chapter.

References to the left or right side of the vehicle assume you are sitting in the driver's seat, facing forward.

Even though we have prepared this manual with extreme care, neither the publisher nor the author can accept responsibility for any errors in, or omissions from, the information given.

NOTE

A **Note** provides information necessary to properly complete a procedure or information which will make the procedure easier to understand.

CAUTION

A **Caution** provides a special procedure or special steps which must be taken while completing the procedure where the Caution is found. Not heeding a Caution can result in damage to the assembly being worked on.

WARNING

A **Warning** provides a special procedure or special steps which must be taken while completing the procedure where the Warning is found. Not heeding a Warning can result in personal injury.

Introduction to the Toyota Kluger

The MCU28R Toyota Kluger was released in 2003 as an all-wheel-drive only and powered by a 3.3 litre V6 (3MZ-FE) petrol engine coupled to a 5-speed automatic transmission.

August 2007 saw the release of the GSU40R two-wheel-drive and GSU45R all-wheel-drive models. A 3.5 litre V6 (2GR-FE) petrol engine was used along with a 5-speed automatic transaxle. On all vehicles, drive is primarily through the front axles until traction is lost, when on all-wheel-drive models, the drive is also then transmitted to the rear wheels via a propeller shaft, rear differential and driveshafts.

Suspension is independent at all four wheels, MacPherson struts being used at the front end and at the rear. The rack-and-pinion steering unit is mounted on the suspension crossmember.

The brakes are disc at the front and rear, with power assist standard. All models are equipped with an anti-lock brake system (ABS).

Vehicle identification numbers

Modifications are a continuing and unpublicised process in vehicle manufacturing. Since spare parts manuals and lists are compiled on a numerical basis, the individual vehicle numbers are essential to correctly identify the component required.

Vehicle Identification Number (VIN)

This very important identification number is stamped on a plate attached to the firewall, on early models, or to the floor in front of the driver seat (see illustration) on late models. It can also be found on the certification label located on the passenger side B-pillar (see illustration).

Certification label

The certification label is attached to passenger side B-pillar (see illustration). The plate contains the name of the manufacturer, the month and year of production, the Gross Vehicle Weight Rating (GVWR), the Gross Axle Weight Rating (GAWR) and the certification statement.

Engine number

The engine identification number is stamped into a machined pad on the left end (passenger side) of the engine block (see illustration).

The Vehicle Identification Number (VIN) location on MCU28R (early) models

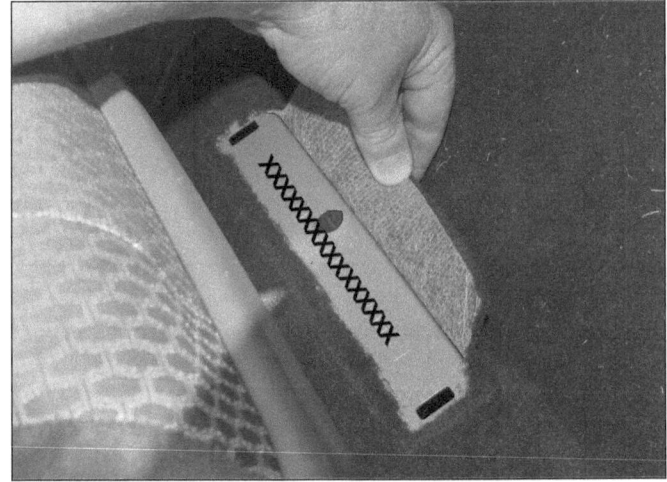

On late models, the VIN is stamped into the floor and viewed after removing a panel in front of the driver seat

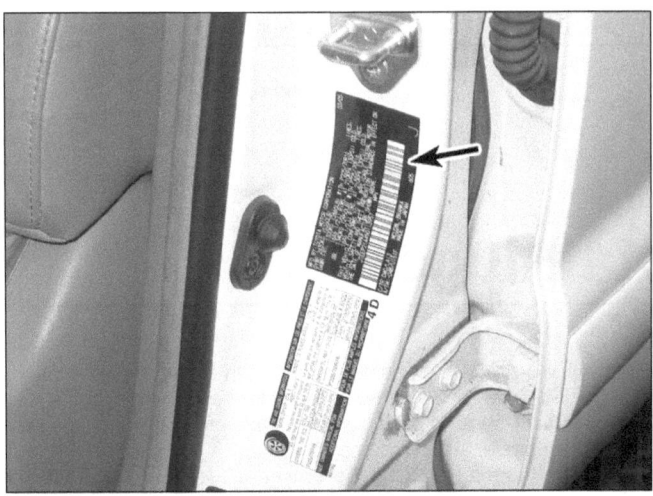

The vehicle certification label is attached to the passenger door B-pillar

The engine serial number is located on the front side of the block, adjacent to the transaxle

Recall information

Vehicle recalls are carried out by the manufacturer in the rare event of a possible safety-related defect. The vehicle's registered owner is contacted with details of the recall. Remedial work is carried out free of charge at a dealer service department.

If you are not the original owner of the vehicle and you wish to determine if a recall has been carried out, contact your local dealer and quote the vehicle identification number (VIN). The dealer will be able to inform you if there are any outstanding recalls on that particular vehicle.

Most vehicles have a form in the owner's manual that can be filled out by subsequent vehicle owners. If this form is submitted to the manufacturer, the owner will receive information about any future vehicle recall notifications.

The recall information below is current at the time of production.

To check for further recall campaigns, visit the Australian Competition and Consumer Commission (ACCC) website which will link you to the Product safety recalls page, or type *http://www.recalls.gov.au/* into your web browser.

Recall date	Recall campaign no.	Models affected	Concern
27 April 2004	2004/6952	MCU28R models between 30 May 2003 and 28 January 2004	A Child Protection Lock (CPL) System is fitted to both of the rear side doors. When an operator of the vehicle closes the door very hard with the CPL lever set to the lock position, there is a possibility that the lever may contact the body panel, causing the CPL lever to move into the unlock position.
11 November 2011	2011/12898	MCU28R models between 1 June 2004 and 31 March 2005	The amount of adhesive agent applied between the outer ring and torsional rubber damper of the crankshaft pulley may be insufficient. There is a possibility that the defect may lead to abnormal noise or sudden illumination of the charging system warning light. In rare cases, the belt for the power steering pump may become detached from the pulley, which could result in a sudden unexpected increase in steering effort.
11 October 2012	2012/13327	GSU40R/GSU45R models between 1 February 2006 and 30 April 2009	The sliding electrical contact module in the driver's-side power window master switch may exhibit a "sticky" feel during operation. This is due to the non-uniform application of lubricating grease, resulting in wear to the internal sliding contact points. In some instances, the switch may become inoperative. In the worst case, if a commercially available lubricant is applied in an attempt to rectify the operation, the switch assembly may over-heat and melt.

Buying parts

Replacement parts are available from many sources, which generally fall into one of two categories - authorised dealer parts departments and independent retail auto parts stores. Our advice concerning these parts is as follows:

Retail auto parts stores: Good auto parts stores will stock frequently needed components which wear out relatively fast, such as clutch components, exhaust systems, brake parts, tune-up parts, etc. These stores often supply new or reconditioned parts on an exchange basis, which can save a considerable amount of money. Discount auto parts stores are often very good places to buy materials and parts needed for general vehicle maintenance such as oil, grease, filters, spark plugs, belts, touch-up paint, bulbs, etc. They also usually sell tools and general accessories, have convenient hours, charge lower prices and can often be found not far from home.

Authorised dealer parts department: This is the best source for parts which are unique to the vehicle and not generally available elsewhere (such as major engine parts, transmission parts, trim pieces, etc.).

Warranty information: If the vehicle is still covered under warranty, be sure that any replacement parts purchased - regardless of the source - do not invalidate the warranty!

To be sure of obtaining the correct parts, have engine and chassis numbers available and, if possible, take the old parts along for positive identification.

Maintenance techniques, tools and working facilities

Maintenance techniques

There are a number of techniques involved in maintenance and repair that will be referred to throughout this manual. Application of these techniques will enable the home mechanic to be more efficient, better organised and capable of performing the various tasks properly, which will ensure that the repair job is thorough and complete.

Fasteners

Fasteners are nuts, bolts, studs and screws used to hold two or more parts together. There are a few things to keep in mind when working with fasteners. Almost all of them use a locking device of some type, either a lockwasher, locknut, locking tab or thread adhesive. All threaded fasteners should be clean and straight, with undamaged threads and undamaged corners on the hex head where the wrench fits. Develop the habit of replacing all damaged nuts and bolts with new ones. Special locknuts with nylon or fibre inserts can only be used once. If they are removed, they lose their locking ability and must be replaced with new ones.

Rusted nuts and bolts should be treated with a penetrating fluid to ease removal and prevent breakage. Some mechanics use turpentine in a spout-type oil can, which works quite well. After applying the rust penetrant, let it work for a few minutes before trying to loosen the nut or bolt. Badly rusted fasteners may have to be chiselled or sawed off or removed with a special nut breaker, available at tool stores.

If a bolt or stud breaks off in an assembly, it can be drilled and removed with a special tool commonly available for this purpose. Most automotive machine shops can perform this task, as well as other repair procedures, such as the repair of threaded holes that have been stripped out.

Flat washers and lockwashers, when removed from an assembly, should always be replaced exactly as removed. Replace any damaged washers with new ones. Never use a lockwasher on any soft metal surface (such as aluminium), thin sheet metal or plastic.

Fastener sizes

For a number of reasons, automobile manufacturers are making wider and wider use of metric fasteners. Therefore, it is important to be able to tell the difference between standard (sometimes called U.S. or SAE) and metric hardware, since they cannot be interchanged.

All bolts, whether standard or metric, are sized according to diameter, thread pitch and length. For example, a standard 1/2 - 13 x 1 bolt is 1/2 inch in diameter, has 13 threads per inch and is 1 inch long. An M12 - 1.75 x 25 metric bolt is 12 mm in diameter, has a thread pitch of 1.75 mm (the distance between threads) and is 25 mm long. The two bolts are nearly identical, and easily confused, but they are not interchangeable.

In addition to the differences in diameter, thread pitch and length, metric and standard bolts can also be distinguished by examining the bolt heads. To begin with, the distance across the flats on a standard bolt head is measured in inches, while the same dimension on a metric bolt is sized in millimetres (the same is true for nuts). As a result, a standard wrench should not be used on a metric bolt and a metric wrench should not be used on a standard bolt. Also, most standard bolts have slashes radiating out from the centre of the head to denote the grade or strength of the bolt, which is an indication of the amount of torque that can be applied to it. The greater the number of slashes, the greater the strength of the bolt. Grades 0 through 5 are commonly used on automobiles. Metric bolts have a property class (grade) number, rather than a slash, moulded into their heads to indicate bolt strength. In this case, the higher the number, the stronger the bolt. Property class numbers 8.8, 9.8 and 10.9 are commonly used on automobiles.

Strength markings can also be used to distinguish standard hex nuts from metric hex nuts. Many standard nuts have dots stamped into one side, while metric nuts are marked with a number. The greater the number of dots, or the higher the number, the greater the strength of the nut.

Metric studs are also marked on their ends according to property class (grade). Larger studs are numbered (the same as metric bolts), while smaller studs carry a geometric code to denote grade.

It should be noted that many fasteners, especially Grades 0 through 2, have no distinguishing marks on them. When such is the case, the only way to determine whether it is standard or metric is to measure the thread pitch or compare it to a known fastener of the same size.

Standard fasteners are often referred to as SAE, as opposed to metric. However, it should be noted that SAE technically refers to a non-metric fine thread fastener only. Coarse thread non-metric fasteners are referred to as USS sizes.

Since fasteners of the same size (both standard and metric) may have different strength ratings, be sure to reinstall any bolts, studs or nuts removed from your vehicle in their original locations. Also, when replacing a fastener with a new one, make sure that the new one has a strength rating equal to or greater than the original.

Tightening sequences and procedures

Most threaded fasteners should be tightened to a specific torque value (torque is the twisting force applied to a threaded component such as a nut or bolt). Overtightening the fastener can weaken it and cause it to break, while undertightening can cause it to eventually come loose. Bolts, screws and studs, depending on the material they are made of and their thread diameters, have specific torque values, many of which are noted in the Specifications at the beginning of each Chapter. Be sure to follow the torque recommendations closely. For fasteners not assigned a specific torque, a general torque value chart

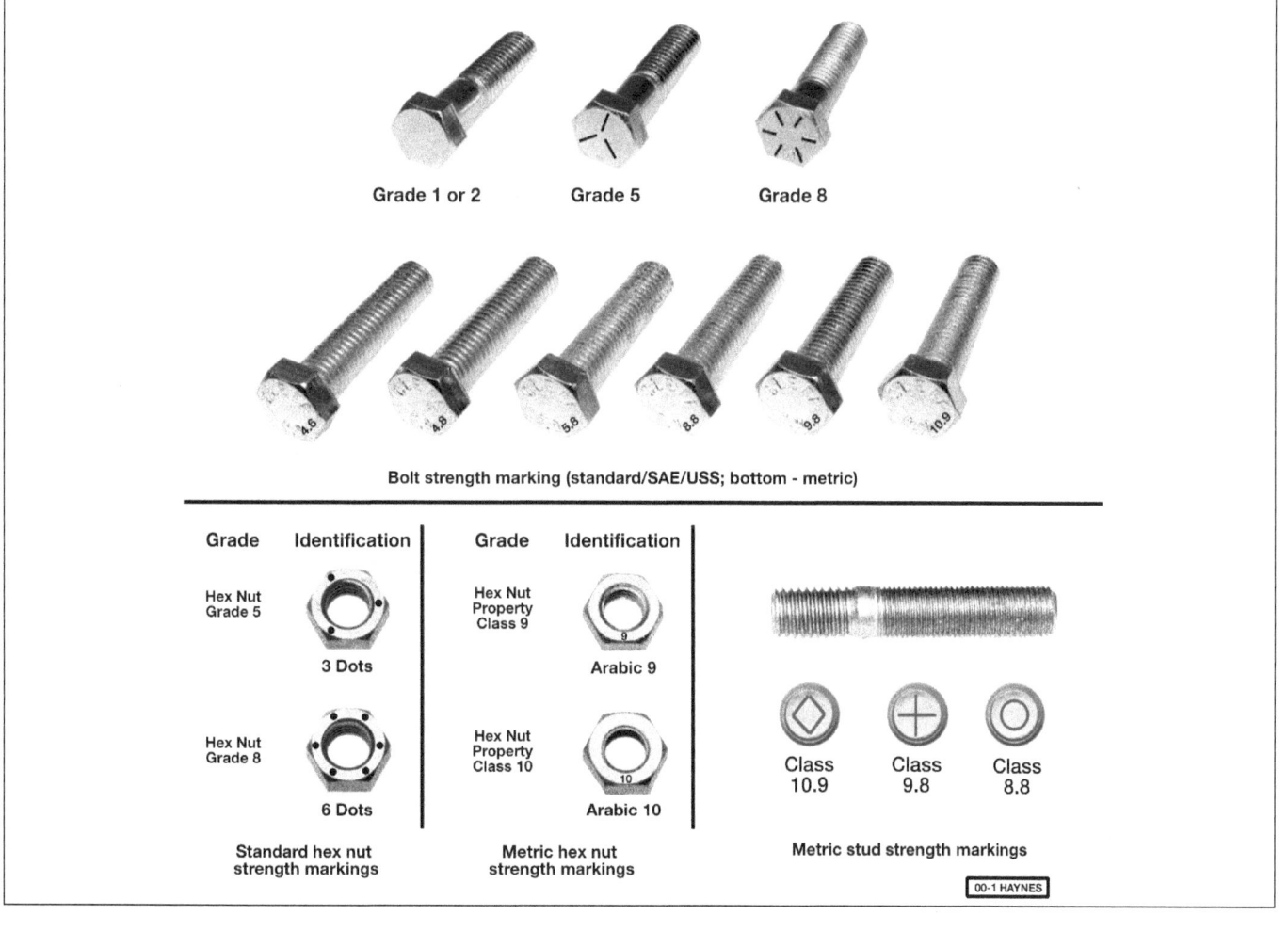

Grade 1 or 2   Grade 5   Grade 8

Bolt strength marking (standard/SAE/USS; bottom - metric)

Grade	Identification
Hex Nut Grade 5	3 Dots
Hex Nut Grade 8	6 Dots

Standard hex nut strength markings

Grade	Identification
Hex Nut Property Class 9	Arabic 9
Hex Nut Property Class 10	Arabic 10

Metric hex nut strength markings

Class 10.9   Class 9.8   Class 8.8

Metric stud strength markings

00-1 HAYNES

is presented here as a guide. These torque values are for dry (unlubricated) fasteners threaded into steel or cast iron (not aluminium). As was previously mentioned, the size and grade of a fastener determine the amount of torque that can safely be applied to it. The figures listed here are approximate for Grade 2 and Grade 3 fasteners. Higher grades can tolerate higher torque values.

Fasteners laid out in a pattern, such as cylinder head bolts, oil pan bolts, differential cover bolts, etc., must be loosened or tightened in sequence to avoid warping the component. This sequence will normally be shown in the appropriate Chapter. If a specific pattern is not given, the following procedures can be used to prevent warping.

Initially, the bolts or nuts should be assembled finger-tight only. Next, they should be tightened one full turn each, in a criss-cross or diagonal pattern. After each one has been tightened one full turn, return to the first one and tighten them all one-half turn, following the same pattern. Finally, tighten each of them one-quarter turn at a time until each fastener has been tightened to the proper torque. To loosen and remove the fasteners, the procedure would be reversed.

Component disassembly

Component disassembly should be done with care and purpose to help ensure that the parts go back together properly. Always

Metric thread sizes	Ft-lbs	Nm
M-6	6 to 9	9 to 12
M-8	14 to 21	19 to 28
M-10	28 to 40	38 to 54
M-12	50 to 71	68 to 96
M-14	80 to 140	109 to 154

Pipe thread sizes		
1/8	5 to 8	7 to 10
1/4	12 to 18	17 to 24
3/8	22 to 33	30 to 44
1/2	25 to 35	34 to 47

U.S. thread sizes		
1/4 - 20	6 to 9	9 to 12
5/16 - 18	12 to 18	17 to 24
5/16 - 24	14 to 20	19 to 27
3/8 - 16	22 to 32	30 to 43
3/8 - 24	27 to 38	37 to 51
7/16 - 14	40 to 55	55 to 74
7/16 - 20	40 to 60	55 to 81
1/2 - 13	55 to 80	75 to 108

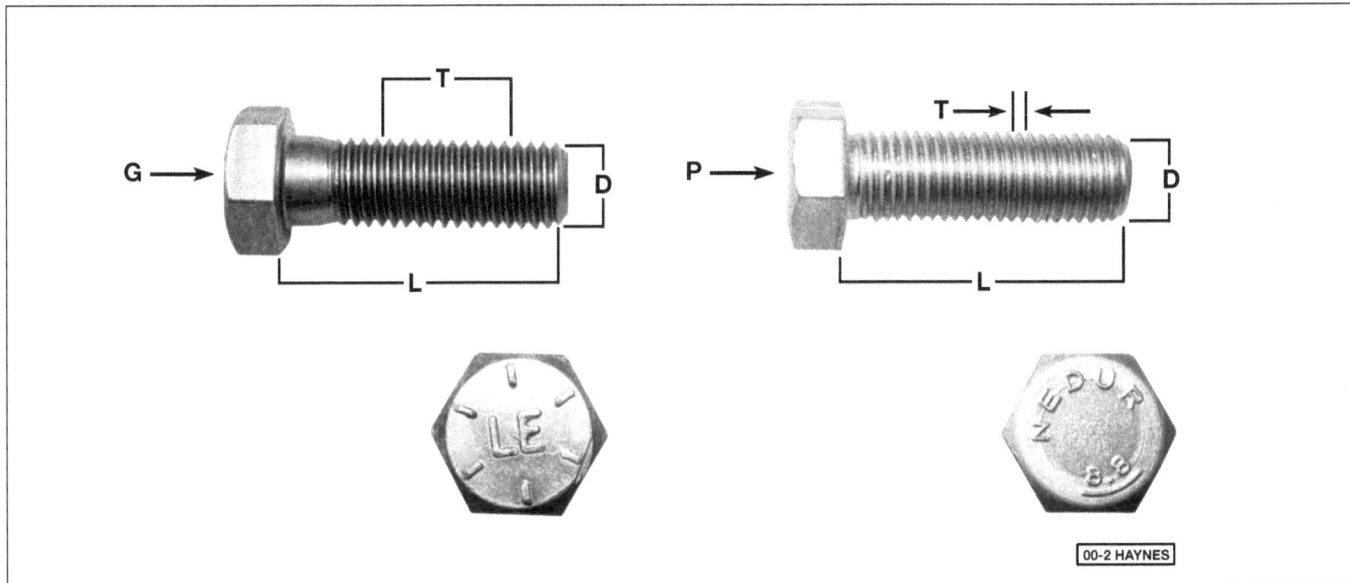

Standard (SAE and USS) bolt dimensions/grade marks   **Metric bolt dimensions/grade marks**

G Grade marks (bolt strength)
L Length (in inches)
T Thread pitch (number of threads per inch)
D Nominal diameter (in inches)

P Property class (bolt strength)
L Length (in millimetres)
T Thread pitch (distance between threads in millimetres)
D Diameter

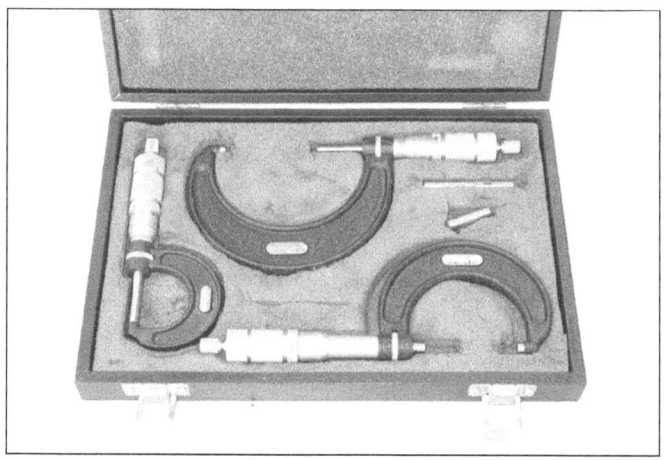

Micrometer set

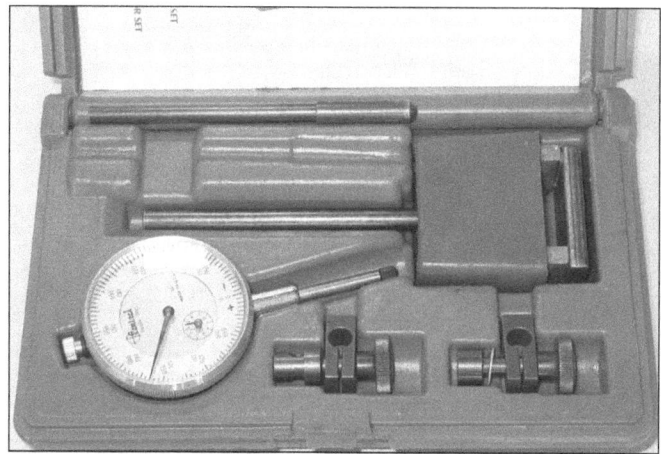

Dial indicator set

keep track of the sequence in which parts are removed. Make note of special characteristics or marks on parts that can be installed more than one way, such as a grooved thrust washer on a shaft. It is a good idea to lay the disassembled parts out on a clean surface in the order that they were removed. It may also be helpful to make sketches or take instant photos of components before removal.

When removing fasteners from a component, keep track of their locations. Sometimes threading a bolt back in a part, or putting the washers and nut back on a stud, can prevent mix-ups later. If nuts and bolts cannot be returned to their original locations, they should be kept in a compartmented box or a series of small boxes. A cupcake or muffin tin is ideal for this purpose, since each cavity can hold the bolts and nuts from a particular area (i.e. oil pan bolts, valve cover bolts, engine mount bolts, etc.). A pan of this type is especially helpful when working on assemblies with very small parts, such as the brakes, valve train or interior dash and trim pieces. The cavities can be marked with paint or tape to identify the contents.

Whenever wiring looms, harnesses or connectors are separated, it is a good idea to identify the two halves with numbered pieces of masking tape so they can be easily reconnected.

Gasket sealing surfaces

Throughout any vehicle, gaskets are used to seal the mating surfaces between two parts and keep lubricants, fluids, vacuum or pressure contained in an assembly.

Many times these gaskets are coated with a liquid or paste-type gasket sealing compound before assembly. Age, heat and pressure can sometimes cause the two parts to stick together so tightly that they are very difficult to separate. Often, the assembly can be loosened by striking it with a soft-face hammer near the mating surfaces. A regular hammer can be used if a block of wood is placed between the hammer and the part. Do not hammer on cast parts or parts that could be easily damaged. With any particularly

stubborn part, always recheck to make sure that every fastener has been removed.

Avoid using a screwdriver or bar to pry apart an assembly, as they can easily mar the gasket sealing surfaces of the parts, which must remain smooth. If prying is absolutely necessary, use an old broom handle, but keep in mind that extra clean up will be necessary if the wood splinters.

After the parts are separated, the old gasket must be carefully scraped off and the gasket surfaces cleaned. Stubborn gasket material can be soaked with rust penetrant or treated with a special chemical to soften it so it can be easily scraped off.

Caution: *Never use gasket removal solutions or caustic chemicals on plastic or other composite components. A scraper can be fashioned from a piece of copper tubing by flattening and sharpening one end. Copper is recommended because it is usually softer than the surfaces to be scraped, which reduces the chance of gouging the part. Some gaskets can be removed with a wire brush, but regardless of the method used, the mating surfaces must be left clean and smooth. If for some reason the gasket surface is gouged, then a gasket sealer thick enough to fill scratches will have to be used during reassembly of the components. For most applications, a non-drying (or semi-drying) gasket sealer should be used.*

Hose removal tips

Warning: *If the vehicle is equipped with air conditioning, do not disconnect any of the A/C hoses without first having the system depressurised by a dealer service department or a service station.*

Hose removal precautions closely parallel gasket removal precautions. Avoid scratching or gouging the surface that the hose mates against or the connection may leak. This is especially true for radiator hoses. Because of various chemical reactions, the rubber in hoses can bond itself to the metal spigot that the hose fits over. To remove a hose, first loosen the hose clamps that secure it to the spigot. Then, with slip-joint pli-

ers, grab the hose at the clamp and rotate it around the spigot. Work it back and forth until it is completely free, then pull it off. Silicone or other lubricants will ease removal if they can be applied between the hose and the outside of the spigot. Apply the same lubricant to the inside of the hose and the outside of the spigot to simplify installation.

As a last resort (and if the hose is to be replaced with a new one anyway), the rubber can be slit with a knife and the hose peeled from the spigot. If this must be done, be careful that the metal connection is not damaged.

If a hose clamp is broken or damaged, do not reuse it. Wire-type clamps usually weaken with age, so it is a good idea to replace them with screw-type clamps whenever a hose is removed.

Tools

A selection of good tools is a basic requirement for anyone who plans to maintain and repair his or her own vehicle. For the owner who has few tools, the initial investment might seem high, but when compared to the spiralling costs of professional auto maintenance and repair, it is a wise one.

To help the owner decide which tools are needed to perform the tasks detailed in this manual, the following tool lists are offered: *Maintenance and minor repair, Repair/overhaul* and *Special.*

The newcomer to practical mechanics should start off with the *maintenance and minor repair* tool kit, which is adequate for the simpler jobs performed on a vehicle. Then, as confidence and experience grow, the owner can tackle more difficult tasks, buying additional tools as they are needed. Eventually the basic kit will be expanded into the *repair and overhaul* tool set. Over a period of time, the experienced do-it-yourselfer will assemble a tool set complete enough for most repair and overhaul procedures and will add tools from the special category when it is felt that the expense is justified by the frequency of use.

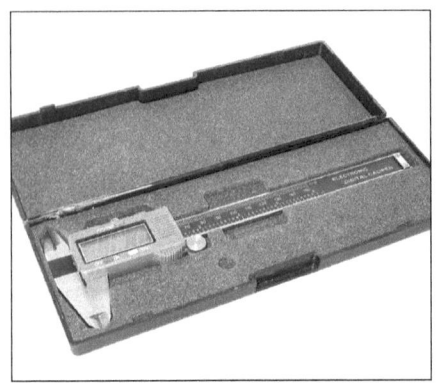

Vernier caliper

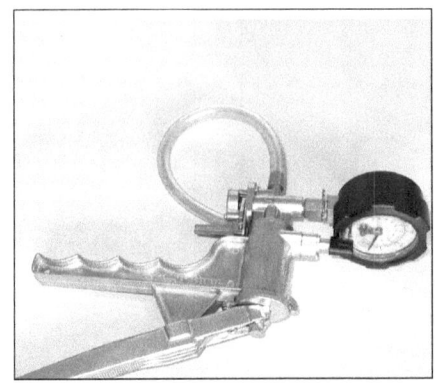

Hand-operated vacuum pump

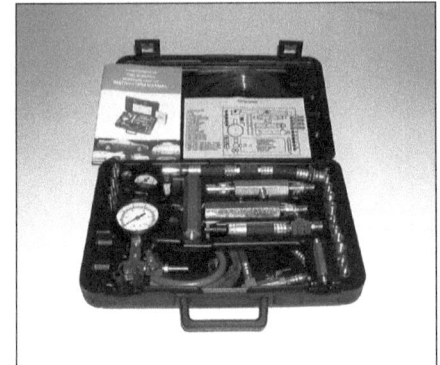

Fuel pressure gauge

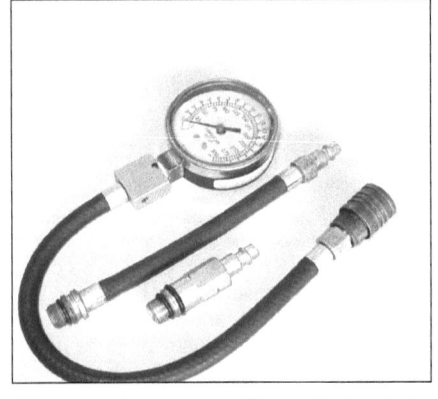

Compression gauge with spark plug hole adapter

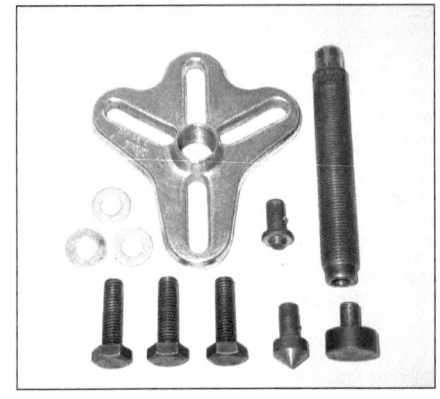

Damper/steering wheel puller

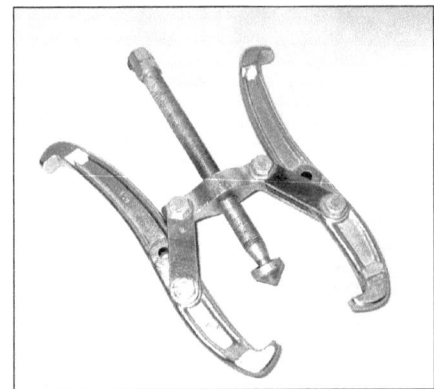

General purpose puller

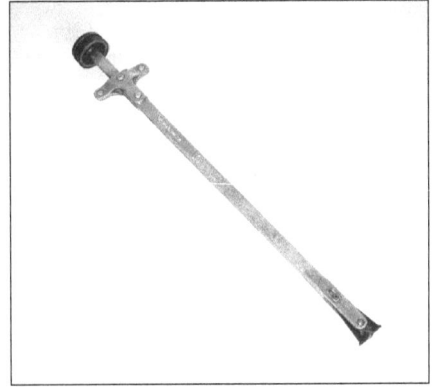

Hydraulic lifter removal tool

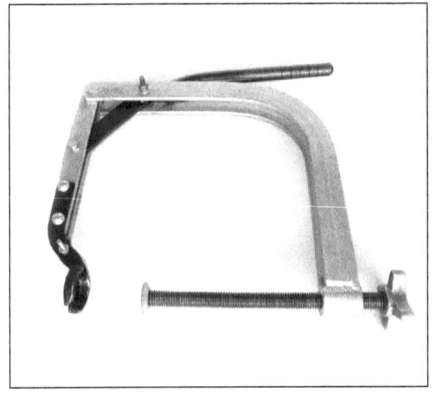

Valve spring compressor

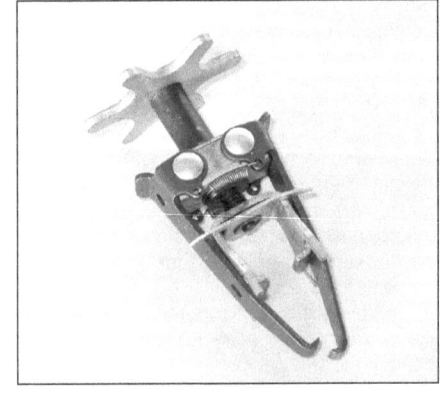

Valve spring compressor

Ridge reamer

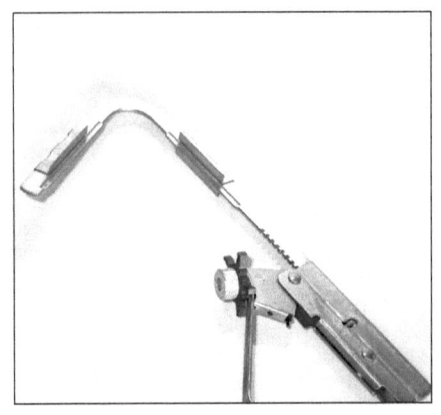

Piston ring groove cleaning tool

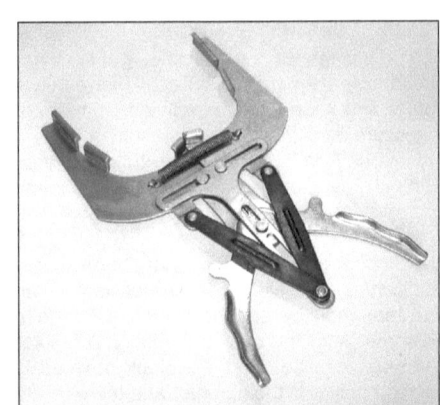

Ring removal/installation tool

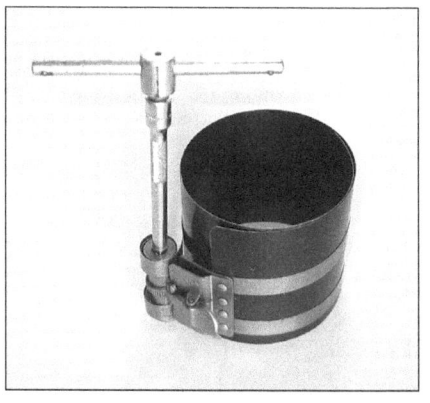

Ring compressor

Cylinder hone

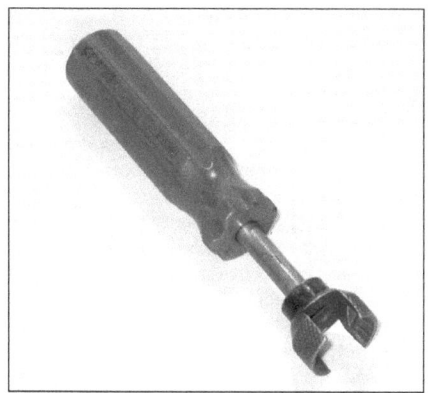

Brake hold-down spring tool

Torque angle gauge

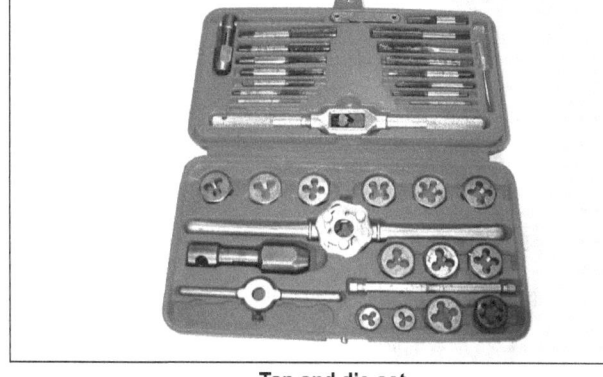

Tap and die set

Maintenance and minor repair tool kit

The tools in this list should be considered the minimum required for performance of routine maintenance, servicing and minor repair work. We recommend the purchase of combination spanners (box-end and open-end combined in one spanner). While more expensive than open end spanners, they offer the advantages of both types of spanner.

Combination spanner set (6 to 19 mm)
Adjustable spanner
Spark plug wrench with rubber insert
Spark plug gap adjusting tool
Feeler gauge set
Brake bleeder wrench
Standard screwdriver
Phillips screwdriver
Combination pliers
Hacksaw and assortment of blades
Tyre pressure gauge
Grease gun
Oil can
Fine emery cloth
Wire brush
Battery post and cable cleaning tool
Oil filter wrench
Funnel (medium size)
Safety goggles
Jackstands (2)
Drain pan

If basic tune-ups are going to be part of routine maintenance, it will be necessary to pur-

chase a good quality stroboscopic timing light and combination tachometer/dwell meter. Although they are included in the list of special tools, it is mentioned here because they are absolutely necessary for tuning most vehicles properly.

Repair and overhaul tool set

These tools are essential for anyone who plans to perform major repairs and are in addition to those in the maintenance and minor repair tool kit. Included is a comprehensive set of sockets which, though expensive, are invaluable because of their versatility, especially when various extensions and drives are available. We recommend the 1/2-inch drive over the 3/8-inch drive. Although the larger drive is bulky and more expensive, it has the capacity of accepting a very wide range of large sockets. Ideally, however, the mechanic should have a 3/8-inch drive set and a 1/2-inch drive set.

Socket set(s)
Reversible ratchet
Extension
Universal joint
Torque wrench (same size drive as sockets)
Ball peen hammer
Soft-face hammer (plastic/rubber)
Standard screwdriver
Standard screwdriver (stubby)
Phillips screwdriver

Phillips screwdriver (stubby - No. 2)
Pliers - vice grip
Pliers - lineman's
Pliers - needle nose
Pliers - snap-ring (internal and external)
Cold chisel
Scribe
Scraper (made from flattened copper tubing)
Counterpunch
Pin punches
Steel rule/straightedge
Allen wrench set (4 to 10 mm)
A selection of files
Wire brush (large)
Jackstands (second set)
Jack (scissor or hydraulic type)

Another tool which is often useful is an electric drill with a chuck capacity of 10 mm and a set of good quality drill bits.

Special tools

The tools in this list include those which are not used regularly, are expensive to buy, or which need to be used in accordance with their manufacturer's instructions. Unless these tools will be used frequently, it is not very economical to purchase many of them. A consideration would be to split the cost and use between yourself and a friend or friends. In addition, most of these tools can be obtained from a tool rental shop on a temporary basis.

This list primarily contains only those tools and instruments widely available to the public, and not those special tools produced by the vehicle manufacturer for distribution to dealer service departments. Occasionally, references to the manufacturer's special tools are included in the text of this manual. Generally, an alternative method of doing the job without the special tool is offered. However, sometimes there is no alternative to their use. Where this is the case, and the tool cannot be purchased or borrowed, the work should be turned over to the dealer service department or an automotive repair shop.

Valve spring compressor
Piston ring groove cleaning tool
Piston ring compressor
Piston ring installation tool
Cylinder compression gauge
Cylinder ridge reamer
Cylinder surfacing hone
Cylinder bore gauge
Micrometers and/or dial calipers
Hydraulic lifter removal tool
Balljoint separator
Universal-type puller
Impact screwdriver
Dial indicator set
Stroboscopic timing light (inductive pick-up)
Hand operated vacuum/pressure pump
Tachometer/dwell meter
Universal electrical multimeter
Cable hoist
Floor jack

Buying tools

For the do-it-yourselfer who is just starting to get involved in vehicle maintenance and repair, there are a number of options available when purchasing tools. If maintenance and minor repair is the extent of the work to be done, the purchase of individual tools is satisfactory. If, on the other hand, extensive work is planned, it would be a good idea to purchase a modest tool set from one of the large retail chain stores. A set can usually be bought at a substantial savings over the individual tool prices, and they often come with a tool box. As additional tools are needed, add-on sets, individual tools and a larger tool box can be purchased to expand the tool selection. Building a tool set gradually allows the cost of the tools to be spread over a longer period of time and gives the mechanic the freedom to choose only those tools that will actually be used.

Tool stores will often be the only source of some of the special tools that are needed, but regardless of where tools are bought, try to avoid cheap ones, especially when buy-ing screwdrivers and sockets, because they won't last very long. The expense involved in renewing cheap tools will eventually be greater than the initial cost of quality tools.

Care and maintenance of tools

Good tools are expensive, so it makes sense to treat them with respect. Keep them clean and in useable condition and store them properly when not in use. Always wipe off any dirt, grease or metal chips before putting them away. Never leave tools lying around in the work area. Upon completion of a job, always check closely under the bonnet for tools that may have been left there so they won't get lost during a test drive.

Some tools, such as screwdrivers, pliers, spanners and sockets, can be hung on a panel mounted on the garage or workshop wall, while others should be kept in a tool box or tray. Measuring instruments, gauges, meters, etc. must be carefully stored where they cannot be damaged by weather or impact from other tools.

When tools are used with care and stored properly, they will last a very long time. Even with the best of care, though, tools will wear out if used frequently. When a tool is damaged or worn out, renew it. Subsequent jobs will be safer and more enjoyable if you do.

How to repair damaged threads

Sometimes, the internal threads of a nut or bolt hole can become stripped, usually from overtightening. Stripping threads is an all-too-common occurrence, especially when working with aluminium parts, because aluminium is so soft that it easily strips out.

Usually, external or internal threads are only partially stripped. After they've been cleaned up with a tap or die, they'll still work. Sometimes, however, threads are badly damaged. When this happens, you've got three choices:

1)   Drill and tap the hole to the next suitable oversise and fit a larger diameter bolt, screw or stud.

2)   Drill and tap the hole to accept a threaded plug, then drill and tap the plug to the original screw size. You can also buy a plug already threaded to the original size. Then you simply drill a hole to the specified size, then run the threaded plug into the hole with a bolt and jam nut. Once the plug is fully seated, remove the jam nut and bolt.

3)   The third method uses a patented thread repair kit like Heli-Coil or Slim-sert. These easy-to-use kits are designed to repair damaged threads in straight-through holes and blind holes. Both are available as kits which can handle a variety of sizes and thread patterns. Drill the hole, then tap it with the special included tap. Refit the Heli-Coil and the hole is back to its original diameter and thread pitch.

Regardless of which method you use, be sure to proceed calmly and carefully. A little impatience or carelessness during one of these relatively simple procedures can ruin your whole day's work and cost you a bundle if you wreck an expensive part.

Working facilities

Not to be overlooked when discussing tools is the workshop. If anything more than routine maintenance is to be carried out, some sort of suitable work area is essential.

It is understood, and appreciated, that many home mechanics do not have a good workshop or garage available, and end up removing an engine or doing major repairs outside. It is recommended, however, that the overhaul or repair be completed under the cover of a roof.

A clean, flat workbench or table of comfortable working height is an absolute necessity. The workbench should be equipped with a vice that has a jaw opening of at least 10 cm.

As mentioned previously, some clean, dry storage space is also required for tools, as well as the lubricants, fluids, cleaning solvents, etc. which soon become necessary.

Sometimes waste oil and fluids, drained from the engine or cooling system during normal maintenance or repairs, present a disposal problem. To avoid pouring them on the ground or into a sewage system, pour the used fluids into large containers, seal them with caps and take them to an authorised disposal site or recycling centre. Plastic jugs, such as old antifreeze containers, are ideal for this purpose.

Always keep a supply of old newspapers and clean rags available. Old towels are excellent for mopping up spills. Many mechanics use rolls of paper towels for most work because they are readily available and disposable. To help keep the area under the vehicle clean, a large cardboard box can be cut open and flattened to protect the garage or shop floor.

Whenever working over a painted surface, such as when leaning over a fender to service something under the bonnet, always cover it with an old blanket or bedspread to protect the finish. Vinyl covered pads, made especially for this purpose, are available at auto parts stores.

Jacking and towing

Warning: *The jack supplied with the vehicle should only be used for changing a tyre. Never work under the vehicle or start the engine while this jack is being used as the only means of support.*

Using the vehicle jack

1   The vehicle should be on level ground. Place the shift lever in Park, if you have an automatic, or Reverse if you have a manual transaxle. Block the wheel diagonally opposite the wheel being changed. Set the parking brake.

2   Remove the spare tyre and jack from stowage. Remove the wheel cover and trim ring (if so equipped) with the tapered end of the wheel nut wrench by inserting and twisting the handle and then prying against the back of the wheel cover. Loosen, but do not remove, the wheel nuts (one-half turn is sufficient).

3   Place the scissors-type jack under the vehicle and adjust the jack height until it engages with the proper jacking point. There is a front and rear jacking point on each side of the vehicle **(see illustrations)**.

4   Turn the jack handle clockwise until the tyre clears the ground. Remove the wheel nuts and pull the wheel off, then install the spare.

5   Install the wheel nuts with the bevelled edges facing in. Tighten them snugly. Don't attempt to tighten them completely until the vehicle is lowered or it could slip off the jack. Turn the jack handle counterclockwise to lower the vehicle. Remove the jack and tighten the wheel nuts in a diagonal pattern.

6   Stow the tyre, jack and wrench. Unblock the wheels.

Floor jack and chassis stands

7   When the vehicle has to be raised using a floor jack, locate the lifting pad of the jack at the front or rear positions **(see illustrations)**.

8   Place wheel chocks under the rear wheels when the front end of the vehicle is raised and under the front wheels when the rear end of the vehicle is raised.

9   Place chassis stands at the points illustrated for the vehicle jack **(see illustrations)**.

Warning: *Never get under a vehicle that is only supported by the jack. Always support the vehicle with chassis stands at the positions shown in the illustrations. Under no circumstances use a floor jack, chassis stands or car ramps on sloping or unstable ground. Always use a flat solid surface, preferably concrete.*

Note: *Insert a wooden or rubber block between the chassis stand and the chassis when the supported surface is flat.*

Towing

10   Two-wheel-drive versions of these vehicles can be towed from the front with the front wheels off the ground, using a wheel lift type tow truck. If towing a two-wheel-drive from the rear or an all-wheel-drive, the wheels on the road must be placed on a dolly. A sling-type tow truck cannot be used, as body damage will result. The best way to tow the vehicle is with a flat-bed car carrier.

11   In an emergency the vehicle can be towed a short distance with a cable or chain attached to the towing eyelet at the front or rear of the vehicle.

Note: *The towing eyelet is in with the vehicle jack and other tools. To install it to the vehicle, remove the plastic cover from the bumper and screw the eyelet into the threaded hole revealed with the cover removed.*

Warning: *Remember that the power steering and power brakes will not work with the engine off.*

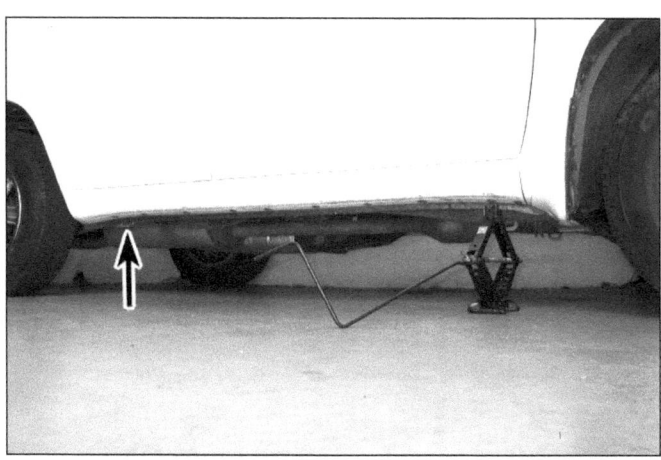

The jack fits over the rocker panel flange, between the two notches (there are two jacking points on each side of the vehicle)

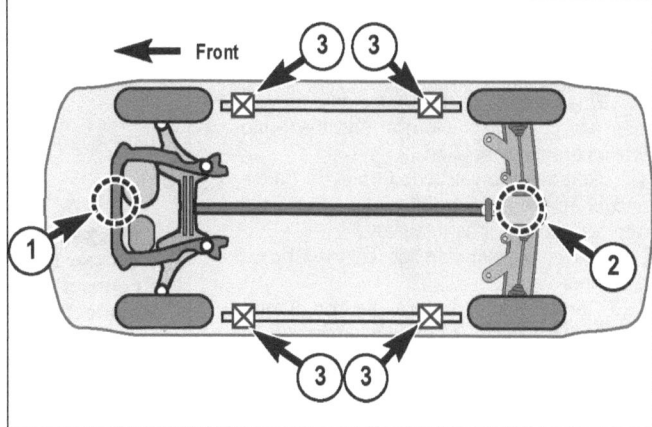

Jacking points

1 Front floor jack jacking point
2 Rear floor jack jacking point
3 Chassis stand locations along the sill panels - the same spot as the vehicle jack jacking point

Booster battery (jump) starting

Warning: *Jump starting a vehicle can be dangerous if the procedure described below is not performed correctly. If any doubt exists, it is recommended that the services of a competent mechanic be obtained.*

The range of vehicles covered by this manual are equipped with complex electronic circuitry which can be damaged by voltage surges. These voltage surges can be generated when jump starting or being jump started by another vehicle.

If available, use jumper leads equipped with a surge protection device and follow the lead manufacturers instructions carefully, particularly regarding the connection and disconnection of the leads.

1   Ensure that the booster battery is 12 volts and the negative terminal is earthed.

2   Ensure that the vehicles are not touching and that the ignition and all accessories on both vehicles are switched Off.

3   Ensure that the transaxles on both vehicles are in Park or Neutral and the handbrakes are firmly applied.

4   Remove the vent caps from the battery and check the electrolyte level. Replenish with distilled water as necessary.

5   Place the vent caps loosely over the cell apertures.

6   Connect one end of the red jumper lead to the positive (+) battery terminal of the booster battery (connection 1) and the other end of the red lead to the positive (+) battery terminal of the discharged battery (connection 2).

Warning: *The battery emits hydrogen gas which is explosive. Do not expose the battery to naked flames or sparks. Do not lean over the battery when connecting the jumper leads. Do not allow the ends of the jumper leads to*

touch one another or any part of the vehicle.

7   Connect one end of the black jumper lead to the negative (–) battery terminal of the booster battery (connection 3) and the other end of the black lead to a good earthing point on the engine of the vehicle with the discharged battery (connection 4).

Note: *Do not connect the jumper lead directly to the negative (–) battery terminal of the discharged battery.*

8   Start the engine on the vehicle with the booster battery and run the engine at a moderate speed for a few minutes.

9   Start the engine on the vehicle with the discharged battery.

10   Leave the engines of both vehicles running for at least 10 minutes. This will partially

charge the discharged battery and reduce the risk of damage to electronic circuitry from voltage surges.

11   Switch the engines of both vehicles Off and disconnect the jumper leads in the reverse order of the connecting sequence.

12   Attempt to start the engine of the vehicle with the discharged battery.

13   If the battery has not charged sufficiently to start the engine, reconnect the jumper leads as previously described and start the engines of both vehicles.

14   Switch On the headlamps of the vehicle with the discharged battery.

15   Disconnect the jumper leads in the reverse order of the connecting sequence. Switch the headlamps Off.

Illustration of jumper lead connections. Connect in the order shown and disconnect in the reverse sequence

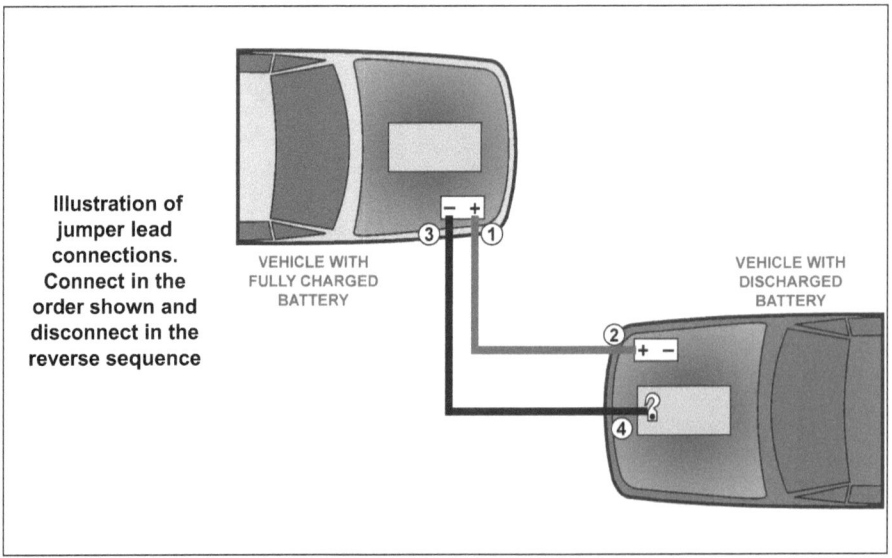

VEHICLE WITH FULLY CHARGED BATTERY

VEHICLE WITH DISCHARGED BATTERY

Automotive chemicals and lubricants

A number of automotive chemicals and lubricants are available for use during vehicle maintenance and repair. They include a wide variety of products ranging from cleaning solvents and degreasers to lubricants and protective sprays for rubber, plastic and vinyl.

Cleaners

Carburettor cleaner and choke cleaner is a strong solvent for gum, varnish and carbon. Most carburettor cleaners leave a dry-type lubricant film which will not harden or gum up. Because of this film it is not recommended for use on electrical components.

Brake system cleaner is used to remove brake dust, grease and brake fluid from the brake system, where clean surfaces are absolutely necessary. It leaves no residue and often eliminates brake squeal caused by contaminants.

Electrical cleaner removes oxidation, corrosion and carbon deposits from electrical contacts, restoring full current flow. It can also be used to clean spark plugs, carburettor jets, voltage regulators and other parts where an oil-free surface is desired.

Demoisturants remove water and moisture from electrical components such as alternators, voltage regulators, electrical connectors and fuse blocks. They are non-conductive and non-corrosive.

Degreasers are heavy-duty solvents used to remove grease from the outside of the engine and from chassis components. They can be sprayed or brushed on and, depending on the type, are rinsed off either with water or solvent.

Lubricants

Motor oil is the lubricant formulated for use in engines. It normally contains a wide variety of additives to prevent corrosion and reduce foaming and wear. Motor oil comes in various weights (viscosity ratings) from 0 to 50. The recommended weight of the oil depends on the season, temperature and the demands on the engine. Light oil is used in cold climates and under light load conditions. Heavy oil is used in hot climates and where high loads are encountered. Multi-viscosity oils are designed to have characteristics of both light and heavy oils and are available in a number of weights from 0W-20 to 20W-50.

Gear oil is designed to be used in differentials, manual transmissions and other areas where high-temperature lubrication is required.

Chassis and wheel bearing grease is a heavy grease used where increased loads and friction are encountered, such as for wheel bearings, balljoints, tie-rod ends and universal joints.

High-temperature wheel bearing grease is designed to withstand the extreme temperatures encountered by wheel bearings in disc brake equipped vehicles. It usually contains molybdenum disulfide (moly), which is a dry-type lubricant.

White grease is a heavy grease for metal-to-metal applications where water is a problem. White grease stays soft under both low and high temperatures (usually from -56 to +106 degrees C), and will not wash off or dilute in the presence of water.

Assembly lube is a special extreme pressure lubricant, usually containing moly, used to lubricate high-load parts (such as main and rod bearings and cam lobes) for initial start-up of a new engine. The assembly lube lubricates the parts without being squeezed out or washed away until the engine oiling system begins to function.

Silicone lubricants are used to protect rubber, plastic, vinyl and nylon parts.

Graphite lubricants are used where oils cannot be used due to contamination problems, such as in locks. The dry graphite will lubricate metal parts while remaining uncontaminated by dirt, water, oil or acids. It is electrically conductive and will not foul electrical contacts in locks such as the ignition switch.

Moly penetrants loosen and lubricate frozen, rusted and corroded fasteners and prevent future rusting or freezing.

Heat-sink grease is a special electrically non-conductive grease that is used for mounting electronic ignition modules where it is essential that heat is transferred away from the module.

Sealants

RTV sealant is one of the most widely used gasket compounds. Made from silicone, RTV is air curing, it seals, bonds, waterproofs, fills surface irregularities, remains flexible, doesn't shrink, is relatively easy to remove, and is used as a supplementary sealer with almost all low and medium temperature gaskets.

Anaerobic sealant is much like RTV in that it can be used either to seal gaskets or to form gaskets by itself. It remains flexible, is solvent resistant and fills surface imperfections. The difference between an anaerobic sealant and an RTV-type sealant is in the curing. RTV cures when exposed to air, while an anaerobic sealant cures only in the absence of air. This means that an anaerobic sealant cures only after the assembly of parts, sealing them together.

Thread and pipe sealant is used for sealing hydraulic and pneumatic fittings and vacuum lines. It is usually made from a Teflon compound, and comes in a spray, a paint-on liquid and as a wrap-around tape.

Chemicals

Anti-seize compound prevents seizing, galling, cold welding, rust and corrosion in fasteners. High-temperature ant-seize, usually made with copper and graphite lubricants, is used for exhaust system and exhaust manifold bolts.

Anaerobic locking compounds are used to keep fasteners from vibrating or working loose and cure only after installation, in the absence of air. Medium strength locking compound is used for small nuts, bolts and screws that may be removed later. High-strength locking compound is for large nuts, bolts and studs which aren't removed on a regular basis.

Oil additives range from viscosity index improvers to chemical treatments that claim to reduce internal engine friction. It should be noted that most oil manufacturers caution against using additives with their oils.

Gas additives perform several functions, depending on their chemical makeup. They usually contain solvents that help dissolve gum and varnish that build up on carburettor, fuel injection and intake parts. They also serve to break down carbon deposits that form on the inside surfaces of the combustion chambers. Some additives contain upper cylinder lubricants for valves and piston rings, and others contain chemicals to remove condensation from the gas tank.

Miscellaneous

Brake fluid is specially formulated hydraulic fluid that can withstand the heat and pressure encountered in brake systems. Care must be taken so this fluid does not come in contact with painted surfaces or plastics. An opened container should always be resealed to prevent contamination by water or dirt.

Weatherstrip adhesive is used to bond weatherstripping around doors, windows and trunk lids. It is sometimes used to attach trim pieces.

Undercoating is a petroleum-based, tar-like substance that is designed to protect metal surfaces on the underside of the vehicle from corrosion. It also acts as a sound-deadening agent by insulating the bottom of the vehicle.

Waxes and polishes are used to help protect painted and plated surfaces from the weather. Different types of paint may require the use of different types of wax and polish. Some polishes utilise a chemical or abrasive cleaner to help remove the top layer of oxidised (dull) paint on older vehicles. In recent years many non-wax polishes that contain a wide variety of chemicals such as polymers and silicones have been introduced. These non-wax polishes are usually easier to apply and last longer than conventional waxes and polishes.

Conversion factors

Length (distance)

Inches (in)	X	25.4	= Millimetres (mm)	X 0.0394	= Inches (in)
Feet (ft)	X	0.305	= Metres (m)	X 3.281	= Feet (ft)
Miles	X	1.609	= Kilometres (km)	X 0.621	= Miles

Volume (capacity)

Cubic inches (cu in; in³)	X	16.387	= Cubic centimetres (cc; cm³)	X 0.061	= Cubic inches (cu in; in³)
Imperial pints (Imp pt)	X	0.568	= Litres (l)	X 1.76	= Imperial pints (Imp pt)
Imperial quarts (Imp qt)	X	1.137	= Litres (l)	X 0.88	= Imperial quarts (Imp qt)
Imperial quarts (Imp qt)	X	1.201	= US quarts (US qt)	X 0.833	= Imperial quarts (Imp qt)
US quarts (US qt)	X	0.946	= Litres (l)	X 1.057	= US quarts (US qt)
Imperial gallons (Imp gal)	X	4.546	= Litres (l)	X 0.22	= Imperial gallons (Imp gal)
Imperial gallons (Imp gal)	X	1.201	= US gallons (US gal)	X 0.833	= Imperial gallons (Imp gal)
US gallons (US gal)	X	3.785	= Litres (l)	X 0.264	= US gallons (US gal)

Mass (weight)

Ounces (oz)	X	28.35	= Grams (g)	X 0.035	= Ounces (oz)
Pounds (lb)	X	0.454	= Kilograms (kg)	X 2.205	= Pounds (lb)

Force

Ounces-force (ozf; oz)	X	0.278	= Newtons (N)	X 3.6	= Ounces-force (ozf; oz)
Pounds-force (lbf; lb)	X	4.448	= Newtons (N)	X 0.225	= Pounds-force (lbf; lb)
Newtons (N)	X	0.1	= Kilograms-force (kgf; kg)	X 9.81	= Newtons (N)

Pressure

Pounds-force per square inch (psi; lbf/in²; lb/in²)	X	0.070	= Kilograms-force per square centimetre (kgf/cm²; kg/cm²)	X 14.223	= Pounds-force per square inch (psi; lbf/in²; lb/in²)
Pounds-force per square inch (psi; lbf/in²; lb/in²)	X	0.068	= Atmospheres (atm)	X 14.696	= Pounds-force per square inch (psi; lbf/in²; lb/in²)
Pounds-force per square inch (psi; lbf/in²; lb/in²)	X	0.069	= Bars	X 14.5	= Pounds-force per square inch (psi; lbf/in²; lb/in²)
Pounds-force per square inch (psi; lbf/in²; lb/in²)	X	6.895	= Kilopascals (kPa)	X 0.145	= Pounds-force per square inch (psi; lbf/in²; lb/in²)
Kilopascals (kPa)	X	0.01	= Kilograms-force per square centimetre (kgf/cm²; kg/cm²)	X 98.1	= Kilopascals (kPa)

Torque (moment of force)

Pounds-force inches (lbf in; lb in)	X	1.152	= Kilograms-force centimetre (kgf cm; kg cm)	X 0.868	= Pounds-force inches (lbf in; lb in)
Pounds-force inches (lbf in; lb in)	X	0.113	= Newton metres (Nm)	X 8.85	= Pounds-force inches (lbf in; lb in)
Pounds-force inches (lbf in; lb in)	X	0.083	= Pounds-force feet (lbf ft; lb ft)	X 12	= Pounds-force inches (lbf in; lb in)
Pounds-force feet (lbf ft; lb ft)	X	0.138	= Kilograms-force metres (kgf m; kg m)	X 7.233	= Pounds-force feet (lbf ft; lb ft)
Pounds-force feet (lbf ft; lb ft)	X	1.356	= Newton metres (Nm)	X 0.738	= Pounds-force feet (lbf ft; lb ft)
Newton metres (Nm)	X	0.102	= Kilograms-force metres (kgf m; kg m)	X 9.804	= Newton metres (Nm)

Vacuum

Inches mercury (in. Hg)	X	3.377	= Kilopascals (kPa)	X 0.2961	= Inches mercury
Inches mercury (in. Hg)	X	25.4	= Millimetres mercury (mm Hg)	X 0.0394	= Inches mercury

Power

Horsepower (hp)	X	745.7	= Watts (W)	X 0.0013	= Horsepower (hp)

Velocity (speed)

Miles per hour (miles/hr; mph)	X	1.609	= Kilometres per hour (km/hr; kph)	X 0.621	= Miles per hour (miles/hr; mph)

Fuel consumption*

Miles per gallon, Imperial (mpg)	X	0.354	= Kilometres per litre (km/l)	X 2.825	= Miles per gallon, Imperial (mpg)
Miles per gallon, US (mpg)	X	0.425	= Kilometres per litre (km/l)	X 2.352	= Miles per gallon, US (mpg)

Temperature

Degrees Fahrenheit = (°C x 1.8) + 32   Degrees Celsius (Degrees Centigrade; °C) = (°F - 32) x 0.56

*It is common practice to convert from miles per gallon (mpg) to litres/100 kilometres (l/100km), where mpg (Imperial) x l/100 km = 282 and mpg (US) x l/100 km = 235

DECIMALS to MILLIMETRES

Decimal	mm	Decimal	mm
0.001	0.0254	0.500	12.7000
0.002	0.0508	0.510	12.9540
0.003	0.0762	0.520	13.2080
0.004	0.1016	0.530	13.4620
0.005	0.1270	0.540	13.7160
0.006	0.1524	0.550	13.9700
0.007	0.1778	0.560	14.2240
0.008	0.2032	0.570	14.4780
0.009	0.2286	0.580	14.7320
		0.590	14.9860
0.010	0.2540		
0.020	0.5080		
0.030	0.7620		
0.040	1.0160	0.600	15.2400
0.050	1.2700	0.610	15.4940
0.060	1.5240	0.620	15.7480
0.070	1.7780	0.630	16.0020
0.080	2.0320	0.640	16.2560
0.090	2.2860	0.650	16.5100
		0.660	16.7640
0.100	2.5400	0.670	17.0180
0.110	2.7940	0.680	17.2720
0.120	3.0480	0.690	17.5260
0.130	3.3020		
0.140	3.5560		
0.150	3.8100		
0.160	4.0640	0.700	17.7800
0.170	4.3180	0.710	18.0340
0.180	4.5720	0.720	18.2880
0.190	4.8260	0.730	18.5420
		0.740	18.7960
0.200	5.0800	0.750	19.0500
0.210	5.3340	0.760	19.3040
0.220	5.5880	0.770	19.5580
0.230	5.8420	0.780	19.8120
0.240	6.0960	0.790	20.0660
0.250	6.3500		
0.260	6.6040		
0.270	6.8580	0.800	20.3200
0.280	7.1120	0.810	20.5740
0.290	7.3660	0.820	21.8280
		0.830	21.0820
0.300	7.6200	0.840	21.3360
0.310	7.8740	0.850	21.5900
0.320	8.1280	0.860	21.8440
0.330	8.3820	0.870	22.0980
0.340	8.6360	0.880	22.3520
0.350	8.8900	0.890	22.6060
0.360	9.1440		
0.370	9.3980		
0.380	9.6520		
0.390	9.9060		
		0.900	22.8600
0.400	10.1600	0.910	23.1140
0.410	10.4140	0.920	23.3680
0.420	10.6680	0.930	23.6220
0.430	10.9220	0.940	23.8760
0.440	11.1760	0.950	24.1300
0.450	11.4300	0.960	24.3840
0.460	11.6840	0.970	24.6380
0.470	11.9380	0.980	24.8920
0.480	12.1920	0.990	25.1460
0.490	12.4460	1.000	25.4000

FRACTIONS to DECIMALS to MILLIMETRES

Fraction	Decimal	mm	Fraction	Decimal	mm
1/64	0.0156	0.3969	33/64	0.5156	13.0969
1/32	0.0312	0.7938	17/32	0.5312	13.4938
3/64	0.0469	1.1906	35/64	0.5469	13.8906
1/16	0.0625	1.5875	9/16	0.5625	14.2875
5/64	0.0781	1.9844	37/64	0.5781	14.6844
3/32	0.0938	2.3812	19/32	0.5938	15.0812
7/64	0.1094	2.7781	39/64	0.6094	15.4781
1/8	0.1250	3.1750	5/8	0.6250	15.8750
9/64	0.1406	3.5719	41/64	0.6406	16.2719
5/32	0.1562	3.9688	21/32	0.6562	16.6688
11/64	0.1719	4.3656	43/64	0.6719	17.0656
3/16	0.1875	4.7625	11/16	0.6875	17.4625
13/64	0.2031	5.1594	45/64	0.7031	17.8594
7/32	0.2188	5.5562	23/32	0.7188	18.2562
15/64	0.2344	5.9531	47/64	0.7344	18.6531
1/4	0.2500	6.3500	3/4	0.7500	19.0500
17/64	0.2656	6.7469	49/64	0.7656	19.4469
9/32	0.2812	7.1438	25/32	0.7812	19.8438
19/64	0.2969	7.5406	51/64	0.7969	20.2406
5/16	0.3125	7.9375	13/16	0.8125	20.6375
21/64	0.3281	8.3344	53/64	0.8281	21.0344
11/32	0.3438	8.7312	27/32	0.8438	21.4312
23/64	0.3594	9.1281	55/64	0.8594	21.8281
3/8	0.3750	9.5250	7/8	0.8750	22.2250
25/64	0.3906	9.9219	57/64	0.8906	22.6219
13/32	0.4062	10.3188	29/32	0.9062	23.0188
27/64	0.4219	10.7156	59/64	0.9219	23.4156
7/16	0.4375	11.1125	15/16	0.9375	23.8125
29/64	0.4531	11.5094	61/64	0.9531	24.2094
15/32	0.4688	11.9062	31/32	0.9688	24.6062
31/64	0.4844	12.3031	63/64	0.9844	25.0031
1/2	0.5000	12.7000	1	1.0000	25.4000

Safety first!

Regardless of how enthusiastic you may be about getting on with the job at hand, take the time to ensure that your safety is not jeopardised. A moment's lack of attention can result in an accident, as can failure to observe certain simple safety precautions. The possibility of an accident will always exist, and the following points should not be considered a comprehensive list of all dangers. Rather, they are intended to make you aware of the risks and to encourage a safety conscious approach to all work you carry out on your vehicle.

Essential DOs and DON'Ts

DON'T rely on a jack when working under the vehicle. Always use approved jackstands to support the weight of the vehicle and place them under the recommended lift or support points.

DON'T attempt to loosen extremely tight fasteners (i.e. wheel nuts) while the vehicle is on a jack - it may fall.

DON'T start the engine without first making sure that the transmission is in Neutral (or Park where applicable) and the parking brake is set.

DON'T remove the radiator cap from a hot cooling system - let it cool or cover it with a cloth and release the pressure gradually.

DON'T attempt to drain the engine oil until you are sure it has cooled to the point that it will not burn you.

DON'T touch any part of the engine or exhaust system until it has cooled sufficiently to avoid burns.

DON'T siphon toxic liquids such as gasoline, antifreeze and brake fluid by mouth, or allow them to remain on your skin.

DON'T inhale brake lining dust - it is potentially hazardous (see *Asbestos* below).

DON'T allow spilled oil or grease to remain on the floor - wipe it up before someone slips on it.

DON'T use loose fitting wrenches or other tools which may slip and cause injury.

DON'T push on wrenches when loosening or tightening nuts or bolts. Always try to pull the wrench toward you. If the situation calls for pushing the wrench away, push with an open hand to avoid scraped knuckles if the wrench should slip.

DON'T attempt to lift a heavy component alone - get someone to help you.

DON'T *rush or take unsafe shortcuts to finish a job.*

DON'T allow children or animals in or around the vehicle while you are working on it.

DO wear eye protection when using power tools such as a drill, sander, bench grinder, etc. and when working under a vehicle.

DO keep loose clothing and long hair well out of the way of moving parts.

DO make sure that any hoist used has a safe working load rating adequate for the job.

DO get someone to check on you periodically when working alone on a vehicle.

DO carry out work in a logical sequence and make sure that everything is correctly assembled and tightened.

DO keep chemicals and fluids tightly capped and out of the reach of children and pets.

DO remember that your vehicle's safety affects that of yourself and others. If in doubt on any point, get professional advice.

Steering, suspension and brakes

These systems are essential to driving safety, so make sure you have a qualified shop or individual check your work. Also, compressed suspension springs can cause injury if released suddenly - be sure to use a spring compressor.

Airbags

Airbags are explosive devices that can **CAUSE** injury if they deploy while you're working on the vehicle. Follow the manufacturer's instructions to disable the airbag whenever you're working in the vicinity of airbag components.

Asbestos

Certain friction, insulating, sealing, and other products - such as brake linings, brake bands, clutch linings, torque converters, gaskets, etc. - may contain asbestos or other hazardous friction material. Extreme care must be taken to avoid inhalation of dust from such products, since it is hazardous to health. If in doubt, assume that they do contain asbestos.

Fire

Remember at all times that gasoline is highly flammable. Never smoke or have any kind of open flame around when working on a vehicle. But the risk does not end there. A spark caused by an electrical short circuit, by two metal surfaces contacting each other, or even by static electricity built up in your body under certain conditions, can ignite gasoline vapours, which in a confined space are highly explosive. Do not, under any circumstances, use gasoline for cleaning parts. Use an approved safety solvent.

Always disconnect the negative battery (-) terminal before working on any part of the fuel system or electrical system. Never risk spilling fuel on a hot engine or exhaust component. It is strongly recommended that a fire extinguisher suitable for use on fuel and electrical fires be kept handy in the garage or workshop at all times. Never try to extinguish a fuel or electrical fire with water.

Fumes

Certain fumes are highly toxic and can quickly cause unconsciousness and even death if inhaled to any extent. Gasoline vapour falls into this category, as do the vapours from some cleaning solvents. Any draining or pouring of such volatile fluids should be done in a well ventilated area.

When using cleaning fluids and solvents, read the instructions on the container carefully. Never use materials from unmarked containers.

Never run the engine in an enclosed space, such as a garage. Exhaust fumes contain carbon monoxide, which is extremely poisonous. If you need to run the engine, always do so in the open air, or at least have the rear of the vehicle outside the work area.

The battery

Never create a spark or allow a bare light bulb near a battery. They normally give off a certain amount of hydrogen gas, which is highly explosive.

Always disconnect the battery ground (-) cable at the battery before working on the fuel or electrical systems.

If possible, loosen the filler caps or cover when charging the battery from an external source (this does not apply to sealed or maintenance-free batteries). Do not charge at an excessive rate or the battery may burst.

Take care when adding water to a non maintenance-free battery and when carrying a battery. The electrolyte, even when diluted, is very corrosive and should not be allowed to contact clothing or skin.

Always wear eye protection when cleaning the battery to prevent the caustic deposits from entering your eyes.

Household current

When using an electric power tool, inspection light, etc., which operates on household current, always make sure that the tool is correctly connected to its plug and that, where necessary, it is properly grounded. Do not use such items in damp conditions and, again, do not create a spark or apply excessive heat in the vicinity of fuel or fuel vapour.

Secondary ignition system voltage

A severe electric shock can result from touching certain parts of the ignition system (such as the spark plug wires) when the engine is running or being cranked, particularly if components are damp or the insulation is defective. In the case of an electronic ignition system, the secondary system voltage is much higher and could prove fatal.

Hydrofluoric acid

This extremely corrosive acid is formed when certain types of synthetic rubber, found in some O-rings, oil seals, fuel hoses, etc. are exposed to temperatures above 400 degrees C. The rubber changes into a charred or sticky substance containing the acid. *Once formed, the acid remains dangerous for years. If it gets onto the skin, it may be necessary to amputate the limb concerned.*

When dealing with a vehicle which has suffered a fire, or with components salvaged from such a vehicle, wear protective gloves and discard them after use.

Troubleshooting

Contents

This section provides an easy reference guide to the more common problems which may occur during the operation of your vehicle. These problems and their possible causes are grouped under headings denoting various components or systems, such as Engine, Cooling system, etc. They also refer you to the chapter and/or section which deals with the problem.

Remember that successful troubleshooting is not a mysterious art practiced only by professional mechanics. It is simply the result of the right knowledge combined with an intelligent, systematic approach to the problem. Always work by a process of elimination, starting with the simplest solution and working through to the most complex - and never overlook the obvious. Anyone can run the gas tank dry or leave the lights on overnight, so don't assume that you are exempt from such oversights.

Finally, always establish a clear idea of why a problem has occurred and take steps to ensure that it doesn't happen again. If the electrical system fails because of a poor connection, check the other connections in the system to make sure that they don't fail as well. If a particular fuse continues to blow, find out why - don't just replace one fuse after another. Remember, failure of a small component can often be indicative of potential failure or incorrect functioning of a more important component or system.

Engine

1   Engine will not rotate when attempting to start

1   Battery terminal connections loose or corroded (Chapter 1).
2   Battery discharged or faulty (Chapter 1).
3   Automatic transaxle not completely engaged in Park (Chapter 7).
4   Broken, loose or disconnected wiring in the starting circuit (Chapters 5 and 12).
5   Starter motor pinion jammed in flywheel ring gear (Chapter 5).
6   Starter solenoid faulty (Chapter 5).
7   Starter motor faulty (Chapter 5).
8   Ignition switch faulty (Chapter 12).
9   Starter pinion or flywheel teeth worn or broken (Chapter 5).

2   Engine rotates but will not start

1   Fuel tank empty.
2   Battery discharged (engine rotates slowly) (Chapter 5).
3   Battery terminal connections loose or corroded (Chapter 1).
4   Leaking fuel injector(s), faulty fuel pump, pressure regulator, etc. (Chapter 4).
5   Fuel not reaching fuel rail (Chapter 4).
6   Ignition components damp or damaged (Chapter 5).

7   Worn, faulty or incorrectly gapped spark plugs (Chapter 1).
8   Broken, loose or disconnected wiring in the starting circuit (Chapter 5).
9   Broken, loose or disconnected wires at the ignition coil(s) or faulty coil(s) (Chapter 5).
10   Faulty camshaft or crankshaft position sensor (Chapter 6).

3   Engine hard to start when cold

1   Battery discharged or low (Chapter 1).
2   Malfunctioning fuel system (Chapter 4).
3   Faulty cold start injector (Chapter 4).
4   Injector(s) leaking (Chapter 4).
5   Faulty coolant temperature sensor (Chapter 6).

4   Engine hard to start when hot

1   Air filter clogged (Chapter 1).
2   Fuel not reaching the fuel injection system (Chapter 4).
3   Corroded battery connections, especially ground (Chapter 1).

5   Starter motor noisy or excessively rough in engagement

1   Pinion or flywheel gear teeth worn or broken (Chapter 5).
2   Starter motor mounting bolts loose or missing (Chapter 5).

6   Engine starts but stops immediately

1   Loose or faulty electrical connections at coil(s) or alternator (Chapter 5).
2   Insufficient fuel reaching the fuel injector(s) (Chapters 1 and 4).
3   Vacuum leak at the gasket between the intake manifold/plenum and throttle body (Chapters 1 and 4).

7   Oil puddle under engine

1   Oil pan gasket and/or oil pan drain bolt washer leaking (Chapter 2).
2   Oil pressure sending unit leaking (Chapter 2).
3   Valve covers leaking (Chapter 2).
4   Engine oil seals leaking (Chapter 2).
5   Oil pump housing leaking (Chapter 2).

8   Engine lopes while idling or idles erratically

1   Vacuum leakage (Chapters 2 and 4).
2   Leaking EGR valve (Chapter 6).
3   Air filter clogged (Chapter 1).
4   Fuel pump not delivering sufficient fuel to the fuel injection system (Chapter 4).
5   Leaking head gasket (Chapter 2).
6   Timing belt and/or sprockets worn (Chapter 2).
7   Camshaft lobes worn (Chapter 2).

9   Engine misses at idle speed

1   Spark plugs worn or faulty (Chapter 1).
2   Faulty spark plug wires (Chapter 1).
3   Vacuum leaks (Chapter 1).
4   Fault in engine management system (Chapter 6).
5   Uneven or low compression (Chapter 2).

10   Engine misses throughout driving speed range

1   Fuel filter clogged and/or impurities in the fuel system (Chapter 1).
2   Low fuel output at the injector(s) (Chapter 4).
3   Faulty or worn spark plugs (Chapter 1).
4   Fault in engine management system (Chapter 6).
5   Faulty emission system components (Chapter 6).
6   Low or uneven cylinder compression pressures (Chapter 2).
7   Weak or faulty ignition coil(s) (Chapter 5).
8   Vacuum leak in fuel injection system, intake manifold/plenum, air control valve or vacuum hoses (Chapter 4).

11   Engine stumbles on acceleration

1   Spark plugs fouled (Chapter 1).
2   Fuel injection system faulty (Chapter 4).
3   Fuel filter clogged (Chapters 1 and 4).
4   Fault in engine management system (Chapter 6).
5   Intake manifold or plenum air leak (Chapters 2 and 4).

12   Engine surges while holding accelerator steady

1   Intake air leak (Chapter 4).
2   Fuel pump faulty (Chapter 4).
3   Loose fuel injector wire harness connectors (Chapter 4).
4   Defective ECM or information sensor (Chapter 6).

13 Engine stalls

1 Fuel filter clogged and/or water and impurities in the fuel system (Chapters 1 and 4).
2 Ignition components damp or damaged (Chapter 5).
3 Faulty emissions system components (Chapter 6).
4 Faulty or incorrectly gapped spark plugs (Chapter 1).
5 Vacuum leak in the fuel injection system, intake manifold or vacuum hoses (Chapters 2 and 4).
6 Valve clearances incorrectly set (Chapter 1).

14 Engine lacks power

1 Fault in engine management system (Chapter 6).
2 Faulty or worn spark plugs (Chapter 1).
3 Fuel injection system malfunction (Chapter 4).
4 Faulty coil(s) (Chapter 5).
5 Brakes binding (Chapter 9).
6 Automatic transaxle fluid level incorrect (Chapter 1).
7 Fuel filter clogged and/or impurities in the fuel system (Chapters 1 and 4).
8 Emissions control systems not functioning properly (Chapter 6).
9 Low or uneven cylinder compression pressures (Chapter 2).
10 Obstructed exhaust system (Chapter 4).

15 Engine backfires

1 Emission control system not functioning properly (Chapter 6).
2 Fault in engine management system (Chapter 6).
3 Faulty spark plug insulator (Chapter 1).
4 Fuel injection system malfunction (Chapter 4).
5 Vacuum leak at fuel injector(s), intake manifold, air control valve or vacuum hoses (Chapters 2 and 4).
6 Valve clearances incorrectly set and/or valves sticking (Chapter 1).

16 Pinging or knocking engine sounds during acceleration or uphill

1 Incorrect grade of fuel.
2 Fault in engine management system (Chapter 6).
3 Fuel injection system faulty (Chapter 4).
4 Improper or damaged spark plug(s) (Chapter 1).
5 Vacuum leak (Chapters 2 and 4).
6 Defective knock sensor (Chapter 6).

17 Engine runs with oil pressure light on

1 Low oil level (Chapter 1).
2 Short in wiring circuit (Chapter 12).
3 Faulty oil pressure sender (Chapter 2).
4 Worn engine bearings and/or oil pump (Chapter 2).

18 Engine continues to run after switching off

1 Excessive engine operating temperature (Chapter 3).
2 Fault in engine management system (Chapter 6).

Engine electrical system

19 Battery will not hold a charge

1 Alternator drivebelt defective or not adjusted properly (Chapter 1).
2 Battery electrolyte level low (Chapter 1).
3 Battery terminals loose or corroded (Chapter 1).
4 Alternator not charging properly (Chapter 5).
5 Loose, broken or faulty wiring in the charging circuit (Chapter 5).
6 Short in vehicle wiring (Chapter 12).
7 Internally defective battery (Chapters 1 and 5).

20 Alternator light fails to go out

1 Faulty alternator or charging circuit (Chapter 5).
2 Alternator drivebelt defective or out of adjustment (Chapter 1).
3 Alternator voltage regulator inoperative (Chapter 5).

21 Alternator light fails to come on when key is turned on

1 Warning light bulb defective (Chapter 12).
2 Fault in the printed circuit, dash wiring or bulb holder (Chapter 12).

Fuel system

22 Excessive fuel consumption

1 Dirty or clogged air filter element (Chapter 1).
2 Fault in engine management system (Chapter 6).
3 Emissions systems not functioning properly (Chapter 6).
4 Fuel injection system not functioning properly (Chapter 4).
5 Low tyre pressure or incorrect tyre size (Chapter 1).

23 Fuel leakage and/or fuel odour

1 Leaking fuel feed or return line (Chapters 1 and 4).
2 Tank overfilled.
3 Evaporative canister filter clogged (Chapters 1 and 6).
4 Fuel injection system not functioning properly (Chapter 4).

Cooling system

24 Overheating

1 Insufficient coolant in system (Chapter 1).
2 Water pump defective (Chapter 3).
3 Radiator core blocked or grille restricted (Chapter 3).
4 Thermostat faulty (Chapter 3).
5 Electric coolant fan blades broken or cracked (Chapter 3).
6 Radiator cap not maintaining proper pressure (Chapter 3).
7 Fault in engine management system (Chapter 6).

25 Overcooling

1 Faulty thermostat (Chapter 3).
2 Inaccurate temperature gauge sending unit (Chapter 3)

26 External coolant leakage

1 Deteriorated/damaged hoses; loose clamps (Chapters 1 and 3).
2 Water pump defective (Chapter 3).
3 Leakage from radiator core or coolant reservoir bottle (Chapter 3).
4 Engine drain or water jacket core plugs leaking (Chapter 2).

27 Internal coolant leakage

1 Leaking cylinder head gasket (Chapter 2).

2   Cracked cylinder bore or cylinder head (Chapter 2).

28 Coolant loss

1   Too much coolant in system (Chapter 1).
2   Coolant boiling away because of over-heating (Chapter 3).
3   Internal or external leakage (Chapter 3).
4   Faulty radiator cap (Chapter 3).

29 Poor coolant circulation

1   Inoperative water pump (Chapter 3).
2   Restriction in cooling system (Chapters 1 and 3).
3   Water pump drivebelt defective/out of adjustment (Chapter 1).
4   Thermostat sticking (Chapter 3).

Automatic transaxle

Note: *Due to the complexity of the automatic transaxle, it is difficult for the home mechanic to properly diagnose and service this component. For problems other than the following, the vehicle should be taken to a dealer or transaxle shop.*

30 Fluid leakage

1   Automatic transaxle fluid is a deep red colour. Fluid leaks should not be confused with engine oil, which can easily be blown onto the transaxle by air flow.
2   To pinpoint a leak, first remove all built-up dirt and grime from the transaxle housing with degreasing agents and/or steam cleaning. Then drive the vehicle at low speeds so air flow will not blow the leak far from its source. Raise the vehicle and determine where the leak is coming from. Common areas of leakage are:

   a *Pan (Chapters 1 and 7)*
   b *Dipstick tube (Chapters 1 and 7)*
   c *Transaxle oil lines (Chapter 7)*
   d *Speed sensor (Chapter 7)*
   e *Differential drain plug (Chapters 1 and 7)*

31 Transaxle fluid brown or has a burned smell

Transaxle fluid overheated (Chapter 1).

32 General shift mechanism problems

1   Chapter 7 deals with checking and adjusting the shift linkage on automatic transaxles. Common problems which may be attributed to poorly adjusted linkage are:

   a *Engine starting in gears other than Park or Neutral.*
   b *Indicator on shifter pointing to a gear other than the one actually being used.*
   c *Vehicle moves when in Park.*
2   Refer to Chapter 7 for the shift linkage adjustment procedure.

33 Transaxle will not downshift with accelerator pedal pressed to the floor

These transaxles are electronically controlled. Check for trouble codes stored in the PCM (see Chapter 6).

34 Engine will start in gears other than Park or Neutral

Transmission Range (TR) sensor malfunctioning (Chapter 6).

35 Transaxle slips, shifts roughly, is noisy or has no drive in forward or reverse gears

There are many probable causes for the above problems, but the home mechanic should be concerned with only one possibility - fluid level. Before taking the vehicle to a repair shop, check the level and condition of the fluid as described in Chapter 1. Correct the fluid level as necessary or change the fluid and filter if needed. If the problem persists, have a professional diagnose the cause.

Driveaxles

36 Clicking noise in turns

Worn or damaged outboard CV joint (Chapter 8).

37 Shudder or vibration during acceleration

1   Excessive toe-in (Chapter 10).
2   Worn or damaged inboard or outboard CV joints (Chapter 8).
3   Sticking inboard CV joint assembly (Chapter 8).

38 Vibration at highway speeds

1   Out-of-balance front wheels and/or tyres (Chapters 1 and 10).
2   Out-of-round front tyres (Chapters 1 and 10).
3   Worn CV joint(s) (Chapter 8).

Brakes

Note: *Before assuming that a brake problem exists, make sure that:*

   a *The tyres are in good condition and properly inflated (Chapter 1).*
   b *The front end alignment is correct.*
   c *The vehicle is not loaded with weight in an unequal manner.*

39 Vehicle pulls to one side during braking

1   Incorrect tyre pressures (Chapter 1).
2   Front end out of alignment (have the front end aligned).
3   Front, or rear, tyres not matched to one another.
4   Restricted brake lines or hoses (Chapter 9).
5   Malfunctioning caliper assembly (Chapter 9).
6   Loose suspension parts (Chapter 10).
7   Loose calipers (Chapter 9).
8   Excessive wear of brake pad material or disc on one side.

40 Noise (high-pitched squeal when the brakes are applied)

Front and/or rear disc brake pads worn out. The noise comes from the wear sensor rubbing against the disc. Replace pads with new ones immediately (Chapter 9).

41 Brake roughness or chatter (pedal pulsates)

1   Excessive lateral runout (Chapter 9).
2   Uneven pad wear (Chapter 9).
3   Defective disc (Chapter 9).

42 Excessive brake pedal effort required to stop vehicle

1   Malfunctioning power brake booster (Chapter 9).
2   Partial system failure (Chapter 9).
3   Excessively worn pads (Chapter 9).
4   Piston in caliper stuck or sluggish (Chapter 9).
5   Brake pads contaminated with oil, grease or brake fluid (Chapter 9).

6   New pads installed and not yet seated. It will take a while for the new material to seat against the disc.

43 Excessive brake pedal travel

1   Partial brake system failure (Chapter 9).
2   Insufficient fluid in master cylinder (Chapters 1 and 9).
3   Air trapped in system (Chapters 1 and 9).

44 Dragging brakes

1   Incorrect adjustment of brake light switch (Chapter 9).
2   Master cylinder pistons not returning correctly (Chapter 9).
3   Restricted brakes lines or hoses (Chapters 1 and 9).
4   Incorrect parking brake adjustment (Chapter 9).

45 Grabbing or uneven braking action

1   Malfunction of proportioning valve (Chapter 9).
2   Malfunction of power brake booster unit (Chapter 9).
3   Binding brake pedal mechanism (Chapter 9).

46 Brake pedal feels spongy when depressed

1   Air in hydraulic lines (Chapter 9).
2   Master cylinder mounting bolts loose (Chapter 9).
3   Master cylinder defective (Chapter 9).

47 Brake pedal travels to the floor with little resistance

1   Little or no fluid in the master cylinder reservoir caused by leaking caliper piston(s) (Chapter 9).
2   Loose, damaged or disconnected brake lines (Chapter 9).
3   Defective master cylinder (Chapter 9).

48 Parking brake does not hold

Parking brake improperly adjusted (Chapters 1 and 9).

Suspension and steering systems

Note: *Before attempting to diagnose the suspension and steering systems, perform the following preliminary checks:*

a   *Tyres for wrong pressure and uneven wear.*
b   *Steering universal joints from the column to the rack and pinion for loose connectors or wear.*
c   *Front and rear suspension and the steering gear assembly for loose or damaged parts.*
d   *Out-of-round or out-of-balance tires, bent rims and loose and/or rough wheel bearings.*

49 Vehicle pulls to one side

1   Mismatched or uneven tyres (Chapter 10).
2   Broken or sagging springs (Chapter 10).
3   Wheel alignment (Chapter 10).
4   Front brake dragging (Chapter 9).

50 Abnormal or excessive tyre wear

1   Wheel alignment (Chapter 10).
2   Sagging or broken springs (Chapter 10).
3   Tyre out of balance (Chapter 10).
4   Worn strut damper (Chapter 10).
5   Overloaded vehicle.
6   Tyres not rotated regularly.

51 Wheel makes a thumping noise

1   Blister or bump on tyre (Chapter 10).
2   Improper strut damper action (Chapter 10).

52 Shimmy, shake or vibration

1   Tyre or wheel out-of-balance or out-of-round (Chapter 10).
2   Loose or worn wheel bearings (Chapters 1, 8 and 10).
3   Worn tie-rod ends (Chapter 10).
4   Worn lower balljoints (Chapters 1 and 10).
5   Excessive wheel runout (Chapter 10).
6   Blister or bump on tyre (Chapter 10).

53 Hard steering

1   Lack of lubrication at balljoints, tie-rod ends and steering gear assembly (Chapter 10).
2   Front wheel alignment (Chapter 10).
3   Low tyre pressure(s) (Chapters 1 and 10).

54 Poor returnability of steering to centre

1   Lack of lubrication at balljoints and tie-rod ends (Chapter 10).
2   Binding in balljoints (Chapter 10).
3   Binding in steering column (Chapter 10).
4   Lack of lubricant in steering gear assembly (Chapter 10).
5   Front wheel alignment (Chapter 10).

55 Abnormal noise at the front end

1   Lack of lubrication at balljoints and tie-rod ends (Chapters 1 and 10).
2   Damaged strut mounting (Chapter 10).
3   Worn control arm bushings or tie-rod ends (Chapter 10).
4   Loose stabiliser bar (Chapter 10).
5   Loose wheel nuts (Chapters 1 and 10).
6   Loose suspension bolts (Chapter 10)

56 Wander or poor steering stability

1   Mismatched or uneven tyres (Chapter 10).
2   Lack of lubrication at balljoints and tie-rod ends (Chapters 1 and 10).
3   Worn strut assemblies (Chapter 10).
4   Loose stabiliser bar (Chapter 10).
5   Broken or sagging springs (Chapter 10).
6   Wheels out of alignment (Chapter 10).

57 Erratic steering when braking

1   Wheel bearings worn (Chapter 10).
2   Broken or sagging springs (Chapter 10).
3   Leaking wheel cylinder or caliper (Chapter 9).
4   Warped brake discs (Chapter 9).

58 Excessive pitching and/or rolling around corners or during braking

1   Loose stabiliser bar (Chapter 10).
2   Worn strut dampers or mountings (Chapter 10).
3   Broken or sagging springs (Chapter 10).
4   Overloaded vehicle.

59 Suspension bottoms

1   Overloaded vehicle.
2   Worn strut dampers (Chapter 10).
3   Incorrect, broken or sagging springs (Chapter 10).

60 Cupped tires

1   Front wheel or rear wheel alignment (Chapter 10).
2   Worn strut dampers (Chapter 10).
3   Wheel bearings worn (Chapter 10).
4   Excessive tyre or wheel runout (Chapter 10).
5   Worn balljoints (Chapter 10).

61 Excessive tyre wear on outside edge

1   Inflation pressures incorrect (Chapter 1).
2   Excessive speed in turns.
3   Front end alignment incorrect (excessive toe-in). Have professionally aligned.
4   Suspension arm bent or twisted (Chapter 10).

62 Excessive tyre wear on inside edge

1   Inflation pressures incorrect (Chapter 1).
2   Front end alignment incorrect (toe-out). Have professionally aligned.
3   Loose or damaged steering components (Chapter 10).

63 Tyre tread worn in one place

1   Tyres out of balance.
2   Damaged wheel. Inspect and replace if necessary.
3   Defective tyre (Chapter 1).

64 Excessive play or looseness in steering system

1   Wheel bearing(s) worn (Chapter 10).
2   Tie-rod end loose (Chapter 10).
3   Steering gear loose (Chapter 10).
4   Worn or loose steering intermediate shaft (Chapter 10).

65 Rattling or clicking noise in steering gear

1   Steering gear loose (Chapter 10).
2   Steering gear defective.

Chapter 1
Tune-up and routine maintenance

Contents

Specifications

Recommended lubricants and fluids

Note: *Listed here are manufacturer recommendations at the time this manual was written. Manufacturers occasionally upgrade their fluid and lubricant specifications, so check with your auto parts store for current recommendations.*

Engine oil
Type	API SL
Viscosity	See table
Capacity [1]	
3MZ-FE engine	
With filter	4.5 litres
Without filter	4.7 litres
2GR-FE engine	
With filter	5.7 litres
Without filter	6.1 litres

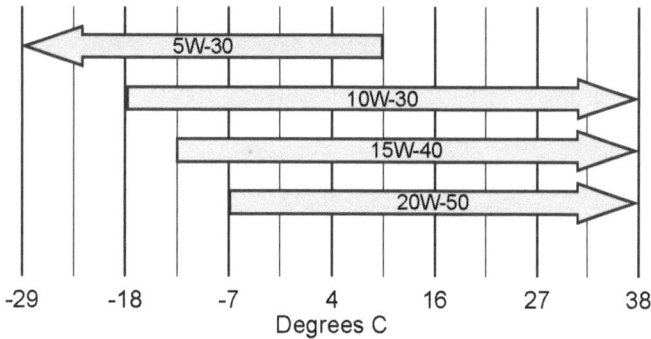

Oil viscosity table - pick the oil viscosity that closest suits the anticipated vehicle operating temperature

Coolant
Type .... Toyota Super Long Life Coolant or equivalent ethylene glycol based non-silicate/non-amine/non-nitrate/non-borate coolant with long-life Hybrid Organic Acid Technology (HOAT)

Capacity [1]
3MZ-FE engine
Without rear heater... 10.1 litres
With rear heater.. 11.4 litres
2GR-FE engine
Without rear heater... 9.5 litres
With rear heater.. 11.7 litres
Automatic transaxle
Type
MCU28R models .... Toyota ATF Type T-IV automatic transmission fluid
GSU40R/GSU45R models .... Toyota ATF Type WS automatic transmission fluid
Capacity (drain and refill) [1]... 3.5 litres
Brake fluid type.. DOT 3 brake fluid
Power steering system fluid... DEXRON II or III
Transfer case (AWD models) [2]
Type
MCU28R models .... API GL-5 SAE 80W-90 hypoid gear oil
GSU40R and GSU45R models .... API GL-5 SAE 90W hypoid gear oil
Capacity .... 0.9 litre
Rear differential (AWD models) [2]
Type .... API GL-5 SAE 90 hypoid gear oil
Capacity [1].. 0.9 litre

[1] All capacities approximate. Add as necessary to bring up to the appropriate level
[2] Toyota recommends API GL-5 SAE 80W-90 hypoid gear oil in temperatures below -18 degrees C

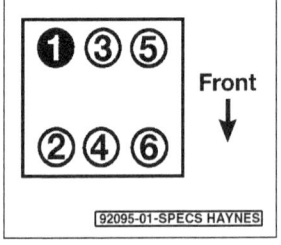

Cylinder numbering - V6
engines

Ignition system
Spark plug type
3MZ-FE engine
Type 1 .... NGK IFR6A11
Type 2 .... Nippondenso SK20R11 or equivalent
2GR-FE engine .... Nippondenso FK20HR11 or equivalent
Spark plug gap .... 1.1 mm
Engine firing order 1-2-3-4-5-6

Valve clearance (engine cold)
3MZ-FE engine
Intake .... 0.15 to 0.25 mm
Exhaust.. 0.25 to 0.35 mm
2GR-FE engine... Hydraulic, non-adjustable

Brakes
Disc brake pad lining thickness (minimum) .... 1.5 mm

Torque specifications   Nm
Automatic transaxle
Pan bolts 7.5
Strainer bolts 11
Drain plug... 47
Drivebelt (2GR-FE engine)
Idler pulley to cylinder block bolt 43
Tensioner pulley bolt (LH thread) .... Not specified
Tensioner bolts 43
Engine oil drain plug
3MZ-FE engine 45
2GR-FE engine 40
Engine oil filter 2GR-FE engine
Filter cap bolt... 25
Filter cap drain plug.. 13
Spark plugs
3MZ-FE engine 25
2GR-FE engine 18
Wheel nuts.. 103

3.3 litre (3MZ-FE) engine compartment (MCU28R model)

1 Battery
2 Automatic transaxle dipstick
3 Radiator cap
4 Engine oil dipstick
5 Upper radiator hose

6 Windshield washer fluid reservoir
7 Engine coolant reservoir
8 Power steering fluid reservoir
9 Engine cover (remove for access to
   spark plugs)

10 Engine oil filler cap
11 Brake fluid reservoir
12 Air filter housing
13 Relay box

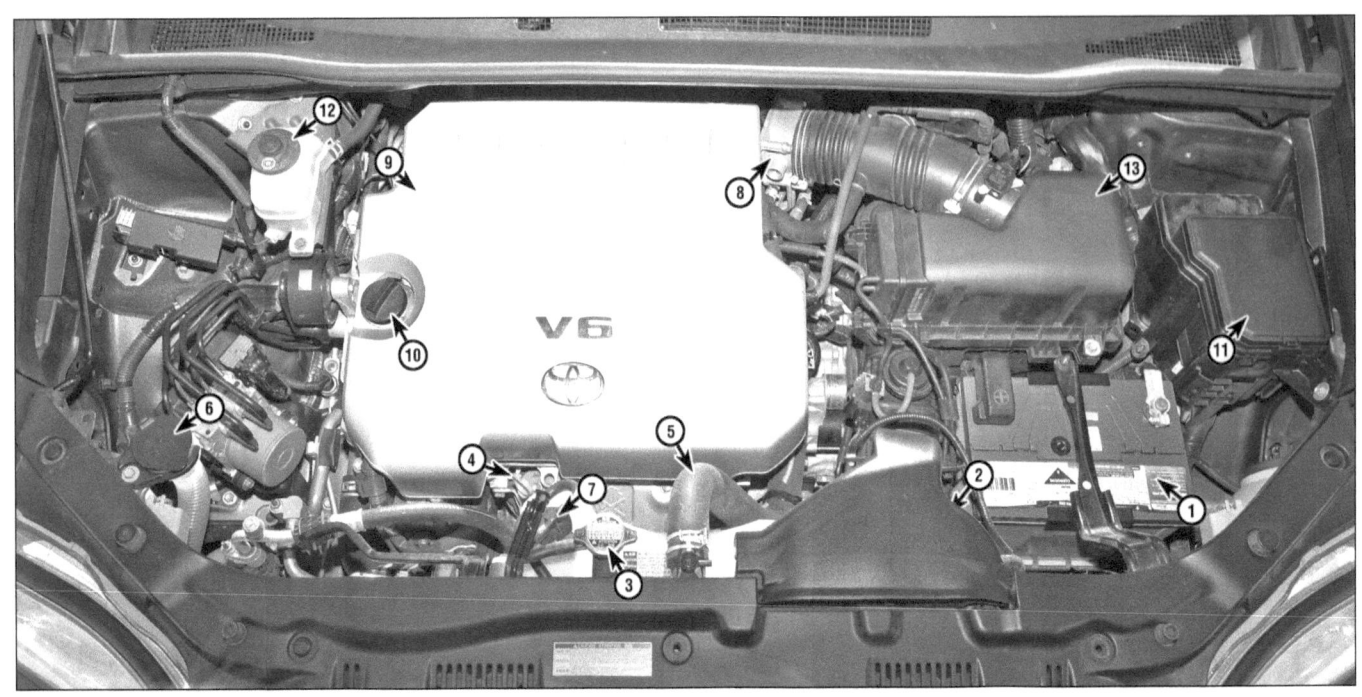

3.5 litre (2GR-FE) engine compartment (GSU40 and GSU45R models)

1 *Battery*
2 *Automatic transaxle dipstick*
3 *Radiator cap*
4 *Engine oil dipstick*
5 *Upper radiator hose*

6 *Windshield washer fluid reservoir*
7 *Engine coolant reservoir*
8 *Throttle body*
9 *Engine cover (remove for access to spark plugs)*

10 *Engine oil filler cap*
11 *Relay box*
12 *Brake fluid reservoir*
13 *Air filter housing*

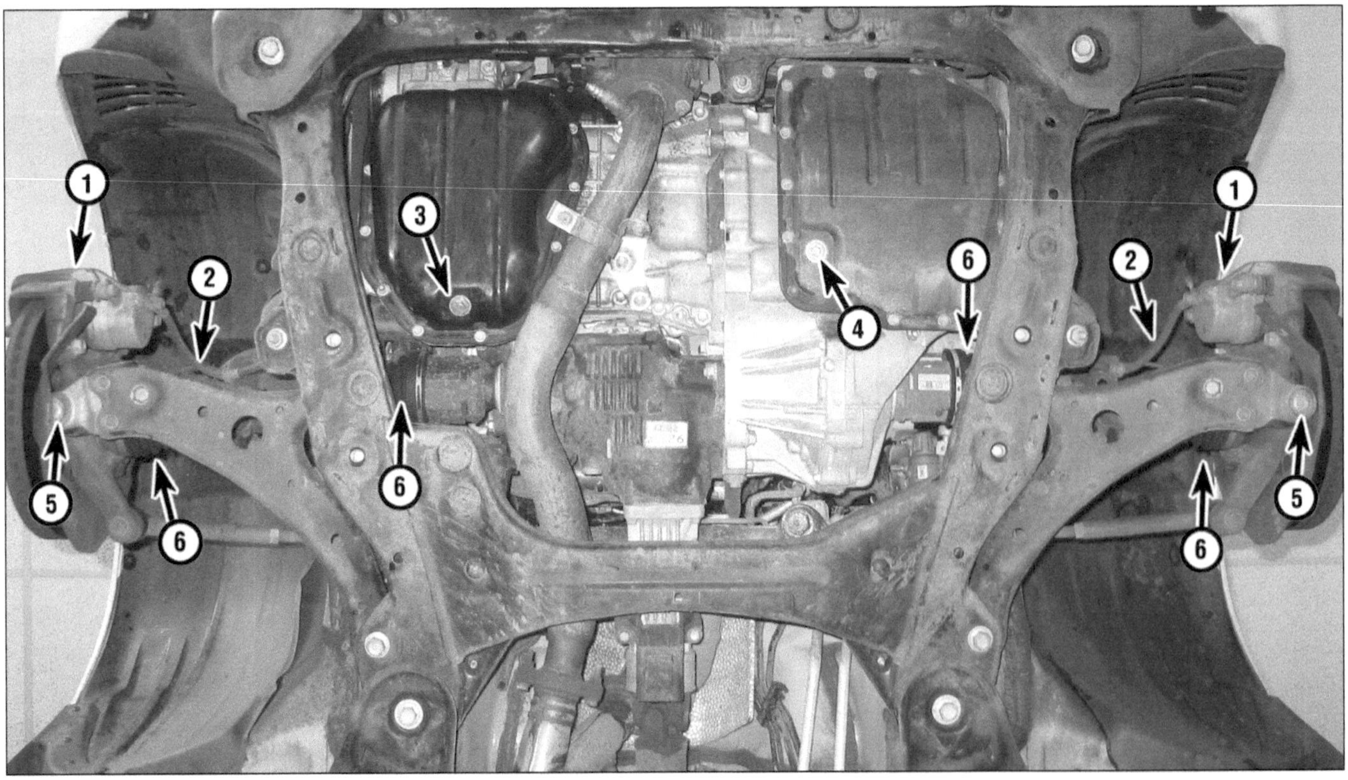

Typical front underside components

1 *Front brake calipers*
2 *Brake hoses*

3 *Engine oil drain plug*
4 *Automatic transaxle drain plug*

5 *Balljoints*
6 *Driveaxle boots*

Typical rear underside components

1 Muffler
2 Outer driveaxle boot
3 Inner driveaxle boot
4 Rear differential drain plug

Maintenance schedule

The maintenance intervals in this manual are provided with the assumption that you, not the dealer, will be doing the work. These are the maintenance intervals recommended by the factory for vehicles that are driven daily. If you wish to keep your vehicle in peak condition at all times, you may wish to perform some of these procedures even more often, especially if the vehicle is being used to carry heavy loads, towing a caravan or heavy trailer or operating in an extreme environment; such as being used off-road or travelling through water or dust. In these cases, it is recommended that the lubricants are changed more frequently and the air filter is checked/cleaned or replaced more often.

Because frequent maintenance enhances the efficiency, performance and resale value of your car, we encourage you to do so. If you drive in dusty areas, tow a trailer, idle or drive at low speeds for extended periods or drive for short distances (less than four miles) in below freezing temperatures, shorter intervals are also recommended.

When your vehicle is new, it should be serviced by a factory authorised dealer service department to protect the factory warranty. In many cases, the initial maintenance check is done at no cost to the owner.

MCU28R models

Every 10,000 km or 6 months

Change the engine oil and oil filter (see Section 6)
Check the engine drivebelt (see Section 21)
Check and service the battery (see Section 7)
Check the power steering fluid level (see Section 4)
Check the driveshaft boots (see Section 13)
Check the tyre condition and pressure (see Section 5)
Check that all of the lights, horn and wipers and washers operate
Inspect (and replace, if necessary) the windshield wiper blades
    (see Section 9)

Every 20,000 km or 12 months

Inspect the exhaust system (see Section 14)
Clean/replace the engine air filter (see Section 15)
Inspect and replace if necessary all underbonnet hoses. Also
    inspect the charcoal canister and the seal on the fuel filler cap,
    as well as the connections between the fuel tank and engine
    (see Section 10)
Check the brake pedal height and freeplay (see Chapter 9).
Check the parking brake adjustment (see Section 12).
Check the brake pipes and hoses (see Sections 10 and 12)
Inspect the suspension and steering components (see Section 13)
Check the transfer case fluid level (see Section 4)
Check the rear differential fluid level (see Section 4)
Clean/replace the cabin air filter (see Section 17)

Every 40,000 km or 24 months

Check the cooling system (see Section 11)
Inspect and replace if necessary all underbonnet hoses. Also
    inspect the seal on the fuel filler cap and connections between
    the fuel tank and engine (see Section 10)
Change the brake fluid (see Section 20)
Check the automatic transaxle fluid level (see Section 4)
Change the rear differential lubricant (AWD models) (see Section
    25)
Change the transfer unit lubricant (AWD models with automatic
    transaxle) (see Section 24)

Every 80,000 km or 48 months

Replace the fuel filter, including the in-tank fuel filter (see Chapter 4)
Inspect and if noisy, adjust the valve clearance (see Section 22)
Replace the engine coolant (see Section 26)

Note: *First replace the coolant when the mileage reaches 160,000 km or 96 months. Then replace the coolant every 80,000 km or 48 months.*

Every 100,000 km or 60 months

Replace the spark plugs (see Section 27)
Check the tightness of the chassis bolts

Every 150,000 km or 90 months

Replace the timing belt (see Chapter 2A)

GSU40R and GSU45R models

Every 10,000 km or 6 months

Change the engine oil and oil filter (see Section 6)
Check the engine drivebelt (see Section 21)
Check the battery electrolyte condition (see Section 7)
Check the battery terminals (see Section 7)
Check and service the battery (see Section 7)
Check the driveshaft boots (see Section 13)
Check the tyre condition and pressure (see Section 5)
Check that all of the lights, horn and wipers and washers operate
Inspect (and replace, if necessary) the windshield wiper blades
   (see Section 9)

Every 20,000 km or 12 months

Inspect the exhaust system (see Section 14)
Clean/replace the engine air filter (see Section 15)
Check the front and rear brake pads (see Section 12)
Check the brake pipes and hoses (see Sections 10 and 12)
Inspect the suspension and steering components (see Section 13)
Check the transfer case fluid level (see Section 4)
Check the rear differential fluid level (see Section 4)
Clean/replace the cabin air filter (see Section 17)

Every 40,000 km or 24 months

Check the cooling system (see Section 11)
Inspect and replace if necessary all underbonnet hoses. Also
   inspect the seal on the fuel filler cap and connections between
   the fuel tank and engine (see Section 10)
Change the brake fluid (see Section 20)
Inspect the charcoal canister and associated hoses (see Chapter 6)
Inspect and replace if necessary all underbonnet hoses (see Section 10)
Check the brake pedal height and freeplay (see Chapter 9)
Check the parking brake adjustment (see Section 12)
Check the automatic transaxle fluid level (see Section 4)
Change the rear differential lubricant (AWD models) (see Section 25)
Change the transfer unit lubricant (AWD models with automatic transaxle) (see Section 24)

Every 80,000 km or 48 months

Replace the fuel filter, including the in-tank fuel filter (see Chapter 4)
Replace the engine coolant (see Section 26)
Note: *First replace the coolant when the mileage reaches 160,000 km or 96 months. Then replace the coolant every 80,000 km or 48 months.*

Every 100,000 km or 60 months

Replace the spark plugs (see Section 27)
Check the tightness of the chassis bolts

2   Introduction

This Chapter is designed to help the home mechanic maintain his vehicle for peak performance, economy, safety and long life.

Included is a master maintenance schedule, followed by sections dealing specifically with each item on the schedule. Visual checks, adjustments, component replacement and other helpful items are included. Refer to the accompanying illustrations of the engine compartment and the underside of the vehicle for the location of various components.

Servicing your vehicle in accordance with the mileage/time maintenance schedule and the following Sections will provide it with a planned maintenance program that should result in a long and reliable service life. This is a comprehensive plan, so maintaining some items but not others at the specified service intervals won't produce the same results.

As you service your vehicle, you will discover that many of the procedures can - and should - be grouped together because of the nature of the particular procedure you're performing or because of the close proximity of two otherwise unrelated components to one another.

For example, if the vehicle is raised for any reason, you should inspect the exhaust, suspension, steering and fuel systems while you're under the vehicle. When you're rotating the tyres, it makes good sense to check the brakes and wheel bearings since the wheels are already removed.

Finally, let's suppose you have to borrow or rent a torque wrench. Even if you only need to tighten the spark plugs, you might as well check the torque of as many critical fasteners as time allows.

The first step of this maintenance program is to prepare yourself before the actual work begins. Read through all sections pertinent to the procedures you're planning to do, then make a list of and gather together all the parts and tools you will need to do the job. If it looks as if you might run into problems during a particular segment of some procedure, seek advice from your local parts man or dealer service department.

3   Tune-up general information

The term tune-up is used in this manual to represent a combination of individual operations rather than one specific procedure.

If, from the time the vehicle is new, the routine maintenance schedule is followed closely and frequent checks are made of fluid levels and high wear items, as suggested throughout this manual, the engine will be kept in relatively good running condition and the need for additional work will be minimised.

More likely than not, however, there will be times when the engine is running poorly due to lack of regular maintenance. This is even more likely if a used vehicle, which has not received regular and frequent maintenance checks, is purchased. In such cases, an engine tune-up will be needed outside of the regular routine maintenance intervals.

The first step in any tune-up or engine diagnosis to help correct a poor running engine would be a cylinder compression check. A check of the engine compression (see Chapter 2C) will give valuable informa-

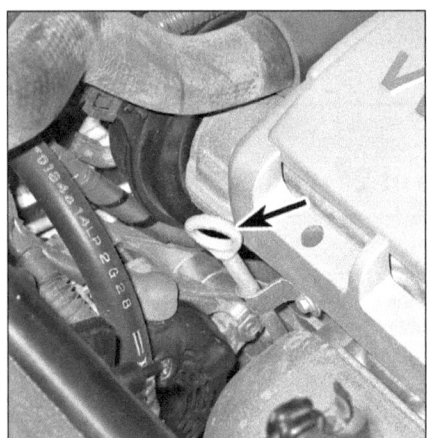

4.2 The engine oil dipstick is mounted on the front (radiator) side of the engine

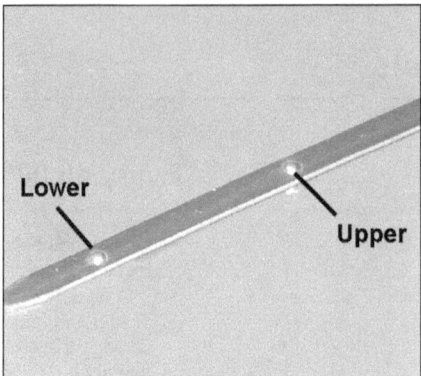

4.4 The oil level should be at or near the upper mark on the dipstick - if it isn't, add enough oil to bring the level to or near the upper mark (it takes 1.5 litres to raise the level from the lower mark to the upper mark)

4.6 The threaded oil filler cap is located on the valve cover - to prevent dirt from contaminating the engine, always make sure the area around this opening is clean before removing the cap

tion regarding the overall performance of many internal components and should be used as a basis for tune-up and repair procedures. If, for instance, a compression check indicates serious internal engine wear, a conventional tune-up will not help the running condition of the engine and would be a waste of time and money. Also in Chapter 2C is information on checking engine vacuum, which also gives information on the engine's state-of-tune and condition.

The following series of operations are those most often needed to bring a generally poor-running engine back into a proper state of tune.

Minor tune-up

Check all engine related fluids (Section 4)
Clean, inspect and test the battery
   (Section 7)
Check all underbonnet hoses (Section 10)
Check the cooling system (Section 11)
Check the air filter (Section 15)
Check and adjust the drivebelts (Section 21)

Major tune-up

All items listed under Minor tune-up, plus . . .
Replace the air filter (Section 15)
Check the fuel system (Section 16)
Replace the spark plugs (Section 27)
Check the charging system (Chapter 5)

---

4   Fluid level weekly checks

---

1   Fluids are an essential part of the lubrication, cooling, brake, clutch and other systems. Because these fluids gradually become depleted and/or contaminated during normal operation of the vehicle, they must be periodically replenished. See Recommended lubricants and fluids and Capacities in this Chapter's Specifications before adding fluid to any of the following components.

Note: *The vehicle must be on level ground*

before fluid levels can be checked.

Engine oil

Refer to illustrations 4.2, 4.4 and 4.6

2   The engine oil level is checked with a dipstick located at the front side of the engine **(see illustration)**. The dipstick extends through a metal tube from which it protrudes down into the engine oil pan.

3   The oil level should be checked before the vehicle has been driven, or about 5 minutes after the engine has been shut off. If the oil is checked immediately after driving the vehicle, some of the oil will remain in the upper engine components, producing an inaccurate reading on the dipstick.

4   Pull the dipstick from the tube and wipe all the oil from the end with a clean rag or paper towel. Insert the clean dipstick all the way back into its metal tube and pull it out again. Observe the oil at the end of the dipstick. At its highest point, the level should be between the lower and upper marks **(see illustration)**.

5   It takes about 1.5 litres to raise the level from the lower mark to the upper mark on the dipstick. Do not allow the level to drop below the lower mark or oil starvation may cause engine damage. Conversely, overfilling the engine (adding oil above the upper mark) may cause oil-fouled spark plugs, oil leaks or oil seal failures.

6   Remove the threaded cap from the valve cover to add oil **(see illustration)**. Use a funnel to prevent spills. After adding the oil, install the filler cap hand tight. Start the engine and look carefully for any small leaks around the oil filter or drain plug. Stop the engine and check the oil level again after it has had sufficient time to drain from the upper block and cylinder head galleys.

7   Checking the oil level is an important preventive maintenance step. A continually dropping oil level indicates oil leakage through damaged seals, from loose connections, or past worn rings or valve guides. If the oil

looks milky in colour or has water droplets in it, a cylinder head gasket may be blown. The engine should be checked immediately. The condition of the oil should also be checked. Each time you check the oil level, slide your thumb and index finger up the dipstick before wiping off the oil. If you see small dirt or metal particles clinging to the dipstick, the oil should be changed (see Section 6).

Engine coolant

Refer to illustrations 4.8a and 4.8b

Warning: *Do not allow antifreeze to come in contact with your skin or painted surfaces of the vehicle. Flush contaminated areas immediately with plenty of water. Don't store new coolant or leave old coolant lying around where it's accessible to children or pets - they're attracted by its sweet smell. Ingestion of even a small amount of coolant can be fatal! Wipe up garage floor and drip pan spills immediately. Keep antifreeze containers covered and repair cooling system leaks as soon as they're noticed.*

8   All models covered by this manual are equipped with a coolant recovery system. The coolant reservoir is connected by a hose to the base of the coolant filler cap **(see illustrations)**. If the coolant heats up during engine operation, coolant can escape through the pressurised filler cap and connecting hose into the reservoir. As the engine cools, the coolant is automatically drawn back into the cooling system to maintain the correct level.

9   The coolant level should be checked regularly. It must be between the Full and Low lines on the tank. The level will vary with the temperature of the engine. When the engine is cold, the coolant level should be at or slightly above the Low mark on the tank. Once the engine has warmed up, the level should be at or near the Full mark. If it isn't, allow the fluid in the tank to cool, then remove the cap from the reservoir and add coolant to bring the level up to the Full line. Use only the

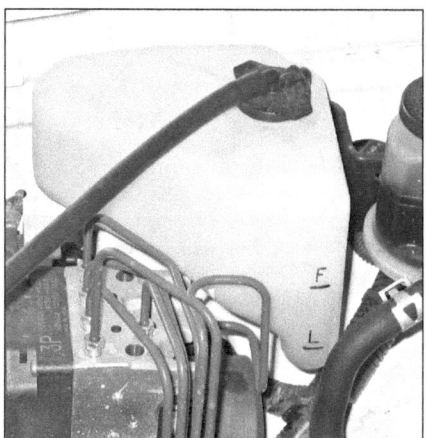

4.8a The coolant reservoir is located at the ride side of the engine compartment on early models. . .

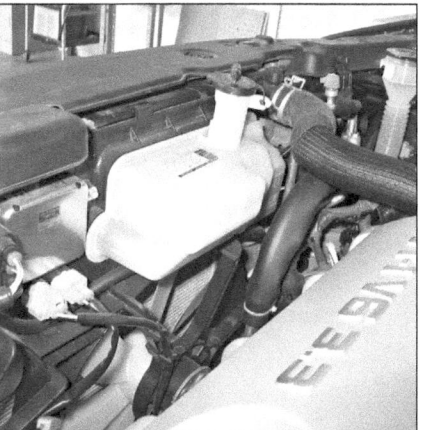

4.8b . . . and on later models it's located on the radiator

4.14 The windshield washer fluid reservoir is located at the right front corner of the engine compartment

type of coolant listed in this Chapter's Speci-fications or in your owner's manual. Do not use supplemental inhibitors or additives. If only a small amount of coolant is required to bring the system up to the proper level, water can be used. However, repeated additions of water will dilute the recommended anti-freeze and water solution. In order to maintain the proper ratio of antifreeze and water, it is advisable to top up the coolant level with the correct mixture.

Note: *The coolant recommended by the manufacturer is premixed to the correct ratio, so water should not be mixed with it when adding coolant. If you're using a non-Toyota coolant, check the container carefully.*

10   If the coolant level drops within a short time after replenishment, there may be a leak in the system. Inspect the radiator, hoses, engine coolant filler cap, drain plugs, air bleeder plugs and water pump. If no leak is evident, have the radiator cap pressure tested.

Warning: *To prevent scalding, use caution when releasing the radiator cap if the engine is warm. Squeeze the upper radiator hose. If resistance is felt, the system is pressurised and the cap should not be removed until the radiator hose can easily be squeezed together. Escaping steam and scalding liquid could cause serious injury.*

Note: *If the engine has overheated allow, the engine to cool for at least 30 minutes and fill the system with coolant while the engine is running to avoid cracking the cylinder heads or block.*

11   If it is necessary to open the radiator cap, wait until the system has cooled completely, then wrap a thick cloth around the cap and turn it to the first stop. If any steam escapes, wait until the system has cooled further, then remove the cap.

12   When checking the coolant level, always note its condition. It should be relatively clear. If it is brown or rust colored, the system should be drained, flushed and refilled. Even if the coolant appears to be normal, the corro-

sion inhibitors wear out with use, so it must be replaced at the specified intervals.

13   Do not allow antifreeze to come in con-tact with your skin or painted surfaces of the vehicle. Flush contacted areas immediately with plenty of water.

Windshield washer fluid

Refer to illustration 4.14

14   Fluid for the windshield washer system is stored in a plastic reservoir which is located at the right front corner of the engine compart-ment **(see illustration)**. In milder climates, plain water can be used to top up the reser-voir, but the reservoir should be kept no more than two-thirds full to allow for expansion should the water freeze. In colder climates, the use of a specially designed windshield washer fluid, available at your dealer and any auto parts store, will help lower the freezing point of the fluid. Mix the solution with water in accordance with the manufacturer's direc-tions on the container. Do not use regular antifreeze. It will damage the vehicle's paint.

Brake fluid

Refer to illustration 4.16

15   The brake master cylinder is mounted in the RH rear corner of the engine compart-ment.

16   To check the fluid level of the brake mas-ter cylinder reservoir, simply look at the MAX and MIN marks on the reservoir **(see illustra-tion)**. The level should be within the specified distance from the maximum fill line.

17   If the level is low, wipe the top of the res-ervoir cover with a clean rag to prevent con-tamination of the brake system before lifting the cover.

18   Add only the specified brake fluid to the brake reservoir (refer to recommended lubri-cants and fluids in this Chapter's Specifica-tions or your owner's manual). Mixing differ-ent types of brake fluid can damage the sys-tem. Fill the brake master cylinder reservoir only to the dotted line - this brings the fluid to the correct level when you put the cover back on.

4.16 The brake fluid should be kept between the Min and Max marks on the reservoir

Warning: *Use caution when filling the reservoir - brake fluid can harm your eyes and damage painted surfaces. Do not use brake fluid that has been opened for more than one year or has been left open. Brake fluid absorbs moisture from the air. Excess moisture can cause a dangerous loss of braking.*

19   While the reservoir cap is removed, inspect the master cylinder reservoir for con-tamination. If deposits, dirt particles or water droplets are present, the system should be drained and refilled (see Section 20).

20   After filling the reservoir to the proper level, make sure the lid is properly seated to prevent fluid leakage and/or system pressure loss.

21   The brake fluid in the master cylinder will drop slightly as the brake pads at each wheel wear down during normal operation. If the master cylinder requires repeated replenish-ing to keep it at the proper level, this is an indi-cation of leakage in the brake system, which should be corrected immediately. Check all brake lines and connections, along with the wheel cylinders and booster (see Section 12 for more information).

4.26 The power steering fluid reservoir is located on the right side of the engine compartment - the reservoir is translucent so the fluid level can be checked either hot or cold without removing the cap - MCU28R models

4.32a The automatic transaxle dipstick on MCU28R models is next to the battery

4.32b On the GSU40R/GSU45R, the transaxle dipstick is below the air intake

22   If, upon checking the master cylinder fluid level, you discover the reservoir empty or nearly empty, the brake system should be thoroughly inspected for leaks (see Chapter 9).

Power steering fluid

Refer to illustrations 4.26

Note: *Models to 2007 are equipped with hydraulic power steering. however, models from 2007 (GSU40R/GSU45R series) have electric power assist steering. These vehicles will not be equipped with a power steering fluid reservoir. Consult with your owner's manual for information on your power steering system.*

23   Unlike manual steering, the power steering system relies on fluid which may, over a period of time, require replenishing.

24   The fluid reservoir for the power steering pump is located on the right (passenger side) inner fender panel near the front of the engine.

25   For the check, the front wheels should be pointed straight ahead and the engine should be off.

26   The reservoir is translucent plastic and the fluid level can be checked visually **(see illustration)**.

27   If additional fluid is required, pour the specified type directly into the reservoir, using a funnel to prevent spills.

28   If the reservoir requires frequent fluid additions, all power steering hoses, hose connections, the power steering pump and the rack and pinion assembly should be carefully checked for leaks.

Automatic transaxle fluid

Refer to illustrations 4.32a, 4.32b and 4.34

29   The level of the automatic transaxle fluid should be carefully maintained. Low fluid level can lead to slipping or loss of drive, while overfilling can cause foaming, loss of fluid and transaxle damage.

30   The transaxle fluid level should only be checked when the transaxle is hot (at its normal operating temperature). If the vehicle has just been driven over 15 kilometres and the fluid temperature is 70 to 80 degrees C, the transaxle is hot.

Caution: *If the vehicle has just been driven for a long time at high speed or in city traffic in hot weather, or if it has been pulling a trailer, an accurate fluid level reading cannot be obtained. Allow the fluid to cool down for about 30 minutes.*

31   If the vehicle has not been driven, park the vehicle on level ground, set the parking brake, then start the engine and bring it to operating temperature. While the engine is idling, depress the brake pedal and move the selector lever through all the gear ranges, beginning and ending in Park.

32   With the engine still idling, remove the dipstick from its tube **(see illustrations)**. Check the level of the fluid on the dipstick and note its condition.

33   Wipe the fluid from the dipstick with a clean rag and reinsert it back into the filler tube until the cap seats.

34   Pull the dipstick out again and note the fluid level **(see illustration)**. If the transmission is cold, the level should be in the COLD or COOL range on the dipstick. If it is hot, the fluid level should be in the HOT range. If the

level is at the low side of either range, add the specified automatic transmission fluid through the dipstick tube with a funnel.

35   Add just enough of the recommended fluid to fill the transmission to the proper level. It takes about 1.5 litres to raise the level from the low mark to the high mark when the fluid is hot, so add the fluid a little at a time and keep checking the level until it is correct.

36   The condition of the fluid should also be checked along with the level. If the fluid at the end of the dipstick (if equipped) is black or a dark reddish brown colour, or if it emits a burned smell, the fluid should be changed (see Section 23). If you are in doubt about the condition of the fluid, purchase some new fluid and compare the two for colour and smell.

Transfer case lubricant (AWD models)

Refer to illustration 4.37

Warning: *If the vehicle is equipped with electronically modulated air suspension, make sure that the height control switch is turned off.*

37   The transfer case does not have a dipstick. To check the fluid level, raise the vehicle and support it securely on jackstands (see Jacking and Towing). On the back side of the

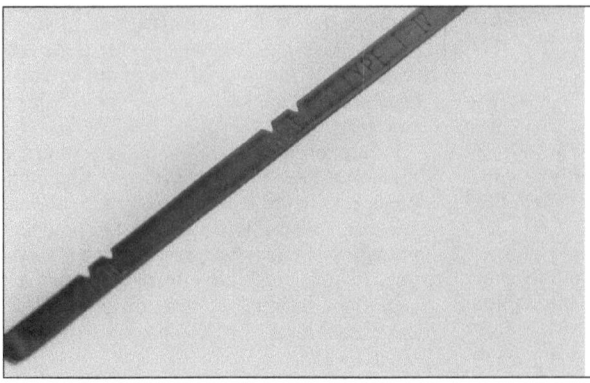

4.34 If the automatic transaxle fluid is cold, the level should be between the lower two notches; if it's at normal operating temperature, the level should be between the upper notches on the dipstick

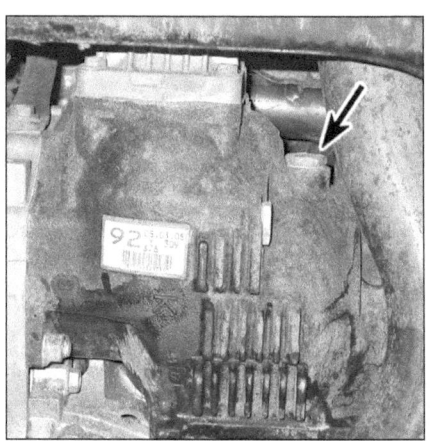

4.37 Location of the transfer case check/ fill plug

transfer case housing, you will see a plug **(see illustration)** - remove it. If the lubricant level is correct, it should be up to the lower edge of the hole.

38   If the transaxle needs more lubricant (if the level is not up to the hole), use a syringe or a gear oil pump to add more. Stop filling the transaxle when the lubricant begins to run out the hole.

39   Install the plug and tighten it securely. Drive the vehicle a short distance, then check for leaks.

Rear differential lubricant level (AWD models)

Refer to illustration 4.41

40   Raise the vehicle and support it securely on jackstands (see Jacking and Towing).

Warning: *If the vehicle is equipped with electronically modulated air suspension, make sure that the height control switch is turned off.*

41   Using the appropriate wrench, unscrew the plug from the rear differential **(see illustration)**.

42   Use your little finger to reach inside the housing to feel the lubricant level. The level should be at or near the bottom of the plug hole. If it isn't, add the recommended lubricant through the plug hole with a syringe or squeeze bottle.

43   Install the plug and tighten it securely. Check for leaks after the first few miles of driving.

---

5   Tyre and tyre pressure checks

Refer to illustrations 5.2, 5.3, 5.4a, 5.4b and 5.8

1   Periodic inspection of the tyres may spare you from the inconvenience of being stranded with a flat tyre. It can also provide you with vital information regarding possible problems in the steering and suspension systems before major damage occurs.

2   Normal tread wear can be monitored with a simple, inexpensive device known as a tread depth indicator **(see illustration)**. When the tread depth reaches approximately 1.5 mm, replace the tyre(s) (preferably long before that).

3   Note any abnormal tread wear **(see illustration)**. Tread pattern irregularities such as cupping, flat spots and more wear on one side than the other are indications of front end alignment and/or balance problems. If any of these conditions are noted, take the vehicle

4.41 Location of the rear differential check/fill plug

5.2 Use a tyre tread depth gauge to monitor tyre wear - they are available at auto parts stores and service stations and cost very little

UNDERINFLATION

INCORRECT TOE-IN OR EXTREME CAMBER

CUPPING

Cupping may be caused by:
- Underinflation and/or mechanical irregularities such as out-of-balance condition of wheel and/or tire, and bent or damaged wheel.
- Loose or worn steering tie-rod or steering idler arm.
- Loose, damaged or worn front suspension parts.

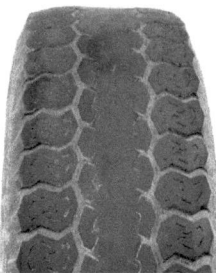

OVERINFLATION

FEATHERING DUE TO MISALIGNMENT

5.3 This chart will help you determine the condition of your tyres, the probable cause(s) of abnormal wear and the corrective action necessary

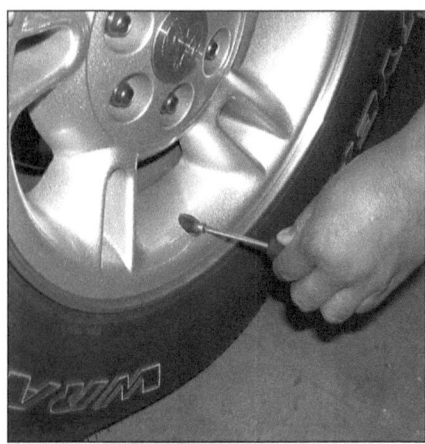

5.4a If a tyre loses air on a steady basis, check the valve core first to make sure it's snug (special inexpensive wrenches are commonly available at auto parts stores)

5.4b If the valve core is tight, raise the corner of the vehicle with the low tyre and spray a soapy water solution onto the tread as the tyre is turned slowly - slow leaks will cause small bubbles to appear

5.8 To extend the life of your tyres, check the air pressure at least once a week with an accurate gauge (don't forget the spare!)

to a tyre shop or service station to correct the problem.

4   Look closely for cuts, punctures and embedded nails or tacks. Sometimes a tyre will hold its air pressure for a short time or leak down very slowly even after a nail has embedded itself into the tread. If a slow leak persists, check the valve stem core to make sure it is tight **(see illustration)**. Examine the tread for an object that may have embedded itself into the tyre or for a "plug" that may have begun to leak (radial tyre punctures are repaired with a plug that is fitted in a puncture). If a puncture is suspected, it can be easily verified by spraying a solution of soapy water onto the puncture area **(see illustration)**. The soapy solution will bubble if there is a leak. Unless the puncture is inordinately large, a tyre shop or gas station can usually repair the punctured tyre.

5   Carefully inspect the inner sidewall of each tyre for evidence of brake fluid leakage. If you see any, inspect the brakes immediately.

6   Correct tyre air pressure adds miles to the lifespan of the tyres, improves mileage

and enhances overall ride quality. Tyre pressure cannot be accurately estimated by looking at a tyre, particularly if it is a radial. A tyre pressure gauge is therefore essential. Keep an accurate gauge in the glovebox. The pressure gauges fitted to the nozzles of air hoses at gas stations are often inaccurate.

7   Always check tyre pressure when the tyres are cold. "Cold," in this case, means the vehicle has not been driven over a mile in the three hours preceding a tyre pressure check. A pressure rise of four to eight pounds is not uncommon once the tyres are warm.

8   Unscrew the valve cap protruding from the wheel or hubcap and push the gauge firmly onto the valve **(see illustration)**. Note the reading on the gauge and compare this figure to the recommended tyre pressure shown on the tyre placard in the glovebox. Be sure to reinstall the valve cap to keep dirt and moisture out of the valve stem mechanism. Check all four tyres and, if necessary, add enough air to bring them up to the recommended pressure levels.

9   Don't forget to keep the spare tyre inflated to the specified pressure (consult your

owner's manual). Note that the air pressure specified for a compact spare is significantly higher than the pressure of the regular tyres.

---

6   Engine oil and oil filter change

Refer to illustrations 6.2 and 6.7

Warning: *If the vehicle is equipped with electronically modulated air suspension, make sure that the height control switch is turned off.*

1   Frequent oil changes are the best preventive maintenance the home mechanic can give the engine, because aging oil becomes diluted and contaminated, which leads to premature engine wear.

2   Make sure that you have all the necessary tools before you begin this procedure **(see illustration)**. You should also have plenty of rags or newspapers handy for mopping up any spills.

3   Park the vehicle on a level spot. Start the engine and allow it to reach its normal operating temperature (the needle on the tem-

---

6.2 These tools are required when changing the engine oil and filter

*1 **Drain pan** - It should be fairly shallow in depth, but wide in order to prevent spills*

*2 **Rubber gloves** - When removing the drain plug and filter, it is inevitable that you will get oil on your hands (the gloves will prevent burns)*

*3 **Breaker bar** - Sometimes the oil drain plug is pretty tight and a long breaker bar is needed to loosen it*

*4 **Socket** - To be used with the breaker bar or a ratchet (must be the correct size to fit the drain plug)*

*5 **Filter wrench** - This is a metal band-type wrench, which requires clearance around the filter to be effective*

*6 **Filter wrench** - This type fits on the bottom of the filter and can be turned with a ratchet or beaker bar (different size wrenches are available for different types of filters)*

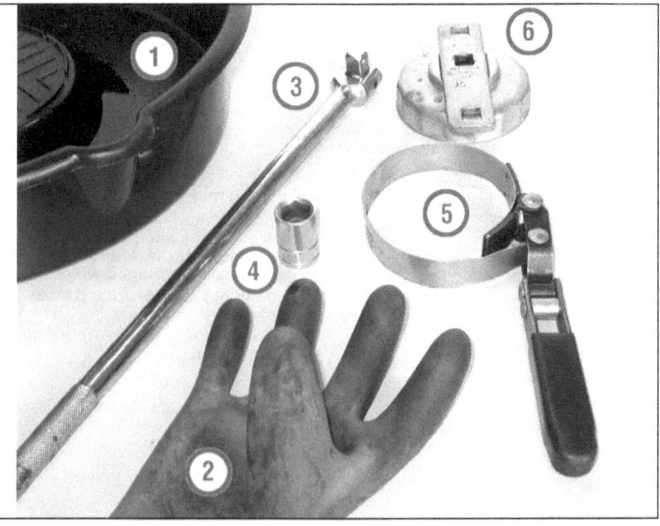

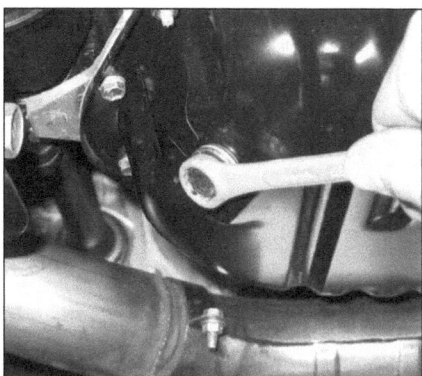

6.7 Use the proper size box-end wrench or socket to remove the oil drain plug without rounding off the corners

6.12 Using a filter tool to loosen a spin-on oil filter. Loosen in an anticlockwise direction - 3.3 litre engines

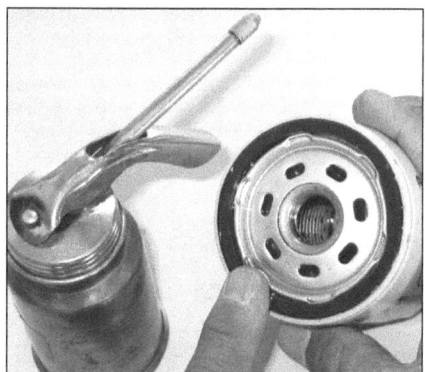

6.14 Lubricate the oil filter gasket with clean engine oil before installing the filter on the engine

perature gauge should be at least above the bottom mark). Warm oil and sludge will flow out more easily. Turn off the engine when it's warmed up.

4   Remove the oil filler cap (see Section 4).
5   Raise the vehicle and support it securely on jackstands (see Jacking and Towing).

Warning: *To avoid personal injury, never get beneath the vehicle when it is supported only by a jack. The jack provided with your vehicle is designed solely for raising the vehicle to remove and replace the wheels. Always use jackstands to support the vehicle when it becomes necessary to place your body underneath the vehicle.*

6   If this is your first oil change, get under the vehicle and familiarise yourself with the location of the oil drain plug. The engine and exhaust components will be warm during the actual work, so try to anticipate any potential problems before the engine and accessories are hot.
7   Being careful not to touch the hot exhaust components, place the drain pan under the drain plug in the bottom of the pan and remove the plug **(see illustration)**. You may want to wear gloves while unscrewing

the plug the final few turns if the engine is really hot.
8   Allow the old oil to drain into the pan. It may be necessary to move the pan farther under the engine as the oil flow slows to a trickle. Inspect the old oil for the presence of metal shavings and chips.
9   After all the oil has drained, wipe off the drain plug with a clean rag. Even minute metal particles clinging to the plug would immediately contaminate the new oil.
10   Clean the area around the drain plug opening, reinstall the plug and tighten it to the torque listed in this Chapter's Specifications.
11   Move the drain pan into position under the oil filter.

3MZ-FE engines

Refer to illustrations 6.12 and 6.14

12   Loosen the oil filter **(see illustration)** by turning it counterclockwise with the filter wrench. Any standard filter wrench should work. Once the filter is loose, use your hands to unscrew it from the block. Just as the filter is detached from the block, immediately tilt the open end up to prevent the oil inside the filter from spilling out.

Warning: *The engine exhaust manifold may still be hot, so be careful.*

13   With a clean rag, wipe off the mounting surface on the block. If a residue of old oil is allowed to remain, it will smoke when the block is heated up. It will also prevent the new filter from seating properly. Also make sure that none of the old gasket remains stuck to the mounting surface. It can be removed with a scraper if necessary.
14   Compare the old filter with the new one to make sure they are the same type. Smear some engine oil on the rubber gasket of the new filter and screw it into place **(see illustration)**.
15   Because over-tightening the filter will damage the gasket, do not use a filter wrench to tighten the filter. Tighten it by hand until the gasket contacts the seating surface, then seat the filter by giving it an additional 3/4 turn. Lower the vehicle.

2GR-FE engines

Refer to illustrations 6.16a, 6.16b and 6.16c

16   Use a ratchet with an extension to remove the plug from the bottom of the oil filter housing, being careful to minimise spillage

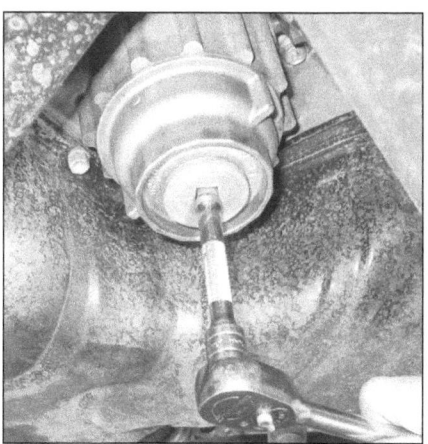

6.16a Use a 3/8-inch drive extension to remove the oil filter housing drain plug - the entire filter housing can be removed instead, but it creates more spillage

6.16b The filter housing can be drained by inserting a blunt tool to lift the drain valve - be sure to have the drain pan centred under the filter

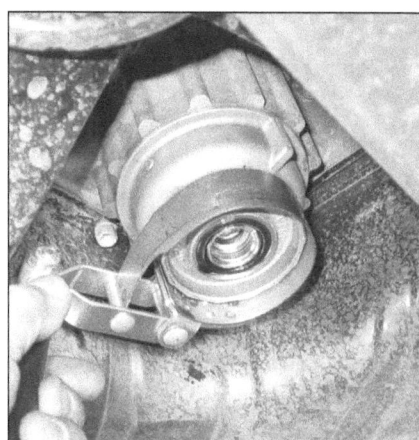

6.16c The main filter housing can usually be unscrewed by hand - if it's stuck you'll have to use an oil filter wrench, but be careful as the housing can be easily damaged

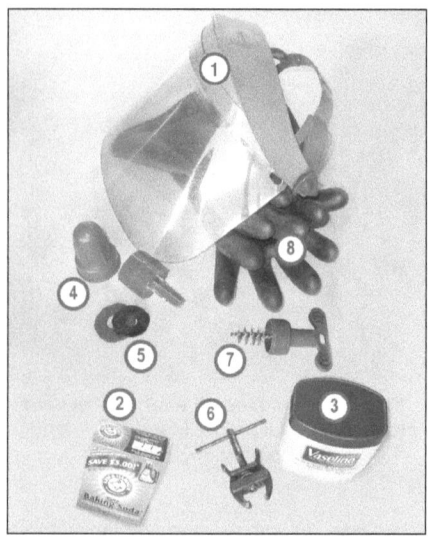

7.1   Tools and materials required for battery maintenance

1   *Face shield/safety goggles* - *When removing corrosion with a brush, the acidic particles can easily fly up into your eyes*
2   *Baking soda* - *A solution of baking soda and water can be used to neutralise corrosion*
3   *Petroleum jelly* - *A layer of this on the battery posts will help prevent corrosion*
4   *Battery post/cable cleaner* - *This wire brush cleaning tool will remove all traces of corrosion from the battery posts and cable clamps*
5   *Treated felt washers* - *Placing one of these on each post, directly under the cable clamps, will help prevent corrosion*
6   *Puller* - *Sometimes the cable clamps are very difficult to pull off the posts, even after the nut/bolt has been completely loosened. This tool pulls the clamp straight up and off the post without damage*
7   *Battery post/cable cleaner* - *Here is another cleaning tool which is a slightly different version of number 4 above, but it does the same thing*
8   *Rubber gloves* - *Another safety item to consider when servicing the battery; remember that's acid inside the battery*

(see illustration). Use a blunt tool to push up the inner valve and allow the canister to drain **(see illustration)**. Unscrew the main oil filter housing. If it's too tight to be removed by hand, you can use an oil filter wrench **(see illustration)**.

Note: *A special tool is available for this that includes a drain hose in order to make the job as clean as possible.*

17   Remove the filter element and the large O-ring from the housing.

7.6a   Battery terminal corrosion usually appears as light, fluffy powder

Note: *Don't use a metal tool to remove the O-ring, as this may scratch the soft housing.*

18   Carefully clean all components and the engine block sealing area. Install a new O-ring and filter, then screw the assembly back onto the engine. Tighten it to the torque listed in this Chapter's Specifications. If you removed the drain plug, clean it thoroughly, install a new O-ring and tighten the plug to the torque listed in this Chapter's Specifications. Lower the vehicle.

All models

19   Add new oil to the engine through the oil filler cap in the valve cover. Use a funnel to prevent oil from spilling onto the top of the engine. Pour 4 litres (3MZ-FE engine) or 5.5 litres (2GR-FE engine) of fresh oil into the engine. Wait a few minutes to allow the oil to drain into the pan, then check the level on the oil dipstick (see Section 4 if necessary). If the oil level is at or near the F mark, install the filler cap hand tight, start the engine and allow the new oil to circulate.
20   Allow the engine to run for about a minute. While the engine is running, look under the vehicle and check for leaks at the oil pan drain plug and around the oil filter. If either is leaking, stop the engine and tighten the plug or filter slightly.
21   Wait a few minutes to allow the oil to trickle down into the pan, then recheck the level on the dipstick and, if necessary, add enough oil to bring the level to the F mark.
22   During the first few trips after an oil change, make it a point to check frequently for leaks and proper oil level.
23   The old oil drained from the engine cannot be reused in its present state and should be discarded. Oil reclamation centres, auto garages and gas stations will normally accept the oil, which can be refined and used again. After the oil has cooled, it can be drained into

a suitable container (capped plastic jugs, topped bottles etc.) for transport to one of these disposal sites.

---

7   Battery check, maintenance and charging

Refer to illustrations 7.1, 7.6a, 7.6b, 7.7a and 7.7b

Warning: *Certain precautions must be followed when checking and servicing the battery. Hydrogen gas, which is highly flammable, is always present in the battery cells, so keep lighted tobacco and all other open flames and sparks away from the battery. The electrolyte inside the battery is actually dilute sulfuric acid, which will cause injury if splashed on your skin or in your eyes. It will also ruin clothes and painted surfaces. When removing the battery cables, always detach the negative cable first and hook it up last!*

Maintenance

1   A routine preventive maintenance program for the battery in your vehicle is the only way to ensure quick and reliable starts. But before performing any battery maintenance, make sure that you have the proper equipment necessary to work safely around the battery **(see illustration)**.
2   There are also several precautions that should be taken whenever battery maintenance is performed. Before servicing the battery, always turn the engine and all accessories off and disconnect the cable from the negative terminal of the battery.
3   The battery produces hydrogen gas, which is both flammable and explosive. Never create a spark, smoke or light a match around the battery. Always charge the battery in a ventilated area.
4   Electrolyte contains poisonous and corrosive sulfuric acid. Do not allow it to get in your eyes, on your skin on your clothes. Never ingest it. Wear protective safety glasses when working near the battery. Keep children away from the battery.
5   Note the external condition of the battery. If the positive terminal and cable clamp on your vehicle's battery is equipped with a rubber protector, make sure that it's not torn or damaged. It should completely cover the terminal. Look for any corroded or loose connections, cracks in the case or cover or loose hold-down clamps. Also check the entire length of each cable for cracks and frayed conductors.
6   If corrosion, which looks like white, fluffy deposits **(see illustration)** is evident, particularly around the terminals, the battery should be removed for cleaning. Loosen the cable clamp bolts with a wrench, being careful to remove the ground cable first, and slide them off the terminals **(see illustration)**. Then disconnect the hold-down clamp bolt and nut, remove the clamp and lift the battery from the engine compartment.

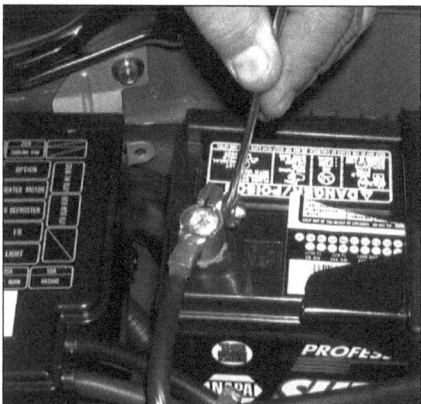

7.6b Removing a cable from the battery post with a wrench - sometimes a pair of special battery pliers are required for this procedure if corrosion has caused deterioration of the nut hex (always remove the ground (-) cable first and hook it up last!)

7.7a When cleaning the cable clamps, all corrosion must be removed (the inside of the clamp is tapered to match the taper on the post, so don't remove too much material)

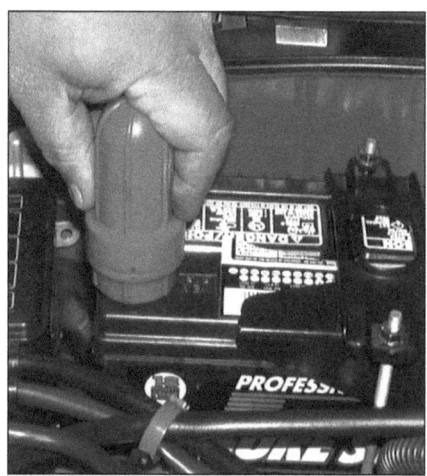

7.7b Regardless of the type of tool used to clean the battery posts, a clean, shiny surface should be the result

7   Clean the cable clamps thoroughly with a battery brush or a terminal cleaner and a solution of warm water and baking soda **(see illustration)**. Wash the terminals and the top of the battery case with the same solution but make sure that the solution doesn't get into the battery. When cleaning the cables, terminals and battery top, wear safety goggles and rubber gloves to prevent any solution from coming in contact with your eyes or hands. Wear old clothes too - even diluted, sulfuric acid splashed onto clothes will burn holes in them. If the terminals have been extensively corroded, clean them up with a terminal cleaner **(see illustration)**. Thoroughly wash all cleaned areas with plain water.

8   Make sure that the battery tray is in good condition and the hold-down clamp bolts are tight. If the battery is removed from the tray, make sure no parts remain in the bottom of the tray when the battery is reinstalled. When reinstalling the hold-down clamp bolts, do not overtighten them.

9   Any metal parts of the vehicle damaged by corrosion should be covered with a zinc-based primer, then painted.

10   Information on removing and installing the battery can be found in Chapter 5. Information on jump starting can be found at the front of this manual. For more detailed battery checking procedures, refer to the Haynes Automotive Electrical Manual.

Charging

Warning: *When batteries are being charged, hydrogen gas, which is very explosive and flammable, is produced. Do not smoke or allow open flames near a battery. Wear eye protection when near the battery during charging. Also, make sure the charger is unplugged before connecting or disconnecting the battery from the charger.*

Note: *The manufacturer recommends the battery be removed from the vehicle for charging because the gas that escapes during*

this procedure can damage the paint. Fast charging with the battery cables connected can result in damage to the electrical system.

11   Slow-rate charging is the best way to restore a battery that's discharged to the point where it will not start the engine. It's also a good way to maintain the battery charge in a vehicle that's only driven a few miles between starts. Maintaining the battery charge is particularly important in the winter when the battery must work harder to start the engine and electrical accessories that drain the battery are in greater use.

12   It's best to use a one or two-amp battery charger (sometimes called a "trickle" charger). They are the safest and put the least strain on the battery. They are also the least expensive. For a faster charge, you can use a higher amperage charger, but don't use one rated more than 1/10th the amp/hour rating of the battery. Rapid boost charges that claim to restore the power of the battery in one to two hours are hardest on the battery and can damage batteries not in good condition. This type of charging should only be used in emergency situations.

13   The average time necessary to charge a battery should be listed in the instructions that come with the charger. As a general rule, a trickle charger will charge a battery in 12 to 16 hours.

14   Remove all the cell caps (if equipped) and cover the holes with a clean cloth to prevent spattering electrolyte. Disconnect the negative battery cable and hook the battery charger cable clamps up to the battery posts (positive to positive, negative to negative), then plug in the charger. Make sure it is set at 12 volts if it has a selector switch.

15   If you're using a charger with a rate higher than two amps, check the battery regularly during charging to make sure it doesn't overheat. If you're using a trickle charger, you can safely let the battery charge overnight after you've checked it regularly for the first

couple of hours.

16   If the battery has removable cell caps, measure the specific gravity with a hydrometer every hour during the last few hours of the charging cycle. Hydrometers are available inexpensively from auto parts stores - follow the instructions that come with the hydrometer. Consider the battery charged when there's no change in the specific gravity reading for two hours and the electrolyte in the cells is gassing (bubbling) freely. The specific gravity reading from each cell should be very close to the others. If not, the battery probably has a bad cell(s).

17   Some batteries with sealed tops have built-in hydrometers on the top that indicate the state of charge by the colour displayed in the hydrometer window. Normally, a bright-colored hydrometer indicates a full charge and a dark hydrometer indicates the battery still needs charging.

18   If the battery has a sealed top and no built-in hydrometer, you can hook up a voltmeter across the battery terminals to check the charge. A fully charged battery should read 12.6 volts or higher after the surface charge has been removed.

19   Further information on the battery and jump starting can be found in Chapter 5 and at the front of this manual.

8   Tyre rotation

Refer to illustrations 8.2a and 8.2b

Warning: *If the vehicle is equipped with electronically modulated air suspension, make sure that the height control switch is turned off.*

1   The tyres should be rotated at the specified intervals and whenever uneven wear is noticed. Since the vehicle will be raised and the tyres removed anyway, check the brakes (see Section 12) at this time.

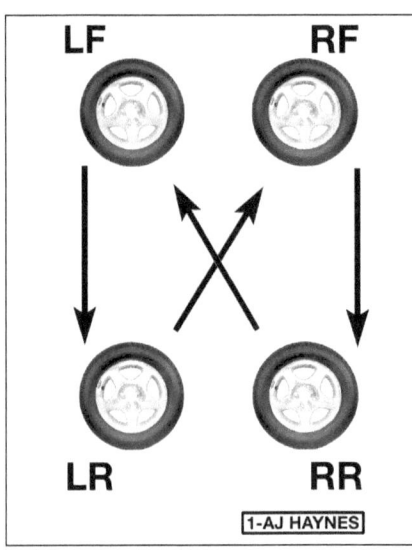

8.2a Four-tyre rotation pattern

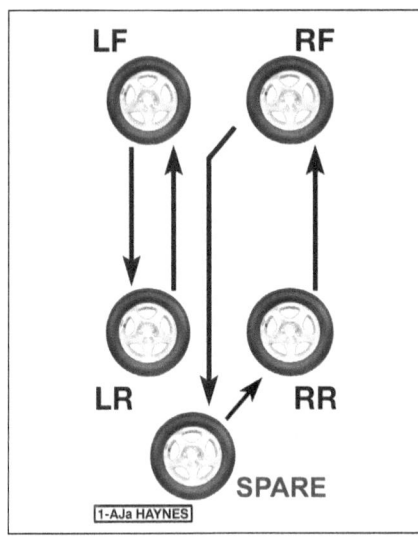

8.2b Five-tyre rotation pattern (to be used only if the spare tyre is the same as the other four)

2   Radial tyres must be rotated in a specific pattern (**see illustrations**).
3   Refer to the information in Jacking and towing at the front of this manual for the proper procedures to follow when raising the vehicle and changing a tyre. If the brakes are to be checked, do not apply the parking brake as stated. Make sure the tyres are blocked to prevent the vehicle from rolling.
4   Preferably, the entire vehicle should be raised at the same time. This can be done on a hoist or by jacking up each corner and then lowering the vehicle onto jackstands placed under the frame rails. Always use four jackstands and make sure the vehicle is firmly supported.
5   After rotation, check and adjust the tyre pressures as necessary and be sure to check the lug nut tightness.
6   For further information on the wheels and tyres, refer to Chapter 10.

9   Wiper blade inspection and replacement

Refer to illustrations 9.5a and 9.5b

1   The wiper and blade assembly should be inspected periodically for damage, loose components and cracked or worn blade elements.
2   Road film can build up on the wiper blades and affect their efficiency, so they should be washed regularly with a mild detergent solution.
3   The action of the wiping mechanism can loosen bolts, nuts and fasteners, so they should be checked and tightened, as necessary, at the same time the wiper blades are checked.
4   If the wiper blade elements are cracked, worn or warped, or no longer clean adequately, they should be replaced with new ones.

5   Lift the arm assembly away from the glass for clearance, press the release lever, then slide the wiper blade assembly out of the hook at the end of the arm (**see illustrations**).
6   Attach the new wiper to the arm. Connection can be confirmed by an audible click.

10   Underbonnet hose check and replacement

Warning: *Replacement of air conditioning hoses must be left to a dealer service department or air conditioning shop that has the equipment to depressurise the system safely. Never remove air conditioning components or hoses until the system has been evacuated and the refrigerant recovered by a dealer service department or air-conditioning shop.*

General

1   High temperatures in the engine compartment can cause the deterioration of the rubber and plastic hoses used for engine, accessory and emission systems operation. Periodic inspection should be made for cracks, loose clamps, material hardening and leaks.
2   Information specific to the cooling system hoses can be found in Section 11.
3   Some, but not all, hoses are secured to the fittings with clamps. Where clamps are used, check to be sure they haven't lost their tension, allowing the hose to leak. If clamps aren't used, make sure the hose has not expanded and/or hardened where it slips over the fitting, allowing it to leak.

Vacuum hoses

4   It's quite common for vacuum hoses, especially those in the emissions system, to be colour coded or identified by colored stripes moulded into them. Various systems require hoses with different wall thickness, collapse resistance and temperature resist-

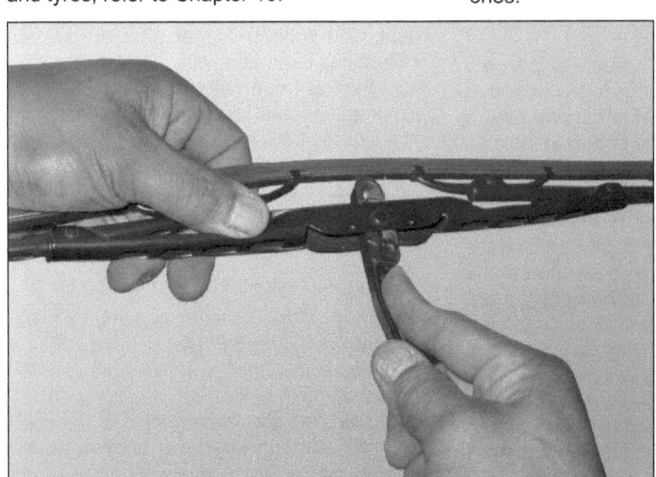

9.5a To release the blade holder, push the release pin . . .

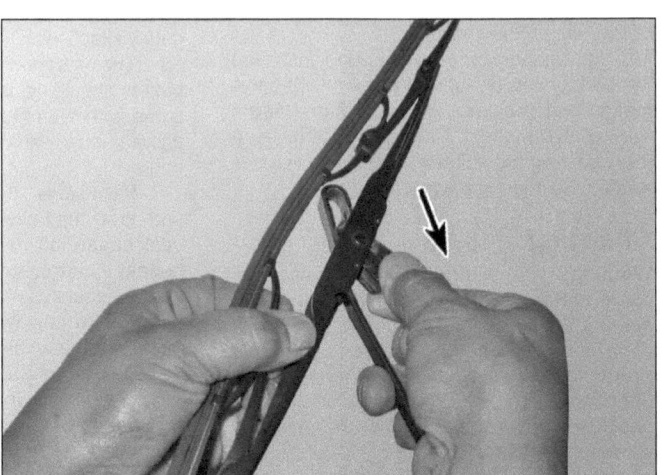

9.5b . . . and pull the wiper blade in the direction of the arrow to separate it from the arm

ance. When replacing hoses, be sure the new ones are made of the same material.

5   Often the only effective way to check a hose is to remove it completely from the vehicle. If more than one hose is removed, be sure to label the hoses and fittings to ensure correct installation.

6   When checking vacuum hoses, be sure to include any plastic T-fittings in the check. Inspect the fittings for cracks and the hose where it fits over the fitting for distortion, which could cause leakage.

7   A small piece of vacuum hose (6 mm inside diameter) can be used as a stethoscope to detect vacuum leaks. Hold one end of the hose to your ear and probe around vacuum hoses and fittings, listening for the "hissing" sound characteristic of a vacuum leak. **Warning:** *When probing with the vacuum hose stethoscope, be very careful not to come into contact with moving engine components such as the drivebelts, cooling fan, etc.*

Fuel hose

Warning: *Gasoline is extremely flammable, so take extra precautions when you work on any part of the fuel system. Don't smoke or allow open flames or bare light bulbs near the work area, and don't work in a garage where a gas-type appliance (such as a water heater or a clothes dryer) is present. Since gasoline is carcinogenic, wear fuel resistant gloves when there's a possibility of being exposed to fuel, and, if you spill any fuel on your skin, rinse it off immediately with soap and water. Mop up any spills immediately and do not store fuel-soaked rags where they could ignite. The fuel system is under constant pressure, so, if any fuel lines are to be disconnected, the fuel pressure in the system must be relieved first. When you perform any kind of work on the fuel system, wear safety glasses and have a Class B type fire extinguisher on hand.*

8   Check all rubber fuel lines for deterioration and chafing. Check especially for cracks in areas where the hose bends and just before fittings, such as where a hose attaches to the fuel filter.

9   High quality fuel line should be used for fuel line replacement. Never, under any circumstances, use unreinforced vacuum line, clear plastic tubing or water hose for fuel lines.

10   Spring-type clamps are commonly used on fuel lines. These clamps often lose their tension over a period of time, and can be "sprung" during removal. Replace all spring-type clamps with screw clamps whenever a hose is replaced.

Metal lines

11   Sections of metal line are often used for fuel line between the fuel pump and fuel injection unit. Check carefully to be sure the line has not been bent or crimped and that cracks have not started in the line.

12   If a section of metal fuel line must be replaced, only seamless steel tubing should

be used, since copper and aluminium tubing don't have the strength necessary to withstand normal engine vibration.

13   Check the metal brake lines where they enter the master cylinder and brake proportioning unit (if used) for cracks in the lines or loose fittings. Any sign of brake fluid leakage calls for an immediate thorough inspection of the brake system.

11   Cooling system check

Refer to illustration 11.4

1   Many major engine failures can be attributed to a faulty cooling system. If the vehicle is equipped with an automatic transaxle, the cooling system also cools the transaxle fluid and thus plays an important role in prolonging transaxle life.

2   The cooling system should be checked with the engine cold. Do this before the vehicle is driven for the day or after the engine has been shut off for at least three hours.

Warning: *Never remove the radiator pressure cap when the engine is running or has just been shut down, because the cooling system is hot. Escaping steam and scalding liquid could cause serious injury.*

3   Remove the radiator pressure cap by turning it to the left until it reaches a stop. If you hear a hissing sound (indicating there is still pressure in the system), wait until it stops. Now press down on the cap with the palm of your hand and continue turning to the left until the cap can be removed. Thoroughly clean the cap, inside and out, with clean water. Also clean the filler neck on the radiator. All traces of corrosion should be removed. The coolant inside the radiator should be relatively transparent. If it's rust colored, the system should be drained and refilled (see Section 26). If the coolant level isn't up to the top, add additional antifreeze/coolant mixture (see Section 4).

4   Carefully check the large upper and lower radiator hoses along with the smaller diameter heater hoses which run from the engine to the bulkhead. Inspect each hose along its entire length, replacing any hose which is cracked, swollen or shows signs of deterioration. Cracks may become more apparent if the hose is squeezed (**see illustration**). Regardless of condition, it's a good idea to replace hoses with new ones every two years.

5   Make sure that all hose connections are tight. A leak in the cooling system will usually show up as white or rust colored deposits on the areas adjoining the leak. If wire-type clamps are used at the ends of the hoses, it may be a good idea to replace them with more secure screw-type clamps.

6   Use compressed air or a soft brush to remove bugs, leaves, etc. from the front of the radiator or air conditioning condenser. Be careful not to damage the delicate cooling fins or cut yourself on them.

7   Every other inspection, or at the first indication of cooling system problems, have the

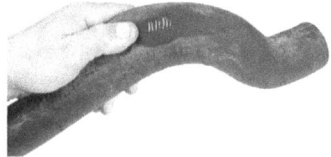

Check for a chafed area that could fail prematurely.

Check for a soft area indicating the hose has deteriorated inside.

Overtightening the clamp on a hardened hose will damage the hose and cause a leak.

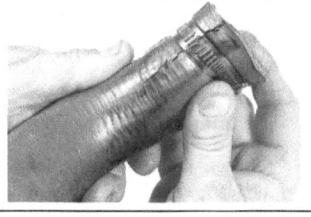

Check each hose for swelling and oil-soaked ends. Cracks and breaks can be located by squeezing the hose.

11.4 Hoses, like drivebelts, have a habit of failing at the worst possible time - to prevent the inconvenience of a blown radiator or heater hose, inspect them carefully as shown here

cap and system pressure tested. If you don't have a pressure tester, most gas stations and garages will do this for a minimal charge.

12   Brake check

Warning: *The dust created by the brake system is harmful to your health. Never blow it out with compressed air and don't inhale any of it. An approved filtering mask should be worn when working on the brakes. Do not, under any circumstances, use petroleum-based solvents to clean brake parts. Use brake system cleaner only!*

Note: *For detailed photographs of the brake system, refer to Chapter 9.*

1   In addition to the specified intervals, the brakes should be inspected every time the wheels are removed or whenever a defect is suspected.

2   Any of the following symptoms could indicate a potential brake system defect: The vehicle pulls to one side when the brake pedal

12.7a You'll find an inspection hole like this in each caliper through which you can view the inner brake pad lining

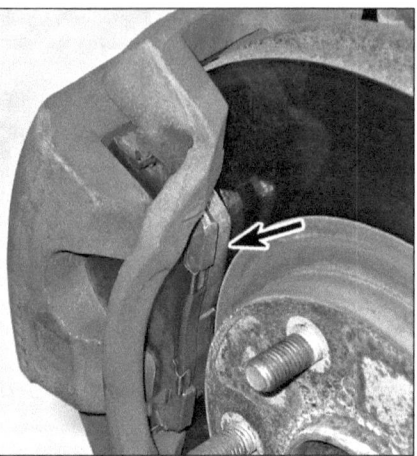

12.7b The outer pad is more easily checked at the edge of the caliper

is depressed; the brakes make squealing or dragging noises when applied; brake pedal travel is excessive; the pedal pulsates; or brake fluid leaks, usually onto the inside of the tyre or wheel.

3   Loosen the wheel nuts.

4   Raise the vehicle and place it securely on jackstands (see Jacking and Towing).

Warning: *If the vehicle is equipped with electronically modulated air suspension, make sure that the height control switch is turned off.*

5   Remove the wheels (see Jacking and towing at the front of this book, or your owner's manual, if necessary).

Disc brakes

Refer to illustrations 12.7a and 12.7b

6   There are two pads (an outer and an inner) in each caliper. The pads are visible with the wheels removed. The vehicles covered by this manual have disc brakes front and rear, with a mechanical, drum-type parking brake mechanism inside the rear discs.

7   Check the pad thickness by looking at each end of the caliper and through the inspection window in the caliper body **(see illustrations)**. If the lining material is less than the thickness listed in this Chapter's Specifications, replace the pads.

Note: *Keep in mind that the lining material is riveted or bonded to a metal backing plate and the metal portion is not included in this measurement.*

8   If it is difficult to determine the exact thickness of the remaining pad material by the above method, or if you are at all concerned about the condition of the pads, remove the caliper(s), then remove the pads from the calipers for further inspection (refer to Chapter 9).

9   Once the pads are removed from the calipers, clean them with brake cleaner and re-measure them with a ruler or a vernier caliper.

10   Measure the disc thickness with a

micrometer to make sure that it still has service life remaining. If any disc is thinner than the specified minimum thickness, replace it (refer to Chapter 9). Even if the disc has service life remaining, check its condition. Look for scoring, gouging and burned spots. If these conditions exist, remove the disc and have it resurfaced (see Chapter 9).

11   Before installing the wheels, check all brake lines and hoses for damage, wear, deformation, cracks, corrosion, leakage, bends and twists, particularly in the vicinity of the rubber hoses at the calipers. Check the clamps for tightness and the connections for leakage. Make sure that all hoses and lines are clear of sharp edges, moving parts and the exhaust system. If any of the above conditions are noted, repair, reroute or replace the lines and/or fittings as necessary (see Chapter 9).

Brake booster check

12   Sit in the driver's seat and perform the following sequence of tests.

13   With the brake fully depressed, start the engine - the pedal should move down a little when the engine starts.

14   With the engine running, depress the brake pedal several times - the travel distance should not change.

15   Depress the brake, stop the engine and hold the pedal in for about 30 seconds - the pedal should neither sink nor rise.

16   Restart the engine, run it for about a minute and turn it off. Then firmly depress the brake several times - the pedal travel should decrease with each application.

17   If your brakes do not operate as described, the brake booster has failed. Refer to Chapter 9 for the replacement procedure.

Parking brake

18   One method of checking the parking brake is to park the vehicle on a steep hill with the parking brake set and the transmission in Neutral (be sure to stay in the vehicle for this

check). If the parking brake cannot prevent the vehicle from rolling, it's in need of attention (see Chapter 9).

13   Steering, suspension and driveaxle boot check

Steering check

Note: *For detailed illustrations of the steering and suspension components, refer to Chapter 10.*

1   With the vehicle on the ground and the front wheels pointed straight ahead, rock the steering wheel gently back and forth. If freeplay is excessive, a front wheel bearing, main shaft yoke, intermediate shaft yoke, lower arm balljoint or steering system joint is worn or the steering gear is out of adjustment or broken. Steering wheel freeplay is the amount of travel (measured at the rim of the steering wheel) between the initial steering input and the point at which the front wheels begin to turn (indicated by slight resistance). Refer to Chapter 10 for the appropriate repair procedure.

2   Other symptoms, such as excessive vehicle body movement over rough roads, swaying (leaning) around corners and binding as the steering wheel is turned, may indicate faulty steering and/or suspension components.

Suspension check

Refer to illustrations 13.7 and 13.8

3   Check the shock absorbers by pushing down and releasing the vehicle several times at each corner. If the vehicle does not come back to a level position within one or two bounces, the shocks/struts are worn and must be replaced. When bouncing the vehicle up and down, listen for squeaks and noises from the suspension components. Additional information on suspension components can be found in Chapter 10.

4   Raise the vehicle with a floor jack and support it securely on jackstands (see Jacking and Towing).

5   Check the tyres for irregular wear patterns and proper inflation. See Section 5 in this Chapter for information regarding tyre wear and Chapter 10 for the wheel bearing replacement procedures.

6   Inspect the universal joint between the steering shaft and the steering gear housing. Check the steering gear housing for lubricant leakage or oozing. Make sure that the dust seals and boots are not damaged and that the boot clamps are not loose. Check the steering linkage for looseness or damage. Check the track rod ends for excessive play. Look for loose bolts, broken or disconnected parts and deteriorated rubber bushings on all suspension and steering components. While an assistant turns the steering wheel from side to side, check the steering components for free movement, chafing and binding. If the steer-

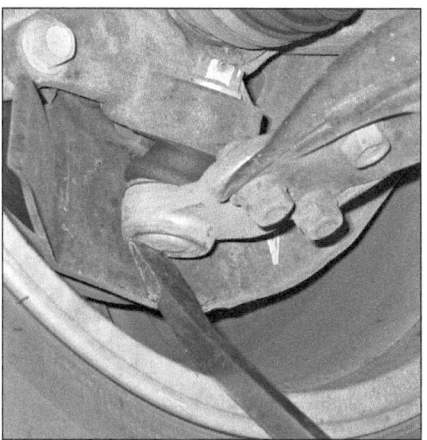

13.7 To check the balljoints attempt to move the lower arm up and down with a prybar to make sure here is no play in the balljoint (if there is, replace it)

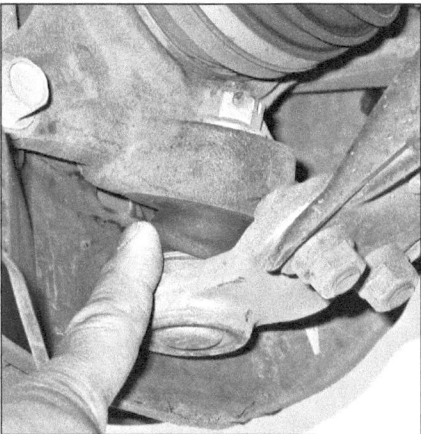

13.8 Push on the balljoint boot to check for tears and grease leaks

13.10 Flex the driveaxle boots by hand to check for tears, cracks and leaking grease

ing components do not seem to be reacting with the movement of the steering wheel, try to determine where the slack is located.

7   Check the balljoints for wear by trying to move each lower arm up and down with a prybar **(see illustration)** to ensure that its balljoint has no play. If any balljoint does have play, replace it. See Chapter 10 for the front balljoint replacement procedure.

8   Inspect the balljoint boots for damage and leaking grease **(see illustration)**. Replace the balljoints with new ones if they are damaged (see Chapter 10).

Driveaxle boot check

Refer to illustration 13.10

9   The driveaxle boots are very important because they prevent dirt, water and foreign material from entering and damaging the constant velocity (CV) joints. Oil and grease can cause the boot material to deteriorate prematurely, so it's a good idea to wash the boots with soap and water.

10   Inspect the boots for tears and cracks as well as loose clamps **(see illustration)**. If there is any evidence of cracks or leaking

lubricant, they must be replaced as described in Chapter 8.

14   Exhaust system check

Refer to illustrations 14.2a and 14.2b

1   With the engine cold (at least three hours after the vehicle has been driven), check the complete exhaust system from its starting point at the engine to the end of the tailpipe. This should be done on a hoist where unrestricted access is available.

2   Check the pipes and connections for evidence of leaks, severe corrosion or damage. Make sure that all brackets and hangers are in good condition and tight **(see illustrations)**.

3   At the same time, inspect the underside of the body for holes, corrosion, open seams, etc. which may allow exhaust gases to enter the passenger compartment. Seal all body openings with silicone or body putty.

4   Rattles and other noises can often be traced to the exhaust system, especially the mounts and hangers. Try to move the pipes, silencer and catalytic converter. If the compo-

nents can come in contact with the body or suspension parts, secure the exhaust system with new mounts.

5   Check the running condition of the engine by inspecting inside the end of the tailpipe. The exhaust deposits here are an indication of engine state-of-tune. If the pipe is black and sooty or coated with white deposits, the engine is in need of a tune-up, including a thorough fuel system inspection.

15   Air filter replacement

Refer to illustrations 15.1 and 15.2

1   The air filter is located inside a housing at the left (driver's) side of the engine compartment. To remove the air filter, release the clamps retaining the two halves of the air filter housing **(see illustration)**.

2   Lift the cover up and remove the air filter element **(see illustration)**.

3   Inspect the outer surface of the filter element. If it is dirty, replace it. If it is only moderately dusty, it can be reused by blowing it clean from the back to the front surface with compressed air.

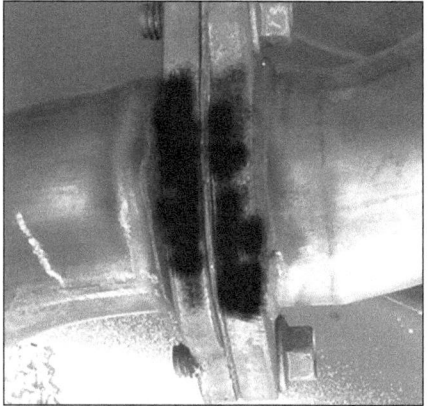

14.2a Soot around the exhaust joints as illustrated is an indicator of a leaking gasket

14.2b Check the exhaust system for damage, or worn rubber hangers

15.1 Release the clamps securing the air filter housing lid

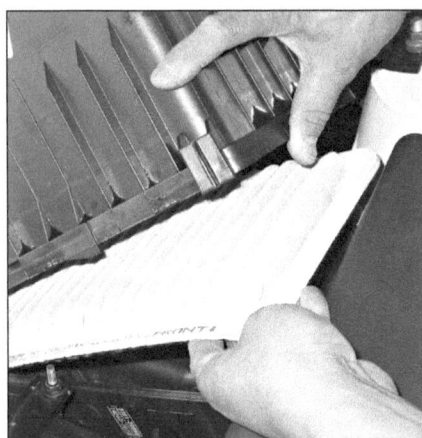

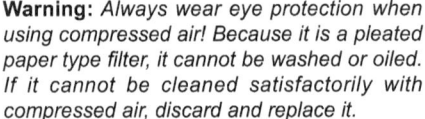

15.2 Lift the cover up and remove the filter

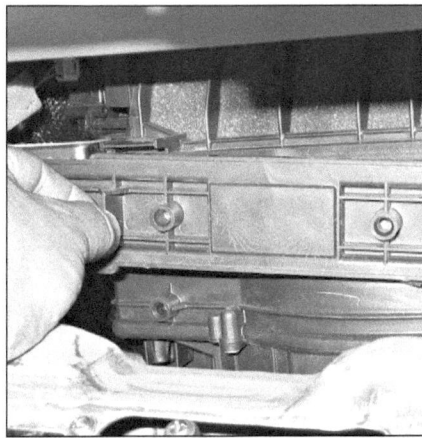

17.3 Release the cabin air filter mounting tabs

18.2 Use a small screwdriver to carefully pry out the old gasket - take care not to damage the cap

Warning: *Always wear eye protection when using compressed air! Because it is a pleated paper type filter, it cannot be washed or oiled. If it cannot be cleaned satisfactorily with compressed air, discard and replace it.*
Caution: *Never drive the vehicle with the air cleaner removed. Excessive engine wear could result and backfiring could even cause a fire under the bonnet.*

4   Installation is the reverse of removal. The hinge tabs on the housing cover must engage properly with the lower part of the housing.

16   Fuel system check

Warning: *Gasoline is extremely flammable, so take extra precautions when you work on any part of the fuel system. Don't smoke or allow open flames or bare light bulbs near the work area, and don't work in a garage where a gas-type appliance (such as a water heater or a clothes dryer) is present. Since gasoline is carcinogenic, wear fuel resistant gloves when there's a possibility of being exposed to fuel, and, if you spill any fuel on your skin, rinse it off immediately with soap and water. Mop up any spills immediately and do not store fuel-soaked rags where they could ignite. The fuel system is under constant pressure, so, if any fuel lines are to be disconnected, the fuel pressure in the system must be relieved first. When you perform any kind of work on the fuel system, wear safety glasses and have a Class B type fire extinguisher on hand.*

1   If you smell fuel while driving or after the vehicle has been sitting in the sun, inspect the fuel system immediately.
2   Remove the fuel filler cap and inspect it for damage and corrosion. The gasket should have an unbroken sealing imprint. If the gasket is damaged or corroded, remove it and install a new one (see Section 18).
3   Inspect the fuel feed and return lines for cracks. Make sure that the threaded flare nut type connectors which secure the metal fuel

lines to the fuel injection system and the banjo bolts which secure the banjo fittings to the in-line fuel filter are tight.
4   Since some components of the fuel system - the fuel tank and part of the fuel feed and return lines, for example - are underneath the vehicle, they can be inspected more easily with the vehicle raised on a hoist. If that's not possible, raise the vehicle and support it securely on jackstands (see Jacking and Towing).
5   With the vehicle raised and safely supported, inspect the fuel tank and filler neck for punctures, cracks and other damage. The connection between the filler neck and the tank is particularly critical. Sometimes a rubber filler neck will leak because of loose clamps or deteriorated rubber. These are problems a home mechanic can usually rectify.
Warning: *Do not, under any circumstances, try to repair a fuel tank (except rubber components). A welding torch or any open flame can easily cause fuel vapours inside the tank to explode.*
6   Carefully check all rubber hoses and metal lines leading away from the fuel tank. Check for loose connections, deteriorated hoses, crimped lines and other damage. Carefully inspect the lines from the tank to the fuel injection system. Repair or replace damaged sections as necessary (see Chapter 4).

17   Cabin air filter replacement

Refer to illustration 17.3

1   There is an air filter in the blower housing that cleans the air before it enters the passenger's compartment.
2   To remove the air filter, remove the glove box (see Chapter 11).
3   Depress the filter cover mounting tabs **(see illustration)**.
4   Lift the cover off and remove the filter.
5   Installation is the reverse of removal.

18   Fuel tank cap gasket inspection and replacement

Refer to illustration 18.2

1   Remove the tank cap and inspect the rubber gasket for cracks or tears.
2   If replacement is necessary, carefully pry the old gasket out of the recess **(see illustration)**. Be very careful not to damage the sealing surface inside the cap.
3   Work the new gasket into the cap recess.
4   Install the cap, then remove it and make sure the gasket seals all the way around.

19   Positive Crankcase Ventilation (PCV) valve check and replacement

1   The PCV valve and hose is located in the valve cover.
2   Disconnect the hose, pull the PCV valve from the cover, then reconnect the hose.
3   With the engine idling at normal operating temperature, place your finger over the valve opening. If there's no vacuum at the valve, check for a plugged hose or valve. Replace any plugged or deteriorated hoses.
4   Turn off the engine. Remove the PCV valve from the valve cover. Blow through the valve from the valve cover (cylinder head) end. If air will not pass through the valve in this direction, replace it with a new one.
5   When purchasing a replacement PCV valve, make sure it's for your particular vehicle and engine size. Compare the old valve with the new one to make sure they're the same.

20   Brake fluid change

Refer to illustration 20.7

The brake fluid should be renewed at intervals specified in Routine Maintenance.

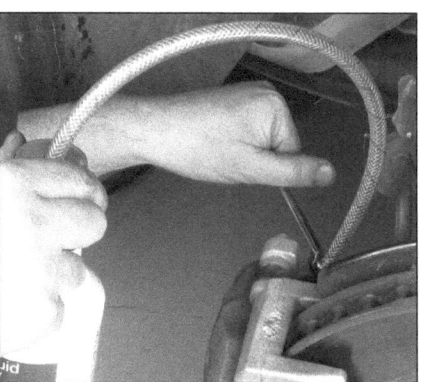

20.7 Bleeding one of the brake calipers

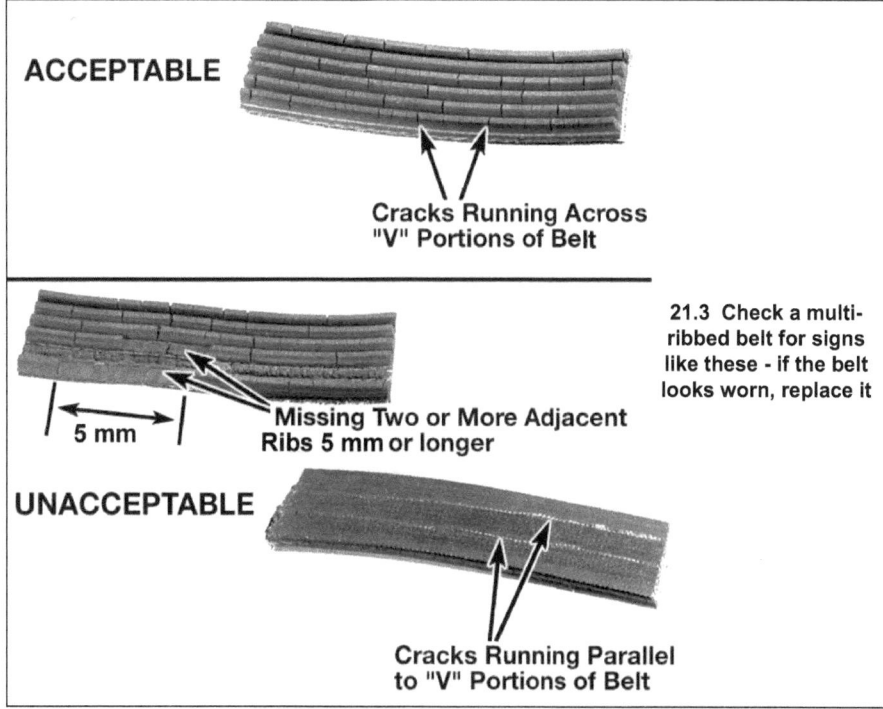

ACCEPTABLE

Cracks Running Across
"V" Portions of Belt

5 mm

Missing Two or More Adjacent
Ribs 5 mm or longer

UNACCEPTABLE

Cracks Running Parallel
to "V" Portions of Belt

21.3 Check a multi-ribbed belt for signs like these - if the belt looks worn, replace it

There are four points in the system where bleeder valves are installed, one on each caliper.

1   Raise the front and rear of the vehicle and support on chassis stands. Refer to the front of this manual for the correct vehicle jacking points. Remove the wheels.
2   Withdraw as much old fluid as possible from the master cylinder, using a syringe or similar.
3   Fill the fluid reservoir with clean brake fluid and maintain at least one third full throughout the entire operation.
4   If fitted, remove the dust cap and attach a transparent hose to the bleeder valve on the left rear caliper. Immerse the other end of the hose in a small amount of brake fluid contained in a clean glass jar held higher than the bleeder valve.

Note: *If desired, a one person bleeding kit may be used. These kits usually consist of a transparent tube with a one way ball valve. With a one person bleeding kit, it is not necessary to close the bleeder valve after each set of pedal strokes, however follow the kit manufacturer's instructions.*

5   Unscrew the bleeder valve one complete turn.
6   Have an assistant depress the brake pedal slowly to the full extent of its travel. Close the bleeder valve and allow the brake pedal to return without assistance.
7   Repeat steps 5 and 6 until a constant stream of new brake fluid, without any air bubbles, is being discharged into the container **(see illustration)**. Hold the pedal down and tighten the bleeder valve. Install the dust cap. Note: Do not allow the fluid level in the reservoir to fall below the one third full level at any time during the operation or air will enter the system and the procedure will have to be repeated. Always use new brake fluid for topping up the reservoir.
8   Perform the bleeding operation, in the same manner, on the remaining bleeder valves in the system. Always work from the longest brake line in the system to the shortest. This means, start with the left rear brake, then the right rear brake, left front and finally the right front brake.

9   Top up the reservoir with the specified brake fluid to the MAX level and install the reservoir cap.
10   If the brake pedal is spongy or travels to the floor, air has entered the system. Repeat the bleeding procedure ensuring that all the air is removed from the brake hydraulic system.

Warning: *Do not operate the vehicle if you are in doubt about the effectiveness of the brake system.*

---

21   Drivebelt check and replacement

Check

Refer to illustration 21.3

1   The drivebelts are located at the front (right side) of the engine and play an important role in the operation of the vehicle and its components. Due to their function and material makeup, belts are prone to failure after a period of time and should be inspected and adjusted periodically to prevent major damage.
2   3MZ-FE engines use two drivebelts; one for the power steering pump and one for the alternator, water pump and air conditioning compressor. 2GR-FE engines use one drivebelt, which is self adjusting.
3   With the engine turned off, open the bonnet and locate the drivebelt(s) at the front of the engine. Use a flashlight to carefully check for a severed core, separation of the adhesive rubber on both sides of the core and for core separation from the belt side. Inspect the ribs for separation from the adhesive rubber and for cracking or separation of the ribs, torn or

worn ribs or cracks in the inner ridges of the ribs **(see illustration)**. Also check for fraying and glazing, which gives the belt a shiny appearance. Inspect both sides of the belt by twisting the belt to check the underside. Use your fingers to feel the belt where you can't see it. If any of the above conditions are evident, replace the belt(s).

Note: *The drivebelt inspection can be made easier by removing the under-vehicle splash shield.*

Drivebelt adjustment - 3MZ-FE engine

Refer to illustration 21.4

4   If the alternator/AC compressor belt must be adjusted, loosen the alternator pivot bolt located on the front, left corner of the block. Loosen the locking bolt and turn the adjusting bolt (see Chapter 5).
5   Measure the belt tension; push firmly with your thumb and see how much the belt moves (deflects) **(see illustration)**. A new belt should deflect approximately 10 to 11 mm and a used belt should deflect approximately 11 to 14 mm.
6   Continue to rotate the belt adjusting bolt until the belt deflects the specified amount.
7   Adjust the power steering pump belt by loosening the adjustment bolt that secures the pump to the slotted bracket and pivot the pump (away from the engine to tighten the belt, toward it to loosen it). Repeat the procedure until the drivebelt tension is correct (see Step 5) and tighten the bolt.

Replacement

Note: *Take the old belt with you when purchasing new ones in order to make a*

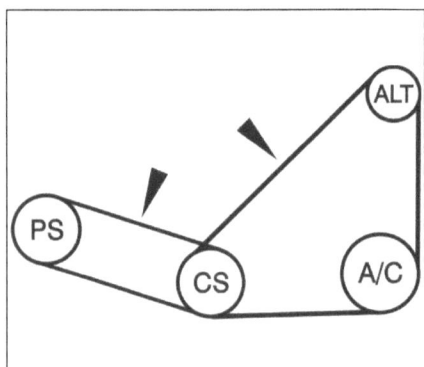

21.4 3MZ-FE engine drive belt routing diagram - Arrows indicate the measuring points for belt deflection

21.11 Using a wrench on the centre bolt of the tensioner, rotate the tensioner to loosen the belt - 2GR-FE engine

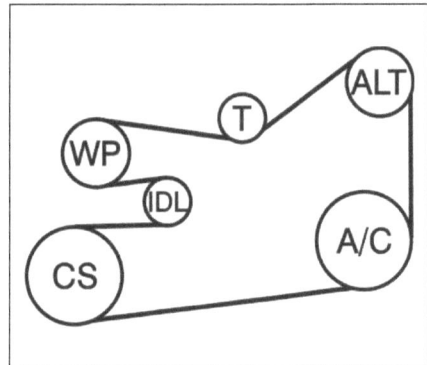

21.14 2GR-FE engine drive belt routing diagram

direct comparison for length, width and design.

8   Disconnect the negative (-) battery terminal (see Chapter 5).
9   Remove the right front wheel.
10   Remove the right side inner guard liner and splash shield (see Chapter 11).

3MZ-FE engine

Note: *Follow the procedure for drivebelt adjustment (see Step 4), but slip the belt off the crankshaft pulley and remove it. It is a good idea to replace both belts at the same time.*

2GR-FE engine

Refer to illustrations 21.11 and 21.14

11   If reusing the belt, place a mark to indicate the direction of rotation of the belt so that it is returned to the engine in the same position.
12   Place a wrench on the bolt in the centre of the tensioner pulley. Rotate the tensioner away from the belt to release tension on the belt **(see illustration)**.

Note: *The tensioner can be locked in the*

retracted position by inserting a suitable sized pin through the lock pin hole **(see illustration 21.19)**.
13   Remove the belt and slowly release the tensioner if it isn't locked.
14   Install the drivebelt. Route it correctly, and make sure that the belt is centred on all of the pulleys.
15   Route the new belt over the pulleys **(see illustration)**, rotating the tensioner to allow the belt to be installed. Release the belt tensioner, ensuring that the belt is properly centred in each pulley.

Note: *New belts are difficult to place into position. It may be easiest to slip the belt over the tensioner pulley and the idler pulley last as you turn the tensioner pulley.*

Drivebelt tensioner replacement

Refer to illustrations 21.17 and 21.19

Note: *This procedure is difficult to do in the vehicle. It will require the use of a socket set*

with universal joint fittings.

16   Disconnect the negative (-) battery terminal (see Chapter 5).
17   Disconnect the wiring from the air condiitioning compressor **(see illustration)**. Remove the bolts retaining the compresser to the engine and manoeuvre it clear of the work area.

Warning: *Do not disconnect the refrigerent lines from the compressor.*

18   With the compressor clear of the work area, remove the alternator (see Chapter 5).
19   Remove the tensioner fasteners and manoeuvre the tensioner from the engine **(see illustration)**.

Note: *On 2GR-FE engines, it will be necessary to remove the air conditioning compressor to access the drivebelt tensioner mounting bolts (see Chapter 5).*

20   Installation is the reverse of removal; be sure the locking pin is seated into the housing. Tighten the fasteners to the torque values listed in this Chapter's Specifications.
21   Install the drivebelt.

21.17 2GR-FE engine A/C compressor location

1   Magnetic clutch wiring connector
2   Compressor lock sensor connector
3   Compressor mounting bolts

21.19 2GR-FE engine drive belt tensioner

1   Tensioner
2   Tensioner pulley bolt
3   Lock pin hole
4   Two of the tensioner assembly retaining bolts

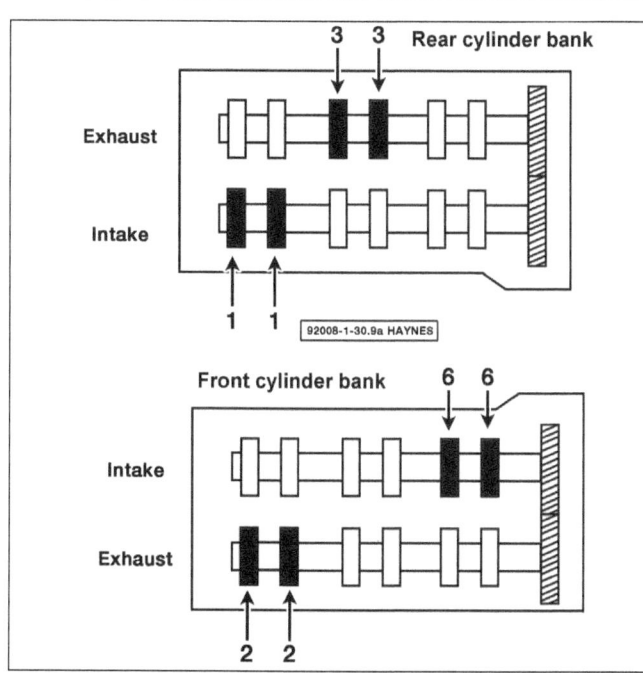

22.5a When the No. 1 piston is at TDC on the compression stroke, the clearance of the indicated valves can be measured

22.5b Measure the clearance for each valve with a feeler gauge of the specified thickness - if the clearance is correct, you should feel a slight drag on the gauge as you pull it out

22 Valve clearance check and adjustment - 3MZ-FE engine

Refer to illustrations 22.5a, 22.5b, 22.6a, 22.6b, 2.7a, 22.7b, 22.7c and 22.8

Note: *This procedure applies to the 3MZ-FE engine only. Valve clearances need only be* checked *if there is a valve tapping sound coming from the engine at idle, indicating excessive valve clearance. Or, if the engine suffers from a rough idle, backfiring and or possible stutter at low speeds - which can be an indicator of valves not completely closing. It is also necessary to use a special lifter tool to compress the valve spring and remove the shim from between the camshaft and lifter. It* is impossible to perform this task without it.

1   Disconnect the negative (-) battery terminal (see Chapter 5).
2   Drain the coolant (see Section 26).
3   Remove the valve covers (see Chapter 2A).
4   Position the No.1 piston at TDC on the compression stroke (see Chapter 2A).
5   Measure the clearance of the indicated valves with a feeler gauge of the specified thickness **(see illustrations)**. Record the clearance of each valve and note which are out of specification. This information will be

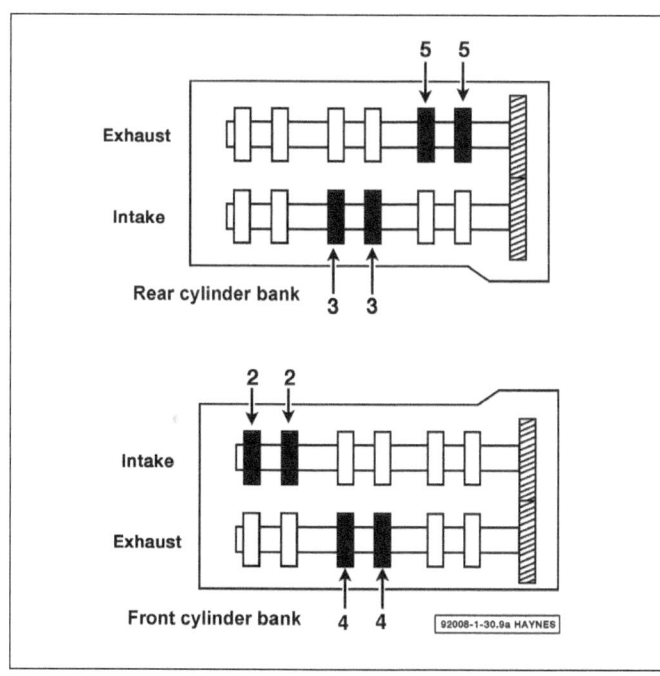

22.6a After the engine has been rotated 240 degrees from No.1 cylinder TDC on the compression stroke, measure the clearance of the indicated valves

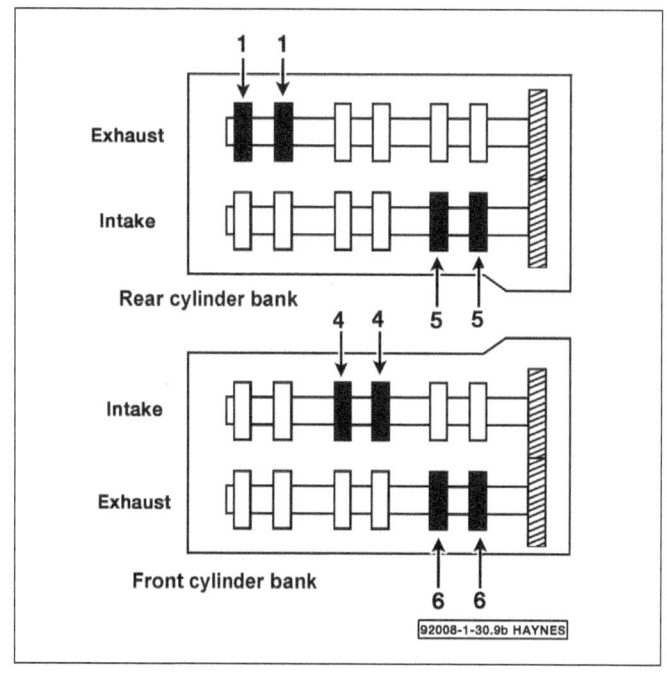

22.6b Rotate the crankshaft an additional 2/3 of a revolution (240 degrees) and measure the clearance of the remaining valves

22.7a Install the lifter tool as shown and squeeze the handles together to depress the lifter, then hold the lifter down with the smaller tool so the shim can be removed . . .

22.7b . . . keeping pressure on the lifter with the smaller tool and remove the shim with a small screwdriver . . .

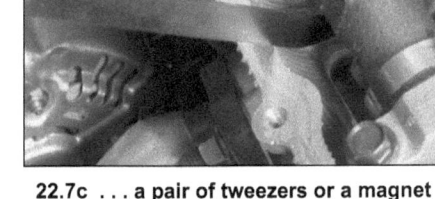

22.7c . . . a pair of tweezers or a magnet as shown here

used later to determine the required replacement shims.

6   Rotate the crankshaft 2/3 turn (240 degrees) clockwise. Measure the valve clearance on the valves shown **(see illustration 22.6a)**. Rotate the crankshaft a further 2/3 turn and measure the clearance on the remaining valves **(see illustration 22.6b)**.

7   After measuring and recording the clearance of each valve, turn the crankshaft pulley until the camshaft lobe above the first valve which you intend to adjust is pointing upward, away from the shim. Position the notch in the lifter toward the spark plug. Then depress the lifter with the special lifter tools **(see illustration)**. Place the special lifter tool in position as shown, with the longer jaw of the tool gripping the lower edge of the cast lifter boss and the upper, shorter jaw gripping the upper edge of the lifter itself. Depress the lifter by squeezing the handles of the lifter tool together, then hold the lifter down with the smaller tool and remove the larger one. Remove the adjusting shim with a small screwdriver or a pair of tweezers **(see illustrations)**. Note that the wire hook on the end of some lifter tool

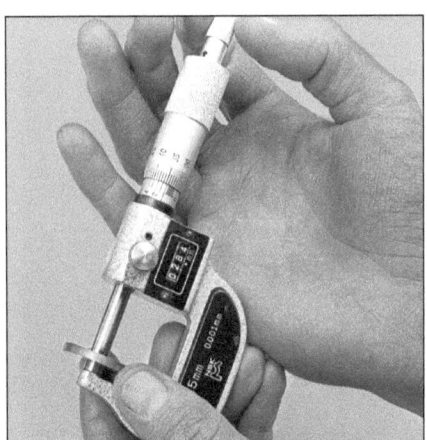

22.8 Measure the shim thickness with a micrometer

handles can be used to clamp both handles together to keep the lifter depressed while the shim is removed.

8   Measure the thickness of the shim with a micrometer **(see illustration)**.

All models

9   To calculate the correct thickness of a replacement shim or lifter that will place the valve clearance within the specified value, use the following formula:

   $N = T + (A - V)$
   T = thickness of the old shim or lifter
   A = valve clearance measured
   N = thickness of the new shim or lifter
   V = desired valve clearance (see this Chapter's Specifications)

10   Select a shim or lifter with a thickness as close as possible to the valve clearance calculated. Shims are available in 17 sizes in increments of 0.050 mm, and range in size from 2.500 mm to 3.300 mm.

Note: *Through careful analysis of the shim or lifter sizes needed to bring the out-of-specification valve clearance within specification, it is often possible to simply move a shim or lifter that has to come out anyway to another lifter requiring a shim or lifter of that particular size, thereby reducing the number of new shims that must be purchased.*

11   Place the special lifter tool in position as shown **(see illustration 22.7a)**, with the longer jaw of the tool gripping the lower edge of the cast lifter boss and the upper, shorter jaw gripping the upper edge of the lifter itself, press down the lifter by squeezing the handles of the lifter tool together and install the new adjusting shim (note that the wire hook on the end of one lifter tool handle can be used to clamp the handles together to keep the lifter depressed while the shim is inserted). Measure the clearance with a feeler gauge to make sure that your calculations are correct.

12   Repeat this procedure until all the valves

which are out of clearance have been corrected.

13   Installation of the spark plugs, valve cover, camshaft(s), accelerator cable bracket, etc. is the reverse of removal.

---

23   Automatic transaxle fluid change

Refer to illustrations 23.7, 23.8a, 23.8b, 23.9 and 23.12

1   At the specified time intervals, the automatic transaxle and differential fluid should be drained and replaced.

Note: *Although the manufacturer doesn't specify it, it is a good idea to clean the transaxle fluid strainer periodically to remove accumulated dirt and metal particles.*

2   Before beginning work, purchase the specified transaxle fluid (see this Chapter's Specifications).

3   Other tools necessary for this job include jackstands to support the vehicle in a raised position, a 10 mm hex bit or Allen wrench, a drain pan capable of holding at least five litres, newspapers and clean rags.

4   The fluid should be drained immediately after the vehicle has been driven. Hot fluid is more effective than cold fluid at removing built up sediment.

Warning: *Fluid temperature can exceed 180 degrees C in a hot transaxle. Wear protective gloves.*

5   After the vehicle has been driven to warm up the fluid, raise it and place it on jackstands for access to the transaxle and differential drain plugs (see Jacking and Towing).

6   Move the necessary equipment under the vehicle, being careful not to touch any of the hot exhaust components.

7   Place the drain pan under the drain plug in the transaxle pan and remove the drain plug **(see illustration)**. Be sure the drain

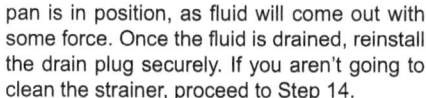

23.7 Remove the automatic transaxle
drain plug

23.8a After loosening the front bolts,
remove the rear pan bolts . . .

23.8b . . . and allow the remaining fluid to
drain out

pan is in position, as fluid will come out with some force. Once the fluid is drained, reinstall the drain plug securely. If you aren't going to clean the strainer, proceed to Step 14.

8   To clean the strainer, remove the front transaxle pan bolts, then loosen the rear bolts and carefully pry the pan loose with a screwdriver and allow the remaining fluid to drain **(see illustrations)**. Once the fluid has drained, remove the bolts and lower the pan.

9   Remove the strainer retaining bolts, disconnect the clip (some models) and lower the strainer from the transaxle **(see illustration)**. Be careful when lowering the strainer as it contains residual fluid.

10   Wash the strainer thoroughly in clean transmission fluid.

11   Place the strainer in position, connect the clip (if equipped) and install the bolts. Tighten the bolts to the torque listed in this Chapter's Specifications.

12   Carefully clean the gasket surfaces of the fluid pan, removing all traces of old gasket material. Noting their location, remove the magnets, wash the pan in clean solvent and dry it with compressed air.

Warning: *Always wear eye protection when*

using compressed air! Be sure to clean and reinstall the magnets in the pan **(see illustration)**.

13   Install a new gasket, place the fluid pan in position and install the bolts in their original positions. Tighten the bolts to the torque listed in this Chapter's Specifications.

14   Lower the vehicle.

15   With the engine off, add new fluid to the transaxle through the dipstick tube (see Recommended fluids and lubricants for the recommended fluid type and capacity). Use a funnel to prevent spills. It is best to add a little fluid at a time, continually checking the level with the dipstick (see Section 4). Allow the fluid time to drain into the pan.

16   Start the engine and shift the gearchange selector into all positions from P through L, then shift the gear change into P and apply the parking brake.

17   With the engine idling, check the fluid level. Add fluid up to the Cool level on the dipstick.

18   Drive the vehicle to warm up the transaxle to normal operating temperature, then recheck the fluid level.

24 Transfer case lubricant change (AWD models)

Refer to illustration 24.2

1   Raise the vehicle and support it securely on jackstands (see Jacking and Towing).

Note: *On GSU45R models, it is recommended to remove the exhaust pipe from adjacent to the check/fill plug to make access easier.*

2   Remove the check/fill plug, then remove the drain plug and drain the lubricant **(see illustration)**.

3   Reinstall the drain plug and tighten it securely.

4   Add new lubricant until it is even with the lower edge of the filler hole. See Recommended lubricants and fluids for the specified lubricant type.

5   Reinstall the check/fill plug and tighten it securely.

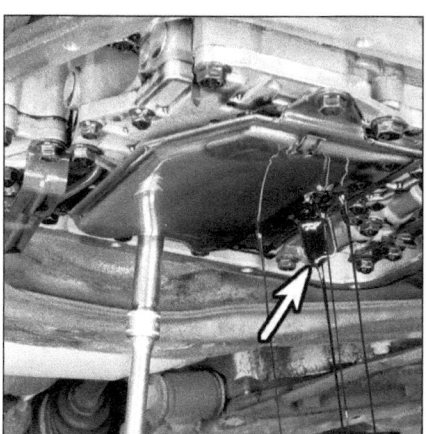

23.9 Remove the strainer bolts and lower
the strainer (be careful, there will be some
residual fluid)

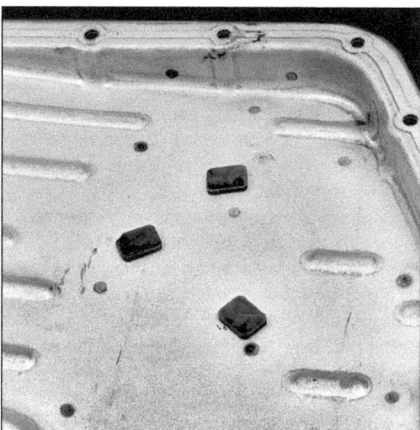

23.12 Noting their locations, remove the
magnets and wash them and the pan in
solvent before installing them

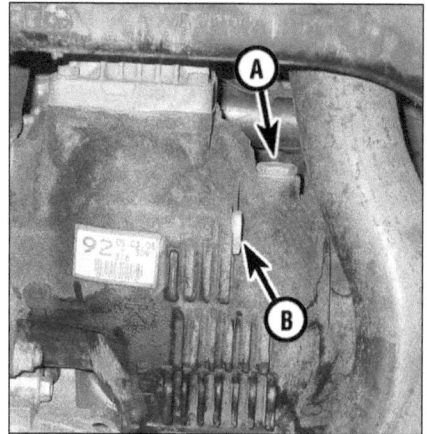

24.2 Location of the transfer case check/
fill plug (A) and drain plug (B)

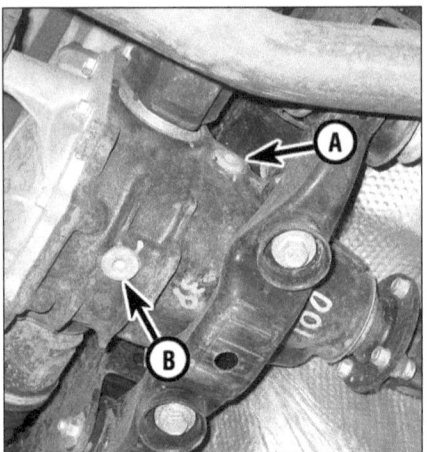

25.2 Location of the rear differential check/fill plug (A) and drain plug (B)

26.4 On most models you will have to remove a splash panel for access to the drain fitting located at the bottom of the radiator

26.5 There is a coolant drain like this located on both the front and rear sides of the block

25   Rear differential lubricant change (AWD models)

Refer to illustration 25.2

1   Raise the rear of the vehicle and support it securely on jackstands (see Jacking and Towing).
2   Remove the check/fill plug, then remove the drain plug and drain the lubricant **(see illustration)**.
3   Reinstall the drain plug and tighten it securely.
4   Add new lubricant until it is even with the lower edge of the filler hole (see Section 4). See Recommended lubricants and fluids for the specified lubricant type.
5   Reinstall the check/fill plug and tighten it securely.

26   Cooling system servicing (draining, flushing and refilling)

Warning: *Wait until the engine is completely cool before beginning this procedure.*
Warning: *Do not allow engine coolant (antifreeze) to come in contact with your skin or painted surfaces of the vehicle. Rinse off spills immediately with plenty of water. Antifreeze is highly toxic if ingested. Never leave antifreeze laying around in an open container or in puddles on the floor; children and pets are attracted by it's sweet smell and may drink it. Check with local authorities about disposing of used antifreeze. Many communities have collection centres which will see that antifreeze is disposed of safely.*
Warning: *To prevent scalding, use caution when releasing the radiator cap if the engine is warm. Squeeze the upper radiator hose. If resistance is felt, the system is pressurised and the cap should not be removed until the radiator hose can easily be squeezed together. Escaping steam and scalding liquid could cause serious injury.*

Caution: *We recommend using a concentrated type coolant that complies with the coolant type listed in Specifications. After flushing the cooling system with clean water, it is near impossible to remove all of the water from the cooling system. Therefore using a pre-mix type coolant is not recommended as the coolant will be diluted by the water remaining in the cooling system - depleting the corrosive and cooling inhibiting chemicals within the coolant. A concentrated coolant will mix with the water already in the system and still maintain the correct chemical balance to be proactive in preventing corrosion buildup and maintaining cooling properties.*

1   Periodically, the cooling system should be drained, flushed and refilled to replenish the antifreeze mixture and prevent formation of rust and corrosion, which can impair the performance of the cooling system and cause engine damage. When the cooling system is serviced, all hoses and the radiator cap should be checked and replaced if necessary.

Draining

Refer to illustrations 26.4, 26.5, 26.8a and 26.8b

2   Apply the parking brake and block the wheels. If the vehicle has just been driven, wait several hours to allow the engine to cool down before beginning this procedure.
3   Once the engine is completely cool, remove the radiator cap.
4   Move a large container under the radiator drain to catch the coolant. Attach a 10 mm inner diameter hose to the drain fitting to direct the coolant into the container (some models are already equipped with a hose), then open the drain fitting (a pair of pliers may be required to turn it) **(see illustration)**.
5   After the coolant stops flowing out of the radiator, move the container under the engine block drain plugs. Loosen the plugs and allow the coolant in the block to drain. There is a drain plug is on each side of the block **(see illustration)**.

6   While the coolant is draining, check the condition of the radiator hoses, heater hoses and clamps (refer to Section 11 if necessary).
7   Replace any damaged clamps or hoses (see Chapter 3).
8   On models with the 2GR-FE engine, loosen the two bleed plugs - one on the cylinder head **(see illustration)** and the other on the top of the radiator hose inlet **(see illustration)**.

Flushing

Refer to illustrations 26.11 and 26.12

9   Once the system is completely drained, remove the thermostat from the engine (see Chapter 3). Then reinstall the thermostat housing without the thermostat. This will allow the system to be flushed.
10   Reinstall the engine block drain plug(s) and tighten the radiator drain plug. Turn your heating system controls to Hot, so that the heater core can be flushed.

26.8a When opened, this bleed valve will allow the air trapped in the cylinder block to escape while filling the cooling system - 2GR-FE engine

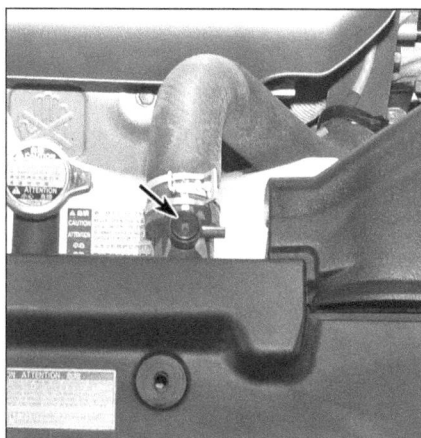

26.8b As with the cylinder head bleed valve, this valve will allow trapped air to escape from the upper radiator hose and radiator top tank - 2GR-FE engine

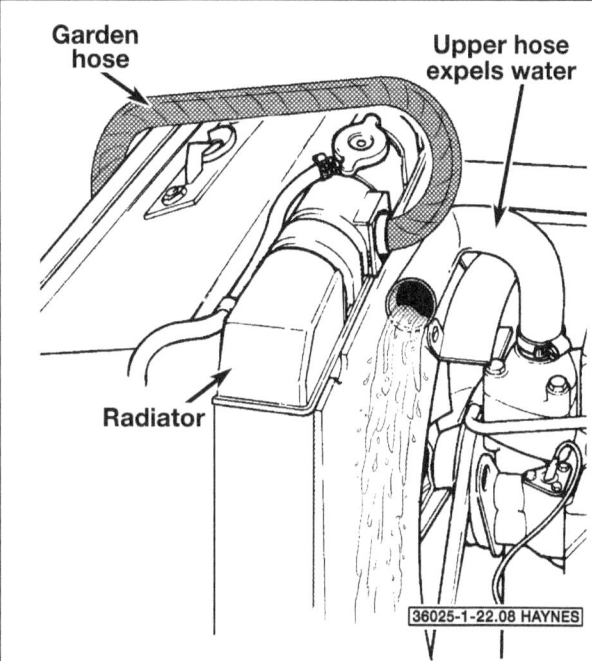

26.11 With the thermostat removed, disconnect the upper radiator hose and flush the radiator and engine block with a garden hose

26.12 The heater core hoses pass through the firewall into the heater core - remove the hoses and flush the core by placing the hose into one of the pipes and flushing it until clean water comes out of the other pipes - 2GR-FE engine shown, 3MZ-FE engine similar

11   Disconnect the upper radiator hose from the radiator. Place a garden hose in the upper radiator inlet, turn the water on and flush the system until the water runs clear out of the upper radiator hose **(see illustration)**.

12   Remove the hoses from the heater core **(see illustration)** and flush fresh water through the heater core until clean and clear water comes out the opposite pipe.

13   In severe cases of contamination or clogging of the radiator, remove the radiator (see Chapter 3) and have a radiator repair facility clean and repair it if necessary. Many deposits can be removed by the chemical action of a cleaner available at auto parts stores. Follow the procedure outlined in the manufacturer's instructions.

Note: *When the coolant is regularly drained and the system refilled with the correct*

antifreeze/water mixture, there should be no need to use chemical cleaners or descalers.

13   After flushing, drain the radiator and remove the block drain plugs once again to drain the water from the system.

Refilling

14   Close and tighten the radiator drain. Install and tighten the block drain plug.

15   Place the heater temperature control in the maximum heat position.

16   Slowly add new coolant to the radiator until it's full. Add coolant to the reservoir up to the lower mark.

Note: *Models with the 2GR-FE engine are equipped with an air bleed valve on the top of the engine in the coolant housing* **(see illustration 26.8a)** *and a second air bleed plug on the neck of the radiator hose connection* **(see illustration 26.8b)**. *Open these plugs when filling the system, then tighten the plugs once coolant begins to flow from them.*

17   Leave the radiator cap off and run the engine in a well-ventilated area until the thermostat opens (coolant will begin flowing through the radiator and the upper radiator hose will become hot).

18   Turn the engine off and let it cool. Add more coolant mixture to bring the level back up to the lip on the radiator filler neck.

19   Squeeze the upper radiator hose to expel air, then add more coolant mixture if necessary. Replace the radiator cap.

20   Start the engine, allow it to reach normal operating temperature and check for leaks.

21   It is good practice to check the coolant level after the next few trips, just in case there was some air trapped in the system and the level has dropped slightly.

27 Spark plug check and replacement

Refer to illustrations 27.1, 27.5, 27.7, 27.8, 27.9a and 27.9b

Note: *Do not adjust the gap on iridium spark plugs. Using a gapping tool on them could damage the iridium plating on the electrodes. These spark plugs are pre-gapped by the manufacturer.*

1   Spark plug replacement requires a spark plug socket that fits onto a ratchet. This socket is lined with a rubber grommet to protect the porcelain insulator of the spark plug and to hold the plug while you insert it into the spark plug hole **(see illustration)**.

2   If you are replacing the plugs, purchase the new plugs and replace each plug one at a time.

Note: *The manufacturer specifies that only iridium-tipped spark plugs be used on these models. When buying new spark plugs, it's essential that you obtain the correct plugs for your specific vehicle. This information can be found in this Chapter's Specifications, on the Vehicle Emissions Control Information label located on the underside of the bonnet or in the owner's manual. If these sources specify different plugs, purchase the spark plug type specified on the label because that information is provided specifically for your engine.*

3   Inspect each of the new plugs for defects. If there are any signs of cracks in the porcelain insulator of a plug, don't use it.

4   Remove the engine cover and, to access the rear bank plugs, it is necessary to remove the upper intake manifold (see Chapter 2A) or (see Chapter 2B).

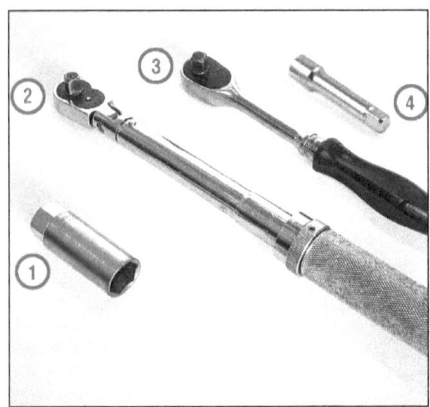

27.1 Tools required for changing spark plugs

1   **Spark plug socket** - *This will have special padding inside to protect the spark plug's porcelain insulator*
2   **Torque wrench** - *Although not mandatory, using this tool is the best way to ensure the plugs are tightened properly*
3   **Ratchet** - *Standard hand tool to fit the spark plug socket*
4   **Extension** - *Depending on model and accessories, you may need special extensions and universal joints to reach one or more of the plugs*

5   Remove the bolts and detach each ignition coil assembly from the spark plugs (**see illustration**).
6   If compressed air is available, blow any dirt or foreign material away from the spark plug area before proceeding.
Warning: *Always wear eye protection when using compressed air!*
7   Remove the spark plug (**see illustration**).
8   Whether you are replacing the plugs at this time or intend to re-use the old plugs, compare each old spark plug with accompanying chart (**see illustration**) to determine the overall running condition of the engine.
9   Apply a small amount of anti-seize compound to the spark plug threads (**see illustration**). It's often difficult to insert spark plugs

27.5 Remove the retaining bolt (A), disconnect the electrical connector (B) and detach the individual coils to reach the spark plugs

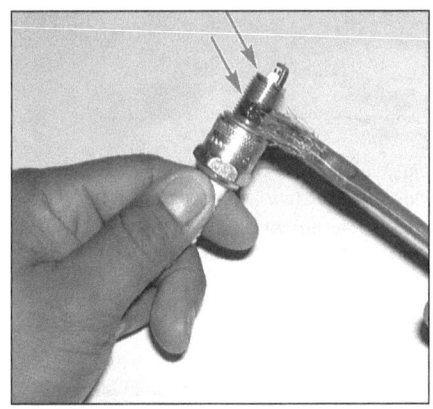

27.9a A light coat of anti-seize compound applied to the threads of the spark plugs will keep the threads in the cylinder head from being damaged the next time the plugs are removed

into their holes without cross-threading them. To avoid this possibility, fit a short piece of rubber hose over the end of the spark plug (**see illustration**). The flexible hose acts as a universal joint to help align the plug with the spark plug hole. Should the plug begin to cross-thread, the hose will slip on the spark

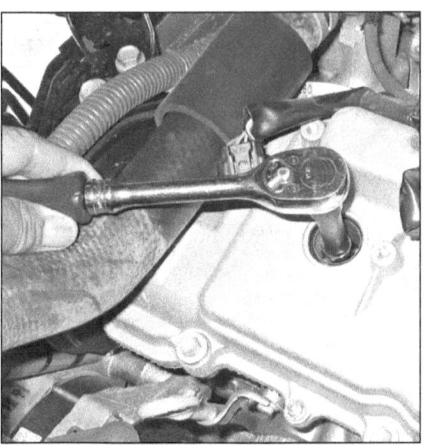

27.7 Because they are deeply recessed, the proper spark plug socket and an extension will be required when removing or installing the spark plugs

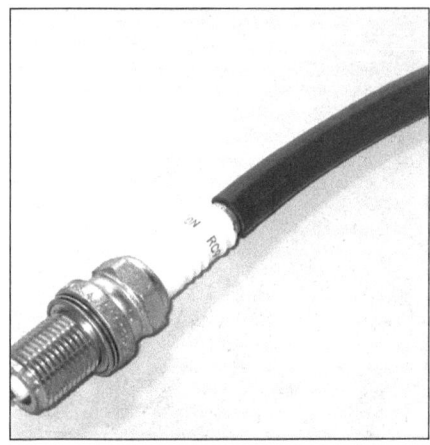

27.9b A section of rubber hose will aid in getting the spark plug threads started

plug, preventing thread damage. Tighten the plug to the torque listed in this Chapter's Specifications.
10   Attach the ignition coil assembly to the new spark plug.

Overheating, burnt electrodes and white blistered appearance, Incorrect plug, engine running too hot or plug loose in engine.

Worn out spark plug indicated by rounded electrodes. Renew.

Black damp deposists indicating incorrect plug type or high oil consumption. May not be firing

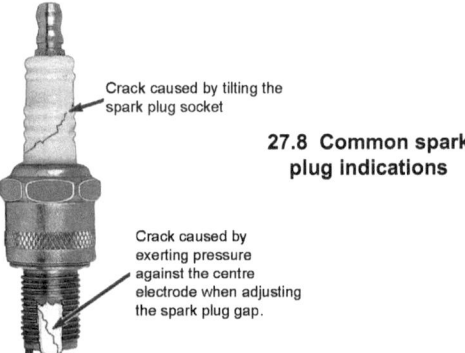

Crack caused by tilting the spark plug socket

27.8 Common spark plug indications

Crack caused by exerting pressure against the centre electrode when adjusting the spark plug gap.

Electrodes

Chapter 2 Part A
3.3L V6 (3MZ-FE) engine

Contents

Specifications

General

Engine code...	3MZ-FE
Displacement..	3.3 litres
Cylinder numbers (timing belt end-to-transaxle end)	
Right (firewall) side..	1-3-5
Left (radiator) side	2-4-6
Firing order..	1-2-3-4-5-6

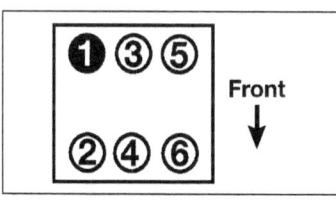

Cylinder numbering

Cylinder head

Warpage limits	
Cylinder head	0.10 mm
Intake manifold...	0.08 mm
Exhaust manifolds...	0.50 mm
Cylinder head bolt diameter (minimum)........................	8.75 mm

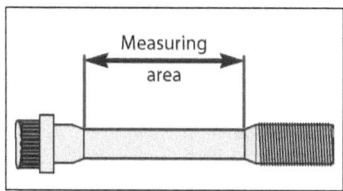

**Renew the cylinder head bolt if
the diameter is less than specified
anywhere in this area**

Camshaft and related components

Valve clearance (engine cold)	
Intake	0.15 to 0.25 mm
Exhaust	0.25 to 0.35 mm
Bearing journal diameter	26.959 to 26.975 mm
Bearing oil clearance	
Intake #4 and #5	0.025 to 0.057 mm
All others	0.025 to 0.062 mm
Service limit..	0.10 mm
Lobe height	
Intake	
Standard	43.132 to 43.232 mm
Service Limit	42.98 mm
Exhaust	
Standard	43.010 to 43.110 mm
Service limit	42.86 mm

Thrust clearance (endplay)	
Standard	0.040 to 0.090 mm
Service limit	0.12 mm
Runout limit (total indicator reading)	0.06 mm
Camshaft gear backlash	
Standard	0.020 to 0.200 mm
Service limit	0.30 mm
Lifters	
Outside diameter	30.966 to 30.976 mm
Bore diameter	31.009 to 31.025 mm
Lifter-to-bore (oil) clearance	
Standard	0.033 to 0.059 mm
Service limit	0.070 mm

Oil pump

Driven rotor-to-pump body clearance	
Standard	0.250 to 0.325 mm
Service limit	0.50 mm
Rotor tip clearance	
Standard	0.060 to 0.180 mm
Service limit	0.30 mm
Rotor side clearance	
Standard	0.030 to 0.090 mm
Service limit	0.15 mm

Torque specifications

	Nm
Crankshaft pulley bolt	220
Camshaft bearing cap bolts	16
Cylinder head bolts (12-point)	
Step 1	54
Step 2	Tighten an additional 90 degrees (1/4 turn)
Cylinder head bolt (recessed)	19
Cylinder head cover - rear	10
Driveplate bolts [1]	83
Exhaust camshaft sprocket bolt	125
Engine mounting bracket bolts/nuts	28
Exhaust manifold nuts	49
Exhaust manifold heat shield bolts	9
Intake camshaft sprocket bolt	125
Intake manifold	
Lower intake manifold bolts/nuts	15
Upper intake manifold bolts/nuts	28
Lower engine crankcase to engine block bolts	
10 mm bolt head	8
12 mm bolt head	20
Oil pan bolts	
Aluminium section	
10 mm bolt head	8
12 mm bolt head	20
Steel section	8
Oil pump mounting bolts	
10 mm bolt head	8
12 mm bolt head	20
14 mm bolt head	43
Oil pump cover screws	10
Oil pick-up tube mounting bolts	8
Timing belt cover (front) bolts	9
Timing belt cover (rear) bolts	9
Timing belt idler	
Upper	43
Lower	34
Timing belt tensioner bolts	27
Rear crankshaft oil seal retainer mounting bolts	8
Valve cover bolts	8
Variable Valve Timing (VVT) system	
Oil control valve filter plug	45
Oil control valve hold-down bolt	8
Intake camshaft actuator retaining nut [2]	150
Water pump	8

[1] Apply thread locking compound to the threads prior to installation
[2] LH thread

3.5 A compression gauge can be used in the number one plug hole to assist in finding TDC

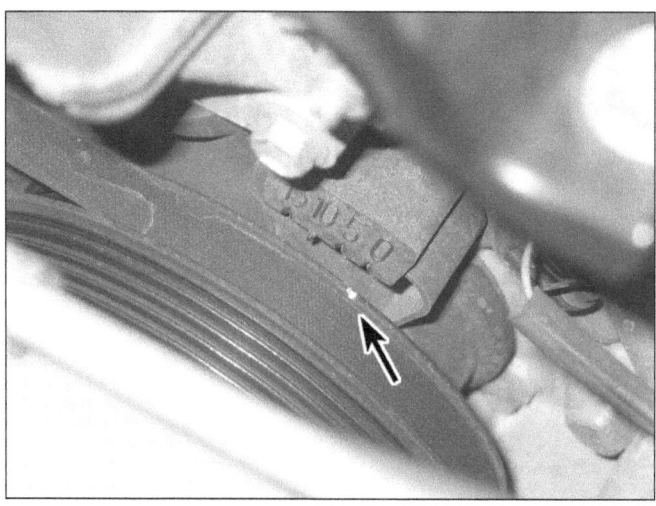

3.6 Turn the crankshaft until the notch in the pulley aligns with the zero on the timing plate

1   General information

The 3.3L, 3MZ-FE engine is a DOHC (dual overhead cam) type with four valves per cylinder (24 in all), an aluminium engine block, distributorless ignition, and two-piece oil pan.

Chapter 2A is devoted to in-vehicle repair procedures for the 3.3L V6 (3MZ-FE) engine. Information concerning engine removal and installation and engine overhaul can be found in Part C (see Chapter 2C).

The following repair procedures are based on the assumption that the engine is installed in the vehicle. If the engine has been removed from the vehicle and mounted on a stand, many of the steps outlined here will not apply.

2   Repair operations possible with the engine in the vehicle

Many major repair operations can be accomplished without removing the engine from the vehicle.

Clean the engine compartment and the exterior of the engine with some type of degreaser before any work is done. It will make the job easier and help keep dirt out of the internal areas of the engine.

Depending on the components involved, it may be helpful to remove the bonnet to improve access to the engine as repairs are performed (refer to Chapter 11 if necessary). Cover the guards to prevent damage to the paint. Special pads are available, but an old bedspread or blanket will also work.

If vacuum, exhaust, oil or coolant leaks develop, indicating a need for gasket or seal replacement, the repairs can generally be made with the engine in the vehicle. The intake and exhaust manifold gaskets, oil pan gasket, crankshaft oil seals and cylinder head gaskets are all accessible with the engine in

place.

Exterior engine components, such as the intake and exhaust manifolds, the oil pan, the oil pump, the water pump, the starter motor, the alternator, and the fuel system components can be removed for repair with the engine in place.

Since the cylinder heads can be removed without pulling the engine, valve component servicing can also be accomplished with the engine in the vehicle. Replacement of the camshafts, timing belt and sprockets is also possible with the engine in the vehicle.

3   Top Dead Centre (TDC) for number one piston - locating

Refer to illustrations 3.5 and 3.6

1   Top Dead Centre (TDC) is the highest point in the cylinder that each piston reaches as it travels up the cylinder bore. Each piston reaches TDC on the compression stroke and again on the exhaust stroke, but TDC generally refers to piston position on the compression stroke.

2   Positioning the piston(s) at TDC is an essential part of many procedures such as valve timing and camshaft and timing belt/sprocket removal.

3   Before beginning this procedure, be sure to place the transaxle in Neutral and apply the parking brake or block the rear wheels. Disable the fuel system by relieving the fuel system pressure (see Chapter 4, Section 2), then disconnect the electrical connectors from the ignition coils (see Chapter 5).

4   In order to bring any piston to TDC, the crankshaft must be turned using one of the methods outlined below. When looking at the front of the engine, normal crankshaft rotation is clockwise.

  a   The preferred method is to turn the crankshaft clockwise with a socket and ratchet attached to the bolt threaded into

the front of the crankshaft.

  b   A remote starter switch, which may save some time, can also be used. Follow the instructions included with the switch. Once the piston is close to TDC, use a socket and ratchet as described in the previous paragraph.

  c   If an assistant is available to turn the ignition switch to the Start position in short bursts, you can get the piston close to TDC without a remote starter switch. Make sure your assistant is out of the vehicle, away from the ignition switch, then use a socket and ratchet as described in Paragraph (a) to complete the procedure.

5   Remove the spark plug and install a compression pressure gauge in the number one spark plug hole. It should be a gauge with a screw-in fitting and a hose at least 150 mm long **(see illustration).**

Caution: *It is possible to check the compression on cylinder number 1 on the V6 engine with the upper intake manifold and throttle body installed on the engine. The spark plugs can remain in the cylinder heads (except for number 1) if all of the ignition coils and the fuel pump have been disabled.*

6   Rotate the crankshaft using one of the methods described above while observing the compression gauge. When the compression stroke of the number one cylinder is reached, compression pressure will begin to show on the gauge; continue to rotate the crankshaft and align the notch on the crankshaft pulley with the 0 mark on the timing plate **(see illustration).** If you go past the marks, release the gauge pressure and rotate the crankshaft around two more revolutions.

7   After the number one piston has been positioned at TDC on the compression stroke, TDC for the remaining cylinders can be located by turning the crankshaft 120 degrees (1/3 turn) at a time and following the firing order (refer to this Chapter's Specifications).

4.2 Remove the oil filler cap, then the three fasteners (A) and the clip (B) to remove the engine cover

4.5a Remove nuts and disconnect the left-hand engine harness . . .

---

4   Valve covers - removal and installation

Removal

Refer to illustrations 4.2, 4.5a, 4.5b and 4.6

1   Disconnect the negative (-) battery terminal (see Chapter 5).
2   Remove the engine cover(s) **(see illustrations)**.
3   Remove the ignition coils (see Chapter 5).
4   Remove the upper intake manifold to access the rear valve cover (see Section 5).
5   Detach the engine wiring harness from the right side of the engine, the number 3 timing belt cover, the rear of the engine and left side of the engine compartment **(see illustrations)**.
6   Remove the retaining bolts and sealing washers, then detach the cover(s) **(see illustration)**. If the cover is stuck to the head, bump the end with a wood block and a ham-

mer to jar it loose. If that doesn't work, try to slip a flexible putty knife between the head and cover to break the seal.

Caution: *Don't pry at the cover-to-head joint or damage to the sealing surfaces may occur, leading to oil leaks after the cover is reinstalled.*

Installation

Refer to illustration 4.9

7   The mating surfaces of the cylinder head and cover must be clean when the cover is installed. Use a gasket scraper to remove all traces of sealant and old gasket material, then clean the mating surfaces with lacquer thinner or acetone. If there's residue or oil on the mating surfaces when the cover is installed, oil leaks may develop.
8   Install new spark plug tube seals.
9   Apply RTV sealant to the gasket/seal joints at the front and rear camshaft-to-head mounts and install the valve cover with a new gasket **(see illustration)**.
10   Tighten the bolts a little at a time to the

torque listed in this Chapter's Specifications.
11   Reinstall the remaining parts, run the engine and check for oil leaks.

---

5   Intake manifold - removal and installation

Warning: *Wait until the engine is completely cool before beginning this procedure.*

Removal

1   Relieve the fuel system pressure (see Chapter 4).
2   Disconnect the negative (-) battery terminal (see Chapter 5).
3   Remove the engine cover **(see illustration 4.2)**.

Upper intake manifold

Refer to illustration 5.6

Note: *The following procedure describes upper intake manifold removal for access to*

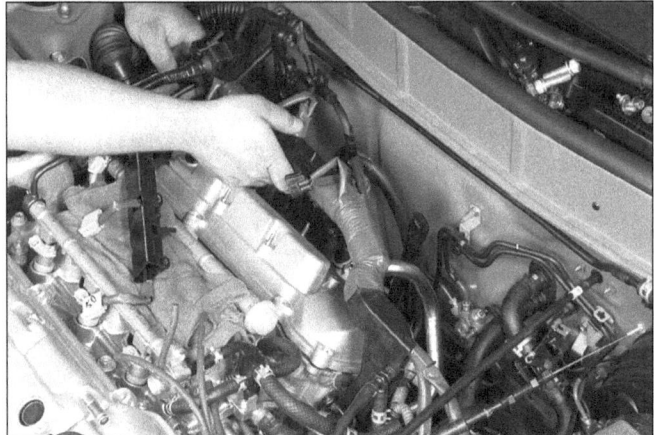

4.5b . . . disconnect the wire clips at the timing belt cover and the five bolts retaining the right-hand harness, then move the harness away from the rear valve cover

4.6 Remove the bolts and sealing washers and remove the valve cover

4.9 Apply RTV sealant to the areas indicated and install the cover with a new gasket

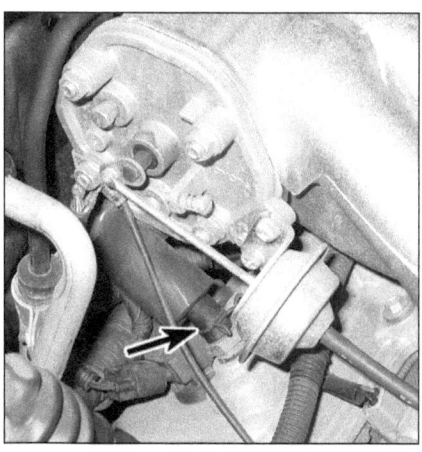

5.6 Location of the PCV hose at the rear valve cover

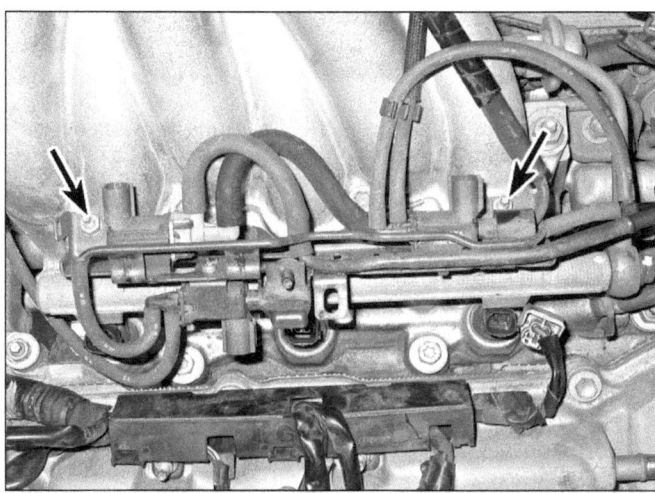

5.7 Remove the nuts, lift the vacuum switching assembly from the upper intake manifold and position the assembly off to the side

5.8 Location of the throttle body mounting nuts (2001 model shown, later models similar)

the rear valve cover, the rear cylinder head and the sensors. However, it is possible to separate the upper intake manifold from the throttle body leaving the air filter housing and the throttle body intact for spark plug removal, compression check and fuel rail servicing.

4   Remove the top cowl/ventilation cover (see Chapter 11) and then remove the windshield wiper arms and the windshield wiper motor (see Chapter 12).

5   Remove the lower cowl cover (see Chapter 11).

6   Disconnect the PCV hose from the valve cover **(see illustration)**.

For spark plug removal

Refer to illustrations 5.7, 5.8, 5.10 and 5.12

7   Disconnect the ground strap, the ACIS system components (see Chapter 6), the electrical connectors and the vacuum lines **(see illustration)** from the upper intake manifold. Label each connector using tape and a marker to ensure correct reassembly.

8   Remove the throttle body mounting nuts **(see illustration)**.

9   Unbolt the upper intake manifold brace(s) at the back of the upper intake manifold assembly.

10   Remove the bolts and nuts mounting the upper intake manifold to the lower intake manifold **(see illustration)**.

11   Remove the two Torx mounting studs (A) from the cylinder head **(see illustration 5.10)**.

12   Move the upper intake manifold to the side and separate it from the throttle body and lower intake manifold **(see illustration)**.

5.10 Location of the upper intake manifold bolts (B) and the mounting nuts (A)

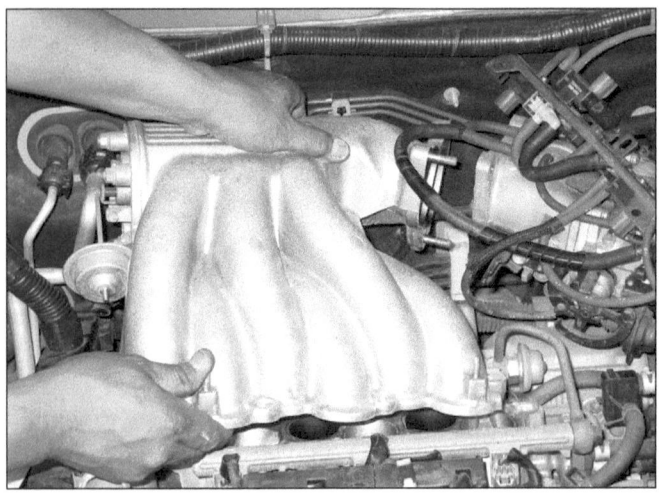

5.12 Slide the upper intake manifold to the side to detach it from the throttle body

5.23 This water transfer hose should be replaced whenever the intake manifold is off for other repairs

For all other procedures

13   Disconnect the ground strap, the ACIS system components (see Chapter 6), the electrical connectors, vacuum lines **(see illustration 5.7)** and coolant bypass hoses from the upper intake manifold/throttle body assembly.

Note: *Clamp-off the coolant hoses before detaching them, or plug them as soon as they are detached. Be prepared for coolant spillage. The throttle body can remain attached to the upper intake manifold unless it is being removed for cleaning or gasket service. Label each connector using tape and a marker to insure correct reassembly.*

14   Remove the air filter housing and air intake ducts (see Chapter 4).

15   Disconnect the electronic throttle control system electrical connector (see Chapter 6) from the throttle body.

16   Remove the strut bar between the two shock towers (see Chapter 10).

17   Unbolt the upper intake manifold brace(s) and the throttle body brace at the back of the upper intake manifold.

18   Remove the bolts and nuts mounting the upper intake manifold to the lower intake manifold and lift the upper intake manifold/throttle body assembly from the engine compartment **(see illustration 5.10)**.

Lower intake manifold

Refer to illustration 5.23

19   Drain the coolant into a clean container (see Chapter 1).

20   Disconnect the electrical connectors from the fuel injectors (see Chapter 4). Also detach the fuel line from the fuel rail (see Chapter 4).

Note: *The intake manifold can be removed with the injectors and fuel rails in place or removed, depending on the work to be done.*

21   Disconnect the heater hoses from the lower intake manifold.

22   Remove the mounting bolts and two nuts following the reverse of the tightening sequence, then detach the lower intake manifold from the engine **(see illustration 5.26)**. If the manifold is stuck, don't pry between

the gasket mating surfaces or damage may result.

23   There is a water transfer hose **(see illustration)** that is exposed only when the intake manifold is removed. Because of the difficulty in getting at this hose for replacement, we recommend that it be replaced with a new hose if the intake manifold is removed for other work.

Installation

Refer to illustrations 5.26 and 5.27

24   Use a scraper to remove all traces of old gasket material and sealant from the lower intake manifold and cylinder heads, then clean the mating surfaces with lacquer thinner or acetone.

25   Install new gaskets, then position the manifold on the engine. Make sure the gaskets haven't shifted, then install the nuts/bolts.

26   Tighten the nuts/bolts, in three or four equal steps, to the torque listed in this Chapter's Specifications. Tighten the bolts in the correct sequence **(see illustration)**.

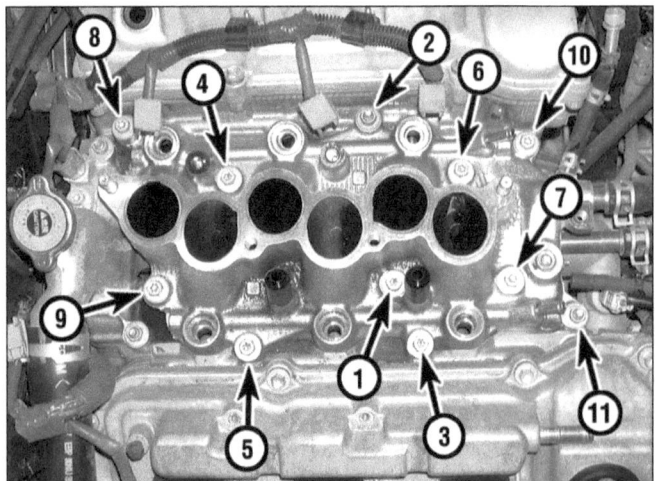

5.26 Bolt tightening sequence for the lower intake manifold

5.27 After the surface of the lower intake manifold has been prepared properly, install a new gasket

6.3 Locations of the engine splash shield fasteners

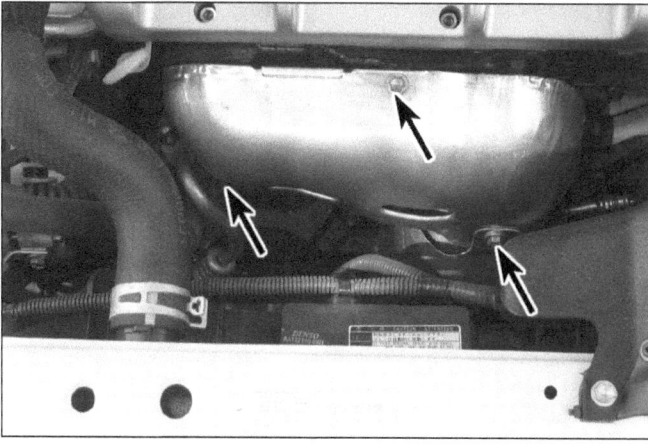

6.5 Remove the exhaust heat shield bolts (not all models are equipped with a heat shield)

27　Install the remaining parts in the reverse order of removal. Use a new gasket between the lower intake manifold and the upper intake manifold **(see illustration)**.
28　Refill the cooling system (see Chapter 1).
29　Run the engine and check for fuel, vacuum and coolant leaks.

6　Exhaust manifold/catalytic converter assemblies - removal and installation

Refer to illustrations 6.3, 6.5 and 6.6

Warning: *The engine must be completely cool before beginning this procedure.*
1　Disconnect the negative (-) battery terminal (see Chapter 5).
2　Spray penetrating oil on the exhaust manifold fasteners and allow it to soak in.
3　If you're removing the rear (firewall side) exhaust manifold, raise the front of the vehicle and support it securely on jackstands (see Jacking and Towing). Then remove the engine splash shields **(see illustration)**.
4　Remove the heated oxygen sensors from the manifold(s) (see Chapter 6).
5　Remove the bolts and the heat shield over the exhaust manifold, on models so equipped **(see illustration)**.
6　Remove the exhaust manifold brace, if equipped **(see illustration)**.
7　Remove the nuts retaining the exhaust pipe(s) to the exhaust manifold(s).
8　Unbolt the exhaust manifold(s) from the cylinder head(s), working from the ends toward the middle. Slip the manifold(s) off the mounting studs.
9　Carefully inspect the manifold(s) and fasteners for cracks and damage.
10　Use a scraper to remove all traces of old gasket material and carbon deposits from the manifold and cylinder head mating surfaces. If the gasket was leaking, check the manifold for warpage on the cylinder head mounting surface by placing a straightedge over the surface and trying to insert a feeler gauge. If

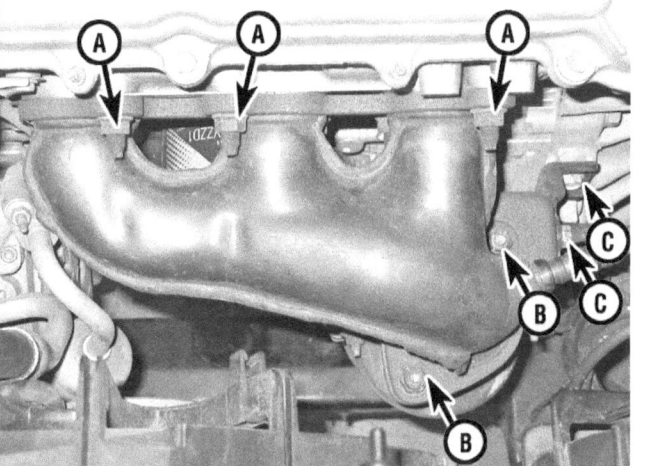

6.6 Location of the front exhaust manifold mounting nuts (A), the exhaust flange nuts (B) and the brace bolts (C) - lower exhaust manifold mounting nuts hidden from view

the clearance exceeds the limit listed in this Chapter's Specifications, have the manifold resurfaced at an automotive machine shop.
11　Position a new gasket over the cylinder head studs.
12　Install the manifold(s) and thread the mounting nuts into place.
13　Working from the centre out, tighten the nuts to the torque listed in this Chapter's Specifications in three or four equal steps.
14　Reinstall the remaining parts in the reverse order of removal. Use new gaskets when connecting the exhaust pipes.
15　Run the engine and check for exhaust leaks.

7　Timing belt and sprockets - removal, inspection and installation

Removal

Refer to illustrations 7.13, 7.14a, 7.14b, 7.16, 7.19, 7.21, 7.23 and 7.25
1　Disconnect the negative (-) battery terminal (see Chapter 5).
2　Remove the top cowl/ventilation cover

(see Chapter 11) and then remove the windshield wiper arms and the windshield wiper motor (see Chapter 12).
3　Remove the lower cowl cover (see Chapter 11).
4　Loosen the wheel nuts on the right front wheel, but don't remove them yet.
5　Raise the front of the vehicle and support it securely on jackstands (see Jacking and Towing).
6　Apply the parking brake and block the rear wheels. Remove the right front wheel.
7　Remove the right front inner guard liner (see Chapter 11).
8　Remove the engine splash shields from below the engine compartment **(see illustration 6.3)**.
9　Position the number one cylinder at TDC (see Section 3).
10　Remove the drivebelts (see Chapter 1).
11　Support the engine with a jack from below and remove the engine movement control rod and its bracket on the engine **(see illustration 16.1f)**. Place a wood block on the jack head and do not place the jack directly under the oil pan drain plug.
12　Remove the power steering pump and position it off to the side without disconnecting the fluid lines. Remove the power steering pump bracket.

13   Remove the upper (number 2) timing belt cover and gasket **(see illustration)**.

Note: *Unclip the wiring harness above the cover and push it back enough to remove the belt cover.*

14   Remove the engine mounting brackets **(see illustrations)**.

15   Remove the alternator bracket **(see illustration 7.14b)**.

16   Check to see if there are installation marks on the timing belt - if you intend to re-use the belt and the marks have been obscured, make new ones **(see illustration)**.

17   Remove the crankshaft pulley bolt. Wedge a large screwdriver into the driveplate ring gear teeth or against a converter bolt to keep the engine from turning, or use a chain wrench to hold the pulley stationary. Use a breaker bar and socket to loosen the pulley bolt.

18   When the crankshaft pulley bolt is loosened, the TDC position of the crankshaft may be disturbed. Check and align again, if necessary.

Note: *The crankshaft timing belt sprocket has a TDC alignment mark that lines up with a mark on the oil pump housing, making it easy to check the TDC alignment even after the crankshaft pulley and lower timing belt cover are removed.*

19   Once the pulley bolt is removed, remove the crankshaft pulley from the crankshaft. The pulley should slide off the crankshaft by hand **(see illustration)**, but if it's stuck, use a bolt-type puller to remove it.

Caution: *Do not use a jaw-type puller - it will damage the pulley/damper assembly. Also, be sure to use the proper adapter to prevent damage to the end of the crankshaft.*

20   Remove the lower (number 1) timing belt cover and gasket.

21   Make sure the camshaft marks are properly aligned with the marks on the rear timing belt cover **(see illustration)**.

22   Rotate the crankshaft counterclockwise approximately 60 degrees BTDC.

Caution: *The engine pistons must be moved*

7.16   If you intend to re-use the belt and the original installation marks are obscured or missing, make new ones

7.13   Remove the number 2 (upper) timing belt cover

7.14a   Remove the mounting bolts and lift the engine mount spacer and side bracket from the engine mount bracket

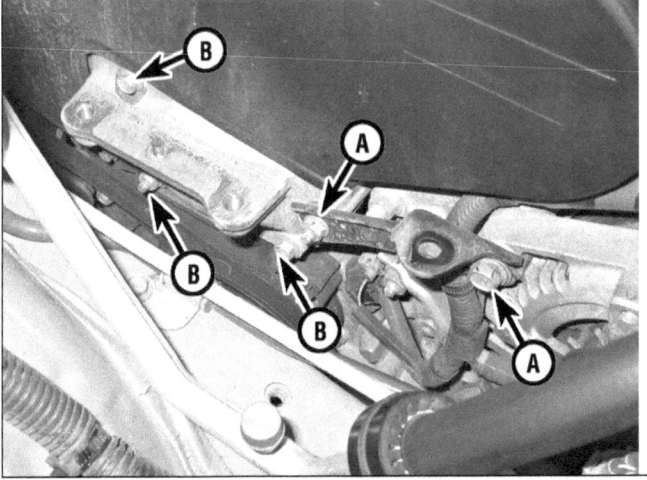

7.14b   First remove the alternator bracket bolts (A) and the bracket, then remove the engine mount bracket bolts (B) and separate the bracket from the engine block

from the TDC number 1 position where they will not accidentally contact the valves when the timing belt tension has been released and the timing belt removed.

Note: *The crankshaft pulley bolt must be installed and tightened enough to be able to rotate the engine in a counterclockwise direction.*

7.19   After loosening the crankshaft pulley with a puller, it should come off by hand

23   Remove the timing belt tensioner **(see illustration)**.

Caution: *Loosen the bolts a little at a time, alternating from side to side until the tension has been released from the timing belt.*

24   Remove the timing belt in the correct order **(see illustration 7.21)**:

   a   *Step 1: Slide the timing belt off the tensioner pulley*
   b   *Step 2: Lift the timing belt over the right side camshaft sprocket*
   c   *Step 3: Slide the timing belt from under the idler pulley*
   d   *Step 4: Lift the timing belt over the left side camshaft sprocket*
   e   *Step 5: Slide the timing belt off the water pump sprocket*
   f   *Step 6: Release the timing belt from the crankshaft sprocket*

25   The camshaft sprockets can be removed at this point. Remove the valve cover(s) (see Section 5) and hold the camshaft with a wrench on the cast-in hex while loosening the sprocket bolt **(see illustration)**. Remove the bolt and detach the sprocket.

26   The crankshaft sprocket can be removed at this point, after removing the sprocket retainer **(see illustration 7.37)**. If it won't

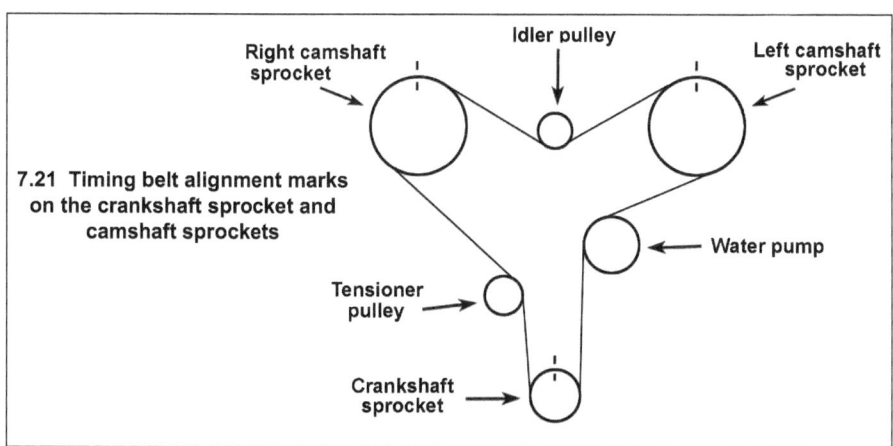

7.21 Timing belt alignment marks on the crankshaft sprocket and camshaft sprockets

Right camshaft sprocket
Idler pulley
Left camshaft sprocket
Water pump
Tensioner pulley
Crankshaft sprocket

7.23 Remove the two bolts and detach the timing belt tensioner

7.25 If the camshaft sprockets are to be removed, hold the hex portion of the camshaft with a wrench while removing the sprocket bolt

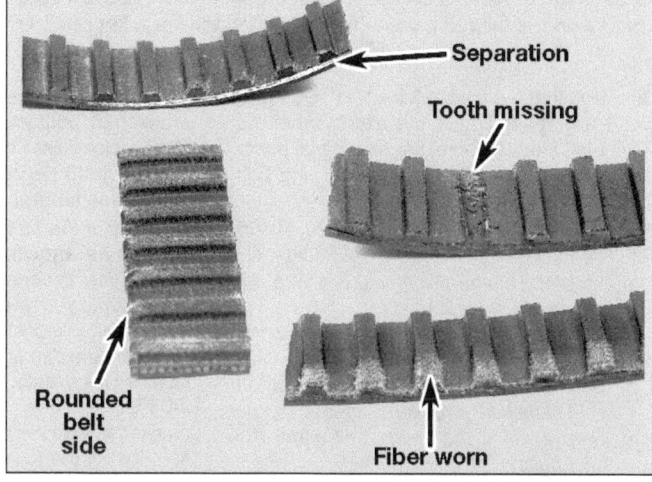

Separation
Tooth missing
Rounded belt side
Fiber worn

7.27 Check the timing belt for cracked or missing teeth - if the belt is cracked or worn, also check the pulleys for nicks or burrs - wear on one side of the belt indicates pulley misalignment problems

come off by hand, a steering wheel type puller may be needed to remove the sprocket. Be careful not to damage the crankshaft sensor portion of the sprocket during the removal process.

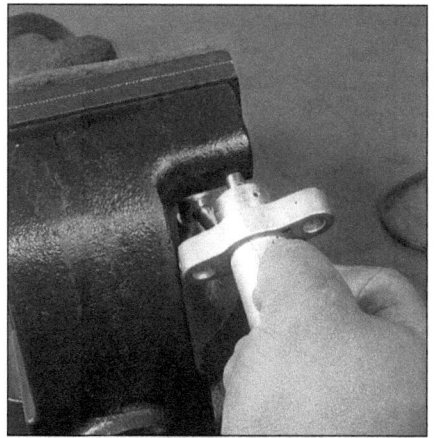

7.29 Check the tensioner for signs of leakage and test for leakdown by forcing it against an immovable object

Inspection

Refer to illustrations 7.27 and 7.29

27   Check the belt for the presence of oil or dirt, and inspect for visible defects **(see illustration).**

28   Check the belt tensioner for visible oil leakage. If there's only a faint trace of oil on the pushrod side, the tensioner seal is in satisfactory condition.

29   Hold the tensioner in both hands and push it forcefully against an immovable object **(see illustration).** If the pushrod moves, replace the tensioner.

30   Check around the crankshaft and camshaft sprockets for any signs of oil leakage. Repair any oil leaks to avoid premature failure of the new timing belt.

31   Check that the idler pulleys turn smoothly.

Installation

Refer to illustrations 7.39 and 7.41

32   Remove all dirt, oil and grease from the timing belt area at the front of the engine.

33   Install the camshaft sprocket(s) (if they

were removed) on the camshaft(s) with the flange side facing OUT. Align the pin hole in the sprocket with the pin in the end of the camshaft. Do not interchange the camshaft sprockets. Install the intake camshaft sprocket onto the intake camshaft and the exhaust camshaft sprocket onto the exhaust camshaft.

34   Install the camshaft sprocket-retaining bolt(s) and tighten it to the torque listed in this Chapter's Specifications.

35   Install the tensioner pulley. Apply thread-locking compound to the first two or three threads of the bolt, then position the pulley and washer and install the bolt. Tighten the bolt to the torque listed in this Chapter's Specifications.

36   Install the upper idler pulley. Tighten the bolt to the torque listed in this Chapter's Specifications. Make sure the pulley turns smoothly.

37   Align the camshaft sprocket alignment marks **(see illustration 7.21).**

38   Install the crankshaft sprocket with the flange side up against the engine. Be careful not to damage the crankshaft sensor portion of the crankshaft sprocket.

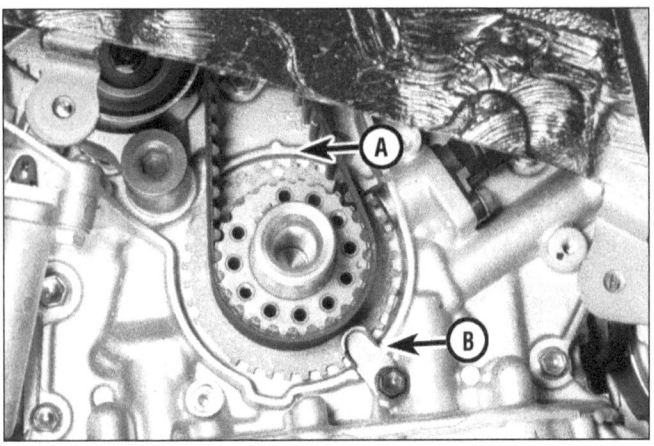

7.39 Align the marks on the crankshaft timing sprocket with the marks on the oil pump case (A), and install the sprocket retainer (B) and bolt

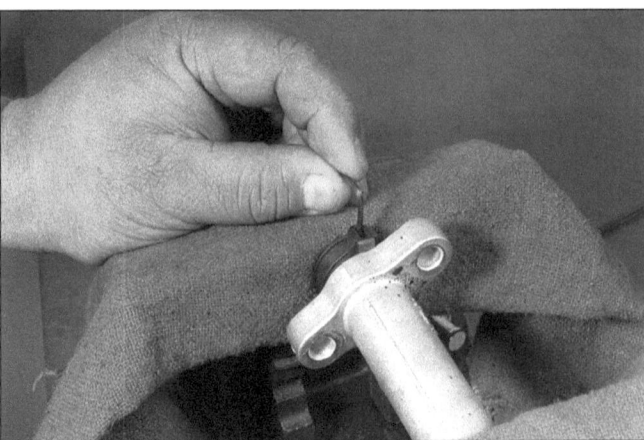

7.41 Restrain the tensioner pushrod by compressing the unit in a vise and inserting a pin approximately 1.5 mm in diameter - make sure the rubber boot is in place

39   Rotate the crankshaft back to TDC number 1 alignment. Check the alignment of the TDC marks on the sprocket and the oil pump housing, and reinstall the retainer and bolt **(see illustration)**.

40   Install the timing belt, starting at the crankshaft sprocket, in the correct order:

a) *Step 1: Engage the timing belt with the crankshaft sprocket*

b) *Step 2: Slide the timing belt over the water pump sprocket*

c) *Step 3: Lift the timing belt over the left side camshaft sprocket*

d) *Step 4: Slide the timing belt under the idler pulley*

e) *Step 5: Lift the timing belt over the right side camshaft sprocket*

f) *Step 6: Slide the timing belt over the tensioner pulley*

41   Using a press or vise, slowly compress the timing belt tensioner pushrod **(see illustration)**. Insert a metal pin, drill bit or Allen wrench through the holes in the pushrod and housing. Remove the tensioner from the press or vise.

42   Install the timing belt tensioner and tighten the bolts to the torque listed in this Chapter's Specifications. Remove the retaining pin.

43   Using a socket and breaker bar on the crankshaft pulley bolt, turn the crankshaft slowly (clockwise) through two complete revolutions (720 degrees). Recheck the timing marks **(see illustration 7.21)**.

Caution: *If the timing marks are not aligned exactly as shown, repeat the timing belt installation procedure. DO NOT start the engine until you're absolutely certain that the timing belt is installed correctly. Serious and costly engine damage could occur if the belt is installed incorrectly.*

44   Slip the belt guide over the end of the crankshaft with the cupped side facing out.

45   Install the lower (number 1) timing belt cover and gasket.

46   Slip the crankshaft (drivebelt) pulley onto the crankshaft, aligning the pulley keyway with the crankshaft key. Install the bolt and tighten it to the torque listed in this Chapter's Specifications. Prevent the crankshaft from turning by using the method described in Step 17.

47   Reinstall the engine movement control rod's mounting bracket (see Section 15).

48   Install the upper (number 2) timing belt cover and gasket.

49   Install the engine movement control rod and braces and tighten the bolts securely (see Section 15).

50   Reinstall the remaining parts in the reverse order of removal.

---

8   Variable Valve Timing (VVT) system - description, check and component replacement

---

Description

Refer to illustration 8.4

Note: *The following procedures apply to the oil control valve, oil filter or intake camshaft sprocket/actuator on either cylinder head.*

1   The VVT system varies intake camshaft timing by directing oil pressure to advance or retard the intake camshaft sprocket/actuator assembly. Changing the intake camshaft timing during certain engine conditions increases engine torque and fuel economy and reduces emissions.

2   System components include the Powertrain Control Module (PCM), an oil control valve (OCV) in each cylinder head, an oil filter for each OCV and an intake camshaft sprocket/actuator assembly.

3   The PCM uses inputs from the vehicle

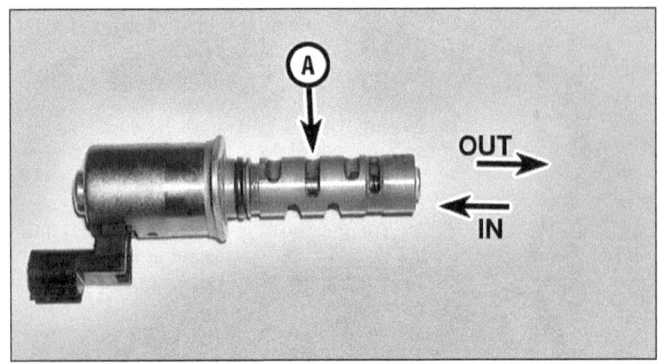

8.4 When voltage is applied, the OCV plunger (A), which you can see through the slots in the housing, should move out; when voltage is cut, the plunger should move in

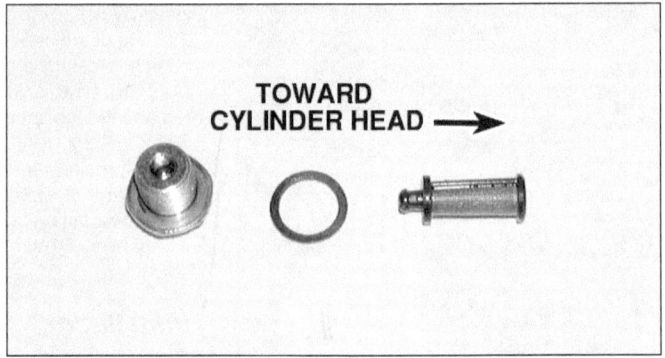

8.8 If you suspect a problem with the VVT system, inspect the OCV filter for obstructions; when you install the filter, use a new O-ring and make sure that the big end of the filter faces toward the head

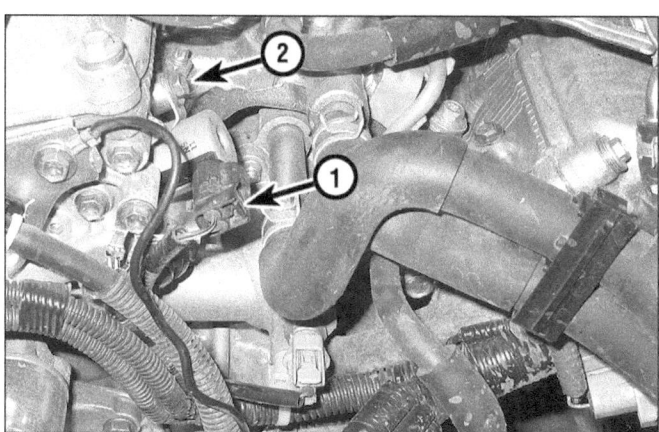

8.9a Location of the oil control valve for the rear cylinder bank

1 Electrical connector   *2 Mounting bolt*

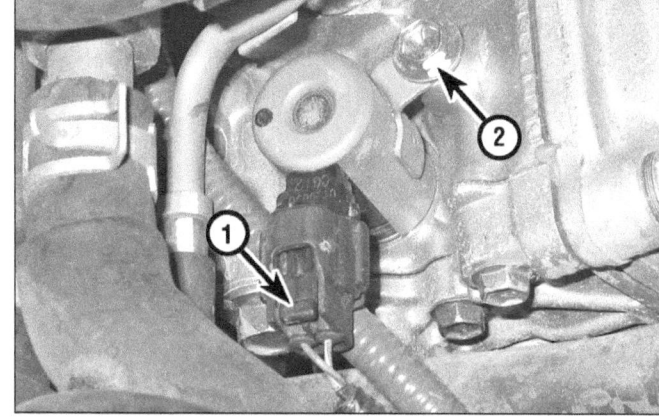

8.9b Location of the oil control valve for the front cylinder bank

1 Electrical connector   *2 Mounting bolt*

speed sensor (VSS), the throttle position sensor (TPS), the mass air flow (MAF) sensor and the engine coolant temperature (ECT) sensor to turn the oil control valve ON or OFF.

4   When the OCV is energised by the PCM, it directs a specified amount of oil pressure from the engine to advance or retard the intake camshaft sprocket/actuator assembly **(see illustration)**.

5   The intake camshaft sprocket/actuator assembly is equipped with an inner hub that is attached to the camshaft. The inner hub consists of a series of fixed vanes. Oil pressure acts against the vanes to rotate the camshaft. By directing the oil to the advance or retard side of the fixed vanes at varying pressure, the OCV controls the amount of camshaft advance or retard.

6   When oil is applied to the advance side of the vanes, the actuator can advance the camshaft up to 21 degrees in a clockwise direction. When oil is applied to the retard side of the vanes, the actuator will start to rotate the camshaft counterclockwise back to 0 degrees, which is the normal position of the actuator during engine operation under no load or at idle. The PCM can also send a signal to the oil control valve to stop oil flow to both (advance and retard) passages to hold camshaft advance in its current position.

7   Under light engine loads, the VVT system retards the camshaft timing to decrease valve overlap and stabilise engine output. Under medium engine loads, the VVT system advances the camshaft timing to increase valve overlap, thereby increasing fuel economy and decreasing exhaust emissions. Under heavy engine loads at low RPM, the VVT system advances the camshaft timing to help close the intake valve faster, which improves low to midrange torque. Under heavy engine loads at high RPM, the VVT system retards the camshaft timing to slow the closing of the intake valve to improve engine horsepower.

Component replacement

Note: *A problem in the VVT oil control valve*

circuit will set a diagnostic trouble code and turn on the CHECK ENGINE light on the dash. Refer to Chapter 6 for accessing trouble codes.

Note: *Most problems in the VVT system originate from the oil control valve(s) and filter(s). Regular engine oil and filter changes are necessary for trouble-free operation of the oil control valve(s).*

Note: *Some checks and inspections of the VVT system require removal of the valve cover and the intake camshaft.*

Oil control valve (OCV) filter

Refer to illustration 8.8

8   A clogged OCV filter screen is often the cause of VVT system problems. Remove the OCV filter from the rear of the cylinder head and then inspect the filter for clogging. Clean the filter if necessary and reinstall it using a new O-ring. Make sure that the big end of the filter faces toward the head **(see illustration)**. Be sure to tighten the filter plug to the torque listed in this Chapter's Specifications.

Oil control valve (OCV)

Refer to illustrations 8.9a and 8.9b

9   To replace the OCV, remove the hold-down bolt and pull the OCV out of the cylinder head **(see illustrations)**. There is one valve at the rear (transaxle end) of each cylinder head. Use a new O-ring when installing the new OCV. Be sure to tighten the OCV hold-down bolt to the torque listed in this Chapter's Specifications.

Camshaft sprocket/actuator assembly

10   Remove the valve cover (see Section 4), the timing belt (see Section 7) and the intake camshaft (see Section 10).

Note: *Do NOT remove the exhaust camshaft or sprocket from the engine.*

11   Mount the camshaft in a bench vise. Secure the camshaft in the vise by clamping up the hexagonal nut part of the cam.

Caution: *Be careful not to damage the camshaft or any of the cam lobes or journals.*

12   Verify that the sprocket/actuator will not rotate from the locked position. The locked position is a neutral position in which the actuator is placed during idle and no load conditions, and anytime that the VVT system is not activated by the PCM.

13   Using brake system cleaner, remove all traces of oil from the front cam journals and the VVT oil control orifices. Apply vinyl tape over all the oil control orifices except the advance side oil port.

14   Apply 100 kPa of air pressure to the advance side oil port and try to rotate the actuator assembly by hand. The actuator should rotate freely, with no obvious binding, for about 30 degrees in the advance angle direction from the locked position.

Note: *It is critical to have an air tight seal between the air gun nozzle and the advance oil port hole, because if air leaks out at the air nozzle, or at any of the other oil control orifices, the lock pin in the actuator won't be forced out of its locating hole. If leakage occurs, apply a little more air pressure to the advance side oil port to force the lock pin from the locating hole.*

15   If the actuator does not rotate freely as described, replace the intake camshaft sprocket/actuator assembly.

16   To replace the sprocket/actuator assembly, put the camshaft in a bench vise and remove the 46 mm nut by turning it clockwise (the nut is reverse-threaded).

17   Remove the sprocket/actuator assembly. If it's hard to pull off the camshaft, tap it lightly with a plastic-tip hammer.

Caution: *Do NOT try to disassemble the sprocket/actuator assembly - it's NOT serviceable.*

18   Lubricate the sprocket/actuator seating surface on the camshaft with clean engine oil. Before installing the sprocket/actuator assembly, make sure that the lock pin (in the camshaft) and lock pin groove (inside the sprocket/actuator) are aligned. Install the sprocket/actuator assembly. Using a NEW

9.4a Removing the front crankshaft oil seal using a self tapping screw, pliers and a block of wood as a fulcrum.

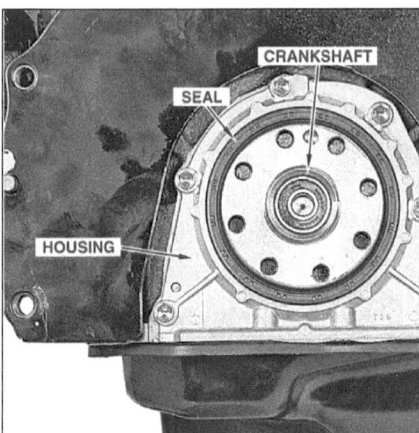

9.4b Rear crankshaft oil seal and associated components

9.4c Removing the rear crankshaft oil seal using a self tapping screw, pliers and a block of wood as a fulcrum.

sprocket/actuator assembly retaining nut, tighten the retaining nut to the torque listed in this Chapter's Specifications (don't forget, it's reverse-threaded).
19 Install the intake camshaft (see Section 10), the timing belt (see Section 7) and the valve cover (see Section 4).

---

9   Oil seals - replacement

Crankshaft oil seal

Refer to illustrations 9.4a, 9.4b and 9.4c

1   To access the front seal, remove the timing belt and crankshaft sprocket (see Section 7).
2   To access the rear seal, remove the transaxle (see Chapter 7) and the drive plate (see Section 14).
3   Using a centre punch, tap a small hole into the front face of the oil seal. Use care not to make the hole too deep and damage the carrier.
4   Screw a self tapping screw into the oil seal. Grip the head of the screw with a pair of pliers and, noting the installed depth of the seal, withdraw the seal from the housing **(see illustrations)**.
5   Clean the bore in the engine and coat the outer edge of the new seal with engine oil or multi-purpose grease. Apply the same grease to the seal lip.
6   Using a seal driver or a socket with an outside diameter slightly smaller than the outside diameter of the seal, carefully drive the new seal into place with a hammer. Make sure it's installed squarely and driven in to the same depth as the original. Check the seal after installation to make sure the spring didn't pop out of place.
7   Reinstall any components removed to access the seals.
8   Run the engine and check for oil leaks at the front seal.

Camshaft oil seals

8   Remove the timing belt and camshaft sprocket(s) (see Section 7).
9   Remove the bolts and detach the rear timing belt cover.
10 Note how far the seal is seated in the bore, then carefully pry it out with a screwdriver. Wrap the screwdriver tip with tape - don't scratch the bore or damage the camshaft (if the camshaft is damaged, the new seal will end up leaking).
11 Clean the bore and coat the outer edge of the new seal with engine oil or multi-purpose grease. Apply multi-purpose grease to the seal lip.
12 Using a seal driver or a socket with an outside diameter slightly smaller than the outside diameter of the seal, carefully drive the new seal into place with a hammer. Make sure it's installed squarely and driven in to the same depth as the original.
13 Reinstall the rear timing belt cover and tighten the bolts.
14 Reinstall the camshaft sprocket(s) and timing belt (see Section 7).
15 Run the engine and check for oil leaks at the camshaft seal.

10.3 Timing marks on the backside of the camshaft gears (typical markings)

---

10   Camshafts and lifters - removal, inspection and installation

---

Note: *Before beginning this procedure, obtain two 6 x 1.0 mm bolts 16 to 20 mm long. They will be referred to as service bolts in the text.*

Removal

Refer to illustrations 10.3, 10.10, 10.12, 10.13 and 10.14

1   Position the engine at TDC (see Section 3), then remove the valve covers (see Section 4), the timing belt and the camshaft sprocket (see Section 7).
2   The following steps apply to the removal of each of the four camshafts. On each head, the exhaust camshaft subgear is secured first, the intake cam removed, then the exhaust camshaft is removed.
3   Make sure the cam timing marks on the drive and driven gears are in alignment **(see illustration)**.

Note: *On the right (rear) cylinder head, align the two dots on the intake camshaft gear with the two dots on the exhaust camshaft gear. On the left (front) cylinder head, align the one dot on the intake camshaft gear with the one dot on the exhaust camshaft gear.*

4   Secure the exhaust camshaft sub-gear to the driven gear with a service bolt installed in the threaded hole **(see illustration 10.12)**.

Caution: *Since the camshaft thrust clearance is minimal, the camshafts must be held level as they are being removed. If they aren't, the portion of the cylinder head next to the cam gears may crack or be damaged by the gear leverage. Before lifting a camshaft out of the head, make certain that the torsional spring force of the sub-gear has been eliminated by the service bolt.*

5   Loosen the intake camshaft bearing cap bolts in 1/4 turn increments until they can be removed by hand. Start with the outer caps and work inward.
6   Remove the bearing caps and gently lift

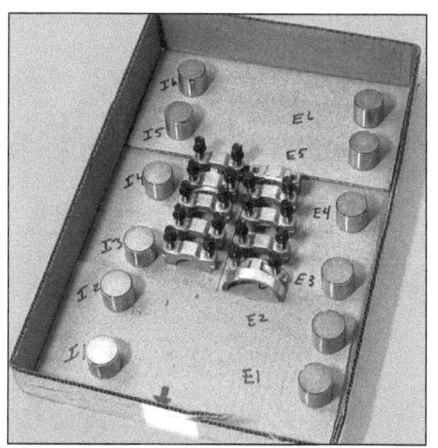

10.10 Mark up a cardboard box to store the lifters/shims and camshaft bearing caps - use a separate box for each set to avoid mix-ups and mark the FRONT, INTAKE and EXHAUST orientation

10.12 With the hex portion of the camshaft held in a vise, use a two-pin spanner to remove the tension from the sub-gear and remove the service bolt, then release the sub-gear

10.13 Remove the snap-ring with a pair of snap-ring pliers

10.14 Remove the wave washer (1), the camshaft sub-gear (2) and the gear spring (3) - exhaust camshaft shown

10.16 Inspect the bearing surfaces in the cylinder head and caps for pits, score marks and abnormal wear

out the intake camshaft. Be sure to keep it level.

7 Loosen the exhaust camshaft bearing cap bolts in 1/4 turn increments until they can be removed by hand. Start with the outer caps and work inward.

8 Remove the exhaust camshaft bearing caps and oil seal and gently lift out the exhaust camshaft. Be sure to keep it level.

9 Repeat the steps for the other cylinder head.

10 Store the bearing caps in the correct order.

Note: *If necessary, the valve lifters and shims can now be removed with a magnetic tool. Be sure to store them separately so they can be reinstalled in their original locations* **(see illustration).**

11 To disassemble an exhaust camshaft gear, mount the cam in a vise with the jaws gripping the large hex on the shaft.

12 Install a second service bolt in the un-threaded hole in the camshaft sub-gear. Using a screwdriver positioned against the service bolt just installed, rotate the sub-gear clockwise and remove the first service bolt. The second bolt isn't needed if you have a two-pin spanner **(see illustration).**

13 Remove the sub-gear snap-ring **(see illustration).**

14 The wave washer, sub-gear and camshaft gear spring can now be removed from the exhaust camshaft **(see illustration).** Be sure to keep the parts from the rear cylinder head cams separate from the front cylinder head parts. The front of the intake camshaft has the VVT assembly, which is secured to the camshaft with a large nut. To remove the VVT assembly, hold the hex portion of the camshaft in a vise and use a breaker bar and 46 mm socket.

Note: *The nut is a left-hand thread. Do NOT remove the nut or the VVT assembly unless either the camshaft or VVT assembly is to be replaced.*

Inspection

Refer to illustrations 10.16, 10.17, 10.18, 10.20 and 10.21

15 Before the camshafts are removed from the engine, check the camshaft endplay by placing a dial indicator with the stem in line with the camshaft and touching the snout. Push the camshaft all the way to the rear and zero the dial indicator. Next, pry the camshaft to the front as far as possible and check the reading on the dial indicator. The distance it moves is the endplay. If the endplay for the intake camshaft is greater than

indicated in this Chapter's Specifications, check the thrust surfaces of the No.1 journal bearing for wear. If the thrust surface is worn, the bearings must be replaced. If the endplay for the exhaust camshaft is greater than indicated in this Chapter's Specifications, the camshaft or the cylinder head (or both) may need to be replaced.

16 With the camshafts removed, visually check the camshaft bearing surfaces in the cylinder head for pitting, score marks, galling and abnormal wear. If the bearing surfaces are damaged, the cylinder head may have to be replaced **(see illustration).**

17 Measure the outside diameter of each camshaft bearing journal and record your measurements **(see illustration).** Compare them to the journal outside diameter in this Chapter's Specifications, then measure the inside diameter of each corresponding camshaft bearing and record the measurements. Subtract each cam journal outside diameter from its respective cam bearing bore inside diameter to determine the oil clearance for each bearing. Compare the results to the specified journal-to-bearing clearance. If any of the measurements fall outside the standard wear limits in this Chapter's Specifications, either the camshaft or the cylinder head (or

10.17 Measure each journal diameter with a micrometer - if any journal measures less than the specified limit, replace the camshaft

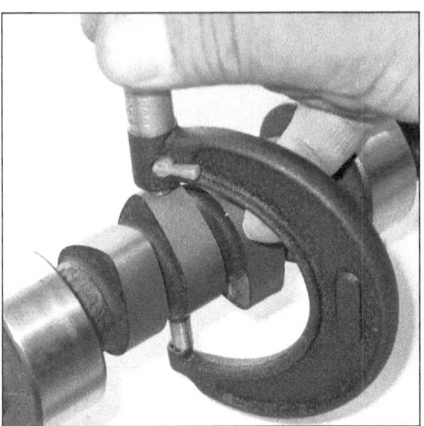

10.18 Measure the lobe heights on each camshaft - if any lobe height is less than the specified allowable minimum, replace that camshaft

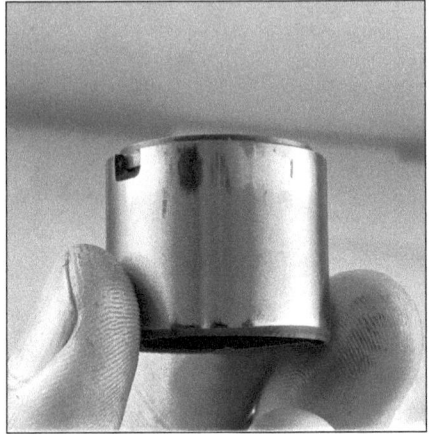

10.20 Wipe off the oil and inspect each lifter for wear and scuffing

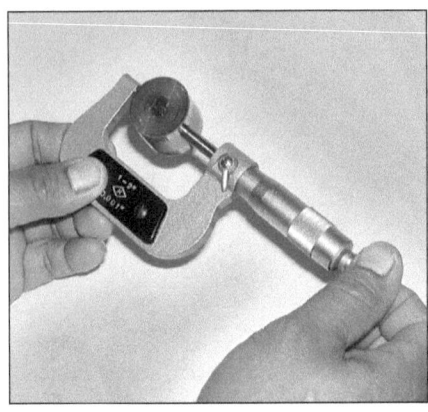

10.21 Measure the outside diameter of each lifter and the inside diameter of each lifter bore to determine the oil clearance measurement

both) must be replaced.

Note: *If precision measuring tools are not available, Plastigage may be used to determine the bearing journal oil clearance.*

18   Using a micrometer, measure the height of each camshaft lobe **(see illustration)**. Compare your measurements with this Chapter's Specifications. If the height for any one lobe is less than the specified minimum, replace the camshaft.

19   Check the camshaft runout by placing the camshaft back into the cylinder head and set up a dial indicator on the center journal. Zero the dial indicator. Turn the camshaft slowly and note the dial indicator readings. If the measured runout exceeds the specified runout, replace the camshaft.

20   Inspect the lifters for scuffing and score marks **(see illustration)**.

21   Measure the outside diameter of each lifter **(see illustration)** and the corresponding lifter bore inside diameter. Subtract the lifter diameter from the lifter bore diameter to determine the oil clearance. Compare it to this Chapter's Specifications. If the oil clearance is excessive, a new cylinder head and/or new lifters will be required.

Installation

16   Reassemble the exhaust camshaft gear(s) by installing the camshaft gear spring, sub-gear, wave washer and snap-ring.

17   Mount the camshaft in a padded vise.

18   Insert a service bolt into the un-threaded hole in the camshaft sub-gear. Using a screwdriver, align the holes of the camshaft driven gear and sub-gear by turning the camshaft sub-gear clockwise. Install a second service bolt in the threaded hole, tightening it to clamp the gears together. Remove the service bolt from the un-threaded hole. Repeat the procedure for the other exhaust camshaft.

19   Apply moly-base grease or engine assembly lube to the lifters, then install them in their original locations in the cylinder heads. Make sure the valve adjustment shims are in place in the lifters, and that all lifters are installed in their original bores.

20   Apply camshaft installation lubricant to the exhaust camshaft lobes, bearing journals and gear thrust faces.

21   Set the exhaust camshaft in place in the cylinder head with the timing mark on the sub-gear facing the centre of the head.

22   Apply a thin coat of RTV sealant to the outer edges of the front bearing cap-to-cylinder head mating surfaces.

23   Install the bearing caps in numerical order with the arrows pointing toward the timing belt end of the engine.

24   Tighten the bearing cap bolts in 1/4 turn increments to the torque listed in this Chapter's Specifications. Start with the centre cap and work your way out to the ends.

25   Refer to Section 9 and install a new camshaft oil seal.

26   Apply camshaft installation lubricant to the intake camshaft lobes, bearing journals and gear thrust faces. If the VVT assembly was removed from the intake camshaft, install it with its groove aligned with the pin on the camshaft. Oil the threads and install a new nut and torque to this Chapter's Specifications.

27   Set the intake camshaft in place in the cylinder head, with the timing mark aligned

with the exhaust camshaft timing mark **(see illustration 10.3)**.

Note: *On the right (rear) cylinder head, align the two dots on the intake camshaft gear with the two dots on the exhaust camshaft gear. On the left (front) cylinder head, align the one dot on the intake camshaft gear with the one dot on the exhaust camshaft gear.*

28   Install the bearing caps in numerical order with the arrows pointing toward the front (timing belt end) of the engine.

29   Tighten the bearing cap bolts in 1/4 turn increments to the torque listed in this Chapter's Specifications. Start with the centre cap and work your way out to the ends.

30   Remove the service bolt from the exhaust camshaft sub-gear.

31   Reinstall the timing belt rear cover, the camshaft sprockets and the timing belt (see Section 8). Before installation, inspect the gasket on the timing belt rear cover. If there is minor damage, repair it with RTV sealant. If there are large sections missing, scrape off the old gasket and install a new one.

32   Reinstall the remaining components in the reverse order of removal.

33   Before reinstalling the valve covers, apply RTV sealant in the areas indicated **(see illustration 4.9)**. Clean the rubber half-circle plugs for the back of the heads and reinstall with new RTV sealant.

34   The remainder of the installation is the reverse of the disassembly sequence.

35   Run the engine, then check for leaks and proper operation.

11   Cylinder heads - removal and installation

Warning: *Wait until the engine is completely cool before beginning this procedure.*

Removal

Refer to illustrations 11.8 and 11.11

1   Disconnect the negative (-) battery terminal (see Chapter 5).

11.8 Remove the bolts and the coolant transfer casting (A) - the transfer hose (B) should be replaced whenever the intake manifold is removed

11.11 Remove the recessed bolt with an 8 mm hex bit

11.20 Be sure the new head gaskets are positioned right side up (check all holes and coolant passages for correct alignment) and over the block dowels

2   Drain the cooling system, including the engine block (see Chapter 1).
3   Remove the upper and lower intake manifolds (see Section 5).
4   Remove the exhaust manifold(s) (see Section 6).
5   Remove the alternator (see Chapter 5). Refer to Chapter 10 and unbolt and set aside the power steering pump.
6   Remove the timing belt, camshaft sprockets and upper idler pulley (see Section 7).
7   Remove the bolts holding the rear timing belt cover and remove it from the engine block and cylinder heads.
8   Disconnect the coolant sensor connectors and remove the water transfer casting

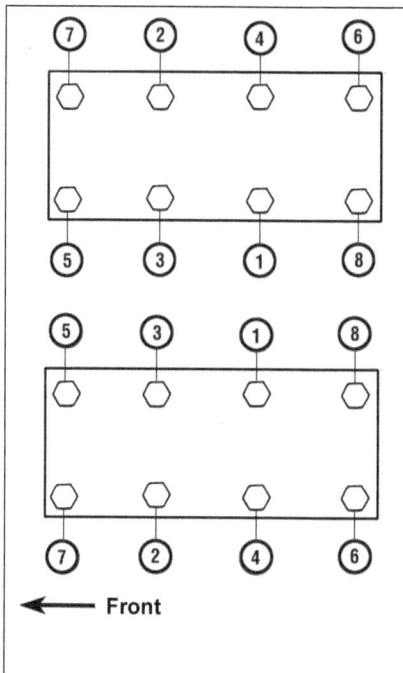

11.23 Cylinder head bolt TIGHTENING sequence

(see illustration).
9   Remove the camshaft(s) from the head(s) you intend to remove (see Section 10). Disconnect the electrical connectors from the camshaft position sensor and the VVT oil control valve (see Section 8).
10   Remove the bolts at the rear of the cylinder heads and move the engine wiring harnesses away from the heads.
11   Using an 8 mm hex bit or Allen wrench, remove the recessed head bolts (one in each head) (see illustration).
12   Using a 12-point socket, loosen the rest of the cylinder head bolts in 1/4 turn increments until they can be removed by hand, along with their hardened washers. Follow the reverse order of the recommended tightening sequence (see illustration 11.23).
13   Lift the cylinder head off the engine block. If the head is stuck, place a wood block against it and strike the wood with a hammer.
Caution: *Don't pry between the head and block. The gasket surfaces may be damaged and leaks could result.*
14   Repeat the procedure for the other head, if necessary.

Installation

Refer to illustrations 11.20 and 11.23
15   The mating surfaces of the cylinder heads and block must be perfectly clean when the heads are installed.
16   Use a gasket scraper to remove all traces of carbon and old gasket material, then clean the mating surfaces with lacquer thinner or acetone. If there's oil on the mating surfaces when the head is installed, the gasket may not seal correctly and leaks could develop. When working on the block, stuff the cylinders with clean shop rags to keep out debris. Use a vacuum cleaner to remove material that falls into the cylinders.
17   Check the block and head mating surfaces for nicks, deep scratches and other damage. If damage is slight, it can be

removed with a file; if it's excessive, machining may be the only alternative.
18   Use a tap of the correct size to chase the threads in the cylinder head bolt holes, then clean the holes with compressed air - make sure that nothing remains in the holes.
Warning: *Wear eye protection when using compressed air!*
19   Mount each bolt in a vise and run a die down the threads to remove corrosion and restore the threads. Dirt, corrosion, sealant and damaged threads will affect torque readings. Measure the diameter of the shoulder area of each head bolt and compare your findings with the value listed in this Chapter's Specifications. Replace any bolts that have stretched too thin.
20   Position the new gaskets over the dowel pins in the block (see illustration).
21   Carefully set the head on the block without disturbing the gasket.
22   Before installing the head bolts, apply a small amount of clean engine oil to the threads.
23   Install the bolts in their original locations and tighten them finger tight. Following the recommended sequence, tighten the bolts to the torque listed in this Chapter's Specifications (see illustration). Don't tighten the recessed bolt at this time.
24   Mark the front of each bolt head with paint. You can also mark the socket you are using.
25   Following the same sequence, tighten each 12-point bolt an additional 1/4 turn (90 degrees) (see illustration 11.23).
26   Tighten the recessed bolt to the torque listed in this Chapter's Specifications.
27   Repeat the entire procedure to install the other cylinder head.
28   The remaining installation steps are the reverse of removal.
29   Refill the cooling system, change the oil and filter (see Chapter 1), run the engine and check for leaks.

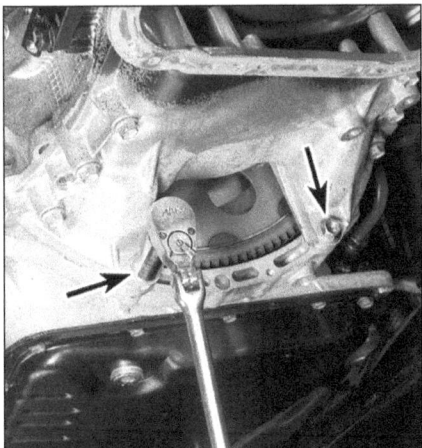

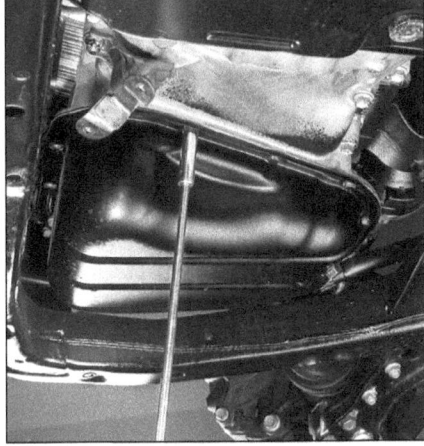

12.7 Remove two bolts and the driveplate cover

12.8 Remove the two bolts securing the aluminium upper pan to the transaxle

12.9 Remove the steel section of the oil pan

12 Oil pan - removal and installation

Removal

Refer to illustrations 12.7, 12.8 and 12.9

1　Remove the bonnet (see Chapter 11).

2　Disconnect the negative (-) battery terminal (see Chapter 5).

3　Raise the vehicle and support it securely on jackstands (see Jacking and Towing).

Warning: *If the vehicle is equipped with electronically modulated air suspension, make sure that the height control switch is turned off.*

4　Remove the engine splash shields **(see illustration 6.3)**.

5　Drain the engine oil and remove the oil filter. The oil pan is a two-part assembly, with an aluminium casting attached to the block and transaxle, and a lower stamped-steel pan section at the bottom.

6　Disconnect the front exhaust pipe from the catalytic converter and the support bracket, and the nuts holding the pipe to the front and rear exhaust manifolds/catalytic converter assemblies.

7　Remove the driveplate cover **(see illustration)**.

8　Remove the two bolts holding the aluminium oil pan section to the transaxle **(see illustration)**.

9　Remove the ten bolts and two nuts securing the steel oil pan section, and detach the steel pan **(see illustration)**. If it's stuck, pry it loose very carefully with a small screwdriver or putty knife. Don't damage the mating surfaces of the pan or oil leaks could develop.

10　Remove the oil pump strainer/pickup **(see illustration 13.4)**.

11　Remove the bolts securing the aluminium oil pan section to the block.

Note: *Some bolts are within the area formerly covered by the steel pan.*

12　Remove the oil pan baffle plate, if equipped.

Installation

Refer to illustration 12.18

13　Use a scraper to remove all traces of old sealant from the block and oil pan. Clean the mating surfaces with lacquer thinner or acetone.

14　Make sure the threaded bolt holes in the block are clean.

15　Check the flange of the steel pan section for distortion, particularly around the bolt holes. If necessary, place the pan on a wood

block and use a hammer to flatten and restore the gasket surface.

16　If the baffle had been removed, reinstall it now.

17　Clean the mating surfaces of the engine block and aluminium pan section, being careful not to gouge the soft metal, which could lead to leaks.

18　Apply a 4 mm wide bead of RTV sealant to the aluminium pan section **(see illustration)**.

19　Install the aluminium pan section within five minutes and uniformly tighten the bolts to the torque listed in this Chapter's Specifications in several passes. Work from the centre out towards the ends of the pan.

20　Inspect the oil pump pick-up/strainer assembly for cracks and a blocked strainer. If the pick-up was removed, clean it with solvent or thinner and install it now, using a new gasket (see Section 13). Tighten the fasteners to the torque listed in this Chapter's Specifications.

21　Apply a 3 to 4 mm wide bead of RTV sealant to the flange of the steel oil pan section.

Note: *The steel pan section must be installed*

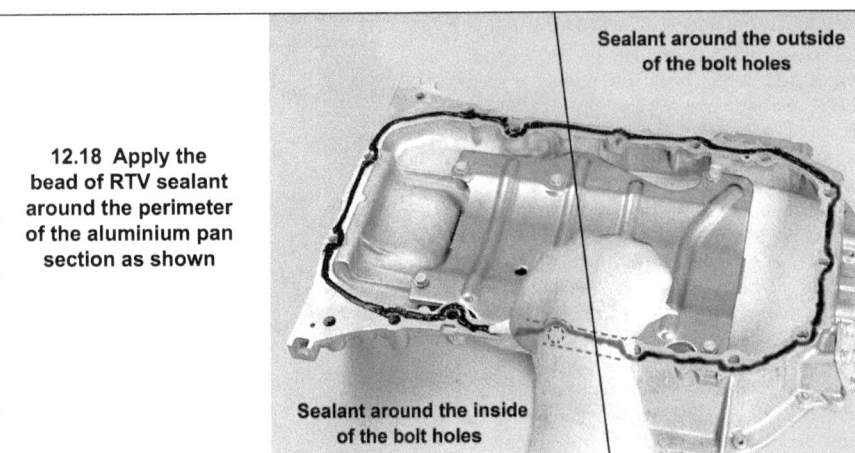

12.18 Apply the bead of RTV sealant around the perimeter of the aluminium pan section as shown

Sealant around the outside of the bolt holes

Sealant around the inside of the bolt holes

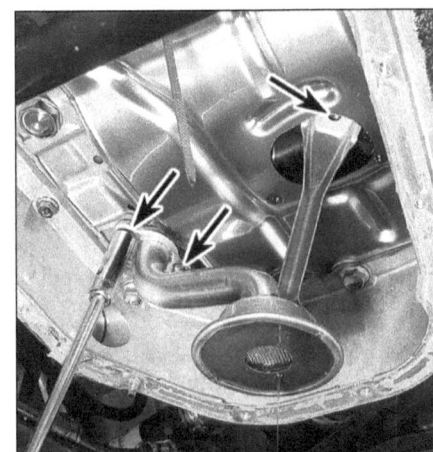

13.4 The oil pick-up tube is held in place with three fasteners

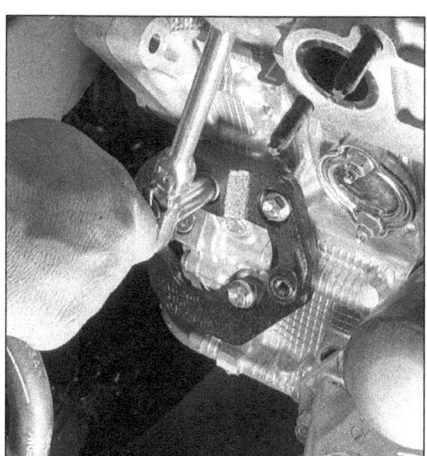

13.7 Unbolt the air conditioning compressor bracket from the block

13.8 Remove the power steering pump adjuster bar and pry the pump away from the oil pump body

13.9 Using a 10 mm hex bit or Allen wrench, remove the timing belt tensioner pulley

within five minutes once the sealant has been applied.

22   Carefully position the steel pan on the aluminium section and install the bolts. Working from the centre out, tighten them to the torque listed in this Chapter's Specifications in three or four steps.

23   The remainder of installation is the reverse of removal. Allow the sealant to set for at least two hours before adding new oil and a new oil filter.

24   Run the engine and check for oil pressure and leaks.

13   Oil pump - removal, inspection and installation

Removal

Refer to illustrations 13.4, 13.7, 13.8, 13.9, 13.11 and 13.12

1   Remove the oil pan (see Section 12).

2   Remove the timing belt (see Section 7).

3   Remove the crankshaft sprocket (see Section 7) and the crankshaft position sensor (see Chapter 6). Place a jack under the

engine. Remove the Engine mounts (see Section 15).

4   Remove the oil pick-up tube **(see illustration)**.

5   Remove the alternator and its bracket (see Chapter 5).

6   Unbolt the air conditioning compressor and set it aside without disconnecting the refrigerant lines.

7   Remove the air conditioning compressor bracket **(see illustration)**.

8   Remove the power steering pump adjusting bracket and pry the pump away from the oil pump body **(see illustration)**.

9   Remove the timing belt tensioner pulley **(see illustration)**.

10   Remove the bolts and detach the oil pump from the engine. You may have to pry carefully between the front main bearing cap and the pump body with a screwdriver.

11   Remove the O-ring. Remove the oil pressure relief valve snap-ring, retainer, spring and valve **(see illustration)**.

Warning: *The spring is tightly compressed - be careful and wear eye protection.*

12   Use a large Phillips screwdriver to remove the screws retaining the body cover to the rear of the oil pump **(see illustration)**.

13   Lift the cover off and remove the pump rotors.

14   Use a scraper to remove all traces of sealant and old gasket material from the pump body and engine block, then clean the mating surfaces with lacquer thinner or acetone.

Inspection

Refer to illustrations 13.17a, 13.17b and 13.17c

15   Clean all components with solvent, then inspect them for wear and damage.

16   Check the oil pressure relief valve sliding surface and valve spring. If either the spring or the valve is damaged, they must be replaced as a set.

17   Check the clearance of the following components with a feeler gauge and compare the measurements to this Chapter's Specifications **(see illustrations)**:

   a *Driven rotor-to-oil pump body clearance*
   b *Rotor side clearance*
   c *Rotor tip clearance*

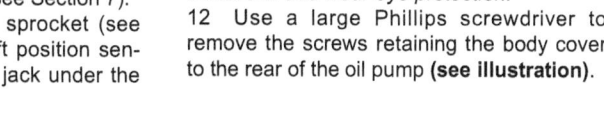

13.11 Remove the oil pressure relief plug, spring and valve

13.12 Use a large Phillips screwdriver or bit to remove the screws retaining the pump cover

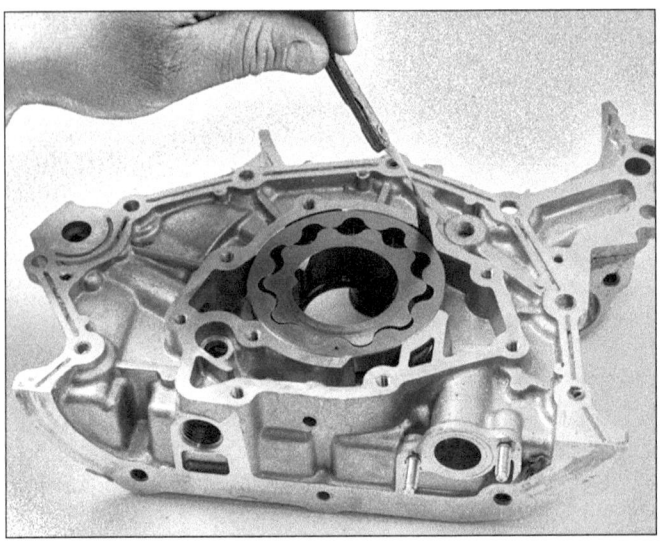

13.17a Measure the driven rotor-to-body clearance with a feeler gauge

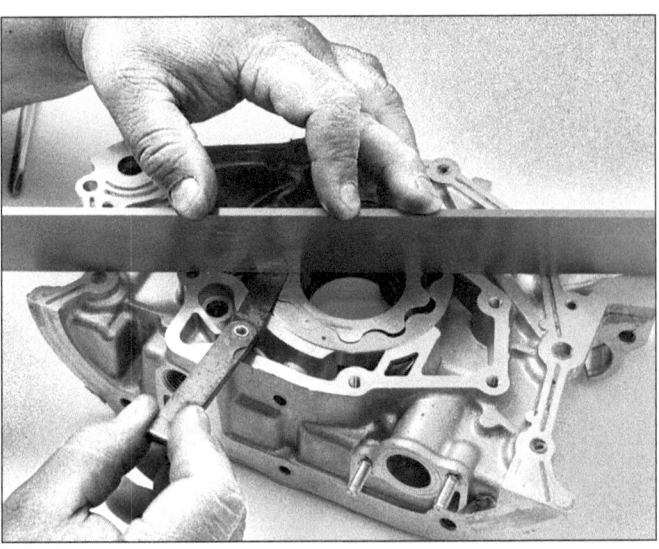

13.17b Measure the rotor side clearance with a precision straightedge and feeler gauge

Installation

Refer to illustration 13.26

18   Pry the old crankshaft seal out with a screwdriver.

19   Apply multi-purpose grease or engine oil to the outer edge of the new seal and carefully drive it into place with a seal driver and a hammer. Also apply multi-purpose grease to the seal lip.

20   Place the drive and driven rotors into the pump body with the marks facing out **(see illustration 13.17c)**.

21   Pack the pump cavity with petroleum jelly and install the cover. Tighten the screws securely following a criss-cross pattern.

22   Lubricate the oil pressure relief valve with engine oil and install the valve components in the pump body.

23   Use acetone or lacquer thinner and a clean rag to remove all traces of oil from the gasket surfaces.

24   Apply a 2 to 3 mm wide bead of anaerobic sealant to the oil pump. Avoid using an excessive amount of sealant, especially around oil passages and bolt holes.

25   Position a new O-ring on the block.

26   Engage the flats on the oil pump drive rotor with the flats on the crankshaft and slide the pump into place **(see illustration)**.

27   Install the oil pump mounting bolts in their original locations and tighten them to the torque listed in this Chapter's Specifications in a criss-cross pattern.

28   Using a new gasket, install the oil pick-up tube and tighten the fasteners to the torque listed in this Chapter's Specifications.

29   Reinstall the remaining parts in the reverse order of removal.

30   Add oil, start the engine and check for oil leaks.

31   Recheck the engine oil level.

14   Driveplate - removal and installation

Note: *There are two spacers used in driveplate mounting, one between the crankshaft flange and the driveplate, the other between the rear face of the driveplate and the driveplate mounting bolts. When removing the driveplate, mark the spacers and reinstall them in the same positions and facing the same way as originally installed.*

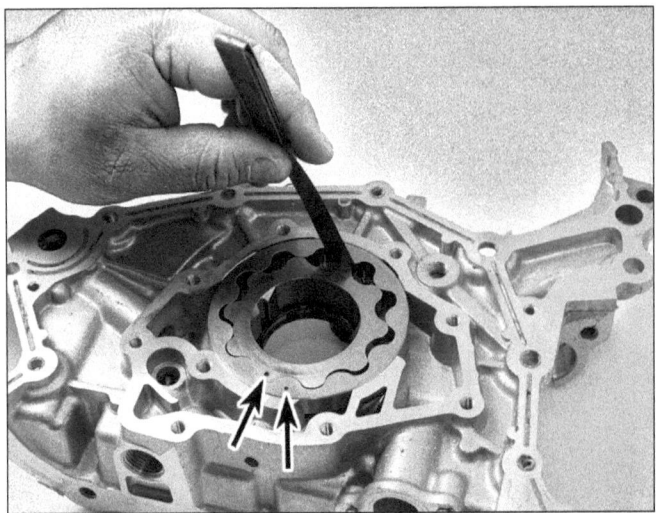

13.17c Measure the rotor tip clearance with a feeler gauge - note the rotor marks are facing out (when the pump body cover is installed, the marks will be against the cover)

13.26 Be sure to install a new O-ring on the block, and align the drive rotor and the crankshaft as the oil pump is installed

14.3 Placing an alignment mark between the crankshaft and driveplate will ensure the driveplate is returned to its original position

14.5 Ensure the spacers are returned to their original positions

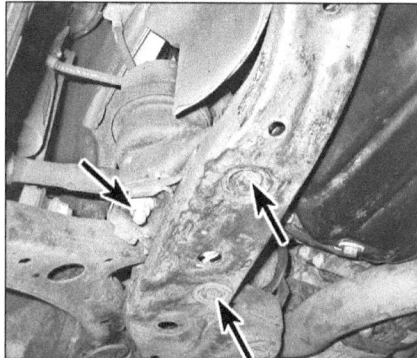

15.9 First remove the access plugs at the subframe, then remove the nuts from the lower engine mount

Removal

Refer to illustrations 14.3 and 14.5

1   Raise the front of the vehicle and support it securely on jackstands (see Jacking and Towing).

2   Remove the transaxle (see Chapter 7). If it's leaking, now would be a very good time to replace the front pump seal/O-ring (automatic transaxle only).

3   Use a centre punch or paint to make alignment marks on the driveplate and crankshaft to ensure correct alignment during reinstallation **(see illustration)**.

4   Remove the bolts that secure the driveplate to the crankshaft. If the crankshaft turns, wedge a screwdriver in the ring gear teeth to jam the driveplate.

5   Remove the driveplate from the crankshaft. This engine has spacers on both sides of the driveplate **(see illustration)**. Keep them with the driveplate.

Installation

6   Inspect the driveplate surface for cracks, especially around the driveplate-to-torque converter bolt holes. Check for cracked and broken ring gear teeth.

7   Clean and inspect the mating surfaces of the driveplate and the crankshaft. If the crank-

shaft rear seal is leaking, replace it before reinstalling the driveplate.

8   Position the driveplate against the crankshaft. Be sure to align the marks made during removal. Note that some engines have an alignment dowel or staggered bolt holes to ensure correct installation. Before installing the bolts, apply thread locking compound to the threads.

9   Wedge a screwdriver in the ring gear teeth to keep the driveplate from turning and tighten the bolts to the torque listed in this Chapter's Specifications. Follow a criss-cross pattern and work up to the final torque in three or four steps.

10   The remainder of installation is the reverse of the removal procedure

---

15   Engine mounts - check and replacement

Refer to illustrations 15.9, 15.10, 15.12, 15.15, 15.18 and 15.21

1   Engine mounts seldom require attention, but broken or deteriorated mounts should be replaced immediately or the added strain placed on driveline components may cause damage or wear.

Check

2   During the check, the engine (or transaxle) must be raised slightly to remove the weight from the mounts.

3   Raise the vehicle and support it securely on jackstands (see Jacking and Towing).

4   Remove the splash shields under the engine and position a jack under the engine oil pan. Place a large block of wood between the jack and the oil pan, then carefully raise the engine just enough to take the weight off the mounts. Do not position the wood block under the oil drain plug.

Warning: *DO NOT place any part of your body under the engine when it is supported only by a jack!*

4   Check the mounts to see if the rubber is cracked, hardened or separated from the bushing in the centre of the mount.

5   Check for relative movement between the mount plates and the engine or frame (use a large screwdriver or pry bar to attempt to move the mounts). If movement is noted, lower the engine and tighten the mount fasteners.

6   Rubber preservative should be applied to the mounts to slow deterioration.

Replacement

7   Disconnect the negative (-) battery terminal (see Chapter 5)

8   Raise the vehicle and support it securely on jackstands, (see Jacking and Towing). Support the engine as described in Step 4.

Note: *If several mounts need replacement, only replace one at a time and tighten them as you go. Do not remove all the mounts at once.*

Driver side (right-hand) lower engine mount

9   Working below the vehicle, remove the nuts securing the mount to the upper and lower brackets **(see illustration)**.

10   Remove the bolts securing the mount to the frame, then raise the engine enough **(see illustration)** to allow removal of the mount.

15.10 Carefully raise the engine until the engine mount studs clear the subframe, remove the nut from the top of the mount and angle the engine mount from the vehicle - it will be necessary to loosen the other mounts at the subframe in order to raise the engine the extra clearance

15.12 Location of the passenger side access plugs and mounting nuts for the left side transaxle mount

15.15 Front engine mount upper nut

Note: *It will be necessary to loosen the mounting nuts on the other Engine mounts at the subframe to allow the engine to be raised enough for clearance for the driver side mount removal.*

11   Installation is the reverse of the removal. Use thread-locking compound on the bolts and be sure to tighten them securely.

Passenger side (left-hand) transaxle mount

12   Working below the vehicle, remove the nut securing the mount to the upper and lower brackets **(see illustration)**.

13   Remove the bolts securing the mount to the frame, then raise the transaxle enough to allow removal of the mount.

Note: *It will be necessary to loosen the mounting nuts on the other Engine mounts at the subframe to allow the engine to be raised*

enough for clearance for the passenger side mount removal.

14   Installation is the reverse of the removal. Use thread-locking compound on the bolts and be sure to tighten them securely.

Front engine mount

15   Remove the fastener securing the mount to the bracket **(see illustration)**.

16   Remove the bolts securing the mount to the frame, then raise the engine enough to allow removal of the mount.

17   Installation is the reverse of the removal. Use thread-locking compound on the bolts and be sure to tighten them securely.

Rear engine mount

18   Working below the vehicle, remove the mount nut and slide the through bolt out of the insulator (see illustration).

19   Remove the bolts securing the mount to the frame, then raise the engine enough to allow removal of the mount.

20   Installation is the reverse of the removal. Use thread-locking compound on the bolts and be sure to tighten them securely.

RH upper mount - engine movement control rod

21   Working in the engine compartment, remove the bolts securing the engine movement control rod and its bracket **(see illustration)**.

22   Installation is the reverse of the removal. Use thread-locking compound on the bolts and be sure to tighten them securely.

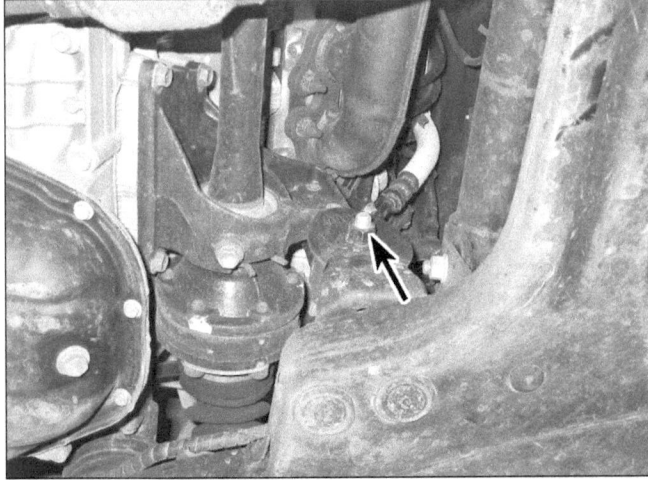

15.18 Location of the rear engine/driveaxle mount through-bolt

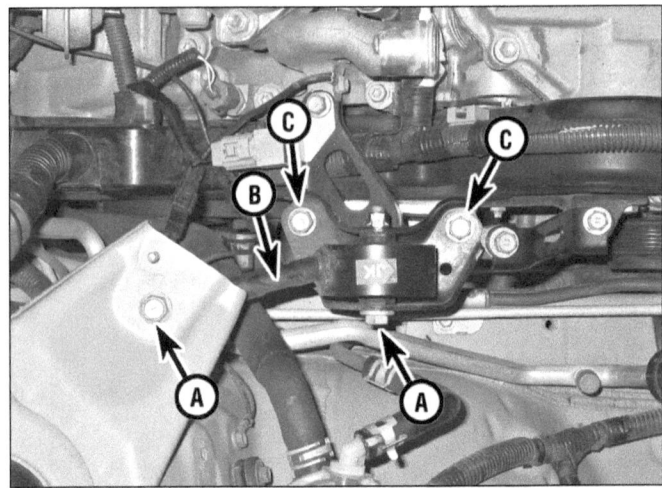

15.21 Remove the movement-control rod bolts (A) and the engine movement control rod (B), then remove the mounting bolts (C) and the engine mounting brace

Chapter 2 Part B
3.5L V6 (2GR-FE) engine

Contents

Specifications

General

Engine designation	2GR-FE
Displacement..	3.5 litres
Cylinder numbers (timing chain end-to-transmission end)	
Rear cylinder bank	1-3-5
Front cylinder bank..	2-4-6
Firing order	1-2-3-4-5-6

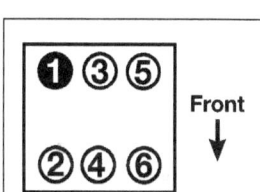

Cylinder locations

Cylinder head

Warpage limits	
Cylinder head - maximum	
Cylinder-to-block surface	0.10 mm
Intake and exhaust manifold surfaces	0.10 mm
Intake manifold - maximum	0.10 mm
Minimum cylinder head bolt diameter - measured 103 mm	
from underside of bolt head **(see illustration)**.................................	10.7 mm

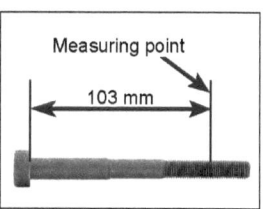

Renew the cylinder head bolt if the diameter is less than specified at the measuring point

Camshaft and related components

Valve clearance	Hydraulic, non-adjustable
Camshaft journal diameter	
No. 1 journal...	35.946 to 35.950 mm
All others	25.959 to 25.975 mm
Bearing oil clearance	
Standard	
No. 1 journal...	0.040 to 0.079 mm
All other journals	0.025 to 0.062 mm
Service limit	
No. 1 journal...	0.10 mm
Others	0.09 mm
Lobe height	
Number 1 and 3 camshafts - Intake	
Standard	44.316 to 44.416 mm
Service limit	44.166 mm
Number 2 and 4 camshafts - Exhaust	
Standard	44.262 to 44.362 mm
Service limit	44.112 mm
Thrust clearance (endplay)	
Standard...	0.08 to 0.13 mm
Service limit...	0.15 mm
Runout limit (total indicator reading)..	0.04 mm

Timing chain

Timing chain (No.1) stretch limit (between 15 pins)	136.9 mm
Timing chain (No.2) stretch limit	137.6 mm
Idler sprocket wear limits	
With No. 1 chain installed..	61.4 mm
Idler sprocket collar diameter...	22.987 to 23.000 mm
Idler sprocket inside diameter	23.020 to 23.030 mm
Oil clearance	
Standard	0.020 to 0.043 mm
Maximum	0.093 mm
Chain tensioner No.2 and No.3 wear limit...	0.90 mm
Chain tensioner slipper wear limit...	0.10 mm
Vibration damper No. 1 and No. 2 wear limit..	0.10 mm

Oil pump

Driven rotor-to-pump body clearance	
Standard-to-maximum..	0.250 to 0.325 mm
Rotor tip clearance	
Standard-to-maximum..	0.06 to 0.16 mm
Rotor side clearance	
Standard-to-maximum..	0.03 to 0.09 mm

Torque specifications

	Nm
Camshaft housing bolts - in sequence **(see illustration 9.18a or 9.18b)**....	28
Camshaft timing sprocket bolt	100
Camshaft bearing cap bolts - in sequence **(see illustration 9.19a or 9.19b)**	
Step 1	10
Step 1	16
Crankshaft pulley bolt...	250
Cylinder head bolts, in sequence **(see illustrations 10.12a and 10.12b)**	
Step 1	36
Step 2	Tighten an additional 90 degrees
Step 3	Tighten an additional 90 degrees
Left cylinder head (two front 14 mm-head bolts).............................	30
Drivebelt idler pulley bolts..	43
Drivebelt tensioner pulley bolt [1]..	Not specified
Drivebelt tensioner mounting bolts	43
Driveplate-to-crankshaft bolts..	83
Engine rear oil seal retainer...	10
Exhaust manifold nuts	21
Intake manifold assembly	
Upper intake manifold bolts..	18
Upper intake manifold nuts	16
Lower intake manifold-to-cylinder head nuts and bolts	21
Oil pan bolts/nuts	
Upper oil pan-to-engine block and front cover	
2 small bolts..	10
Other bolts...	21
Lower oil pan-to-upper oil pan..	10
Engine oil drain plug...	40
Oil pan-to-transaxle bolts	43
Oil pick-up tube nuts...	10
Oil pump assembly	
Oil pump cover bolts	9
Oil pump relief valve plug..	49
Timing chain cover - in sequence **(see illustration 7.40)**	
Small bolts/nuts..	21
Large bolt (Bolt B #24)	43
Timing chain tensioner bolts	
Chain tensioner No.1	10
Chain tensioner No.2 and No.3..	21
Timing chain guide bolts...	23
Timing chain idler sprocket shaft	60
Valve cover fasteners	
Small bolts..	10
Large bolts	21

[1] *LH thread*

3.6 Turn the crankshaft until the notch in the pulley aligns with the zero on the timing plate

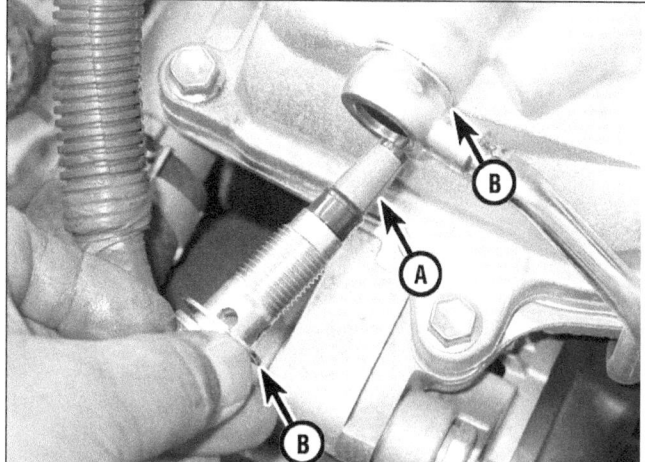

4.9 Take care with the oil filter (A) and the sealing washers (B) when disconnecting the oil line from the valve cover

1   General information

Chapter 2B covers the 3.5L (2GR-FE) V6 engine. Information concerning engine removal and installation and engine overhaul can be found in Part C (see Chapter 2C).

Most of the repair procedures are based on the assumption that the engine is installed in the vehicle. If the engine has been removed from the vehicle and mounted on a stand, many of the steps outlined in this chapter will not apply.

2   Repair operations possible with the engine in the vehicle

1   Some major repair operations can be accomplished without removing the engine from the vehicle. Clean the engine compartment and the exterior of the engine with some type of degreaser before any work is done. It will make the job easier and help keep dirt out of the internal areas of the engine.

2   Depending on the components involved, it may be helpful to remove the bonnet to improve access to the engine as repairs are performed (refer to Chapter 11 if necessary). Cover the fenders to prevent damage to the paint. Special pads are available, but an old bedspread or blanket will also work.

3   The cowl assembly is removable and must be taken out for access to any components in the upper rear of the engine compartment. Refer to Section 4.

4   If vacuum, exhaust, oil or coolant leaks develop, indicating a need for gasket or seal replacement, the repairs can sometimes be made with the engine in the vehicle.

5   Although some major components can be removed with the engine in place, it is usually easier to first lower the engine/transaxle assembly out of the vehicle. Because of this, most procedures in this Section do not have details for in-the-vehicle service.

3   Top Dead Centre (TDC) for number one piston - locating

Refer to illustration 3.6

1   Top Dead Centre (TDC) is the highest point in the cylinder that each piston reaches as it travels up the cylinder bore. Each piston reaches TDC on the compression stroke and again on the exhaust stroke, but TDC generally refers to piston position on the compression stroke.

2   Positioning the piston(s) at TDC is an essential part of many procedures such as valve adjustment and camshaft and timing chain/sprocket removal.

3   Before beginning this procedure, be sure to place the transaxle in Neutral and apply the parking brake or block the rear wheels. Disable the fuel system by relieving the fuel system pressure (see Chapter 4, Section 2), then disconnect the electrical connectors from the ignition coils (see Chapter 5).

4   In order to bring any piston to TDC, the crankshaft must be turned using one of the methods outlined below. When looking at the front of the engine, normal crankshaft rotation is clockwise.

   a   *The preferred method is to turn the crankshaft with a socket and ratchet attached to the bolt threaded into the front of the crankshaft. Turn the bolt in a clockwise direction only.*

   b   *If an assistant is available to turn the ignition switch to the Start position in short bursts, you can get the piston close to TDC without a remote starter switch. Make sure your assistant is out of the vehicle, away from the ignition switch, then use a socket and ratchet as described in Paragraph (a) to complete the procedure.*

5   Install a compression pressure gauge in the number one spark plug hole (see Chapter 2C). It should be a gauge with a screw-in fitting and a hose at least 200 mm long.

6   Rotate the crankshaft using one of the methods described above while observing the compression gauge. When TDC for the compression stroke of number one cylinder is reached, compression pressure will show on the gauge as the marks on the crankshaft pulley are beginning to line up (see illustration). If you go past the marks, release the gauge pressure and rotate the crankshaft around two more revolutions.

7   After the number one piston has been positioned at TDC on the compression stroke, TDC for the next cylinder in the firing order can be located by turning the crankshaft another 120 degrees (refer to the firing order in this Chapter's Specifications).

4   Valve covers - removal and installation

Refer to illustrations 4.9, 4.10 and 4.11

1   Disconnect the negative (-) battery terminal (see Chapter 5).

2   Remove the windshield wiper arms, side seals and plastic cowl (see Chapter 12).

3   Remove the wiper motor and linkage (see Chapter 12).

4   Remove the cowl assembly (see Chapter 11).

5   Pull up on the front side of the engine top cover to detach it from the two front retainers. After the front is detached, pull up on the back retainer and remove the engine cover.

Caution: *Do not pull up on the front and rear at the same time or the cover can be damaged.*

6   Disconnect the hose from the PCV valve.

7   Remove the upper intake manifold (see Section 5).

8   Remove the ignition coils (see Chapter 5). Disconnect the wiring from the sensors and actuators and secure the wiring harnesses out of the way.

9   Disconnect the oil line from the end of each valve cover (see illustration). Carefully set aside the oil control valve filter when

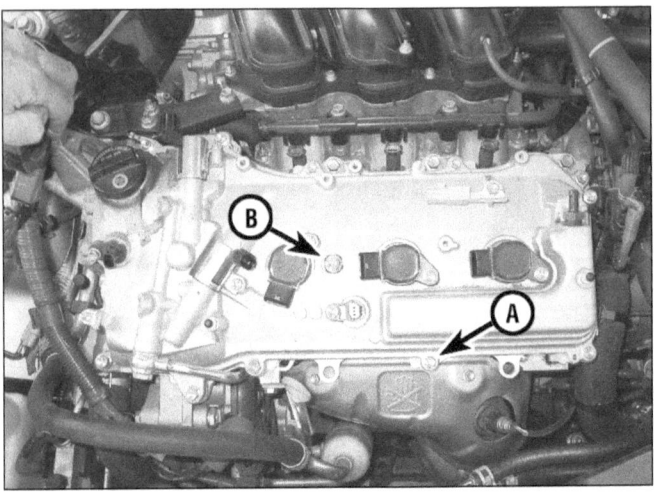

4.10 The valve cover is retained with 11 perimeter bolts (A) and a central bolt (B)

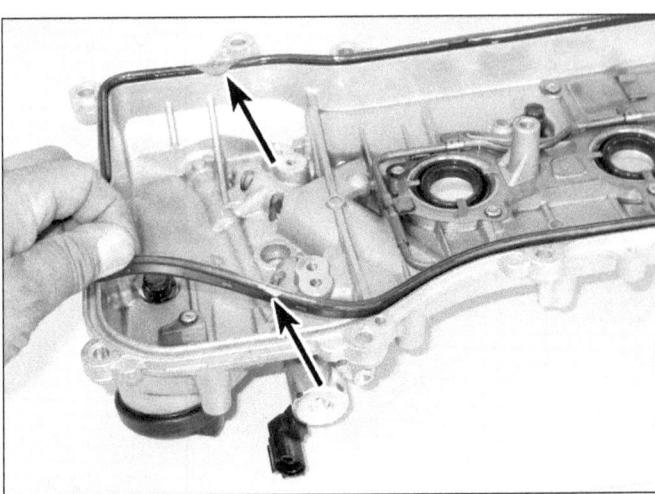

4.11 Make sure that the gasket is fully seated into the valve cover groove, and that the spark plug tube seals are seated as well; arrows indicate areas where sealant was applied on the joint between the timing chain cover and the cylinder head - clean old sealant from the gasket before reusing it

you remove the upper banjo bolt from the valve cover. The sealing washers should be replaced with new ones if they're worn.

10 Remove the valve cover bolts and remove the valve cover **(see illustration)**.

11 Check the three small round interior gaskets as well as the large perimeter gasket **(see illustration)**. They should be replaced with new ones if they show signs of deterioration.

12 Installation is the reverse of removal. Thoroughly clean all sealing surfaces prior to putting the new gaskets in place.

13 Apply dabs of RTV sealant to the joints where the timing chain cover meets the cylinder heads.

14 Evenly tighten the valve cover nuts and bolts to the torque listed in this Chapter's Specifications.

15 Start the engine and check for oil leaks around the edges of the valve cover.

5   Intake manifold - removal and installation

Warning: *Wait until the engine is completely cool before beginning this procedure.*

Upper intake manifold

Refer to illustrations 5.6 and 5.7

Note: *Toyota refers to the upper intake manifold as the intake air surge tank. If you're buying a gasket for the upper intake manifold at a dealer parts department, use the Toyota terminology.*

1 Disconnect the negative (-) battery terminal (see Chapter 5).

Warning: *If you plan on removing the lower intake manifold, relieve the fuel system pressure before disconnecting the battery (see Chapter 4, Section 2).*

2 Disconnect all hoses and the wiring from the throttle body (see Chapter 4). The coolant

hoses can be pinched off to avoid draining the cooling system. Label the hoses to avoid confusion later.

3 Remove the windshield wiper arms and motor (see Chapter 12), side seals and plastic cowl (see Chapter 12).

4 Remove the throttle body bracket, the upper intake manifold brace and the throttle body (see Chapter 4).

5 Disconnect all wiring and hoses from the upper intake manifold.

6 Remove the intake manifold mounting fasteners and remove the upper intake manifold **(see illustration)**.

7 Check the condition of the upper intake manifold gasket **(see illustration)**. If it isn't cracked, hardened or flattened, it can be reused.

8 Installation is the reverse of removal. Tighten the upper intake manifold mounting bolts and nuts to the torque listed in this Chapter's Specifications. Start with the inner bolts and work outward in a circular pattern.

5.6 Upper intake manifold fasteners

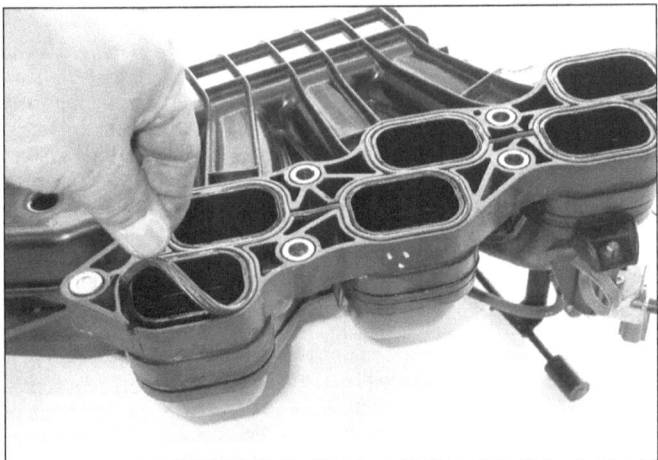

5.7 Check the condition of the upper intake manifold gasket, replacing it if necessary

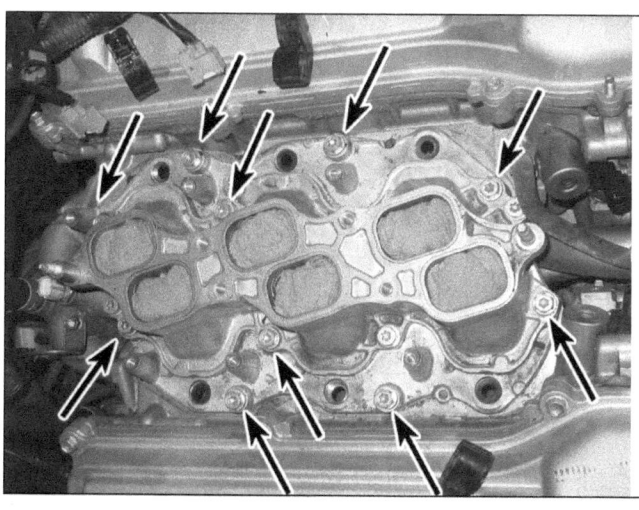

5.13 Lower intake manifold mounting bolts

Lower intake manifold

Refer to illustration 5.13

Note: *Toyota refers to the lower intake manifold as simply the "intake manifold." If you're buying a gasket for the lower intake manifold at a dealer parts department, use the Toyota terminology.*

9   Remove the upper intake manifold (see Steps 1 through 7).

10   If you're removing the lower intake manifold to replace it, remove the fuel rail now (see Chapter 4).

11   If you're just removing the lower intake manifold to replace the gaskets, it's not necessary to remove the fuel rail, but you'll have to disconnect the fuel line connection (see Chapter 4).

12   Remove the interfering brace.

13   Unscrew the bolts and remove the lower intake manifold **(see illustration)**.

14   Remove and discard the old lower intake manifold gaskets. Clean off all traces of old gasket material from the mating surfaces of the manifold and cylinder heads, then wipe the surfaces with brake system cleaner.

15   Installation is the reverse of removal. Use new gaskets and tighten the lower intake manifold bolts a little at a time, in a criss-cross pattern working from the centre bolts outward, to the torque listed in this Chapter's Specifications.

6   Exhaust manifolds - removal and installation

Warning: *The engine must be completely cool before beginning this procedure.*

Note: *The following procedure applies to either exhaust manifold.*

1   Disconnect the electrical connectors from the left upstream oxygen sensor.

2   Remove the bolts that secure the exhaust manifold support bracket and remove it.

3   Disconnect any interfering wire clamps.

4   Remove the heat shield from the front exhaust manifold.

5   Evenly loosen the nuts that secure each exhaust manifold and remove the exhaust manifold.

6   Remove and discard the old exhaust manifold gasket.

7   Installation is the reverse of removal. Use a new gasket and install it with the oval-shaped protruding tip facing in the correct direction. For the left (driver's side) manifold, the tip must face to the rear; on the right manifold, it must face to the front.

8   Tighten the exhaust manifold nuts a little at a time, working from the centre nuts outward, to the torque listed in this Chapter's Specifications.

7   Timing chains and sprockets - removal, inspection and installation

Removal

Refer to illustrations 7.3a, 7.3b, 7.6, 7.8a, 7.8b, 7.8c, 7.8d and 7.9

Warning: *Wait until the engine is completely cool before beginning this procedure.*

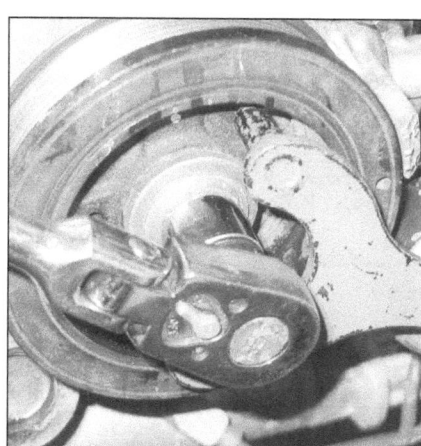

7.3a Hold the crankshaft pulley with a pin spanner while removing the bolt

Caution: *The timing system is complex, and severe engine damage will occur if you make any mistakes. Do not attempt this procedure unless you are highly experienced with this type of repair. If you are at all unsure of your abilities, be sure to consult an expert. Double-check all your work and be sure everything is correct before you attempt to start the engine.*

Note: *The manufacturer recommends removing the engine and transaxle assembly to perform this procedure (see Chapter 2C).*

1   Remove the engine/transaxle assembly (see Chapter 2C).

2   Remove the drivebelt, unbolt the drive-belt tensioner (see Chapter 1), remove the idler pulley bolts and remove the two idler pulleys.

3   Set the engine to TDC (see Section 3). Remove the crankshaft pulley **(see illustrations)**.

4   Remove the four timing chain cover bolts from the front of the upper oil pan.

5   Remove the water inlet (see Chapter 3). Remove the O-ring and gasket from the water inlet and discard them.

6   Remove the timing chain cover mounting fasteners and remove the timing chain cover. There are only a few spots where you can safely pry the cover off without damaging it **(see illustration)**. Do NOT pry the timing chain cover loose at any other spot or you will damage the sealing surface of the cover.

Note: *There are three different sized bolts used on the timing chain cover* **(see illustration 7.40).**

7   After removing the timing chain cover, carefully pry out the old crankshaft seal with a screwdriver (see Section 8). Make sure that you don't scratch the seal bore. If you want to inspect or replace any oil pump parts, refer to Section 12.

7.3b If the crankshaft pulley can't be removed by hand, use a puller that bolts to the hub of the pulley, not a jaw-type puller. Also, be sure to use the correct adapter between the nose of the crankshaft and the puller screw, so as not to damage the threads in the crankshaft

7.6 The timing chain cover can be pried loose at the lower corners and at the upper corners; prying anywhere else may damage the cover

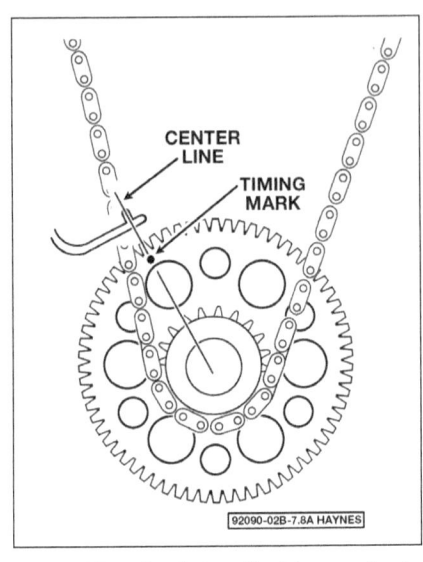

7.8a Align the dot on the trigger wheel with the rib on the block - this should set the engine at TDC

7.8b The exhaust camshaft sprocket of the left (front) cylinder head with the engine at TDC

Note: *Keep track of the locations of all of the bolts. They are of different lengths and can't be interchanged.*

7.8c The intake camshaft sprocket of the left (front) cylinder head with the engine at TDC

8   Verify that the piston in the No. 1 cylinder is near TDC on its compression stroke. If not, install the crankshaft pulley bolt, then rotate the crankshaft until the dot on the crankshaft

position trigger wheel (the toothed wheel behind the lower crankshaft sprocket) is at the 11 o'clock position and is aligned with the rib on the engine block **(see illustration)**. You can also temporarily install the front cover and the crankshaft pulley and set the pulley at the 0 degree mark. Verify that the timing marks on the camshaft timing sprockets are aligned with their corresponding marks on top of the front camshaft bearing caps **(see illustrations)**. If the marks are not aligned, rotate the crankshaft another 360 degrees and recheck the marks.

9   Turn the stopper plate on the No. 1 tensioner clockwise and push in the tensioner plunger **(see illustration)**. To lock the plunger in this position, turn the stopper plate counterclockwise and insert a drill or punch (1.27 mm) through the holes in the stopper plate and the tensioner body. Remove the

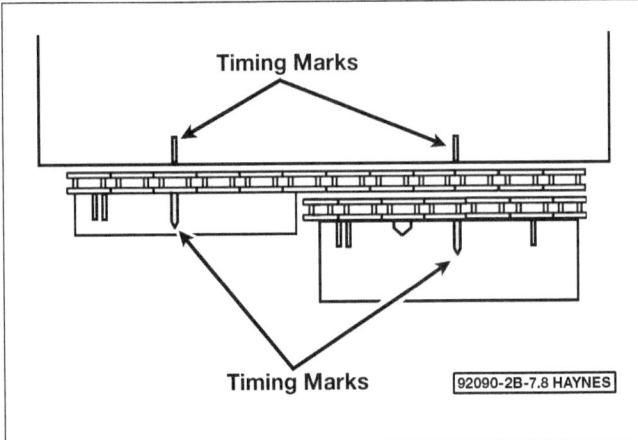

7.8d Alignment marks for the right (rear) camshaft sprockets

7.9 To lock the tensioner in the retracted position, rotate the stopper plate clockwise and push the plunger in, then rotate the stopper plate counterclockwise and insert a pin through the hole in the stopper plate and the tensioner body

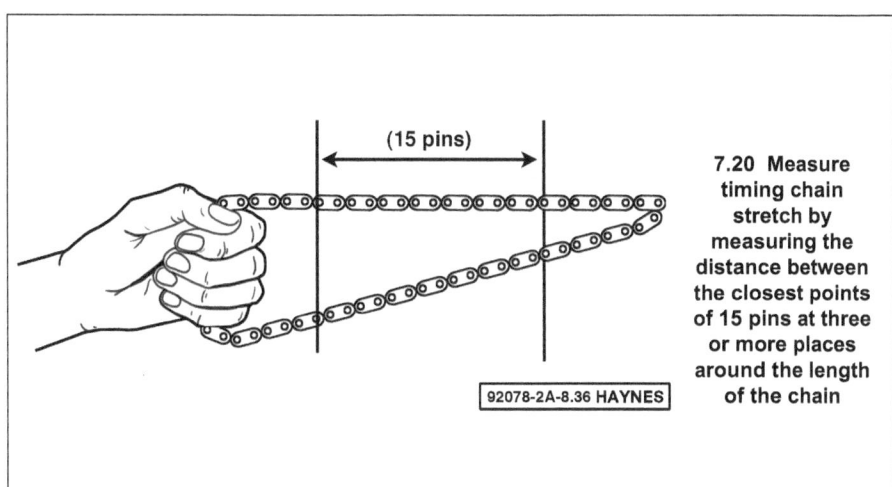

7.20 Measure timing chain stretch by measuring the distance between the closest points of 15 pins at three or more places around the length of the chain

92078-2A-8.36 HAYNES

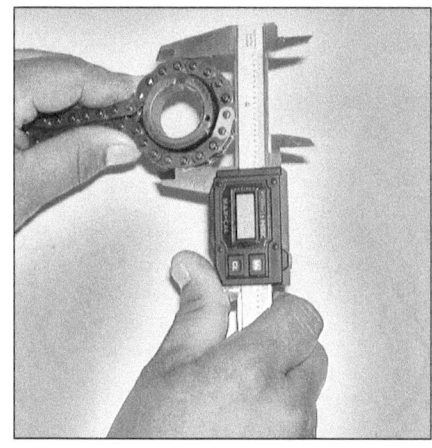

7.21 Wrap the chain around each of the timing chain sprockets and measure the diameter of the sprockets across the chain rollers. If the measurement is less than the minimum sprocket diameter, replace the chain and the timing sprockets

tensioner mounting bolts and the No. 1 tensioner.

Note: *The No. 1 tensioner is the tensioner for the main timing chain.*

10   Remove the chain tensioner slipper.

11   Using a 10 mm hex wrench, unscrew the idler sprocket shaft and remove the idler shaft, sprocket and collar. Note which side of the sprocket faces out.

12   Remove the chain vibration dampers.

13   Note the positions of the timing marks on each camshaft sprocket and the crankshaft sprocket. Make sketches or take pictures. Remove the No. 1 (main) timing chain.

Caution: *While the No. 1 timing chain is removed, DO NOT ROTATE THE CRANKSHAFT!*

14   Remove the crankshaft timing chain sprocket.

15   Compress chain tensioner No. 2 and insert a drill bit or punch (1.27 mm) into the hole.

Note: *Timing chain No. 2 and the No. 2 chain tensioner are on the right (rear) cylinder head. Timing chain No. 3 and the No. 3 tensioner are on the left (front) cylinder head.*

16   Hold the hex on the exhaust camshaft with a wrench and unscrew the two bolts that secure the camshaft timing sprockets to the camshafts. Remove the sprockets and chain as an assembly. Keep the components in a re-sealable plastic bag to ensure that none of these components is mixed with the other timing chain set.

Caution: *Don't attempt to disassemble the adjustable intake sprocket assembly. If disassembled, it will have to be replaced.*

17   Remove the chain tensioner No. 2 mounting bolt and remove chain tensioner No. 2. Store the tensioner in the plastic bag with the other No. 2 timing chain components.

18   To remove the No. 3 timing chain and tensioner, repeat these Steps. Again, store the components in a re-sealable plastic bag.

Caution: *DO NOT ROTATE THE CRANKSHAFT while the timing chains are removed!*

Inspection

Refer to illustrations 7.20 and 7.21

19   Inspect all parts of the timing chain assembly for wear and damage. Inspect the three timing chains for loose pins, cracks, and worn rollers and side plates. Inspect the sprockets for hook-shaped, chipped and/or broken teeth.

20   Inspect timing chain No. 1 for stretching. To measure timing chain stretch, measure the distance between 15 pins at three or more places around the length of the chain **(see illustration)**. Measure between the inside of the rollers and compare your measurements with the distance listed in this Chapter's Specifications.

21   Measure the diameter of each timing chain sprocket and idler sprocket with the appropriate timing chain installed on the sprocket **(see illustration)**. The sprocket diameter, with the chain in place, should not exceed the dimensions listed in this Chapter's Specifications.

22   Measure the idler sprocket oil clearance as follows. First, measure the diameter of the idler sprocket collar with a micrometer and record your measurement. Then measure the inside diameter of the idler sprocket and record that measurement as well. Subtract the idler sprocket collar diameter from the inside diameter of the idler sprocket and compare the result with the clearance listed in this Chapter's Specifications. If the clearance is excessive, replace the idler sprocket and/or collar, as necessary.

23   Some scoring and wear of the timing chain tensioners and vibration dampers is normal, but excessive wear will increase chain noise, accelerate chain and sprocket wear and could damage the engine if a chain jumps timing. Inspect chain tensioners No. 2 and 3, the timing chain tensioner slipper and the timing chain vibration dampers for excessive wear. If the measured chain wear for any of these components exceeds the depth listed in this Chapter's Specifications, replace the component.

24   Check the chain tensioners for correct operation. On the No. 1 tensioner, raise

the ratchet pawl and verify that the plunger moves smoothly in and out of the tensioner, then release the ratchet pawl and verify that it prevents the plunger from sliding back into the tensioner. Also verify that the plungers on the No. 2 and No. 3 tensioners move in and out smoothly.

Installation

Refer to illustrations 7.26, 7.28, 7.33a, 7.33b and 7.40

Caution: *Before starting the engine, carefully rotate the crankshaft by hand through at least two full revolutions (use a socket and breaker bar on the crankshaft pulley centre bolt). If you feel any resistance, STOP! There is something wrong - most likely, valves are contacting the pistons. You must find the problem before proceeding.*

25   Push in the tensioner plunger on chain tensioner No. 2 and insert a drill or punch (1.27 mm diameter) into the hole of the tensioner to lock the plunger in the retracted position. Install the tensioners and tighten the mounting bolts to the torque listed in this Chapter's Specifications.

26   Install the No. 2 (right bank inner) timing chain on the camshaft sprockets. Make sure that the yellow mark links on the chain are aligned with the single timing dots or lines on the camshaft sprockets **(see illustration)**.

27   Align the yellow links on the No. 2 timing chain with the timing marks on the bearing caps and install timing chain No. 2 and the camshaft sprockets as an assembly. Install the two bolts that secure the timing sprockets to the camshafts. Immobilise the hex on the exhaust camshaft with an adjustable wrench and tighten these two bolts to the torque listed in this Chapter's Specifications. Remove the drill or punch that was used to lock the tensioner plunger in its retracted position and verify that the plunger tensions the chain.

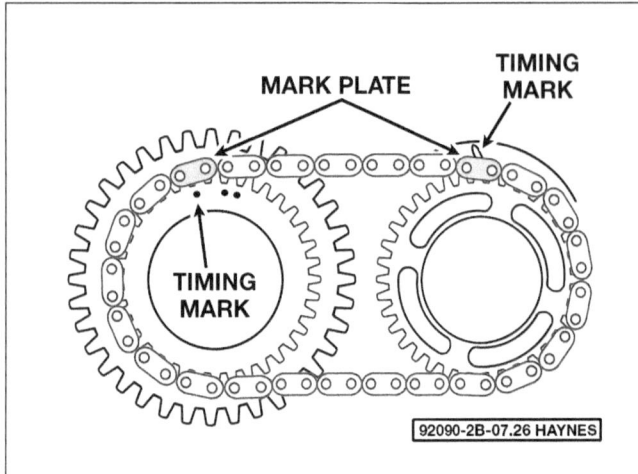

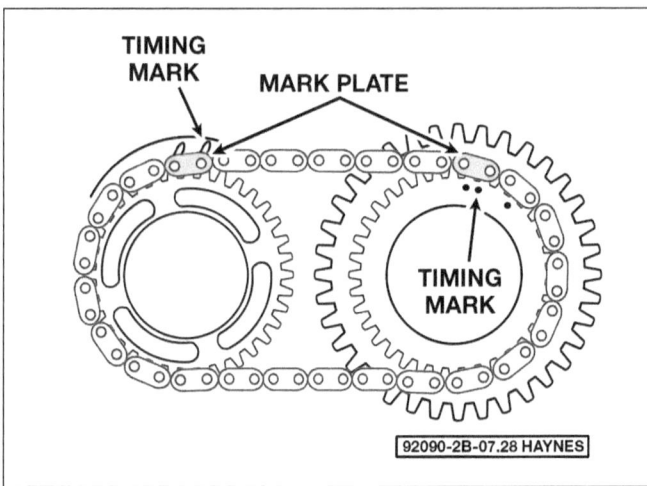

7.26 The small No. 2 timing chain maintains the alignment of the intake and exhaust camshaft sprockets of the right (rear) cylinder head; set the yellow links on the single line and single dot of the camshaft sprockets

7.28 Set the yellow links of the No. 3 timing chain of the left (front) cylinder head on the double lines and double dots of the camshaft sprockets

28   Install the other inner timing chain by repeating Steps 25 through 27. Align the yellow links with the double line or dot marks on the sprockets **(see illustration)**. Also align its yellow links with the marks on the bearing caps.

29   Install the chain guides and tighten the bolts to the torque listed in this Chapter's Specifications.

30   Install the crankshaft timing sprocket on the crankshaft. Align the timing sprocket keyway with the keys on the crankshaft.

31   Apply a light coat of engine oil to the bearing surface of the idler sprocket collar. Install the idler sprocket collar, sprocket and shaft. Make sure that the teeth on the idler sprocket are facing forward. Tighten the idler sprocket shaft to the torque listed in this Chapter's Specifications.

32   Verify that the timing marks on the camshaft timing sprockets are aligned with their corresponding marks on top of the front camshaft bearing caps.

33   Install the long timing chain (No. 1) on the camshaft timing sprockets and on the idler sprocket. Turn the camshaft sprockets to remove the slack in the upper part of the chain, then install the chain over the crankshaft sprocket. Make sure that the yellow link is aligned with the timing dot on the crankshaft timing sprocket (it's near the 3 o'clock position) and that the orange links are aligned with the timing marks on the intake camshaft sprockets **(see illustrations)**. There is a dot on the crankshaft position trigger wheel (the toothed wheel behind the lower crankshaft sprocket) that must be at the 11 o'clock position and aligned with the rib on the engine block **(see illustration 7.8a)**.

34   Turn the stopper plate on the No. 1 tensioner clockwise and push in the tensioner plunger. To lock the plunger in this position,

turn the stopper plate counterclockwise and insert a drill or punch (1.27 mm) through the holes in the stopper plate and the tensioner. Install the tensioner and tighten the tensioner mounting bolts to the torque listed in this Chapter's Specifications. Remove the drill or punch that you inserted into chain tensioner No. 1 and verify that it tensions timing chain No. 1.

Caution: *Carefully rotate the crankshaft by hand through at least two full revolutions (use a socket and breaker bar on the crankshaft pulley centre bolt). If you feel any resistance, STOP! There is something wrong - most likely, valves are contacting the pistons. You must find the problem before proceeding.*

35   Remove all old RTV sealant from the gasket mating surfaces of the timing chain cover and from the front of the cylinder heads and engine block.

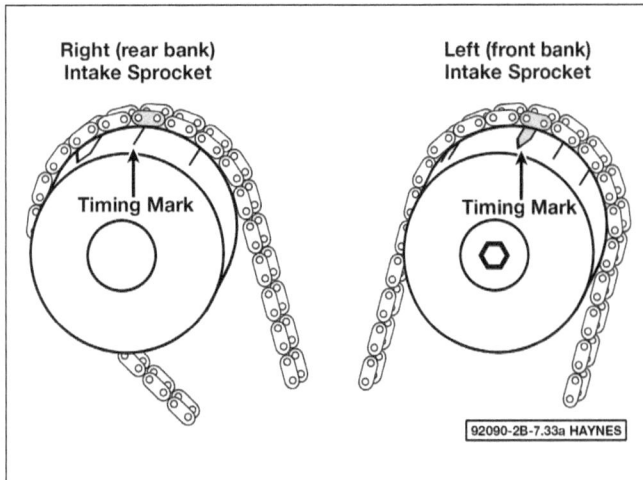

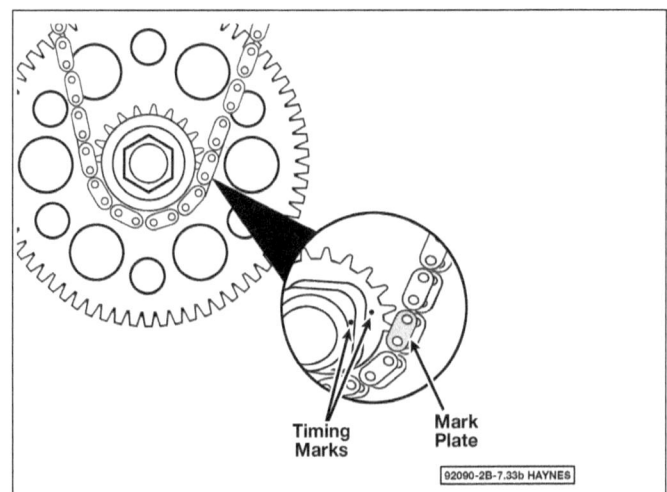

7.33a The orange links of the No. 1 (main) timing chain must align with the correct marks on each intake sprocket - the rear single line on the right (rear bank) head and the large arrowhead on the left (front bank) head

7.33b The lower yellow link of the No. 1 timing chain aligns with the dots on the crankshaft at about the two o'clock position

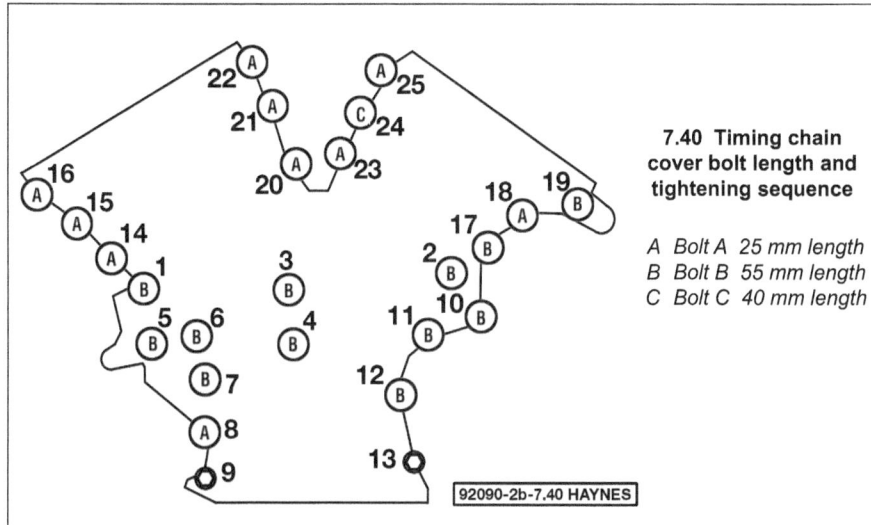

7.40 Timing chain cover bolt length and tightening sequence

A Bolt A 25 mm length
B Bolt B 55 mm length
C Bolt C 40 mm length

92090-2b-7.40 HAYNES

36   Install a new crankshaft oil seal in the timing chain cover (see Section 8).
37   Install a new O-ring on the left cylinder head.
38   Apply gray RTV sealant on the timing chain cover in all areas where the cover seals to the engine block and oil pan. These beads should be about 3 to 4.5 mm wide. Get sealant into the corners where the oil pan meets the engine block and avoid getting any on the O-rings.
Caution: *Once you have installed the sealant on the engine and timing chain cover you have three minutes to install the cover. If you take longer than that, the sealant might not set up properly, so you'll have to remove the sealant and re-apply it.*
39   Rotate the flats on the oil drive rotor to align it with the square part of the crankshaft timing sprocket and slide the timing chain cover into place.
40   Install all of the cover bolts in the same locations they were removed from, tightening them as you go. Tighten all of the bolts in the proper sequence to the torque listed in this Chapter's Specifications **(see illustration)**.

Caution: *Do not put long bolts in short holes or vice versa.*
41   Install and tighten the four oil pan bolts that go into the timing chain cover.
42   The remainder of installation is the reverse of removal.
43   Install the engine/transaxle assembly (see Chapter 2C).
44   Refill the engine with oil and coolant (see Chapter 1).
45   Reconnect the negative battery terminal (see Chapter 5).
46   Start the engine and check for leaks.

8   Crankshaft front oil seal - replacement

Refer to illustrations 8.2 and 8.4
1   Remove the crankshaft pulley (see Section 7).
2   Carefully pry the seal out of the timing chain cover with a screwdriver or seal removal tool **(see illustration)**. If you use a

screwdriver, wrap tape around the tip - don't scratch the housing bore or damage the crankshaft (if the crankshaft is damaged, the new seal will end up leaking).
3   Clean the bore in the timing chain cover and coat the lip and the outer edge of the new seal with engine oil or multi-purpose grease.
4   Using a seal driver or a socket with an outside diameter slightly smaller than the outside diameter of the seal, carefully drive the new seal into place with a hammer **(see illustration)**. Make sure it's installed squarely and driven in flush with the surface of the timing chain cover. Check the seal after installation to make sure the spring didn't pop out of place.
5   Reinstall the crankshaft pulley, tightening the bolt to the torque listed in this Chapter's Specifications.
6   Run the engine and check for oil leaks at the front seal.

9   Camshafts, rocker arms and valve adjusters - removal, inspection and installation

Removal

Note: *The manufacturer recommends removing the engine and transaxle assembly to perform this procedure (see Chapter 2C).*

Note: *The following procedure is not for beginners. Please read the entire procedure carefully before deciding whether this is a job that you want to tackle at home.*
1   Remove the engine and transaxle (see Chapter 2C).
2   Drain the engine oil and coolant (see Chapter 1).
3   Remove the timing chains and sprockets (see Section 7).
4   Before removing the camshafts from the right (rear bank) cylinder head, check to make sure that the nose of the intake cam lobe for the No. 1 cylinder is facing toward 12 o'clock, and the nose of the exhaust cam lobe is facing approximately 3 o'clock (the locating pins at the front of the camshaft should be at 12 o'clock for the exhaust cam and approximately 1:30 for the intake cam).
5   Gradually loosen and remove the 8 (smaller) bearing cap bolts in the reverse of the tightening sequence **(see illustrations 9.19a and 9.19b)**.
6   Gradually loosen and remove the remaining 12 housing bolts in the reverse of the tightening sequence **(see illustrations 9.18a and 9.18b)**.
7   Remove all five bearing caps and remove the intake and exhaust camshafts. Keep all of the components in the correct order. One way to do this is to put them in a box and label the cap numbers with a utility marker pen.
8   Carefully pry the camshaft housing from the top of the cylinder head.

8.2 Pry the seal out of the timing chain cover, being careful not to scratch the crankshaft

8.4 Lubricate the seal lip and drive the new crankshaft seal into place with a large socket or piece of pipe and a hammer

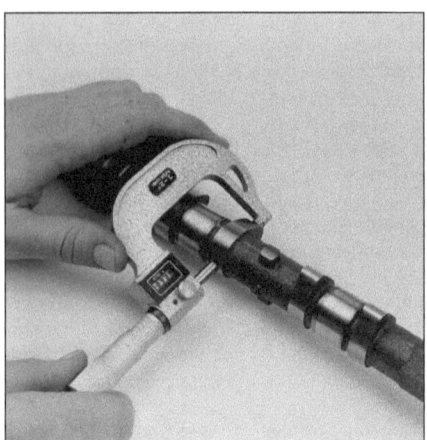

9.12 Measure the lobe heights on each camshaft - if any lobe height is less than the specified allowable minimum, replace that camshaft

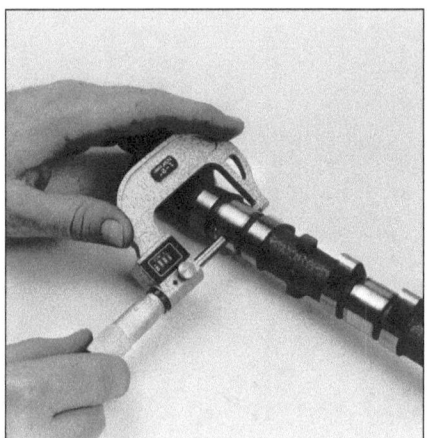

9.13 Measure each journal diameter with a micrometer - if any journal measures less than the specified limit, replace the camshaft

9.14 Compare the width of the crushed Plastigage to the scale on the envelope to determine the oil clearance

Caution: *Use a screwdriver wrapped with tape to avoid scratching the parts.*

9   Remove all of the rocker arms and lash adjusters and put them in the same box with the cam bearing caps. Every component should be marked or labelled so that it can be returned to its original location.

10   If you're removing the camshafts from the front bank cylinder head, repeat Steps 5 through 9. Make sure that the front camshaft lobes on the intake cam are positioned at 9 o'clock and the exhaust cam at 1 o'clock (the locating pins at the front of the camshaft should be at 12 o'clock for both cams).

Caution: *DO NOT ROTATE THE CRANKSHAFT while the timing chains and camshafts are removed!*

Inspection

Refer to illustrations 9.12, 9.13 and 9.14

11   Inspect each rocker and lash adjuster arm for wear.

12   Visually examine the cam lobes and bearing journals for score marks, pitting, galling and evidence of overheating (blue, dis-

coloured areas). Look for flaking away of the hardened surface layer of each lobe. Using a micrometer, measure the height of each camshaft lobe **(see illustration)**. Compare your measurements with this Chapter's Specifications. If the height for any one lobe is less than the specified minimum, replace the camshaft.

13   Using a micrometer, measure the diameter of each journal at several points **(see illustration)**. Compare your measurements with this Chapter's Specifications. If the diameter of any one journal is less than specified, replace the camshaft.

14   Check the oil clearance for each camshaft journal as follows:

Note: *Don't turn the camshaft while the Plastigage is in place.*

a   Clean the bearing caps and the camshaft journals with brake system cleaner.
b   Carefully lay the camshaft(s) in place in the cylinder head. Don't install the lifters and don't use any lubrication.
c   Lay a strip of Plastigage on each journal.

d   Install the bearing caps with the arrows pointing toward the front (timing chain end) of the engine.
e   Tighten the bolts to the torque listed in this Chapter's Specifications in 1/4 turn increments.
f   Remove the bolts and detach the caps.
g   Compare the width of the crushed Plastigage (at its widest point) to the scale on the Plastigage envelope **(see illustration)**.
h   If the clearance is greater than specified, replace the camshaft and/or cylinder head.
i   Scrape off the Plastigage with your fingernail or the edge of a credit card - don't scratch or nick the journals or bearing caps.

Installation

Refer to illustrations 9.16a, 9.16b, 9.18a, 9.18b, 9.19a and 9.19b

15   Lightly lubricate the lash adjuster bores and the adjusters themselves with clean engine oil, then install them in the same bores

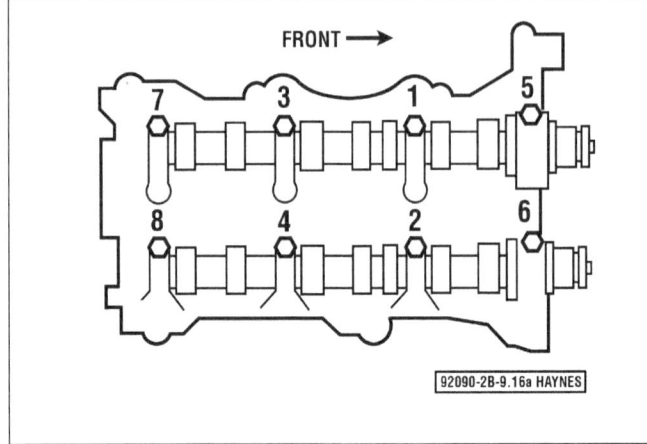

9.16a Snugly tighten the (small) camshaft cap bolts of the right (rear) cylinder head in this sequence

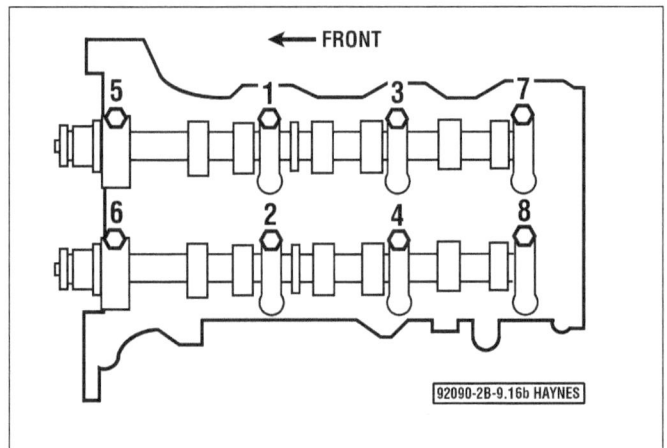

9.16b Snugly tighten the (small) camshaft cap bolts of the left (front) cylinder head in this sequence

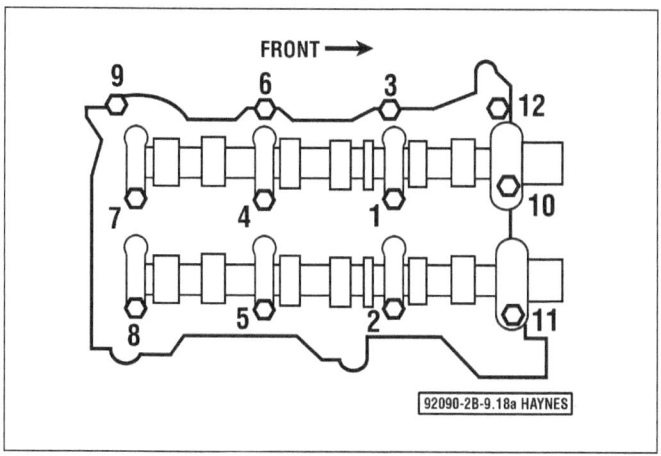

9.18a Camshaft housing bolt tightening sequence - right (rear) cylinder head

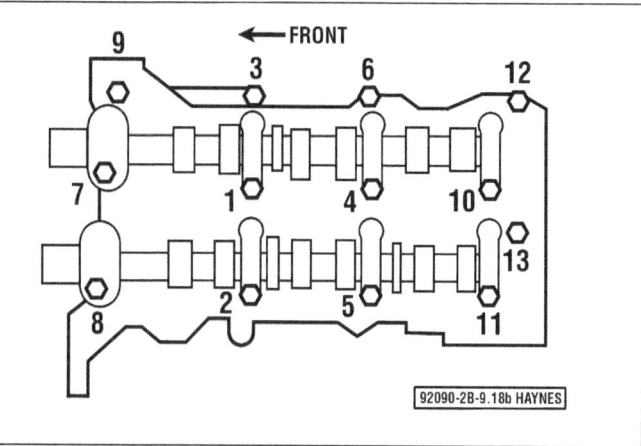

9.18b Camshaft housing bolt tightening sequence - left (front) cylinder head

from which they were removed. Install the rocker arms in their original positions, oiling all wear points as you do so.

16 Right side (rear cylinder bank): Lubricate the camshaft journals and lobes with camshaft installation lubricant. Install the camshafts on the right camshaft housing so that the locating pin of the exhaust camshaft is at 12 o'clock and the intake camshaft's locating pin is rotated approximately 45 degrees to 1:30. Apply a light coat of engine oil to the upper bearing caps, then install them in their correct locations. Tighten the bolts snug at this time in the correct sequence (see illustrations).

17 Thoroughly clean the sealing surfaces of the bottom of the camshaft bearing support and the top of the cylinder head. Apply a continuous 3 to 5 mm bead of RTV silicone sealer to the surface of the top of the cylinder head that mates with the camshaft bearing housing.

18 Set the camshaft housing assembly into place. Install the 12 mounting bolts and tighten them in the correct sequence to the torque listed in this Chapter's Specifications (see illustrations).

19 Install the remaining (smaller) bearing cap bolts, then tighten them in the correct sequence to the torque listed in this Chapter's Specifications (see illustrations).

20 Left side (front cylinder bank): Lightly lubricate the camshaft journals with camshaft installation lubricant. Install the camshafts on the left cylinder head so that the locating pin of each camshaft is in the 12 o'clock position. Proceed as with the right cylinder head.

Note: There are 13 bolts in the camshaft housing instead of 12.

21 The remainder of installation is the reverse of removal. Install the timing chains, the timing chain cover and all of the components attached to the cover (see Section 7).

Caution: Carefully rotate the crankshaft by hand through at least two full revolutions (use a socket and breaker bar on the crankshaft pulley centre bolt). If you feel any resistance, STOP! There is something wrong - most likely valves are contacting the pistons. You must find the problem before proceeding.

22 Refill the engine with oil and coolant (see Chapter 1), reconnect the cable to the negative battery terminal, start the engine and

check for leaks.

Note: It may take a few minutes for lifter clatter to disappear.

10 Cylinder heads - removal and installation

Warning: The engine must be completely cool before starting this procedure.

Caution: New cylinder head bolts should be used when installing the cylinder head.

Note: This procedure applies to either cylinder head.

Note: The manufacturer recommends removing the engine and transaxle assembly to perform this procedure (see Chapter 2C).

Removal

1 Remove the camshafts and the camshaft housings (see Section 9).

2 Remove the exhaust manifolds (see Section 6).

3 If you're removing the left cylinder head,

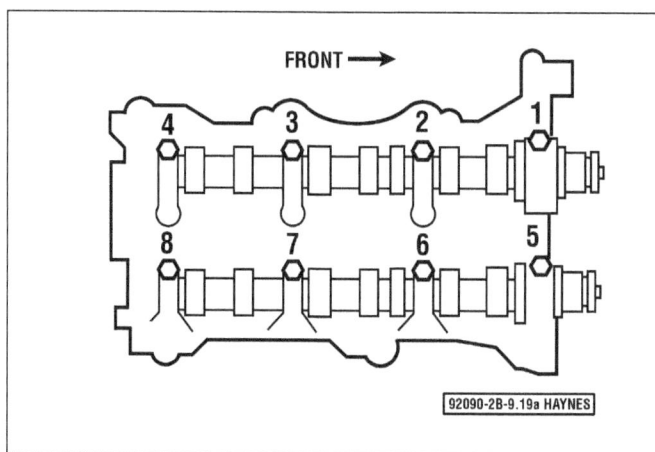

9.19a Camshaft bearing cap bolt tightening sequence - small bolts - for the right (rear) cylinder head

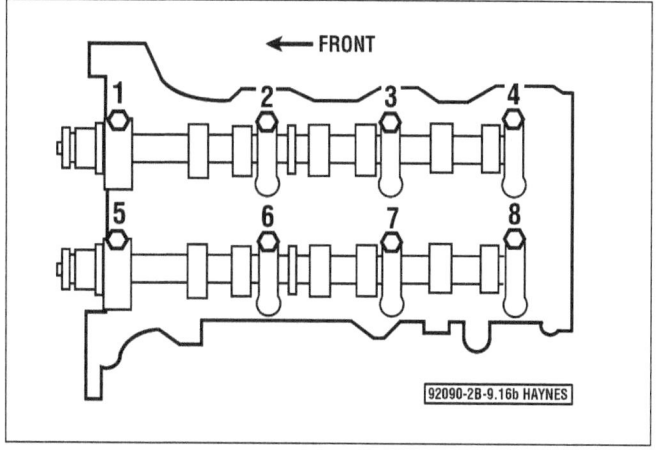

9.19b Camshaft cap bolt tightening sequence - small bolts - for the left (front) cylinder head

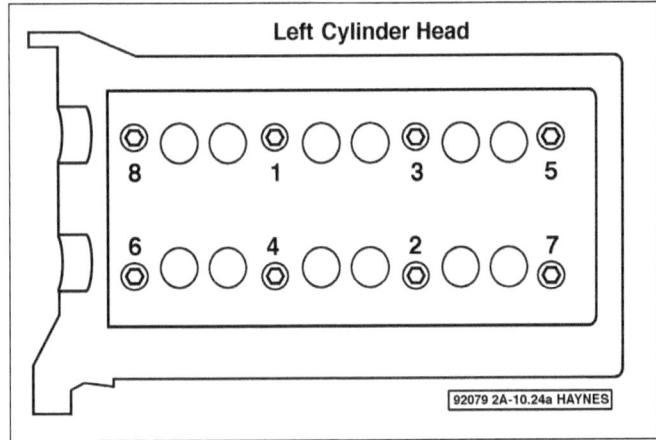

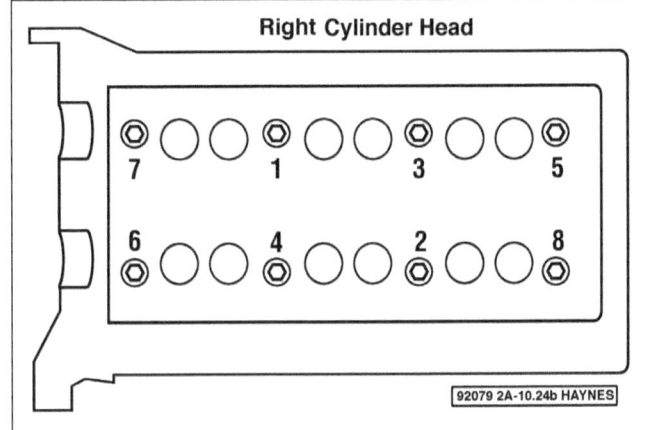

10.12a Cylinder head bolt tightening sequence - left (front bank) cylinder head

10.12b Cylinder head bolt tightening sequence - right (rear bank) cylinder head

gradually loosen and remove the two front bolts.

4   Remove the cylinder head bolts gradually and evenly, in the order opposite that of the tightening sequence, then remove the cylinder head from the engine block.

5   Remove and discard the old cylinder head gasket.

Installation

Refer to illustrations 10.12a, 10.12b and 10.14

6   The mating surfaces of the cylinder heads and the block must be perfectly clean as the heads are installed.

7   Use a gasket scraper to remove all traces of carbon and old gasket material, then clean the mating surfaces with brake system cleaner. If there's oil on the mating surfaces when the head is installed, the gasket may not seal correctly and leaks could develop.

8   When working on the block, stuff the cylinders with clean shop rags to keep out debris. Use a vacuum cleaner to remove material that falls into the cylinders.

9   Check the block and head mating surfaces for nicks, deep scratches and other damage. If damage is slight, it can be removed with a file; if it's excessive, machining may be the only alternative.

10   Use a tap of the correct size to chase the threads in the cylinder head bolt holes, then clean them with compressed air - make sure that nothing remains in the holes.

Warning: *Wear eye protection when using compressed air!*

11   Position the cylinder head gasket on the engine block so that the lot number stamp is on the centre upper edge of the gasket facing up. Carefully place the cylinder head on the head gasket.

12   Apply a light coat of oil to the new cylinder head bolts, then install and tighten them (don't forget the washers!) gradually and evenly, in the proper sequence **(see illustrations)**, to the initial torque listed in this Chapter's Specifications.

13   After tightening all eight bolts to the ini-

tial torque, put a paint mark on the front edge of each bolt (the edge facing toward the front of the engine), then retighten each bolt, in the same sequence, another 90 degrees. Repeat this one more time so that the bolts have turned 180 degrees from the initial torque. Make sure to use the proper sequence.

14   If you're installing the left cylinder head, install the two front head bolts and tighten them in the correct sequence to the torque listed in this Chapter's Specifications **(see illustration)**.

15   If you removed both cylinder heads, install the other cylinder head now.

16   Install the intake and exhaust camshafts (see Section 9).

17   Install the camshaft timing oil control valve, the oil control valve filter and the VVT-i sensor (see Chapter 6).

18   Install the timing chains, the timing chain cover and all components attached to the cover (see Section 7).

19   The remainder of installation is the reverse of removal.

20   Install the engine/transaxle assembly (see Chapter 2C). Refill the engine with oil and coolant (see Chapter 1).

21   Reconnect the cable to the negative bat-

tery terminal, start the engine and check for leaks.

---

11   Oil pan - removal and installation

Note: *The manufacturer recommends removing the engine and transaxle assembly to perform this procedure (see Chapter 2C).*

Removal

1   Drain the engine oil (see Chapter 1).

2   Remove the bolts and nuts that secure oil pan No. 2 (the smaller stamped steel pan) to the larger cast aluminium oil pan.

3   Oil pan No. 2 will probably be stuck to the oil pan with RTV sealant. Try tapping it loose with a rubber-tipped mallet. If you're unable to knock it loose, carefully cut the sealant with a putty knife and a hammer. Make sure that you don't damage the mating surfaces of the two pans.

4   Remove the two oil pump pickup tube/ strainer mounting nuts and the brace bolt. Remove the pickup/strainer assembly.

5   Remove the 16 bolts and two nuts that

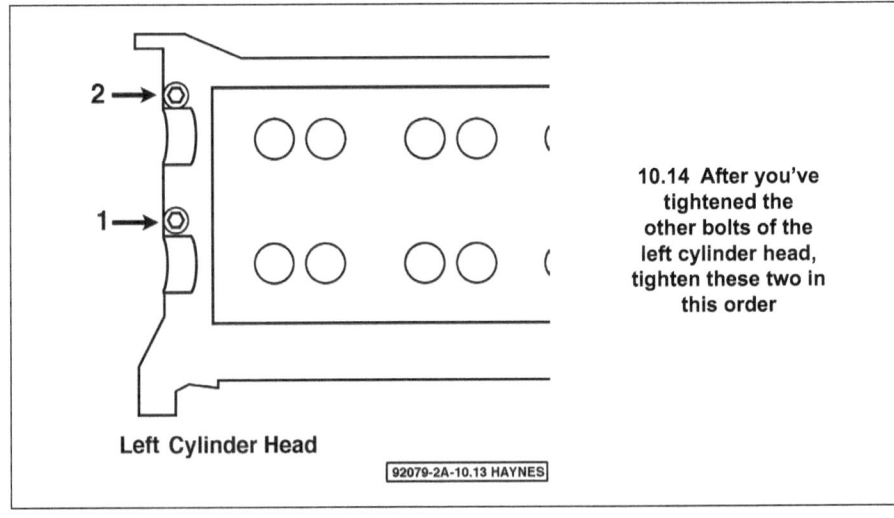

10.14 After you've tightened the other bolts of the left cylinder head, tighten these two in this order

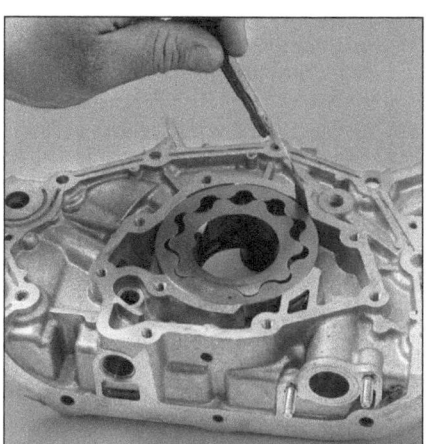

12.6a Measure the driven rotor-to-body clearance with a feeler gauge

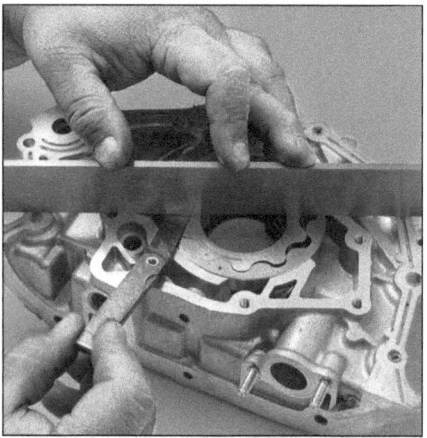

12.6b Measure the rotor side clearance with a precision straightedge and feeler gauge

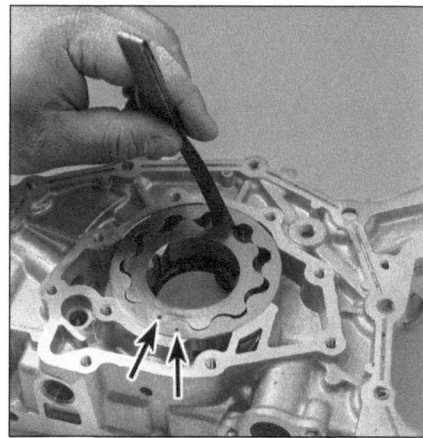

12.6c Measure the rotor tip clearance with a feeler gauge - note the rotor marks are facing out (when the pump body cover is installed, the marks will be against the cover)

secure oil pan No. 1 to the engine block.

6   Carefully pry the oil pan loose from the engine block.

Caution: *Only pry in the small cutout areas along the side of the pan.*

7   Remove the two O-rings from the bottom of the engine block. The sheet metal baffle plate can be removed at this time if necessary.

Installation

8   Install the baffle plate if you removed it. Tighten the fasteners to the torque listed in this Chapter's Specifications.

9   Use a scraper to remove all traces of old sealant from the block and oil pan. Clean the mating surfaces with brake system cleaner.

10   Make sure the threaded holes in the block are clean. Install new O-rings to the block, holding them in place with clean grease if required.

11   Check the flange of the steel oil pan for distortion around the bolt holes. If necessary, place it on a wood block and use a hammer to flatten and restore the gasket surface.

12   Inspect the strainer for cracks or blockage. Clean it with solvent and install it using a new gasket. Tighten the fasteners to the torque listed in this Chapter's Specifications.

13   Apply a 3 mm bead of RTV sealant to the upper oil pan flange.

14   Position the pan onto the block and install the fasteners. Working from the centre out, tighten the fasteners to the torque listed in this Chapter's Specifications in several steps.

15   After you have installed the aluminium portion of the oil pan, apply a bead of RTV sealant to the flange of the No. 2 oil pan, carefully position it on the upper oil pan and install the bolts. Working from the centre out, tighten them to the torque listed in this Chapter's Specifications in several steps.

16   The remainder of installation is the reverse of removal. Add oil and install a new

filter (see Chapter 1). Run the engine and check for leaks.

---

12 Oil pump - removal, inspection and installation

Removal

1   Remove the timing chain cover (see Section 7). The oil pump is on the inside of the cover.

2   Remove the relief valve plug using a 27 mm socket. Slide out the spring and the relief valve.

3   Remove the oil pump cover bolts and remove the oil pump cover. Remove the oil pump drive rotor and driven rotor.

Inspection

Refer to illustrations 12.6a, 12.6b and 12.6c

4   Clean all components with solvent, then inspect them for wear and damage. Check that the oiled relief valve falls easily through its bore without sticking.

5   Check the oil pressure relief valve sliding surface and valve spring. If either the spring or the valve is damaged, they must be replaced as a set.

6   Check the clearance of the following components with a feeler gauge and compare the measurements to this Chapter's Specifications **(see illustrations)**:

   a   Driven rotor-to-oil pump body
   b   Rotor side clearance
   c   Rotor tip clearance

7   Replace any worn parts or replace the entire oil pump assembly.

Installation

8   Pry the old crankshaft seal out of the timing chain cover with a screwdriver.

9   Apply multi-purpose grease or engine oil to the outer edge of the new crank seal and

carefully drive it into place with a deep socket and a hammer. Apply multi-purpose grease or engine oil to the seal lip.

10   Apply a coat of petroleum jelly to the pump drive and driven rotors, then place the two rotors into position in the timing chain cover. Make sure that the pump marks (dimples) are facing out, toward the pump cover and away from the timing chain cover.

11   Pack the pump cavity with petroleum jelly (this will help to prime the pump) and install the cover. Tighten the cover bolts to the torque listed in this Chapter's Specifications.

12   Lubricate the oil pressure relief valve with clean engine oil and insert the valve, then the spring, into the pump cover. Screw in the plug and tighten it to the torque listed in this Chapter's Specifications.

13   Install the timing chain cover (see Section 7).

14   The remainder of installation is the reverse of removal. Add oil and install a new filter (see Chapter 1). Run the engine and check for leaks.

---

13 Driveplate - removal and installation

Removal

1   Remove the engine/transmission assembly from the vehicle (see Chapter 2C), then remove the transaxle from the engine (see Chapter 7).

2   Make alignment marks on the driveplate and crankshaft to ensure correct alignment during reinstallation.

3   Remove and discard the old bolts securing the driveplate to the crankshaft. If the crankshaft turns, wedge a screwdriver in the ring gear teeth to hold the driveplate.

4   Remove the driveplate from the crankshaft. Support it while removing the last bolt. Automatic transmission equipped vehicles

14.4 Drive the new seal into the retainer with a wood block or a section of pipe - make sure that you don't cock the seal in the retainer bore

have spacers on both sides of the driveplate. Keep them with the driveplate.

Installation

5   Clean the driveplate to remove grease and oil. Inspect the surface for cracks. Check for cracked or broken ring gear teeth.

6   Clean and inspect the mating surfaces of the driveplate and the crankshaft. If the crankshaft rear seal is leaking, replace it before reinstalling the driveplate (see Section 14).

7   Position the driveplate against the crankshaft. Align the marks made during removal. Note that some engines have an alignment dowel or staggered bolt holes to ensure correct installation. Before installing the new bolts, apply thread-locking compound to the threads.

8   Wedge a screwdriver in the ring gear teeth to keep it from turning and tighten the bolts to the torque listed in this Chapter's Specifications. Follow a criss-cross pattern and work up to the final torque in three or four steps.

9   The remainder of installation is the reverse of removal.

14   Rear main oil seal - replacement

Refer to illustration 14.4

Note: *This procedure assumes that the engine has been removed from the vehicle.*

1   Remove the engine/transmission assembly from the vehicle (see Chapter 2C), then remove the transaxle from the engine (see Chapter 7). Remove the driveplate (see Section 13).

2   The seal can be replaced without removing the oil pan or seal retainer. The easiest method involves using a seal-removal tool. If this tool isn't available, you can use a sharp knife to cut the lip off the old seal while carefully avoiding scratching the crankshaft. With the lip gone, use a screwdriver wrapped with tape to pry the seal out.

3   Lubricate the crankshaft seal journal and the lip of the new seal with multi-purpose grease.

4   Evenly drive the new seal into the retainer with a wood block or a section of pipe slightly smaller in diameter than the outside diameter of the seal **(see illustration)**. The new seal should be approximately flush with the surface of the retainer.

5   The remainder of installation is the reverse of removal.

15   Engine mounts - check and replacement

1   Engine mounts seldom require attention, but broken or deteriorated mounts should be replaced immediately or the added strain placed on the driveline components may cause damage or wear.

Check

2   During the check, the engine must be raised slightly to remove the weight from the mounts.

3   Raise the vehicle and support it securely on jackstands (see Jacking and Towing), then position a jack under the engine oil pan. Place a large wood block between the jack head and the oil pan, then carefully raise the engine just enough to take the weight off the mounts. Do not position the wood block under the drain plug.

Warning: *DO NOT place any part of your body under the engine when it's supported only by a jack!*

4   Check the mounts to see if the rubber is cracked, hardened or separated from the metal plates. Sometimes the rubber will separate from the bushing in the centre of the mount.

5   Check for relative movement between the mount plates and the engine or frame (use a large screwdriver or prybar to attempt to move the mounts).

6   If movement is noted, lower the engine and tighten the mount fasteners.

Replacement

7   Raise the vehicle and support it securely on jackstands (if not already done). Support the engine as described in Step 3.

8   To remove an engine mount, remove the fasteners, raise the engine and detach the mount. The engine can be raised with an engine hoist, or with a floor jack and wood block placed under the oil pan.

Note: *Even if only one mount is being replaced, remove the mount-to-engine bracket nut from the other mount (this will allow the engine to be raised far enough for mount removal).*

9   Installation is the reverse of removal. Use non-hardening thread locking compound on the mount bolts/nuts and be sure to tighten them securely.

Chapter 2 Part C
General engine overhaul procedures

Contents

Specifications

General

Displacement
    3MZ-FE 3.3L V6 .... 3,311cc
    2GR-FE 3.5L V6 .... 3,456cc
Cylinder compression pressure
    Standard
        3MZ-FE .... 1,500 kPa
        2GR-FE .... 1,300 kPa
    Minimum compression pressure .... 1,000 kPa
        3MZ-FE .... 1,000 kPa
        2GR-FE .... 980 kPa
    Variation between cylinders .... 100 kPa
Oil pressure
    3MZ-FE engine
        At curb idle .... Above 29 kPa
        At 3,000 rpm .... 245 to 539 kPa
    2GR-FE engine
        At curb idle .... Above 80 kPa
        At 3,000 rpm .... Above 380 kPa

Connecting rod

Connecting rod bearing cap bolt wear dimensions (see illustration 0.1)

    Standard diameter.. 7.2 to 7.3 mm

    Minimum diameter... 7.0 mm

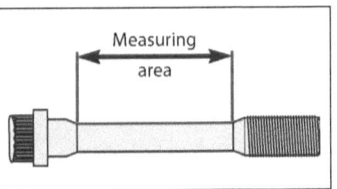

0.1 Renew the bolt if the diameter is less than specified anywhere in this area

Crankshaft

Main bearing cap bolt wear dimensions

    3MZ-FE engine (see illustration 0.1)

        Standard diameter .... 7.5 to 7.6 mm

        Minimum diameter .... 7.2 mm

    2GR-FE engine (see illustration 0.2)

        Standard diameter .... 10.8 to 11.0 mm

        Minimum diameter .... 10.7 mm

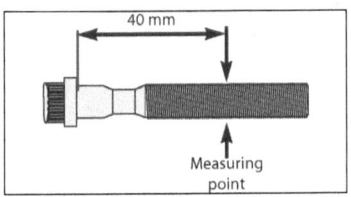

0.2 Renew the main bearing cap bolt if the diameter is less than specified in the measuring point area

Torque specifications

                                                                      Nm

Connecting rod bearing cap bolts

    Step 1 25

    Step 2 .... Tighten an additional 90 degrees (1/4 turn)

Main bearing cap bolts (see illustrations 0.3 and 0.4)

    3MZ-FE engine

        Step 1 (12-point bolts) 22

        Step 2 (12-point bolts) .... Tighten an additional 90 degrees (1/4 turn)

        Step 3 (side-bolts)... 27

    2GR-FE engine

        Step 1 61

        Step 2 .... Tighten an additional 90 degrees (1/4 turn)

        Step 3 (side-bolts)... 52

    Water inlet housing mounting bolts 10

    Subframe mounting bolts.. See Chapter 10

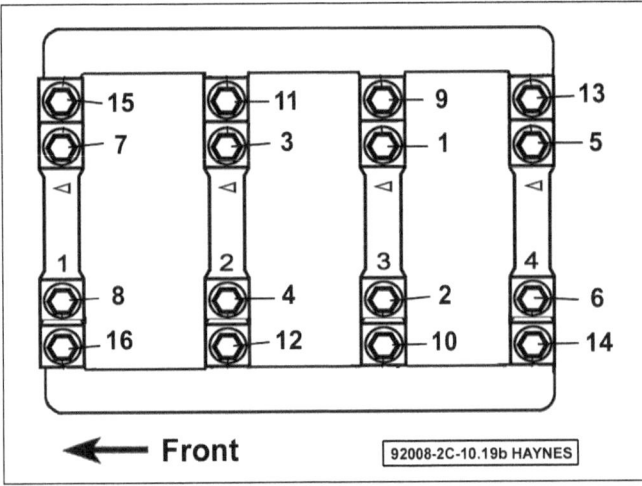

0.3 Main bearing cap bolt tightening sequence

Note: On 2GR-FE engines, the inner rows of bolts are 100 to 102 mm long, the outer row of bolts are 105.5 to 107.5 mm long

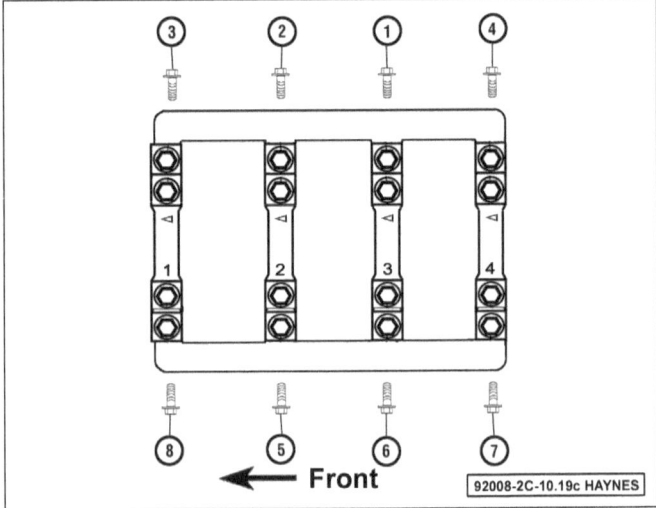

0.4 Main bearing cap side-bolt tightening sequence

Note: On 2GR-FE engines, the bolts labelled 4 and 7 are 45 mm long. The remainder are 30 mm long

2.2a On 3MZ-FE engines, the oil pressure sending unit is located at the front of the engine, above the crankshaft position sensor

2.2b On 2GR-FE V6 models, the oil pressure sending unit is located next to the oil filter

1 General information - engine overhaul

Overhauling an engine is a difficult and time-consuming task. Special tools and knowledge are required. For these reasons, we recommend that engine overhaul is best left to a professional engine rebuilder. A competent engine rebuilder will handle the inspection of your old parts and offer advice concerning the reconditioning or replacement of the original engine.

Be aware that some engine builders can only rebuild the engine you bring them, which can take several weeks, while other rebuilders have rebuilt exchange engines in stock. If time is an issue, an exchange engine may be the best solution. If an exchange engine is fitted, check with your state registry authority as some insist the engine number on the new engine is included on your registration and insurance details.

An engine overhaul involves restoring the internal parts to the specifications of a new engine. During an overhaul, the piston rings are replaced and the cylinder walls are reconditioned (rebored and/or honed). If a rebore is done by an automotive machine shop, new oversize pistons will also be installed. The main bearings and connecting rod bearings are generally replaced with new ones and, if necessary, the crankshaft may be reground to restore the journals. Generally, the valves are serviced as well, since they're usually in less-than-perfect condition at this point. The end result should be a like-new engine that will give many trouble-free miles.

For those with engine overhaul experience and access to the necessary tools who wish to undertake the overhaul themselves, engine specifications have been included at the start of this chapter. Also included in this chapter are general information and diagnostic testing procedures for determining the overall mechanical condition of your engine.

It is important to establish the condition of the cylinder block. Never purchase parts or have machine work done on other components until the block has been thoroughly inspected by a professional machine shop.

The following Sections have been written to help you determine whether your engine needs to be overhauled and how to remove and install it once you've determined it needs to be rebuilt. For information concerning in-vehicle engine repair, see Chapter 2A for the 3MZ-FE engine or see Chapter 2B for the 2GR-FE engine.

The Specifications included relate to engine overhaul. Refer to the previous Engine chapters for additional engine Specifications.

It's not always easy to determine when, or if, an engine should be completely overhauled, because a number of factors must be considered.

High mileage is not necessarily an indication that an overhaul is needed, while low mileage doesn't preclude the need for an overhaul. Frequency of servicing is probably the most important consideration. An engine that has had regular and frequent oil and filter changes, as well as other required maintenance, will most likely give many thousands of miles of reliable service. Conversely, a neglected engine may require an overhaul very early in its service life.

Excessive oil consumption is an indication that piston rings, valve seals and/or valve guides are in need of attention. Make sure that oil leaks aren't responsible before deciding that the rings and/or valve guides are bad. Perform a cylinder compression check to determine the extent of the work required (see Section 3).

Check the oil pressure with a gauge installed in place of the oil pressure sending unit and compare it to this chapter's Specifications (see Section 2). If it's extremely low, the bearings and/or oil pump are probably worn out.

Loss of power, rough running, knocking or metallic engine noises, excessive valve train noise and high fuel consumption rates may also point to the need for an overhaul, especially if they're all present at the same time. If a complete tune-up doesn't remedy the situation, major mechanical work is the only solution.

Note: *Critical cooling system components such as the hoses, drivebelts, thermostat and water pump should be replaced with new*

parts when an engine is overhauled. The radiator should be checked carefully to ensure that it isn't clogged or leaking (see Chapter 3). If you purchase a rebuilt engine or short block, some rebuilders will not warranty their engines unless the radiator has been professionally flushed.

2 Oil pressure check

Refer to illustrations 2.2a, 2.2b, 2.2c and 2.3

1 Low engine oil pressure can be a sign of an engine in need of rebuilding. A low oil pressure indicator (often called an "idiot light") is not a test of the oiling system. Such indicators only come on when the oil pressure is dangerously low. Even a factory oil pressure gauge in the instrument panel is only a relative indication, although much better for driver information than a warning light. A better test is with a mechanical (not electrical) oil pressure gauge.

2 Locate the oil pressure indicator sending unit on the engine block **(see illustrations)**.

3 Unscrew and remove the oil pressure sending unit and then screw in the hose for your oil pressure gauge **(see illustration)**. If necessary, install an adapter fitting. Use Tef-

2.3 The oil pressure can be checked by removing the sending unit and installing a pressure gauge in its place

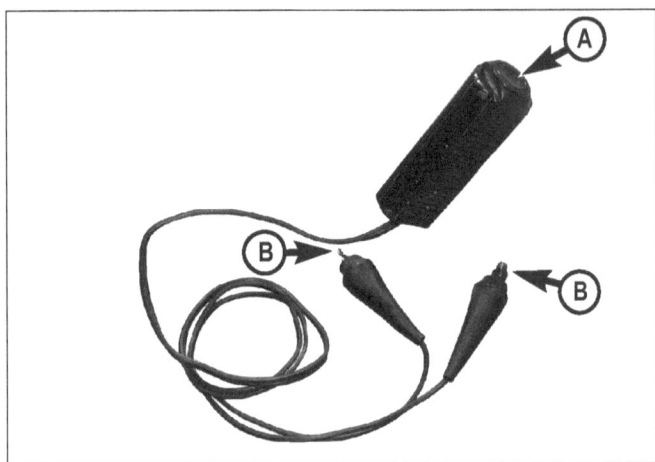

3.6a Typical remote starter switch (A) and alligator clips (B)

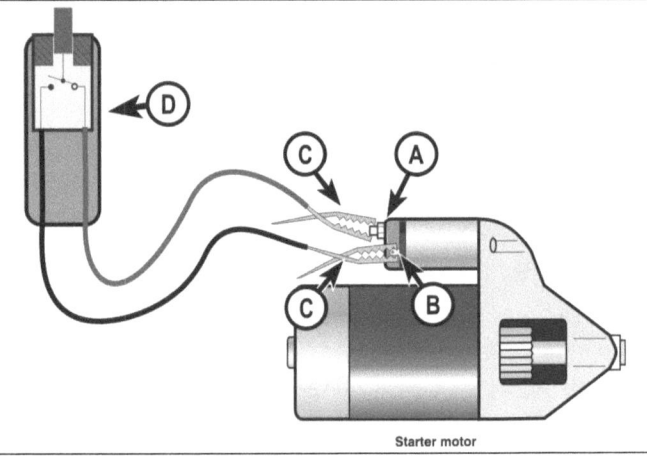

Starter motor

3.6b Illustration showing how to connect the remote starter switch. Connect one alligator clip to the large terminal on the starter motor that goes to the battery (A). Connect the second terminal to the solenoid terminal after disconnecting the wire from the solenoid (B). Ensure the alligator clips (C) are not touching. When the switch (D) is pressed, the starter motor will operate

lon tape or thread sealant on the threads of the adapter and/or the fitting on the end of your gauge's hose.

4   Connect an accurate tachometer to the engine, according to the tachometer manufacturer's instructions.

5   Check the oil pressure with the engine running (normal operating temperature) at the specified engine speed, and compare it to this Chapter's Specifications. If it's extremely low, the bearings and/or oil pump are probably worn out.

3   Cylinder compression check

Refer to illustrations 3.6a, 3.6b, 3.7a, 3.7b and 3.7c

Note: *When doing a compression check, the ignition and fuel systems must be isolated to prevent the engine from starting while the compression gauge is installed. Due to the complexity of disabling the fuel and ignition*

system on these engines, it is recommended that a remote starter be used. A remote starter connects to the starter motor. One end connects to the large battery supply terminal and the other end connects to the small solenoid terminal. When the button on the remote starter is pressed, the starter motor will energise and rotate the engine. Doing the compression test this way means the ignition can remain Off preventing raw fuel being injected into the engine and passing through to the catalytic converter – damaging the converter. It also prevents the engine management system from setting fault codes about low fuel pressure or no ignition signals at the coils. A remote starter can be purchased from your local auto parts retailer.

1   A compression check will tell you what mechanical condition the upper end (pistons,

rings, valves, head gaskets) of the engine is in. Specifically, it can tell you if the compression is down due to leakage caused by worn piston rings, defective valves and seats or a blown head gasket.

Note: *The engine must be at normal operating temperature and the battery must be fully charged for this check.*

2   Begin by cleaning the area around the spark plugs before you remove them. Compressed air should be used, if available. The idea is to prevent dirt from getting into the cylinders as the compression check is being done.

3   Remove all of the spark plugs from the engine (see Chapter 1).

4   Block the throttle wide open.

5   Install the compression gauge in the number one spark plug hole.

3.7a The remote starter wiring connected to the starter motor

3.7b Checking the engine compression using the remote starter to crank the engine - note the clamp holding the throttle open

3.7c Use a compression gauge with a threaded fitting for the spark plug hole, not the type that requires hand pressure to maintain the seal - be sure to open the throttle valve as far as possible during the test

6   Install a remote starter to the starter motor following the instructions supplied with the tool **(see illustrations)**.

7   Crank the engine over at least seven compression strokes and watch the gauge **(see illustration)**. The compression should build up quickly in a healthy engine. Low compression on the first stroke, followed by gradually increasing pressure on successive strokes, indicates worn piston rings. A low compression reading on the first stroke, which doesn't build up during successive strokes, indicates leaking valves or a blown head gasket (a cracked head could also be the cause). Deposits on the undersides of the valve heads can also cause low compression. Record the highest gauge reading obtained.

8   Repeat the procedure for the remaining cylinders, turning the engine over for the same length of time for each cylinder, and compare the results to this Chapter's Specifications.

9   If the readings are below normal, add some engine oil (about three squirts from a plunger-type oil can) to each cylinder, through the spark plug hole, and repeat the test.

10   If the compression increases after the oil is added, the piston rings are definitely worn. If the compression doesn't increase significantly, the leakage is occurring at the valves or head gasket. Leakage past the valves may be caused by burned valve seats and/or faces or warped, cracked or bent valves.

11   If two adjacent cylinders have equally low compression, there's a strong possibility the head gasket between them is blown. The appearance of coolant in the combustion chambers or the crankcase would verify this condition.

12   If one cylinder is about 20-percent lower than the others, and the engine has a slightly rough idle, a worn exhaust lobe on the camshaft could be the cause.

13   If the compression is unusually high, the combustion chambers are probably coated with carbon deposits. If that's the case, the cylinder heads should be removed and decarbonised.

14   If compression is way down or varies greatly between cylinders, it would be a good idea to have a leak-down test performed by an automotive repair shop. This test will pinpoint exactly where the leakage is occurring and how severe it is.

---

4   Vacuum gauge diagnostic checks

Refer to illustrations 4.4 and 4.6

1   A vacuum gauge provides inexpensive but valuable information about what is going on in the engine. You can check for worn rings or cylinder walls, leaking head or intake manifold gaskets, incorrect carburettor adjustments, restricted exhaust, stuck or burned valves, weak valve springs, improper ignition or valve timing and ignition problems.

2   Unfortunately, vacuum gauge readings are easy to misinterpret, so they should be used in conjunction with other tests to confirm the diagnosis.

3   Both the absolute readings and the rate of needle movement are important for accurate interpretation. Most gauges measure vacuum in inches of mercury (in-Hg). The following references to vacuum assume the diagnosis is being performed at sea level. As elevation increases (or atmospheric pressure decreases), the reading will decrease. For every 1,000 foot increase in elevation above approximately 2000 feet, the gauge readings will decrease about one inch of mercury.

4   Connect the vacuum gauge directly to the intake manifold vacuum, not to ported (throttle body) vacuum **(see illustration)**. Be sure no hoses are left disconnected during the test or false readings will result.

5   Before you begin the test, allow the engine to warm up completely. Block the wheels and set the parking brake. With the transmission in Park, start the engine and allow it to run at normal idle speed.

Warning: *Keep your hands and the vacuum gauge clear of the fans and drivebelts.*

6   Read the vacuum gauge; an average, healthy engine should normally produce about 17 to 22 in-Hg with a fairly steady needle **(see illustration)**. Refer to the following vacuum gauge readings and what they indicate about the engine's condition:

7   A low steady reading usually indicates a leaking gasket between the intake manifold and cylinder head(s) or throttle body, a leaky vacuum hose, late ignition timing or incorrect camshaft timing. Check ignition timing with a timing light and eliminate all other possible causes, utilizing the tests provided in this Chapter before you remove the timing chain cover to check the timing marks.

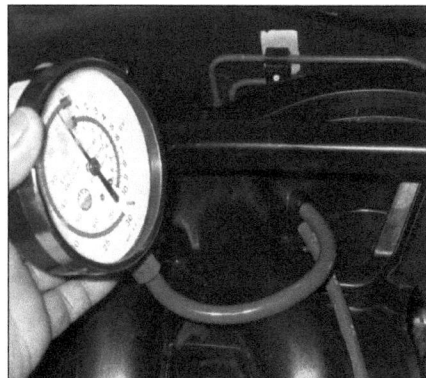

4.4 A simple vacuum gauge can be handy in diagnosing engine condition and performance

4.6 Typical vacuum gauge readings

6.1 After tightly wrapping water-vulnerable components, use a spray cleaner on everything, with particular concentration on the greasiest areas, usually around the valve cover and lower edges of the block. If one section dries out, apply more cleaner

6.2 Depending on how dirty the engine is, let the cleaner soak in according to the directions and then hose off the grime and cleaner. Get the rinse water down into every area you can get at; then dry important components with a hair dryer or paper towels

8   If the reading is three to eight inches below normal and it fluctuates at that low reading, suspect an intake manifold gasket leak at an intake port or a faulty fuel injector.

9   If the needle has regular drops of about two-to-four inches at a steady rate, the valves are probably leaking. Perform a compression check or leak-down test to confirm this.

10   An irregular drop or down-flick of the needle can be caused by a sticking valve or an ignition misfire. Perform a compression check or leak-down test and read the spark plugs.

11   A rapid vibration of about four in-Hg vibration at idle combined with exhaust smoke indicates worn valve guides. Perform a leak-down test to confirm this. If the rapid vibration occurs with an increase in engine speed, check for a leaking intake manifold gasket or head gasket, weak valve springs, burned valves or ignition misfire.

12   A slight fluctuation, say one inch up and down, may mean ignition problems. Check all the usual tune-up items and, if necessary, run the engine on an ignition analyser.

13   If there is a large fluctuation, perform a compression or leak-down test to look for a weak or dead cylinder or a blown head gasket.

14   If the needle moves slowly through a wide range, check for a clogged PCV system, incorrect idle fuel mixture, throttle body or intake manifold gasket leaks.

15   Check for a slow return after revving the engine by quickly snapping the throttle open until the engine reaches about 2,500 rpm and let it shut. Normally the reading should drop to near zero, rise above normal idle reading (about 5 in-Hg over) and then return to the previous idle reading. If the vacuum returns slowly and doesn't peak when the throttle is snapped shut, the rings may be worn. If there is a long delay, look for a restricted exhaust system (often the muffler or catalytic converter). An easy way to check this is to tem-

porarily disconnect the exhaust ahead of the suspected part and redo the test.

5   Engine rebuilding alternatives

The do-it-yourselfer is faced with a number of options when purchasing a rebuilt engine. The major considerations are cost, warranty, parts availability and the time required for the rebuilder to complete the project. The decision to replace the engine block, piston/connecting rod assemblies and crankshaft depends on the final inspection results of your engine. Only then can you make a cost effective decision whether to have your engine overhauled or simply purchase an exchange engine for your vehicle.

Some of the rebuilding alternatives include:

Individual parts - If the inspection procedures reveal that the engine block and most engine components are in reusable condition, purchasing individual parts and having a rebuilder rebuild your engine may be the most economical alternative. The block, crankshaft and piston/connecting rod assemblies should all be inspected carefully by a machine shop first.

Short block - A short block consists of an engine block with a crankshaft and piston/connecting rod assemblies already installed. All new bearings are incorporated and all clearances will be correct. The existing camshafts, valve train components, cylinder head and external parts can be bolted to the short block with little or no machine shop work necessary.

Long block - A long block consists of a short block plus an oil pump, oil pan, cylinder head, valve cover, camshaft and valve train components, timing sprockets and chain or gears and timing cover. All components are installed with new bearings, seals and gaskets incorporated throughout. The installation

of manifolds and external parts is all that's necessary.

Low mileage used engines - Some companies now offer low mileage used engines which is a very cost effective way to get your vehicle up and running again. These engines often come from vehicles that have been in totalled in accidents or come from other countries that have a higher vehicle turn over rate. A low mileage used engine also usually has a similar warranty like the newly remanufactured engines.

Give careful thought to which alternative is best for you and discuss the situation with local automotive machine shops, auto parts dealers and experienced rebuilders before ordering or purchasing replacement parts.

6   Engine removal - methods and precautions

Refer to illustrations 6.1, 6.2, 6.3 and 6.4

If you've decided that an engine must be removed for overhaul or major repair work, several preliminary steps should be taken. Read all removal and installation procedures carefully prior to committing to this job.

Locating a suitable place to work is extremely important. Adequate work space, along with storage space for the vehicle, will be needed. If a shop or garage isn't available, at the very least a flat, level, clean work surface made of concrete or asphalt is required.

Cleaning the engine compartment and engine before beginning the removal procedure will help keep tools clean and organised **(see illustrations 6.1 and 6.2).**

An engine hoist will also be necessary. Make sure the hoist is rated in excess of the combined weight of the engine and transaxle. Safety is of primary importance, considering the potential hazards involved in removing the engine from the vehicle.

6.3 Get an engine hoist that's strong enough to easily lift your engine in and out of the engine compartment; an adapter, like the one shown here, can be used to change the angle of the engine as it's being removed or installed

A vehicle hoist will be necessary for engine removal, since on these models the subframe must be removed and the engine/transaxle assembly must be lowered from the engine compartment, then the vehicle is raised and the powertrain unit is removed from under the vehicle. If the necessary equipment is not available, the engine will have to be removed by a qualified automotive repair facility.

If you're a novice at engine removal, get at least one helper. One person cannot easily do all the things you need to do to remove a big heavy engine and transaxle assembly from the engine compartment. Also helpful is to seek advice and assistance from someone who's experienced in engine removal.

Plan the operation ahead of time. Arrange for or obtain all of the tools and equipment you'll need prior to beginning the job **(see illustrations 6.3 and 6.4)**. Some of the equipment necessary to perform engine removal and installation safely and with relative ease are (in addition to a vehicle hoist and an engine hoist) a heavy duty floor jack (preferably fitted with a transaxle jack head adapter), complete sets of wrenches and sockets as described in the front of this manual, wooden blocks, plenty of rags and cleaning solvent for mopping up spilled oil, coolant and petrol.

Plan for the vehicle to be out of use for quite a while. A machine shop can do the

6.4 Get an engine stand sturdy enough to firmly support the engine while you're working on it. Stay away from three-wheeled models - they have a tendency to tip over more easily, so get a four-wheeled unit

work that is beyond the scope of the home mechanic. Machine shops often have a busy schedule, so before removing the engine, consult the shop for an estimate of how long it will take to rebuild or repair the components that may need work.

---

7 Engine - removal and installation

Warning: *The models covered by this manual are equipped with Supplemental Restraint Systems (SRS), more commonly known as airbags. Always disable the airbag system before working in the vicinity of airbag system components to avoid the possibility of accidental employment of the airbag, which could cause personal injury (see Chapter 12).*

Warning: *Gasoline is extremely flammable, so take extra precautions when you work on any part of the fuel system. Don't smoke or allow open flames or bare light bulbs near the work area, and don't work in a garage where a gas type appliance (such as a water heater or a clothes dryer) is present. Since gasoline is carcinogenic, wear fuel resistant gloves when there's a possibility of being exposed to fuel and if you spill any fuel on your skin, rinse it off immediately with soap and water. Mop up any spills immediately and do not store fuel soaked rags where they could ignite. The fuel system is under constant pressure, so if any fuel lines are to be disconnected, the fuel pressure in the system must be relieved first (see Chapter 4 for more information). When you perform any work on the system, wear safety glasses and have a Class B fire extinguisher on hand.*

Note: *Engine removal on these vehicles is a difficult job, especially for the do-it-yourself mechanic working at home. Because of the vehicle's design, the manufacturer states that*

the engine and transaxle have to be removed as a unit from the bottom of the vehicle, not the top. With a floor jack and jackstands, the vehicle can't be raised high enough or supported safely enough for the engine/transaxle assembly to slide out from underneath. The manufacturer recommends that removal of the engine/transaxle assembly only be performed with the use of a frame-contact type vehicle hoist.

Note: *Keep in mind that during this procedure you'll have to adjust the height of the vehicle with the vehicle hoist to perform certain operations.*

Removal

Refer to illustrations 7.15, 7.30a, 7.30b and 7.38

1   Park the vehicle on a frame-contact type vehicle hoist, then engage the arms of the hoist with the jacking points of the vehicle. Raise the hoist arms until they contact the vehicle, but not so much that the wheels come off the ground.
2   Relieve the fuel system pressure (see Chapter 4).
3   On GSU40R/GSU45R, remove the top cowl/ventilation cover (see Chapter 11).
4   On GSU40R/GSU45R, remove the windshield wiper arms and the windshield wiper motor (see Chapter 12).
5   On GSU40R/GSU45R, remove the lower cowl cover (see Chapter 11).
6   Remove the battery and battery tray (see Chapter 5).
7   Remove the air filter housing and air intake duct (see Chapter 4).
8   Disconnect the wiring from the throttle body (see Chapter 4).
9   Disconnect the shift cable from the transaxle (see Chapter 7).
10   Remove the alternator (see Chapter 5).
11   Remove the air conditioning compressor without disconnecting the refrigerant lines (see Chapter 3).

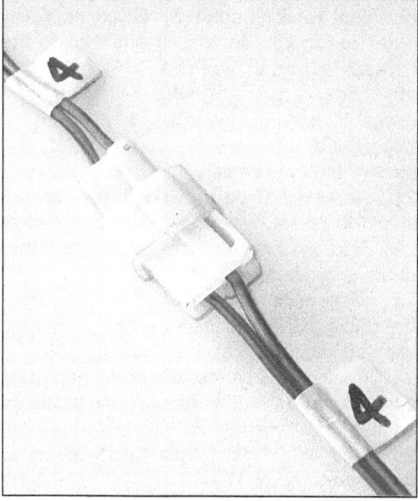

7.15 Label both ends of each wire or hose before disconnecting it

7.29a Remove the transaxle bellhousing access cover bolts . . .

7.29b . . . then remove the torque converter bolts

12   Secure the compressor out of the way (but not to the subframe).

13   Disconnect the intermediate shaft from the steering gear (see Chapter 10).

14   Disconnect the fuel feed hose from the fuel rail (see Chapter 4). Plug the line and fitting.

15   Clearly label and disconnect all vacuum lines, emissions hoses, electrical connectors and ground straps connecting the engine and transaxle to the vehicle. Masking tape and/or a touch up paint applicator work well for marking items **(see illustration)**. Take instant photos or sketch the locations of components and brackets, if necessary.

16   On MCU28R models, using a suction gun, remove as much fluid from the power steering fluid reservoir as possible. Detach the power steering hose from the return line.

17   Working on the engine mounts, remove the engine movement control rod (see Chapter 2A), or (see Chapter 2B). Also remove its mounting bracket from the cylinder head.

18   Disconnect the electrical harness from the main fuse/relay box in the engine compartment (see Chapter 5). Disconnect any other electrical connectors attached to the harness leading to the PCM.

19   Loosen the front wheel nuts and the driveshaft/hub nuts (see Chapter 8).

20   Raise the vehicle on the hoist and remove the front wheels.

21   Remove the under-vehicle splash shield(s) (see Chapter 2A), or (see Chapter 2B). Also remove the inner guard liners and guard apron seals (see Chapter 11).

22   Disconnect the stabiliser bar links from the stabiliser bar and the tie-rod ends from the steering knuckles (see Chapter 10).

23   Remove the driveshafts (see Chapter 8).

24   On AWD models, remove the propeller shaft (see Chapter 8).

25   On AWD models, drain the transfer case fluid (see Chapter 1).

26   Drain the engine coolant (see Chapter 1).

27   Drain the engine oil (see Chapter 1).

28   Drain the transaxle fluid (see Chapter 1).

29   Remove the driveplate-to-torque converter bolts **(see illustrations)**. Also disconnect the transaxle fluid cooler hoses from the transmission fluid cooler (see Chapter 7).

30   Disconnect the fluid lines from the power steering pump. Also detach the pressure and return lines from the power steering gear.

31   Unbolt the exhaust pipe(s) from the exhaust manifold/catalytic converter assemblies (see Chapter 2A or 2B).

32   Remove the front portion of the exhaust system (see Chapter 4).

33   Lower the vehicle and disconnect the radiator hoses and heater hoses from the engine. Remove the radiator (see Chapter 3).

34   Support the engine/transaxle assembly from above with a hoist. Attach the hoist chain to the lifting brackets. If no lifting brackets or hooks are present, lifting hooks may be available from your local auto parts store or dealer parts department. If not, you will have to fasten the chains to some substantial parts of the engine - ones that are strong enough to take the weight, but in locations that will provide good balance. If you're attaching a chain to a stud on the engine, or are using a bolt passing through the chain and into a threaded hole, place a washer between the nut or bolt head and the chain and tighten the nut or bolt securely.

Warning: *Do not place any part of your body under the engine/transaxle when it's supported only by a hoist or other lifting device.*

35   Take up the slack until there is slight tension on the hoist. Position the chain on the hoist so it balances the engine and the transaxle level with the vehicle.

Note: *Depending on the design of the engine hoist, it may be helpful to position the hoist from the side of the vehicle, so that when the engine/transaxle assembly is lowered, it will fit between the legs of the hoist.*

Note: *The sling or chain must be long enough to allow the engine hoist to lower the engine/*

transaxle assembly to the ground, without letting the hoist arm contact the vehicle.

36   Support the subframe with a pair of floor jacks. Recheck to be sure that there aren't any hoses or wiring between the subframe and the vehicle. Unbolt the engine mounts from the subframe (see Chapter 2A or 2B), remove the subframe mounting bolts (see Chapter 10) and lower it to the floor, then remove it out from underneath the vehicle.

Warning: *This can be tricky, depending on the design of the engine hoist, but it is imperative that the subframe be supported securely before its mounting bolts are removed.*

37   Recheck to be sure nothing is still connecting the engine or transaxle to the vehicle. Disconnect and label anything still remaining.

38   Lower the engine/transaxle assembly **(see illustration)**. Once the engine/transaxle assembly is on the floor, disconnect the engine hoist and raise the vehicle until it clears the engine/transaxle assembly.

39   Reconnect the chain or sling to support the engine and transaxle.

40   Raise the engine/transaxle assembly, then support the engine with blocks of wood or another floor jack, while leaving the sling or chain attached. Support the transaxle with another floor jack, preferably one with a transaxle jack head adapter. At this point the transfer case can be unbolted and removed (AWD models - see Chapter 7). Be very careful to ensure that the components are supported securely so they won't topple off their supports during disconnection.

41   Remove the transaxle-to-engine bolts and separate the transaxle from the engine.

42   Reconnect the lifting chain to the engine, then raise the engine and attach it to an engine stand.

Installation

43   Installation is the reverse of removal, noting the following points:

   a   *Check the engine/transaxle mounts. If they're worn or damaged, replace them.*

7.38 After the subframe has been removed, lower the engine/transaxle unit to the floor

b   Attach the transaxle to the engine (see Chapter 7).

c   When installing the subframe, tighten the subframe mounting bolts to the torque listed in the Chapter 10 Specifications.

d   Tighten the driveshaft/hub nuts to the torque listed in the Chapter 8 Specifications. Tighten all steering and suspension fasteners to the torque listed in the Chapter 10 Specifications. Tighten the wheel nuts to the torque listed in the Chapter 1 Specifications.

e   Refill the engine coolant, oil, power steering and transaxle fluids (see Chapter 1).

f   Reconnect the battery (see Chapter 5).

g   Run the engine and check for proper operation and leaks. Shut off the engine and recheck fluid levels.

8   Initial start-up and break-in after installation

Warning: Have a fire extinguisher handy when starting the engine for the first time.

1   Once the engine has been installed in the vehicle, double-check the engine oil and coolant levels.

2   It is good mechanical practice to crank the engine with the spark plugs removed to get oil circulating around the engine without the engine being under load. To do this, remove the spark plugs from the engine and crank it for about 10-seconds with a 15-second break and then repeat the procedure. Do this several times. While doing this it is imperative that the fuel injection and ignition systems are disabled. A procedure to crank the engine is covered in the engine compression check procedure (see Section 3).

Caution: Ensure the fuel and ignition system is disabled before cranking the engine.

3   Install the spark plugs hook up the plug wires and restore the ignition system and fuel pump functions.

4   Start the engine. It may take a few moments for the fuel system to build up pressure, but the engine should start without a great deal of effort.

5   After the engine starts, it should be allowed to warm up to normal operating temperature. While the engine is warming up, make a thorough check for fuel, oil and coolant leaks.

6   Shut the engine off and recheck the engine oil and coolant levels.

7   Drive the vehicle to an area with minimum traffic, accelerate from 50 to 80 km/h, then allow the vehicle to slow to 50 km/h with the throttle closed. Repeat the procedure 10 or 12 times. This will load the piston rings and cause them to seat properly against the cylinder walls. Check again for oil and coolant leaks.

8   Drive the vehicle gently for the first 800 km (no sustained high speeds) and keep a constant check on the oil level. It is not unusual for an engine to use oil during the break-in period.

9   At approximately 800 to 1,000 km change the oil and filter.

10   For the next few hundred kilometres, drive the vehicle normally. Do not pamper it or abuse it.

11   After 3,000 km, change the oil and filter again and consider the engine broken in.

Chapter 3
Cooling, heating and air conditioning systems

Contents

Specifications

General

Radiator cap opening	
New cap	93 to 122 kPa
Used cap - minimum opening pressure	78 kPa
Thermostat rating	
Opens	80 to 84 degrees C
Fully open...	95 degrees C

Torque specifications

	Nm
Drivebelt tensioner pulley bolt (2GR-FE engine) [1]	Not specified
Drivebelt tensioner bolts (2GR-FE engine)..	43
Drivebelt idler pulley bolts (2GR-FE engine)	43
Thermostat housing bolts	
3MZ-FE engine	8
2GR-FE engine	10
Water pump bolts/nuts	
3MZ-FE engine	8
2GR-FE engine **(see illustration 7.35)**	
Bolts A..	21
Bolts B	10
Bolts C	10
Water inlet pipe-to-thermostat housing (3MZ-FE engine)	20
Water pump pulley (2GR-FE engine)	21

[1] LH thread

1   General information

Warning: *To prevent scalding, use caution when releasing the radiator cap if the engine is warm. Squeeze the upper radiator hose. If resistance is felt, the system is pressurised and the cap should not be removed until the radiator hose can easily be squeezed together. Escaping steam and scalding liquid could cause serious injury.*

Engine cooling system

Refer to illustrations 1.1a, 1.1b and 1.2

All vehicles covered by this manual employ a pressurised engine cooling system with thermostatically controlled coolant circulation **(see illustration)**. An impeller type water pump mounted on the front of the block pumps coolant through the engine. The coolant flows around each cylinder and toward the rear of the engine. Cast-in coolant passages direct coolant around the intake and exhaust ports, near the spark plug areas and in proximity to the exhaust valve guides.

A wax pellet-type thermostat is located in the thermostat housing near the front of the engine **(see illustration)**. During warm up, the closed thermostat prevents coolant from circulating through the radiator. When the engine reaches normal operating temperature, the thermostat opens and allows hot coolant to travel through the radiator, where it

is cooled before returning to the engine.

The cooling system is sealed by a pressure-type radiator cap. This raises the boiling point of the coolant, and the higher boiling point of the coolant increases the cooling efficiency of the radiator. If the system pressure exceeds the cap pressure relief value, the excess pressure in the system forces the spring-loaded valve inside the cap off its seat and allows the coolant to escape through the overflow tube into a coolant reservoir. When the system cools, the excess coolant is automatically drawn from the reservoir back into the radiator.

The coolant reservoir serves as both the point at which fresh coolant is added to the cooling system to maintain the proper fluid level and as a holding tank for overheated coolant.

This type of cooling system is known as a closed design because coolant that escapes past the pressure cap is saved and reused.

Heating system

The heating system consists of a blower fan and heater core located within the heater box, the inlet and outlet hoses connecting the heater core to the engine cooling system and the heater/air conditioning control head on the dashboard. Hot engine coolant is circulated through the heater core. When the heater mode is activated, a flap door opens to expose the heater box to the passenger com-

partment. A fan switch on the control head activates the blower motor, which forces air through the core, heating the air.

Air conditioning system

The air conditioning system consists of a condenser mounted in front of the radiator, an evaporator mounted adjacent to the heater core under the dashboard, a compressor mounted on the engine, a receiver-drier which contains a high pressure relief valve and the plumbing connecting all of the above.

A blower fan forces the warmer air of the passenger compartment through the evaporator core (sort of a radiator-in-reverse), transferring the heat from the air to the refrigerant. The liquid refrigerant boils off into low-pressure vapour, taking the heat with it when it leaves the evaporator. The compressor keeps refrigerant circulating through the system, pumping the warmed coolant through the condenser where it is cooled and then circulated back to the evaporator.

Some models are equipped with an optional Automatic Air Conditioning system. With this system, you select the desired interior temperature with a knob on the controls, similar to setting the temperature on a home heating/cooling thermostat, and the system automatically adds the right blend of cool or warm air to maintain this temperature. The system has sensors that detect both the interior and outside temperature.

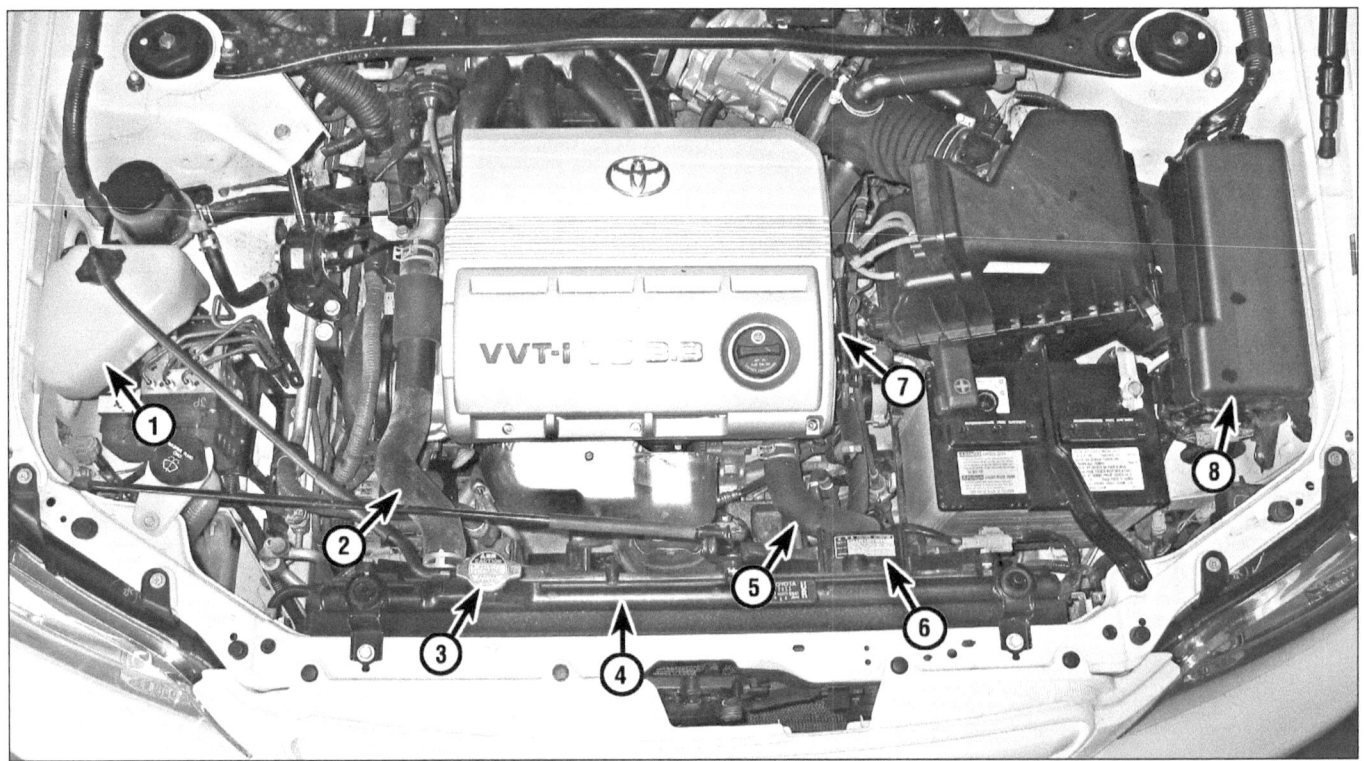

1.1a 3.3L (3MZ-FE) engine cooling system component locations

1 *Coolant reservoir*	4 *Radiator*
2 *Upper radiator hose*	5 *Lower radiator hose*
3 *Radiator cap*	6 *Cooling fans*

7 *Thermostat (vicinity shown)*
8 *Fuse and relay box*

1.1b 3.5L (2GR-FE) engine cooling system component locations

1 Coolant reservoir
2 Upper radiator hose
3 Radiator cap
4 Radiator

5 Lower radiator hose
6 Cooling fans
7 Thermostat
8 Fuse and relay box

9   Radiator bleed valve
10 Cylinder head bleed valve
11 Coolant temperature sensor

2   Antifreeze - general information

Refer to illustration 2.4

Warning: *Do not allow antifreeze to come in contact with your skin or painted surfaces of the vehicle. Rinse off spills immediately with*

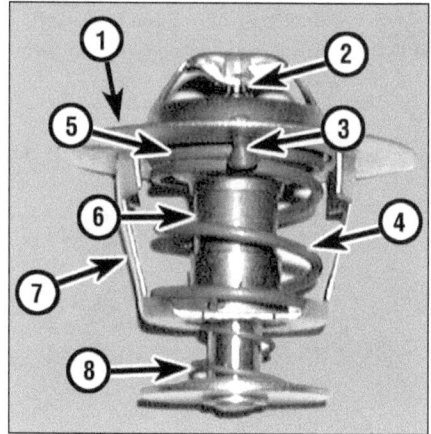

1.2 A typical thermostat

1 Flange
2 Piston
3 Jiggle valve
4 Main coil spring
5 Valve seat
6 Valve
7 Frame
8 Secondary coil spring

plenty of water. Antifreeze is highly toxic if ingested. Never leave antifreeze lying around in an open container or in puddles on the floor; children and pets are attracted by its sweet smell and may drink it. Check with local authorities on disposing of used antifreeze. Many communities have collection centres that will see that antifreeze is disposed of safely. Never dump used antifreeze on the ground or into drains.

Note: *Non-toxic coolant is available at local auto parts stores. Although the coolant is non-toxic when fresh, proper disposal of used coolant is still required.*

The cooling system should be filled with a water/ethylene-glycol based antifreeze solution, which will prevent freezing down to at least -20 degrees C, or lower if local climate requires it. It also provides protection against corrosion and increases the coolant boiling point.

The cooling system should be drained, flushed and refilled at least every other year (see Chapter 1). The use of antifreeze solutions for periods of longer than two years is likely to cause damage and encourage the formation of rust and scale in the system. If your tap water is hard (contains a lot of dissolved minerals), use distilled water with the antifreeze.

Before adding antifreeze to the system, check all hose connections, because antifreeze tends to leak through very minute openings. Engines do not normally consume

coolant. Therefore, if the level goes down, find the cause and correct it.

The exact mixture of antifreeze-to-water that you should use depends on the relative weather conditions. The mixture should contain at least 50 percent antifreeze, but should never contain more than 70-percent antifreeze. Consult the mixture ratio chart on the antifreeze container before adding coolant. Hydrometers are available at most auto parts stores to test the ratio of antifreeze to water **(see illustration)**. Use antifreeze which meets the vehicle manufacturer's specifications.

2.4 An inexpensive hydrometer can be used to test the condition of your coolant

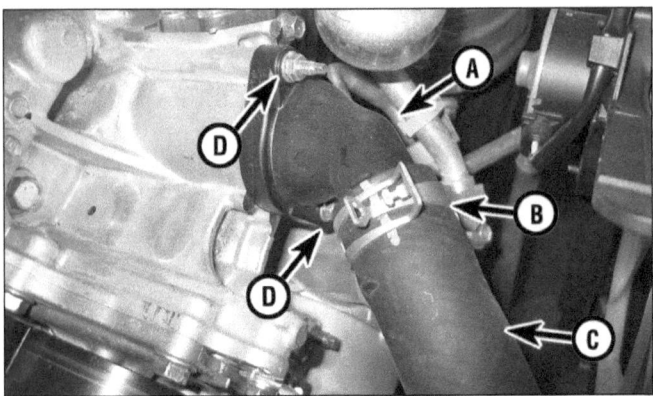

3.2 Typical thermostat details

A   *Thermostat housing*
B   *Radiator hose spring clamp*
C   *Radiator hose*

D   *Thermostat housing nuts*

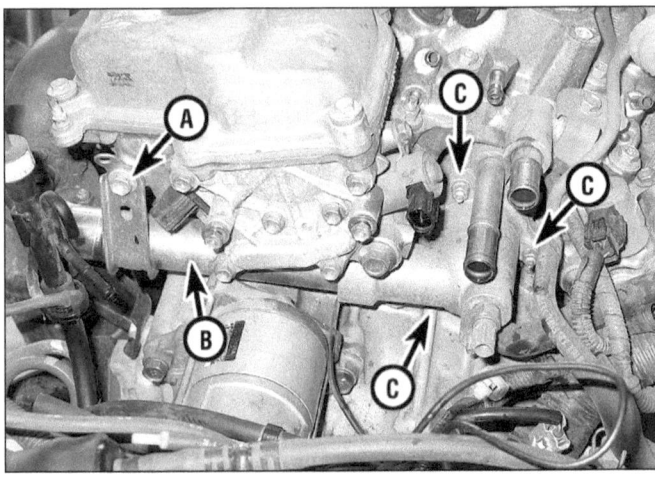

3.13 Water inlet pipe mounting fastener (A), pipe (B) and thermostat housing mounting fasteners (C) - 3MZ-FE engine

3   Thermostat - check and replacement

Warning: *To prevent scalding, use caution when releasing the radiator cap if the engine is warm. Squeeze the upper radiator hose. If resistance is felt, the system is pressurised and the cap should not be removed until the radiator hose can easily be squeezed together. Escaping steam and scalding liquid could cause serious injury.*

General check

Refer to illustration 3.2

1   Before assuming the thermostat is responsible for a cooling system problem, check the coolant level (see Chapter 1), drive-belt tension (see Chapter 1) and temperature gauge (or light) operation.
2   If the engine takes a long time to warm up (as indicated by the temperature gauge or heater operation), the thermostat is probably stuck open. Replace the thermostat with a new one **(see illustration)**.

3   If the engine runs hot, use your hand to check the temperature of the lower radiator hose. If the hose is not hot, but the engine is, the thermostat is probably stuck in the closed position, preventing the coolant inside the engine from escaping to the radiator. Replace the thermostat.
Caution: *Do not drive the vehicle without a thermostat. The computer may stay in open loop and emissions and fuel economy will suffer.*
4   If the lower radiator hose is hot, it means that the coolant is flowing and the thermostat is open. Consult the Troubleshooting Section at the front of this manual for further diagnosis.

Thermostat test

5   A more thorough test of the thermostat can only be made when it is removed from the vehicle (see below). If the thermostat remains in the open position at room temperature, it is faulty and must be replaced.
6   To test it fully, suspend the (closed) thermostat on a length of string or wire in a

container of cold water, with a thermometer (cooking type that reads beyond 100 degrees C). A clear Pyrex cooking container is easiest to use.
7   Heat the water on a stove while observing the temperature and the thermostat. Neither should contact the sides of the container.
8   Note the temperature when the thermostat begins to open and when it is fully open. Compare the temperatures to the Specifications in this Chapter. The number stamped into the thermostat is generally the fully-open temperature. Some manufacturers provide Specifications for the beginning-to-open temperature, the fully-open temperature, and sometimes the amount the valve should open.
9   If the thermostat doesn't open and close as specified, or sticks in any position, replace it.

Replacement

Refer to illustrations 3.13, 3.16a and 3.16b

10   Disconnect the negative (-) battery terminal (see Chapter 5).
11   Remove the engine cover.

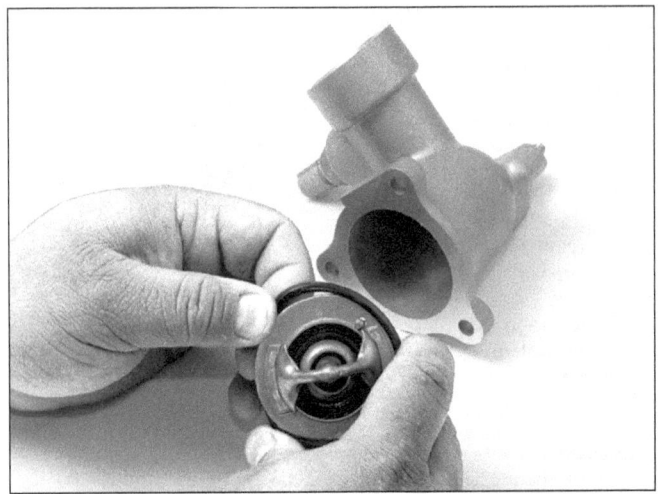

3.16a The thermostat seal fits around the edge of the thermostat

3.16b Note the position of the thermostat and how the seal is installed around it

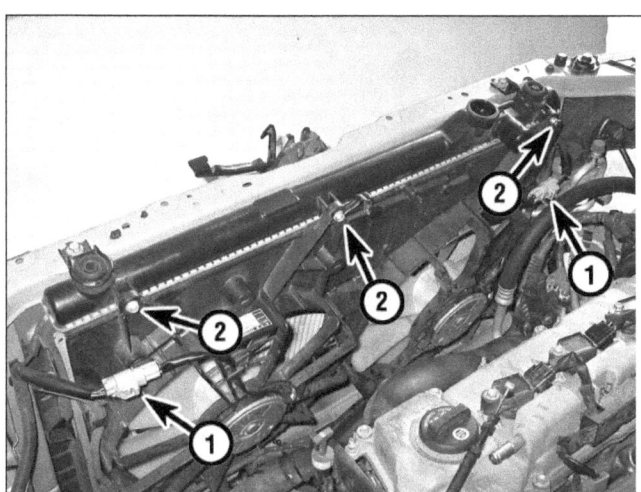

4.3a Engine cooling fan mounting details:

1   Fan motor connectors
2   Fan assembly mounting fasteners (top shown, bottom similar)

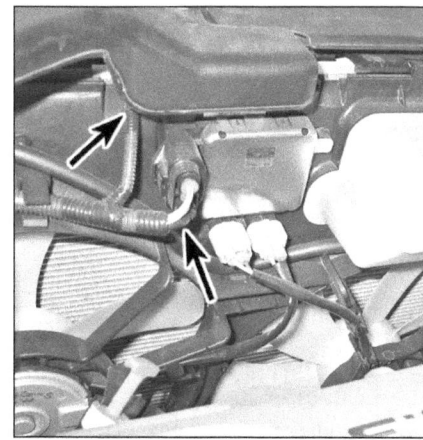

4.3b Disconnect these harnesses from the fan shroud

12   Drain the engine coolant (see Chapter 1). Disconnect the radiator hose from the thermostat housing or water inlet pipe.
13   On 3MZ-FE engines, proceed as follows:
  a   Remove the air filter (see Chapter 4).
  b   Unbolt the water inlet pipe and remove the pipe and O-ring **(see illustration)**.
14   Disconnect the radiator hose from the thermostat housing.
15   Remove the thermostat housing mounting fasteners and housing from the coolant inlet housing. Remove the thermostat, noting the direction in which it was installed in the housing, and thoroughly clean the sealing surfaces.
16   Install a new gasket to the thermostat **(see illustration)**. Install the thermostat into the inlet housing, with the jiggle valve positioned at the highest point **(see illustration)**. Install the thermostat housing.
17   Tighten the housing fasteners to the torque listed in this Chapter's Specifications. The remainder of installation is the reverse of removal.
18   Refill the cooling system (see Chapter 1). Run the engine and check for leaks and proper operation.

4   Engine cooling fans - removal and installation

Refer to illustrations 4.3a, 4.3b, 4.5 and 4.6

Warning: *Do not start this procedure until the engine is completely cool. Do not allow antifreeze to come in contact with your skin or painted surfaces of the vehicle. Rinse off spills immediately with plenty of water. Antifreeze is highly toxic if ingested. Never leave antifreeze lying around in an open container or in puddles on the floor; children and pets are attracted by its sweet smell and may drink it. Check with local authorities on disposing of used antifreeze. Many communities have collection centres, which will see that antifreeze is disposed of safely. Never dump used antifreeze on the ground or into drains.*

Warning: *The models covered by this manual are equipped with Supplemental Restraint Systems (SRS), more commonly known as airbags. Always disarm the airbag system before working in the vicinity of any airbag system component to avoid the possibility of*

accidental deployment of the airbag, which could cause personal injury (see Chapter 12).

Note: *On most models, the manufacturer's procedure for engine cooling fan removal involves removing the radiator and fan assembly together and then separating them afterwards. It is possible to remove the engine cooling fans without removing the radiator.*

1   Disconnect the cable from the negative terminal of the battery (see Chapter 5). Drain the cooling system (see Chapter 1), then detach the upper radiator hose from the radiator.
2   Remove the air intake duct (see Chapter 4), the plastic cover over the radiator support, and the bonnet release latch (see Chapter 11). Remove the six mounting bolts (two on each end and two in the middle) for the radiator support and then remove the support.
3   Disconnect the electrical connectors for both fan motors **(see illustration)**.

Note: *On GSU40R/GSU45R models, disconnect the electrical connectors to the fan electronic control unit (ECU) and any other harness connectors attached to the fan shroud* **(see illustration)**.

4   Remove the fan/shroud mounting fasteners from the radiator, remove any hoses or wiring harnesses that may be attached to it and then lift out of the vehicle **(see illustration 4.3a)**.
5   Hold the fan blades and remove the fan retaining nut **(see illustration)**.
6   Unbolt the fan motor from the shroud **(see illustration)**.
7   Installation is the reverse of removal. Tighten the radiator support mounting bolts to the torque listed in this Chapter's Specifications. Refill the cooling system (see Chapter 1).

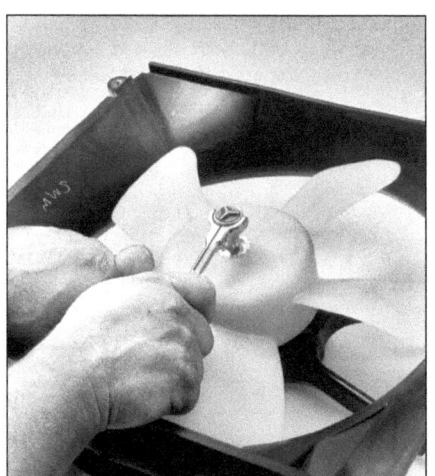

4.5 Remove the fan from the motor

4.6 Remove the screws and separate the motor from the shroud

5.6a   Radiator support cover (1) and mounting fasteners (2) on GSU40R/GSU45R models

5.6b   Removing the radiator support from above the radiator - GSU40R/GSU45R models

5   Radiator and coolant reservoir - removal and installation

Warning: *Do not start this procedure until the engine is completely cool. Do not allow antifreeze to come in contact with your skin or painted surfaces of the vehicle. Rinse off spills immediately with plenty of water. Antifreeze is highly toxic if ingested. Never leave antifreeze lying around in an open container or in puddles on the floor; children and pets are attracted by its sweet smell and may drink it. Check with local authorities on disposing of used antifreeze. Many communities have collection centres, which will see that antifreeze is disposed of safely. Never dump used antifreeze on the ground or into drains.*

Warning: *The models covered by this manual are equipped with Supplemental Restraint Systems (SRS), more commonly known as airbags. Always disarm the airbag system before working in the vicinity of any airbag system component to avoid the possibility of accidental deployment of the airbag, which could cause personal injury (see Chapter 12).*

Note: *Non-toxic coolant is available at local auto parts stores. Although the coolant is non-toxic when fresh, proper disposal of used coolant is still required.*

Radiator

Removal

Refer to illustrations 5.6a, 5.6b, 5.9 and 5.11

1   Disconnect the negative (-) battery terminal (see Chapter 5).
2   Drain the cooling system (see Chapter 1).
3   Remove the engine cover.

Note: *On 2GR-FE engines, pull up on the front side of the engine top cover to detach it from the two front retainers. After the front is detached, pull up on the back retainer and remove the engine cover. Do not pull up on the front and rear at the same time or the cover can be damaged.*

4   Remove the air intake duct(s) from above the radiator (see Chapter 4).
5   Remove the engine splash shields from below the radiator.
6   On GSU40R/GSU45R models, proceed as follows:

   *a Remove the radiator support cover **(see illustration).***
   b Remove the fasteners and remove the front grille and bonnet lock (see Chapter 11).
   c Remove the air intake duct retaining bolts and disconnect the duct from the air-cleaner housing. Remove from the vehicle.
   d Remove the bolt retaining the battery cooling duct and the bolt retaining the A/C hose bracket to the support cover.
   *e Disconnect the horn electrical connectors, remove the mounting bolts for the radiator support cover and the mounting brackets and lift the assembly clear of the work area **(see illustration).***
   f Remove the bolts now visible retaining the A/C condenser to the top of the radiator.

7   Detach the upper and lower radiator hoses from the radiator and the coolant reservoir hose from the radiator filler neck.
8   On GSU40R/GSU45R models, remove the battery (see Chapter 5).
9   Disconnect the transaxle cooler lines from the radiator **(see illustration)**. Place a drip pan underneath to catch the fluid, and cap the fittings.
10   Disconnect the electrical connectors for the engine cooling fans (see Section 4) and detach any wires or brackets from the fan shroud and radiator.
11   On MCU28R models, remove the upper radiator mounting brackets.
12   Carefully remove the radiator and fan shroud as an assembly **(see illustration)**.
13   Remove the cooling fans from the radiator (see Section 4). On GSU40R/GSU45R models, remove the two bolts and remove the coolant reservoir from the fan shroud also.

5.9   Detach the automatic transaxle cooler lines

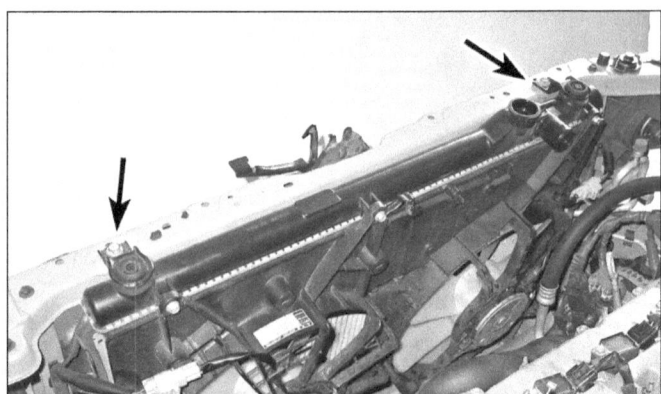

5.11   Radiator bracket mounting bolts - MCU28R models

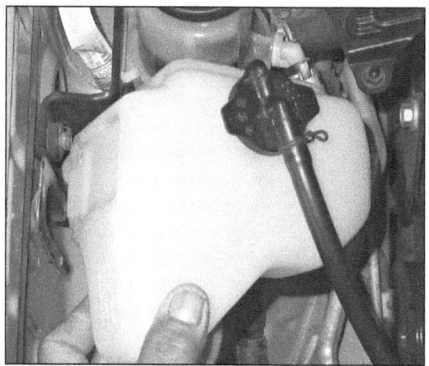

5.19a Pull the coolant reservoir up and out of its bracket to remove it on MCU28R models

5.19b Coolant reservoir fasteners on GSU40R/GSU45R models

14   With the radiator removed, it can be inspected for leaks, damage and internal blockage. If in need of repairs, have a professional radiator shop perform the work, as special techniques are required.
15   Bugs and dirt can be cleaned from the radiator with compressed air and a soft brush. Don't bend the cooling fins as this is done.
Warning: *Wear eye protection.*

Installation

16   Installation is the reverse of removal. Be sure the rubber mounts are correctly in place.
17   After installation, fill the cooling system with the proper mixture of antifreeze and water (see Chapter 1).
18   Start the engine and check for leaks. Allow the engine to reach normal operating temperature, indicated by the upper radiator hose becoming hot. Recheck the coolant level and add more if required.
19   Check the automatic transaxle fluid level and add fluid as needed (see Chapter 1).

Coolant reservoir

Refer to illustrations 5.19a and 5.19b

19   On MCU28R models, the coolant reservoir simply pulls up and out of the bracket on the inner guard **(see illustration)**. On GSU40R/GSU45R models, it is retained by two bolts to the fan shroud **(see illustration)**.
20   Pour the coolant into a container. Wash out and inspect the reservoir for cracks and chafing. Replace it if damaged.
21   Installation is the reverse of removal.

6   Water pump - check

Note: *On MCU28R models with the 3MZ-FE engine, the water pump is driven by the timing belt. Inspection is only possible once the timing belt covers are removed (see Chapter 2A). It is good mechanical practice to renew the water pump as a matter of course when the timing belt is replaced as it is not uncommon for it to leak once the timing belt tension has been relieved and re-applied with a new timing belt.*

1   A failure in the water pump can cause serious engine damage due to overheating.
2   Water pumps are equipped with weep or vent holes. If a failure occurs in the pump seal, coolant will leak from this hole. In most cases it will be necessary to use a flashlight to find the hole on the water pump by looking through the space behind the pulley just below the water pump shaft. A slight gray discolouration around the weep hole is normal, while dark brown stains indicate a problem.
3   If the water pump shaft bearings fail, there may be a howling sound at the front of the engine while it is running. Bearing wear can be felt if the water pump pulley is rocked up and down. Do not mistake drivebelt slippage, which causes a squealing sound, for water pump failure. Spray automotive drivebelt dressing on the belts to eliminate the belt as a possible cause of the noise.

7   Water pump - removal and installation

Warning: *Do not start this procedure until the engine is completely cool. Do not allow antifreeze to come in contact with your skin or painted surfaces of the vehicle. Rinse off spills immediately with plenty of water. Antifreeze is highly toxic if ingested. Never leave antifreeze lying around in an open container or in puddles on the floor; children and pets are attracted by its sweet smell and may drink it. Check with local authorities on disposing of used antifreeze. Many communities have collection centres, which will see that antifreeze is disposed of safely. Never dump used antifreeze on the ground or into drains.*

Note: *Non-toxic coolant is available at local auto parts stores. Although the coolant is non-toxic when fresh, proper disposal of used coolant is still required.*

1   Disconnect the negative (-) battery terminal (see Chapter 5).
2   Drain the cooling system (see Chapter 1).

3MZ-FE engine

Refer to illustrations 7.4, 7.5 and 7.7

3   Remove the timing belt, camshaft sprockets (see Chapter 2A) and the number 2 idler pulley (above the water pump).
4   Remove the number 3 timing belt cover **(see illustration)**.
5   Remove the water pump retaining bolts/nuts, and separate the pump from the engine.

Note: *There are two long studs that hold the engine mounting bracket and the water pump. The studs have a small hex-head that is used to remove the stud **(see illustration)**. It may be necessary to remove one or both of these studs to remove the water pump. If the stud is stuck, remove it with locking pliers and replace it with a new one of the same length.*

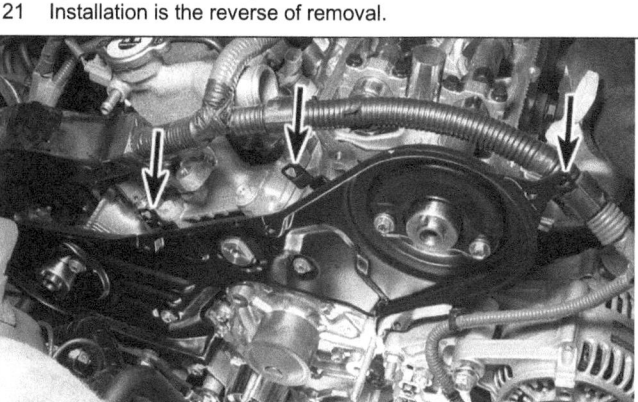

7.4 Release the three wiring harness clips, pull the harness back and remove the number 3 timing belt cover - 3MZ-FE engine

7.5 3MZ-FE engine water pumps have two long studs - one or both may have to be removed with a small wrench to allow water pump removal

6   Thoroughly clean all sealing surfaces, removing all traces of old gaskets, sealer and O-rings. Remove any traces of oil with acetone or lacquer thinner and a clean rag.

7   These models use a metal and rubber gasket **(see illustration)**.

8   The reminder of installation is the reverse of removal. Tighten the water pump bolts/nuts in several steps to the torque listed in this Chapter's Specifications.

9   Refill the cooling system (see Chapter 1) and run the engine, checking for leaks and proper operation.

2GR-FE engine

Refer to illustrations 7.19, 7.21, 7.23 and 7.24

Note: *Removing the water pump will require a floor jack or engine hoist to raise and lower the engine. Once all the components are removed from the timing chain cover, there will be enough clearance to remove the water pump with the pulley (bolts removed), but not separately.*

10   Remove the engine covers, radiator support trim cover and the inner guard splash shield on the right side (see Chapter 11).

11   Remove the drivebelt (see Chapter 1).

12   Remove the engine harness ground connector.

7.7 On 3MZ-FE engines, a new metal/rubber gasket is used when installing the water pump

13   Remove the upper front engine mount bracket and the engine movement control rod (see Chapter 2B).

14   Remove the rear engine mounts and insulators (see Chapter 2B).

15   Remove the front engine mounts and insulators (see Chapter 2B).

7.19 Using a pin spanner to hold the water pump pulley, remove the pulley mounting bolts

16   Place a floor jack with a wooden block under the engine oil pan for support. Remove the front engine mounting bracket. There will be little clearance to access the bolts; it will be necessary to use an open end spanner and to raise and lower the engine for access.

17   Remove both the front and rear drivebelt idler pulley assemblies. Keep them in order; note that the larger of the washers goes under the head of the pulley bolt, and the smaller goes between the pulley and the engine block.

18   Remove the bolt and the drivebelt tensioner pulley.

Caution: *Rotate the drivebelt tensioner pulley bolt CLOCKWISE to loosen.*

19   Hold the water pump pulley with a special pin-spanner **(see illustration)**. If you don't have one, you can use a chain wrench or strap wrench instead, as long as you wrap a section of old drivebelt around it for protection. Remove the pulley mounting bolts.

20   Remove the coolant inlet housing and gasket.

21   Remove the water pump mounting bolts **(see illustration)**, then remove the water pump/pulley and gasket.

Note: *The bolts that secure the water pump are of three different lengths. Make note of where each bolt is located so it may be reinstalled in the same location.*

22   Thoroughly clean all sealing surfaces, removing all traces of old gasket and sealer.

23   Install a new gasket to the water pump **(see illustration)**. Install the water pump and tighten the bolts and nuts to the torque listed in this Chapter's Specifications.

24   Install new gasket and O-ring to the water inlet housing **(see illustration)**.

25   The remainder of installation is the reverse of removal. Tighten the bolts to the torque listed in this Chapter's Specifications.

26   Refill the cooling system (see Chapter 1) and run the engine, checking for leaks and proper operation.

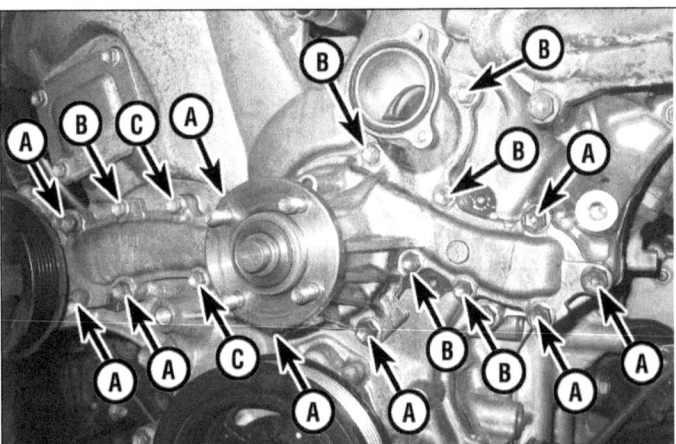

7.21 Locations of the different length water pump mounting bolts - 2GR-FE engine

7.23 Install a new gasket and clean the surface of the timing chain cover thoroughly - 2GR-FE engine

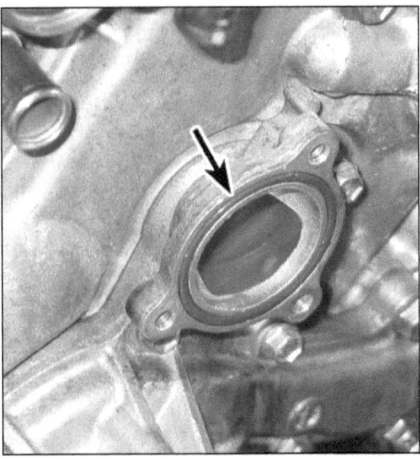

7.24 After installing the water pump, replace the inlet housing O-ring with a new one - 2GR-FE engine

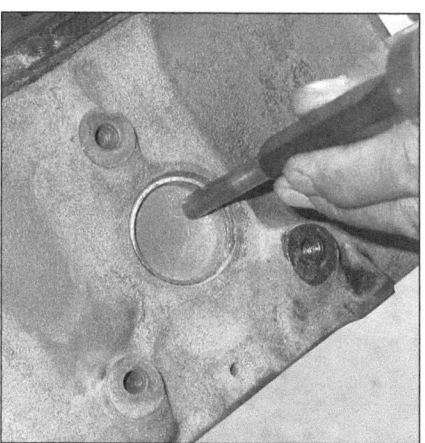

8.3 Tap the edge of the welch plug into the block . . .

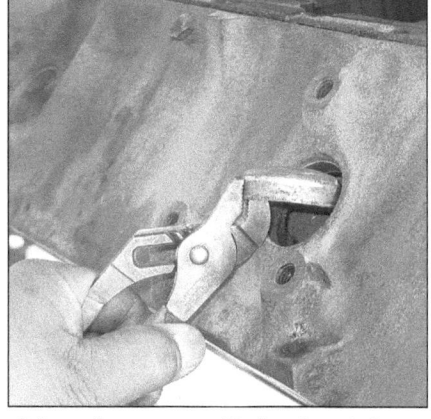

8.4 . . . then, use multigrip pliers to lever the old welch plug from the block

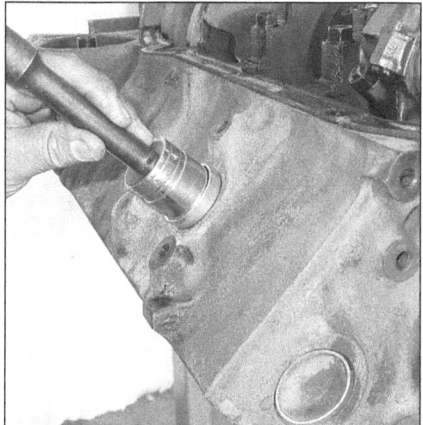

8.7 Use a socket that sits around the edge of the welch plug to tap it squarely into the block

8 Welch plugs - replacement

To facilitate the casting of the cylinder block and cylinder heads, a number of openings were made during manufacture. These openings are sealed with welch plugs.

The welch plugs will have to be renewed when cleaning the water jackets or when they become defective due to corrosion.

Note: *If a welch plug is found to be corroded, it is advisable to renew all the welch plugs.*

To renew

Refer to illustrations 8.3, 8.4 and 8.7

1　Drain the cooling system as previously described.

2　Remove the necessary engine components or accessories to gain ample working space around the damaged plug.

Note: *To access the welch plugs in the rear of the cylinder head and the rear of the cylinder block, it will be necessary to remove the engine.*

3　Using a punch and hammer, tap the welch plug on its outer circumference into its opening **(see illustration)**.

4　Grasp the edge of the welch plug with a pair of multigrip pliers and using the shoulder of the pliers as a fulcrum, lever the plug out of its opening **(see illustration)**.

5　Thoroughly clean and dry the welch plug opening.

6　Lightly smear the edge of the new welch plug and the opening with a suitable jointing compound, such as Loctite No 2.

7　Place the new welch plug onto the opening and using a large socket or piece of tubing fitting neatly inside the rim of the welch plug, tap the plug squarely into the opening **(see illustration)**.

Note: *The welch plug must be entered squarely into its opening or leakage may occur.*

8　Install the components which were removed to gain access to the welch plug.

9　Refill the cooling system as previously described. With the radiator cap installed, run the engine until it reaches normal operating temperature and check for coolant leaks. Rectify as necessary.

9 Coolant temperature indicator - check

Warning: *Wait until the engine is completely cool before beginning this procedure.*

1　The coolant temperature indicator system consists of a temperature gauge on the dash and a sensor mounted on the engine. On all models, an Engine Coolant Temperature (ECT) sensor (see Chapter 6), which is

an information sensor for the Powertrain Control Module (PCM), provides a signal to the PCM which controls and actuates the temperature gauge.

2　If an overheating indication has occurred, first check the coolant level in the system (see Chapter 1) and that the coolant mixture is correct (see Section 2). Also, refer to the Troubleshooting section at the beginning of this book before assuming that the temperature indicator is faulty.

3　Start the engine and warm it up for 10 minutes. If the temperature gauge has not moved from the C position, check the wiring harness connections going to the instrument cluster.

4　If there is a problem with the ECT sensor, it is very likely that the Check Engine lamp will be illuminated and the sensor or circuit will need repair (see Chapter 6).

10 Blower motor - removal and installation

Refer to illustrations 10.4 and 10.5

Warning: *The models covered by this manual are equipped with Supplemental Restraint Systems (SRS), more commonly known as airbags. Always disarm the airbag system before working in the vicinity of any airbag system component to avoid the possibility of accidental deployment of the airbag, which could cause personal injury (see Chapter 12).*

Note: *Some models have a rear heater assembly with a blower motor. The motor can be serviced in the same manner as the front motor. See Section 12 for removal of the rear heater core, which is necessary for access to the blower motor.*

1　Disconnect the negative (-) battery terminal (see Chapter 5).

2　The blower unit is located under the dash and below the glove box.

3　Remove the LH lower dash panel (just below the glove box), if equipped (see Chapter 11).

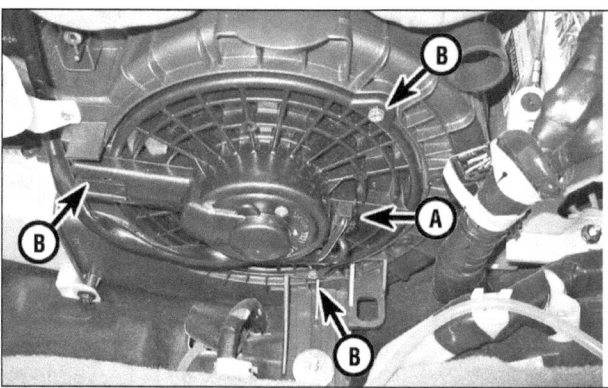

10.4 Blower motor details

A *Blower motor connector*
B *Blower motor mounting screws*

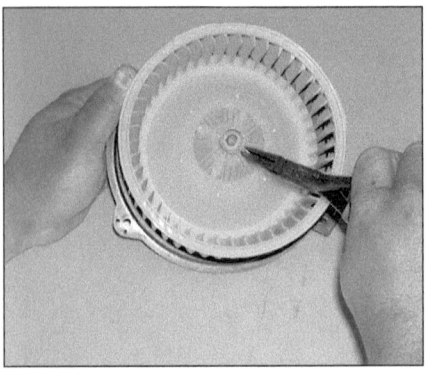

10.5 Use pliers to release and remove the clip, then lift the blower fan off the motor shaft

4   To remove the blower, remove the blower unit retaining screws and lower the unit from the housing **(see illustration)**.
5   If the motor is being replaced, transfer the fan to the new motor prior to installation **(see illustration)**.
6   Installation is the reverse of removal. Check for proper operation.

11   Heater and air conditioning control assembly - removal and installation

Refer to illustrations 11.3, 11.4, 11.5 and 11.6

Warning: *The models covered by this manual are equipped with Supplemental Restraint Systems (SRS), more commonly known as airbags. Always disarm the airbag system before working in the vicinity of any airbag system component to avoid the possibility of accidental deployment of the airbag, which could cause personal injury (see Chapter 12).*
1   Disconnect the negative (-) battery terminal (see Chapter 5).
2   Remove the centre trim panel around the control assembly (see Chapter 11), exposing the four mounting fasteners.
3   Remove the mounting screws for the

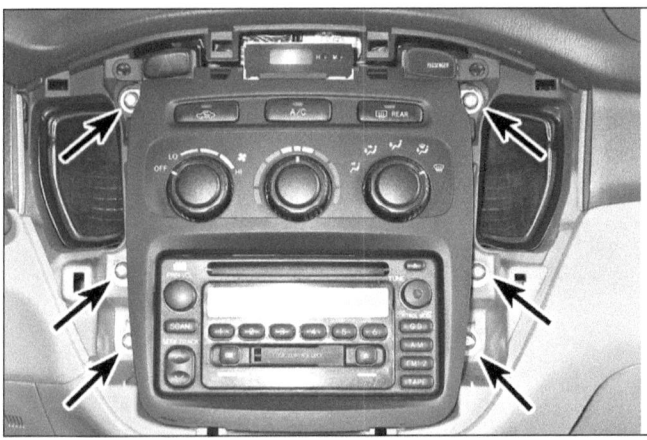

11.3 Control assembly mounting fasteners - MCU28R models

control assembly and the audio unit **(see illustration)**.
4   Pull the assembly out slightly and disconnect all electrical connectors for the control assembly and the audio unit **(see illustration)**.
5   Detach the audio unit from the control assembly by removing the mounting bracket screws from the control assembly **(see illustration)**. On other models, the control unit can be separated in a similar fashion.
6   On models equipped with rear heating, there is an additional control switch mounted in the rear trim **(see illustration)**.
7   Installation is the reverse of the removal procedure.
8   Run the engine and check for proper functioning of the heater and air conditioning.

12   Heater core - removal and installation

Front heater core

Refer to illustrations 12.7a, 12.7b, 12.12, 12.13, 12.14, 12.15a, 12.15b, 12.17 and 12.18

Warning: *The models covered by this manual are equipped with Supplemental Restraint*

Systems (SRS), more commonly known as airbags. Always disarm the airbag system before working in the vicinity of any airbag system component to avoid the possibility of accidental deployment of the airbag, which could cause personal injury (see Chapter 12).*
Warning: *Do not allow antifreeze to come in contact with your skin or painted surfaces of the vehicle. Rinse off spills immediately with plenty of water. Antifreeze is highly toxic if ingested. Never leave antifreeze lying around in an open container or in puddles on the floor; children and pets are attracted by its sweet smell and may drink it. Check with local authorities on disposing of used antifreeze. Many communities have collection centres which will see that antifreeze is disposed of safely. Never dump used antifreeze on the ground or into drains.*
Warning: *Wait until the engine is completely cool before beginning this procedure.*
Note: *Non-toxic coolant is available at local auto parts stores. Although the coolant is non-toxic when fresh, proper disposal of used coolant is still required.*
Note: *Removal of the heater core is a difficult procedure for the home mechanic. There are numerous fasteners involved, some of which can be difficult to access, and we recommend*

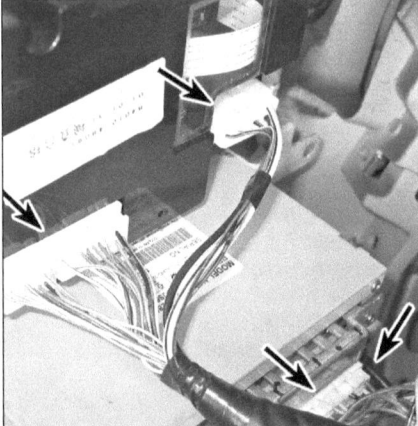

11.4 Unplug the connectors from the rear of the control assembly and audio unit - MCU28R models

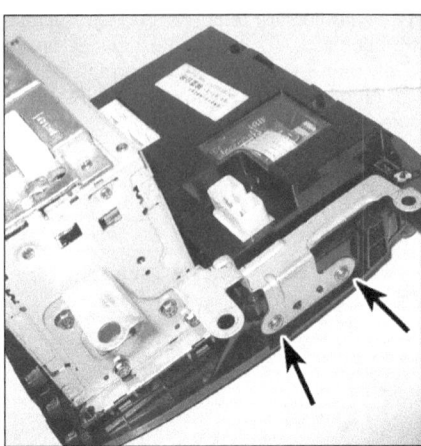

11.5 Mounting bracket fasteners - MCU28R models

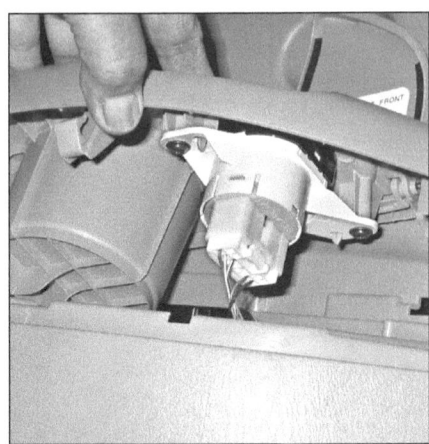

11.6 Carefully pry out the trim panel to access the control switch - MCU28R models

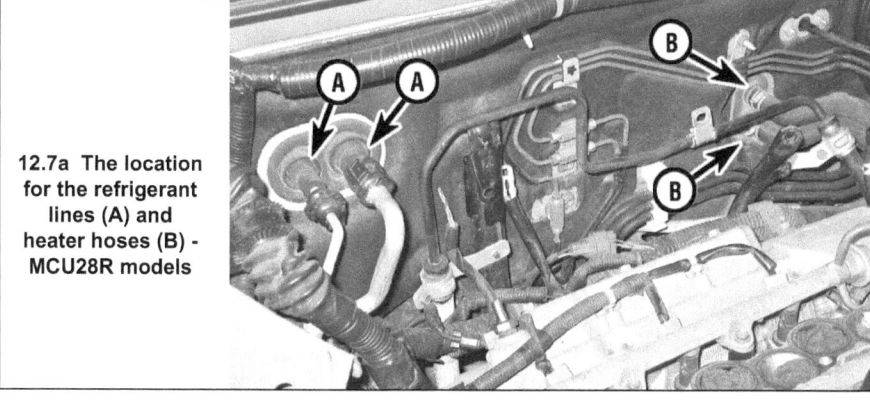

12.7a The location for the refrigerant lines (A) and heater hoses (B) - MCU28R models

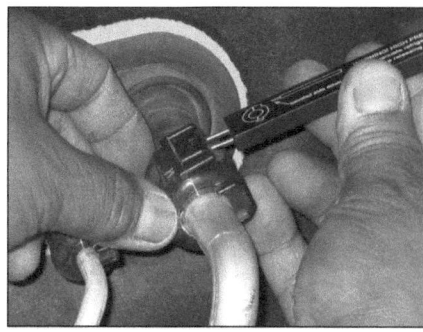

12.7b Using a special tool to release the clamp on the refrigerant lines

12.12 The cross-cowl tube brace and shift cable mounting fasteners - MCU28R models

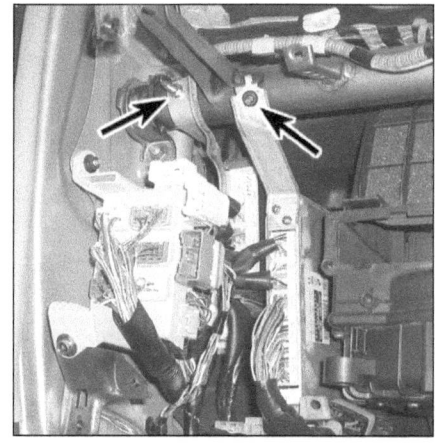

12.13 Mounting fasteners for the PCM and body control module on the cross-cowl tube - MCU28R models

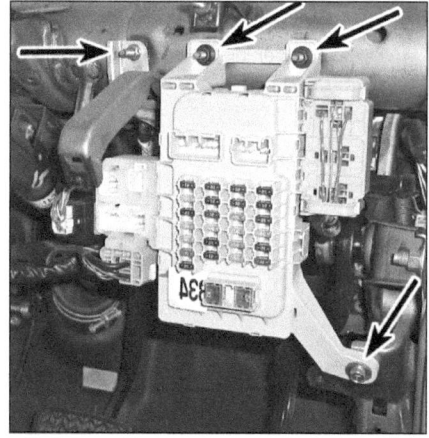

12.14 Mounting fasteners for the fuse and relay box and skid control module on the cross-cowl tube- MCU28R models

that you have considerable mechanical experience before performing a heater core replacement.

1   Take the vehicle to a dealer service department or automotive air conditioning shop and have the air conditioning system discharged and the refrigerant recovered.

2   Disconnect the negative (-) battery terminal (see Chapter 5).

3   Drain the cooling system (see Chapter 1).

4   The factory procedure for removal of the heater core involves removal of the heater/

evaporator housing, which requires complete removal of the instrument panel and support tube.

5   Remove the floor console and instrument panel (see Chapter 11).

6   Remove the windshield wiper motor and cowl tray from the engine compartment (see Chapter 11).

7   From the engine side of the firewall, disconnect the refrigerant lines to the evaporator, then twist the coolant hoses off the heater core tubes **(see illustrations)**.

8   If the hoses are stuck, cut the hoses off and cut the remaining hose from the metal

heater core tubes.

9   Detach the steering column from the support tube (see Chapter 10).

10   Remove the shift lever (see Chapter 7).

11   Pull the carpet back enough to remove the floor air ducts coming from the heater/ evaporator housing.

12   Detach the shift cable from the cross-cowl tube brace. Unscrew the mounting fasteners for each brace and remove them **(see illustration)**.

13   Detach the PCM and the body control module from the left side of the cross-cowl tube **(see illustration)**.

14   Detach the instrument panel fuse and relay box and the ABS module from the cross-cowl tube **(see illustration)**. On GSU40R/ GSU45R models, remove the power steering control module from on top of the RH side of the support tube.

15   Remove the mounting bolts for the cross-cowl tube and carefully remove it **(see illustrations)**.

Note: *On GSU40R/GSU45R models, there are two fasteners for the cross-cowl tube in the engine compartment side of the firewall.*

Note: *Make certain that none of the wiring harnesses are damaged while removing the tube.*

16   Remove any small air ducts on the heater/evaporator housing.

12.15a The cross-cowl mounting fasteners on the right side - MCU28R models

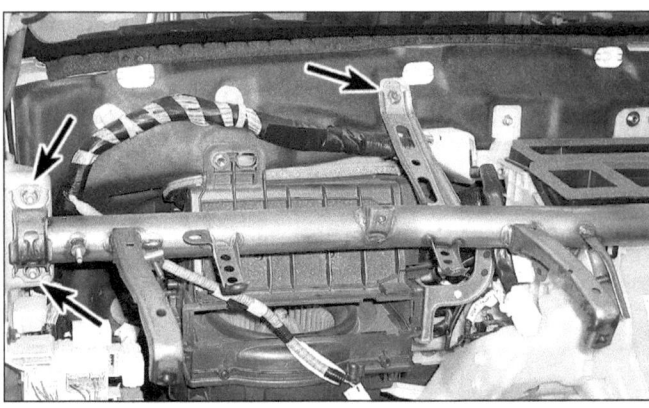

12.15b The cross-cowl mounting fasteners on the left side - MCU28R models

12.17 Mounting fasteners for the heater/evaporator housing (one hidden - vicinity given) - MCU28R models

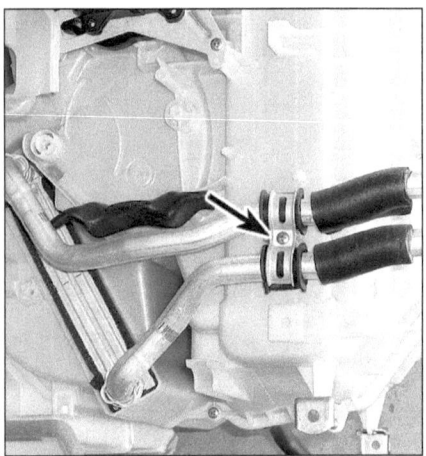

12.18 Heater core tube retainer and mounting fastener - MCU28R models

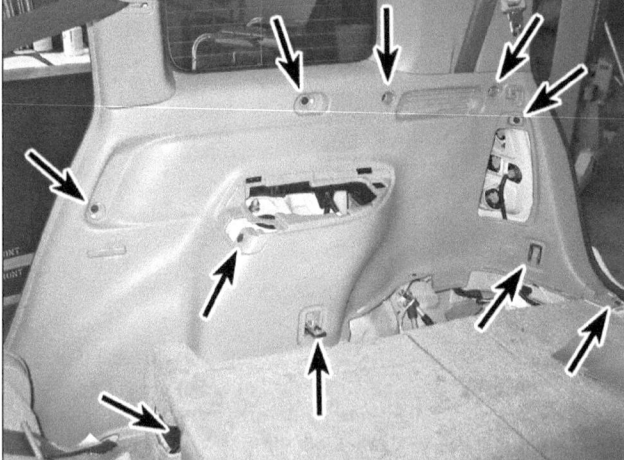

12.26a The right rear panel fastener locations

17 Disconnect any wiring harnesses attached to the heater/evaporator housing and then remove the mounting fasteners for the housing and carefully pull it away from the firewall until the tubes for the heater core and evaporator are clear of the openings (**see illustration**).

18 Remove the retaining clamp securing the heater core tubes to the side of the hous-

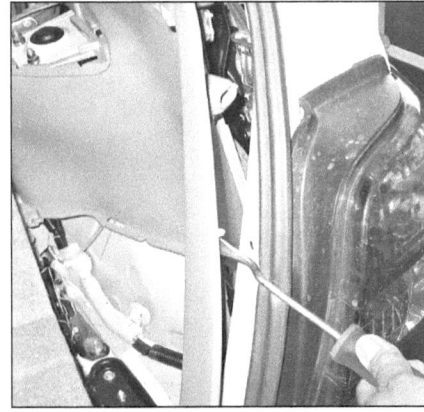

12.26b Separate the panel from the body by carefully prying with a trim panel tool

ing and then slide the heater core out of the housing (**see illustration**).

19 Installation is the reverse order of removal. Use new O-rings to seal the evaporator refrigerant connections. Make sure all of the cross-cowl support tube mounting fasteners are tightened securely before installing the instrument panel pad.

20 Refill the cooling system (see Chapter 1).

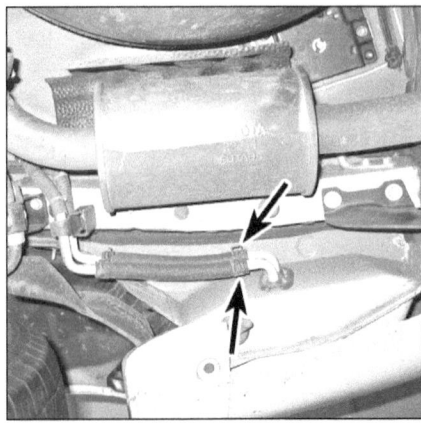

12.27 Disconnect the hoses from the heater core tubes

Rear heater core

Refer to illustrations 12.26a, 12.26b, 12.27, 12.29 and 12.30

Note: *The rear heater is only fitted to select models.*

21 Remove the right rear floor panel.

22 Pull the weatherstripping away from the bottom and right side of the rear door area.

23 Remove the trim from the back edge of the carpet.

24 Remove the small box that was covered by the right rear floor panel.

25 Remove the bottom trim and the weather-stripping for the right rear door.

26 Remove the various fastener covers and fasteners, then remove the right rear trim panel (**see illustrations**).

27 Disconnect the heater hoses from beneath the vehicle (**see illustration**).

Note: *Pinch the hoses off to avoid fluid loss before disconnecting them.*

28 Remove the air ducts.

29 Remove the plate for the heater assembly and disconnect the electrical connectors (**see illustration**).

30 Remove the mounting fasteners for the heater assembly and then carefully remove it (**see illustration**).

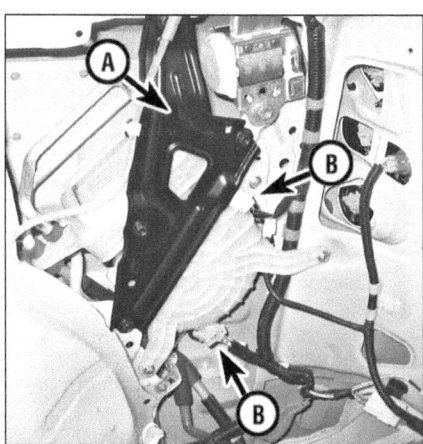

12.29 Remove the plate that covers the heater assembly (A) and disconnect the electrical connectors (B)

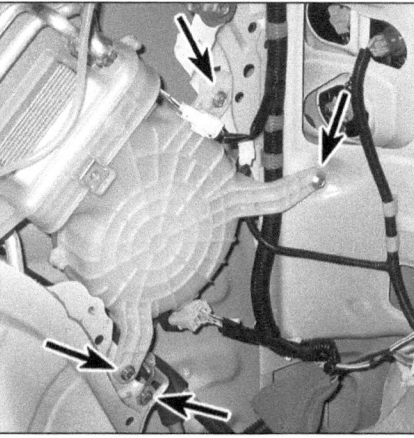

12.30 Mounting fasteners for the heater assembly

13.8 Place an accurate thermometer in the centre dash vent, turn the air conditioning on and check the output temperature

31   Disassemble the heater assembly and remove the heater core.

32   Installation is the reverse of removal. Check the coolant level and check the hose connections for any leaks.

---

13   Air conditioning and heating system - check and maintenance

---

Air conditioning system

Warning: *The air conditioning system is under high pressure. Do not loosen any hose fittings or remove any components until the system has been discharged. Air conditioning refrigerant must be properly discharged into an EPA-approved recovery/recycling unit by a dealer service department or an automotive air conditioning repair facility. Always wear eye protection when disconnecting air conditioning system fittings.*

1   The following maintenance checks should be performed on a regular basis to ensure that the air conditioner continues to operate at peak efficiency.

  a *Inspect the condition of the compressor drivebelt. If it is worn or deteriorated, replace it (see Chapter 1).*
  b *Check the drivebelt tension and, if necessary, adjust it (see Chapter 1).*
  c *Inspect the system hoses. Look for cracks, bubbles, hardening and deterioration. Inspect the hoses and all fittings for oil bubbles or seepage. If there is any evidence of wear, damage or leakage, replace the hose(s).*
  d *Inspect the condenser fins for leaves, bugs and any other foreign material that may have embedded itself in the fins. Use a fin comb or compressed air to remove debris from the condenser.*
  e *Make sure the system has the correct refrigerant charge.*

2   It's a good idea to operate the system

for about ten minutes at least once a month. This is particularly important during the winter months because long term non-use can cause hardening, and subsequent failure, of the seals.

3   Because of the complexity of the air conditioning system and the special equipment necessary to service it, in-depth troubleshooting and repairs are beyond the scope of this manual. However, simple component replacement procedures are provided in this Chapter.

4   The most common cause of poor cooling is simply a low system refrigerant charge. If a noticeable drop in system cooling ability occurs, one on the following quick checks will help you determine whether the refrigerant level is low.

Check

Refer to illustration 13.8

5   Warm the engine up to normal operating temperature.

6   Place the air conditioning temperature selector at the coldest setting and put the blower at the highest setting. Open the doors (to make sure the air conditioning system doesn't cycle off as soon as it cools the passenger compartment).

7   After the system reaches operating temperature, feel the two pipes connected to the evaporator at the firewall.

8   The pipe (thinner tubing) leading from the condenser outlet to the evaporator should be cold, and the evaporator outlet line (the thicker tubing that leads back to the compressor) should be slightly colder. If the evaporator outlet is considerably warmer than the inlet, the system needs a charge. Insert a thermometer in the centre air distribution duct **(see illustration)** while operating the air conditioning system - the temperature of the output air should be 3 to 5 degrees C below the ambient air temperature (down to approximately 5 degrees C). If the ambient (outside) air temperature is very high, say 40 degrees C, the duct air temperature may be as high as 15 degrees C, but generally the air condition-

ing is 3 to 5 degrees C cooler than the ambient air. If the air isn't as cold as it used to be, the system probably needs a charge. Further inspection or testing of the system is beyond the scope of the home mechanic and should be left to a professional.

Heating systems

Refer to illustration 13.13

9   If the air coming out of the heater vents isn't hot, the problem could stem from any of the following causes:

  a *The thermostat is stuck open, preventing the engine coolant from warming up enough to carry heat to the heater core. Replace the thermostat (see Section 3).*
  b *A heater hose is blocked, preventing the flow of coolant through the heater core. Feel both heater hoses at the firewall. They should be hot. If one of them is cold, there is an obstruction in one of the hoses or in the heater core, or the heater control valve is shut. Detach the hoses and back flush the heater core with a water hose. If the heater core is clear but circulation is impeded, remove the two hoses and flush them out with a garden hose.*
  c *If flushing fails to remove the blockage from the heater core, the core must be replaced (see Section 12).*

10   If the blower motor speed does not correspond to the setting selected on the blower switch, the problem could be a bad fuse, circuit, blower relay, speed switch or blower resistor.

11   If there isn't any air coming out of the vents:

  a *Turn the ignition ON and activate the fan control. Place your ear at the heating/air conditioning register (vent) and listen. Most motors are audible. Can you hear the motor running?*
  b *If you can't (and have already verified that the blower switch and the blower motor resistor are good), the blower*

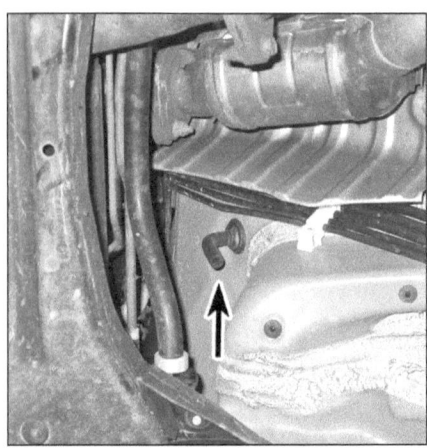

13.13 This drain hose from the heater/air conditioning unit should be kept clear to allow drainage of condensation (shown from under the vehicle)

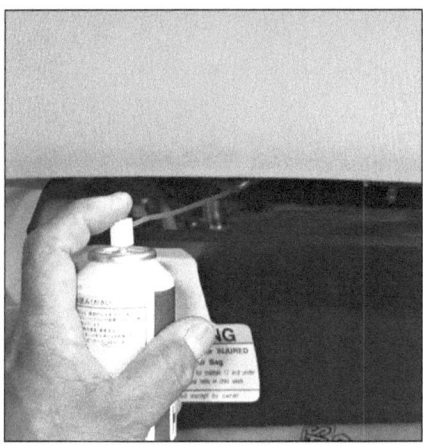

13.17 Remove the cabin air filter, then insert the disinfectant spray nozzle - be sure to support the nozzle so it doesn't get tangled up in the blower fan!

motor itself is probably bad (see Section 9).

12   If the carpet under the heater core is damp, or if antifreeze vapour or steam is coming through the vents, the heater core is leaking. Remove it (see Section 12) and install a new unit (most radiator shops will not repair a leaking heater core).

13   Inspect the drain hose from the heater/evaporator, which exits the body under the floor **(see illustration)**. If there is a humid mist coming from the system ducts, this hose may be plugged with leaves or road debris.

Eliminating air conditioning odours

Refer to illustration 13.17

14   Unpleasant odours that often develop in air conditioning systems are caused by the growth of a fungus, usually on the surface of the evaporator core. The warm, humid environment there is a perfect breeding ground for mildew to develop.

15   The evaporator core on most vehicles is difficult to access, and factory dealerships have a lengthy, expensive process for eliminating the fungus by opening up the evaporator case and using a powerful disinfectant and rinse on the core until the fungus is gone. You can service your own system at home, but it takes something much stronger than basic household germ-killers or deodorisers.

16   Aerosol disinfectants for automotive air-conditioning systems are available in most auto parts stores, but remember when shopping for them that the most effective treatments are also the most expensive. The basic procedure for using these sprays is to start by running the system in the RECIRC mode for ten minutes with the blower on its highest speed. Use the highest heat mode to dry out the system and keep the compressor from engaging by disconnecting the wiring connector at the compressor (see Section 14).

17   The disinfectant can usually comes with

a long spray hose. Remove the cabin air filter, point the nozzle inside the hole and spray according to the manufacturer's recommendations **(see illustration)**. Follow the manufacturer's recommendations for the length of spray and waiting time between applications.

18   Once the evaporator has been cleaned, the best way to prevent the mildew from coming back again is to make sure your evaporator housing drain tube is clear **(see illustration 12.13)** and to run the defrost cycle briefly to dry the evaporator out after a long drive with the air conditioning on.

14   Air conditioning compressor - removal and installation

Refer to illustrations 14.6

Warning: *The air conditioning system is under high pressure. Do not loosen any hose fittings or remove any components until the system has been discharged. Air conditioning refrigerant must be properly discharged into*

an EPA-approved recovery/recycling unit by a dealer service department or an automotive air conditioning repair facility. Always wear eye protection when disconnecting air conditioning system fittings.

Caution: *The receiver/drier should be replaced whenever the compressor is replaced.*

1   Have the refrigerant discharged by an automotive air conditioning technician.

2   Disconnect the negative (-) battery terminal (see Chapter 5).

3   Remove the drivebelt from the compressor (see Chapter 1).

4   Remove the splash shield from below the engine compartment.

5   Remove the radiator (see Section 5).

6   Detach the wiring connector and the refrigerant lines **(see illustration)**.

7   Unbolt the compressor and lift it from the vehicle **(see illustration 14.6)**.

8   If a new or rebuilt compressor is being installed, follow the directions, which come with it regarding the proper level of oil prior to installation.

9   Installation is the reverse of removal.

10   Replace any O-rings with new ones specifically made for the purpose and lubricate them with refrigerant oil.

11   Have the system evacuated, recharged and leak tested by the shop that discharged it.

15   Air conditioning condenser - removal and installation

Refer to illustrations 15.4 and 15.5

Warning: *The air conditioning system is under high pressure. Do not loosen any hose fittings or remove any components until the system has been discharged. Air conditioning refrigerant must be properly discharged into an EPA-approved recovery/recycling unit by a dealer service department or an automotive air conditioning repair facility. Always wear eye protection when disconnecting air conditioning system fittings.*

14.6 Compressor details

1 Refrigerant line fittings
2 Electrical connector
3 Mounting bracket
4 Mounting fasteners

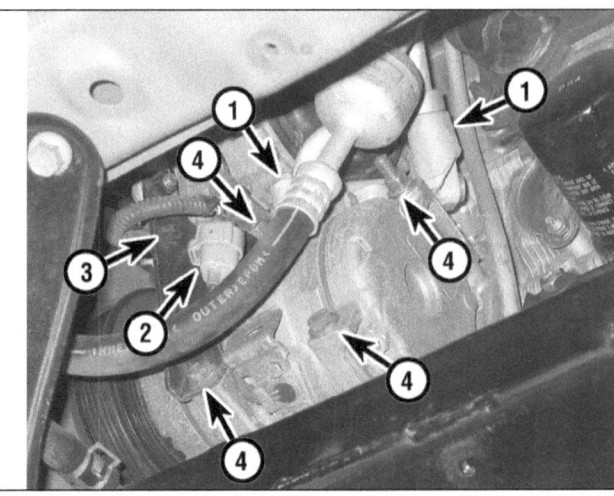

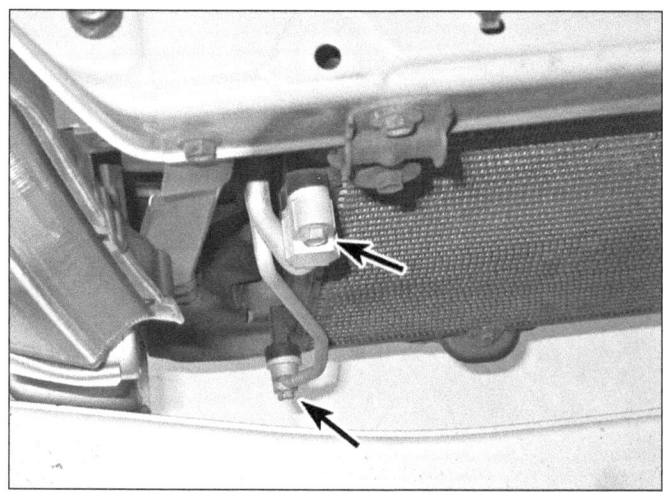

15.4 Condenser line fittings

15.5 Condenser mounting bracket fasteners

Caution: *The receiver/drier should be replaced whenever the condenser is replaced.*

1   Have the refrigerant discharged by an air conditioning technician.

2   Remove the radiator grill (see Chapter 11).

3   On GSU40R/GSU45R models, remove the radiator support panel (see Section 5) or the radiator upper mounts on MCU28R models..

4   Disconnect the inlet and outlet fittings **(see illustration)**. Cap the open fittings immediately to keep moisture and dirt out of the system.

5   Remove the mounting fasteners **(see illustration)**. Push the radiator back toward the engine, then push the condenser rearward until it's free of the radiator support and can be pulled up and out of the vehicle.

6   Install the condenser, brackets and bolts, making sure the rubber cushions fit on the mounting points properly.

7   Reconnect the refrigerant lines, using new O-rings where needed.

8   Reinstall the remaining parts in the reverse order of removal.

9   Have the system evacuated, charged and leak tested by the shop that discharged it.

Chapter 4
Fuel and exhaust systems

Contents

Specifications

Fuel system

Fuel system pressure	304 to 343 kPa
Fuel system hold pressure (after five minutes)	147 kPa minimum
Fuel injector resistance (approximate)	
3MZ-FE engine	13.4 to 14.2 ohms
2GR-FE engine	11.6 to 12.5 ohms
Fuel pump resistance	0.2 to 3.0 ohms
Fuel pump resistor resistance	0.30 to 0.34 ohms

Torque specifications

	Nm
Fuel rail mounting bolts/nuts	
3MZ-FE engine	10
2GR-FE engine	21
Pulsation damper	
3MZ-FE engine	33
2GR-FE engine	Not applicable
Fuel crossover pipe banjo bolt	
3MZ-FE engine	33
2GR-FE engine	Not applicable
Throttle body mounting bolts/nuts	
3MZ-FE engine	11
2GR-FE engine	10

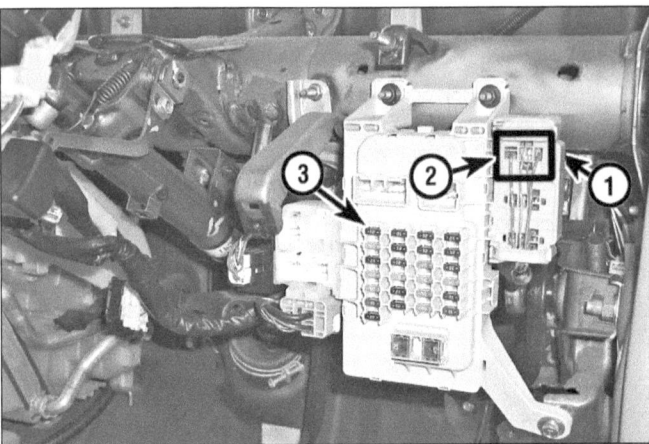

2.2 The circuit opening relay faces toward the front of the vehicle (1). The outline (2) illustrates its location; (3) indicates the EFI fuse location - models with the 3MZ-FE engine

2.3 To access the fuel pump relay (1) remove the upper cover and then the upper frame from the fuse and relay box; the circuit opening relay is contained within this combined relay unit (2), apart from replacing the fuses on top, this assembly is non-servicable and is replaced as an assembly, if faulty - models with the 2GR-FE engine

1   General information

The fuel system consists of the fuel tank, the electric in-tank fuel pump, the fuel pressure regulator (an integral part of the pump), the fuel pulsation damper, the fuel rail, the fuel injectors and the fuel lines connecting the pump to the fuel rail. The injectors are turned on and off by the Powertrain Control Module (PCM). The amount of time the injectors are open (On) dictates how much fuel is injected into the engine for combustion. This process is controlled by the PCM (see Chapter 6). The fuel pump operation is also controlled by the PCM. The pump will be momentarily activated once the ignition is switched On allowing the fuel system to pressurise. The pump will then stop and only begin to operate again once the engine begins to crank. The PCM will continue to run the fuel pump until the ignition is switched Off, or the PCM no longer receives a cranking signal from the engine camshaft position sensors. This is a safety feature to prevent the fuel pump to continue to pump fuel if the vehicle has been involved in an accident. If the PCM no longer receives signals to say the engine is running (no camshaft position sensor signals), the fuel pump is shut down. If the engine has stalled for some reason, once the ignition is switched Off and then the engine is restarted, the fuel pump should once again begin to operate.

The PCM controls the fuel pump operation by energising the circuit opening relay.

On models with the 2GR-FE engine, the fuel pump operates at two speeds. The low speed is used for low engine speeds and idle and is achieved by energising a second relay called the fuel pump relay. This relay will direct power from the circuit opening relay through the fuel pump relay and then through a resistor before reaching the fuel pump. This slows the operation of the fuel pump down and reduces fuel pressure, helping with emissions. When higher engine speeds or loads are needed, the PCM de-energises the fuel pump relay and full battery voltage flows from a second circuit, bypassing the resistor to the fuel pump, increasing the fuel pump speed and pressure.

The fuel system electrical circuits are protected by the fuses.

The air intake system consists of the air filter housing, the air intake duct, the throttle body and the intake manifold. The intake manifold is covered in Chapter 2A for the 3MZ-FE engine (see Chapter 2A), or in Chapter 2B for the 2GR-FE engine (see Chapter 2B).

Sequential Electronic Fuel Injection (SFI) system

The Electronic Fuel Injection (EFI) or Sequential Electronic Fuel Injection (SFI) system uses timed impulses to inject the fuel directly into the intake port of each cylinder in the ignition firing order. The Powertrain Control Module (PCM) controls the injectors. The PCM monitors various engine parameters and delivers the exact amount of fuel required into the intake ports. The throttle body controls the amount of air drawn into the engine.

Fuel pump and lines

Fuel is circulated from the in-tank fuel pump to the fuel rail through a fuel line running along the underside of the vehicle. Various sections of the fuel line are either rigid metal or nylon, or flexible fuel hose. The various sections of the fuel hose are connected by quick-connect fittings. An electric fuel pump/fuel level sending unit is located inside the fuel tank. The fuel pressure regulator is also located in the fuel tank and is an integral part of the fuel pump/fuel level sending unit.

The circuit opening relay is equipped with a primary and secondary voltage circuit. The primary circuit is controlled by the PCM and the secondary circuit is linked directly to the EFI main relay from the ignition switch. With the ignition switch ON (engine not running),

the PCM will ground the relay for two seconds. During cranking, the PCM grounds the fuel pump relay as long as the Camshaft Position (CMP) sensor sends its position signal. If there are no reference pulses, the fuel pump will shut off after two seconds.

Exhaust system

The exhaust system consists of the exhaust manifold(s), the exhaust pipes, the catalytic converters, a muffler, and a tail pipe.

Two catalytic converters are used - one below each exhaust manifold For more information about the catalytic converters, refer to Chapter 6.

2   Fuel pressure relief procedure

Refer to illustrations 2.2 and 2.3

Warning: *Petrol is extremely flammable, so take extra precautions when you work on any part of the fuel system. Don't smoke or allow open flames or bare light bulbs near the work area, and don't work in a garage where a fuel-type appliance (such as a water heater or a clothes dryer) is present. Since petrol is carcinogenic, wear fuel resistant gloves when there's a possibility of being exposed to fuel, and, if you spill any fuel on your skin, rinse it off immediately with soap and water. Mop up any spills immediately and do not store fuel-soaked rags where they could ignite. The fuel system is under constant pressure, so, if any fuel lines are to be disconnected, the fuel pressure in the system must be relieved first. When you perform any kind of work on the fuel system, wear safety glasses and have a Class B type fire extinguisher on hand.*

1   Remove the fuel cap to release any pressure in the fuel tank.

2   On MCU28R models with the 3MZ-FE engine, remove the circuit opening relay from

3.4a Removing the EFI fuse. Arrow indicates the EFI relay location - models with the 3MZ-FE engine (check the fuse/relay box cover to verify the location of the EFI fuse on your vehicle)

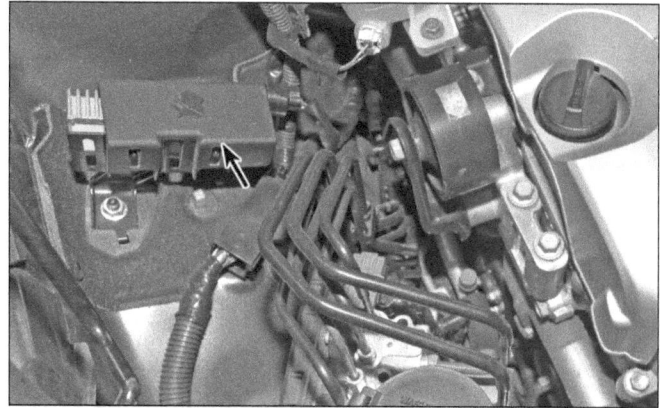

3.4b The fuel pump resistor is mounted to the RH inner guard - models with the 2GR-FE engine

the interior fuse and relay box **(see illustration)**.

3   On GSU40R/GSU45R models with the 2GR-FE engine, remove the fuel pump relay from the engine compartment fuse and relay box **(see illustration)**.

4   Start the engine and allow it to run until it stops, then turn the ignition key to OFF.

5   Disconnect the negative (-) battery terminal (see Chapter 5).

6   The fuel system pressure is now relieved, and you can now safely open fuel line fittings anywhere in the system. But even though there is no longer any pressure in the system, it's still a good idea to wrap a shop rag around a fitting before opening it to soak up any fuel that leaks out.

3   Fuel pump/fuel pressure - check

Warning: *Petrol is extremely flammable, so take extra precautions when you work on any part of the fuel system. See the Warning in Section 2.*

General checks

Refer to illustrations 3.4a and 3.4b

1   Make sure that there is adequate fuel in the fuel tank.

2   Verify the fuel pump actually runs. Have an assistant turn the ignition switch to ON - you should hear a brief whirring noise for about two seconds as the pump comes on and pressurises the system.

3   It should be possible to momentarily hear the fuel pump operate through the fuel filler neck as soon as the ignition is switched On.

4   If the fuel pump makes no sound:

a   *On models with the 3MZ-FE engine, check the IGN fuse and the circuit opening (C/OPN)* **(see illustration 2.2)** *and the EFI fuse and EFI relay, which is in the engine compartment fuse and relay box* **(see illustration)**. *If the fuse and relay are OK, check the wiring back to the fuel pump. If voltage is present at the fuel pump electrical connector for a couple of seconds when the ignition key is turned on, the fuel pump is defective.*

b   *On models with the 2GR-FE engine, check the ignition (IGN) fuse, in the interior fuse and relay box; the fuel pump relay* **(see illustration 2.3)** *and the fuel pump resistor* **(see illustration)**. *Compare the resistance between the resistor terminals with Specifications and renew if necessary.*

5   On models with the 2GR-FE engine, a combined relay unit housing several fuses, the circuit opening relay, the EFI relay and the air/fuel ratio sensor relay is contained in the engine compartment fuse and relay box **(see illustration 2.3)**. To remove the combined relay unit and to test the circuit opening and EFI relay circuits, proceed as follows:

a   *Remove the upper cover and then the upper frame from the fuse and relay box*

b   *Using two small flat-bladed screwdrivers, release the tabs from each end of the combined relay unit* **(see illustration)**.

c   *Lift the combined relay unit up and out of the fuse and relay box* **(see illustration)**.

d   *Disconnect the wiring connectors* **(see illustration 3.5b)**.

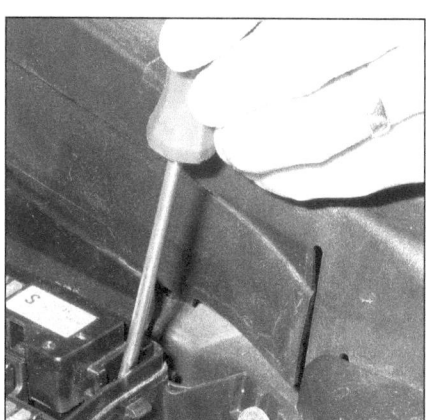

3.5a Releasing one of the tangs from the combined relay unit - 2GR-FE engines

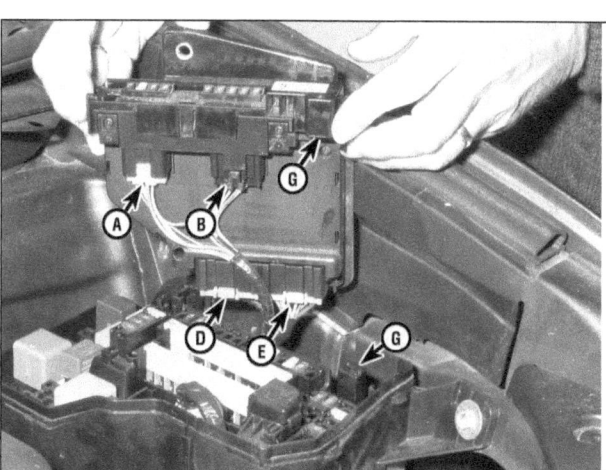

3.5b Combined relay unit partially removed showing each connector (labelled) - 2GR-FE engine. Note connector G automatically disconnects when the unit is removed

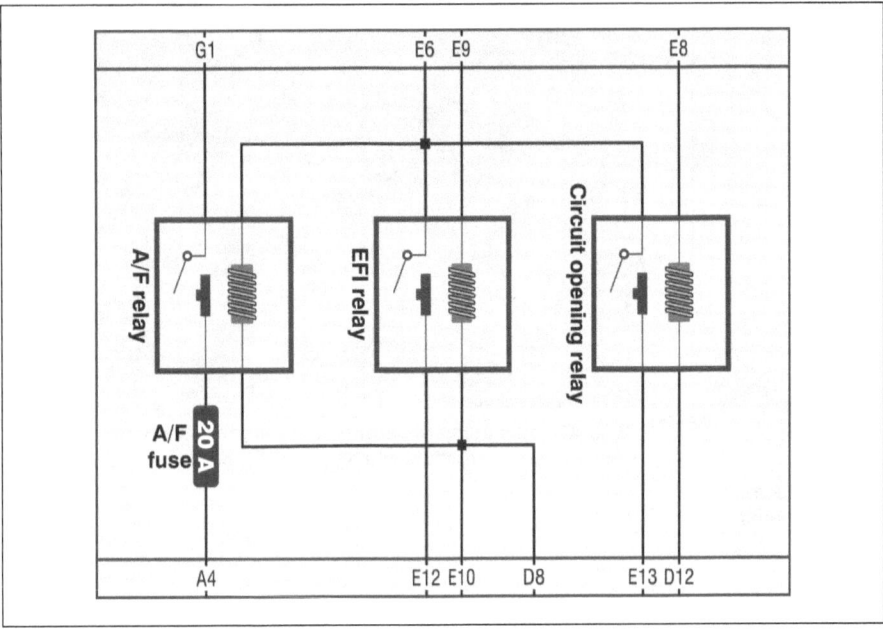

3.5c Illustration showing the relay internal circuits for testing

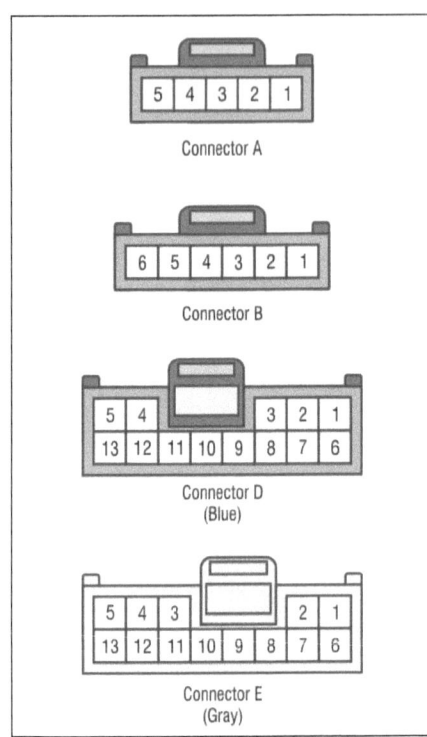

3.5d The combined relay unit connector terminal identification. Note that the connector labels here coincide with the labels on illustration 3.5b and also on the edge of the illustration 3.5c

e   *Using an ohmmeter, and a 12 volt power supply, check the condition of each relay within the combined relay unit.*

Note: *Chapter 12 has an explanation of how to use an ohmmeter (see Chapter 12).*

f   *Refer to the table below and check that continuity is available between the relay control circuits.*

Terminals	Continuity
E6 and E10	Yes
E9 and E10	Yes
E8 and D12	Yes

g   *Apply power to one of the relay control circuits and check that there is continuity between that relays power circuit.*

Note: *See illustration 3.5b for the position of connector G1.*

Apply power to	Continuity should exist between
E6 and E10	G1 and A4
E9 and E10	E6 and E12
E8 and D12	E6 and E13

h   *If the relay fails one of the tests, renew the combined relay unit.*

6   Connect the wiring back onto the combined relay unit and slide it back into the engine bay fuse and relay box until the retainers click into place.

Fuel pump pressure check

Refer to illustrations 3.8, 3.10a, 3.110b and 3.10c

7   Relieve the fuel system pressure (see Section 2).

8   To test the fuel pressure you will need a fuel pressure gauge capable of measuring the fuel pressure in the range listed in this Chapter's Specifications, a fuel pressure test hose and an adapter to connect into the fuel supply line.

Note: *On models with the 3MZ-FE engine, a banjo fitting with the same diameter and thread pitch as the banjo bolt that secures the crossover line between the two fuel rails (**see illustration**) is required. On models with the 2GR-FE engine, a fitting for the fuel pressure gauge with connections to go between the*

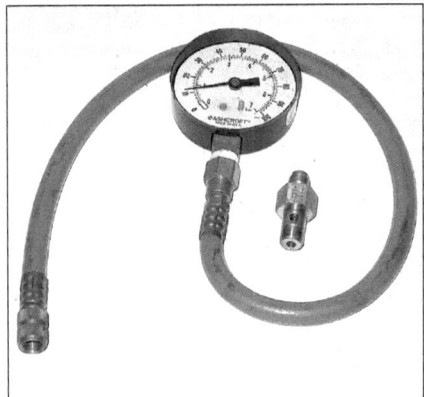

3.8 To test the fuel pressure on V6 models you'll need a fuel pressure gauge, a hose and an adapter that will screw into the same hole in the end of the front fuel rail as the banjo bolt that secures the crossover line between the two fuel rails

fuel rail and the fuel supply line fitting are required.

9   Remove the engine cover.

Note: *On 2GR-FE engines, pull up on the front side of the engine top cover to detach it from the two front retainers. After the front is detached, pull up on the back retainer and remove the engine cover. Do not pull up on the front and rear at the same time or the cover can be damaged.*

10   On models with the 3MZ-FE engine, unscrew the banjo bolt that secures the crossover line to the left end of the front fuel rail **(see illustration)**. Using the same two sealing washers on both sides of the banjo fitting, screw the adapter into the fuel rail in place of the banjo bolt, then connect the fuel pressure test hose to the adapter **(see illustrations)**.

11   On models with the 2GR-FE engine, proceed as follows:

a   *Disconnect the PCV valve hose and the breather hose from the upper intake manifold.*

b   *Using a screwdriver, remove the cover from the fuel line fitting (**see illustration**).*

c   *Clean around the fitting with compressed air or carburettor cleaner before disconnecting the fuel supply line (see Section 4) from the fuel rail (**see illustration**).*

d   *Using the appropriate fittings, connect the fuel pressure gauge into the fuel supply line and to the fuel rail.*

12   Turn off all accessories and turn the ignition switch to ON. The fuel pump should run

3.10a To connect a fuel pressure gauge to the 3MZ-FE engine, remove this banjo bolt from the left end of the front fuel rail. The banjo bolt connects the crossover tube (A) to the front fuel rail, which must remain connected to the fuel rail for this test

3.10b Screw the adapter into the front fuel rail of the V6 engine (make sure that there are still sealing washers on both sides of the banjo fitting) . . .

3.10c . . . then connect the fuel pressure test hose to the adapter

for about two seconds to pressurise the system. Note the reading on the gauge. After the pump stops running, the pressure should hold steady. After five minutes it should not drop below the minimum listed in this Chapter's Specifications.

13   Start the engine and let it idle at normal operating temperature. The pressure should remain the same. If all the pressure readings are within the limits listed in this Chapter's Specifications, the system is operating correctly.

14   If the fuel pressure is not within specifications, check the following:

a   *If the pressure is higher than specified, replace the fuel pressure regulator (see Section 6).*

b   *If the pressure is lower than specified, inspect the fuel line from the fuel tank to the fuel rail for a kinked or pinched line that would cause a restriction.*

c   *If the fuel lines are in good shape, inspect the fuel filter. Remove the fuel pump/fuel level sending unit (see Section 5) and inspect the condition of the fuel filter (see Section 6).*

d   *If the pressure is still low, most likely the fuel pressure regulator or the fuel pump is defective. In this situation, we recommend replacing both the fuel pressure regulator and the fuel pump (see Sections 5 and 6).*

e   *Another possibility of low fuel pressure is a leaking fuel injector, but that would most likely set a trouble code and turn on the CHECK ENGINE light (because the fuel mixture would be too rich).*

15   After testing is complete, relieve the fuel pressure (see Section 2) and remove the fuel pressure gauge.

16   Reconnect the crossover line to the front fuel rail (3MZ-FE engine) or reconnect the fuel supply line to the to the fuel rail and install the cover (2GR-FE engine).

17   Start the engine and check for leaks.

4   Fuel lines and fittings - general information and disconnection

1   Relieve the fuel pressure before servicing fuel lines or fittings (see Section 2), then disconnect the negative (-) battery terminal (see Chapter 5) before proceeding.

2   The fuel supply line connects the fuel pump in the fuel tank to the fuel rail on the engine. The evaporative emission (EVAP) system lines connect the fuel tank to the EVAP canister and connect the canister to the intake manifold.

3   Whenever you're working under the vehicle, be sure to inspect all fuel and evaporative emission lines for leaks, kinks, dents and other damage. Always replace a damaged fuel or EVAP line immediately.

4   If you find signs of dirt in the lines during disassembly, disconnect all lines and blow them out with compressed air. Inspect the fuel strainer on the fuel pump pick-up unit for damage and deterioration.

Steel tubing

5   It is critical that the fuel lines be replaced with lines of equivalent type and specification.

6   Some steel fuel lines have threaded fittings. When loosening these fittings, hold the stationary fitting with a wrench while turning the tube nut.

Plastic tubing

7   When replacing fuel system plastic tubing, use only original equipment replacement plastic tubing.

Caution: *When removing or installing plastic fuel line tubing, be careful not to bend or twist it too much, which can damage it. Also, plastic fuel tubing is NOT heat resistant, so keep it away from excessive heat*

Flexible hoses

8   When replacing fuel system flexible hoses, use only original equipment replacements.

9   Don't route fuel hoses (or metal lines) within 100 mm of the exhaust system or within 250 mm of the catalytic converter. Make sure that no rubber hoses are installed directly against the vehicle, particularly in places where there is any vibration. If allowed to touch some vibrating part of the vehicle, a hose can easily become chafed and it might start leaking. A good rule of thumb is to maintain a minimum of 5 mm clearance around a hose (or metal line) to prevent contact with the vehicle underbody.

5   Fuel pump/fuel level sending unit - removal and installation

Refer to illustrations 5.1a, 5.1b, 5.2a, 5.2b, 5.4, 5.7a, 5.7b, 5.8a, 5.8b, 5.9a, 5.9b, 5.9c, 5.11, 5.13a and 5.13b

Warning: *Petrol is extremely flammable, so take extra precautions when you work on any part of the fuel system. See the Warning in Section 2.*

5.1a Releasing one of the vertical panel clips - 2GR-FE engine

Disconnecting Fuel Line Fittings

Two-tab type fitting; depress both tabs with your fingers, then pull the fuel line and the fitting apart

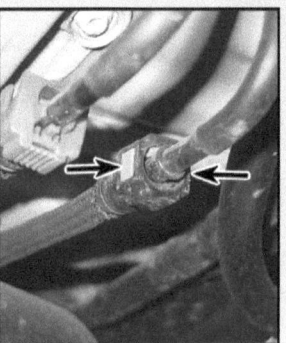

On this type of fitting, depress the two buttons on opposite sides of the fitting, then pull it off the fuel line

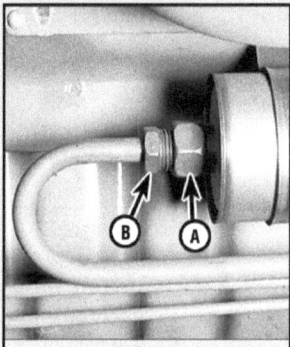

Threaded fuel line fitting; hold the stationary portion of the line or component (A) while loosening the tube nut (B) with a flare-nut wrench

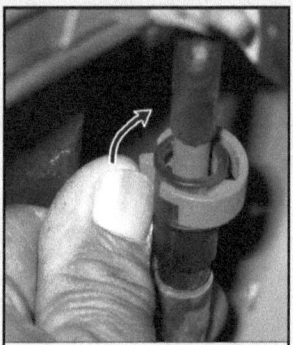

Plastic collar-type fitting; rotate the outer part of the fitting

Metal collar quick-connect fitting; pull the end of the retainer off the fuel line and disengage the other end from the female side of the fitting . . .

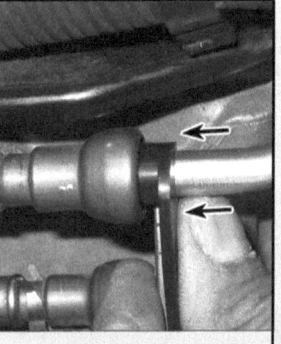

. . . insert a fuel line separator tool into the female side of the fitting, push it into the fitting and pull the fuel line off the pipe

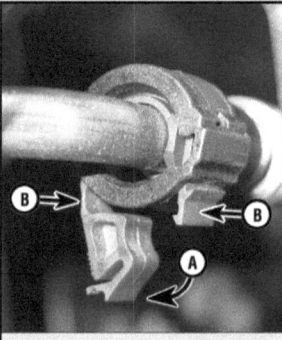

Some fittings are secured by lock tabs. Release the lock tab (A) and rotate it to the fully-opened position, squeeze the two smaller lock tabs (B) . . .

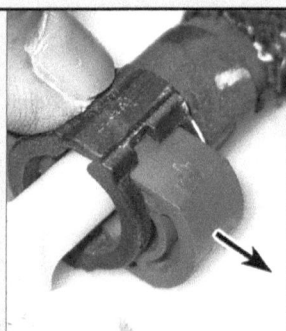

. . . then push the retainer out and pull the fuel line off the pipe

Spring-lock coupling; remove the safety cover, install a coupling release tool and close the tool around the coupling . . .

. . . push the tool into the fitting, then pull the two lines apart

Hairpin clip type fitting: push the legs of the retainer clip together, then push the clip down all the way until it stops and pull the fuel line off the pipe

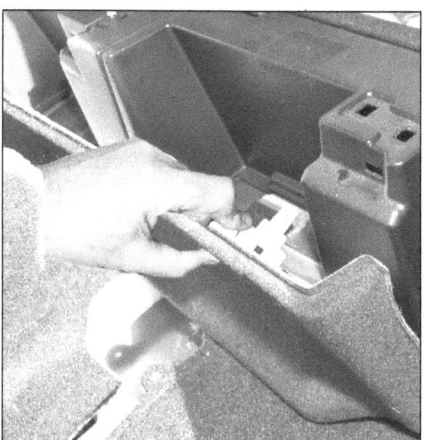

5.1b Removing the vertical panel from behind the rear seats - 2GR-FE engine

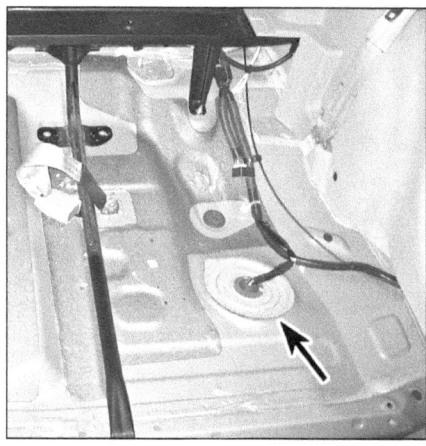

5.2a Service hole cover inside the LH rear door opening

5.2b Using a trim removal tool to lift up the service hole cover

5.4 To disconnect the fuel pump/fuel level sending unit electrical connector, depress this release tab (you might have to use a small pair of needle nose pliers - it's stiff) and pull up

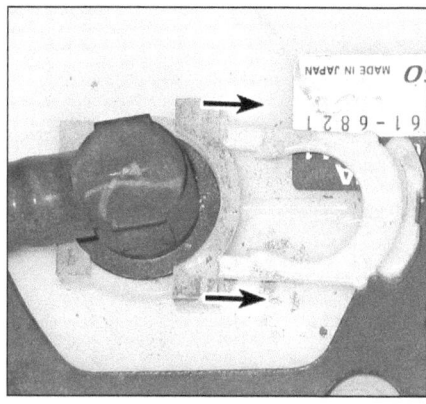

5.7a To disconnect the fuel supply line fitting from the fuel pump outlet pipe, remove this clip . . .

5.7b . . . then pull the fitting straight up. Before reconnecting the fitting, inspect the O-ring inside the fitting. If the O-ring is damaged, replace it

1   Remove the rear seats (see Chapter 11). Remove the vertical panel retaining clips and manoeuvre it from the vehicle **(see illustrations)**. Fold the rear of the carpet toward the front seats exposing the service hole cover.
2   Remove the fuel pump/sending unit floor service hole cover **(see illustrations)**.

3   Relieve the fuel system pressure (see Section 2) and remove the fuel tank cap.

Note: *As you have access to the fuel pump electrical connector, it is easier to remove the connector with the engine running to depressurise the fuel system.*

4   Disconnect the fuel pump electrical connector **(see illustration)**.
5   Disconnect the negative (-) battery terminal (see Chapter 5).
6   Clean around the top of the sender unit and fuel tank to prevent dirt entering the tank once the sender unit assembly is removed.

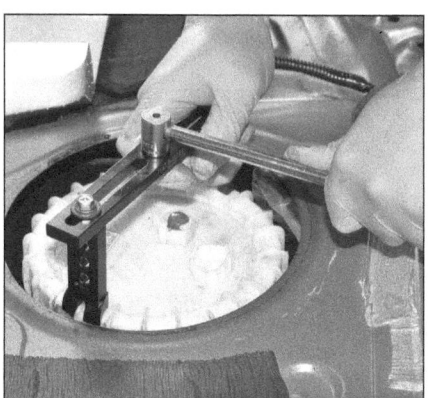

5.8a Use a special tool to rotate the fuel pump module retaining ring

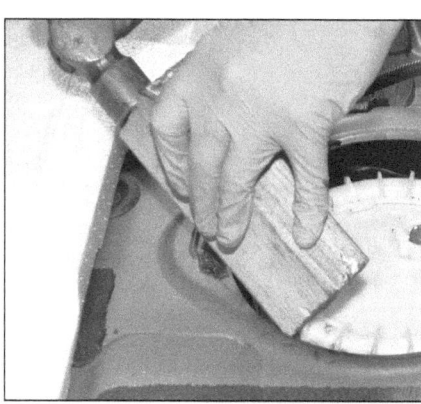

5.8b If the ring cannot be rotated with the special tool, use a piece of timber and a hammer to tap the ring loose

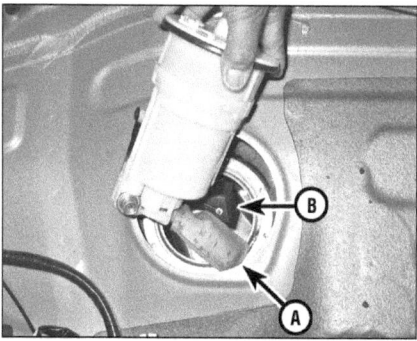

5.9a Angling the pump/sending unit assembly to protect the fuel inlet strainer (A) and the sending unit float (B), carefully lift the fuel pump/fuel level sending unit from the fuel tank . . .

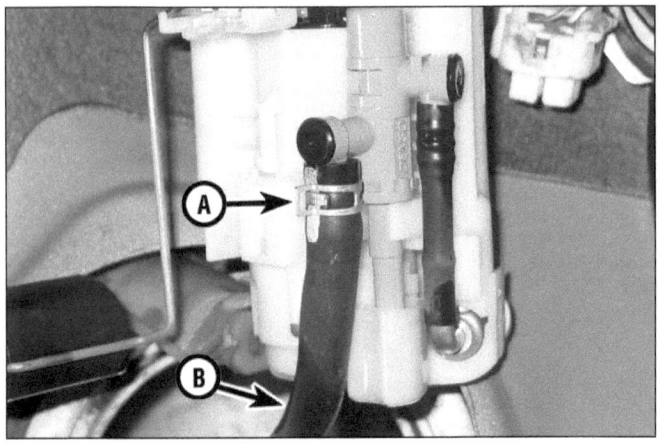

5.9b . . . loosen and slide back this spring-type hose clamp (A) and disconnect the hose (B) from the underside of the pump - 3MZ-FE engine

5.9c Removing the pump/sending unit assembly - 2GR-FE engine.
Note: *Have a container ready to place the unit in to prevent fuel spilling inside the vehicle*

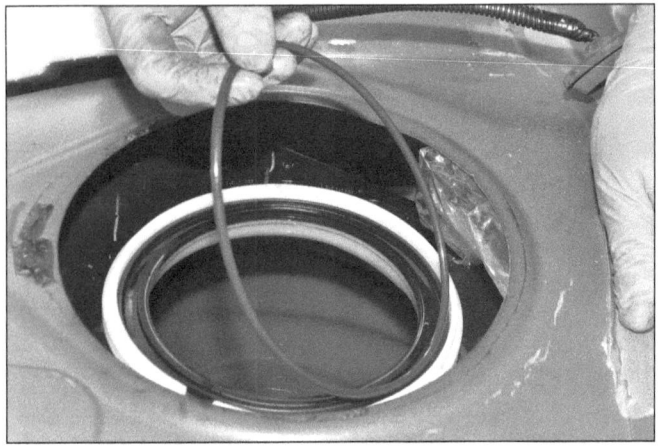

5.11 Removing the O-ring from the fuel tank opening

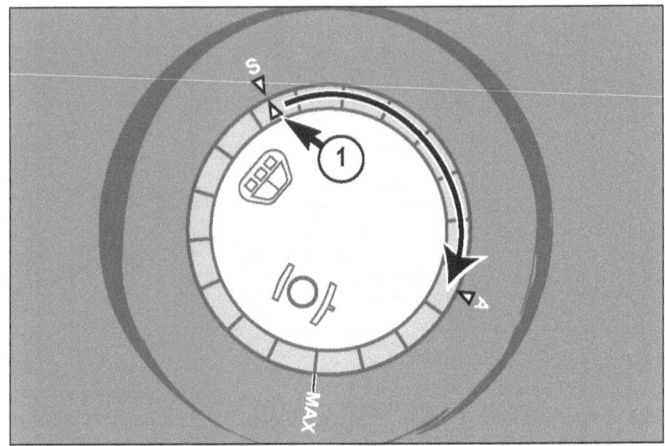

5.13a When installing the retaining ring, align the triangle mark on the retaining ring with the "S" mark on the fuel tank. From that point, tighten the retaining ring 1-1/2 turns. The triangle mark must be positioned between the "A" and MAX marks on the fuel tank - 3MZ-FE engine

7   Disconnect the fuel supply line from the top of the fuel pump unit **(see illustrations)**.
8   Unscrew the retaining ring using a fuel pump/sender removal tool **(see illustration)**.

Note: *On these vehicles, the retaining ring can be extremely tight and a removal tool may not be enough to remove the ring. If necessary use a piece of timber and a hammer to tap*

around the ring in an anticlockwise direction to loosen it before using the tool to unscrew it from the fuel tank.

9   Carefully lift the fuel pump/fuel level sending unit assembly from the fuel tank **(see illustrations)**.

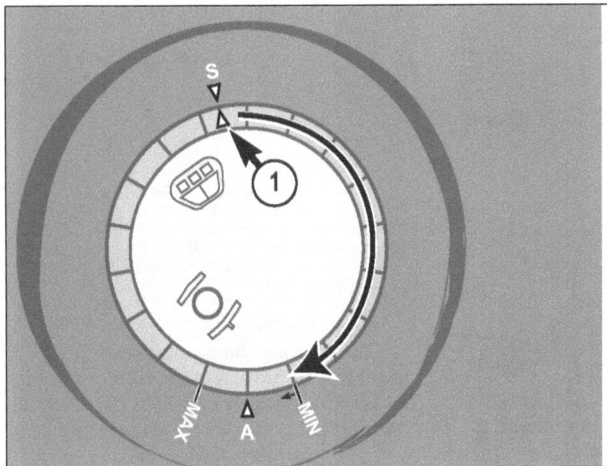

5.13b When installing the retaining ring, align the triangle mark on the retaining ring with the "S" mark on the fuel tank. From that point, tighten the retaining ring 1-1/2 turns. The triangle mark must be positioned between the MIN and MAX marks on the fuel tank - 2GR-FE engine

10   Inspect the fuel pump inlet strainer for contamination. If it's dirty, try cleaning the strainer with some clean solvent and an old toothbrush. If the strainer is too dirty to be cleaned while it's installed, remove it from the fuel pump/fuel level sending unit (see Section 6) and try cleaning it again. If you still can't clean it adequately, replace it.
11   Remove the O-ring from the top of the fuel tank **(see illustration)**.
12   Install a new O-ring to the top of the fuel tank and lubricate it with some fuel.
13   When installing the retaining ring, align the triangle mark on the retaining ring with the "S" mark on the fuel tank. From that point, tighten the retaining ring 1-1/2 turns. The triangle mark must be positioned between the "A" and the MAX marks on the fuel tank - models with the 3MZ-FE engine **(see illustration)** or, between the MIN and MAX marks on the fuel tank **(see illustration)** - models with the 2GR-FE engine.
14   The remainder of installation is the reverse of removal.

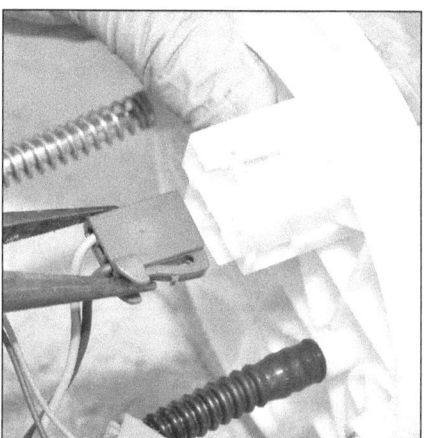

6.3 Disconnecting one of the wiring connectors from the underside of the top cover

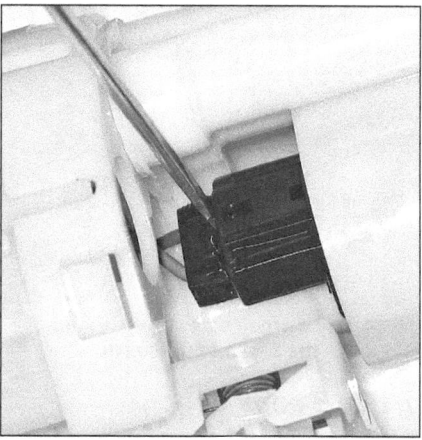

6.6a To disconnect the fuel pump electrical connector, depress this locking tab and pull out the connector

6.6b To remove the fuel pump from the fuel filter housing, pull it out the bottom

6 Fuel pump/filter/fuel level sending unit - component replacement

Warning: *Petrol is extremely flammable, so take extra precautions when you work on any part of the fuel system. See the Warning in Section 2.*

Note: *Once you have removed the fuel pump/ fuel level sending unit from the fuel tank, you can replace the entire assembly, or you can disassemble it and replace the fuel inlet strainer, the fuel pressure regulator, the fuel return jet tube, the fuel pump, the fuel filter or the fuel level sending unit.*

1   Remove the sending unit assembly from the fuel tank (see Section 5).

2   Drain any residual petrol from the fuel pump/fuel level sending unit, then place the fuel pump/fuel level sending unit on a clean workbench. Make sure that the work area is well-ventilated, because there will be some petrol evaporating from the pump/sending unit for awhile.

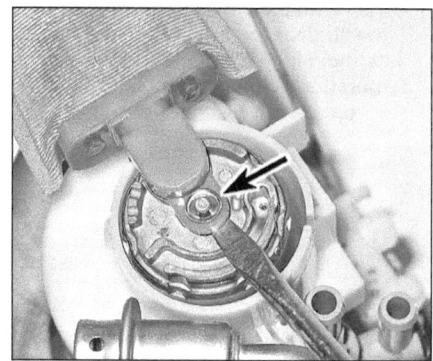

6.7 The pickup filter is secured to the lower end of the fuel pump by this E-clip. To detach the strainer from the pump, insert a screwdriver between the strainer mounting flange and the pump and carefully pry the strainer and the E-clip loose (don't try to pry the E-clip off by itself - it's too difficult to slip a screwdriver under it)

3MZ-FE engine

Refer to illustrations 6.3, 6.6a, 6.6b, 6.7, 6.10 and 6.11

3   Disconnect the wiring from the underside of the top cover **(see illustration)**.

4   Use a flat-bladed screwdriver to release the four-clips retaining the reservoir to the suction plate assembly.

5   Slide the reservoir down and from the assembly.

6   Disconnect the wiring from the top of the

fuel pump **(see illustration)**. Release the two tabs at the top of the fuel pump and pull the pump from the suction plate assembly **(see illustration)**.

7   Remove the fuel pump inlet strainer **(see illustration)** from the lower end of the fuel pump.

8   Working at the bottom of the filter housing, release the clips and lift the fuel tube assembly which contains the fuel pressure regulator from the bottom of the reservoir.

9   If necessary, disconnect the wiring from

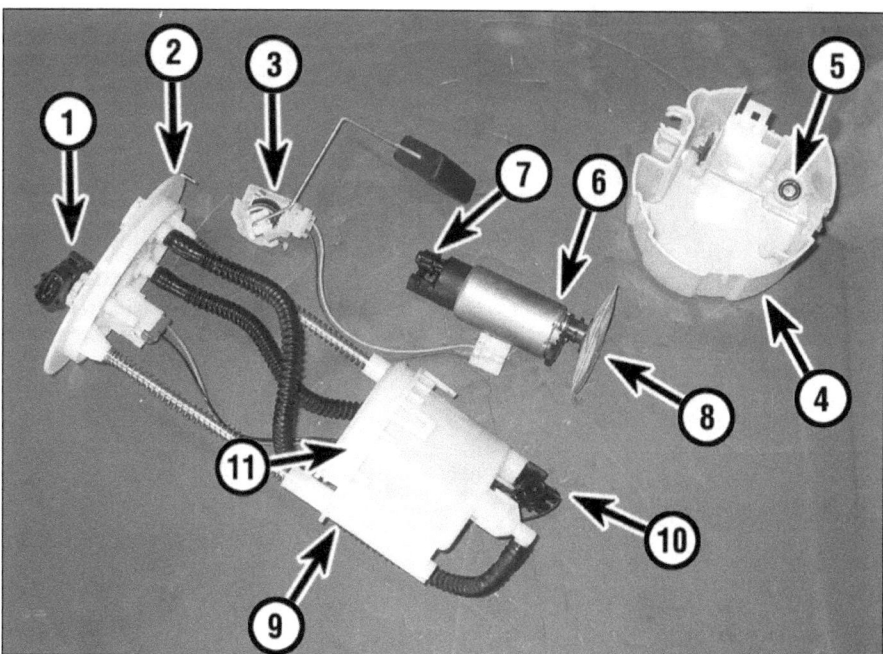

6.10 Exploded view of the fuel pump/fuel level sending unit module - 3MZ-FE engine

1 Main harness connector
2 Mounting flange
3 Fuel level sending unit
4 Fuel pump reservoir
5 O-ring (always replace)
6 Fuel pump

7 Fuel pump spacer
8 Strainer (fuel pump inlet filter)
9 Fuel filter assembly (sealed, cannot be replaced separately from the housing)
10 Fuel pressure regulator
11 Suction plate

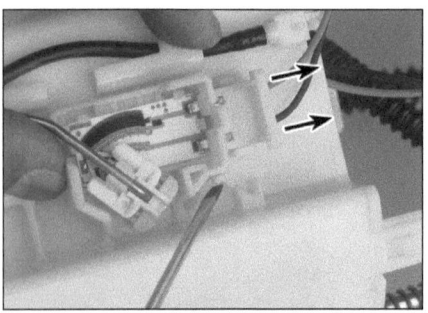

6.11 Release the tab and slide the sender unit up and from the reservoir

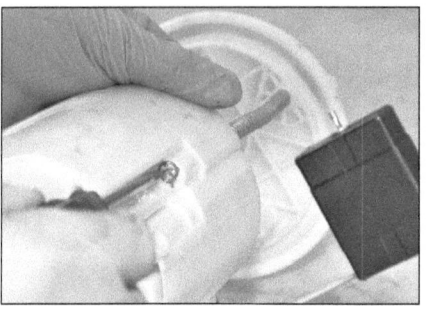

6.14 Use a small screwdriver to remove the E-clip from the rod

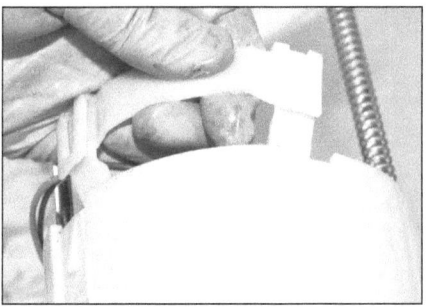

6.15 Removing the filter bracket from the reservoir

the fuel tube and if it needs renewal, remove the spring clip and then remove the fuel pressure regulator from the end of the fuel tube.

Note: *Check the condition of the two O-rings on the fuel pressure regulator and renew if necessary.*

10   Release the clips and separate the fuel filter assembly from the suction plate assembly **(see illustration)**.

11   If necessary, detach the fuel gauge sending unit from the pump reservoir by releasing the lock tab and moving the sending unit down **(see illustration)**.

12   Assembly is a reverse of dismantling, ensure that all O-rings are lubricated with clean fuel or oil.

2GR-FE engine

Refer to illustration 6.14, 6.15, 6.16a, 6.16b, 6.16c, 6.18a, 6.18b, 6.18c, 6.18d, 6.18e, 6.18f, 6.18g and 6.18h

13   Disconnect the wiring from the underside of the top cover **(see illustration 6.3)**.

14   Remove the E-clip retaining the bottom reservoir to the pin **(see illustration)**.

15   Slide the reservoir down from the two pins and then lift the filter bracket from the side of the reservoir **(see illustration)**.

16   Lift the filter/pump assembly from the reservoir **(see illustration)**. Working at the pickup filter, release the clips **(see illustration)** and remove the pickup filter from the bottom of the pump and fuel pressure regulator **(see illustration)**.

17   To detach the fuel gauge sending unit from the pump reservoir, release the lock tab and move the sending unit down **(see illustration 6.11)**.

18   If replacing the fuel pump or filter assembly, proceed as follows:

Note: *If renewing a faulty fuel pump, we recommend installing a new strainer and filter assembly at the same time.*

a   Remove the bracket from the top of the filter **(see illustration)** and remove the fuel pressure regulator using a screwdriver from the bottom of the filter housing **(see illustration)**.

Note: *Check the condition of the two O-rings on the fuel pressure regulator and renew if necessary.*

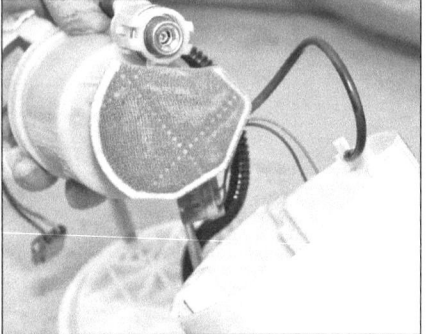

6.16a Remove the filter and pump assembly from the reservoir

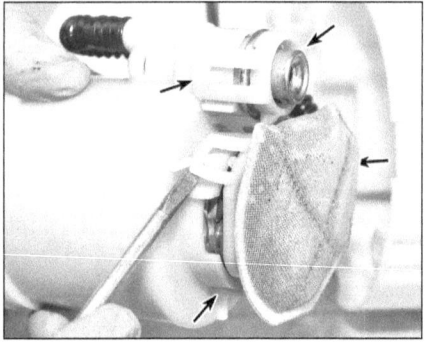

6.16b Arrows indicate the clips retaining the pickup filter to the bottom of the filter housing

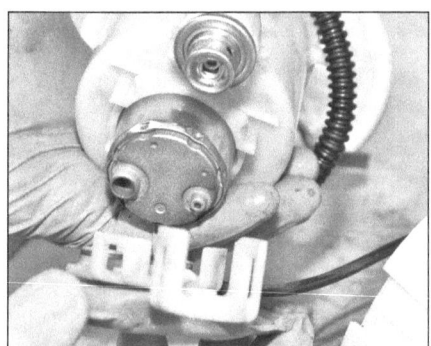

6.16c With the clips released, remove the strainer from the bottom of the filter housing - clean the strainer with carburettor cleaner and replace if it still appears to be contaminated

6.18a Unclip the bracket from the top of the old filter

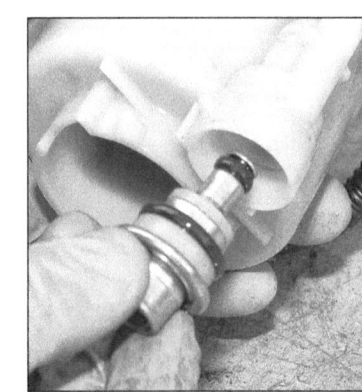

6.18b Remove the fuel pressure regulator from the fuel filter housing

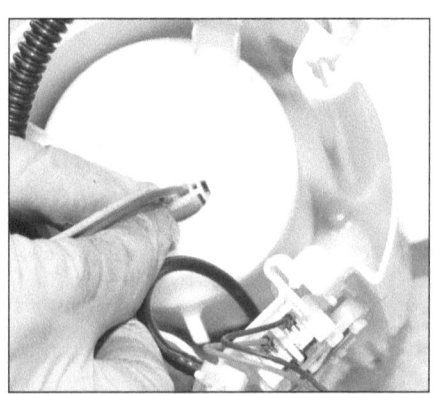

6.18c Disconnect the fuel pump wiring

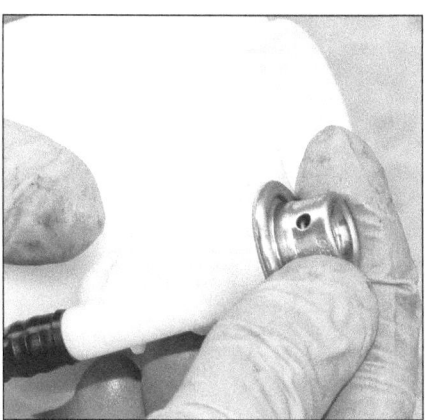

6.18d Install the fuel pressure regulator into the new filter assembly

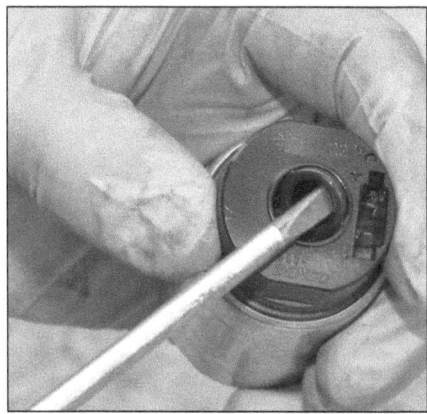

6.18e If the new filter assembly is supplied with an O-ring, remove and discard this fuel pump outlet O-ring

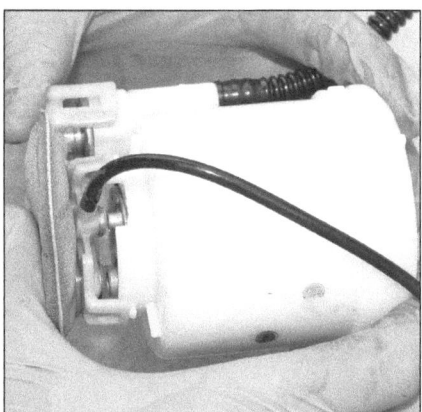

6.18f Installing the strainer onto the bottom of the filter housing

6.18g Ensure the pickup hose is guided between the filter and the side of the reservoir to prevent it kinking

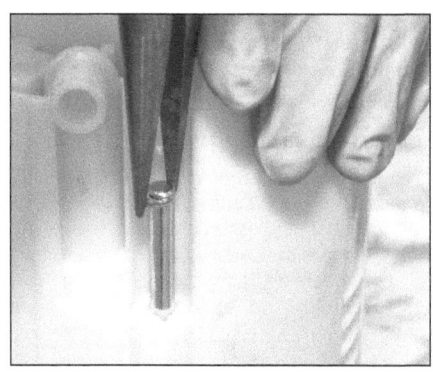
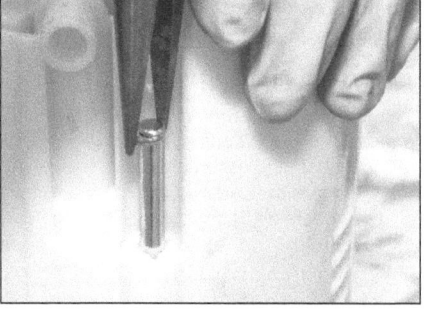

6.18h Use long-nosed pliers to install the E-clip

g Install the spring onto the long rod and engage the rods into the holes in the reservoir. Guide the pickup hose down between the side of the reservoir and the filter assembly **(see illustration)**.

h Turn the assembly upside down and push the reservoir toward the top cover until the long rod has protruded sufficiently to install the E-clip **(see illustration)**. Install the E-clip.

19 Reconnect the wiring to the top cover.

7 Fuel tank - removal and installation

Warning: *Petrol is extremely flammable, so take extra precautions when you work on any part of the fuel system. See the Warning in Section 2.*

1 Relieve the fuel system pressure (see Section 2). Remove the fuel filler cap to relieve fuel tank pressure.

2 Disconnect the negative (-) battery terminal (see Chapter 5).

3 Remove the fuel pump/fuel level sending unit assembly (see Section 5).

b Disconnect the wiring from the top of the fuel pump **(see illustration)**.

c Slide the fuel pump from bottom of the filter housing and discard the O-ring from the top of the fuel pump outlet **(see illustration)**.

Note: *Genuine filters are supplied with a new O-ring to go into the fuel pump outlet port.*

d Lubricate the O-rings on the fuel pressure regulator with clean fuel and slide the regulator into the new filter housing **(see illustration)**.

e Install the fuel pump into the new filter. You will feel the top of the pump and O-ring clip into the filter housing.

f Install the strainer over the bottom of the fuel pressure regulator and pump. Ensure all of the clips engage the filter housing.

7.8a To detach the left and right fuel tank protectors from the fuel tank on a 2WD model, remove these fasteners (typical)

7.8b To detach the fuel tank protector from the fuel tank on a AWD model, remove these fasteners (typical)

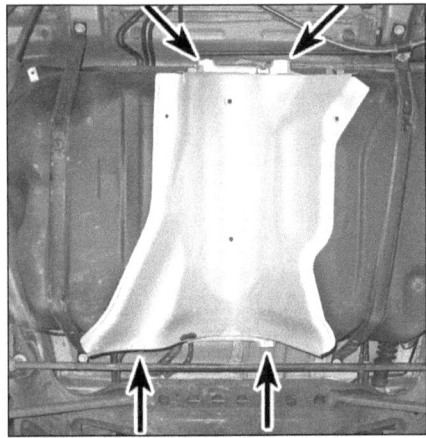

7.9a To detach the heat shield from the fuel tank on a 2WD model, remove these fasteners (typical)

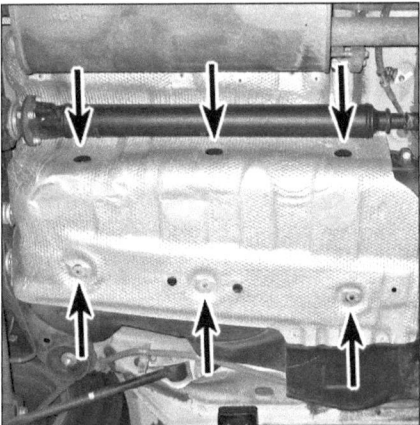

7.9b To detach the heat shield from the fuel tank on a AWD model, remove these fasteners (typical)

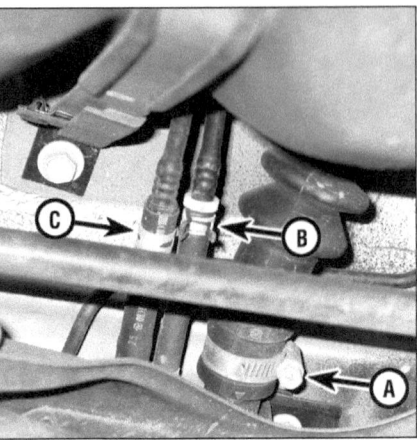

7.10 Loosen the screw-type hose clamp (A) and disconnect the fuel filler neck hose from the fuel tank filler neck pipe, then loosen the two spring-type clamps (B and C) and disconnect the two EVAP hoses

Note: *If the tank is nearly empty, it is only necessary, to disconnect the fuel supply line and the fuel pump/sender unit wiring connector from the top of the fuel tank (see Section 5).*

4   If the tank is full or nearly full, with the fuel pump/sender unit assembly removed, siphon the fuel into an approved container with a siphoning kit. Siphoning kits are available at most auto parts stores.

Warning: *Do not start the siphoning action by mouth!*

5   Raise the vehicle and support it securely on jackstands (see Jacking and Towing).

MCU28R models

Refer to illustrations 7.8a, 7.8b, 7.9a, 7.9b and 7.10

6   Remove the centre part of the exhaust system (the downstream catalytic converter to the tailpipe behind the muffler - see Section 15).

7   On AWD models, remove the propeller shaft (see Chapter 10).

8   Remove the fuel tank protector(s) **(see illustrations)**.

9   Remove the fuel tank heat shield **(see illustrations)**.

10   Disconnect the fuel filler neck hose and the two smaller hoses next to it **(see illustration)**.

GSU40R/GSU45R models

11   Working on the vehicle under-body, remove the front, centre floor cover and the rear exhaust pipe assembly (see Chapter 4).

12   Remove the centre exhaust pipe assembly (see Section 15).

13   Remove the exhaust pipe support bracket.

2WD models

14   Remove the mounting clips and nuts and lower the fuel tank heat shield.

AWD models

15   Remove the rear propeller shaft (see Chapter 8).

16   Remove the mounting bolts and remove the heat shield.

17   Remove the rear subframe with the differential and lower it from the vehicle (see Chapter 10).

All models

Refer to illustration 7.19

18   Support the fuel tank securely.

19   Remove the bolts from the fuel tank retaining straps **(see illustration)**.

20   Carefully lower the tank about 150 mm or so and verify that all electrical harnesses, fuel lines and EVAP system hoses are disconnected.

21   Carefully lower the fuel tank to the ground.

22   Installation is the reverse of removal. Tighten the fuel tank strap bolts securely.

---

8   Fuel tank cleaning and repair - general information

1   Any repairs to the fuel tank or filler neck should be done by a professional with experience in this critical and potentially dangerous work. Even after cleaning and flushing of the fuel system, explosive fumes can remain and ignite during repair of the tank.

2   If the fuel tank is removed from the vehicle, it should not be placed in an area where sparks or open flames could ignite the fumes coming out of the tank. Be especially careful inside garages where a fuel-type appliance is located, because it could cause an explosion.

---

9   Air filter housing - removal and installation

Air intake duct and resonators

Refer to illustrations 9.2 and 9.4

1   Remove the engine cover (see *Intake manifold - removal and installation* in Chapter 2).

2   Disconnect the Positive Crankcase Ventilation (PCV) fresh air inlet hose **(see illustration)** from the air intake duct.

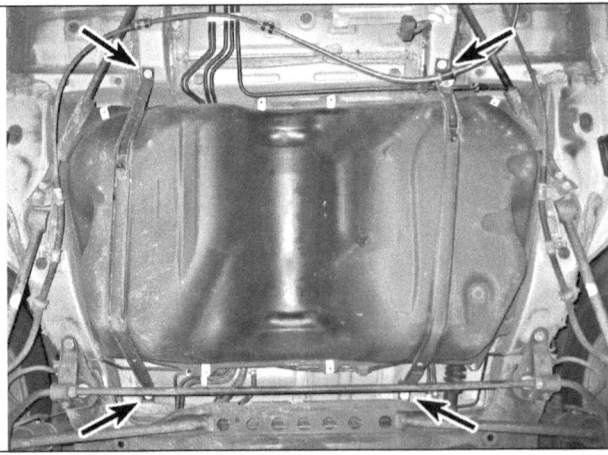

7.19 To detach the fuel tank from the vehicle, remove these four fuel tank strap bolts (2WD model shown, AWD models similar)

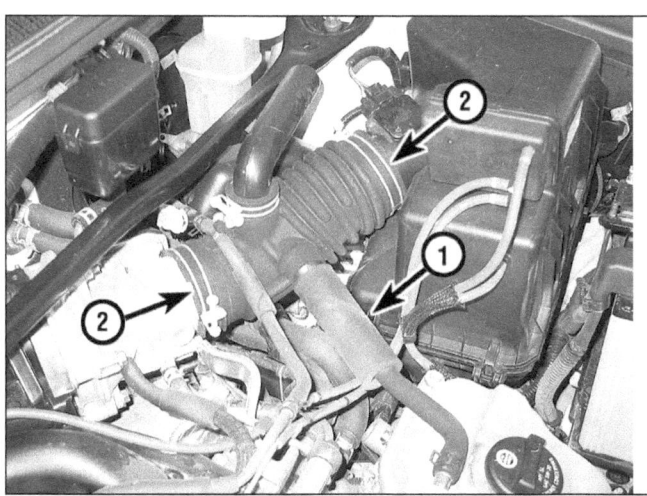

9.2 To remove the air intake duct, disconnect the PCV fresh air inlet hose (1) and loosen the hose clamps (2) at both ends of the duct, then pull the duct off the air filter housing and the throttle body (V6 model shown)

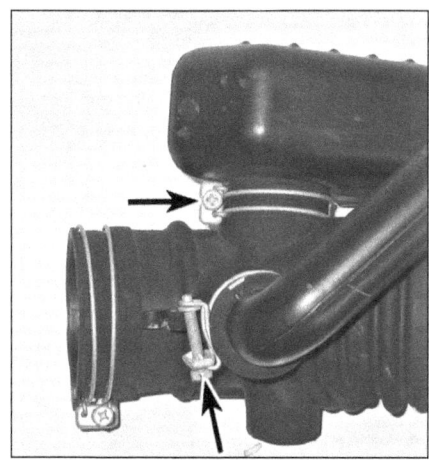

9.4 To remove the resonators, loosen the hose clamps and pull the resonators out of the air intake duct (V6 model shown)

3   Loosen the hose clamps at both ends of the air intake duct and remove the duct.

4   If you're replacing the air intake duct, remove the resonators **(see illustration)** and install them on the new intake duct.

5   Installation is the reverse of removal.

Air filter housing

Refer to illustration 9.7

6   Remove the air filter housing cover and remove the filter element (see Chapter 1).

7   Remove the air filter housing mounting bolts **(see illustration)**.

8   Remove the air filter housing.

9   Installation is the reverse of removal.

---

10   Sequential Electronic Fuel Injection (SFI) system - general information

The SFI system consists of the fuel tank, the electric in-tank fuel pump, the fuel pressure regulator (an integral component of the fuel pump), the EFI main relay, the circuit opening relay (fuel pump relay), the fuel rail and the fuel injectors. The induction system consists of the air filter housing, the air intake

9.7 To detach the air filter housing, remove these three bolts (V6 model shown)

duct and the throttle body. The throttle bodies are PCM-controlled electronic units. The PCM monitors the angle of the accelerator pedal with a sensor at the pedal assembly and directs a solenoid in the throttle body to alter the angle of the throttle valve in the throttle body in accordance with this data. Because they're all parts of the engine management system, the SFI system and the various emission control systems used on these vehicles are closely linked. For information about the emission control systems, see Chapter 6. The SFI system is easy to understand if you divide it into three sub-systems: the air intake system, the electronic control system and the fuel delivery system.

Air intake system

The air intake system consists of the air filter housing, the air intake duct, the resonators, the throttle body and the intake manifold The resonators are oddly shaped appendages clamped to the air intake duct. They function as accumulators, or reservoirs, that help to quiet the flow of air through the air intake duct. The replacement procedures for all of these components are covered in this chapter except the intake manifolds, which are covered in the Engine chapters (see Chapter 2A) for models with the 3MZ-FE engine and (see Chapter 2B) for models with the 2GR-FE engine.

The throttle bodies are equipped with the Electronic Throttle Control System-intelligent (ETCS-i) system. The single-barrel throttle bodies on these models are electronic units; they don't use an accelerator cable to open and close the throttle valve. Instead, a DC motor opens and closes the throttle valve inside one of these units in response to commands from the Powertrain Control Module (PCM). The PCM monitors the position, or angle, of the accelerator pedal with the Accelerator Pedal Position (APP) sensor, then commands the DC motor inside the throttle body to open or close the throttle plate accordingly. These throttle bodies have a Throttle Position (TP) sensor, but, unlike earlier units, it's an integral component of the throttle body, and not removable. There is no Idle Speed Con-

trol (ISC) valve on these units. The idle speed control function is handled by the PCM. For more information about the ETCS-i, the APP sensor and the PCM (see Chapter 6).

Electronic control system

The information sensors, Powertrain Control Module (PCM) and output actuators, and the various emission control system employed on these vehicles, are described in Chapter 6.

Fuel delivery system

The fuel delivery system consists of the fuel pump, the fuel pressure regulator, the fuel filter, the fuel lines, the pulsation damper, the fuel rail and the fuel injectors. The in-tank fuel pump is an electric in-line type. Fuel is drawn through an inlet strainer into the pump, flows through the fuel pressure regulator, passes through the fuel filter and is delivered to the injectors. The fuel pressure regulator maintains a constant fuel pressure to the injectors.

The injectors are solenoid-actuated, constant stroke, pintle types consisting of a solenoid, plunger, needle valve and housing. When current is applied to the solenoid coil, the needle valve is raised off its seat and pressurised fuel squirts out of the injector body through the nozzle. The injection quantity is determined by the *pulse width*, i.e. the length of time that the pintle valve is open, which is controlled by the length of time during which current is supplied to the solenoid coil. Because injector timing determines opening and closing intervals, which in turn determines the air-fuel mixture ratio, injector timing must be precise.

The EFI main relay, located in the engine compartment relay/fuse box, supplies power to the fuel pump relay (circuit opening relay) from the ignition key. The PCM controls the grounding signal to the fuel pump in response to the starting and camshaft position signals at start-up.

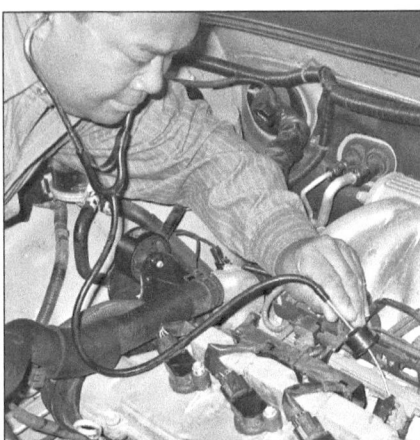

11.7 Using a stethoscope, listen to each fuel injector and verify that it's making a clicking sound when the engine is running

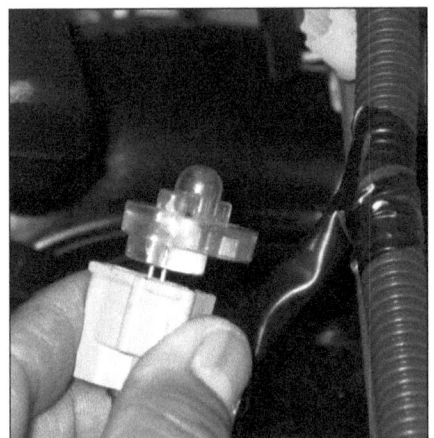

11.8 Plug the "Noide" light into the electrical connector for each fuel injector and verify that it blinks with the engine running

11.9 Turn the mode knob on your digital multimeter to the appropriate resistance range, touch the probes of the meter to the two terminals on each injector and measure the resistance, which should be within the range listed in this Chapter's Specifications

11   Fuel injection system - check

Refer to illustrations 11.7, 11.8 and 11.9

Warning: *Petrol is extremely flammable, so take extra precautions when you work on any part of the fuel system. See the Warning in Section 2.*

1   Check all electrical connectors, especially ground connections, for the system. Loose connectors and poor grounds can cause many engine control system problems.

2   Verify that the battery is fully charged because the Powertrain Control Module (PCM) and sensors cannot operate properly without adequate supply voltage.

3   Refer to Chapter 1 and check the air filter element. A dirty or partially blocked filter will reduce performance and economy.

4   Check fuel pump operation (see Section 3). If the fuel pump fuse is blown, replace it and see if it blows again. If it does, look for a short in the wiring harness to the fuel pump.

5   Inspect the vacuum hoses connected to the intake manifold for damage, deterioration and leakage.

6   Remove the air intake duct from the throttle body and check for dirt, carbon, varnish, or other residue in the throttle body, particularly around the throttle plate. If it's dirty, refer to the Emissions chapter and troubleshoot the PCV and EGR systems for the cause of excessive varnish buildup (see Chapter 6).

7   With the engine running, place an automotive stethoscope against each injector, one at a time, and listen for a clicking sound that indicates operation **(see illustration)**. If you don't have a stethoscope, you can place the tip of a long screwdriver against the injector and listen through the handle.

8   If an injector does not seem to be operating electrically (not clicking), purchase a special injector test light (sometimes called a "Noide" light) and install it into the injector wiring harness connector **(see illustration)**.

Start the engine and see if the Noide light flashes. If it does, the injector is receiving proper voltage. If it doesn't flash, further diagnosis is necessary. You might want to have it checked by a dealership service department or other qualified repair shop.

9   With the engine off and the fuel injector electrical connectors disconnected, measure the resistance of each injector with an ohmmeter **(see illustration)**. Refer to this Chapter's Specifications for the correct resistance. Refer to Chapter 6 for other system checks.

12   Throttle body - check, removal and installation

Check

Refer to illustration 12.1

1   Remove the air intake duct from the throttle body and check for carbon and residue build-up. If it is dirty, clean it with aerosol carburettor cleaner (make sure the can specifically states that it is safe with oxygen sensor systems and catalytic converters) and a toothbrush **(see illustration)**.

Caution: *Do not clean the Throttle Position (TP) sensor with the solvent.*

Removal and installation

Warning: *Wait until the engine is completely cool before beginning this procedure.*

Refer to illustrations 12.9a and 12.9b

2   Disconnect the negative (-) battery terminal (see Chapter 5).

3   On models with the 3MZ-FE engine, remove the strut brace (see Chapter 10).

4   Remove the engine cover.

Note: *On 2GR-FE engines, pull up on the front side of the engine top cover to detach it from the two front retainers. After the front is detached, pull up on the back retainer and remove the engine cover. Do not pull up on the front and rear at the same time or the cover can be damaged.*

5   Remove the air intake duct (see Section 9).

6   Disconnect the electrical connector from the throttle body.

7   Clamp off the coolant hoses to the throttle body to minimise coolant loss.

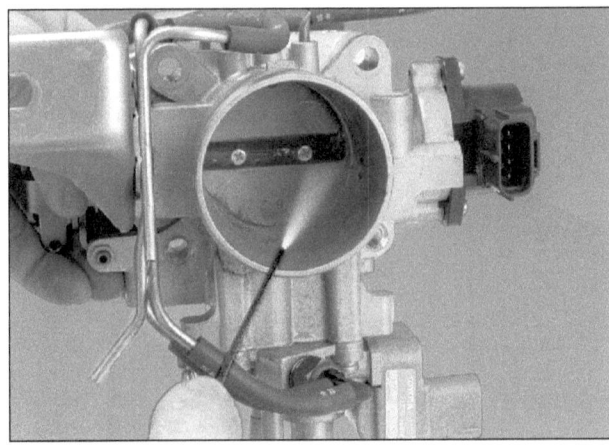

12.1 With the engine off, use aerosol carburettor cleaner, a toothbrush and a shop rag to clean the throttle body bore. Open the throttle plate so that you can clean behind it. (Make sure that the carb cleaner won't damage catalysts and oxygen sensors)

12.9a Throttle body and adapter - 3MZ-FE engine

1 Air intake duct	4 Vacuum hoses
2 Throttle body	5 Adapter
3 Coolant hoses	

12.9b Throttle body - 2GR-FE engine

1 Throttle body	3 Electrical connector
2 Coolant hoses	4 Mounting bolts

8   Disconnect the coolant hoses from the throttle body **(see illustration 12.6)**. Plug the coolant hoses to prevent coolant leakage.

9   Remove the throttle body mounting bolts **(see illustrations)** and remove the throttle body. Discard the gasket.

10   On models with the 3MZ-FE engine, if necessary remove the vacuum hose and remove the adapter from the upper intake manifold that the throttle body is secured to. Discard the gaskets.

11   Installation is the reverse of removal. Use a new gasket and tighten the throttle body mounting bolts to the torque listed in this Chapter's Specifications. Check the coolant level, adding as necessary (see Chapter 1).

13 Fuel pulsation damper - replacement

Warning: *Petrol is extremely flammable, so take extra precautions when you work on any*

part of the fuel system. See the Warning in Section 2.

1   Relieve the fuel pressure (see Section 2).

2   Disconnect the negative (-) battery terminal (see Chapter 5).

4   Remove the engine cover.

Note: *On 2GR-FE engines, pull up on the front side of the engine top cover to detach it from the two front retainers. After the front is detached, pull up on the back retainer and remove the engine cover. Do not pull up on the front and rear at the same time or the cover can be damaged.*

3MZ-FE engine

Refer to illustration 13.5

5   The pulsation damper **(see illustration)** is screwed onto the fuel rail for the rear cylinder bank. Simply unscrew the damper from the fuel rail.

6   Remove and discard the old sealing washers.

7   Installation is the reverse of removal. Install new sealing washers and tighten the damper to the torque listed in this Chapter's Specifications.

2GR-FE engine

Warning: *Wait until the engine is completely cold before beginning this procedure.*

8   The pulsation damper is attached to the rear bank fuel rail **(see illustration)**.

9   Drain the engine coolant (see Chapter 1).

10   Remove the upper intake manifold (see Chapter 2B).

11   Remove the pressure clip and withdraw the fuel pulsation damper from the fuel rail.

12   Install a new O-ring onto the damper and install the assembly into the fuel rail **(see illustration)**.

19   Installation is the reverse of removal.

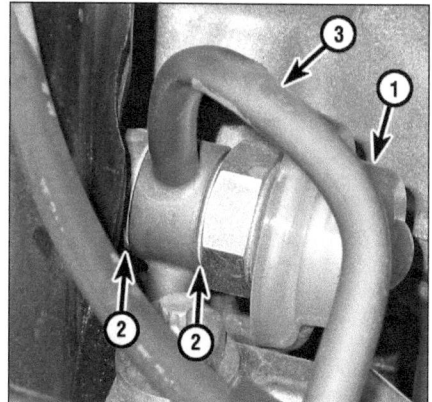

13.5 Pulsation damper (1), sealing washers (2) and crossover tube (3) - 3MZ-FE engine

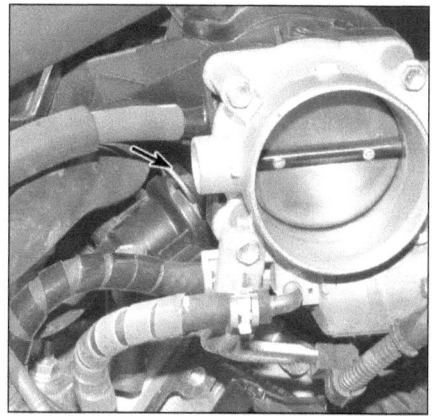

13.8 Pulsation damper location - 2GR-FE engine

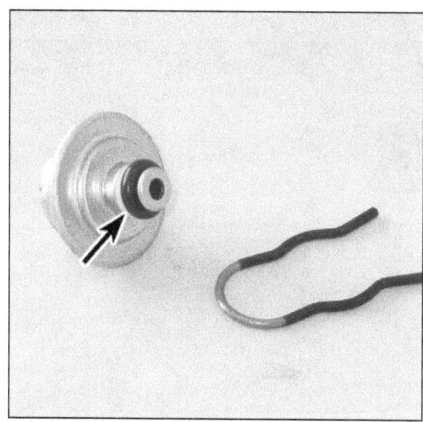

13.12 Ensure the O-ring is not damaged and lubricate with some fuel before installing the damper

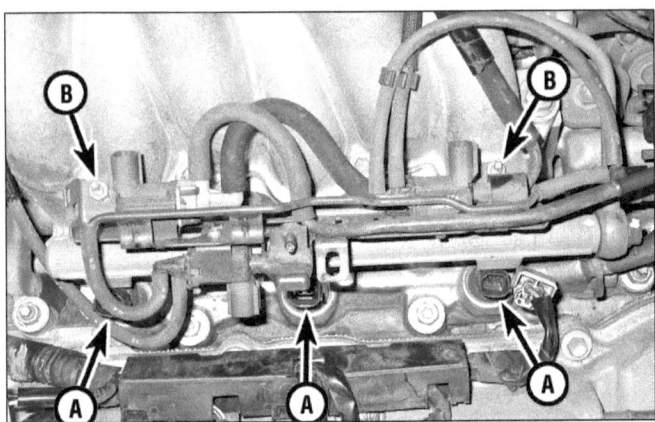

14.7a Disconnect the electrical connectors (A) from the fuel injectors on the front cylinder head. To detach the Vacuum Switching Valve (VSV) mounting bracket from the intake manifold, remove these two nuts (B) - 3MZ-FE engine

14.7b Front fuel rail components - 2GR-FE engine

1 Front fuel rail   *3 Front bank of injectors*
2 Fuel rail fasteners

14   Fuel rail and injectors - removal and installation

Refer to illustrations 14.7a, 14.7b, 14.15, 14.16, 14.17, 14.18 and 14.19

Warning: *Petrol is extremely flammable, so take extra precautions when you work on any part of the fuel system. See the Warning in Section 2.*

1   Relieve the fuel pressure (see Section 2).
2   Disconnect the negative (-) battery terminal (see Chapter 5).
3   Remove the engine cover.

Note: *On 2GR-FE engines, pull up on the front side of the engine top cover to detach it from the two front retainers. After the front is detached, pull up on the back retainer and remove the engine cover. Do not pull up on the front and rear at the same time or the cover can be damaged.*

4   Remove the air intake duct (see Section 9).
5   On models with the 3MZ-FE engine, remove the strut brace (see Chapter 10).

6   Remove the intake manifold (see Chapter 2B) or (see Chapter 2C).
7   Disconnect the electrical connectors from the injectors on the front cylinder head **(see illustrations)**.

3MZ-FE engine

Note: *On 3MZ-FE engines, the fuel rail is a two-piece assembly. The front fuel rail houses the fuel injectors for the cylinders in the front head. The rear fuel rail houses the fuel injectors for the cylinders in the rear head. We recommend replacing all injector O-rings even when only one injector O-ring or seal is leaking. On most fuel rails you have to remove the entire assembly anyway, so replace all of the O-rings/seals at one time to avoid having to remove the fuel rail later to replace another O-ring and/or seal. However, if the leak is occurring at only one front cylinder injector, please note that you do have the option to remove the front fuel rail without removing the rear fuel rail, which means that you won't have to remove the intake manifold. Conversely, you can also remove the rear fuel rail without removing the front fuel rail, though you will have to remove the intake manifold to*

do so. Finally, our recommendation is of that anytime any injector develops a leak it's a good idea to remove all of the injectors and replace all of the O-rings and/or seals. And removing the intake manifold isn't very difficult on these vehicles.

8   Remove the Vacuum Switching Valve (VSV) mounting bracket from the intake manifold **(see illustration 14.7a)** and set the bracket aside. Don't disconnect any of the vacuum hoses.
9   If you're going to remove the entire fuel rail assembly, disconnect the fuel supply line from the fuel rail (see Section 4).
10   If you're only going to remove the front fuel rail, disconnect the metal crossover tube that connects the front fuel rail to the rear fuel rail by removing the banjo bolt from the front fuel rail **(see illustration 3.8)**. If you're going to remove the rear fuel rail, then remove the pulsation damper from the rear fuel rail **(see illustration 13.5)** and remove the crossover tube. Remove and discard the old sealing washers (use new ones during reassembly).
11   If you're just removing the front fuel rail and injectors, remove the front fuel rail mounting bolts **(see illustration 15.15)** and remove the front fuel rail and injectors by lifting the assembly straight up.
12   To remove the fuel injectors and replace the injector O-rings, refer to Steps 17 and 18 below.
13   If you're going to remove the entire fuel rail assembly (or just the rear fuel rail), remove the intake manifold (see Chapter 2A).

All models

14   On 2GR-FE engines, remove the intake manifold (see Chapter 2B).
15   Disconnect the electrical connectors from the rear fuel rail **(see illustration)**.
16   Remove the fuel rail mounting bolts **(see illustration)**.
17   Remove the fuel rail and the fuel injectors as a single assembly **(see illustration)**.
18   Remove the fuel injectors from the fuel rail **(see illustration)**.

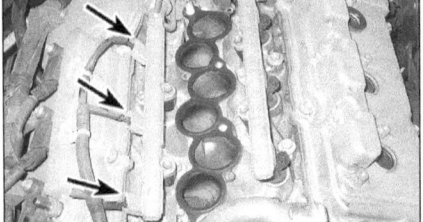

14.15 Disconnect the electrical connectors from the rear fuel injectors - 3MZ-FE engine

14.16 To detach the fuel rail assembly from the intake manifold, remove these bolts - 3MZ-FE engine

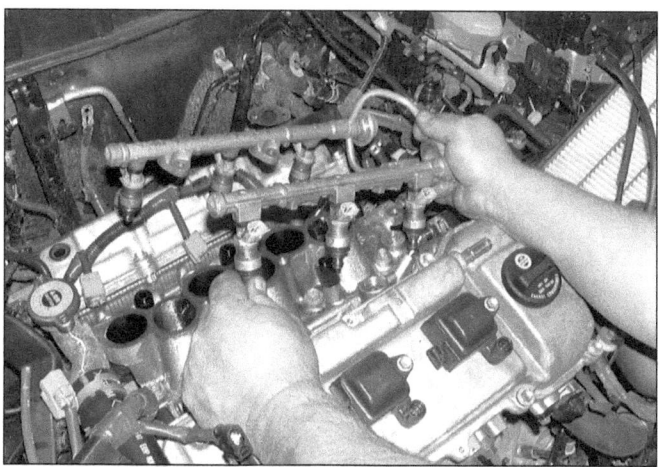

14.17 Remove the fuel rail and injectors as a single assembly

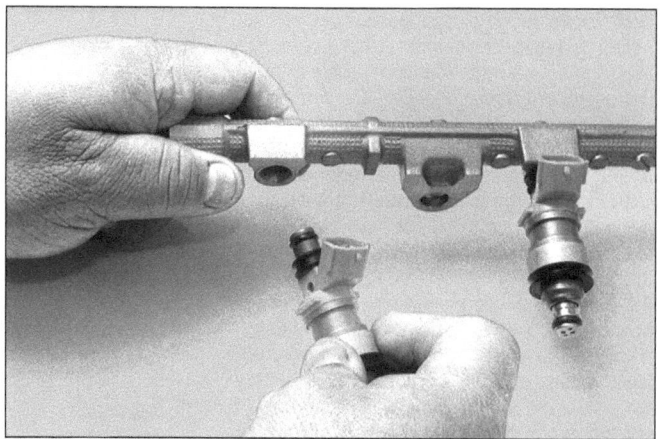

14.18 To remove each fuel injector from the fuel rail, simultaneously twist and pull it out of the fuel rail

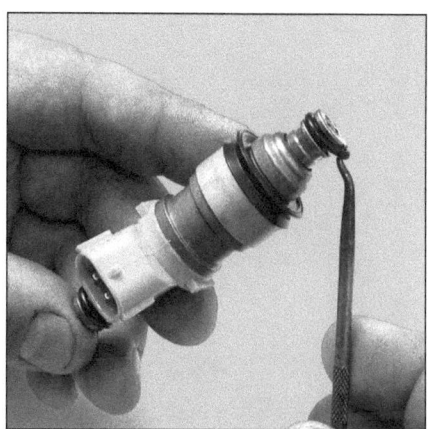

14.19 If you plan to reinstall the original injectors, remove and discard the old O-rings and grommets and replace them with new ones

19   If you intend to re-use the same injectors, replace the grommets and O-rings **(see illustration)**.

20   Installation is the reverse of removal. Be sure to use new injector O-rings and tighten the fuel rail mounting bolts to the torque listed in this Chapter's Specifications.

15 Exhaust system servicing - general information

Refer to illustrations 15.1a, 15.1b and 15.1c

Warning: *Inspect and repair exhaust system components only after the system components have cooled down.*

1   The exhaust system consists of the exhaust manifold(s), the catalytic converters, the muffler, the tailpipe and the exhaust pipes that connect these components together, as well as the brackets, hangers and clamps that support and secure these components. The exhaust system is attached to the body with mounting brackets and rubber hangers **(see illustration)**. If any of these parts are damaged or deteriorated, excessive noise and vibration will be transmitted to the body. The exhaust system is divided into various sections, which are bolted together. Some of these sections consist of several components welded together into one assembly. For example, the centre part of the exhaust system, which is also the longest single section, includes the downstream catalytic converter and the pre-muffler **(see illustrations)**. If either of these components is damaged, you will have to replace the entire assembly, or have the old catalyst or muffler cut off and a new unit welded in. You'll also have to remove the centre exhaust pipe assembly in order to remove the fuel tank.

2   Conducting regular inspections of the exhaust system will keep it safe and quiet.

15.1a Each section of the exhaust system (this is the rear muffler section) is suspended by rubber exhaust hangers. Over time these hangers can become dried out, then crack or tear. Always inspect the exhaust hangers whenever you're servicing anything under the vehicle, and replace them immediately if they're damaged or worn out

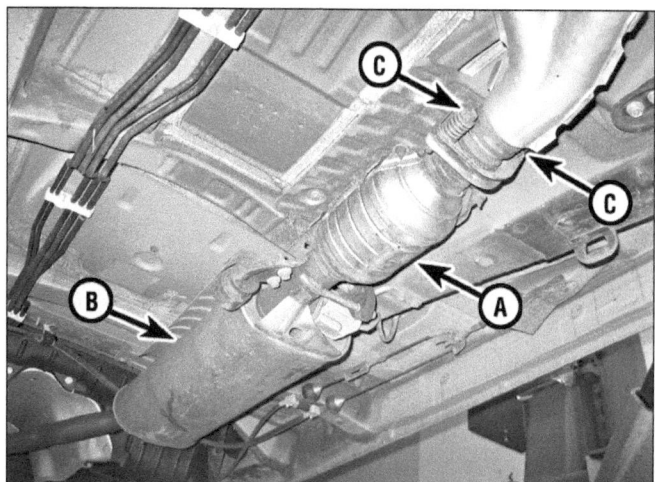

15.1b The centre exhaust pipe assembly is the longest and biggest section of the exhaust system. It consists of the downstream catalytic converter (A) and the forward muffler (B). To unbolt the forward end of the centre exhaust pipe assembly, remove these two bolts (C)

Look for damaged or bent parts, open seams, holes, loose connections, excessive corrosion or other damage that could allow exhaust fumes to enter the vehicle. Do not repair deteriorated exhaust system components - replace them.

3   If the exhaust system components are extremely corroded or rusted together, they will probably have to be cut from the exhaust system. The convenient way to accomplish this is to have a muffler repair shop remove the corroded sections with a cutting torch. If, however, you want to save money by doing it yourself and you don't have an oxy/acetylene welding outfit with a cutting torch, simply cut off the old components with a hacksaw. If you have compressed air, you can also use special pneumatic cutting chisels. If you do decide to tackle the job at home, be sure to wear eye protection to protect your eyes from metal chips, and wear work gloves to protect your hands.

4   Here are some simple guidelines to apply when repairing the exhaust system:

  a *Work from the back to the front when removing exhaust system components.*

  b *Apply penetrating oil to the exhaust system component fasteners to make them easier to remove.*

  c *Use new gaskets, hangers and clamps when installing exhaust system components. Unless the fasteners are in good condition, it's also a good idea to replace*

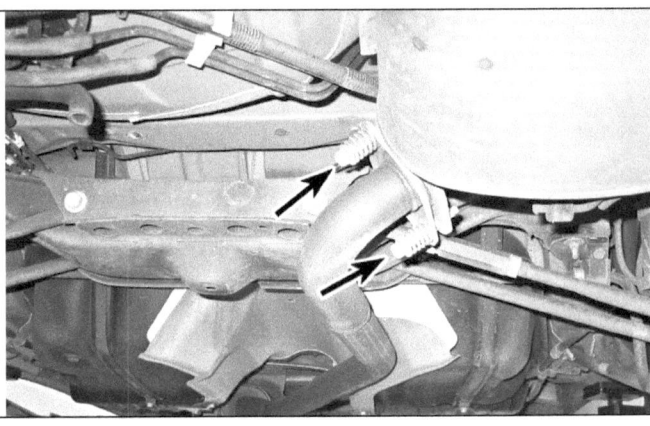

15.1c To unbolt the rear end of the centre exhaust pipe assembly, remove these two bolts

them as well. Even if you're successful in unscrewing rusted fasteners, they will be even more difficult to unscrew the next time that you need to do so, and they might break the next time that they're loosened or tightened.

  d *Apply anti-seize compound to the threads of all exhaust system fasteners during reassembly. Be sure to allow sufficient clearance between newly installed parts and all points on the underbody to avoid overheating the floor pan and possibly damaging the interior carpet and insulation. Pay particularly close attention to the catalytic converter and its heat shield.*

Warning: *The catalytic converter operates at very high temperatures and takes a long time to cool. Wait until it's completely cool before attempting to remove the converter. Failure to do so could result in serious burns.*

Chapter 5   Engine electrical systems

Contents

Specifications

Charging system

Battery voltage	12.5 12.9 volts
Charging voltage	13.2 to 14.8 volts

Torque specifications

	Nm
Alternator	
B+ Terminal	10
Mounting bolts	
3MZ-FE engine	
Lock bolt	18
Pivot bolt	58
2GR-FE engine	43
Ignition coils	
3MZ-FE engine	8
2GR-FE engine	10
Starter motor	
B+ Terminal	10
Mounting bolts	37

1   General information

The engine electrical systems include all ignition, charging and starting components. Because of their engine-related functions, these components are considered separately from chassis electrical devices like the lights, instruments, etc.

Be very careful when working on the engine electrical components. They are easily damaged if checked, connected or handled improperly. The alternator is driven by an engine drivebelt which could cause serious injury if your hands, hair or clothes become entangled in it with the engine running. Both the starter and alternator are connected directly to the battery and could arc or even cause a fire if mishandled, overloaded or shorted out.

Never leave the ignition switch on for long periods of time with the engine off. Don't disconnect the battery cables while the engine is running. Correct polarity must be maintained when connecting battery cables from another source, such as another vehicle, during jump starting. Always disconnect the negative cable first and hook it up last or the battery may be shorted by the tool being used to loosen the cable clamps.

Additional safety related information on the engine electrical systems can be found in Safety First near the front of this manual. It should be referred to before beginning any operation included in this Chapter.

2   Battery - disconnection

Refer to illustration 2.2

Caution: *Always disconnect the negative (-) battery terminal FIRST and hook it up LAST or the battery may be shorted by the tool being used to loosen the cable clamps.*

Some systems on the vehicle require battery power to be available at all times, either to maintain continuous operation (alarm system, power door locks, etc.), or to maintain control unit memory (radio station presets, powertrain control module and other control units). When the battery is disconnected, the power that maintains these systems is cut. So, before you disconnect the battery, please note that on a vehicle with power door locks,

2.2 By disconnecting the negative battery terminal first, you are negating the possibility of shorting the spanner against the body of the vehicle while loosening the battery terminal - which could happen if you loosen the positive terminal first

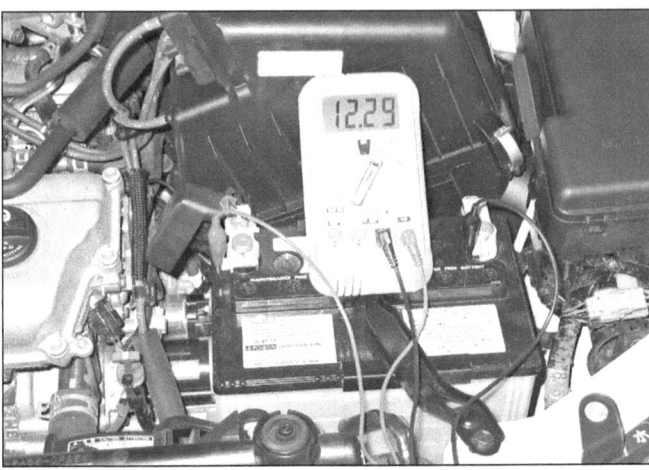

3.3 To test the open circuit voltage of the battery, touch the black probe of the voltmeter to the negative terminal and the red probe to the positive terminal of the battery. A fully charged battery should read at least 12.6 volts

it's a wise precaution to remove the key from the ignition and to keep it with you, so that it does not get locked inside if the power door locks should engage accidentally when the battery is reconnected!

Devices known as "memory-savers" are available to avoid some of these problems. However there is always a risk of shorting a circuit within the vehicle while carrying out any work - resulting in a very expensive repair bill if one of the control modules is damaged, or the Supplement Restraint System (SRS) or airbags are accidently deployed. It is for this reason that we do not recommend using any form of memory saving device.

Warning: *If you're going to work near any of the airbag system components, the battery MUST be disconnected and a memory saver must NOT be used. If a memory saver is used, power will be supplied to the airbag, which means that it could accidentally deploy and cause serious personal injury.*

1   Prior to disconnecting the battery, if possible, leave a window open and remove the key from the vehicle. On models with a power back door, ensure the door is closed.

Note: *Failure to close the back door will result in having to initialise the power back door module (see Section 5).*

2   To disconnect the battery for service procedures requiring power to be cut from the vehicle, loosen the negative battery terminal and disconnect the cable from the battery **(see illustration)**.

Caution: *Isolate the cable end to prevent it from coming into accidental contact with the battery terminal.*

2   When reconnecting the battery terminal, ensure the inside of the cable end and the battery terminal are clean (see Chapter 1) before installing the terminal back onto the battery. Tighten the terminal bolt securely.

3   Some systems will now need to be initialised (see Section 5).

3   Battery - check and replacement

Check

Refer to illustrations 3.3 and 3.4

1   Disconnect the negative battery cable, then the positive cable from the battery.

2   Check the battery state of charge. Visually inspect the indicator eye on the top of the battery; if the indicator eye is black in colour, charge the battery (see Chapter 1).

3   Next perform an open voltage circuit test using a digital voltmeter **(see illustration)**.

Note: *The battery's surface charge must be removed before accurate voltage measurements can be made. Turn on the high beams for ten seconds, then turn them off, and let the vehicle stand for two minutes. With the engine and all accessories turned off, touch the negative probe of the voltmeter to the negative terminal of the battery and the positive probe to the positive terminal of the battery. The battery voltage should be about 12.5 to 12.9 volts. If the battery is less than the specified voltage, charge the battery before proceeding to the next test. Do not proceed with the battery load test unless the battery charge is correct.*

4   Perform a battery load test. An accurate check of the battery condition can only be performed with a load tester (available at most auto parts stores). This test evaluates the ability of the battery to operate the starter and other accessories during periods of heavy load (current draw). Install a special battery load-testing tool onto the terminals **(see illustration)**. Load test the battery according to the manufacturer's instructions for the particular tool. This tool utilises a carbon pile to increase the load demand (amperage draw) on the battery. Maintain the load on the battery for 15 seconds or less and observe that the battery voltage does not drop below 9.6 volts. If the battery condition is weak or defec-

tive, the tool will indicate this condition immediately.

Note: *Cold temperatures will cause the minimum voltage reading to drop slightly. Follow the chart given in the manufacturer's instructions to compensate for cold climates. Minimum load voltage for freezing temperatures (0 degrees C) should be approximately 9.1 volts.*

Replacement

Refer to illustrations 3.5 and 3.8

5   Disconnect the negative battery terminal, then the positive terminal from the battery **(see illustration)**.

6   Remove the battery hold-down clamp **(see illustration 2.2)**.

7   Lift out the battery. Be careful - it's heavy.

Note: *Battery straps and handlers are available at most auto parts stores for a reasonable price. They make it easier to remove and carry the battery.*

3.4 Some battery load testers are equipped with an ammeter that enables you to dial in the battery load (shown). Less expensive testers only have a load switch and voltmeter

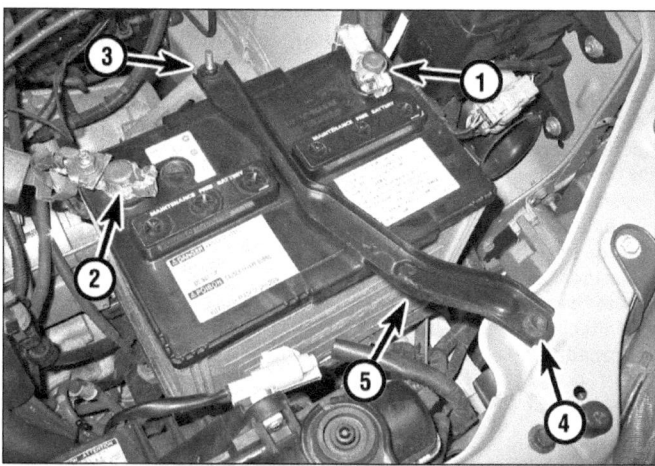

3.5 To remove the battery, disconnect the cable from the negative battery terminal (1), disconnect the cable from the positive terminal (2), then remove the nut (3) and bolt (4) and remove the hold-down clamp (5)

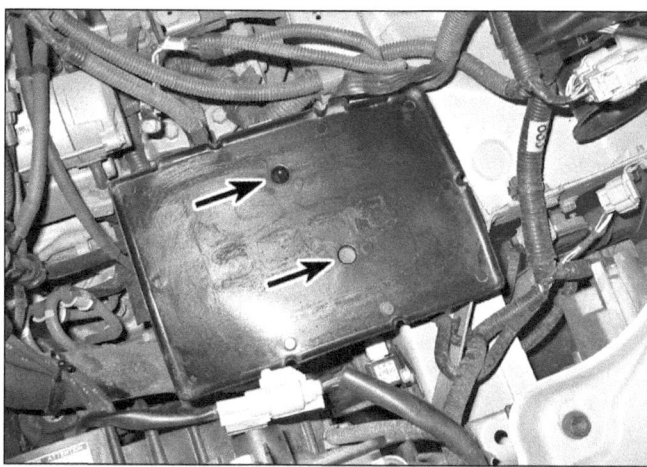

3.8 To detach the plastic battery tray from the tray support bracket underneath, simply pull these two locator pins from their holes in the bracket

8   While the battery is out, remove the battery tray **(see illustration)** and inspect it for corrosion.

9   If there's corrosion on the battery tray, wash the tray thoroughly in clean water. If the tray is cracked or damaged, replace it. When installing the tray, make sure that you push the two locator pins down into their corresponding holes in the tray support bracket until they're fully seated.

10   If you are replacing the battery, make sure you get one that's identical, with the same dimensions, amperage rating, cold cranking rating, etc.

11   Installation is the reverse of removal.

4   Battery cables - check and renewal

Refer to illustrations 4.4a and 4.4b

Caution: *If the stereo in your vehicle is equipped with an anti-theft system, make sure you have the correct activation code before disconnecting the battery.*

1   Periodically inspect the entire length of each battery cable for damage, cracked or burned insulation and corrosion. Poor battery cable connections can cause starting problems and decreased engine performance.

2   Check the cable-to-terminal connections at the ends of the cables for cracks, loose wire strands and corrosion. The presence of white, fluffy deposits under the insulation at the cable terminal connection is a sign that the cable is corroded and should be renewed. Check the terminals for distortion, missing mounting bolts and corrosion.

3   When renewing the cables, always disconnect the negative battery terminal first and hook it up last or the battery may be shorted by the tool used to loosen the cable clamps. Even if only the positive cable is being renewed, be sure to disconnect the negative cable from the battery first.

4   Disconnect and remove the cable. Make sure the renewal cable is the same length and diameter **(see illustrations)**.

5   Clean the threads of the solenoid or earth connection with a wire brush to remove rust and corrosion. Apply a light coat of petroleum jelly to the threads to prevent future corrosion.

6   Attach the cable to the solenoid or earth connection and tighten the mounting nut/bolt securely.

7   Before connecting the new cable to the battery, make sure that it reaches the battery post without having to be stretched. Clean the battery posts thoroughly and apply a light coat of petroleum jelly to prevent corrosion.

8   Connect the positive terminal first, followed by the negative terminal.

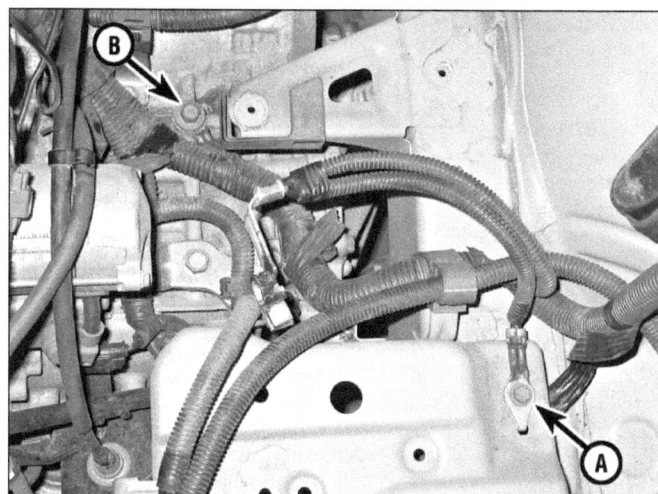

4.4a The battery ground cable is bolted to the battery tray support bracket (A) and to the transaxle (B) - MCU28R models shown, GSU40R/GSU45R models similar

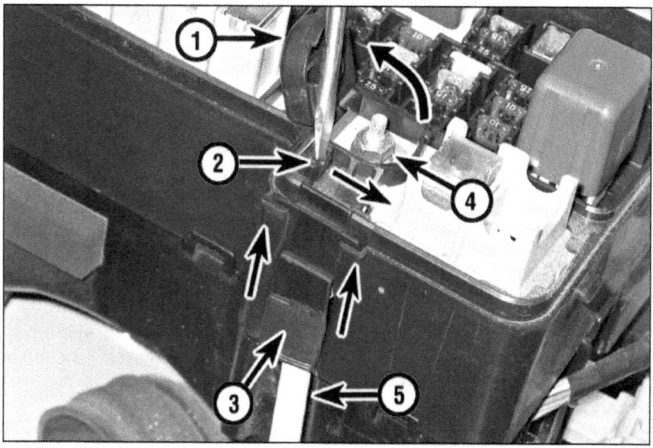

4.4b The battery starter cable is connected to the engine compartment fuse and relay box. To disconnect it, flip up the cover (1), pry the tab (2) loose with a screwdriver, lift up and remove the cable cover (3), then remove the nut (4) and disconnect the cable (5) from the terminal - MCU28R models shown, GSU40R/GSU45R models similar

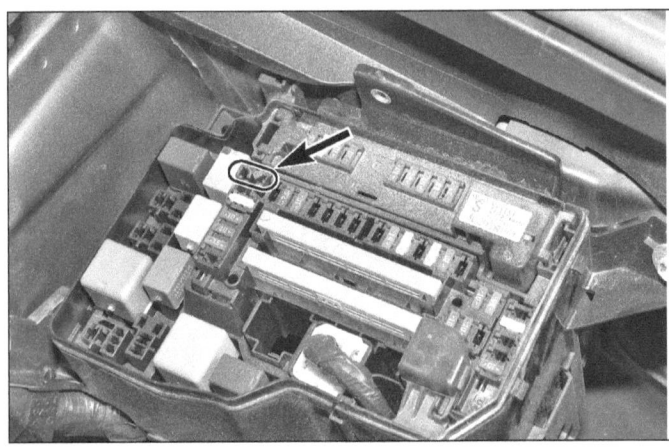

5.1 Locate the SHORT fuse location (arrow) in the engine compartment fuse/relay box and install the fuse into the proper location to activate the Smart Key initialization procedure

5   System initialization

Initialise the following systems after reconnecting or replacing the battery, or after recharging a low battery

Starting system with Smart Key

In vehicles equipped with the Smart Key system, the engine may not start and/or the steering wheel may not unlock after recharging or jump starting a low battery. Confirm that the SHORT fuse is installed into the proper slot **(see illustration)**. Move the shift lever to the Neutral position, turn the ignition key OFF and open the driver's side door. By opening the driver's side door, the initialization procedure has started. Depress the brake pedal and press the START STOP switch.

Power windows

The power window system might not operate correctly, or at all, and the jam protection function will not operate correctly, after you reconnect or replace the battery or recharge a low battery. At this time, the power window switch indicator lights will flash. To initialise the system:

MCU28R models

1   Switch ignition On and check that the door lock switch on the driver door panel is in the Unlocked position.
2   Open the driver door window about halfway.
3   Close the driver door window and continue to hold the button up for an extra second.
4   Fully open the driver door window and continue to hold the button down for an extra second.
5   The power window Auto function should now work. If not, repeat the procedure.

GSU40R/GSU45R models

6   Switch ignition On and check that the door lock switch on the driver door panel is in the Unlocked position.

7   Open the driver door window about halfway.
8   Close the driver door window and continue to hold the button down for an extra second.
9   Fully open the driver door window. When fully opened release the switch momentarily then, press the switch back down and continue to hold the button down for an extra second.
10   The power window Auto function should now work.

Note: *The power window switch light should now stop flashing and be illuminated. If not, repeat the procedure.*

Moon roof system

The moon roof might not operate correctly, or at all, and the jam protection function will not operate correctly, after you reconnect or replace the battery or recharge a low battery. If this condition occurs, initialise the moon roof as follows. Push down and hold the slide control switch toward the TILT UP switch. The moon roof will tilt up and down, then slide open and close. After the moon roof slides to its closed position, release the switch. Verify that the moon roof now functions normally. If it doesn't, have it checked by a dealer service department.

Power back door system

The power back door system might not operate correctly, or at all, after you reconnect or replace the battery or recharge a low battery. To initialise the power back door system, simply close the back door completely, by hand. If the power back door still doesn't operate correctly after closing it by hand, have the system checked. A scan tool with activation function is needed to check the system.

Electronic power steering system - GSU40R/GSU45R models

If the power steering is not functioning correctly after reconnecting the battery, initialise the system as follows:

6   Ignition system - general information and precautions

1   All models covered by this manual are equipped with a computer-controlled electronic ignition system. The ignition system includes the Camshaft Position (CMP) sensor, the Crankshaft Position (CKP) sensor, various other information sensors, the Powertrain Control Module (PCM), four or six coil-over-plug ignition coils with integral igniters, and the spark plugs. There is no distributor and there are no spark plug wires.
2   When working on the ignition system, take the following precautions:

  a   *Do not keep the ignition switch on for more than 10 seconds if the engine will not start.*
  b   *Always connect a tachometer in accordance with the manufacturer's instructions. Some tachometers may be incompatible with this ignition system. Consult an auto parts counter person before buying a tachometer for use with this vehicle.*
  c   *Never allow the ignition coil terminals to touch ground. Grounding the coil could result in damage to the igniter and/or the ignition coil.*
  d   *Do not disconnect the battery when the engine is running.*

7   Ignition system - check

Warning: *Because of the high voltage generated by the ignition system, be extremely cautious when servicing or checking ignition components. This not only includes the ignition coils and spark plugs but test equipment as well.*

1   Relieve the fuel system pressure (see Chapter 4). Keep the fuel system disabled while performing the ignition system checks.
2   If the engine turns over but won't start, disconnect each ignition coil from its corresponding spark plug (see Section 8) and attach it to a calibrated ignition tester **(see illustration)**. Calibrated ignition testers are available at most auto parts stores.
3   Crank the engine and watch the tester to see if bright blue, well-defined sparks occur.
4   If sparks occur, sufficient voltage is reaching the spark plug to fire it. Repeat this test at each spark plug to verify that all the ignition coils are functioning. If there is no spark at a plug, the ignition coil for that plug is probably bad. However, the plug itself might be fouled, so remove and check the plug as described in Chapter 1. If a number of plugs are fouled, it's a good idea to install a set of new spark plugs so that the plug gaps are uniform and the electrodes are all in the same condition.
5   If no sparks or intermittent sparks occur at all of the plugs, check for battery voltage

7.2 To use this type of calibrated ignition tester, unbolt and remove the ignition coil (don't disconnect the electrical connector), plug the tester into the boot at the lower end of the coil, clip the tester to a convenient ground and operate the starter with the ignition turned to ON. If there's enough power to fire the plug, sparks will be visible between the electrode tip and the tester body

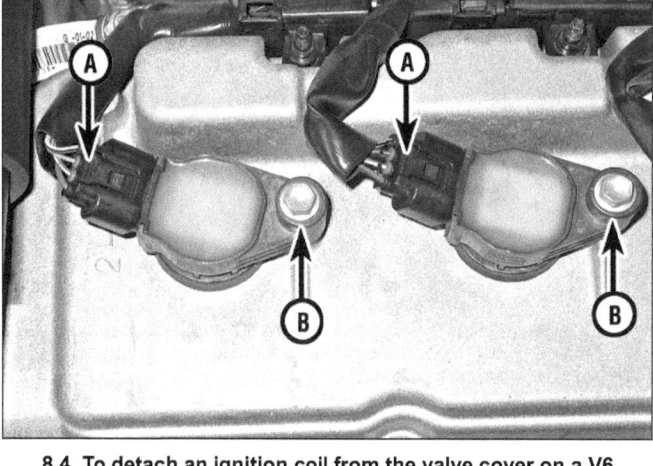

8.4 To detach an ignition coil from the valve cover on a V6 engine, depress the release tab (A) and disconnect the electrical connector, then remove the coil mounting bolt

to the ignition coils. If battery voltage is not present, check the ignition system fuse. The ignition fuse is located in the engine compartment fuse and relay box. It might be labelled as "IGN," as "AM" or as some other acronym. Refer to the fuse guide in your owner's manual for the name and number of the ignition fuse.

6   Use a code-reading tool or a scan tool to check for any stored Diagnostic Trouble Codes (DTCs) related to the ignition system, the Camshaft Position (CMP) sensor, the Crankshaft Position (CKP) sensor, other sensors or and/or the Powertrain Control Module (PCM).

8   Ignition coils - replacement

Note: *There is no published primary or secondary resistance specifications for the ignition coil/igniter units used on these models.*

1   Disconnect the negative battery terminal (see Section 2).
2   Remove the engine cover.

Note: *On 2GR-FE engines, pull up on the front side of the engine top cover to detach it from the two front retainers. After the front is detached, pull up on the back retainer and remove the engine cover. Do not pull up on the front and rear at the same time or the cover can be damaged.*

3   If you're going to remove/replace an ignition coil on the rear cylinder head, remove the upper intake manifold (see Chapter 2A) or (see Chapter 2B).
4   Disconnect the electrical connector from the ignition coil, then remove the mounting bolt **(see illustration)**.

5   Pull the coil straight up and out of the valve cover **(see illustration)**.
6   Installation is the reverse of removal.

9   Charging system - general information and precautions

The charging system includes the alternator, an internal voltage regulator, the discharge warning light, the battery, a fusible link and the wiring between all the components. The charging system supplies electrical power for the ignition system, the lights, the radio, etc. The alternator is driven by a drivebelt at the front of the engine. The voltage regulator limits the alternator's voltage to a preset value to prevent power surges and circuit overloads during peak voltage output.

The discharge warning light on the instrument cluster should come on when the ignition key is turned to START, then it should go off immediately. If it remains on, or if it comes on during vehicle operation, there is a malfunction in the charging system.

The charging system doesn't ordinarily require periodic maintenance. However, the drivebelt, battery and wires and connections should be inspected at the intervals outlined in Chapter 1. Be very careful when making electrical circuit connections to a vehicle equipped with an alternator and note the following:

a   *When reconnecting wires to the alternator from the battery, be sure to note the polarity.*
b   *Before using arc-welding equipment to repair any part of the vehicle, disconnect the wires from the alternator and the battery terminals.*

c   *Never start the engine with a battery charger connected.*
d   *Always disconnect both battery leads before using a battery charger.*
e   *The alternator is driven by an engine drivebelt that could cause serious injury if your hand, hair or clothes become entangled in it with the engine running.*
f   *Because the alternator is connected directly to the battery, it could arc or cause a fire if overloaded or shorted out.*
g   *Wrap a plastic bag over the alternator and secure it with rubber bands before steam cleaning the engine.*

10   Charging system - check

1   If a malfunction occurs in the charging circuit, do not immediately assume that the alternator is causing the problem. First, check the following items:

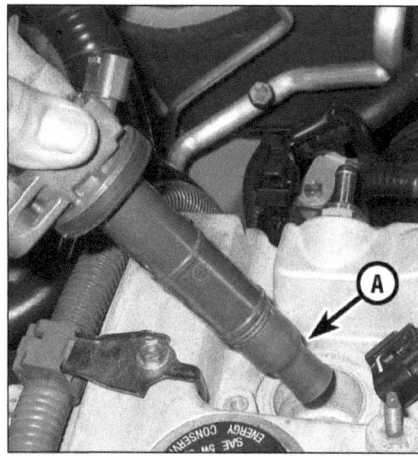

8.5 To remove an ignition coil, pull the coil straight up and out. Make sure the boot (A) is in good condition and fully seated before installing the coil

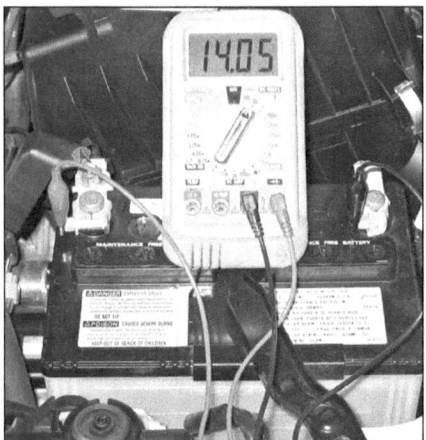

10.3 To check charging voltage, connect a voltmeter to the battery terminals and check the battery voltage with the engine running

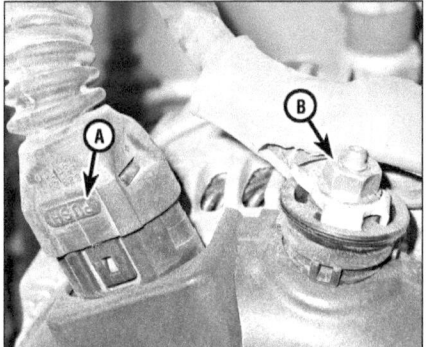

11.3 To disconnect the electrical connector from the alternator, push the release tab (A) in the area indicated and pull off the connector. To disconnect the battery cable from the B+ terminal, pull back the insulator and unscrew the nut (B) - 3MZ-FE engine

5   If the voltage rises above 15.0 volts in either test, the regulator is defective.
6   If the indicated voltage reading is less than the specified charge voltage, the alternator is probably defective. Have the charging system checked at a dealer service department or other properly equipped repair facility.

Note: *An auto-electrician can bench test an alternator off the vehicle to determine its serviceability.*

---

11   Alternator - removal and installation

Removal

1   Disconnect the negative battery terminal (see Section 1).
2   Remove the alternator drivebelt (see Chapter 1).

3MZ-FE engine

Refer to illustrations 11.3 and 11.4.

3   Disconnect the electrical connectors from the alternator **(see illustration)**.
4   Loosen the alternator pivot bolt and lock bolt, then loosen the adjustment bolt **(see illustration)**.
5   Remove the lock bolt and the pivot bolt and remove the alternator.

2GR-FE engine

Refer to illustrations 11.13 and 11.14.

Warning: *Wait until the vehicle is completely cool before beginning this procedure.*

6   Raise the vehicle and support it securely on jackstands (see Jacking and Towing).
7   Remove the inner guard moulding and splash shield (see Chapter 11).
8   Drain the engine coolant (see Chapter 1).
9   Remove the engine cover.

Note: *Pull up on the front side of the engine top cover to detach it from the two front retainers. After the front is detached, pull up*

a   *Make sure the battery cable clamps are clean and tightly secured to the battery terminals.*
b   *Test the condition of the battery (see Section 2). If it does not pass all the tests, replace it.*
c   *Check the external alternator wiring and connections.*
d   *Check the drivebelt condition and tension (see Chapter 1).*
e   *Check the alternator mounting bolts for tightness.*
f   *Run the engine and check the alternator for abnormal noise.*
g   *Check the fusible link (see Chapter 12). If it's burned, determine the cause and repair the circuit.*
h   *Check the discharge warning indicator light on the instrument cluster. It should illuminate when the ignition key is turned to ON (engine not running). If it doesn't, check the circuit between the alternator and the discharge warning indicator light (see the Wiring Diagrams at the end of Chapter 12).*

i   *Check the fuses that are in series with the charging system circuit (see the Wiring Diagrams at the end of Chapter 12).*

2   With the ignition key off, check the battery voltage with no accessories operating. It should be at least 12.6 volts **(see illustration 3.2)**. It may be slightly higher if the engine had been operating within the last hour.
3   Connect an ammeter to the charging system following the tool manufacturer's instructions. Start the engine, and check the battery voltage and amperage. It should now be approximately 13.2 to 14.8 volts **(see illustration)**.
4   Load the battery by turning on the high beam headlights and the air conditioning system and place the blower fan on HIGH. Raise the engine speed to 2,000 rpm and check the voltage and amperage. If the charging system is working properly the voltage should stay above 13.5 volts and the amperage should be 30 amps or more (depending on the condition of the battery, it could be less than 30 amps).

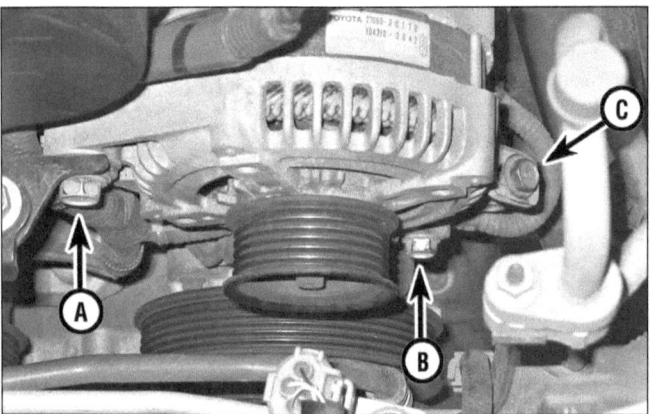

11.4 Alternator mounting details - 3MZ-FE engine

A *Pivot bolt*
B *Lock bolt*
C *Adjustment bolt*

11.13 Alternator upper mounting bolt (1), B+ terminal (2) and regulator connector (3) - 2GR-FE engine

11.14 2GR-FE engine alternator mounting bolts

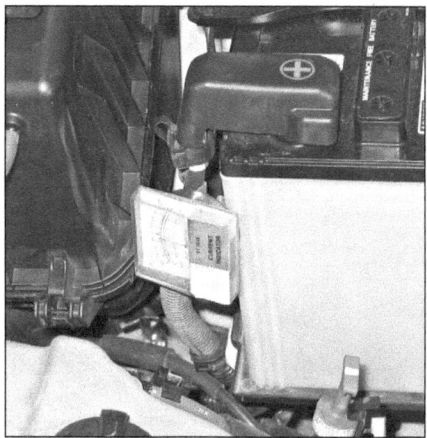

13.3 To use an inductive ammeter, simply hold the ammeter over the positive or negative cable (whichever is more accessible)

on the back retainer and remove the engine cover. Do not pull up on the front and rear at the same time or the cover can be damaged.

10   Remove the battery (see Section 3).

11   Remove the air filter housing intake ducts and the air filter housing (see Chapter 4).

12   Remove the radiator (see Chapter 3).

13   Disconnect the electrical connectors from the alternator **(see illustration)**.

14   Loosen the alternator mounting bolts and bracket and remove the alternator from the engine **(see illustration)**.

Installation

15   If you're replacing the alternator, take the old alternator with you when purchasing a replacement unit. Make sure that the new/rebuilt unit is identical to the old alternator. Look at the terminals - they should be the same in number, size and locations as the terminals on the old alternator. Finally, look at the identification markings - they will be stamped in the housing or printed on a tag or plaque affixed to the housing. Make sure that these numbers are the same on both alternators.

16   If the replacement alternator doesn't have a pulley installed, you might have to switch the pulley from the old unit to the replacement unit. When buying a new or rebuilt alternator, ask about the shop's policy regarding pulley swapping. Some shops will perform this service for free.

17   Installation is the reverse of removal. After the alternator is installed, adjust the drivebelt tension (see Chapter 1), then check the charging voltage to verify that the alternator is operating correctly (see Section 10).

12 Starting system - general information and precautions

The starting system consists of the battery, the starter motor, the starter solenoid and the electrical circuit connecting the com-

ponents. The solenoid is mounted directly on the starter motor. The solenoid/starter motor assembly is installed on the upper part of the transaxle bellhousing.

When the ignition key is turned to the START position, the starter solenoid is actuated through the starter control circuit. The starter solenoid then connects the battery to the starter. The battery supplies the electrical energy to the starter motor, which does the actual work of cranking the engine.

Always observe the following precautions when working on the starting system:

a   Excessive cranking of the starter motor can overheat it and cause serious damage. Never operate the starter motor for more than 15 seconds at a time without pausing to allow it to cool for at least two minutes.

b   The starter is connected directly to the battery and could arc or cause a fire if mishandled, overloaded or short-circuited.

c   Always detach the cable from the negative terminal of the battery before working on the starting system.

13 Starter motor and circuit - check

Refer to illustrations 13.3 and 13.4

1   If a malfunction occurs in the starting circuit, do not immediately assume that the starter is causing the problem. First, check the following items:

a   Make sure the battery cable clamps, where they connect to the battery, are clean and tight.

b   Check the condition of the battery cables (see Section 4). Replace any defective battery cables with new parts.

c   Test the condition of the battery (see Section 3). If it does not pass all the tests, replace it with a new battery.

d   Check the starter solenoid wiring and connections. Refer to the wiring diagrams at the end of Chapter 12.

e   Check the starter mounting bolts for tightness.

f   Check the fusible link (see Chapter 12). If it's burned, determine the cause and repair the circuit.

g   Check the operation of the Park/Neutral switch. Make sure the shift lever is in PARK or NEUTRAL). Refer to Chapter 7 for the Park/Neutral switch check and adjustment procedure. Refer to Chapter 12 wiring diagrams, if necessary, when performing circuit checks. These systems must operate correctly to provide battery voltage to the ignition solenoid.

h   Check the operation of the starter relay. The starter relay is located in the fuse/relay box inside the engine compartment. Refer to Chapter 12 for the relay testing procedure.

2   If the starter does not actuate when the ignition switch is turned to the start position, check for battery voltage to the solenoid. This will determine if the solenoid is receiving the correct voltage signal from the ignition switch. Connect a test light or voltmeter to the starter solenoid positive terminal and while an assistant turns the ignition switch to the start position. If voltage is not available, refer to the wiring diagrams in Chapter 12 and check all the fuses and relays in series with the starting system. If voltage is available but the starter motor does not operate, remove the starter (see Section 14) and bench test it (see Step 4).

3   If the starter turns over slowly, check the starter cranking voltage and the current draw from the battery. This test must be performed with the starter assembly on the engine. Crank the engine over (for 10 seconds or less) and observe the battery voltage. It should not drop below 8.5 volts. Also, observe the current draw using an ammeter **(see illustration)**. It should not exceed 400 amps or drop below 250 amps. If the starter motor cranking amp values are not within the correct range, replace it with a new unit. There are several conditions that may affect the starter cranking potential. The battery must be in good condition and the battery cold-cranking rating must not be under-rated for the particular application. Be sure to check the battery specifications carefully. The battery terminals and cables must be clean and not corroded.

4   If the starter is receiving voltage but does not activate, remove and check the starter/solenoid assembly on the bench **(see illustration)**. Most likely the solenoid is defective. In some rare cases, the engine may be seized so be sure to try and rotate the crankshaft pulley (see Chapter 2A) or (see Chapter 2B) before proceeding. With the starter/solenoid assembly mounted in a vise on the bench, install one jumper cable from the negative battery terminal to the body of the starter. Install the other jumper cable from the positive battery terminal to the B+ terminal on

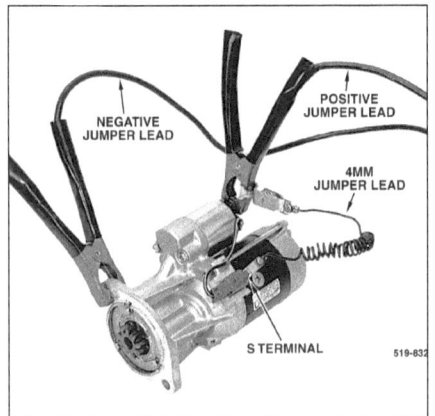

13.4 Starter motor bench testing details

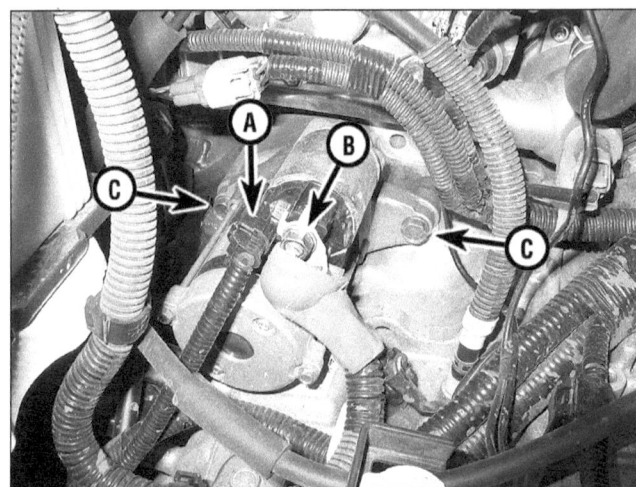

14.4 Disconnect the electrical connector (A) and the battery starter cable (B), then remove the starter mounting bolts (C) and remove the starter

the starter. Install a starter switch and apply battery voltage to the solenoid S terminal (for 10 seconds or less) and see if the solenoid plunger, shift lever and overrunning clutch extends and rotates the pinion drive. If the pinion drive extends but does not rotate, the solenoid is operating but the starter motor is defective. If there is no movement but the solenoid clicks, the solenoid and/or the starter motor is defective. If the solenoid plunger extends and rotates the pinion drive, the starter/solenoid assembly is working properly.

14   Starter motor - removal and installation

Refer to illustration 14.4

1   Disconnect the negative battery terminal (see Section 3).
2   Remove the battery and the battery tray (see Section 3).
3   Remove the air filter housing and the air intake duct (see Chapter 4).

4   Disconnect the electrical connectors and remove the starter mounting bolts **(see illustration)**, then remove the starter.
5   Installation is the reverse of removal. Tighten the starter mounting bolts to the torque listed in this Chapter's Specifications.

Chapter 6
Emissions and engine control systems

Contents

Specifications

Camshaft position sensor resistance	
2GR-FE engine	Note specified
3MZ-FE engine	
Cold	835 to 400 ohms
Hot	1,060 to 1,645 ohms
Crankshaft position sensor resistance	
Cold	1,630 to 2,740 ohms
Hot	2,065 to 3,225 ohms

Torque specifications

	Nm
Knock sensor(s)(retaining nuts)	20
Oxygen sensors	44

1   General information

To prevent pollution of the atmosphere from incompletely burned and evaporating gases, and to maintain good driveability and fuel economy, a number of emission control systems are incorporated. They include the:

On-Board Diagnostic (OBD) II system
Electronic Fuel Injection (EFI) system
Evaporative Emissions Control (EVAP) system
Positive Crankcase Ventilation (PCV) system
Catalytic converter

The Sections in this Chapter include general descriptions, checking procedures within the scope of the home mechanic and component replacement procedures (when possible) for each of the systems listed above.

Before assuming that an emissions control system is malfunctioning, check the fuel and ignition systems carefully. The diagnosis of some emission control devices requires specialised tools, equipment and training. If checking and servicing become too difficult or if a procedure is beyond your ability, consult a dealer service department or other repair shop. Remember, the most frequent cause of emissions problems is simply a loose or broken wire or vacuum hose, so always check the hose and wiring connections first.

This doesn't mean, however, that emissions control systems are particularly difficult to maintain and repair. You can quickly and easily perform many checks and do most of the regular maintenance at home with common tune-up and hand tools.

Pay close attention to any special precautions outlined in this Chapter. It should be noted that the illustrations of the various systems may not exactly match the system installed on your vehicle because of changes made by the manufacturer during production or from year-to-year.

2   On-Board Diagnostic (OBD) system and trouble codes

Scan tool information

Refer to illustration 2.2

1   Hand-held scan tools are the most powerful and versatile tools for analysing engine management systems used on later model vehicles. Previously a scan tool would cost many thousand dollars. However, the price has come down and a scan tool capable of reading stored fault codes on this vehicle is available from most auto parts stores at a fairly reasonable price. If you are thinking of purchasing a scan tool, check that it will be compatible with your vehicle. Scan tools are sold with software loaded that can interface with the vehicles on-board engine management systems. If a fault is detected, which will be evident if the Check Engine lamp on the

1.1 Emissions and engine control system components – MCU28R models with the 3.3 litre (3MZ-FE) engine

1 Engine cover	5 Intake air control valve	8 Crankshaft position sensor
2 Throttle body	6 Fuse and relay box	9 Mass Airflow Sensor (MAF)
3 Air intake duct	7 Coolant temperature sensor and	
4 Air filter	camshaft position sensor	

1.2 Emissions and engine control system components – GSU40R/GSU45R models with the 3.5 litre (2GR-FE) engine

1 Mass Airflow Sensor (MAF)
2 Throttle body
3 Crankshaft position (CKP) sensor (hidden)
4 Camshaft position (CMP) sensor - No.2 bank exhaust camshaft
5 Camshaft position (CMP) sensor - No.2 bank intake camshaft
6 Camshaft position (CMP) sensor - No.1 bank intake camshaft
7 Camshaft timing oil control valve - No.2 bank exhaust camshaft
8 Camshaft timing oil control valve - No.2 bank intake camshaft
9 Coolant temperature sensor
10 Canister purge solenoid valve
11 Air intake control valve
12 Fuse and relay box
13 Fuel pump resistor (see Chapter 4)

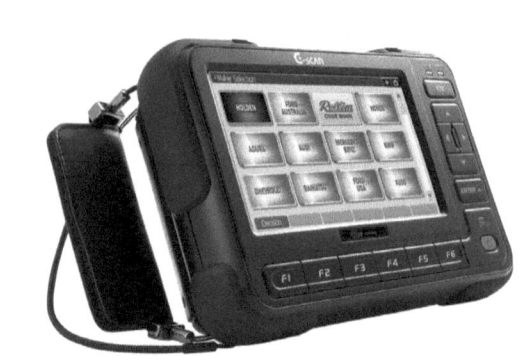

2.2 Scanners like this G-Scan are powerful diagnostic aids - programmed with comprehensive diagnostic information, they can tell you just about anything you want to know about your engine management system

dashboard illuminates while the vehicle is running at any time, a scan tool is the only way to discover what area of the vehicle the fault is located. The software preloaded on the scan tool must be compatible with the vehicle being tested.

2   With models covered by this manual containing a mandated emission control system (OBD-II), a specially designed scanner has been developed. Several tool manufacturers have released OBD-II scan tools for the home mechanic. Many workshops have more expensive type tools that are capable of doing many more interface tasks with the vehicle's on-board systems **(see illustration)**.

OBD system general description

3   All models are equipped with the second generation OBD-II system. This system consists of an on-board computer known as the Powertrain Control Module (PCM), and information sensors, which monitor various functions of the engine and send data to the PCM. This system incorporates a series of diagnostic monitors that detect and identify fuel injection and emissions control systems faults and store the information in the computer memory. This updated system also tests sensors and output actuators, diagnoses drive cycles, freezes data and clears codes. This powerful diagnostic computer must be accessed using the new OBD-II scan tool and 16 pin Data Link Connector (DLC) located under the driver's dash area. The PCM is the "brain" of the electronically controlled fuel and emissions system. It receives data from a number of sensors and other electronic components (switches, relays, etc.). Based on the information it receives, the PCM generates output signals to control various relays, solenoids (i.e. fuel injectors) and other actuators. The PCM is specifically calibrated to optimise the emissions, fuel economy and driveability of the vehicle.

4   It isn't a good idea to attempt diagnosis or replacement of the PCM or emission control components at home while the vehicle is under warranty. Because of a Federally mandated warranty which covers the emissions system components and because any

owner-induced damage to the PCM, the sensors and/or the control devices may void this warranty, take the vehicle to a dealer service department if the PCM or a system component malfunctions.

Information sensors

Note: *The following list provides a brief description of the function, operation and location of each of the important information sensors. We use the standard sensor terminology recommended by the Society of Automotive Engineers (SAE). Where Toyota uses other names for some sensors we provide the Toyota name as well.*

6   **Throttle Pedal Position sensor** - All models covered by this manual are equipped with an Electronic Throttle Control System - intelligent (ETCS-i). The ETCS-i system dispenses with a conventional throttle cable by using an electronic throttle body instead of a conventional cable-operated throttle body. The Powertrain Control Module (PCM) controls the position of the throttle plate with a solenoid that's located in the throttle body. The PCM's commands are based on the inputs that it receives from the Throttle pedal position sensor, which is located at the top of the throttle pedal assembly. Its electrical output signal, which is proportional to the angle of the throttle pedal, is used by the ETCS-i system to determine the corresponding opening angle of the throttle plate inside the throttle body.

7   **Camshaft Position (CMP) sensor** - A CMP sensor monitors the position of the camshaft and tells the Powertrain Control Module (PCM) when the piston in the No.1 cylinder is on its compression stroke. The PCM uses the CMP sensor signal to synchronise the sequential firing of the fuel injectors. Two CMP sensors, one for each cylinder head are fitted to models with the 3MZ-FE engine and four sensors are used on models with the 2GR-FE engine. The CMP sensors are referred to my the manufacturer as VVT sensors. For more information about the Variable Valve Timing-intelligent (VVT-i) system, refer to Section 4 (see Section 4) and the Engine chapters (see Chapter 2A) or (see Chapter 2B).

The CMP sensor is a *variable reluctance* (pick-up coil) type sensor that generates an analog (sine wave) signal pulse each time that a boss on the timing rotor passes by the sensor. The timing rotors are located on the backside of the VVT-i controllers, which are mounted on the left ends of the camshafts (intake only for models with the 3MZ-FE engine). There are three bosses on the timing rotor. As the timing rotor rotates with the camshaft, the CMP sensor generates a voltage output each time one of the bosses on the rotor passes by the sensor. The intake camshaft rotates once for each two rotations of the crankshaft, so there are three voltage outputs for every two rotations of the crankshaft. The PCM uses these voltage outputs to determine the position of the intake camshaft.

8   **Crankshaft Position (CKP) sensor** - Like the CMP sensor, the CKP sensor is a variable reluctance (pick-up coil) type sensor that generates an analog (sine wave) signal pulse each time that a boss on the timing rotor passes by the sensor. The CKP sensor is located on the front of the engine, next to the crankshaft pulley, and the timing rotor is mounted on the back of the crankshaft sprocket. All timing rotors have 36 evenly spaced teeth, with two missing, i.e. there are 34 actual teeth and a blank space for the other two. As the crankshaft rotates, each tooth on the timing rotor moves past the CKP sensor. As each tooth moves past the sensor, the magnetic flux in the sensor coil changes because the air gap between the sensor and the timing rotor changes. This change in magnetic flux induces a voltage pulse in the sensor, and this pulse is sent to the PCM as an output signal. And the blank space with the missing teeth indicates Top Dead Centre (TDC).

The CKP sensor is the primary sensor that provides ignition information to the PCM. The PCM uses the CKP sensor to determine crankshaft position (which piston will be at TDC next) and crank speed (rpm), both of which it needs to synchronise the ignition system.

9   **Engine Coolant Temperature (ECT) sensor** - The ECT sensor measures the temperature of the engine coolant. The ECT sensor is a thermistor, i.e. its resistance decreases as the temperature increases, and its resistance increases as the temperature decreases. This type of thermistor is also referred to as a Negative Temperature Coefficient (NTC) thermistor. This variable resistance produces an analogous voltage drop across the sensor terminals, thus providing an electrical signal to the PCM that accurately reflects the engine coolant temperature.

The ECT sensor is a critical sensor because it tells the PCM when the engine is warmed up sufficiently to go into closed loop operation. And once the engine is in closed loop, the PCM also uses the ECT sensor to control fuel injector pulse width and ignition timing, and it uses the ECT sensor signal to determine when to purge the EVAP system.

10   **Intake Air Temperature (IAT) sensor** - The IAT sensor is used by the PCM to calculate air density, which is one of the variables that it must know in order to calculate injector pulse width and adjust ignition timing (to prevent spark knock when air intake temperature is high). Like the ECT sensor, the IAT sensor is a Negative Temperature Coefficient (NTC) type thermistor, whose resistance decreases as the temperature increases. The IAT sensor is an integral component of the Mass Air Flow (MAF) sensor, which is located on the air filter housing.

11   **Knock sensor** - The knock sensor monitors engine vibration caused by detonation. Basically, a knock sensor converts engine vibration to an electrical signal. When the knock sensor detects a knock in one of the cylinders, it signals the PCM so that the PCM can retard ignition timing accordingly. The knock sensor contains a piezoelectric material, a certain type of piezoresistive crystal, that has the ability to produce a voltage when subjected to a mechanical stress. The piezoelectric crystal in the knock sensor vibrates constantly and produces an output signal that's proportional to the intensity of the vibration. As the intensity of the vibration increases, so does the voltage of the output signal. When the intensity of the crystal's vibration reaches a specified threshold, the PCM stores that value in its memory and retards ignition timing in all cylinders (the PCM does not selectively retard timing only at the affected cylinder). The PCM doesn't respond to the knock sensor's input when the engine is idling; it only responds when the engine reaches a specified speed.

The two knock sensors are located in the valley between the cylinder heads. To access the sensors, the upper and lower intake manifolds must be removed.

12   **Mass Air Flow/Intake Air Temperature (MAF/IAT) sensor** - The MAF sensor is the principal means by which the PCM monitors intake airflow. It uses a hot-wire sensing element to measure the amount of air entering the engine. Air passing over the hot wire causes it to cool down. The hot wire's temperature is maintained at 200 degrees-C above the ambient temperature by electrical current supplied to the wire and controlled by the PCM. A constantly "cold" wire located right next to the hot wire measures the ambient air temperature.) As intake air passes through the MAF sensor and over the hot wire, it cools the wire, and the control system immediately corrects the temperature back to its constant value. The current required to maintain the specified constant temperature value is used by the PCM as an indicator of airflow.

The functions of the MAF and the Intake Air Temperature (IAT) sensors are combined into one assembly. The MAF/IAT sensor is located on top of the air filter housing.

13   **Oxygen sensors** - Oxygen sensors generate a voltage signal that varies in accordance with the amount of oxygen in the exhaust stream. The PCM uses the data from the upstream oxygen sensor to calculate the injector pulse width. The downstream oxygen sensor monitors the oxygen content of the exhaust gases as they exit the catalytic converters. This information is used by the PCM to predict catalyst deterioration and/or failure. One job of the catalytic converter is to store excess oxygen. As long as the catalyst is functioning correctly, the downstream sensor should show little activity because there should be little oxygen exiting the catalyst. But as the catalyst deteriorates, its ability to store oxygen is compromised. When the output signal from the downstream sensor starts to look like the output signal from the upstream sensor, the PCM stores a DTC and turns on the MIL to let you know that it's time to replace the catalyst.

Four oxygen sensors are used: one in each exhaust manifold before the catalytic converter, and one in each down pipe after the catalytic converter.

14   **Power Steering Pressure (PSP) sensor** (fitted to models with the 3MZ-FE engine only) - The PSP sensor monitors the hydraulic pressure of the power steering fluid in the power steering system. The PSP sensor provides a voltage input to the PCM that varies in accordance with changes in the hydraulic pressure. The PCM uses the input signal from the PSP sensor to elevate the idle speed when the engine is already under some other load, such as the air conditioning compressor, while manoeuvring the vehicle at low speed, such as parking or stop-and-go driving. The PSP sensor also signals the PCM to adjust the air assist injector solenoid valve during high-load situations such as parking. The PSP sensor is located at the power steering pump. It's screwed into the top of the banjo bolt that connects the power steering pressure hose banjo fitting to the pump.

15   **Throttle Position (TP) sensor** - The TP sensor, which is located on the throttle body, is a rotary potentiometer, which is a type of variable resistor, that produces a variable voltage signal in proportion to the opening angle of the throttle plate. The PCM sends 5 volts to the TP sensor. As the plate opens and closes, the resistance of the TP sensor changes with it, altering the signal back to the PCM. The output voltage of the TP sensor is about 0.6 volt at idle (closed throttle plate) to 4.5 volts at wide-open throttle. This variable signal enables the PCM to calculate the position (opening angle) of the throttle plate. The PCM uses the TP sensor input, along with other sensor inputs, to adjust fuel injector pulse-width and ignition timing. The sensor forms part of the Electronic Throttle Control-intelligent (ETCS-i) system. The TP sensor is an integral part of the electronic throttle body and is not serviceable separately.

16   **Transmission Range (TR) sensor** - Like the Park/Neutral Position (PNP) switch that it replaces, the TR sensor prevents you from starting the engine unless the automatic transaxle is in Park or Neutral, and it activates the back-up lights when you put the shift lever in Reverse. Unlike a PNP or inhibitor switch, however, the TR sensor also tells the PCM what gear the transaxle is in. The PCM uses this information to determine what gear the transaxle should be in based on the load, engine speed, vehicle speed, etc. and to determine when to upshift and downshift the transaxle. The TR sensor is mounted on the front of the transaxle.

17   **Transmission speed sensors** - There are two speed sensors on all transaxles: the **Input Turbine Speed Sensor**, or **Input Shaft RPM Sensor**, and the **Counter Gear Speed Sensor**, or **Counter Gear RPM Sensor**. The speed sensors are variable reluctance (pickup coil) type sensors that generate an analog (sine wave) signal pulse each time that a boss on a timing rotor passes by the sensor. Both sensors are located on top of the transaxle. The PCM uses the signal from the Input Turbine Speed Sensor to monitor input turbine or input shaft speed. And it uses the signal from the Counter Gear Speed Sensor to monitor counter gear or output shaft speed. The PCM constantly compares these two speeds to its map (program) for the transaxle in order to determine shift scheduling, Torque Converter Clutch (TCC) engagement scheduling and optimal hydraulic pressure for various hydraulically-controlled components inside the transaxle. Both of the speed sensors are located on top of the transaxle. The Input Turbine Speed Sensor is unit located on the left (driver's) end of the transaxle; the Counter Gear Speed Sensor is located to the right of the Input Turbine Speed Sensor, closer to the bellhousing.

18   **Vapour pressure sensor** - The vapour pressure sensor is a component of the Evaporative Emission Control (EVAP) system. It's located on top of the fuel tank. The vapour pressure sensor monitors the pressure of fuel vapours inside the tank. When the vapour pressure exceeds the upper threshold, the vapour pressure sensor signals the PCM, which opens the Vacuum Switching Valve (VSV) for the pressure switching valve, allowing the fuel vapours to migrate to the EVAP canister, where they are stored until they're purged.

Powertrain Control Module (PCM)

19   Based on the information that it receives from the information sensors described above, the PCM adjusts fuel injector pulse width, idle speed, ignition spark advance, ignition coil dwell, EVAP canister purge operation and a lot of other things. It does so by controlling the *output actuators*. The following list provides a brief description of the function, location and operation of each of the important output actuators.

Output actuators

20   **Camshaft timing oil control valve** - The camshaft timing oil control valve is a component of the Variable Valve Timing-intelligent (VVT-i) system, which alters valve timing in response to engine operating conditions in order to improve torque, increase

fuel economy and decrease emissions. The intake valves are advanced or retarded by a hydraulic device known as the VVT-i controller, which is mounted on the end of each camshaft. The camshaft timing oil control valve houses a spool valve that controls the flow of oil to the advance or retard side of the controller on each intake cam. A coil inside the oil control valve controls the spool valve. There are two camshaft timing oil control valves on 3MZ-FE engines, one on each intake camshaft. On 2GR-FE engines, there is one on each camshaft (four in total). For more information about the VVT-i system, refer to the Engine chapters (see Chapter 2A) or (see Chapter 2B).

21   **Canister purge valve** - The canister purge valve is a component of the Evaporative Emission Control (EVAP) system. When the engine is cold or still warming up, no captive fuel vapours are allowed to escape from the EVAP canister. After the engine is warmed up, the PCM energises the canister purge valve, which regulates the flow of these vapours from the canister to the intake manifold. The rate of vapour flow is regulated by the purge valve in response to commands from the PCM, which controls the duty cycle of the valve. On models with the 3MZ-FE engine, the valve is mounted to the rear fuel rail. On models with the 2GR-FE engine, the valve is mounted above the starter motor. For more information about the EVAP system, see Section 19.

22   **Electronic Throttle Body** - The Electronic Throttle Control System-intelligent (ETCS-i) does not use a conventional throttle cable-actuated throttle body. Instead, they use an electronic throttle body that is controlled by the Powertrain Control Module (PCM). The throttle plate inside the throttle body is opened and closed by a PCM-controlled throttle motor. There is no cruise control cable and no Idle Air Control (IAC) valve. Cruise control and idle speed are handled electronically by the PCM. The electronic throttle body has a Throttle Position (TP) sensor, but it's an integral part of the throttle body and cannot be replaced separately from the throttle body assembly. The PCM determines the correct throttle plate angle by processing the input signal from the throttle pedal position sensor the throttle pedal (see throttle pedal position sensor in paragraph 6).

23   **Fuel injectors** - The PCM opens the fuel injectors sequentially (in firing order sequence). The PCM also controls the injector pulse width, which is the interval of time during which each injector is open. The pulse width of an injector (measured in milliseconds) determines the amount of fuel delivered. For more information on the fuel system and the fuel injectors, including injector replacement, refer to Chapter 4.

24   **EFI relay** - The EFI relay, when grounded by the PCM, provides battery voltage to various powertrain management components. On models with the 2GR-FE engine, the EFI relay is contained within the combined relay unit. test procedures for these models are covered in the Fuel and Exhaust Systems chapter (see Chapter 4) under the Fuel Pump/Fuel Pressure - Check heading.

24   **A/F sensor relay** - The A/F sensor relay, when grounded by the PCM, provides battery voltage to the heater circuits for each A/F ratio - or upstream oxygen - sensor. On models with the 2GR-FE engine, the A/F sensor relay is contained within the combined relay unit. Test procedures for these models are covered in the Fuel and Exhaust Systems chapter (see Chapter 4) under the Fuel Pump/Fuel Pressure - Check heading.

25   **Circuit opening relay** - The circuit opening relay, when grounded by the PCM, provides battery voltage to the fuel pump. The circuit opening relay locations and description are shown in the Fuel and Exhaust Systems chapter (see Chapter 4). On models with the 2GR-FE engine, the circuit opening relay is contained within the combined relay unit. Test procedures for these models are covered in the Fuel and Exhaust Systems chapter (see Chapter 4) under the Fuel Pump/Fuel Pressure - Check heading.

26   **Fuel pump relay** - Fitted to models with the 2GR-FE engine, is mounted in the engine compartment fuse and relay box. On these models, the fuel pump operates at two speeds. The low speed is used for low engine speeds and idle and is achieved by energising the fuel pump relay. This relay will direct power from the circuit opening relay through the fuel pump relay and then through a resistor before reaching the fuel pump. This slows the operation of the fuel pump down and reduces fuel pressure, helping with emissions. When higher engine speeds or loads are needed, the PCM de-energises the fuel pump relay and full battery voltage flows from a second circuit, bypassing the resistor to the fuel pump, increasing the fuel pump speed and pressure.

27   **Ignition coil(s)** - All ignition coils used by the vehicles covered in this manual are the coil-over-plug type. Each spark plug has its own coil, mounted directly over the plug. There are no spark plug wires, and there is no separate ignition control module. The Powertrain Control Module (PCM) handles this function. For more information about the ignition coils, refer to the Engine Electrical chapter (see Chapter 5).

28   **Intake air control valve(s)** - The intake air control valve is contained within the upper intake manifold. It is a PCM controlled valve that will redirect the intake air path within the manifold to increase torque at low speed and reduce engine noise at high speed. On models with the 3MZ-FE engine, it is a vacuum operated unit with a vacuum switching valve allowing vacuum to flow to the valve when commanded by the PCM.

On models with the 2GR-FE engine, the valve is electronically controlled and is accompanied by a valve at the air filter housing that also redirects the flow of air through either of two paths to improve airflow into eh engine at different engine speeds. This valve is vacuum controlled with a vacuum switching valve operated by the PCM.

Obtaining trouble codes

Refer to illustration 2.31

30   The PCM illuminates the CHECK ENGINE light (also called the Malfunction Indicator Light) on the dash if it recognises a component fault for two consecutive drive cycles. It will continue to turn on the light until the PCM does not detect any malfunction for three or more consecutive drive cycles.

31   To extract the Diagnostic Trouble Codes (DTCs) you will need an OBD-II scan tool **(see illustration 2.2)**. Plug the scan tool into the PCM's data link connector **(see illustration)**, which is located under the steering column.

32   With the scan tool connected, follow the instructions included with the scan tool to extract all the diagnostic codes.

2.31 The 16-pin Data Link Connector (DLC) is located under the steering column

Information Sensors

Accelerator Pedal Position (APP) sensor - as you press the accelerator pedal, the APP sensor alters its voltage signal to the PCM in proportion to the angle of the pedal, and the PCM commands a motor inside the throttle body to open or close the throttle plate accordingly

Camshaft Position (CMP) sensor - produces a signal that the PCM uses to identify the number 1 cylinder and to time the firing sequence of the fuel injectors

Crankshaft Position (CKP) sensor - produces a signal that the PCM uses to calculate engine speed and crankshaft position, which enables it to synchronize ignition timing with fuel injector timing, and to detect misfires

Engine Coolant Temperature (ECT) sensor - a thermistor (temperature-sensitive variable resistor) that sends a voltage signal to the PCM, which uses this data to determine the temperature of the engine coolant

Fuel tank pressure sensor - measures the fuel tank pressure and controls fuel tank pressure by signaling the EVAP system to purge the fuel tank vapors when the pressure becomes excessive

Intake Air Temperature (IAT) sensor - monitors the temperature of the air entering the engine and sends a signal to the PCM to determine injector pulse-width (the duration of each injector's on-time) and to adjust spark timing (to prevent spark knock)

Knock sensor - a piezoelectric crystal that oscillates in proportion to engine vibration which produces a voltage output that is monitored by the PCM. This retards the ignition timing when the oscillation exceeds a certain threshold

Manifold Absolute Pressure (MAP) sensor - monitors the pressure or vacuum inside the intake manifold. The PCM uses this data to determine engine load so that it can alter the ignition advance and fuel enrichment

Mass Air Flow (MAF) sensor - measures the amount of intake air drawn into the engine. It uses a hot-wire sensing element to measure the amount of air entering the engine

Oxygen sensors - generates a small variable voltage signal in proportion to the difference between the oxygen content in the exhaust stream and the oxygen content in the ambient air. The PCM uses this information to maintain the proper air/fuel ratio. A second oxygen sensor monitors the efficiency of the catalytic converter

Throttle Position (TP) sensor - a potentiometer that generates a voltage signal that varies in relation to the opening angle of the throttle plate inside the throttle body. Works with the PCM and other sensors to calculate injector pulse width (the duration of each injector's on-time)

Photos courtesy of Wells Manufacturing, except APP and MAF sensors.

Diagnostic Trouble Codes

Code	Setting parameters
P0010	Intake variable cam timing solenoid short or open circuit - Bank 1; Variable cam timing circuit at PCM does not alter when solenoid circuit is switched On or Off.
P0011	Intake variable cam timing solenoid over-advanced - Bank 1; Actual valve timing is over-advanced and PCM cannot retard timing.
P0012	Intake variable cam timing solenoid over-retarded - Bank 1; Actual valve timing is over-retarded and PCM cannot advance timing.
P0013	Exhaust variable cam timing solenoid short or open circuit - Bank 1; Variable cam timing circuit at PCM does not alter when solenoid circuit is switched On or Off.
P0014	Exhaust variable cam timing solenoid over-advanced - Bank 1; Actual valve timing is over-advanced and PCM cannot retard timing.
P0015	Exhaust variable cam timing solenoid over-retarded - Bank 1; Actual valve timing is over-retarded and PCM cannot advance timing.
P0016	Valve timing out of sequence - Bank 1, Sensor 1; Camshaft position sensor and crankshaft position sensor signals are indicating that cam timing is out.
P0017	Valve timing out of sequence - Bank 1, Sensor 2; Camshaft position sensor and crankshaft position sensor signals are indicating that cam timing is out.
P0018	Valve timing out of sequence - Bank 2, Sensor 1; Camshaft position sensor and crankshaft position sensor signals are indicating that cam timing is out.
P0019	Valve timing out of sequence - Bank 2, Sensor 2; Camshaft position sensor and crankshaft position sensor signals are indicating that cam timing is out.
P0020	Intake variable cam timing solenoid short or open circuit - Bank 2; Variable cam timing circuit at PCM does not alter when solenoid circuit is switched On or Off.
P0021	Intake variable cam timing solenoid over-advanced - Bank 2; Actual valve timing is over-advanced and PCM cannot retard timing.
P0022	Intake variable cam timing solenoid over-retarded - Bank 2; Actual valve timing is over-retarded and PCM cannot advance timing.
P0023	Exhaust variable cam timing solenoid short or open circuit - Bank 2; Variable cam timing circuit at PCM does not alter when solenoid circuit is switched On or Off.

Code	Setting parameters
P0024	Exhaust variable cam timing solenoid over-advanced - Bank 2; Actual valve timing is over-advanced and PCM cannot retard timing.
P0025	Exhaust variable cam timing solenoid over-retarded - Bank 2; Actual valve timing is over-retarded and PCM cannot advance timing.
P0031	Oxygen sensor heater circuit low -Bank 1, Sensor 1; Heater driver circuit remains low, regardless whether heater circuit is switched On or Off.
P0032	Oxygen sensor heater circuit high - Bank 1, Sensor 1; Heater driver circuit remains high, regardless whether heater circuit is switched On or Off.
P0037	Oxygen sensor heater circuit low -
P0038	Oxygen sensor heater circuit high - Bank 1, Sensor 2; Heater driver circuit remains high, regardless whether heater circuit is switched On or Off.
P0051	Oxygen sensor heater circuit low - Bank 2, Sensor 1; Heater driver circuit remains low, regardless whether heater circuit is switched On or Off.
P0052	Oxygen sensor heater circuit high - Bank 2, Sensor 1; Heater driver circuit remains high, regardless whether heater circuit is switched On or Off.
P0057	Oxygen sensor heater circuit low - Bank 2, Sensor 2; Heater driver circuit remains low, regardless whether heater circuit is switched On or Off.
P0058	Oxygen sensor heater circuit high - Bank 2, Sensor 2; Heater driver circuit remains high, regardless whether heater circuit is switched On or Off.
P0100	Air flow sensor volume signal out of range; Air volume signal below minimum or above maximum signal operating range.
P0101	Air flow sensor volume signal error; Air volume signal within limits, but inconsistent with operating conditions indicated by other sensor inputs.
P0102	Air flow sensor volume signal low; Air volume signal below minimum signal operating voltage range during key On engine running (KOER) test.
P0103	Air flow sensor volume signal high; Air volume signal above maximum signal operating range during self test.
P0110	Intake air temperature sensor signal error - Bank 1, Sensor 1; Intake air temperature signal inconsistent with operating conditions indicated by other sensor inputs.

Code	Setting parameters
P0111	Intake air temperature sensor signal out of range - Bank 1, Sensor 1; Intake air temperature signal below minimum or above maximum signal operating voltage range.
P0112	Intake air temperature sensor signal low - Bank 1, Sensor 1; Intake air temperature signal indicating approximately 140°C (short circuit).
P0113	Intake air temperature sensor signal high - Bank 1, Sensor 1; Intake air temperature signal indicating approximately -40°C (open circuit).
P0115	Coolant temperature sensor signal out of range - Sensor 1; Coolant temperature signal below minimum or above maximum signal operating voltage range.
P0116	Coolant temperature sensor signal error - Sensor 1; Coolant temperature signal inconsistent with operating conditions indicated by other sensor inputs.
P0117	Coolant temperature sensor signal low - Sensor 1; Coolant temperature signal below minimum signal operating voltage range during key On engine running (KOER) test.
P0118	Coolant temperature sensor signal high - Sensor 1; Coolant temperature signal above maximum signal operating range during self test.
P011B	Coolant temperature and intake air temperature sensor signal mismatch; PCM detects an excessive difference between coolant temperature sensor signal and intake air temperature sensor signal.
P0120	TPS signal error - Sensor 1; Throttle position sensor (TPS) signal inconsistent with operating conditions indicated by other sensor inputs.
P0121	TPS signal out of range - Sensor 1; Throttle position sensor (TPS) signal below minimum or above maximum signal operating voltage range.
P0122	TPS signal low - Sensor 1; Throttle position sensor (TPS) signal below minimum signal is consistently below minimum signal operating voltage range during self test.
P0123	TPS signal - high - Sensor 1; Throttle position sensor (TPS) signal above maximum signal operating range during self test.
P0125	Coolant temperature, insufficient temperature for closed loop fuel control; Excessive time taken to enter closed loop fuel control, due to insufficient coolant temperature signal increase.
P0128	Cooling system not reaching temperature to allow thermostat to open; According to signals from coolant temperature sensor, engine not reaching temperature high enough to open thermostat.

Code	Setting parameters
P0136	Oxygen sensor signal error - Bank 1, Sensor 2; Oxygen sensor signal remains high (rich) or low (lean) or signal only changes by a small amount.
P0137	Oxygen sensor signal low - Bank 1, Sensor 2; Oxygen sensor signal is constantly low, indicating lean mixture.
P0138	Oxygen sensor signal high - Bank 1, Sensor 2; Oxygen sensor signal is constantly high, indicating rich mixture.
P0139	Oxygen sensor signal slow to respond - Bank 1, Sensor 2; Oxygen sensor signal takes too long to change from low (lean) to high (rich), or high to low.
P013A	Oxygen sensor signal slow to change from rich to lean - Bank 1, Sensor 2; Oxygen sensor signal takes too long to change from high (rich) to low (lean).
P013C	Oxygen sensor signal slow to change from rich to lean - Bank 2, Sensor 2; Oxygen sensor signal takes too long to change from high (rich) to low (lean).
P0141	Oxygen sensor heater circuit malfunction - Bank 1, Sensor 2; Oxygen sensor heater driver circuit does not alter when heater circuit is switched On or Off.
P0156	Oxygen sensor signal error - Bank 2, Sensor 2; Oxygen sensor signal remains high (rich) or low (lean) or signal only changes by a small amount.
P0157	Oxygen sensor signal low - Bank 2, Sensor 2; Oxygen sensor signal is constantly low, indicating lean mixture.
P0158	Oxygen sensor signal high - Bank 2, Sensor 2; Oxygen sensor signal is constantly high, indicating rich mixture.
P0159	Oxygen sensor signal slow to respond - Bank 2, Sensor 2; Oxygen sensor signal takes too long to change from low (lean) to high (rich), or high to low.
P015A	Oxygen sensor signal slow to respond - Bank 1, Sensor 1; Oxygen sensor signal takes too long to change from low (lean) to high (rich).
P015B	Oxygen sensor signal slow to respond - Bank 1, Sensor 1; Oxygen sensor signal takes too long to change from high (rich) to low (lean).
P015C	Oxygen sensor signal slow to respond - Bank 2, Sensor 1; Oxygen sensor signal takes too long to change from low (lean) to high (rich).
P015D	Oxygen sensor signal slow to respond - Bank 2, Sensor 1; Oxygen sensor signal takes too long to change from high (rich) to low (lean).

Code	Setting parameters
P0161	Oxygen sensor heater circuit malfunction - Bank 2, Sensor 2; Oxygen sensor heater driver circuit does not alter when heater circuit is switched On or Off.
P0171	System too lean - Bank 1; PCM has reached long and short term fuel trim limits, but oxygen sensor signal still indicating lean mixture.
P0172	System too rich - Bank 1; PCM has reached long and short term fuel trim limits, but oxygen sensor signal still indicating rich mixture.
P0174	System too lean - Bank 2; PCM has reached long and short term fuel trim limits, but oxygen sensor signal still indicating lean mixture.
P0175	System too rich - Bank 2; PCM has reached long and short term fuel trim limits, but oxygen sensor signal still indicating rich mixture.
P0220	TPS signal error - Sensor 2; No 2 TPS signal inconsistent with operating conditions indicated by other sensor inputs.
P0222	TPS signal low - Sensor 2; No 2 TPS signal below approximately 0.2 volts.
P0223	TPS signal high - Sensor 2; No 2 TPS signal above approximately 4.8 volts.
P0230	Fuel pump relay driver circuit malfunction; Fuel pump relay driver circuit at PCM does not alter when relay circuit is switched On or Off.
P0300	Random multiple cylinder misfire detected; Sudden change in crankshaft and camshaft position sensor signals indicating a random cylinder misfire.
P0301	No 1 cylinder misfire detected; Sudden change in crankshaft and camshaft position sensor signals indicating a cylinder misfire at No 1 cylinder.
P0302	No 2 cylinder misfire detected; Sudden change in crankshaft and camshaft position sensor signals indicating a cylinder misfire at No 2 cylinder.
P0303	No 3 cylinder misfire detected; Sudden change in crankshaft and camshaft position sensor signals indicating a cylinder misfire at No 3 cylinder.
P0304	No 4 cylinder misfire detected; Sudden change in crankshaft and camshaft position sensor signals indicating a cylinder misfire at No 4 cylinder.
P0305	No 5 cylinder misfire detected; Sudden change in crankshaft and camshaft position sensor signals indicating a cylinder misfire at No 5 cylinder.
P0306	No 6 cylinder misfire detected; Sudden change in crankshaft and camshaft position sensor signals indicating a cylinder misfire at No 6 cylinder.

Code	Setting parameters
P0325	Knock sensor signal missing - Bank 1, Sensor 1; Knock sensor signal missing.
P0327	Knock sensor signal low - Bank 1, Sensor 1; Knock sensor signal is excessively low.
P0328	Knock sensor signal high - Bank 1, Sensor 1; Knock sensor signal remains high.
P0330	Knock sensor signal missing - Bank 2, Sensor 2; Knock sensor signal missing.
P0332	Knock sensor signal low - Bank 2, Sensor 2; Knock sensor signal is excessively low.
P0333	Knock sensor signal high - Bank 2, Sensor 2; Knock sensor signal remains high.
P0335	Crankshaft position sensor signal error or missing - Bank 1, Sensor 1; No crankshaft position sensor signal received at PCM while cranking engine or after engine has started.
P0336	Crankshaft position sensor signal out of range - Bank 1, Sensor 1; Pattern of crankshaft position sensor signal changes, or change in time period between missing tooth portion of crankshaft position sensor signal and camshaft position sensor signal.
P0339	Crankshaft position sensor signal intermittent - Bank 1, Sensor 1; Crankshaft position sensor signal missing while engine speed is above 1,000 rpm.
P0340	Camshaft position sensor signal error - Bank 1, Sensor 1; Camshaft position sensor signal not synchronised with crankshaft position sensor signal.
P0342	Camshaft position sensor signal low - Bank 1, Sensor 1; PCM receives crankshaft position sensor signals, but no camshaft position sensor signal.
P0343	Camshaft position sensor signal high - Bank 1, Sensor 1; Camshaft position sensor signal circuit remains high.
P0345	Camshaft position sensor signal error - Bank 2, Sensor 1; Camshaft position sensor signal not synchronised with crankshaft position sensor signal.
P0347	Camshaft position sensor signal low - Bank 2, Sensor 1; PCM receives crankshaft position sensor signals, but no camshaft position sensor signal.
P0348	Camshaft position sensor signal high - Bank 2, Sensor 1; Camshaft position sensor signal circuit remains high.
P0351	No 1 ignition coil feedback signal; Ignition feedback signal from No 1 ignition coil missing.
P0352	No 2 ignition coil feedback signal; Ignition feedback signal from No 2 ignition coil missing.

Code	Setting parameters
P0353	No 3 ignition coil feedback signal; Ignition feedback signal from No 3 ignition coil missing.
P0354	No 4 ignition coil feedback signal; Ignition feedback signal from No 4 ignition coil missing.
P0355	No 5 ignition coil feedback signal; Ignition feedback signal from No 5 ignition coil missing.
P0356	No 6 ignition coil feedback signal; Ignition feedback signal from No 6 ignition coil missing.
P0365	Camshaft position sensor signal error - Bank 1, Sensor 2; Camshaft position sensor signal not synchronised with crankshaft position sensor signal.
P0367	Camshaft position sensor signal low - Bank 1, Sensor 2; PCM receives crankshaft position sensor signals, but no camshaft position sensor signal.
P0368	Camshaft position sensor signal high - Bank 1, Sensor 2; Camshaft position sensor signal circuit remains high.
P0390	Camshaft position sensor signal error - Bank 2, Sensor 2; Camshaft position sensor signal not synchronised with crankshaft position sensor signal.
P0392	Camshaft position sensor signal low - Bank 2, Sensor 2; PCM receives crankshaft position sensor signals, but no camshaft position sensor signal.
P0393	Camshaft position sensor signal high - Bank 2, Sensor 2; Camshaft position sensor signal circuit remains high.
P0420	Catalyst operating efficiency below threshold - Bank 1; Catalyst continually running below efficiency threshold.
P0430	Catalyst operating efficiency below threshold - Bank 2; Catalyst continually running below efficiency threshold.
P043E	Evaporative emission system leak -detection reference orifice low flow; Evaporative emission system flow sensors have detected a low flow vapour leak in the system.
P043F	Evaporative emission system leak -detection reference orifice high flow; Evaporative emission system flow sensors have detected a high flow vapour leak in the system.
P0441	Evaporative emission system purge flow incorrect; Purge vacuum flow from canister purge solenoid to charcoal canister below minimum or above maximum signal operating voltage range.
P0442	Evaporative emission system small leak; Fuel tank pressure signal is not indicating a significant tank pressure change when canister purge solenoid is energised.

Code	Setting parameters
P0443	Canister purge solenoid circuit fault; Canister purge solenoid circuit at PCM does not alter when solenoid circuit is switched On or Off.
P0446	Evaporative emission system vent control solenoid circuit fault; Vent control solenoid circuit at PCM does not alter when solenoid circuit is switched On or Off.
P0450	Evaporative emission system pressure sensor/switch signal error; Evaporative emission system pressure signal inconsistent with operating conditions indicated by other sensor inputs.
P0451	Evaporative emission system pressure sensor/switch signal out of range; Evaporative emission system pressure signal either below minimum or above maximum signal operating voltage range.
P0452	Evaporative emission system pressure sensor/switch signal low; Evaporative emission system pressure signal below minimum signal operating range during self test.
P0453	Evaporative emission system pressure sensor/switch signal high; Evaporative emission system pressure signal above maximum signal operating range during self test.
P0455	Evaporative emission system major leak; PCM detects a major leak in evaporative emission system resulting in no flow along vacuum circuit.
P0456	Evaporative emission system minor leak; PCM detects a minor leak in evaporative emission system resulting in no flow along vacuum circuit.
P0500	Vehicle speed sensor signal missing - Sensor 1; Vehicle speed sensor signal missing while other sensors are indicating vehicle to be travelling.
P0503	Vehicle speed sensor signal high or intermittent - Sensor 1; Vehicle speed signal is high or intermittently missing or corrupt.
P0504	Stop lamp switch circuit mismatch - Sensor 1 - Sensor 2; Both pedal switch circuits to PCM have power available at same time, or are missing power at same time.
P0505	Idle speed out of range; Engine idle speed cannot be controlled by PCM.
P0560	PCM constant power supply error; PCM constant power supply is either excessively lower or higher than voltage being received at PCM ignition supply, or is missing altogether.
P0604	Internal PCM error RAM access; Internal PCM fault in Random Access Memory (RAM).
P0606	Internal PCM processor error; Code indicates an internal PCM error.

Code	Setting parameters
P0607	Internal PCM performance error; Code indicates an internal PCM error.
P0617	Starter relay circuit high; Starter relay circuit at PCM remains high regardless whether relay circuit is switched On or Off.
P0630	VIN programming error - ECM/PCM; Vehicle identification number (VIN) not programmed into PCM/ECM, or doesn't match TCM.
P0657	Actuator power supply circuit malfunction - Circuit A; Current draw on actuator power supply circuit at PCM does not alter when PCM commands shift solenoids or actuators to energise.
P0660	Variable intake air solenoid circuit open - Bank 1; PCM detects an open circuit in variable intake air solenoid circuit.
P0710	TFT sensor signal error - Sensor 1; Transmission fluid temperature (TFT) signal inconsistent with operating conditions indicated by other sensor inputs.
P0711	TFT sensor signal out of range - Sensor 1; Transmission fluid temperature (TFT) signal is above maximum or below minimum signal operating voltage range during self test.
P0712	TFT sensor signal low - Sensor 1; Transmission fluid temperature (TFT) signal below minimum signal operating range during self test.
P0713	TFT sensor signal high - Sensor 1; Transmission fluid temperature (TFT) signal above maximum signal operating range during self test.
P0717	Turbine/input shaft speed signal missing - Sensor 1; PCM/TCM receiving transmission speed sensor signal from output shaft speed sensor, but no signal from turbine/input shaft speed sensor.
P0724	Brake/stop lamp switch signal high - Sensor 2; Brake pedal signal is constantly high.
P0741	Torque converter/Damper clutch solenoid stuck Off; Torque converter/damper clutch solenoid circuit stuck in Off position.
P0746	Pressure control solenoid A solenoid stuck Off; Pressure control solenoid A circuit stuck in Off position.
P0748	Pressure control solenoid A solenoid circuit malfunction; Pressure control solenoid A circuit at PCM does not alter when solenoid circuit is switched On or Off.
P0750	Shift solenoid A circuit open; PCM detects an open circuit on shift solenoid A circuit.
P0753	Shift solenoid A circuit malfunction; Shift solenoid A circuit at PCM does not alter when solenoid circuit is switched On or Off.

Code	Setting parameters
P0755	Shift solenoid B circuit open; PCM detects an open circuit on shift solenoid B circuit.
P0758	Shift solenoid B circuit malfunction; Shift solenoid B circuit at PCM does not alter when solenoid circuit is switched On or Off.
P0765	Shift solenoid D circuit open; PCM detects an open circuit on the shift solenoid D circuit.
P0766	Shift solenoid D stuck Off; Shift solenoid D circuit stuck in Off position.
P0768	Shift solenoid D circuit malfunction; Shift solenoid D circuit at PCM does not alter when solenoid circuit is switched On or Off.
P0770	Shift solenoid E circuit open; PCM detects an open circuit on the shift solenoid E circuit.
P0773	Shift solenoid E circuit malfunction; Shift solenoid E circuit at PCM does not alter when solenoid circuit is switched On or Off.
P0776	Shift solenoid B stuck Off; Shift solenoid B circuit stuck in Off position.
P0778	Shift solenoid B circuit malfunction; Shift solenoid B circuit at PCM does not alter when solenoid circuit is switched On or Off.
P0793	Counter gear speed signal missing - Sensor 1; Counter gear speed sensor missing while output shaft speed sensor indicating vehicle movement.
P0982	Shift solenoid D circuit low; Shift solenoid D circuit remains low, regardless whether solenoid circuit is switched On or Off.
P0983	Shift solenoid D circuit high; Shift solenoid D circuit remains high, regardless whether solenoid circuit is switched On or Off.
P1660	Air intake control valve circuit malfunction; PCM detects an open or short circuit in the air intake control valve circuit with ignition On.
P2102	Throttle control motor circuit low - Circuit 1 or A; Throttle control motor circuit at PCM remains low, regardless whether motor circuit is switched On or Off.
P2103	Throttle control motor circuit high - Circuit 1 or A; Throttle control motor circuit at PCM remains high, regardless whether motor circuit is switched On or Off.
P2111	Throttle control motor stuck open; TPS signals indicate throttle stuck open and PCM cannot control it with throttle control motor.
P2112	Throttle control motor stuck closed; TPS signals indicate throttle stuck closed and PCM cannot control it with throttle control motor.
P2118	Throttle control motor power supply missing; Throttle control motor power supply from PCM missing.

Code	Setting parameters
P2119	Throttle control motor throttle position cannot be controlled; Throttle angle varying from PCM desired throttle position.
P2120	Throttle pedal position sensor signal error - Circuit D (Sensor 1); Throttle pedal position sensor signal inconsistent with operating conditions indicated by other sensor inputs.
P2121	Throttle pedal position sensor signal out of range - Circuit D (Sensor 1); Throttle pedal position sensor signal is fluctuating rapidly and is inconsistent with operating conditions indicated by other sensor inputs.
P2122	Throttle pedal position sensor signal low - Circuit D (Sensor 1); Throttle pedal position sensor main signal indicating a voltage less than 0.2 volts for more than 1 second.
P2123	Throttle pedal position sensor signal high - Circuit D (Sensor 1); Throttle pedal position sensor signal remains above 4.5 volts for more than 1 second when other sensor inputs indicate it should be lower.
P2125	Throttle pedal position sensor signal error - Circuit E (Sensor 2); Throttle pedal position sensor signal inconsistent with operating conditions indicated by other sensor inputs.
P2127	Throttle pedal position sensor signal low - Circuit E (Sensor 2); Throttle pedal position sensor main signal indicating a voltage less than 0.2 volts for more than 1 second.
P2128	Throttle pedal position sensor signal high - Circuit E (Sensor 2); Throttle pedal position sensor signal remains above 4.5 volts for more than 1 second when other sensor inputs indicate it should be lower.
P2135	Throttle pedal position sensor signal mismatch between sensors 1 and 2; PCM detects too much difference between signals from sensor 1 or A and sensor 2 or B throttle pedal position sensor signals.
P2138	Throttle pedal position sensor signal mismatch between sensors 1 and 2; PCM detects too much difference between signals from sensor 1 or D and sensor 2 or E throttle pedal position sensor signals.
P2195	Oxygen sensor signal stuck lean - Bank 1, Sensor 1; Oxygen sensor signal remains in the low (lean) region, during power enrichment mode.
P2196	Oxygen sensor signal stuck rich - Bank 1, Sensor 1; Oxygen sensor signal remains in the high (rich) region, during fuel cut-off mode.
P2197	Oxygen sensor signal stuck lean - Bank 2, Sensor 1; Oxygen sensor signal remains in the low (lean) region, during power enrichment mode.

Code	Setting parameters
P2198	Oxygen sensor signal stuck rich - Bank 2, Sensor 1; Oxygen sensor signal remains in the high (rich) region, during fuel cut-off mode.
P2237	Oxygen sensor high circuit out of range - Bank 1, Sensor 1; Oxygen sensor high circuit signal is above maximum or below minimum signal operating voltage range during self test.
P2238	Oxygen sensor high circuit low - Bank 1, Sensor 1; Oxygen sensor high circuit is consistently below minimum signal operating voltage range during self test.
P2239	Oxygen sensor high circuit high - Bank 1, Sensor 1; Oxygen sensor high circuit is consistently above maximum signal operating voltage range during self test.
P2240	Oxygen sensor high circuit open - Bank 1, Sensor 1; PCM detects an open oxygen sensor high circuit.
P2241	Oxygen sensor high circuit low - Bank 2, Sensor 1; Oxygen sensor high circuit is consistently below minimum signal operating voltage range during self test.
P2242	Oxygen sensor high circuit high - Bank 2, Sensor 1; Oxygen sensor high circuit is consistently above maximum signal operating voltage range during self test.
P2252	Oxygen sensor low circuit low - Bank 1, Sensor 1; Oxygen sensor low circuit is consistently below minimum signal operating voltage range during self test.
P2253	Oxygen sensor low circuit high - Bank 1, Sensor 1; Oxygen sensor low circuit is consistently above maximum signal operating voltage range during self test.
P2255	Oxygen sensor low circuit low - Bank 2, Sensor 1; Oxygen sensor low circuit is consistently below minimum signal operating voltage range during self test.
P2256	Oxygen sensor low circuit high - Bank 2, Sensor 1; Oxygen sensor low circuit is consistently above maximum signal operating voltage range during self test.
P2A00	Oxygen sensor signal out of range - Bank 1, Sensor 1; Oxygen sensor signal is above maximum or below minimum signal operating voltage range during self test.
P2A03	Oxygen sensor signal out of range - Bank 2, Sensor 1; Oxygen sensor signal is above maximum or below minimum signal operating voltage range during self test.

3.2 The throttle pedal position sensor forms part of the throttle pedal assembly

4.3a Front bank camshaft position sensor location - 3MZ-FE engine

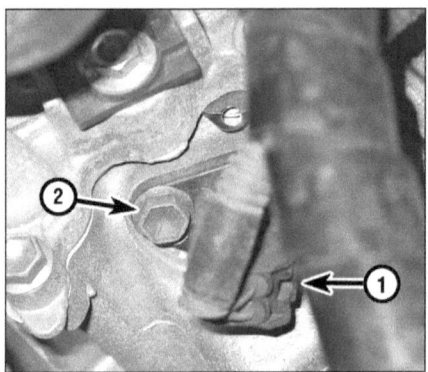

4.3b The CMP sensor the rear cylinder head is accessible through the left wheel housing after you remove the wheel. To remove the sensor, depress the release tab (1) and disconnect the electrical connector, then remove the sensor mounting bolt (2)

3   Throttle pedal position sensor - replacement

Refer to illustration 3.2

Note: *The throttle pedal position sensor is located at the upper end of the throttle pedal assembly. The throttle pedal position sensor and the throttle pedal are removed as a single assembly.*

1   Disconnect the negative (-) battery terminal (see Chapter 5).
2   Disconnect the throttle pedal position sensor electrical connector.
3   Remove the throttle pedal mounting bolts and remove the pedal assembly.
4   Installation is the reverse of removal. Be sure to tighten the throttle pedal assembly mounting bolts securely.

4   Camshaft Position (CMP) sensor - replacement

Refer to illustrations 4.3a, 4.3b, 4.3c and 4.4

Note: *There are two CMP sensors on 3MZ-FE engines, one for each intake camshaft. The CMP sensors are located on the left (passenger) end of the cylinder heads. Refer to Engine (see Chapter 2A) for more information*

Note: *On 2GR-FE engines, four VVT sensors are used to monitor the positions of the camshafts (intake and exhaust). Refer to Engine (see Chapter 2B) for more information.*

1   Disconnect the negative (-) battery terminal (see Chapter 5).
2   Remove the engine cover.

Note: *On 2GR-FE engines, pull up on the front side of the engine top cover to detach it*

from the two front retainers. After the front is detached, pull up on the back retainer and remove the engine cover. Do not pull up on the front and rear at the same time or the cover can be damaged.

3   Disconnect the electrical connector from the CMP sensor **(see illustrations)**.
4   Remove the CMP sensor mounting bolt **(see illustration)** and remove the sensor.
5   Installation is the reverse of removal.

5   Crankshaft Position (CKP) sensor - replacement

1   Disconnect the negative (-) battery terminal (see Chapter 5).

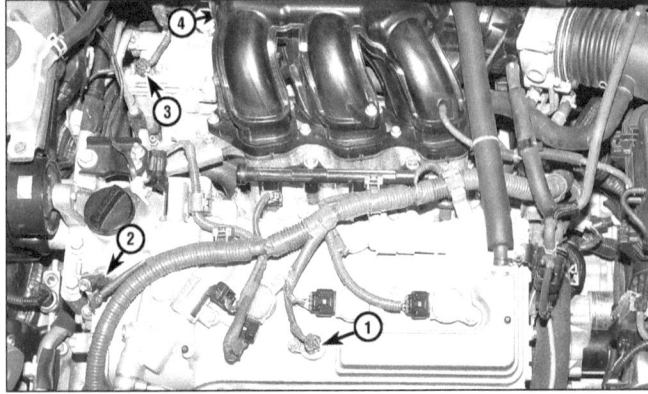

4.3c Camshaft position sensor locations - 2GR-FE engines

1   *Camshaft position (CMP) sensor - No.2 bank exhaust camshaft*
2   *Camshaft position (CMP) sensor - No.2 bank intake camshaft*
3   *Camshaft position (CMP)*

sensor - No.1 bank intake camshaft
4   *Camshaft position (CMP) sensor - No.1 bank exhaust camshaft (this is in a similar position to (1) on the rear bank*

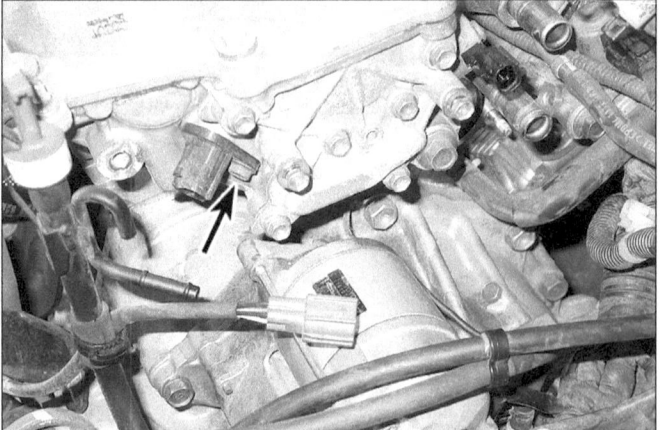

4.4 Connector removed showing the camshaft position sensor retaining bolt - 3MZ-FE engine

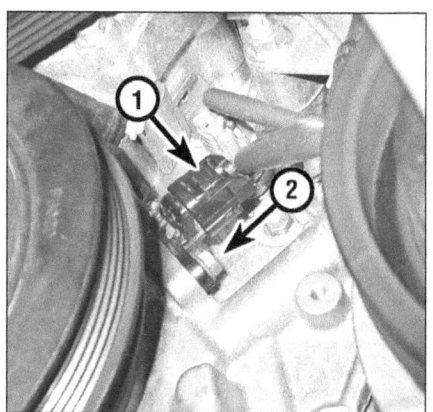

5.2 To remove the CKP sensor depress
this release tab (1) and disconnect the
electrical connector from the sensor, then
remove the sensor mounting bolt (2) -
3MZ-FE engine

3MZ-FE engine

Refer to illustration 5.2

2   Disconnect the electrical connector from
the CKP sensor **(see illustration)**.
3   Remove the CKP sensor mounting bolt
and remove the CKP sensor.
4   Installation is the reverse of removal.

2GR-FE engine

Refer to illustration 5.8

Note: *The CKP sensor is between the A/C
compressor and the engine.*

5   Remove the drivebelt (see Chapter 1).
6   Remove the alternator (see Chapter 5).
7   Remove the bolt that secures the air
conditioning suction line at the front of the
engine, disconnect the electrical connector from the air conditioning compressor and
unbolt the compressor (see Chapter 3).

Warning: *Do NOT disconnect the air
conditioning hoses from the compressor.
Move the compressor aside and support it
with wire or rope.*

8   Disconnect the CKP sensor electrical
connector **(see illustration)**.

6.3b ECT sensor location on the left end
of the engine on the coolant crossover
between the cylinder heads - 2GR-FE
engine

5.8 CKP sensor electrical connector (A)
and mounting bolt (B) - 2GR-FE engine

9   Remove the crankshaft position sensor
retaining bolt and remove the sensor.
10   Installation is the reverse of removal.
Tighten the CKP sensor retaining bolt
securely.

6   Engine Coolant Temperature (ECT) sensor - replacement

Refer to illustrations 6.3a, 6.3b and 6.5

Warning: *Wait until the engine is completely
cool before beginning this procedure.*
Caution: *Handle the ECT sensor with care. A
damaged ECT sensor will affect the operation
of the entire fuel injection system.*

1   Disconnect the negative (-) battery terminal (see Chapter 5).
2   Partially drain the cooling system (see
Chapter 1).
3   Disconnect the electrical connector from
the ECT sensor **(see illustrations)**.
4   Unscrew the ECT sensor from the water
outlet casting.
5   Seal the threads of the ECT sensor with
Teflon tape **(see illustration)**.
6   Installation is the reverse of removal.

6.5 To prevent leaks, wrap the threads of
the ECT sensor with Teflon tape

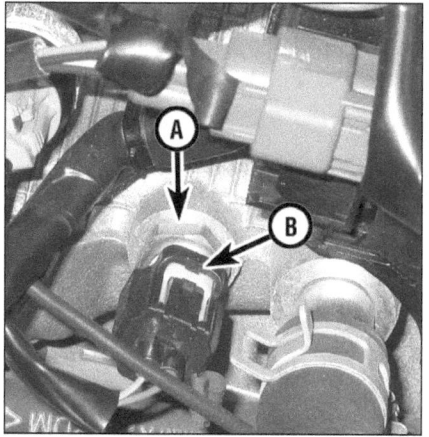

6.3a ECT sensor electrical connector (1)
and the sensor (2) - 3MZ-FE engine

Tighten the ECT sensor securely. Refill the
cooling system (see Chapter 1).

7   Knock sensor - replacement

Refer to illustration 7.4

Warning: *Wait until the engine is completely
cool before beginning this procedure.*

Note: *The knock sensors are located in the
valley between the cylinder heads. To access
them, remove the intake manifold.*

1   Disconnect the negative (-) battery terminal (see Chapter 5).
2   Remove the upper and lower intake
manifolds (see Chapter 2A) or (see Chapter 2B).
3   On models with the 3MZ-FE engine,
remove the water transfer hose **(see illustration 5.23)** (see Chapter 2A).
4   Disconnect the electrical connectors
from the knock sensors **(see illustration)**.
5   Remove the knock sensor retaining nuts.

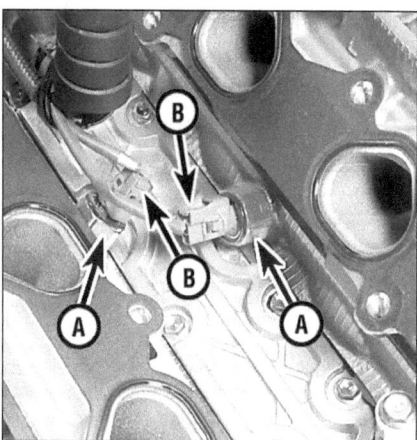

7.4 To remove the knock sensors (A),
depress the release tabs (B) on the
electrical connectors and disconnect
the connectors, then unscrew the knock
sensors (early model shown later models
are secured by a retaining nut)

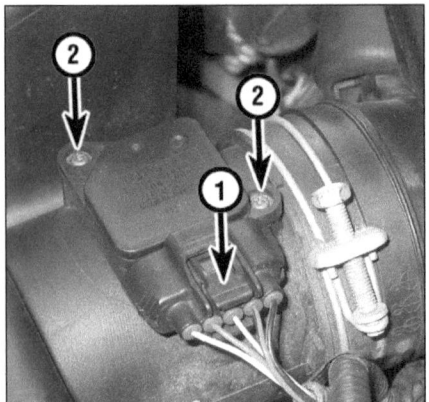

8.2 To disconnect the electrical connector from the MAF sensor, depress the release tab (1) and pull off the connector, then remove the sensor mounting screws (2) and remove the sensor from the air filter housing

6   When installing the knock sensors, angle the electrical terminals of the sensors slightly below the horizontal. Installation is otherwise the reverse of removal. Tighten the knock sensors or the knock sensor retaining nuts to the torque listed in this Chapter's Specifications.

---

8   Mass Air Flow/Intake Air Temperature (MAF/IAT) sensor - replacement

---

Refer to illustration 8.2

Note: *The MAF/IAT sensor is located on top of the air filter housing.*

1   Disconnect the negative (-) battery terminal (see Chapter 5).
2   Disconnect the electrical connector from the MAF sensor **(see illustration)**.
3   Remove the MAF sensor mounting screws and remove the MAF sensor.
4   Remove and discard the old MAF sensor O-ring.
5   Installation is the reverse of removal. Be sure to use a new O-ring.

---

9   Oxygen sensors - replacement

General information

1   Use special care when servicing an oxygen sensor:

Oxygen sensors have a permanently attached pigtail and electrical connector that can't be removed from the sensor. Damage to or removal of the pigtail or the electrical connector will ruin the sensor.

9.3a The upstream oxygen sensor (A) for the front cylinder head on a V6 engine is located on the front exhaust manifold. To find the electrical connector, trace the electrical harness to the connector (B) and disconnect it, then unscrew the sensor from the manifold - 3MZ-FE engine

Keep grease, dirt and other contaminants away from the electrical connector and the oxygen sensor.
Do not use cleaning solvents of any kind on an oxygen sensor.
Do not drop or roughly handle an oxygen sensor.

Replacement

Note: *Because it is installed in the exhaust manifold or catalytic converter, both of which contract when cool, an oxygen sensor might be very difficult to loosen when the engine is cold. Rather than risk damage to the sensor, start and run the engine for a minute or two, then shut it off. Be careful not to burn yourself during the following procedure.*

Upstream oxygen sensor

Refer to illustrations 9.3a, 9.3b and 9.5

Note: *The upstream oxygen sensors are located on the exhaust manifolds, above the Catalytic converter.*

2   Disconnect the negative (-) battery terminal (see Chapter 5).

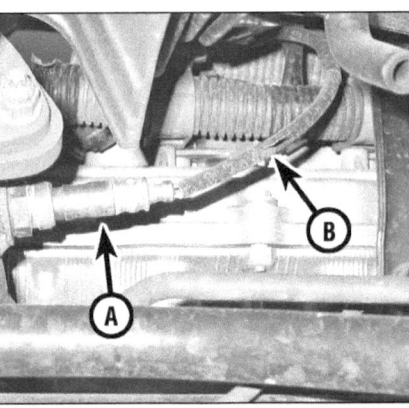

9.3b The upstream oxygen sensor (A) for the rear cylinder head on a V6 engine is located on the rear exhaust manifold. To find the electrical connector, trace the electrical harness (B) up to the connector and disconnect it, then unscrew the sensor from the manifold - 3MZ-FE engine

3   Disconnect the upstream oxygen sensor electrical connector **(see illustrations)**.
4   If you're replacing the upstream oxygen sensor for the rear exhaust manifold, raise the front of the vehicle and support it securely on jackstands (see Jacking and Towing).
5   Unscrew the oxygen sensor from the exhaust manifold **(see illustration)**.
6   Installation is the reverse of removal. Coat the threads of the oxygen sensor with anti-seize compound and tighten it to the torque listed in this Chapter's Specifications.

Downstream oxygen sensor(s)

Note: *There are two downstream oxygen sensors fitted just below the catalytic converter flanges*

7   Disconnect the negative (-) battery terminal (see Chapter 5).
8   Raise the vehicle and support it securely on jackstands (see Jacking and Towing).
9   Locate the downstream oxygen sensor and trace the sensor electrical harness to the sensor connector.
10   Unscrew the oxygen sensor.

9.5 After disconnecting the electrical connector for the downstream oxygen sensor, carefully unscrew the sensor with an oxygen sensor socket (shown) or with a large wrench (oxygen sensor sockets are handy where you don't have room to manoeuvre a wrench)

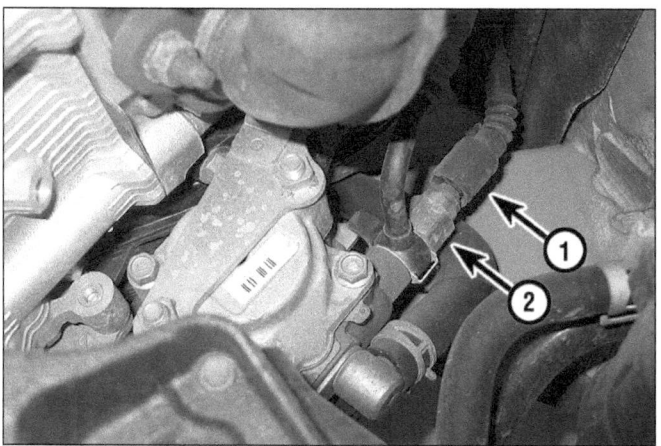

10.1 On models with the 3MZ-FE engine, the Power Steering Pressure (PSP) sensor is screwed into the banjo fitting for the high-pressure line connection at the power steering pump. To remove the PSP sensor, disconnect the electrical connector (1), then unscrew the sensor from the banjo fitting (2)

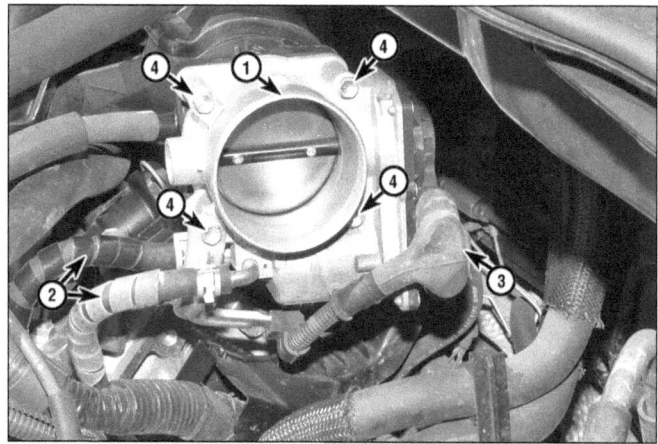

11.1 The throttle position sensor forms part of the throttle body - 2GR-FE engine shown, 3MZ-FE engine similar

1 Throttle body
2 Coolant hoses

3 Throttle control motor and position sensor electrical connector
4 Mounting bolts

11   Installation is the reverse of removal. Coat the threads of the oxygen sensor with anti-seize compound and tighten it to the torque listed in this Chapter's Specifications.

10   Power Steering Pressure (PSP) sensor - replacement

Refer to illustration 10.1

Note: *This procedure is applicable to models with the 3MZ-FE engine.*

Note: *The PSP sensor is located at the power*

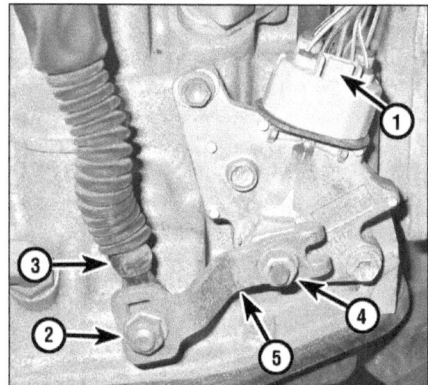

12.3 First, unplug the electrical connector and remove the control shaft lever from the TR sensor:

1   *Depress this release tab and disconnect the electrical connector from the TR sensor*
2   *Remove this nut . . .*
3   *. . . and disconnect the shift control cable from the control shaft lever*
4   *Remove this nut . . .*
5   *. . . and remove the control shaft lever from the manual valve shaft*

steering pump, screwed into the top of the banjo bolt connecting the pressure hose to the pump.

1   Disconnect the electrical connector from the PSP sensor **(see illustration)**.
2   Place a drain pan under the power steering pump, then unscrew the PSP sensor from the banjo bolt. Be prepared for some power steering fluid to leak out.
3   Installation is the reverse of removal. Check the power steering fluid level (see Chapter 1) and add fluid as necessary.

11   Throttle Position (TP) sensor - replacement

Refer to illustration 11.1

1   The throttle position sensor is an integral part of the electronic throttle body **(see illustration)**, and is not removable. It is replaced as an assembly with the throttle body (see Chapter 4).

12   Transmission Range (TR) sensor - replacement

Removal

Refer to illustrations 12.3 and 12.6

Note: *The TR sensor is located on the front of the transaxle.*

1   Disconnect the negative (-) battery terminal (see Chapter 5).
2   Raise the vehicle and place it securely on jackstands (see Jacking and Towing).
3   Disconnect the electrical connector from the TR sensor **(see illustration)**.
4   Remove the nut that secures the shift control cable to the control shaft lever and disconnect the cable from the lever.
5   Remove the nut and washer that secures the control shaft lever to the manual valve shaft and remove the control shaft lever from the manual valve shaft.

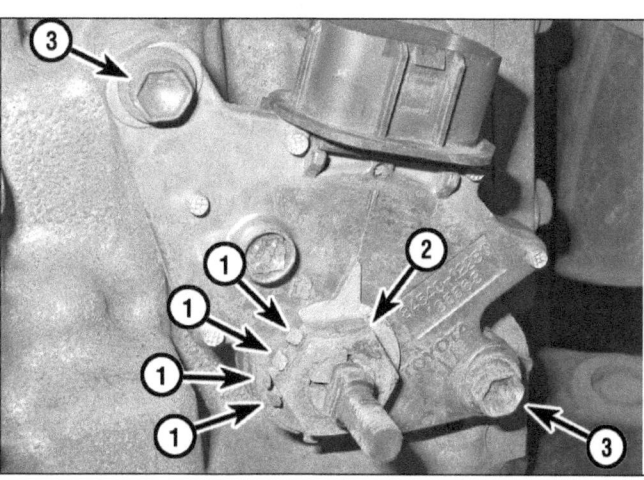

12.6 To detach the TR sensor from the transaxle:

1   *Pry open the lock plate tabs*
2   *Remove the manual valve shaft nut*
3   *Remove the TR sensor mounting bolts and remove the sensor*

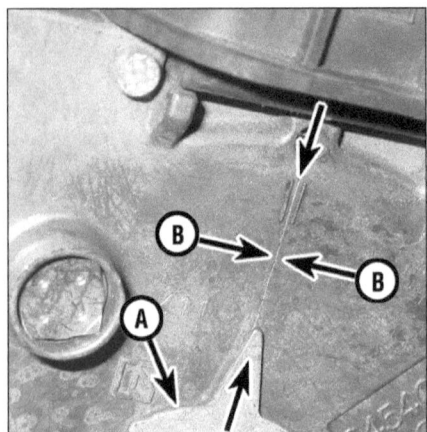

**12.11 To adjust the TR sensor, align
the pointer on the lockplate (A) with the
neutral basic line (B) on the transaxle case**

6   Pry open the lockplate tabs **(see illustration)** and remove the manual valve shaft
nut.
7   Remove the TR sensor mounting bolts
and remove the TR sensor.

Installation

Refer to illustration 12.11

8   To install the TR sensor, slide it onto the
manual valve shaft, then loosely install the
mounting bolts.
9   Install a new lockplate and the manual
valve shaft nut on the manual valve shaft.
10   Install the control shaft lever on the manual valve shaft, turn it anticlockwise through
the gears - it will click as it changes to the
next gear - until it stops, then turn it clockwise
two clicks. It's now in the Neutral position.
11   Align the pointer on the lockplate with
the Neutral basic line **(see illustration)**.
12   Install a new lockplate, install the manual
valve shaft nut, tighten it securely, then bend
the lockplate tabs up against the nut.
13   The remainder of installation is the

**13.4b To replace the Counter Gear Speed
Sensor, depress this release tab (1) and
disconnect the electrical connector, then
remove the sensor mounting bolt (2)**

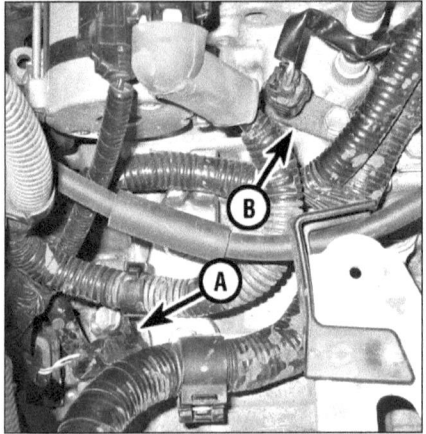

**13.3 Transmission speed
sensor locations:**

A *Input Turbine Speed Sensor*
B *Counter Gear Speed Sensor*

reverse of removal.

---

13   Transmission speed sensors - replacement

---

*Refer to illustrations 13.3, 13.4a, 13.4b
and 13.5*

Note: *The transmission speed sensors are
located on top of the transaxle. The Input
Turbine Speed Sensor is the unit located on
the left (driver's) end of the transaxle; the
Counter Gear Speed Sensor is located to the
right of the Input Turbine Speed Sensor,
closer to the bellhousing.*

1   Remove the battery (see Chapter 5).
2   Remove the air intake duct (see *Air filter housing - removal and installation* in the
Fuel and Exhaust system chapter) (see Chapter 4).
3   Locate the speed sensor that you want
to replace **(see illustration)**.
4   To replace a sensor, disconnect the

**13.5 Remove and discard the old
transmission speed sensor O-ring.
Always use a new O-ring when
installing either speed sensor**

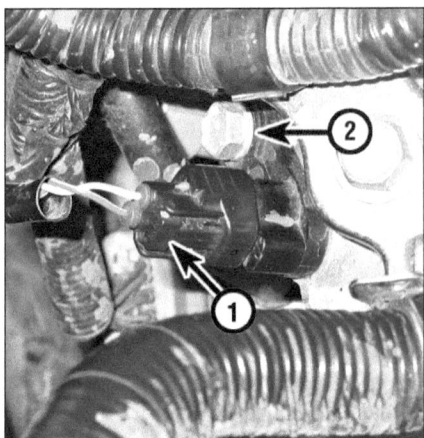

**13.4a To replace the Input Turbine Speed
Sensor, depress the release tab (1) and
disconnect the electrical connector, then
remove the sensor mounting bolt (2)**

electrical connector, then remove the sensor
mounting bolt **(see illustrations)**.
5   Remove the old sensor O-ring **(see
illustration)** and discard it.
6   Installation is the reverse of removal.

---

14   Powertrain Control Module (PCM) - replacement

Refer to illustrations 14.3 and 14.4

Warning: *The models covered by this manual
are equipped with Supplemental Restraint
systems (SRS), more commonly known as
airbags. Always disable the airbag system
before working in the vicinity of any airbag
system component to avoid the possibility of
accidental deployment of the airbag, which
could cause personal injury (see Chapter 12).*
Caution: *To avoid electrostatic discharge
damage to the PCM, handle the PCM only by
its case. Do not touch the electrical terminals
during removal and installation. If available,*

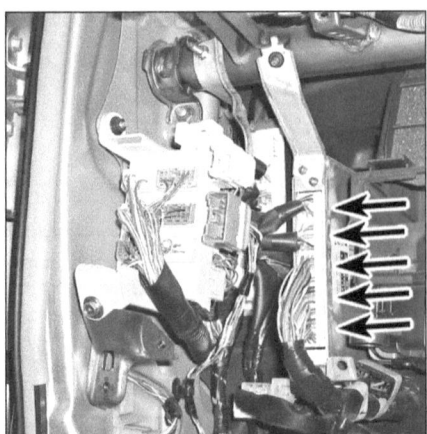

**14.3 To remove the PCM, disconnect the
electrical connectors . . .**

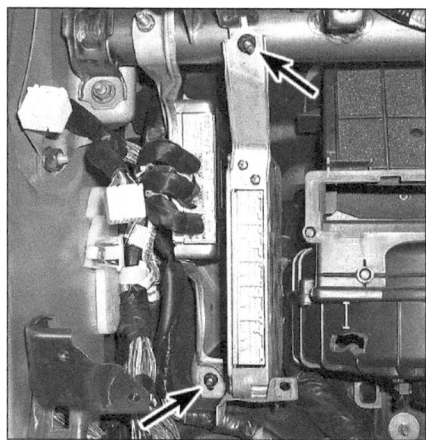

14.4 ... then remove the upper and lower mounting bracket nuts

15.2 Acoustic Control Induction System (ACIS) components - 3MZ-FE engine

A VSV for ACIS actuator
B ACIS control valve actuator
C ACIS control valve

ground yourself to the vehicle with an anti-static ground strap, available at computer supply stores.

Note: *The PCM is located inside the passenger compartment behind the glove box, to the left of the heater blower case.*

1   Disconnect the negative (-) battery terminal (see Chapter 5).
2   Remove the glove box assembly (see Chapter 11).
3   Disconnect the electrical connectors from the PCM **(see illustration)**.
4   Remove the upper and lower PCM mounting bracket nuts **(see illustration)** and carefully remove the PCM.

Caution: *Avoid any static electricity damage to the computer by grounding yourself to the body before touching the PCM and using a special anti-static pad to store the PCM on once it is removed.*

5   Installation is the reverse of removal.

15   Air Control Induction System (ACIS) - description and component replacement

Refer to illustrations 15.2 and 15.3

1   The Acoustic Control Induction System (ACIS) varies the effective length of the intake manifold runners in response to engine speed and the angle of the throttle plate inside the throttle body. This capability increases efficiency and power at low and high speeds.
2   On models with the 3MZ-FE engine, the ACIS consists of an PCM-controlled Vacuum Switching Valve (VSV), and an actuator. The VSV is a PCM controlled-device that controls the intake vacuum applied to the actuator. The actuator is a vacuum diaphragm that uses a pushrod and bellcrank to open and close the intake air control valve. The intake air control valve is fastened to the driver side of the plenum **(see illustration)**.
3   On models with the 2GR-FE engine, the ACIS consists of an electronic control valve that is actuated by the PCM **(see illustration)**.

4   On all models:
a   At low-to-medium speeds, the PCM activates the ASIC assembly, closing the intake air control valve and increasing the length of the intake manifold and improving intake efficiency.
b   At higher speeds, the PCM deactivates the ASIC assembly. The actuator opens the intake air control valve, decreasing the length of the intake manifold and improving engine power.

Component replacement

Note: *Only models with the 3MZ-FE engine have replaceable components. On models with the 2GR-FE engine, the assembly must be renewed with the upper intake manifold (see Chapter 2B).*

5   Remove the engine cover.

Vacuum Switching Valves (VSVs)
6   Disconnect the electrical connector **(see illustration 15.2)**.
7   Clearly label, then disconnect both hoses from the VSV.
8   Remove the VSV mounting bolt.

15.3 The ACIS control valve is part of the upper intake manifold and cannot be renewed separately - 2GR-FE engine

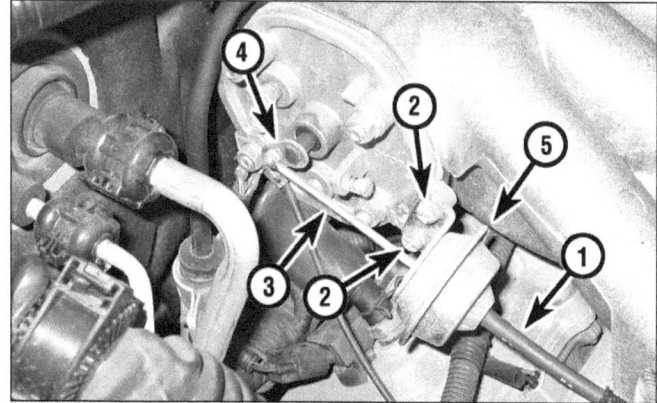

15.10 Intake manifold actuator removal and installation details:

1   Vacuum source hose (from VSV)
2   Actuator mounting bolts
3   Actuator rod
4   Actuator lever
5   ACIS control valve actuator

15.11 To disconnect the intake manifold actuator rod from the actuator lever, remove this E-clip with a small screwdriver

9　Installation is the reverse of removal.

ACIS control valve actuator

Refer to illustrations 15.10 and 15.11

10　Disconnect the vacuum hose **(see illustration)**.
11　Remove the E-clip retaining the rod to the ACIS control valve **(see illustration)** and disconnect the lever from the valve.
12　Remove the actuator mounting bolts and manoeuvre the actuator valve from the engine.
13　Installation is the reverse of removal.

ACIS control valve

14　Remove the control valve actuator.
15　Remove the three mounting bolts and mounting nut.
16　Rotate the lever anticlockwise so that the control valve is closed before removing it from the plenum.
17　Installation is a reversal of removal, ensuring a new gasket is used and the lever is rotated to close before installing the control valve into the upper intake manifold.

16　Catalytic converters - replacement

Note: *The catalytic converters are incorporated into each exhaust manifold. On models with the 3MZ-FE engine, refer to Engine Part A (see Chapter 2A). For models with the 2GR-FE engine, refer to Engine Part B (see Chapter 2B) for the exhaust manifold replacement procedure.*

General description

1　The catalytic converter is an emission control device installed in the exhaust system that reduces pollutants from the exhaust gas stream. The system works in three parts. It firstly reduces the levels of hydrocarbon (HC) and carbon monoxide (CO) by adding oxygen to the exhaust stream to produce water

vapour (H_2O) and carbon dioxide (CO_2) It also works to lower the levels of oxides of nitrogen (NOx) by removing oxygen from the exhaust gases to produce nitrogen (N) and oxygen.
2　The amount of oxygen entering the catalyst is critical to its operation because without oxygen it cannot convert harmful pollutants into harmless compounds. The catalyst is most efficient at capturing and storing oxygen when it converts the exhaust gases of an intake charge that's mixed at the ideal (stoichiometric) air/fuel ratio of 14.7:1. If the air/fuel ratio is leaner than stoichiometric for an extended period of time, the catalyst will store even more oxygen. But if the air/fuel ratio is richer than stoichiometric for any length of time, the oxygen content in the catalyst can become totally depleted. If this condition occurs, the catalyst will not convert anything!
3　Because the catalyst's ability to store oxygen is such an important factor in its operation, it can also be considered a factor in the catalyst's eventual inability to do its job. The PCM monitors the oxygen content going into and coming out of the catalyst by comparing the voltage signals from the upstream and downstream oxygen sensors. When the catalyst is functioning correctly, there is very little oxygen to monitor at the outlet end of the catalyst because it's capturing, storing and releasing oxygen as needed to convert HC, CO and NOx into more benign substances. If the catalyst isn't doing its job, the downstream oxygen sensor tells the PCM that the oxygen content in the catalysed exhaust gases is going up. When the amount of oxygen exiting the catalyst reaches a specified threshold, the PCM stores a Diagnostic Trouble Code (DTC) and turns on the Malfunction Indicator Light (MIL), also known as the CHECK ENGINE light.

17　Variable Valve Timing-intelligent system - description and component replacement

Description

1　There are two types of system: a Variable Valve Timing-intelligent (VVT-i) system used on 3MZ-FE engines and the dual Variable Valve Timing-intelligent (VVT-i) system used on all 2GR-FE engines.
2　The VVT-I system varies intake and exhaust (if equipped) camshaft timing to produce valve timing that is optimised for the driving conditions. The VVT-i system achieves this by using engine oil pressure to advance or retard the controller on the front end of each intake camshaft(s) and exhaust camshaft(s) on all 2GR-FE engines.
3　The VVT-i system on the 3MZ-FE engines consists of two CMP sensors, CKP sensor, camshaft timing oil control valves, Powertrain Control Module (PCM) and one controller for each intake camshaft sprocket/ actuator assembly. The dual VVT-I system on 2GR-FE consists of four VVT sensors, a

CKP sensor, four camshaft timing oil control valves, Powertrain Control Module (PCM) and four controllers (two intake and two exhaust camshaft sprocket/actuator assemblies).
4　Each controller consists of a timing rotor (for the VVT-i sensor), a housing with an impeller-type vane inside it, a lock pin and the actual timing chain sprocket for the intake camshaft. The vane is fixed on the end of the camshaft.
5　The camshaft timing oil control valve is an ECM-controlled device that controls and directs the flow of oil to the advance or retard passages leading to the controller. There is one oil control valve for each camshaft. A spring-loaded spool valve inside the oil control valve directs oil pumped into the valve toward either the advance outlet or the retard outlet port, depending on the engine condition.

Component replacement

Camshaft timing oil control valve(s)

Refer to illustrations 17.10a, 17.10b and 17.10c

Note: *3MZ-FE engines use two camshaft timing control valve. 2GR-FE engines use four timing oil control valves.*

6　Disconnect the negative (-) battery terminal (see Chapter 5).
7　Remove the engine cover.

Note: *On 2GR-FE engines, pull up on the front side of the engine top cover to detach it from the two front retainers. After the front is detached, pull up on the back retainer and remove the engine cover. Do not pull up on the front and rear at the same time or the cover can be damaged.*

8　On models with the 3MZ-FE engine, remove the upper intake manifold (see Chapter 2A).
9　On models with the 2GR-FE engine, remove the upper intake manifold (see Chapter 2B).
10　Disconnect the electrical connector from the camshaft timing oil control valve **(see illustrations)**.

17.10a Location of the Oil Control Valve for the front cylinder bank - 3MZ-FE engine

1 Electrical connector　2 Mounting bolt

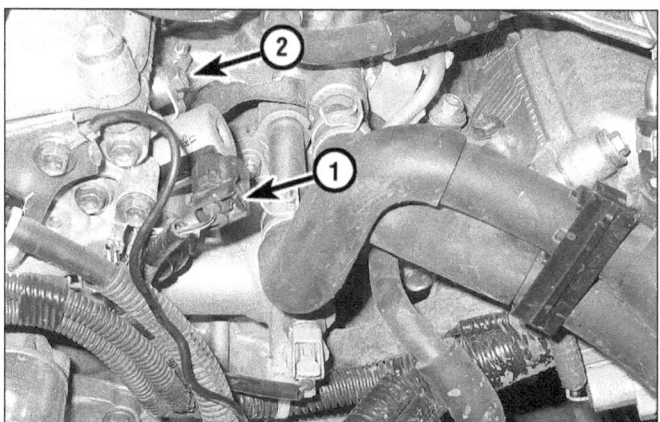

17.10b Location of the Oil Control Valve for the rear cylinder bank - 3MZ-FE engine

1 Electrical connector   2 Mounting bolt

11   Remove the camshaft timing oil control valve mounting bolt and remove the oil control valve from the valve cover.
12   Installation is the reverse of removal.

---

18   Evaporative emissions control (EVAP) system - description and component replacement

Warning: *Petrol and petrol vapours are extremely flammable, so take extra precautions when you work on any part of the fuel system. Don't smoke or allow open flames or bare light bulbs near the work area, and don't work in a garage where a gas-type appliance (such as a water heater or clothes dryer) is present. Since petrol is carcinogenic, wear fuel-resistant gloves when there's a possibility of being exposed to fuel, and, if you spill any fuel on your skin, rinse it off immediately with soap and water. Mop up any spills immediately and do not store*

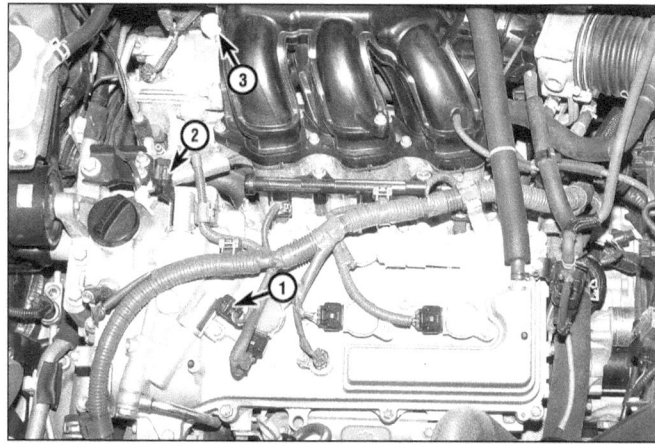

17.10c Three of the four Oil Control Valves - 2GR-FE engine

1 Oil control valve - No.2 bank exhaust camshaft
2 Oil control valve - No.2
    bank intake camshaft
3 Oil control valve - No.1 bank intake camshaft

fuel-soaked rags where they could ignite. When you perform any kind of work on the fuel system, wear safety glasses and have a Class B type fire extinguisher on hand.

EVAP canister purge valve

Refer to illustrations 18.2a and 18.2b

Note: *On models with 3MZ-FE engines, the EVAP canister purge valve is mounted to the intake manifold toward the timing belt end of the engine. On models with the 2GR-FE engine, it is mounted to the LH side of the engine, above the starter motor.*

1   Remove the engine cover.

Note: *On 2GR-FE engines, pull up on the front side of the engine top cover to detach it from the two front retainers. After the front is detached, pull up on the back retainer and remove the engine cover. Do not pull up on the front and rear at the same time or the cover can be damaged.*

2   Disconnect the electrical connector from the purge valve (**see illustrations**).
3   Disconnect the EVAP hoses from the purge valve.
4   Remove the purge valve mounting bolt and remove the purge valve.
5   Installation is the reverse of removal.

EVAP canister

Refer to illustrations 18.8

6   Remove the engine cover.

Note: *On 2GR-FE engines, pull up on the front side of the engine top cover to detach it from the two front retainers. After the front is detached, pull up on the back retainer and remove the engine cover. Do not pull up on the front and rear at the same time or the cover can be damaged.*

7   Remove the air cleaner top cover and the air intake (see Chapter 1).
8   Disconnect the hoses from the EVAP canister (**see illustration**).

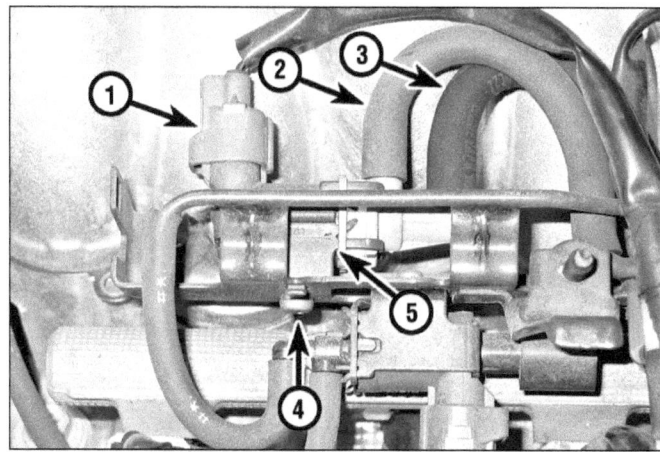

18.2a EVAP canister purge valve assembly - 3MZ-FE engine

1 Electrical connector
2 EVAP hose (coming from the EVAP canister)
3 EVAP purge hose
4 Mounting fastener
5 EVAP canister purge valve

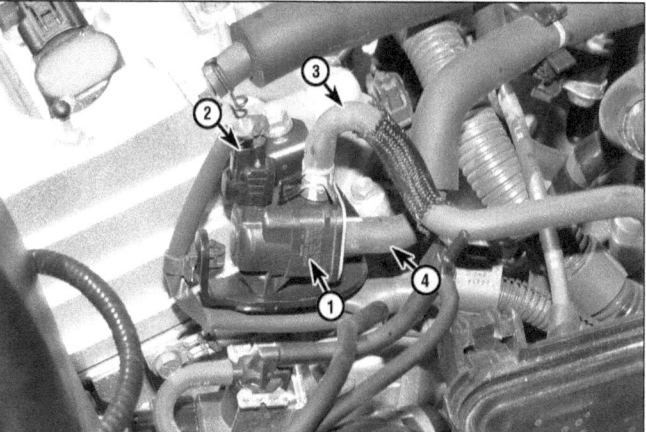

18.2b EVAP canister purge valve assembly - 2GR-FE engine

1 EVAP canister purge valve
2 Electrical connector
3 EVAP hose (coming from the EVAP canister)
4 EVAP purge hose

18.8 EVAP canister - 2GR-FE engine, 3MZ-FE engine similar

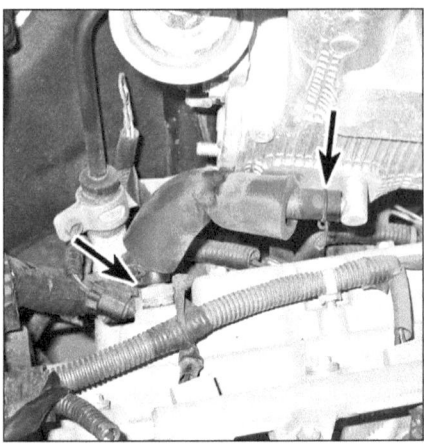

19.1a On 3MZ-FE engines, the PCV valve is located at the right rear corner of the rear valve cover, and the crankcase ventilation hose (or PCV hose) connects the PCV valve to a pipe on the underside of the manifold (the manifold has been disconnected and raised up in this photo so that you can see the connection to the manifold)

9   Remove the EVAP canister mounting bolts to detach the canister.
10   Installation is the reverse of removal.

19   Positive Crankcase Ventilation (PCV) system - system description

Refer to illustrations 19.1a and 19.1b

1   The Positive Crankcase Ventilation (PCV) system **(see illustration)** reduces hydrocarbon emissions by directing blow-by gases and crankcase vapours into the intake manifold, where they're mixed with intake air before drawn into the combustion chambers where they're consumed along with the air/fuel mixture. The PCV system does this by circulating fresh air from the air filter housing through a series of hoses into the crankcase, where the fresh air mixes with blow-by gases before being drawn from the crankcase by intake vacuum, through the PCV valve and then into the intake manifold.
2   During idle and part-throttle conditions, intake manifold vacuum is high. Blow-by gases and crankcase vapours flow from the crankcase through the PCV valve and the crankcase ventilation hose (also known as the PCV hose) into the intake manifold. The strong intake manifold vacuum also pulls fresh air from the air intake duct or the air filter housing through the fresh air inlet hose into the crankcase.

3   There is no scheduled maintenance interval for the PCV valve or the PCV system hoses. But over time the PCV system might become less efficient as an oily residue of sludge builds up inside the PCV valve and the hoses. One symptom of a clogged PCV system is leaking seals. When crankcase vapours can't escape, pressure builds inside the bottom end and eventually causes crankshaft seals to leak. So anytime that you're changing the oil filter, air filter, fuel filter, spark plugs, etc. it's a good idea to pull off the PCV hoses and inspect them. If the hoses are clogged, remove them and clean them out. If they're cracked, torn or deteriorated, replace them.
4   Checking and replacement of the PCV valve is covered in Chapter 1.

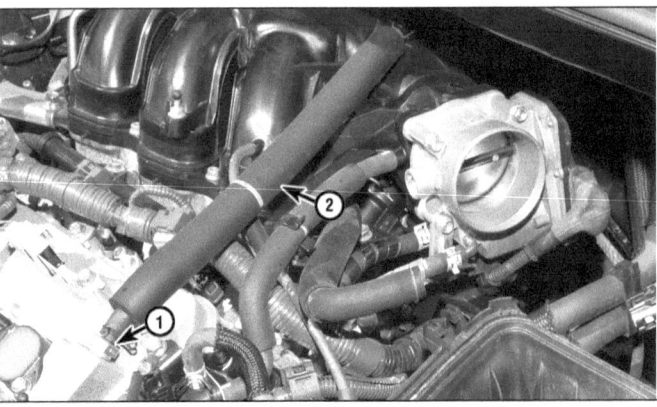

19.1b PCV valve (1) and hose (2) on the 2GR-FE engine

Chapter 7 Automatic transaxle

Contents

Specifications

Transaxle models
Two-wheel-drive (2WD) ... U151E
All-wheel-drive (AWD) ... U151F
Transfer case model ... MF2A

Torque specifications — Nm

Subframe bolts ... See Chapter 10
Transverse engine/transfer case mounting bracket bolts
MCU28R models ... 34
GSU40R/GSU45R models ... 64
Transfer case-to-engine bolts/nuts ... 69
Transaxle-to-engine bolts (Refer to illustration 9.7)
Bolts A ... 64
Bolts B ... 46
Bolts C
MCU28R models ... 37
GSU40R/GSU45R models ... 43
Torque converter to driveplate bolts ... 41

1 General information

All models are fitted with a 5-speed electronically controlled automatic transaxle. All-wheel-drive models have a transfer case attached between the RHF driveshaft and the front differential. The transfer case is bolted to the front differential and has a drive gear and pinion that allows drive from the front differential to be transferred not only to the RHF driveshaft, but also to a propeller shaft that transfers drive to the rear axle as well.

The traction control system eliminates wheel slip by applying brake to any spinning wheels, transferring drive to the other wheels using the ABS system.

Due to the complexity of the automatic transaxles covered in this manual and to the specialised equipment necessary to perform most service operations, this Chapter contains only those procedures related to removal and installation. Transmission and transfer case fluid level checks and change are covered in the Routine Maintenance chapter (see Chapter 1). The transmission and front differential are lubricated by the same oil. The one level check and lubricant change procedure covers both.

If the transaxle requires major repair work, it should be left to a dealer service department or an automotive or transmission shop. You can, however, remove and install the transaxle yourself and save the expense, even if a transmission shop does the repair work (provided that a proper diagnosis has been made prior to removal).

2 Diagnosis - general

Automatic transaxle malfunctions may be caused by five general conditions:

a poor engine performance
b improper adjustments
c hydraulic malfunctions
d mechanical malfunctions
e malfunctions in the computer or its signal network

Diagnosis of these problems should always begin with a check of the easily repaired items: fluid level and condition (see Chapter 1), battery terminal cleanliness and security (see Chapter 1) and battery and charging system condition (see Chapter 5). Also check the transmission range (TR) sensor adjustment (see Chapter 6). Next, perform a road test to determine if the problem has been corrected or if more diagnosis is necessary. If the problem persists after the preliminary tests and corrections are completed, additional diagnosis should be done by a dealer service department or transmission shop. Refer to the Troubleshooting section at the front of this manual for information on symptoms of transaxle problems.

Preliminary checks

1   Drive the vehicle to warm the transaxle to normal operating temperature.
2   Check the fluid level as described in Chapter 1:

   a *If the fluid level is unusually low, add enough fluid to bring the level within the designated area of the dipstick, then check for external leaks (see below).*
   b *If the fluid level is abnormally high, drain off the excess, then check the drained fluid for contamination by coolant. The presence of engine coolant in the automatic transaxle fluid indicates that a failure has occurred in the internal radiator walls that separate the coolant from the transaxle fluid (see Chapter 3).*
   c *If the fluid is foaming, drain it and refill the transaxle, then check for coolant in the fluid, or a high fluid level.*

3   Check the engine idle speed.

Note: *If the engine is malfunctioning, do not proceed with the preliminary checks until it has been repaired and runs normally.*

4   Inspect the shift cable (see Section 3). Make sure that it's properly adjusted and that the linkage operates smoothly.

Fluid leak diagnosis

5   Most fluid leaks are easy to locate visually. Repair usually consists of replacing a seal or gasket. If a leak is difficult to find, the following procedure may help.
6   Identify the fluid. Make sure it's automatic transaxle fluid and not engine oil or brake fluid (automatic transaxle fluid is a deep red colour).
7   Try to pinpoint the source of the leak. Drive the vehicle several miles, then park it over a large sheet of cardboard. After a minute or two, you should be able to locate the leak by determining the source of the fluid dripping onto the cardboard.
8   Make a careful visual inspection of the suspected component and the area immediately around it. Pay particular attention to gasket mating surfaces. A mirror is often helpful for finding leaks in areas that are hard to see.
9   If the leak still cannot be found, clean the suspected area thoroughly with a degreaser or solvent, then dry it.
10   Drive the vehicle for 10 to 15-minutes at normal operating temperature and varying speeds. After driving the vehicle, visually inspect the suspected component again.
11   Once the leak has been located, the cause must be determined before it can be properly repaired. If a gasket is replaced but the sealing flange is bent, the new gasket will not stop the leak. The bent flange must be straightened.
12   Before attempting to repair a leak, check to make sure that the following conditions are corrected or they may cause another leak.

Note: *Some of the following conditions cannot be fixed without highly specialised tools and expertise. Such problems must be referred to a transmission shop or a dealer service department.*

Gasket leaks

13   Check the pan periodically. Make sure the bolts are tight, no bolts are missing, the gasket is in good condition and the pan is flat (dents in the pan may indicate damage to the valve body inside).
14   If the pan gasket is leaking, the fluid level or the fluid pressure may be too high, the vent may be plugged, the pan bolts may be too tight, the pan sealing flange may be warped, the sealing surface of the transaxle housing may be damaged, the gasket may be damaged or the transaxle casting may be cracked or porous. If sealant instead of gasket material has been used to form a seal between the pan and the transaxle housing, it may be the wrong sealant.

Seal leaks

15   If a transaxle seal is leaking, the fluid level or pressure may be too high, the vent may be plugged, the seal bore may be damaged, the seal itself may be damaged or improperly fitted, the surface of the shaft protruding through the seal may be damaged or a loose bearing may be causing excessive shaft movement.
16   Make sure the dipstick tube seal is in good condition and the tube is properly seated. Periodically check the area around the speedometer gear or sensor for leakage. If fluid is evident, check the O-ring for damage.

Case leaks

17   If the case itself appears to be leaking, the casting is porous and will have to be repaired or replaced.
18   Make sure the oil cooler hose fittings are tight and in good condition.

Fluid comes out vent pipe or fill tube

19   If this condition occurs, the transaxle is overfilled, there is coolant in the fluid, the case is porous, the dipstick is incorrect, the vent is plugged or the drain-back holes are plugged.

---

3   Shift cable - replacement and adjustment

Replacement

Refer to illustrations 3.6, 3.7, 3.8, 3.10, 3.11 and 3.12

1   Disconnect the negative (-) battery terminal (see Chapter 5).

3.6 Remove the nut and disconnect the shift cable from the manual lever on the side of the transaxle

3.7 Remove the large C-clip cable retainer from the bracket on the side of the transaxle

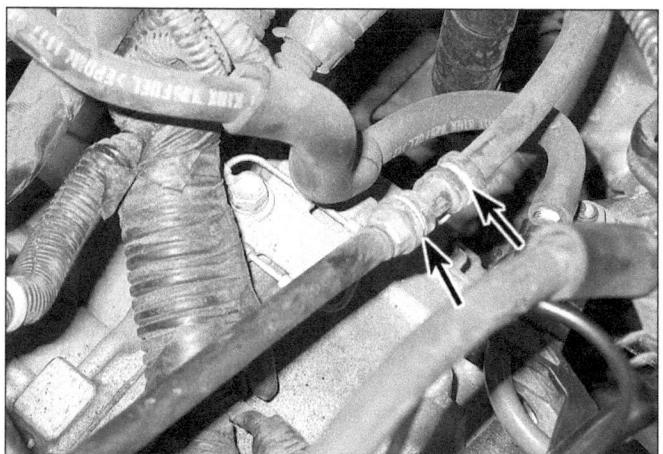

3.8 Remove the shift cable from the wire hanger on the top of the transaxle

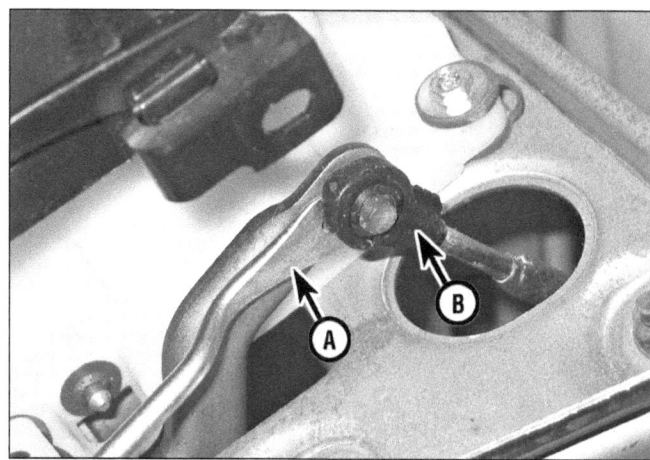

3.10 Use a trim panel tool (A) to separate the shift cable from the shift lever (B) at the centre console

3.11 Remove the two mounting nuts and bolts at the centre console

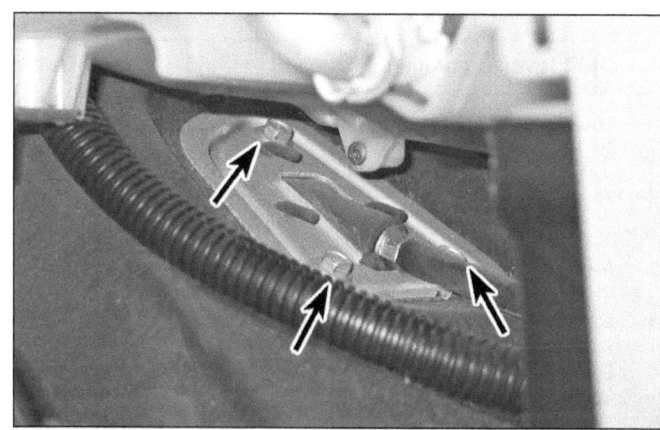

3.12 Remove the bolts from the shift cable bracket at the firewall

2   Remove the centre console trim panel (see Chapter 11).

3   Remove the floor carpet and the instrument panel centre lower trim panel (see Chapter 11).

4   Remove the battery and the battery tray (see Chapter 5).

5   Remove the air filter housing and the air intake ducts (see Chapter 4).

6   Disconnect the shift cable from the manual lever on the transaxle **(see illustration)**.

7   Remove the large C-clip cable retainer **(see illustration)** from the bracket located on the side of the transaxle.

8   Remove the shift cable from the wire hanger **(see illustration)**.

9   On GSU40R/GSU45R models, remove the air conditioning unit (see Chapter 3).

10   Disconnect the shift cable from the shift lever assembly on the centre console **(see illustration)**.

11   On MCU28R models, working on the side of the centre console, remove the two mounting bolts **(see illustration)**.

Note: *GSU40R/GSU45R models are equipped with a stopper cap that secures the cable to the shift lever assembly. Rotate the stopper cap anticlockwise, lift the cap and slide the cable from the shift lever bracket.*

12   Remove the bolts from the shift cable bracket at the firewall **(see illustration)**.

13   Pull the cable through the floor.

14   Installation is the reverse of removal.

15   Be sure to adjust the cable when you're done (see Steps 16 through 21).

Adjustment

Refer to illustration 3.19

16   When the shift lever inside the vehicle is moved from the NEUTRAL position to other positions, it should move smoothly and accurately to each position and the shift indicator should indicate the correct gear position. If the indicator isn't aligned with the correct position, adjust the shift cable as follows:

17   Remove the battery and the battery tray (see Chapter 5).

18   Disconnect the shift cable from the manual lever on the transaxle.

19   Move the manual lever on the transaxle down into PARK (fully downward), then return it two notches to the NEUTRAL position **(see illustration)**.

20   While holding the manual lever in the NEUTRAL position, tighten the shift cable adjustment bolt.

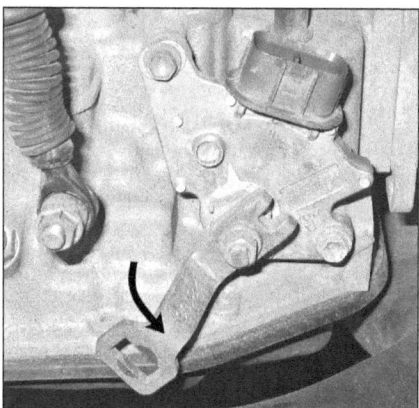

3.19 To adjust the shift cable, push the manual lever all the way DOWN, return it two clicks to the Neutral position, place the shift lever inside the vehicle at the Neutral position, then tighten the swivel nut

21   Check the operation of the transaxle in each shift lever position (try to start the engine in each gear - the starter should operate in the Park and Neutral positions only).

4.5 Disconnect the shift lever electrical connectors from the shift lever assembly at the centre console

4.6 Location of the shift lever mounting bolts - MCU28R models

4   Shift lever - replacement

1   Disconnect the negative (-) battery terminal (see Chapter 5).

MCU28R models

Refer to illustrations 4.5 and 4.6

2   Remove the centre console trim panel (see Chapter 11).
3   Remove the floor carpet and the lower trim panel (see Chapter 11).
4   Disconnect the shift cable from the shift lever at the console (see Section 3).
5   Disconnect the shift lever electrical connectors **(see illustration)**.
6   Remove the mounting bolts and separate the shift lever from the console **(see illustration)**.
7   The remainder of installation is the reverse of removal.

GSU40R/GSU45R models

8   Remove the shift lever knob by rotating it anticlockwise.
9   Remove the four clips and lift the console panel from the shift lever assembly.
10   Remove the two clips and lift the trim panel from below the radio.
11   Remove the front door cowl side trim panels and the scuff plates from the right and left door openings (see Chapter 11).
12   Remove the centre console trim panel (see Chapter 11).
13   Remove the glove compartment door assembly (see Chapter 11).
14   Remove the floor carpet and the lower trim panel (see Chapter 11).
15   Disconnect the shift cable from the shift lever at the console (see Section 3).
16   Disconnect the shift lever electrical connectors.
17   Remove the mounting bolts and separate the shift lever from the console.
18   The remainder of installation is the reverse of removal.

5   Brake Transmission Shift Interlock (BTSI) system - description, replacement and adjustment

Warning: *The models covered by this manual are equipped with a Supplemental Restraint System (SRS), more commonly known as airbags. Always disable the airbag system before working in the vicinity of any airbag system component to avoid the possibility of accidental deployment of the airbag(s), which could cause personal injury (see Chapter 12). Do not use a memory saving device to preserve the PCM or radio memory when working on or near airbag system components.*

Description

1   The Brake Transmission Shift Interlock (BTSI) system incorporates two solenoid-operated devices; one mounted next to the ignition key lock cylinder and the other mounted on the shift lever assembly under the centre console. The solenoid mounted on the shift lever assembly is also equipped with a Shift Lock Module that receives information from the brake pedal switch and the transaxle range (TR) sensor for proper activation of the key lock solenoid (ignition lock cylinder) and the shift lock module (console shift lever). The shift lock module locks the shift lever in the PARK position when the ignition key is in the LOCK position. When the ignition key is in the RUN position, a magnetic holding device is energised. When the system is functioning correctly, the only way to unlock the shift lever and move it out of PARK is to depress the brake pedal. The BTSI system also prevents the ignition key from being turned to the LOCK position unless the shift lever is fully located in the PARK position.

Check

2   Verify that the ignition key can be removed only in the PARK position.

3   When the shift lever is in the PARK position, you should be able to rotate the ignition key from OFF to LOCK. But when the shift lever is in any gear position other than PARK (including NEUTRAL), you should not be able to rotate the ignition key to the LOCK position.
4   You should not be able to move the shift lever out of the PARK position when the ignition key is turned to the OFF position.
5   You should not be able to move the shift lever out of the PARK position when the ignition key is turned to the RUN or START position until you depress the brake pedal.
6   You should not be able to move the shift lever out of the PARK position when the ignition key is turned to the ACC or LOCK position.
7   Once in gear, with the ignition key in the RUN position, you should be able to move the shift lever between gears, or put it into NEUTRAL, without depressing the brake pedal.
8   If the BTSI system doesn't operate as described, try adjusting it as follows.

Replacement

9   Disconnect the negative (-) battery terminal (see Chapter 5).

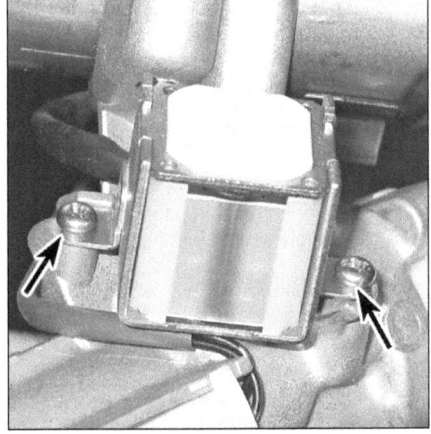

5.12 Location of the key lock solenoid mounting screws

5.15 Twist the console bulb holder anticlockwise to remove it from the side of the indicator base

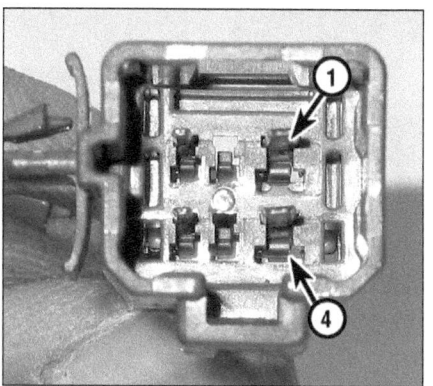

5.16 Use a small jeweller's screwdriver to separate pins 1 and 4 from the backside of the connector and remove the two-wire harness

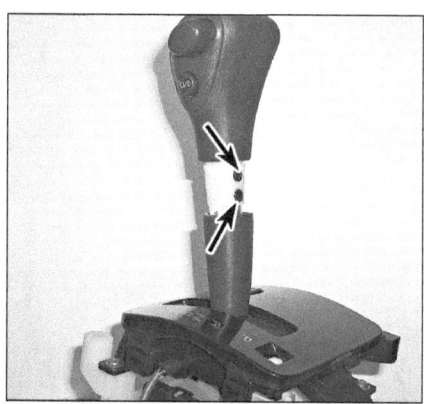

5.17 Remove the two set screws and lift the shift lever knob from the shaft

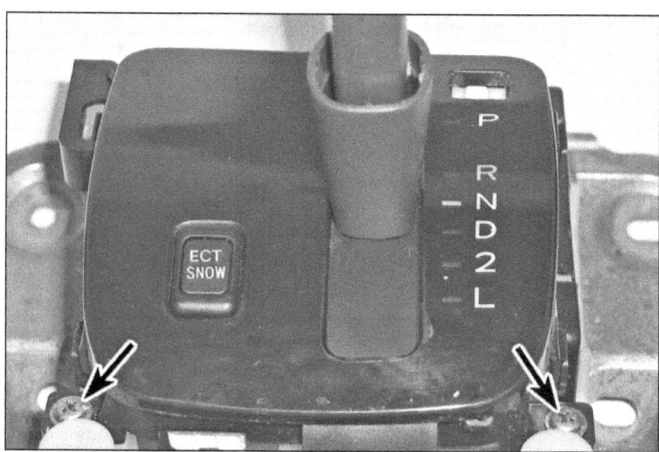

5.18 Remove the indicator cover base mounting screws

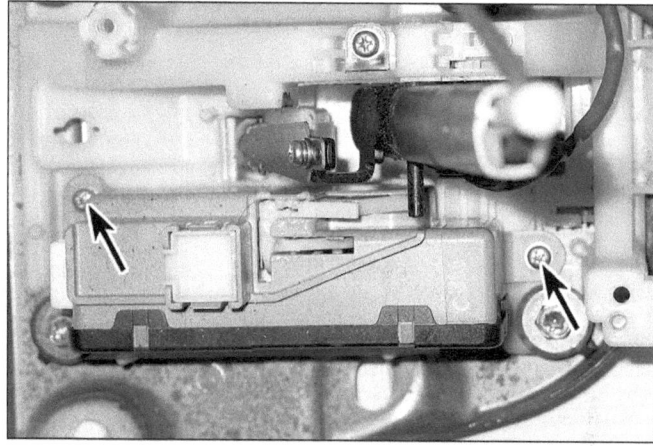

5.19 Location of the shift lock module mounting screws

Key lock solenoid

Refer to illustration 5.12

10   Remove the steering column trim covers (see Chapter 11).

11   Access the ignition key lock cylinder and disconnect the key lock solenoid electrical connector.

12   Remove the key lock solenoid mounting screws **(see illustration)** and separate the solenoid from the ignition key lock cylinder.

13   Installation is the reverse of removal.

Shift lock module

MCU28R models

Refer to illustrations 5.15, 5.16, 5.17, 5.18 and 5.19

14   Remove the shift lever assembly (see Section 4).

15   Remove the console bulb connector **(see illustration)**.

16   Separate the shift overdrive harness pins from the main connector **(see illustration)**.

17   Remove the two set screws and separate the shift lever knob button from the shaft **(see illustration)**.

18   Remove the indicator cover base mounting screws **(see illustration)**.

19   Remove the shift lock module mounting screws **(see illustration)** and separate the shift lock module from the assembly.

20   Installation is the reverse of removal.

GSU40R/GSU45R models

Refer to illustration 5.25

21   Remove the shift lever assembly (see Section 4).

22   Remove the console bulb connector.

23   Remove the position indicator slide cover.

24   Remove the position indicator lower housing.

25   On multi-mode type shift lever systems, separate the harness pins from the main connector **(see illustration)**.

26   Remove the shift lock module mounting screws and separate the shift lock module from the assembly.

27   Installation is the reverse of removal.

Transmission Range (TR) sensor

28   The transmission range sensor incorporates the Park/Neutral function as well as the backup light switch and transmission gear position information to the PCM. The Park/Neutral function of the switch prevents the engine from starting in any gear other than Park or Neutral. If the engine starts with the shift lever in any position other than Park or Neutral, adjust the switch. The transmission position switch is also an information sensor for the electronic controlled transaxle. When the shift lever is placed in position (Park/Neutral), the transmission range sensor sends a voltage signal to the PCM. Refer to Chapter 6 for the replacement procedure.

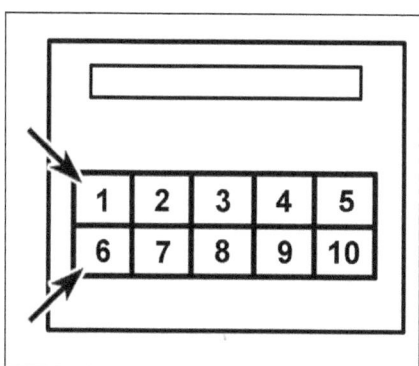

5.25 Use a small jeweller's screwdriver to separate pins 1 and 6 from the backside of the connector and remove the two-wire harness

5.30 Location of the shift lock override button - MCU28R models, other models similar

6.4 Carefully pry out the old driveshaft seal with a prybar, screwdriver or a special seal removal tool; make sure you don't gouge or nick the surface of the seal bore

Shift lock override feature

Refer to illustration 5.30

29   In the event the Brake Transmission Shift Interlock (BTSI) system fails and the shift lever cannot be moved out of gear, the system is equipped with an override feature. The BTSI system can be bypassed and the shift lever can be used in manual operation with the parking brake ON and the engine OFF.

30   Locate the override button alongside the shift lever on the centre console **(see illustration)**, carefully pry the protective cover off, turn the ignition switch to LOCK position, press the override button and shift the select lever into NEUTRAL.

6   Driveshaft oil seals - replacement

Refer to illustrations 6.4 and 6.6

1   Fluid leaks occasionally occur due to wear of the driveshaft oil seals. Replacement

of these seals is relatively easy, since the repairs can be performed without removing the transaxle from the vehicle.

2   The driveshaft oil seals are located in either sides of the transaxle, where the driveshaft shaft is splined into the differential. If leakage at the seal is suspected, raise the vehicle and support it securely on jackstands (see Jacking and Towing). If the seal is leaking, fluid will be found on the side of the transaxle.

3   Remove the driveshaft (see Chapter 8). If you're replacing the right side driveshaft seal, remove the intermediate shaft and the driveshaft assembly as a single unit.

4   Using a screwdriver or prybar, carefully pry the oil seal out of the transaxle bore **(see illustration)**.

5   If the oil seal cannot be removed with a screwdriver or prybar, a special oil seal removal tool (available at auto parts stores) will be required.

6   Using a seal driver or a large deep socket as a drift, install the new oil seal. Drive it into the bore squarely and make sure that it is completely seated **(see illustration)**. Lubri-

cate the lip of the new seal with multi-purpose grease.

7   Install the driveshaft assembly (see Chapter 8). Be careful not to damage the lip of the new seal.

7   Transaxle fluid cooler - removal and installation

Refer to illustrations 7.4 and 7.6

1   Remove the radiator grille (see Chapter 11).

2   Remove the left side inner fender splash shield (see Chapter 11).

3   Remove the front bumper (see Chapter 11).

4   Remove the cooling duct from the transaxle fluid cooler **(see illustration)**.

5   Detach the transaxle fluid cooler lines from the transaxle fluid cooler.

6   Remove the mounting bolts **(see illustration)** and lift the transaxle fluid cooler from the front fender area.

7   Installation is the reverse of removal.

6.6 Drive in the new driveshaft seal with a large socket or a special seal installer

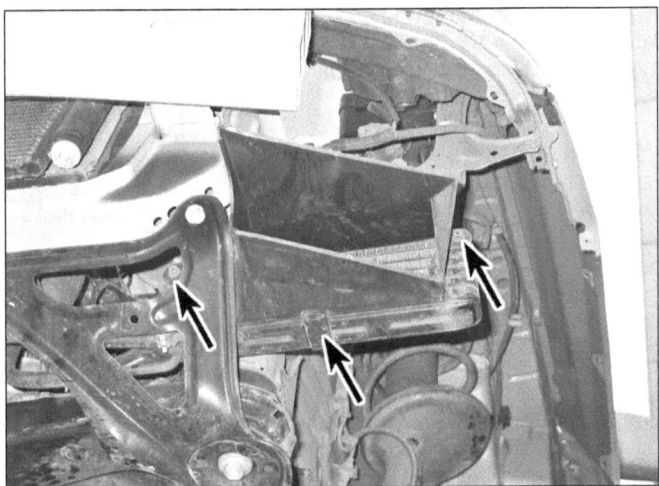

7.4 Remove the cooling duct from the transaxle fluid cooler

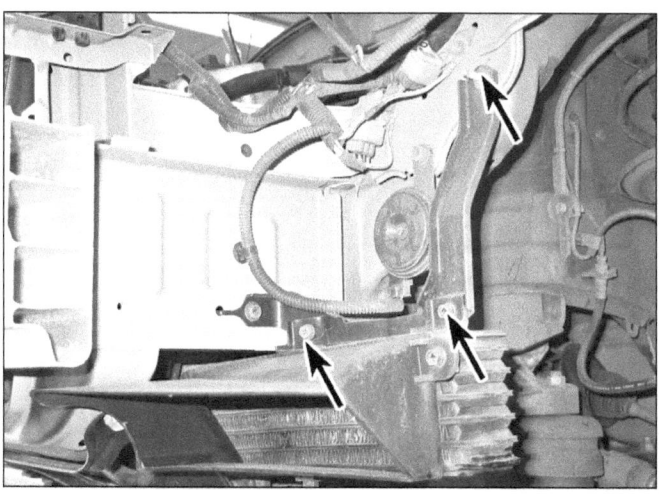

7.6 Location of the transaxle fluid cooler mounting bolts

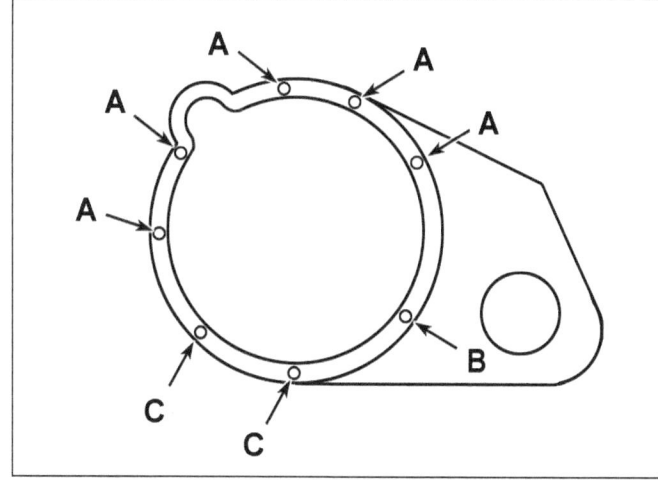

9.7 Transaxle-to-engine bolt locations and identification

8 Transfer case - removal and installation

1 Remove the engine/transaxle assembly with the transfer case attached (see Chapter 2C).
2 Remove the transverse engine mounting bracket from the transfer case and engine.
3 Remove the transfer case mounting bolts and nuts.
4 Separate the transfer case from the engine/transaxle assembly.
5 Installation is the reverse of removal.

9 Automatic transaxle - removal and installation

Note: *The following procedure requires the engine and transaxle to be removed as a unit, then separated once they are out of the vehicle (see Chapter 2C for the engine/transaxle removal procedure).*

Removal

1 Remove the engine/transaxle assembly (see Chapter 2C).
2 On AWD models, remove the transfer case (see Section 8).
3 Remove the transaxle-to-engine bolts **(see illustration 9.7)** and separate the transaxle from the engine.
4 Check the engine and transaxle mounts (see Chapter 2A) or (see Chapter 2B). If any of these components are worn or damaged, replace them.

Installation

Refer to illustrations 9.7a and 9.7b

5 If removed, install the torque converter on the transaxle input shaft. Make sure the converter hub splines are properly engaged with the splines on the transaxle input shaft.
6 With an assistant holding the torque converter in place inside the transaxle, mate the transaxle to the engine and install a couple of the transaxle-to-engine bolts. Do not use excessive force to install the transaxle - if something binds and the transaxle won't mate with the engine, alter the angle of the transaxle slightly until it does mate.
Caution: *Do NOT use transaxle-to-engine bolts to force the engine and transaxle into alignment. Doing so could crack or damage major components. If you experience difficulties, have an assistant help you line up the dowel pins on the block with the transaxle. Some wiggling of the engine and/or the transaxle will probably be necessary to secure proper alignment of the two. Turn the converter to align the bolt holes in the converter with the bolt holes in the driveplate. Install the converter-to-driveplate bolts.*

Note: *Install all of the bolts before tightening any of them.*

7 Install the remaining transaxle-to-engine bolts. Tighten all of the bolts to the torque listed in this Chapter's Specifications **(see illustration).**
8 On AWD models, install the transfer case (see Section 8).
9 Install the engine/transaxle assembly (see Chapter 2C).
10 Reinstall the remaining components in the reverse order of removal.

11 Remove all jacks and hoists and lower the vehicle. Tighten the wheel nuts to the torque listed in the Chapter 1 Specifications. Tighten the driveshaft/hub nuts to the torque listed in the Chapter 8 Specifications.
12 Add the specified type and amount of engine oil and transaxle fluid (see Chapter 1).
13 Connect the negative battery cable. Run the engine, cycle the transaxle through the gears, then check the fluid level (see Chapter 1). Check for proper operation and leaks.
14 Road test the vehicle to check for proper transaxle operation and fluid leakage. Recheck the fluid level.

10 Automatic transaxle overhaul - general information

In the event of a problem occurring, it will be necessary to establish whether the fault is electrical, mechanical or hydraulic in nature, before repair work can be contemplated. Diagnosis requires detailed knowledge of the transaxle's operation and construction, as well as access to specialised test equipment, and so is deemed to be beyond the scope of this manual. It is therefore essential that problems with the automatic transaxle are referred to a dealer service department or other qualified repair facility for assessment.

Note that a faulty transaxle should not be removed before the vehicle has been diagnosed by a knowledgeable technician equipped with the proper tools, as troubleshooting must be performed with the transaxle installed in the vehicle.

Chapter 8   Driveline

Contents

Specifications

General

Rear differential pinion shaft bearing preload (AWD models)

With used bearing	0.6 to 0.9 Nm
With new bearing	1.1 to 1.7 Nm

Torque specifications

	Nm
Driveshaft/hub nut	294
Propeller shaft (AWD models)	
Flange-to-rear differential bolts	74
Centre support bearing bolts	37
Rear CV joint-to-rear flange	
MCU28R models	29
GSU45R models	26
Rear CV joint flange-to-centre propeller shaft and rear centre bearing	
Step 1	182
Step 2	Loosen
Step 3	69
Rear differential (AWD models)	
To-mounting bracket bolts	103
Pinion flange nut	
Initial	108
Maximum	235
Rear mounting bolts-to-subframe	95
Mounting bracket-to-suspension member - mounting bolts	137

1   General information

The information in this Chapter deals with the components from the rear of the engine to the front wheels, except for the transaxle, which is dealt with in the previous Chapter. For the purposes of this Chapter, these components are grouped into two categories - propeller shaft and driveshafts. Separate Sections within this Chapter offer general descriptions and checking procedures for components in each of the two groups.

Since nearly all the procedures covered in this Chapter involve working under the vehicle, make sure it's securely supported on sturdy jackstands or on a hoist where the vehicle can be easily raised and lowered.

2   Driveshafts - removal and installation

Front

Removal

Refer to illustrations 2.1, 2.2 and 2.7

1   Remove the wheel cover or hub cap. Unstake the nut with a punch or chisel (see illustration).

2   Break the hub nut loose with a socket and large breaker bar (see illustration).

3   Loosen the wheel nuts, raise the vehicle and support it securely on jackstands (see Jacking and Towing). Remove the wheel. Drain the transaxle lubricant (see Chapter 1).

4   Remove the nuts and bolt securing the balljoint to the control arm, then pry the control

2.1 If the driveshaft nut is staked, use a centre punch to unstake it (wheel removed for clarity)

2.2 Loosen the driveshaft/hub nut with a long breaker bar

2.7 To separate the inner end of the driveshaft from the transaxle, pry on the CV joint housing like this with a large screwdriver or prybar - you may need to give the prybar a sharp rap with a brass hammer

arm down and separate the lower control arm from the balljoint (see Chapter 10). Now remove the driveshaft/hub nut.

5   Swing the knuckle/hub assembly out (away from the vehicle) until the end of the driveshaft is free of the hub.

Note: *If the driveshaft splines stick in the hub, tap on the end of the driveshaft with a plastic hammer. Support the outer end of the driveshaft with a piece of wire to avoid unnecessary strain on the inner CV joint.*

6   If you're working on the right-side shaft on a four-cylinder model, remove the bolts from the support bearing bracket. If you're working on a V6 model, remove the snap-ring from the support bearing of the intermediate shaft using a pair of pliers.

7   Carefully pry the inner end of the driveshaft from the transaxle - or, on models so equipped, the intermediate shaft - using a large screwdriver or prybar positioned between the transaxle or bearing support and the CV joint housing **(see illustration)**. Support the CV joints and carefully remove the driveshaft from the vehicle.

Installation

Refer to illustrations 2.8a and 2.8b

8   Pry the old spring clip from the inner end of the driveshaft and install a new one **(see illustrations)**. Lubricate the differential or intermediate shaft seal with multi-purpose grease and raise the driveshaft into position while supporting the CV joints.

9   Insert the splined end of the inner CV joint or the intermediate shaft into the differential side gear and make sure the spring clip locks in its groove. If you're installing a driveshaft/intermediate shaft assembly, install the centre support bearing bolts or snap-ring, as applicable.

10   Apply a light coat of multi-purpose grease to the outer CV joint splines, pull out on the strut/steering knuckle assembly and install the stub axle into the hub.

11   Reconnect the balljoint to the lower control arm and tighten the nuts (see the torque specifications in Chapter 10).

12   Install a new driveshaft/hub nut. Tighten the hub nut securely, but don't try to tighten it to the actual torque specification until you've lowered the vehicle to the ground.

13   Grasp the inner CV joint housing (not the driveshaft) and pull out to make sure the driveshaft has seated securely in the transaxle. If the inner CV joint-to-flange bolts were removed, tighten them to the torque listed in this Chapter's Specifications.

14   Install the wheel and wheel nuts, then lower the vehicle.

15   Tighten the wheel nuts to the torque listed in the Chapter 1 Specifications. Tighten the hub nut to the torque listed in this Chapter's Specifications. Stake the nut to the groove in the driveshaft, using a hammer and punch.

16   Refill the transaxle with the recommended type and amount of lubricant (see Chapter 1).

Rear (AWD models)

Removal

17   Remove the wheel cover or hub cap. Unstake the nut with a punch or chisel **(see illustration 2.1)**.

18   Break the hub nut loose with a socket and large breaker bar **(see illustration 2.2)**.

19   Loosen the wheel nuts, raise the vehicle and support it securely on jackstands (see Jacking and Towing). Remove the wheel.

20   Remove the ABS sensor lead clamps and the parking brake cable bracket from the trailing arm.

21   Remove the bolts that secure the control arms to the rear knuckle (see Chapter 10).

22   Remove the driveshaft nut, then pull the driveshaft assembly out of the rear knuckle. Make sure you don't damage the lip of the inner rear knuckle seal. If the splines on the outer CV joint spindle hang up on the splines in the hub, knock them loose with a hammer and punch.

Caution: *Don't let the driveshaft hang by the inner CV joint.*

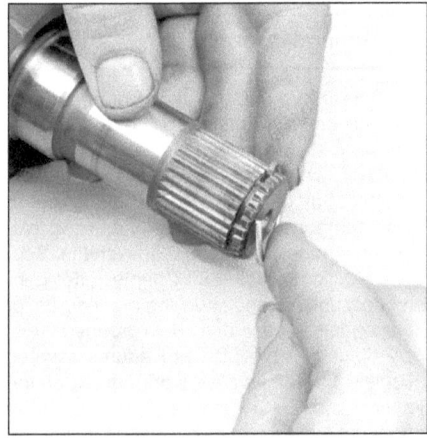

2.8a Pry the old spring clip from the inner end of the driveshaft with a small screwdriver or awl

2.8b To install the new spring clip, start one end in the groove and work the clip over the shaft end, into the groove

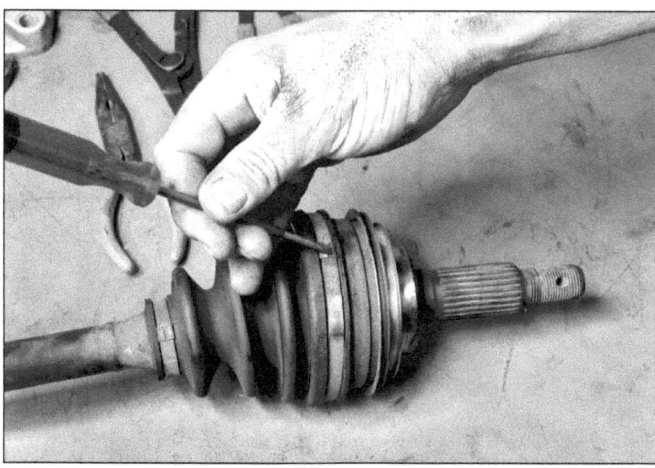

3.3 Lift the tabs on the boot clamps with a small screwdriver, then open the clamps

3.4 Remove the boot from the inner CV joint and slide the joint housing from the tripod

23   Carefully pry the inner end of the driveshaft from the differential using a large screwdriver or prybar positioned between the differential and the CV joint housing. Support the CV joints and carefully remove the driveshaft from the vehicle.

Installation

24   Pry the old spring clip from the inner end of the driveshaft and install a new one **(see illustrations 2.8a and 2.8b)**. Lubricate the differential or intermediate shaft seal with multi-purpose grease and raise the driveshaft into position while supporting the CV joints.

25   Insert the splined end of the inner CV joint or the intermediate shaft into the differential and make sure the spring clip locks in its groove.

26   Apply a light coat of multi-purpose grease to the outer CV joint splines, pull out on the rear knuckle assembly and install the stub axle into the hub.

27   Reconnect the control arms to the rear knuckle (see the torque specifications in Chapter 10).

28   Install a new driveshaft/hub nut. Tighten the hub nut securely, but don't try to tighten it to the actual torque specification until you've lowered the vehicle to the ground.

3.6 Remove the snap-ring with a pair of snap-ring pliers

29   Grasp the inner CV joint housing (not the driveshaft) and pull out to make sure the driveshaft has seated securely in the transaxle.

30   Install the wheel and wheel nuts, then lower the vehicle.

31   Tighten the wheel nuts to the torque listed in the Chapter 1 Specifications. Tighten the hub nut to the torque listed in this Chapter's Specifications. Stake the nut to the groove in the driveshaft, using a hammer and punch.

32   Refill the transaxle with the recommended type and amount of lubricant (see Chapter 1).

---

3   Driveshaft boot - replacement

Disassembly

Refer to illustrations 3.3, 3.4, 3.6 and 3.7

Note: *If the CV joint boots must be replaced, explore all options before beginning the job. Complete rebuilt driveshafts are available on an exchange basis, which eliminates much time and work. Whichever route you choose to take, check on the cost and availability of parts before disassembling the vehicle.*

Note: *Some auto parts stores carry 'split' type replacement boots, which can be installed without removing the driveshaft from the vehicle. This is a convenient alternative; however, the driveshaft should be removed and the CV joint disassembled and cleaned to ensure the joint is free from contaminants such as moisture and dirt which will accelerate CV joint wear. Do NOT disassemble the outboard CV joint.*

1   Remove the driveshaft (see Section 2).

2   Mount the driveshaft in a vise with wood lined jaws (to prevent damage to the driveshaft). Check the CV joint for excessive play in the radial direction, which indicates worn parts. Check for smooth operation throughout the full range of motion for each CV joint. If a

boot is torn, disassemble the joint, clean the components and inspect for damage due to loss of lubrication and possible contamination by foreign matter.

3   Using a small screwdriver, pry the retaining tabs of the clamps up to loosen them and slide them off **(see illustration)**.

4   Using a screwdriver, carefully pry up on the edge of the outer boot and push it away from the CV joint. Old and worn boots can be cut off. Pull the inner CV joint boot back from the housing and slide the housing off the tripod **(see illustration)**.

5   Mark the tripod and driveshaft to ensure that they are reassembled properly.

6   Remove the tripod joint snap-ring with a pair of snap-ring pliers **(see illustration)**.

7   Use a hammer and a brass punch to drive the tripod joint from the driveshaft **(see illustration)**.

8   If you haven't already cut them off, remove both boots.

Note: *Do NOT disassemble the outboard CV joint. If you're working on a right side driveshaft, you'll also have to cut off the clamp*

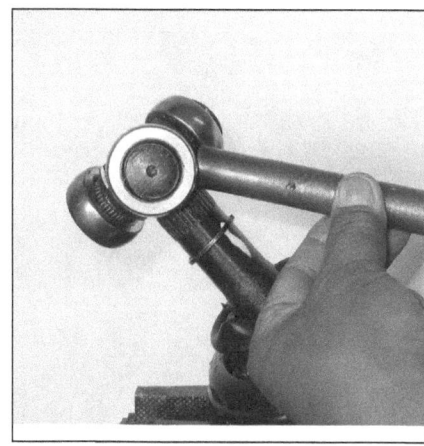

3.7 Drive the tripod joint from the driveshaft with a brass punch and hammer; be careful not to damage the bearing surfaces or the splines on the shaft

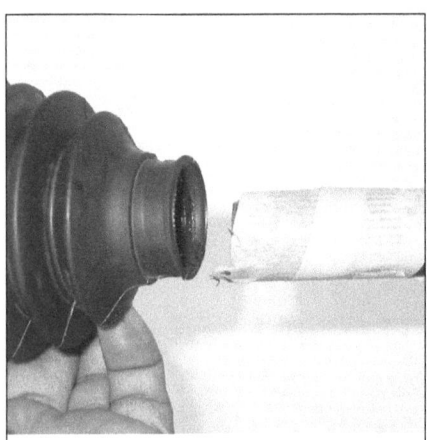

3.10a　Wrap the splined area of the driveshaft with tape to prevent damage to the boots when removing or installing them

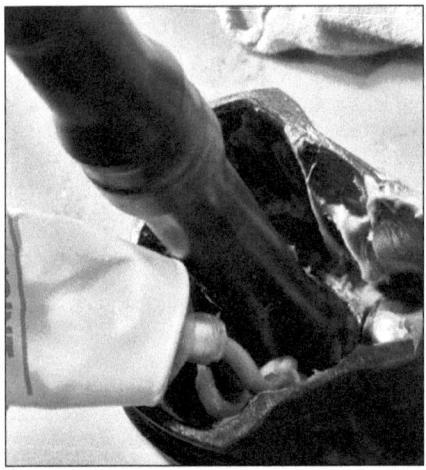

3.10d　Install the boot clamps onto the driveshaft, then insert the tripod into the housing, followed by the rest of the grease

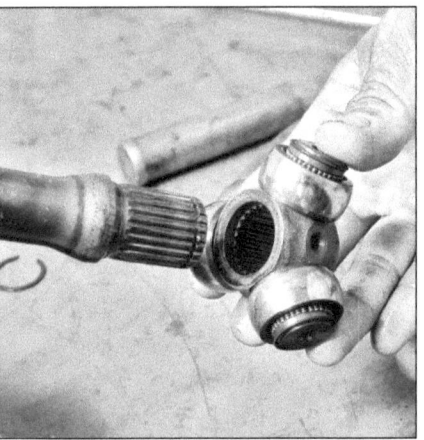

3.10b　Install the tripod with the recessed portion of the splines facing the driveshaft

for the dynamic damper and slide the damper off.

Note: *The damper may have to be pressed off with a hydraulic press. Also, before removing the damper, measure its position from the end of the driveshaft - when reassembling, it must be returned to the same spot.*

Check

9　Thoroughly clean all components, including the outer CV joint assembly, with solvent until the old CV joint grease is completely removed. Inspect the bearing surfaces of the inner tripods and housings for cracks, pitting, scoring and other signs of wear. It's not possible to inspect the bearing surfaces of the inner and outer races of the outer CV joint, but you can at least check the surfaces of the ball bearings themselves. If they're in good shape, so are the races; if they're not, neither are the races. If the inner CV joint is worn, you can buy a new inner CV joint and install it on the old driveshaft; if the outer CV joint is worn, you'll have to purchase a new

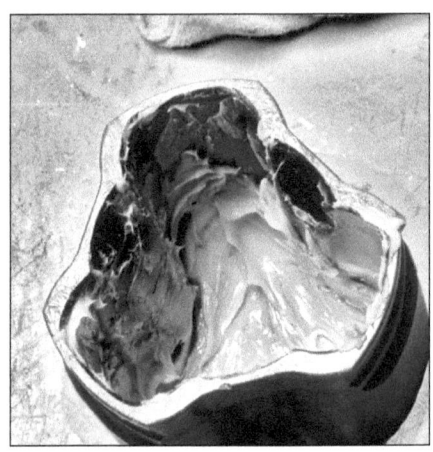

3.10c　Place grease at the bottom of the CV joint housing

outer CV joint and driveshaft (they're sold pre-assembled).

Reassembly

Refer to illustrations 3.10a, 3.10b, 3.10c, 3.10d, 3.12a, 3.12b, 3.12c and 3.12d

10　Wrap the splines on the inner end of the driveshaft with electrical or duct tape to protect the boots from the sharp edges of the splines. Slide the clamps and boot(s) onto the driveshaft, then place the tripod on the shaft. Apply grease to the tripod assembly and inside the housing. Insert the tripod into the housing and pack the remainder of the grease around the tripod **(see illustrations)**.

11　Slide the boot into place, making sure both ends seat in their grooves. Adjust the length of the driveshaft, positioning it midway through its travel.

12　Equalise the pressure in the boot, then tighten and secure the boot clamps **(see illustrations)**.

13　Install the driveshaft assembly (see Section 2).

3.12a　Equalise the pressure inside the boot by inserting a small, dull screwdriver between the boot and the outer race

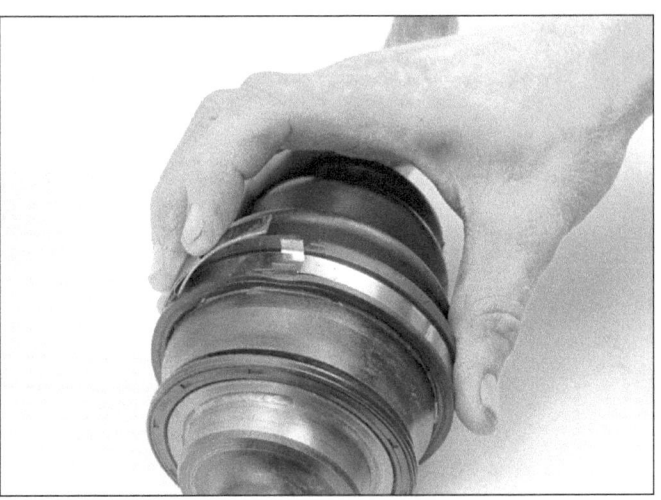

3.12b　To install the new clamps, bend the tang down . . .

3.12c ... then tap the tabs over to hold it in place

3.12d If your replacement boot came with crimp-type clamps, a special tool such as this one (available at most auto parts stores) will be required to tighten them properly

4 Propeller shaft (AWD models) - check, removal and installation

Check

1   Raise the rear of the vehicle and support it securely on jackstands (see Jacking and Towing). Block the front wheels to keep the vehicle from rolling off the stands. Release the parking brake and place the transmission in Neutral.

2   Crawl under the vehicle and visually inspect the propeller shaft. Look for any dents or cracks in the tubing. If any are found, the propeller shaft must be replaced.

3   Check for oil leakage at the front and rear of the propeller shaft. Leakage where the propeller shaft connects to the transfer case indicates a defective transfer case seal. Leakage where the propeller shaft connects to the differential indicates a defective pinion seal.

4   While under the vehicle, have an assistant rotate a rear wheel so the propeller shaft will rotate. As it does, make sure the univer-

sal joints are operating properly without binding, noise or looseness. Listen for any noise from the centre bearing, indicating it's worn or damaged. Also check the rubber portion of the centre bearing for cracking or separation.

5   The universal joints can also be checked with the propeller shaft motionless, by gripping your hands on either side of the joint and attempting to twist the joint. Any movement at all in the joint is a sign of considerable wear. Lifting up on the shaft will also indicate movement in the universal joints. If the joints are worn, front or rear portion of the propeller shaft must be replaced as an assembly.

6   Finally, check the propeller shaft mounting bolts at the ends to make sure they're tight.

Removal and installation

Refer to illustrations 4.8 and 4.10

7   Raise the rear of the vehicle and support it securely on jackstands (see Jacking and Towing). Block the front wheels to prevent the vehicle from rolling. Place the transmission in Neutral with the parking brake off.

8   Make reference marks on the propeller shaft flange and the differential pinion flange in line with each other **(see illustration)**. This is to make sure the propeller shaft is reinstalled in the same position to preserve the balance.

9   Remove the rear universal joint bolts. Turn the propeller shaft (or wheels) as necessary to bring the bolts into the most accessible position. Remove the four bolts, nuts and washers.

10   Mark the position of the centre support bearings, then unbolt the centre support bearings from the floorpan **(see illustration)**.

11   Pull out the front of the propeller shaft from the transaxle and remove the propeller shaft assembly.

12   Lubricate the lips of the transfer case seal with multi-purpose grease. Carefully guide the intermediate shaft yoke into the transfer case and then install the mounting bolts through the centre support bearing, but don't tighten them yet.

13   Reconnect the propeller shaft to the pinion flange. Be sure to align the marks and

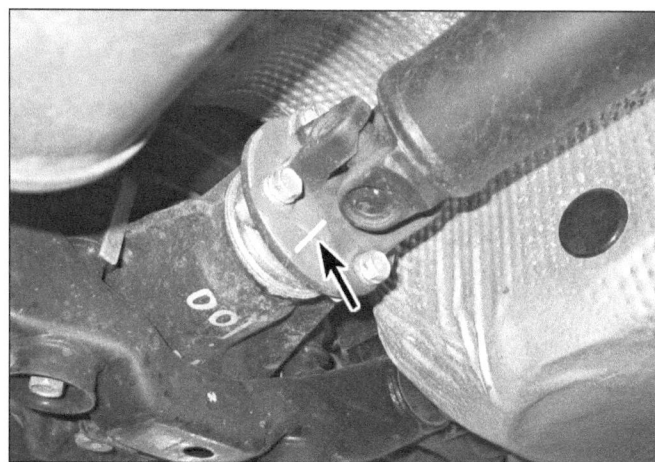

4.8 Mark the relationship of the propeller shaft to the differential pinion flange, then using a back-up wrench to hold each bolt, break loose all four bolts

4.10 Remove the fasteners securing the propeller shaft centre support bearings

tighten the fasteners to the torque listed in this Chapter's Specifications.

14   Reconnect the centre support bearings. Align the marks and tighten the fasteners to the torque listed in this Chapter's Specifications.

5   Differential (AWD models) - removal and installation

Refer to illustration 5.7

1   Raise the rear of the vehicle and support it securely on jackstands (see Jacking and Towing). Block the front wheels to prevent the vehicle from rolling. Place the transmission in Neutral with the parking brake off.
2   Drain the differential lubricant (see Chapter 1).
3   Remove the driveshafts from the from the differential (see Section 2).
4   Mark the relationship of the propeller shaft to the pinion flange, then unbolt the propeller shaft from the flange (see Section 4). Suspend the propeller shaft with a piece of wire (don't let it hang by the centre support bearing).
5   Remove the rear exhaust pipe assembly (see Chapter 4).
6   Remove the rear subframe and differential assembly (see Chapter 10).
7   Support the differential with a floor jack. Remove the mounting bracket and differential mounting bolts **(see illustration)**. Slowly lower the jack and remove the differential out from under the vehicle.
8   Installation is the reverse of the removal procedure. Tighten all fasteners to the torque values listed in this Chapter's Specifications. Fill the differential with the proper lubricant (see Chapter 1).

6   Differential oil seals (AWD models) - removal and installation

Pinion oil seal

Removal

1   Raise the rear of the vehicle and support it securely on jackstands (see Jacking and Towing). Block the front wheels to prevent the vehicle from rolling. Place the transmission in Neutral with the parking brake off.

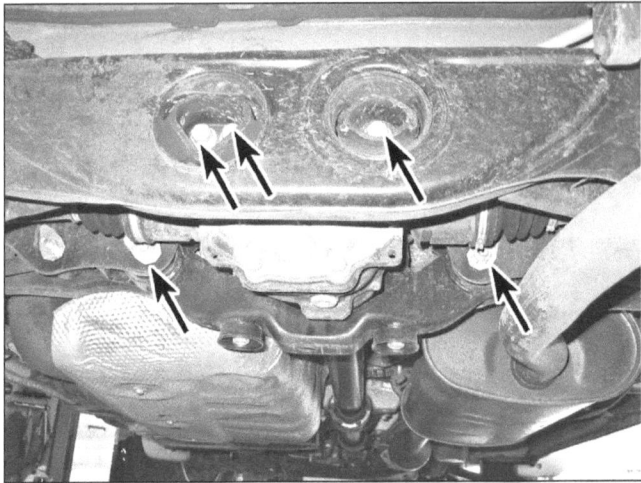

5.7 Differential mounting bolts

2   Mark the relationship of the propeller shaft to the pinion flange, then unbolt the propeller shaft from the flange (see Section 4). Suspend the propeller shaft with a piece of wire (don't let it hang by the centre support bearing).
3   Using a hammer and a punch, unstake the pinion flange nut.
4   A flange holding tool will be required to keep the companion flange from moving while the self-locking pinion nut is loosened. A chain wrench will also work.
5   Remove the pinion nut.
6   Withdraw the flange. It may be necessary to use a two-jaw puller engaged behind the flange to draw it off. Do not attempt to pry or hammer behind the flange or hammer on the end of the pinion shaft.
7   Pry out the old seal and discard it.

Installation
8   Lubricate the lips of the new seal and fill the space between the seal lips with wheel bearing grease, then tap it evenly into position with a seal installation tool or a large socket. Make sure it enters the housing squarely and is tapped in to its full depth.
9   Install the pinion flange; if necessary, tighten the pinion nut to draw the flange into place. Do not try to hammer the flange into position. Tighten the nut to the initial torque listed in this Chapter's Specifications.
10   Using a small torque wrench (dial or beam-type), measure the torque required to rotate the pinion and tighten the nut in small increments (no more than 12.2 Nm) until it matches the pinion shaft bearing preload

listed in this Chapter's Specifications. If the maximum torque listed in this Chapter's Specifications is reached before the specified preload is obtained, the bearing spacer in the differential must be replaced.
11   Once the proper preload is reached, stake the collar of the nut into the slot in the pinion shaft.
12   Reconnect the propeller shaft to the pinion flange (see Section 4). Check the differential lubricant level and add some, if necessary, to bring it to the appropriate level (see Chapter 1).

Driveshaft oil seals
13   Raise the rear of the vehicle and support it securely on jackstands (see Jacking and Towing). Block the front wheels to prevent the vehicle from rolling. Place the transmission in Neutral with the parking brake off.
14   Remove the driveshafts (see Section 2).
15   Carefully pry out the side gear shaft oil seal with a seal removal tool or a large screwdriver; make sure you don't scratch the seal bore.
16   Using a seal installer or a large deep socket as a drift, install the new oil seal. Drive it into the bore squarely and make sure it's completely seated.
17   Lubricate the lip of the new seal with multi-purpose grease, then install the driveshafts (see Section 2). Be careful not to damage the lip of the new seal.
18   Check the differential lubricant level and add some, if necessary, to bring it to the appropriate level (See Chapter 1).

Chapter 9
Brakes

Contents

Specifications

General

Brake fluid type	DOT 3
Brake pedal	
Height	
MCU28R models	160 to 170 mm
GSU40R/GSU45R models	166 to 176 mm
Freeplay	
MCU28R models	2 to 3 mm
GSU40R/GSU45R models	1 to 6 mm
Reserve	
MCU28R models	More than 92 mm
GSU40R/GSU45R models	More than 98 mm
Brake switch clearance	
MCU28R models	0.5 to 2.6 mm
GSU40R/GSU45R models	0.5 to 2.4 mm
Power brake booster pushrod-to-master cylinder piston clearance	0 mm

Disc brakes

Minimum brake pad thickness	See Chapter 1
Disc minimum thickness	Cast into disc
Disc runnout limit	
Front..	0.05 mm
Rear	0.15 mm
Parking brake shoe thickness	
Standard...	2.5 mm
Minimum..	1.0 mm

Torque specifications

	Nm
Caliper mounting bolts	
Front caliper	34
Rear caliper	34
Caliper bracket mounting bolts	
Front	
MCU28R models	107
GSU40R/GSU45R models	104
Rear	78
Brake hose-to-caliper banjo bolt	
MCU28R	30
GSU40R/GSU45R models	
Front brakes..	30
Rear brakes...	33
Master cylinder-to-brake booster nuts	13
Power brake booster mounting nuts	13
Wheel nuts..	See Chapter 1

1   General information

The vehicles covered by this manual are equipped with hydraulically operated front and rear disc brake systems. These disc type brakes are self-adjusting and automatically compensate for pad wear.

Hydraulic system

The hydraulic system consists of two separate circuits. The master cylinder has separate reservoirs for the two circuits, and, in the event of a leak or failure in one hydraulic circuit, the other circuit will remain operative.

Power brake booster

The power brake booster, utilizing engine manifold vacuum and atmospheric pressure to provide assistance to the hydraulically operated brakes, is mounted on the firewall in the engine compartment.

Parking brake

The parking brake operates the rear brakes only, through cable actuation. It's activated by a pedal mounted on the left-side kick panel.

Service

After completing any operation involving disassembly of any part of the brake system, always test-drive the vehicle to check for proper braking performance before resuming normal driving. When testing the brakes, perform the tests on a clean, dry, flat surface. Conditions other than these can lead to inaccurate test results.

Test the brakes at various speeds with both light and heavy pedal pressure. The vehicle should stop evenly without pulling to one side or the other. Avoid locking the brakes, because this slides the tires and diminishes braking efficiency and control of the vehicle.

Tires, vehicle load and wheel alignment are factors which also affect braking performance.

Precautions

There are some general cautions and warnings involving the brake system on this vehicle:

a *Use only brake fluid conforming to DOT 3 specifications.*
b *The brake pads and linings contain fibres which are hazardous to your health if inhaled. Whenever you work on brake system components, clean all parts with brake system cleaner. Do not allow the fine dust to become airborne. Also, wear an approved filtering mask.*
c *Safety should be paramount whenever any servicing of the brake components is performed. Do not use parts or fasteners which are not in perfect condition, and be sure that all clearances and torque specifications are adhered to. If you are at all unsure about a certain procedure, seek professional advice. Upon completion of any brake system work, test the brakes carefully in a controlled area before putting the vehicle into normal service. If a problem is suspected in the brake system, don't drive the vehicle until it's fixed.*
d *Clean up any spilled brake fluid immediately and then wash the area with large amounts of water. This is especially true for any finished or painted surfaces.*

2   Anti-lock Brake System (ABS) - general information

1   The Anti-lock Brake System (ABS) is designed to maintain vehicle steerabilty, directional stability and optimum deceleration under severe braking conditions and on most road surfaces. It does so by monitoring the rotational speed of each wheel and controlling the brake line pressure to each wheel during braking. This prevents the wheel from locking up. The ABS system is primarily designed to prevent wheel lockup during

2.2 The ABS actuator assembly (mounted in the right front portion of the engine compartment. It contains both the actuator and control unit in one assembly - GSU40R/GSU45R models shown, MCU28R model similar

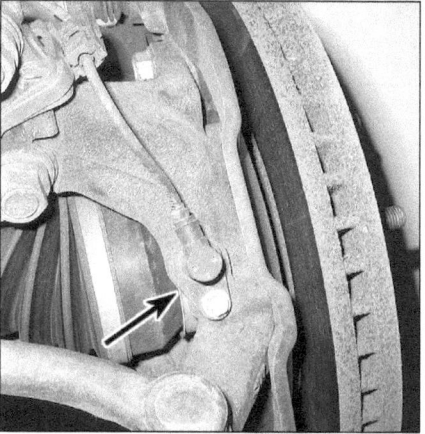

2.12a Front wheel speed sensor - rear wheel speed sensor on AWD models similar

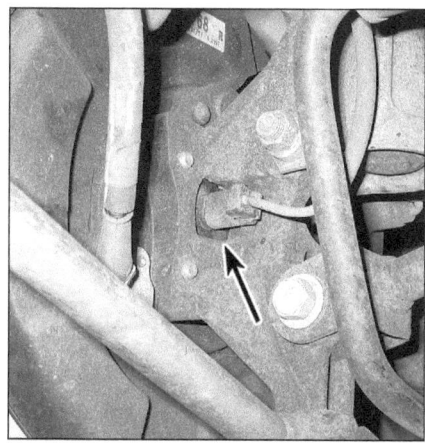

2.12b The rear wheel speed sensor connector on a front-wheel-drive model (the sensor itself is incorporated into the rear hub and bearing assembly)

heavy braking, but the information provided by the wheel speed sensors of the ABS system is shared with several optional systems that use the data to control vehicle handling. EBD (Electronic Brakeforce Distribution), varies the front-to-rear and side-to-side braking balance under different vehicle loads. The traction control system controls only the front (driving) wheels, and is designed to automatically adjust front wheel speed when starting or accelerating on slippery surfaces. The VSC system (Vehicle Skid Control) affects your car's handling during cornering, using information from the ABS sensors and the yaw-rate sensor (which senses the side-to-side tilt of the vehicle). When the skid-control ECU senses oversteer or understeer, it reduces engine power and selectively applies the brakes.

Components

Actuator assembly

Refer to illustration 2.2

2   The actuator assembly is mounted in the engine compartment and consists of an electric hydraulic pump and solenoid valves **(see illustration)**.

  a *The electric pump provides hydraulic pressure to charge the reservoirs in the actuator, which supplies pressure to the braking system. The pump and reservoirs are housed in the actuator assembly.*

  b *The solenoid valves modulate brake line pressure during ABS operation.*

Speed sensors

3   These sensors are located at each wheel and generate small electrical pulsations when the toothed sensor rings are turning, sending a signal to the electronic controller indicating wheel rotational speed.

4   The front speed sensors are mounted to the front steering knuckle in close relationship to the toothed sensor rings, which are integral with the front driveaxle outer CV joints.

5   The rear wheel sensors are bolted to the rear suspension knuckles. The sensor rings are integrated with the rear hub assemblies.

ABS computer

6   The ABS computer is mounted with the actuator and is the brain for the ABS system. The function of the computer is to accept and process information received from the wheel speed sensors to control the hydraulic line pressure, avoiding wheel lock up. The computer also constantly monitors the system, even under normal driving conditions, to find faults within the system.

Diagnosis and repair

7   If a dashboard warning light comes on and stays on while the vehicle is in operation, the ABS system requires attention. Although special electronic ABS diagnostic testing tools are necessary to properly diagnose the system, you can perform a few preliminary checks before taking the vehicle to a dealer service department.

  a *Check the brake fluid level in the reservoir.*

  b *Verify that the computer electrical connectors are securely connected.*

  c *Check the electrical connectors at the hydraulic control unit.*

  d *Check the fuses.*

  e *Follow the wiring harness to each wheel and verify that all connections are secure and that the wiring is undamaged.*

8   If the above preliminary checks do not rectify the problem, the vehicle should be diagnosed by a dealer service department or other qualified repair shop. Due to the complexity of this system, all actual repair work must be done by a qualified automotive technician.

Warning: *Do NOT try to repair an ABS wiring harness. The ABS system is sensitive to even the smallest changes in resistance. Repairing the harness could alter resistance values and cause the system to malfunction. If the ABS wiring harness is damaged in any way, it must be replaced.*

Caution: *Make sure the ignition is turned off before unplugging or reattaching any electrical connections.*

Wheel speed sensor - removal and installation

Refer to illustrations 2.12a and 2.12b

9   Loosen the wheel nuts, raise the vehicle and support it securely on jackstands (see Jacking and Towing). Remove the wheel.

Warning: *If the vehicle is equipped with an electronically modulated air suspension, make sure that the height control switch is turned off before raising the vehicle.*

10   Make sure the ignition key is turned to the Off position.

11   Trace the wiring back from the sensor, detaching all brackets and clips while noting its correct routing, then disconnect the electrical connector.

12   For front wheel speed sensors on all models and rear wheel speed sensors on AWD models, remove the mounting bolt and carefully pull the sensor out from the knuckle **(see illustration)**. The rear wheel speed sensor on front-wheel-drive models is integrated with the rear hub and cannot be removed without removing the hub **(see illustration)**. See Chapter 10 for the rear hub removal procedure.

13   Installation is the reverse of the removal procedure. Tighten the mounting fastener securely.

14   Install the wheel and wheel nuts, tightening them securely. Lower the vehicle and tighten the wheel nuts to the torque listed in the Chapter 1 Specifications.

3.5 Before removing the caliper, slowly depress the piston in the caliper bore by using a large C-clamp between the outer brake pad and the back of the caliper

3.6a Always wash the brakes with brake cleaner before disassembling anything

3   Disc brake pads - replacement

Refer to illustrations 3.5, 3.6a through 3.6p and 3.7a through 3.7n

Warning: *Disc brake pads must be replaced on both front or rear wheels at the same time - never replace the pads on only one wheel. Also, the dust created by the brake system is harmful to your health. Never blow it out with compressed air and don't inhale any of it. An approved filtering mask should be worn when working on the brakes. Do not, under any circumstances, use petroleum-based solvents to clean brake parts. Use brake system cleaner only!*

Note: *This procedure applies to both the front and rear disc brakes.*

Note: *The manufacturer recommends replacing the pad shims and wear indicators whenever the pads are replaced.*

1   Remove the cap from the brake fluid reservoir.

2   Loosen the wheel nuts, raise the front or rear of the vehicle and support it securely on jackstands (see Jacking and Towing). Block the wheels at the opposite end.

3   Remove the wheels. Work on one brake assembly at a time, using the assembled brake for reference if necessary.

4   Inspect the brake disc carefully as outlined in Section 5. If machining is necessary, follow the information in that Section to remove the disc, at which time the pads can be removed as well.

5   Push the piston back into its bore to provide room for the new brake pads. A C-clamp can be used to accomplish this **(see illustration)**. As the piston is depressed to the bottom of the caliper bore, the fluid in the master cylinder will rise. Make sure that it doesn't overflow. If necessary, siphon off some of the fluid.

6   If you're replacing the front brake pads, follow the accompanying photos, beginning with illustration 3.6a. Be sure to stay in order and read the caption under each illustration.

3.6b Remove the lower caliper bolt. To detach the caliper completely, remove both caliper bolts but do not let the caliper hang by the brake hose

7   If you're replacing the rear brake pads, wash the brake assembly **(see illustration 3.6a)**, then follow the accompanying photos

3.6c Pivot the caliper up (be careful not to damage the boot for the upper slide pin). . .

3.6d . . . and secure it to the strut bracket with a piece of wire; do not allow the caliper to hang by the flexible brake hose

3.6e Remove inner pad . . .

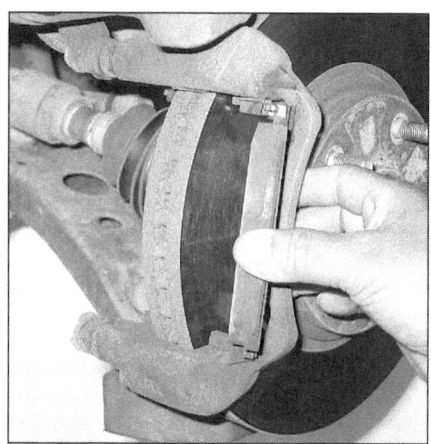

3.6f . . . and the outer pad

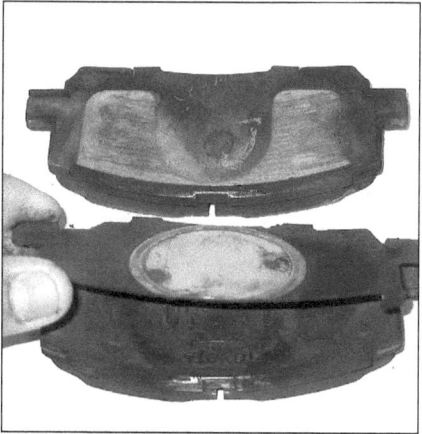

3.6g Remove the shim(s) from each brake pad, noting the order and position (some pads may only have one shim). The manufacturer recommends shim replacement when the pads are replaced

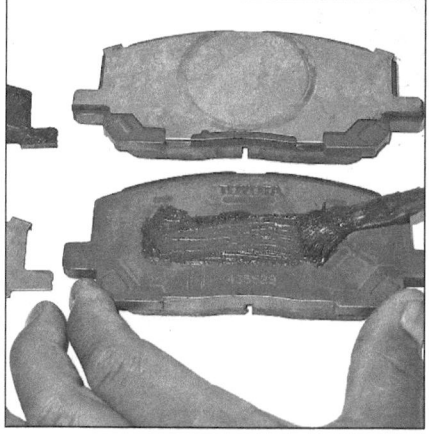

3.6h Apply a thin film of disc brake grease in between the shims and the back of the brake pads

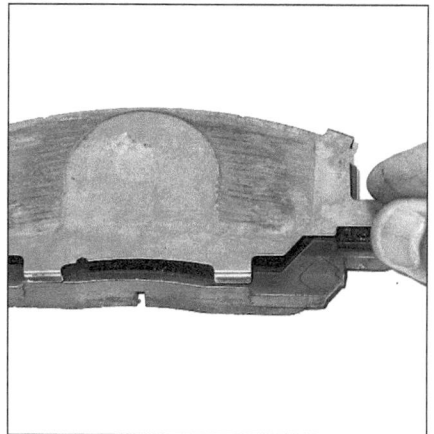

3.6i Place the shims on the pads in the correct order and position as the original ones. If necessary, refer to the installed pads on the other side of the vehicle if there is any question about shim placement

3.6j Remove the upper and lower pad support plates; make sure they are a tight fit and aren't worn. If necessary, replace them

3.6k Install the upper and lower pad support plates

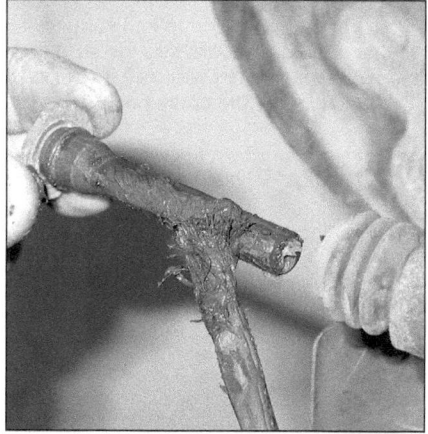

3.6l Pull out the upper and lower sliding pins and clean them. Apply a coat of high-temperature grease to the pins and reinstall them. Be careful not to damage the pin boots, replace any boots that are worn or damaged

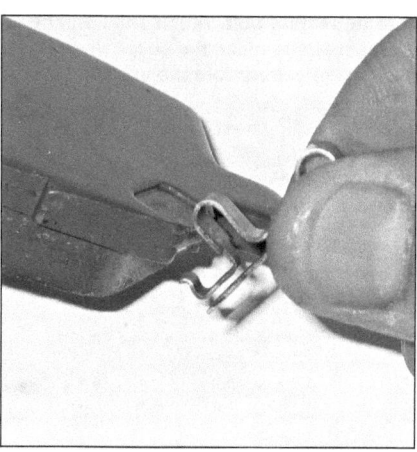

3.6m Place a new wear indicator on the new inner pad; the manufacturer recommends wear indicator replacement when the pads are replaced

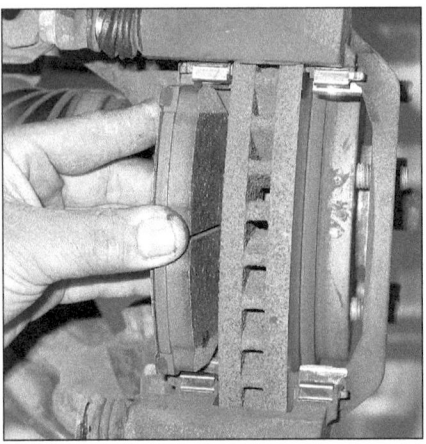

3.6n Install the inner pad, making sure that the ends are seated correctly on the pad support plates

3.6o Install the outer pad, making sure that the ends are seated correctly on the pad support plates

3.6p Install the caliper and tighten the caliper bolts to the torque listed in this Chapter's Specifications

beginning with illustration 3.7a. Be sure to stay in order and read the caption under each illustration.

8   When reinstalling the caliper, be sure to tighten the mounting bolts to the torque listed

in this Chapter's Specifications. After the job has been completed, firmly depress the brake pedal a few times to bring the pads into contact with the disc. Check the level of the brake fluid, adding some if necessary. Check the

operation of the brakes carefully before placing the vehicle into normal service.

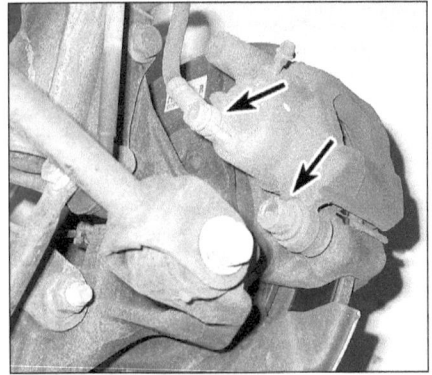

3.7a Wash the brake with brake system cleaner (see illustration 3.6a), then remove the caliper retaining bolt (lower arrow); the upper arrow points to the brake hose banjo fitting bolt, which shouldn't be unscrewed unless the caliper is being removed from the vehicle

3.7b Pivot the caliper up and support it in that position. Secure it to the strut coil spring with a piece of wire and do not let it hang by the brake hose.

3.7c Remove the inner brake pad . . .

3.7d . . . and the outer brake pad

3.7e Remove the upper and lower pad support plates; make sure they are a tight fit and aren't worn. If necessary, replace them

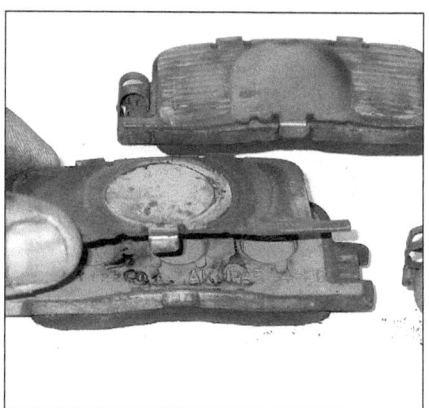

3.7f Remove the shim(s) and pad wear indicator from each brake pad, noting the order and position (some pads may only have one shim). The manufacturer recommends shim and indicator replacement when the pads are replaced

3.7g Replace the wear indicator on each brake pad

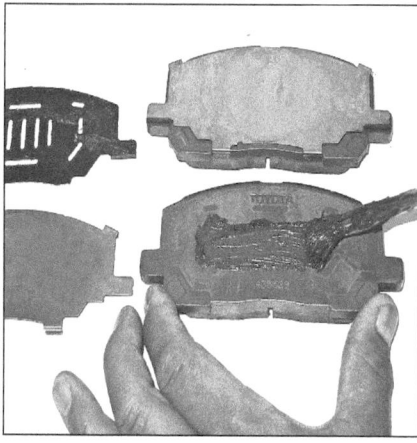

3.7h Apply a thin film of disc brake grease between the shims and the back of the brake pads

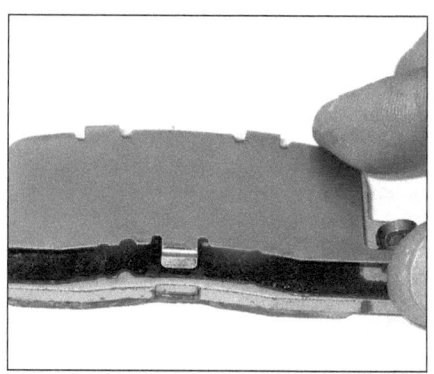

3.7i Replace the shim(s) on each pad in the original position as the old ones. If necessary, refer to the installed pads on the other side of the vehicle if there is any question about shim placement

3.7j Install the pad support plates onto the caliper bracket, then install the inner brake pad

3.7k Install the outer brake pad

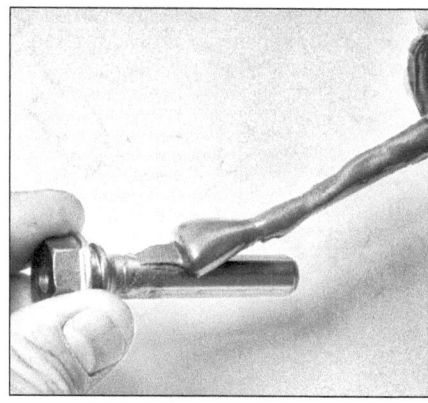

3.7l Pull out the upper and lower sliding pins and clean them. Apply a coat of high-temperature grease to the pins and then reinstall them. Be careful not to damage the pin boots (replace any boots that are worn or damaged). On some models, the pin will be exposed by simply removing the caliper from the bracket. Be careful not to damage the pin boot when removing the caliper

3.7m Install the guide pins and the caliper and pivot the caliper down over the new pads. Install the caliper-retaining bolt(s) and tighten it to the torque listed in this Chapter's Specifications

3.7n If you have difficulty installing the caliper over the new pads, use a C-clamp to bottom the piston in its bore, then try again - it should now slip over the pads. Install the caliper and tighten the caliper bolt(s) to the torque listed in this Chapter's Specifications

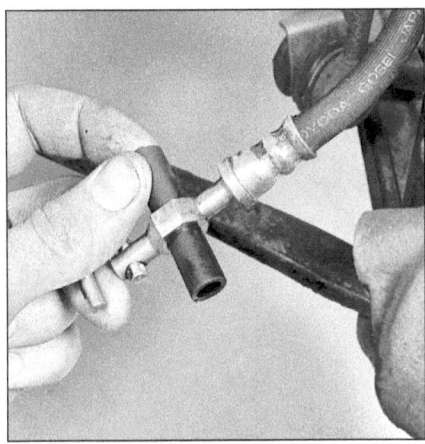

4.2 Using a piece of rubber hose of the appropriate size, plug the brake line banjo fitting to prevent brake fluid from leaking out and to prevent dirt and moisture from contaminating the fluid in the hose

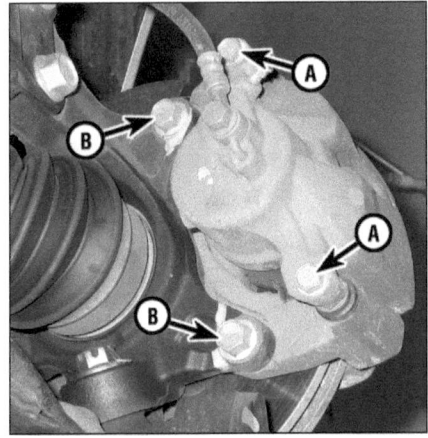

4.3 Front brake caliper mounting details (rear caliper similar)

A   Caliper mounting bolts
B   Caliper bracket mounting bolts

5.2a To remove the front caliper bracket from the steering knuckle, remove these two bolts

---

4   Disc brake caliper - removal and installation

Warning: *Dust created by the brake system is harmful to your health. Never blow it out with compressed air and don't inhale any of it. An approved filtering mask should be worn when working on the brakes. Do not, under any circumstances, use petroleum-based solvents to clean brake parts. Use brake system cleaner only!*

Note: *Always replace the calipers in pairs - never replace just one of them.*

Removal

Refer to illustrations 4.2 and 4.3

1   Loosen the wheel nuts, raise the vehicle and support it securely on jackstands (see Jacking and Towing). Remove the wheels.

Warning: *If the vehicle is equipped with an electronically modulated air suspension, make sure that the height control switch is turned off before raising the vehicle.*

2   Remove the brake hose banjo bolt and disconnect the hose from the caliper. Plug the hose to keep contaminants out of the brake system and to prevent losing any more brake fluid than is necessary **(see illustration)**.

Note: *If you're just removing the caliper for access to other components, don't detach the hose.*

3   Remove the caliper mounting bolts **(see illustration)**.

4   Remove the caliper. If necessary, remove the caliper bracket from the steering knuckle or rear knuckle (see illustrations 5.2a and 5.2b).

Installation

5   Install the caliper by reversing the removal procedure. Tighten the caliper mounting bolts (and bracket bolts, if removed) to the

torque listed in this Chapter's Specifications. Install new sealing washers on either side of the brake hose banjo fitting, then tighten the banjo bolt to the torque listed in this Chapter's Specifications.

6   Bleed the brake system (see Section 8).

7   Install the wheels and wheel nuts. Lower the vehicle and tighten the wheel nuts to the torque listed in the Chapter 1 Specifications.

---

5   Brake disc - inspection, removal and installation

Inspection

Refer to illustrations 5.2a, 5.2b, 5.3, 5.4a, 5.4b, 5.5a and 5.5b

1   Loosen the wheel nuts, raise the vehicle and support it securely on jackstands (see Jacking and Towing). Remove the wheel and install the wheel nuts to hold the disc in place. If the rear brake disc is being worked on, release the parking brake.

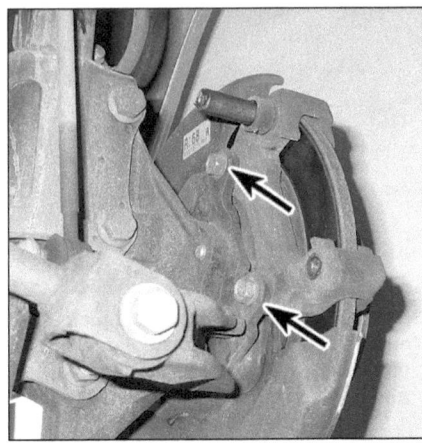

5.2b To remove the rear caliper bracket from the knuckle, remove these two bolts

2   Remove the brake caliper as outlined in Section 4. It isn't necessary to disconnect the brake hose. After removing the caliper bolts, suspend the caliper out of the way with a piece of wire **(see illustration 3.6d)**. Remove the caliper bracket mounting bolts and then remove the bracket **(see illustrations)**.

3   Visually inspect the disc surface for score marks and other damage. Light scratches and shallow grooves are normal after use and may not always be detrimental to brake operation, but deep scoring - over 1.0 mm - requires disc removal and refinishing by an automotive machine shop. Be sure to check both sides of the disc **(see illustration)**. If pulsating has been noticed during application of the brakes, suspect disc runout.

4   To check disc runout, place a dial indicator at a point about 20 mm from the outer edge of the disc **(see illustration)**. Set the indicator to zero and turn the disc. The indicator reading should not exceed the specified allowable runout limit. If it does, the disc should be refinished by an automotive machine shop.

5.3 The brake pads on this vehicle were obviously neglected, as they wore down completely and cut deep grooves into the disc - wear this severe means the disc must be replaced

5.4a Use a dial indicator to check disc runout; if the reading exceeds the maximum allowable runout limit, the disc will have to be machined or replaced

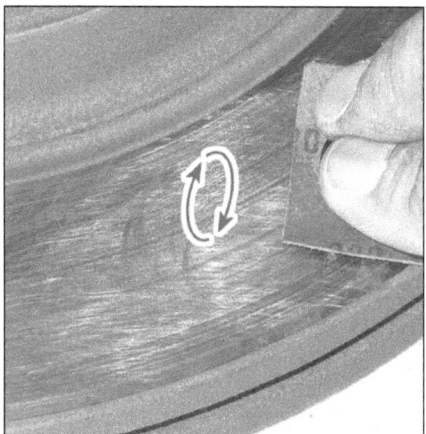

5.4b Using a swirling motion, remove the glaze from the disc surface with sandpaper or emery cloth

5.5a The minimum wear dimension is cast into the back side of the disc (typical)

5.5b Use a micrometer to measure disc thickness

5.6a If the rear disc is difficult to remove, remove this plug . . .

5.6b . . . insert a screwdriver through the hole (the hole must be at the 6 o'clock position, because that's where the adjuster is located) and rotate the adjuster to back the parking brake shoes away from the drum surface in the disc

Note: *Professionals recommend resurfacing the discs whenever the pads are replaced regardless of the dial indicator reading, as this will impart a smooth finish and ensure a perfectly flat surface, eliminating any brake pedal pulsation or other undesirable symptoms. At the very least, if you elect not to have the discs resurfaced, remove the glaze from the surface with sandpaper or emery cloth using a swirling motion* **(see illustration)**.

5   It's absolutely critical that the disc not be machined to a thickness under the specified minimum allowable refinish thickness. The minimum wear (or discard) thickness is cast into the inside of the disc **(see illustration)**. The disc thickness can be checked with a micrometer **(see illustration)**.

Removal

Refer to illustrations 5.6a and 5.6b

6   Remove the wheel nuts that were put on to hold the disc in place and slide the disc off the hub. If the rear disc won't come off, it may be interfering with the parking brake shoes;

remove the plug **(see illustration)** and rotate the adjuster to back the parking brake shoes away from the drum surface within the disc **(see illustration)**.

Installation

7   Place the disc in position over the threaded studs.
8   Install the caliper bracket, tightening the bolts to the torque listed in this Chapter's Specifications.
9   Install the caliper, tightening the bolts to the torque listed in this Chapter's Specifications. Bleeding won't be necessary unless the brake hose was disconnected from the caliper.
10   If you're installing a rear disc, adjust the parking brake shoes as described in Section 10.
11   Install the wheel and wheel nuts. Lower the vehicle and tighten the wheel nuts to the torque listed in the Chapter 1 Specifications. Depress the brake pedal a few times to bring the brake pads into contact with the disc. Check the operation of the brakes carefully before driving the vehicle.

6   Master cylinder - removal and installation

Removal

Refer to illustration 6.5

Caution: *Brake fluid will damage paint or finished surfaces. Cover all body parts and be careful not to spill fluid during this procedure. Clean up any spilled brake fluid immediately and then wash the area with large amounts of water.*

1   Remove the engine cover.

Note: *On 2GR-FE engines, pull up on the front side of the engine top cover to detach it from the two front retainers. After the front is detached, pull up on the back retainer and remove the engine cover. Do not pull up on the front and rear at the same time or the cover can be damaged.*

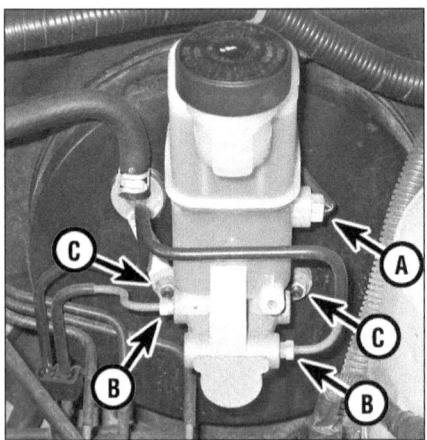

6.5 Master cylinder installation details

A *Electrical connector*
B *Brake line fittings*
C *Mounting nuts*

6.11 The best way to bleed air from the master cylinder before installing it on the vehicle is with a pair of bleed tubes

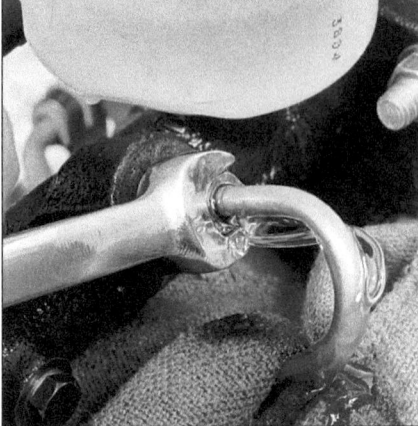

6.19 Loosen the fittings on the master cylinder to bleed it when it is installed on the vehicle (typical shown)

2   Remove the strut brace from between the strut towers, if equipped (see Chapter 10).
3   On GSU40R/GSU45R models, proceed as follows:

    a *Disconnect the negative (-) battery terminal (see Chapter 5).*
    b *Remove the windshield wiper arms, side seals and plastic cowl (see Chapter 12).*
    c *Remove the wiper motor and linkage (see Chapter 12).*
    d *Remove the cowl assembly (see Chapter 11).*

4   Remove as much fluid as possible from the reservoir with a syringe.

Note: *On GSU40R/GSU45R models, the reservoir is not directly attached to the master cylinder. Drain the reservoir and detach any hoses and then remove it for access.*

5   Unplug the electrical connector for the brake fluid level warning switch **(see illustration)**.
6   Place rags under the fittings and prepare caps or plastic bags to cover the ends of the lines once they're disconnected.
7   Loosen the fittings at the ends of the brake lines where they enter the master cylinder. To prevent rounding off the flats, use a flare-nut wrench, which wraps around the fitting hex **(see illustration 6.19)**.
8   Carefully move the brake lines away from the master cylinder and plug the ends to prevent contamination.
9   Remove the nuts attaching the master cylinder to the power booster. Pull the master cylinder off the studs to remove it. Again, be careful not to spill fluid or bend the brake lines as this is done **(see illustration 6.5)**.

Installation

Refer to illustrations 6.11 and 6.19

10   Bench bleed the new master cylinder before installing it. Because it will be necessary to depress the master cylinder piston and, at the same time, control flow from the

brake line outlets, it is recommended that the master cylinder be mounted in a vise.
11   Attach a pair of master cylinder bleeder tubes to the outlet ports of the master cylinder **(see illustration)**.

Note: *On models that have a detached reservoir, feed the bleeder tubes back into the master cylinder where the reservoir hoses connect. On models with an auxiliary type reservoir, place the bleeder tubes into the small tank mounted on the master cylinder.*

12   Fill the reservoir with brake fluid of the recommended type (see Chapter 1).
13   Slowly push the pistons into the master cylinder (a large Phillips screwdriver can be used for this) - air will be expelled from the pressure chambers and into the reservoir. Because the tubes are submerged in fluid, air can't be drawn back into the master cylinder when you release the pistons.
14   Repeat the procedure until no more air bubbles are present.
15   Remove the bleed tubes, one at a time, and install plugs in the open ports to prevent fluid leakage and air from entering. If installing a new master cylinder, adjust the booster pushrod length (see Section 9).
16   Install the reservoir cover, then install the master cylinder over the studs on the power brake booster and tighten the attaching nuts only finger tight at this time.
17   Thread the brake line fittings into the master cylinder. Since the master cylinder is still a bit loose, it can be moved slightly in order for the fittings to thread in easily. Do not strip the threads as the fittings are tightened.
18   Tighten the mounting nuts to the torque listed in this Chapter's Specification and then the brake line fittings securely.
19   Fill the master cylinder reservoir with fluid, then bleed the master cylinder and the brake system as described in Section 8. To bleed the cylinder on the vehicle, have an assistant pump the brake pedal several times slowly and then hold the pedal to the floor.

Loosen the fitting nut to allow air and fluid to escape. Repeat this procedure on both fittings until the fluid is clear of air bubbles **(see illustration)**.

Caution: *Have plenty of rags on hand to catch the fluid - brake fluid will ruin painted surfaces.*

20   If it was necessary to remove the master cylinder-to-ABS actuator brake lines, also bleed the lines at the ABS actuator.
21   The remainder of installation is the reverse of removal. Test the operation of the brake system carefully before placing the vehicle into normal service.

Warning: *Do not operate the vehicle if you are in doubt about the effectiveness of the brake system. On models equipped with ABS, it is possible for air to become trapped in the anti-lock brake system hydraulic control unit, so, if the pedal continues to feel spongy after repeated bleedings or the BRAKE or ANTI-LOCK light stays on, have the vehicle towed to a dealer service department or other qualified shop to be bled with the aid of a scan tool.*

7   Brake hoses and lines - inspection and replacement

Inspection

1   About every six months, with the vehicle raised and supported securely on jackstands, the rubber hoses which connect the steel brake lines with the front and rear brake assemblies should be inspected for cracks, chafing of the outer cover, leaks, blisters and other damage. These are important and vulnerable parts of the brake system and inspection should be complete. A light and mirror will be helpful for a thorough check. If a hose exhibits any of the above conditions, replace it with a new one.

7.3 Unscrew the brake line threaded fitting with a flare-nut wrench to protect the fitting corners from being rounded off

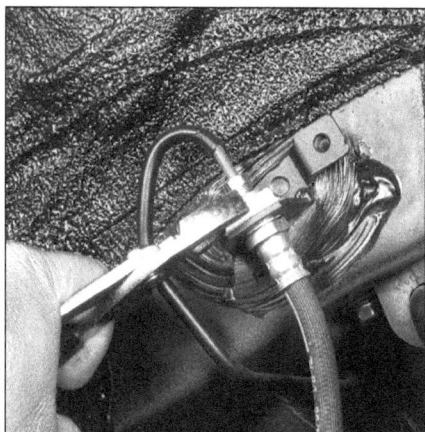

7.4 Remove the brake hose-to-brake line U-clip with a pair of pliers

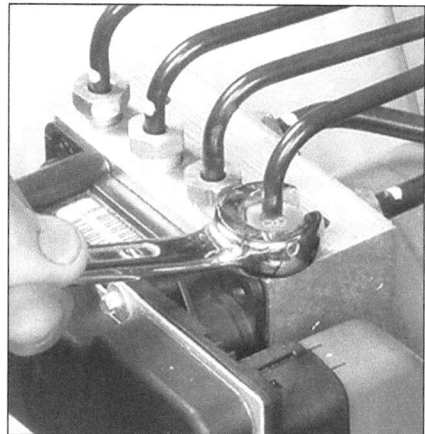

8.5 Bleeding air from one of the ABS brake modulator pipe fittings

Replacement

Front brake hose

Refer to illustrations 7.3 and 7.4

2   Loosen the wheel nuts, raise the vehicle and support it securely on jackstands (see Jacking and Towing). Remove the wheel.

Warning: *If the vehicle is equipped with an electronically modulated air suspension, make sure that the height control switch is turned off before raising the vehicle.*

3   At the frame bracket, unscrew the brake line fitting from the hose **(see illustration)**. Use a flare-nut wrench to prevent rounding off the corners.

4   Remove the U-clip from the female fitting at the bracket with a pair of pliers **(see illustration)**, then pass the hose through the bracket.

5   At the caliper end of the hose, remove the banjo fitting bolt, then separate the hose from the caliper. Note that there are two copper sealing washers on either side of the fitting - they should be replaced with new ones during installation.

6   Remove the fastener from the strut bracket and then detach the hose from it.

7   To install the hose, pass the caliper fitting end through the strut bracket, then connect the fitting to the caliper with the banjo bolt and new sealing washers. Make sure the locating lug on the fitting is engaged with the hole in the caliper, then tighten the bolt to the torque listed in this Chapter's Specifications.

8   Push the metal support into the strut bracket and install the U-clip. Make sure the hose isn't twisted between the caliper and the strut bracket.

9   Route the hose into the frame bracket, again making sure it isn't twisted, then connect the brake line fitting, starting the threads by hand. Install the clip and E-ring, if equipped, then tighten the fitting securely.

10   Bleed the caliper (see Section 8).

11   Install the wheel and wheel nuts, lower the vehicle and tighten the wheel nuts to the torque listed in the Chapter 1 Specifications.

Rear brake hose

12   Perform Steps 2, 3 and 4 above, then repeat Steps 3 and 4 at the other end of the hose. Be sure to bleed the caliper (see Section 8).

Metal brake lines

13   When replacing brake lines, be sure to use the correct parts. Don't use copper tubing for any brake system components. Purchase genuine steel brake lines from a dealer or auto parts store.

14   Prefabricated brake line, with the tube ends already flared and fittings installed, is available at auto parts stores and dealer parts departments.

15   When installing the new line, make sure it's securely supported in the brackets and has plenty of clearance between moving or hot components.

16   After installation, check the master cylinder fluid level and add fluid as necessary. Bleed the brake system (see Section 8) and test the brakes carefully before driving the vehicle in traffic.

---

8   Brake hydraulic system - bleeding

Refer to illustrations 8.5 and 8.7

Warning: *Use only specified brake fluid (see Chapter 1).*

Warning: *Wear eye protection when bleeding the brake system. If the fluid comes in contact with your eyes, immediately rinse them with water and seek medical attention.*

Note: *Bleeding the brake system is necessary to remove any air that's trapped in the system when it's opened during removal and refitting of a hose, line, caliper or master cylinder. The procedure for changing the brake fluid is covered in Chapter 1.*

1   Bleeding of the hydraulic system is necessary to remove air whenever it is introduced into the brake system.

2   Have an assistant on hand, as well as a supply of new brake fluid, an empty clear container, a length of clear plastic tubing to fit over the bleed valve and a spanner to open and close the bleed valve.

3   Remove the cap from the brake fluid reservoir and add fluid, if necessary (see Chapter 1). Don't allow the fluid level to drop too low during this procedure - check it frequently. Reinstall the cap.

4   Raise the front of the vehicle and support it securely on jackstands (see Jacking and Towing).

5   If any lines between the master cylinder and each brake caliper have been removed, proceed as follows:

  a *Have an assistant pump the brake pedal several times to deplete any vacuum in the vacuum booster.*

  b *While an assistant holds the brake pedal depressed, loosen one of the pipe fittings from the master cylinder **(see illustration 6.19)**. Any trapped air in the pipe should escape along with some fluid. Tighten the pipe fitting while the pedal is still depressed and then have the assistant raise the brake pedal. Repeat this until only fluid is expelled from the fitting.*

  c *Repeat the procedure on the other master cylinder outlet pipes.*

  d *Follow the pipes from the master cylinder to the ABS brake modulator assembly and again loosen each inlet pipe fitting – that is the pipe that comes from the master cylinder to the modulator assembly. Bleed the air from these fittings **(see illustration)**.*

  e *Finally bleed the air from the modulator outlet fittings.*

  f *Once this is done, you are ready to move on to bleeding the air from the each caliper.*

6   Beginning at the LH rear brake, loosen the bleed valve slightly, then tighten it to a point where it's snug but can still be loosened quickly and easily.

7   Place one end of the tubing over the bleed valve and submerge the other end in

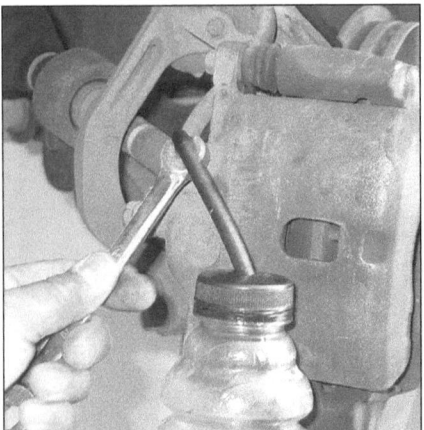

8.7 When bleeding the brakes, a hose is connected to the bleeder valve at the caliper or wheel cylinder and then submerged in brake fluid. Air will be seen as bubbles in the tube and container. All air must be expelled before moving to the next wheel

9.14a Measure the distance that the pushrod protrudes from the brake booster at the master cylinder mounting surface (including the gasket)

brake fluid in the container **(see illustration)**.

8   Open the bleed valve and have your assistant slowly depress the brake pedal and hold the pedal firmly depressed. Watch for air bubbles to exit the submerged end of the tube. When the fluid flow slows, tighten the nipple, then have your assistant slowly release the pedal. Wait five seconds before proceeding.

9   Repeat Step 8 until no more air is seen leaving the tube, then tighten the bleed valve and proceed to the RH rear brake bleed valve. Repeat the bleeding procedure at this bleed valve and tighten securely when no more air is expelled.

10   Continue the bleeding procedure next on the LH front bleed valve and finish at the RH front bleed valve in that order. Be sure to check the fluid in the master cylinder reservoir

9.11 Power brake booster mounting details:

1 Mounting fasteners
2 Return spring
3 Clevis retaining clip
4 Clevis pin

frequently.

11   Lower the vehicle and check the fluid level in the brake fluid reservoir, adding fluid as necessary.

12   Never use old brake fluid. It contains moisture which will allow the fluid to boil, rendering the brakes useless. When bleeding, make sure the fluid coming out of the bleeder is not only free of bubbles, but clean also.

13   Refill the fluid reservoir with new fluid at the end of the operation.

14   Check the operation of the brakes. The pedal should feel solid when depressed, with no sponginess. If necessary, repeat the entire process.

Warning: *Do not operate the vehicle if you are in doubt about the effectiveness of the brake system.*

---

9   Power brake booster - check, removal and installation

Operating check

1   Depress the brake pedal several times with the engine off and make sure there's no change in the pedal reserve distance.

2   Depress the pedal and start the engine. If the pedal goes down slightly, operation is normal.

Airtightness check

3   Start the engine and turn it off after one or two minutes. Depress the brake pedal slowly several times. If the pedal depresses less each time, the booster is airtight.

4   Depress the brake pedal while the engine is running, then stop the engine with the pedal depressed. If there's no change in the pedal reserve travel after holding the pedal for 30 seconds, the booster is airtight.

Removal

Refer to illustration 9.11

5   Power brake booster units shouldn't be disassembled. They require special tools not normally found in most automotive repair stations or shops. They're fairly complex and, because of their critical relationship to brake performance, should be replaced with a new one.

6   Disconnect the negative (-) battery terminal (see Chapter 5).

7   On GSU40R/GSU45R models, remove the engine and transaxle assembly (see Chapter 2C).

Note: *It is not possible to remove the booster assembly on these models with the engine in place*

8   Remove the brake master cylinder (see Section 6).

9   Carefully disconnect the vacuum hose from the brake booster.

10   Inside the vehicle, remove the knee bolster and the brace behind it (see Chapter 11).

Warning: *The GSU40R/GSU45R models have a knee airbag as part of the knee bolster. Ensure the battery is disconnected before attempting to remove the bolster panel.*

11   Remove the brake pedal return spring near the top of the brake pedal. Remove the clevis pin-retaining clip with pliers and then pull out the pin **(see illustration)**.

12   Remove the four fasteners holding the brake booster to the firewall and the brake pedal return spring. Then slide the booster straight out from the firewall until the studs clear the holes **(see illustration 9.11)**.

Installation

Refer to illustrations 9.14a, 9.14b, 9.14c and 9.14d

13   Installation procedures are basically the reverse of removal. Tighten the booster mounting nuts to the torque listed in this Chapter's Specifications.

14   If a new power brake booster unit is being installed, check the pushrod clearance **(see illustration)** as follows:

*a   Measure the distance that the pushrod protrudes from the master cylinder mounting surface on the front of the power brake booster, including the gasket (if equipped) **(see illustration)**. Write down this measurement. This is dimension A.*

*b   Measure the distance from the mounting flange to the end of the master cylinder **(see illustration)**. Write down this measurement. This is dimension B.*

*c   Measure the distance from the end of the master cylinder to the bottom of the pocket in the piston **(see illustration)**. Write down this measurement. This is dimension C.*

d   Subtract measurement B from measurement C, then subtract measurement A from the difference between B and C. This is the pushrod clearance.

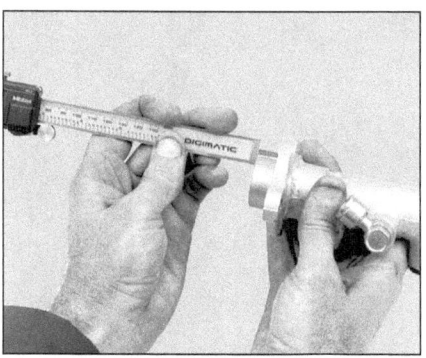

9.14b Measure the distance from the mounting flange to the end of the master cylinder

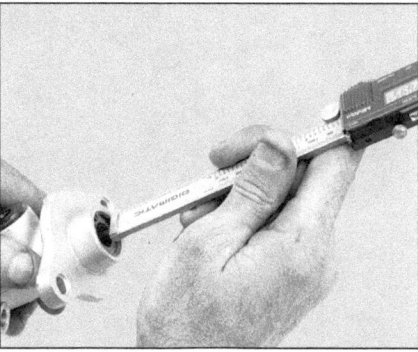

9.14c Measure the distance from the piston pocket to the end of the master cylinder

9.14d To adjust the length of the booster pushrod, hold the serrated portion of the rod with a pair of pliers and turn the adjusting screw in or out, as necessary, to achieve the desired setting

10.4 Before disassembling it, be sure to wash the parking brake assembly with brake cleaner

10.5a Remove the rear parking brake shoe return spring from the anchor pin . . .

10.5b . . . and unhook it from the rear shoe

e   *Compare your calculated pushrod clearance to the pushrod clearance listed in this Chapter's Specifications. If necessary, adjust the pushrod length to achieve the correct clearance* **(see illustration 9.14d)**.

15   After the final installation of the master cylinder and brake hoses and lines, brake pedal height and freeplay must be adjusted and the system must be bled. See the appropriate Sections of this Chapter for the procedures.

10   Parking brake shoes - inspection and replacement

Refer to illustrations 10.4 and 10.5a through 10.5u

Warning: *Dust created by the brake system is hazardous to your health. Never blow it out with compressed air and don't inhale any of it. An approved filtering mask should be worn when working on the brakes. Do not, under any circumstances, use petroleum-based*

solvents to clean brake parts. Use brake system cleaner only!

Warning: *Parking brake shoes must be replaced on both wheels at the same time - never replace the shoes on only one wheel.*

1   Remove the brake disc (see Section 5).
2   Inspect the thickness of the lining material on the shoes. If the lining has worn down to 1.00 mm or less, the shoes must be replaced.
3   Remove the hub and bearing assembly (see Chapter 10).

Note: *It is possible to perform the shoe replacement procedure without removing the hub and bearing assembly, although working room is limited.*

4   Wash off the brake parts with brake system cleaner **(see illustration)**.
5   Follow the accompanying illustrations for the brake shoe replacement procedure **(see illustrations 10.5a through 10.5u)**. Be sure to stay in order and read the caption under each illustration.
6   Install the brake disc. Temporarily thread three of the wheel nuts onto the studs to hold the disc in place.
7   Remove the hole plug from the brake disc. Adjust the parking brake shoe clearance by turning the adjuster star wheel with a brake adjusting tool or screwdriver until the shoes contact the disc and the disc can't be turned **(see illustrations 5.6a and 5.6b)**. Back off

10.5c Remove the front parking brake shoe return spring from the anchor pin . . .

10.5d . . . and unhook it from the front shoe

10.5e Remove the rear shoe hold-down spring and pull out the pin

10.5f Remove the shoe strut from between the shoes

10.5g Remove the front shoe hold-down spring and pull out the pin

10.5h Remove the adjuster and the tension spring (the tension spring, which is not visible in this photo, is behind the adjuster and is attached to both shoes)

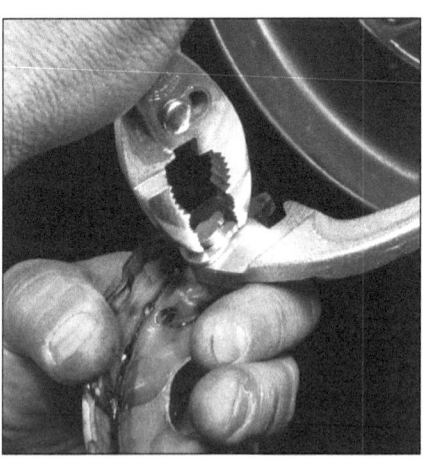

10.5i Pop the C-washer off the pivot pin on the back of the rear shoe . . .

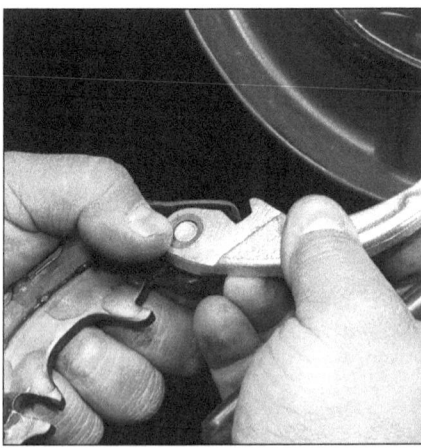

10.5j . . . and pull the parking brake lever off the pivot pin

the adjuster eight notches, then install the hole plug.

8   Install the caliper bracket **(see illustra-** tion 5.2b) and brake caliper (see Section 4). Be sure to tighten the bolts to the torque listed in this Chapter's Specifications.

9   Install the wheel and tighten the wheel nuts to the torque specified in Chapter 1.

10   Set the parking brake and count the number of clicks that it travels. It should be between about five to seven clicks - if it's not, adjust the parking brake (see Section 11).

10.5k Apply a thin coat of high-temperature grease to the contact surfaces of the backing plate

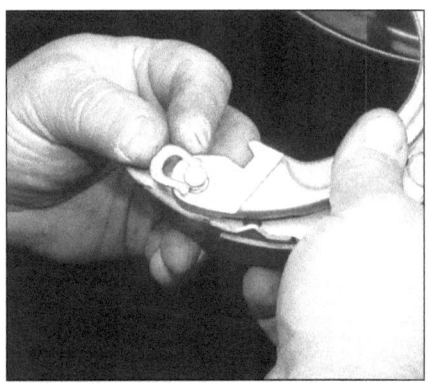

10.5l Slide the parking brake lever onto the pivot pin and install a new C-washer

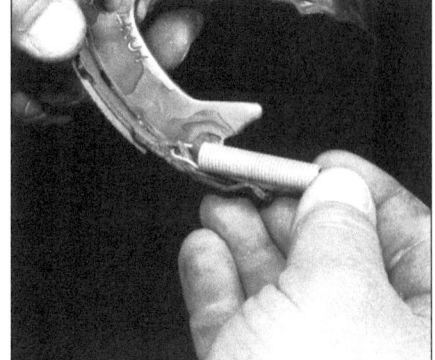

10.5m Attach the tension spring to the back side of the rear shoe . . .

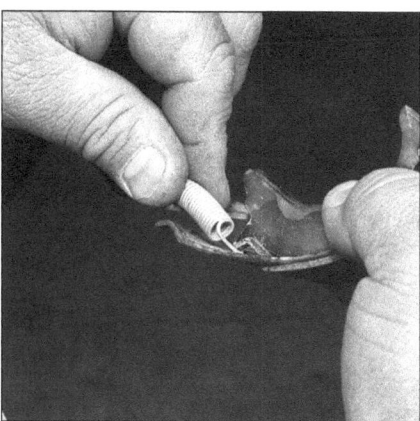

10.5n . . . and to the back side of
the front shoe

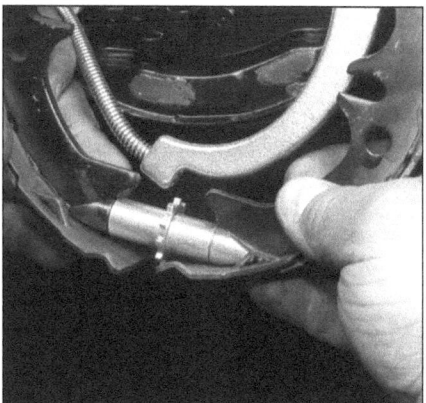

10.5o Flip the shoes around and install
the adjuster; make sure both ends of the
adjuster are properly engaged with
the shoes as shown

10.5p Place the shoes in position and
install the strut and spring as shown;
make sure the ends of the strut are
properly engaged with the
shoes as shown

10.5q Install the front shoe
return spring . . .

10.5r . . . and the rear shoe return spring

10.5s Install the rear shoe
hold-down spring

11 Parking brake - adjustment

Refer to illustration 11.3

1   Slowly depress the parking brake pedal
all the way and count the number of clicks. It

should take about five to seven clicks to apply
the parking brake. If it travels less than five
clicks, there's a chance the parking brake
might not be releasing completely. If it travels more than seven clicks, the parking brake
may not hold adequately on an incline, allowing the car to roll.

2   Release the pedal.
3   The parking brake adjustment is performed at the pedal assembly **(see illustration)**.
4   Loosen the locknut(s) and tighten or
loosen the adjuster nut. Tighten the locknut(s)
after the desired travel is attained.

10.5t . . . and the front shoe
hold-down spring

10.5u This is how the parking brake
assembly should look when you're done!

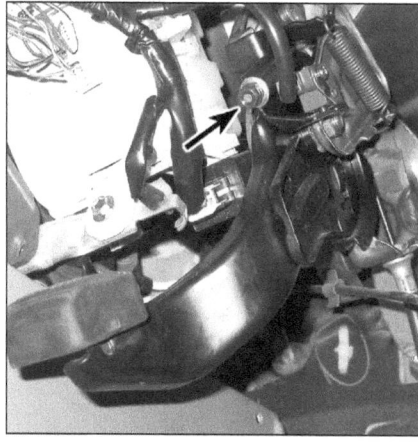

11.3 The location of the parking brake
cable adjuster and locknut

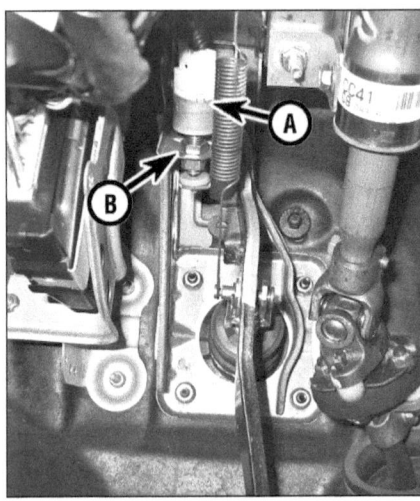

12.1 The brake light switch (A) is located at the top of the brake pedal. Loosen the locknut (B) and then unscrew the switch from its bracket

12   Brake light switch - removal, installation and adjustment

Removal and installation

Refer to illustration 12.1

1   The brake light switch is located on a bracket at the top of the brake pedal **(see illustration)**.
2   Disconnect the wiring harness at the brake light switch.
3   Loosen the locknut and unscrew the switch from the pedal bracket.
4   Installation is the reverse of removal.

Adjustment

Refer to illustration 12.6

5   Check and, if necessary, adjust brake pedal height (see Chapter 1).
6   Loosen the switch locknut, adjust the switch so that the distance the plunger protrudes is within the range listed in this Chapter's Specifications **(see illustration)**. (If you're unable to measure this distance, adjust the plunger so that it lightly contacts the pedal stop.) Tighten the locknut.
7   Plug the electrical connector into the switch. Make sure the brake lights come on when the brake pedal is depressed and go off when the pedal is released. If not, repeat the adjustment procedure until the brake lights function properly.

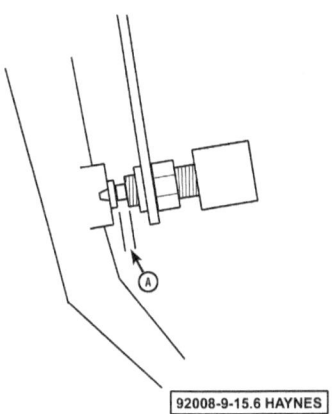

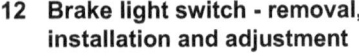

12.6 To adjust the brake light switch, loosen the locknut and rotate the switch until the plunger distance (dimension A) is within the range listed in this Chapter's Specifications, then tighten the locknut

8   Check and, if necessary, adjust brake pedal freeplay (see Section 13).

13   Brake pedal - adjustment

Pedal height

Refer to illustration 13.1

1   The height of the brake pedal is the distance the pedal sits off the floor **(see illustration)**. If the pedal height is not within Specifications, it must be adjusted.
2   To adjust the brake pedal, loosen the locknut and back the pushrod out for clearance. Turn the pushrod to adjust the pedal height in the middle of the specified range, then retighten the locknut **(see illustration 13.1)**.
3   At the brake pedal, loosen the locknut on the brake switch and retract the switch. Before measuring the brake pedal height, make sure the pedal is in the fully-returned position. Measure the pedal height and adjust if necessary (see Step 2).
4   Adjust the brake pedal switch by turning it clockwise until the switch body just contacts the pedal arm, then rotate it counter-clockwise to gain the specified clearance at the beginning of this Chapter and tighten the switch locknut.

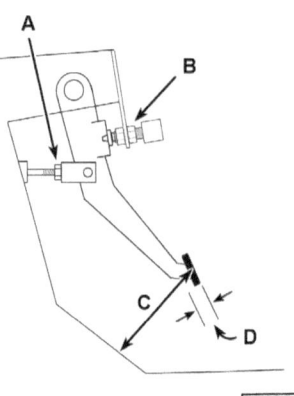

13.1 Brake pedal height and freeplay measuring and adjustment points

A   *Clevis locknut*
B   *Brake light switch adjusting nut/locknut*
C   *Pedal height measurement point*
D   *Freeplay measurement point*

Pedal freeplay

5   The freeplay is the pedal slack, or the distance the pedal can be depressed before it begins to have any effect on the brake system **(see illustration 13.1)**. If the pedal freeplay is not within the specified range, it must be adjusted.
6   To adjust the pedal freeplay, loosen the locknut on the pushrod. Then back out the pushrod to adjust the freeplay to the specified range, then retighten the locknut.
7   Before adjusting brake pedal freeplay, depress the brake pedal several times (with the engine off). Measure the freeplay and adjust if necessary. Loosen the locknut on the pushrod, then back off the pushrod to adjust the pedal freeplay to the specified range and retighten the locknut.

Brake pedal reserve distance

8   With the parking brake released and the engine running, depress the pedal with normal braking effort and have an assistant measure the distance from the centre of the pedal pad to the floor. Compare the measurement to the reserve distance listed in this Chapter's Specifications. If the distance is less than specified, refer to troubleshooting section of this book.

Chapter 10
Suspension and steering systems

Contents

Specifications

Torque specifications

	Nm
Front suspension	
Balljoint	
Balljoint-to-steering knuckle nut	123
Balljoint-to-control arm nuts/bolts	
MCU28R models	127
GSU40R/GSU45R models	92
Control arm-to-subframe bolts	
Front two bolts	200
Rear bolt	206
Stabiliser bar	
Stabiliser bar link nuts	74
Stabiliser bar bushing/retainer bolts	
MCU28R models	16
GSU40R/GSU45R models	29
Strut assembly	
Upper mounting nuts	
MCU28R models	80
GSU40R/GSU45R models	85
Damper shaft nut	
MCU28R models	49
GSU40R/GSU45R models	70
Steering knuckle bolts/nuts	
MCU28R models	230
GSU40R/GSU45R models	290
Subframe mounting bolts	
Large bolts	85
Small bolts	32

Torque specifications   Nm

Rear suspension

Hub and bearing assembly-to-rear knuckle bolts	75
Stabiliser bar	
Stabiliser bar link nuts	39
Stabiliser bar bushing/retainer bolts	
MCU28R models	
LH side	54
RH side	19
GSU40R/GSU45R models	19
Strut assembly	
Strut upper mounting nuts	58
Damper shaft nut	
MCU28R models	55
GSU40R/GSU45R models	49
Steering knuckle bolts/nuts	
MCU28R models	180
GSU40R/GSU45R models	290
Suspension arms	
Strut rod pivot bolts	80
Suspension arm No.1	
Crossmember pivot bolt	
Except GSU40R (2WD) models	80
GSU40R (2WD) models	120
Rear knuckle pivot bolt	112
Suspension arm No.2	
Crossmember pivot bolt	
Except GSU40R (2WD) models	100
GSU40R (2WD) models	120
Rear knuckle pivot bolt	112
Subframe mounting bolts	
MCU28R models	
Front nuts	115
Rear nut/bolts	181
GSU40R (2WD) models	
Rear bolts	55
Front large stud-to-body	17
Front large stud nut to front stopper bracket and subframe	55
Front stopper bracket-to-body nut	38
GSU45R (AWD) models	
Front nuts	115
Rear nut/bolts	181

Steering system

Airbag module retaining screws	9
Steering wheel nut	50
Steering gear mounting bolts/nuts	70
Steering shaft universal joint pinch bolt	35
Tie-rod end-to-steering knuckle nut	49
Power steering pump	
Mounting bolts	43
Pressure line banjo bolt	52
Wheel nuts	See Chapter 1

* Tighten with backup wrench on bolt and torque wrench on nut

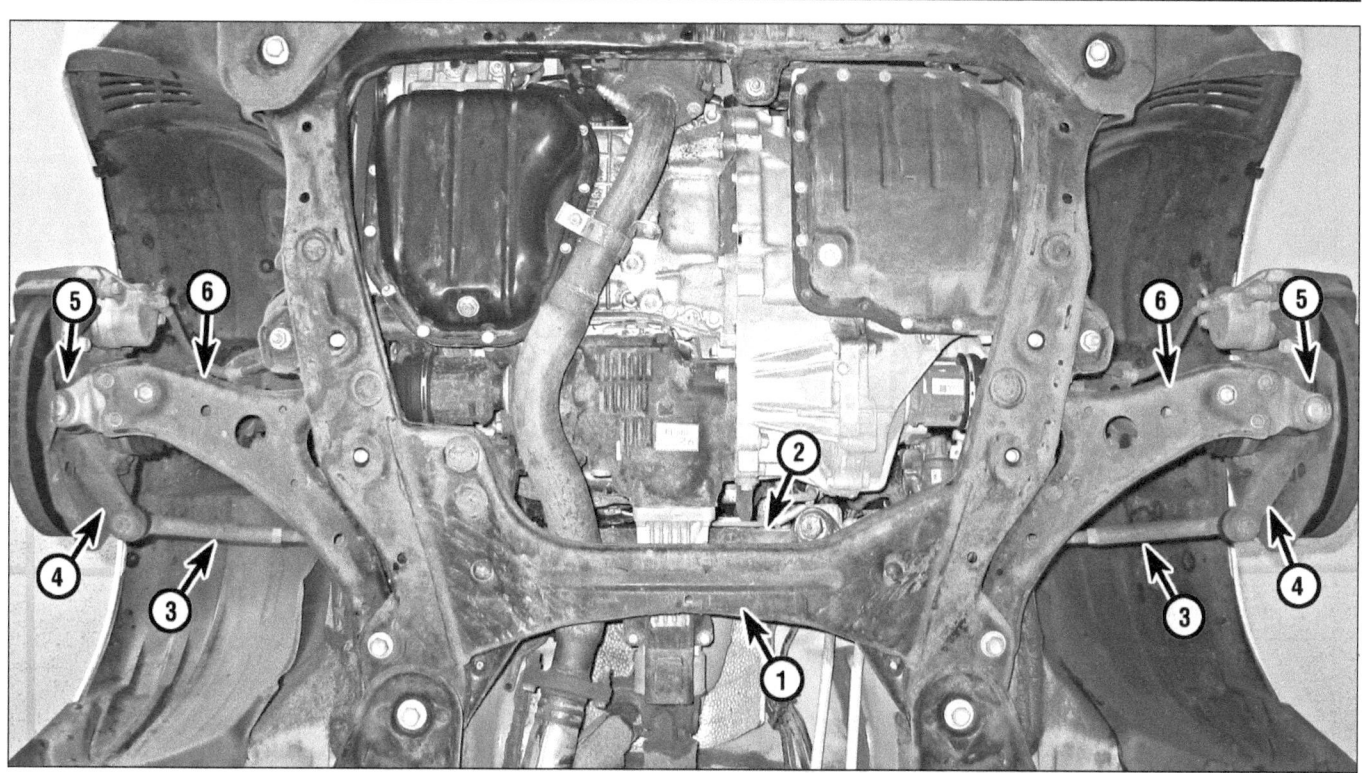

1.1 Typical front suspension and steering components

1 Subframe
2 Steering gear

3 Tie-rod end
4 Steering knuckle

5 Balljoint
6 Control arm

1.2 Rear suspension components - 2007 and earlier models

1 Rear suspension crossmember
2 Suspension arm (no. 2)

3 Rear knuckle
4 Strut rod

5 Suspension arm (no. 1)

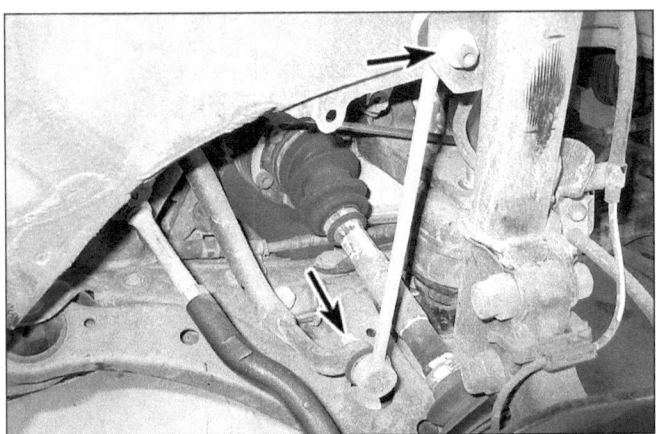

2.3 To detach the stabiliser bar link from the bar, remove the lower nut; if you're removing the strut (or replacing the link), remove the upper nut

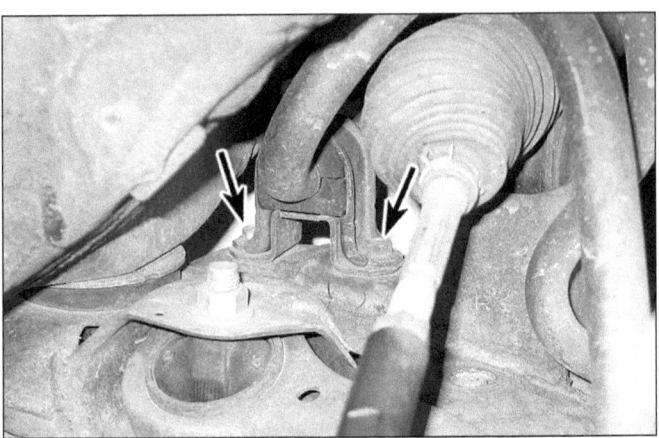

2.4 Bushing retainer fasteners

1   General information

Refer to illustrations 1.1 and 1.2

The front suspension is a MacPherson strut design. The upper end of each strut is attached to the vehicle's body strut support. The lower end of the strut is connected to the upper end of the steering knuckle. The steering knuckle is attached to a balljoint mounted on the outer end of the suspension control arm **(see illustration)**.

The rear suspension uses trailing arms, coil springs, and upper and lower suspension arms locating the rear knuckle. A shock absorber mounts between the rear knuckle and body.

The power-assisted rack-and-pinion steering gear, which is located behind the engine/transaxle assembly, is mounted on the engine cradle. The steering gear actuates the tie-rods, which are attached to the steering knuckles. The steering column is designed to collapse in the event of an accident.

Frequently, when working on the suspension or steering system components, you may come across fasteners that seem impossible to loosen. These fasteners on the underside of the vehicle are continually subjected to water, road grime, mud, etc., and can become rusted or "frozen," making them extremely difficult to remove. In order to unscrew these stubborn fasteners without damaging them (or other components), be sure to use lots of penetrating oil and allow it to soak in for a while. Using a wire brush to clean exposed threads will also ease removal of the nut or bolt and prevent damage to the threads. Sometimes a sharp blow with a hammer and punch will break the bond between nut and bolt threads, but care must be taken to prevent the punch from slipping off the fastener and ruining the threads. Heating the stuck fastener and surrounding area with a torch sometimes helps too, but isn't recommended because of the obvious dangers associated with fire. Long breaker bars and extension, or "cheater,"

pipes will increase leverage, but never use an extension pipe on a ratchet - the ratcheting mechanism could be damaged. Sometimes tightening the nut or bolt first will help to break it loose. Fasteners that require drastic measures to remove should always be replaced with new ones.

Since most of the procedures dealt with in this Chapter involve jacking up the vehicle and working underneath it, a good pair of jackstands will be needed. A hydraulic floor jack is the preferred type of jack to lift the vehicle, and it can also be used to support certain components during various operations.

Warning: *Never, under any circumstances, rely on a jack to support the vehicle while working on it. Whenever any of the suspension or steering fasteners are loosened or removed they must be inspected and, if necessary, replaced with new ones of the same part number or of original equipment quality and design. Torque specifications must be followed for proper reassembly and component retention. Never attempt to heat or straighten any suspension or steering components. Instead, replace any bent or damaged part with a new one.*

2   Stabiliser bar bushings and links (front) - removal and installation

Refer to illustrations 2.3 and 2.4

Note: *Stabiliser bar removal involves removing the steering gear and then removing the stabiliser bar out the left wheel arch. If one becomes damaged, it is most likely the result of an accident that was severe enough to damage other major components (such as the subframe itself). Damage this severe will require the services of an auto body shop.*

1   Loosen the front wheel nuts, then raise the front of the vehicle and support it securely on jackstands (see Jacking and Towing).

2   Remove the front wheels.
3   Disconnect the stabiliser bar links from the bar **(see illustration)**. If the ballstud turns with the nut, use an Allen wrench to hold the stud.
4   Detach both stabiliser bar bushing retainers from the subframe **(see illustration)**.
5   While the stabiliser bar is detached, slide off the retainer bushings and inspect them. If they're cracked, worn or deteriorated, replace them. It's also a good idea to inspect the stabiliser bar link. To check it, flip the balljoint stud side-to-side five or six times and then install the nut. Using a small torque wrench, turn the nut continuously one turn every two to four seconds and note the torque reading on the fifth turn. It should be about 0.05 to 2.00 Nm. If it isn't, replace the link assembly.
6   Clean the bushing area of the stabiliser bar with a stiff wire brush to remove any rust or dirt.
7   Lubricate the inside and outside of the new bushings with vegetable oil (used in cooking) to simplify reassembly.

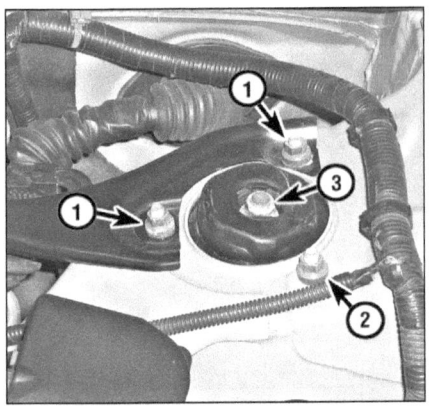

3.1 Mounting fasteners for one side of the strut brace (1). Do NOT remove the third nut (2) or loosen or remove the strut damper shaft nut (3) - MCU28R models

Caution: *Don't use petroleum or mineral-based lubricants or brake fluid - they will lead to deterioration of the bushings.*

Note: *These bushings are split so that you can install them without having to slide them onto the ends of the stabiliser bar. Install the bushings with the slit in each bushing facing towards the rear of the vehicle.*

8   Install the links, tightening the link nuts to the torque listed in this Chapter's Specifications.

9   Install the retainers and bolts, tightening the bolts to the torque listed in this Chapter's Specifications.

3   Strut brace - removal and installation

Refer to illustration 3.1

1   Remove the two strut upper mounting nuts that retain the strut brace from each front strut **(see illustration)**. Do not remove the third nut as this will hold the strut in place.

2   Lift the strut brace from the vehicle.

3   Reinstall the removed nuts and tighten securely.

4   When installing the brace, remove the two nuts again from each strut and install the brace onto the strut upper mounting studs.

5   Install the upper mounting nuts and tighten to the specified torque.

4   Strut assembly (front) - removal, inspection and installation

Removal

Refer to illustrations 4.3, 4.6 and 4.8

1   Loosen the wheel nuts, raise the vehicle and support it securely on jackstands (see Jacking and Towing). Remove the wheel. Support the control arm with a floor jack.

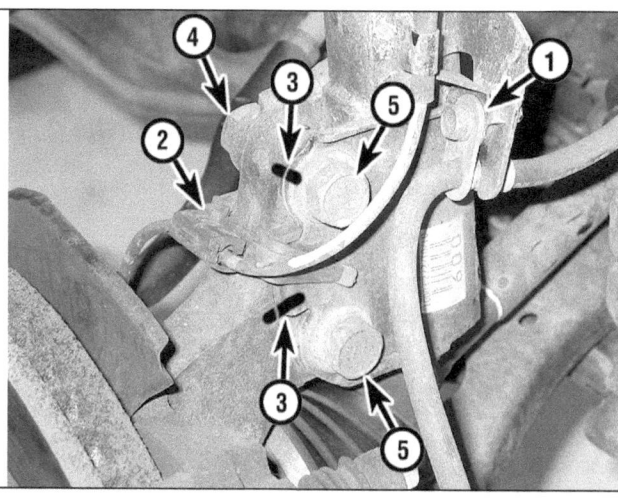

4.3 Strut mounting details at the lower bracket

1 *Brake hose bracket*
2 *ABS harness bracket*
3 *Marks to preserve camber alignment*
4 *Mounting nuts (one shown)*
5 *Mounting bolts*

2   Disconnect the stabiliser bar link from the strut **(see illustration 2.4)**.

3   Remove the brake hose bracket and the wheel speed sensor wiring harness from the strut **(see illustration)**.

4   Mark the position of the steering knuckle to the strut to help preserve the camber alignment adjustment. Remove the strut-to-knuckle nuts and knock the bolts out with a hammer and punch **(see illustration 4.3)**.

5   Separate the strut from the steering knuckle. Be careful not to overextend the inner CV joint. Also, don't let the steering knuckle fall outward, as the brake hose could be damaged.

6   On GSU40R/GSU45R models, proceed as follows:

  a *Remove the windshield wiper arms* **(see illustration)**, *side seals and plastic cowl (see Chapter 12).*

  b *Remove the wiper motor and linkage (see Chapter 12).*

  c *Remove the cowl assembly (see Chapter 11).*

7   If the strut is to be disassembled, loosen, but do not remove, the damper shaft nut (in the centre).

8   Support the strut and spring assembly with one hand (or have an assistant hold it) and remove the three strut-to-shock tower nuts **(see illustration)**. Remove the assembly out from the inner guard.

Note: *MCU28R models have a strut brace between the tops of the two strut towers that is retained by the same nuts that secure the strut to the body. The brace can be removed without removing each strut if necessary.*

Inspection

10   Check the strut body for leaking fluid, dents, cracks and other obvious damage that would warrant repair or replacement.

11   Check the coil spring for chips or cracks in the spring coating (this can cause premature spring failure due to corrosion). Inspect the spring seat for cuts, hardness and general deterioration.

12   If any undesirable conditions exist, proceed to the strut disassembly procedure (see Section 5).

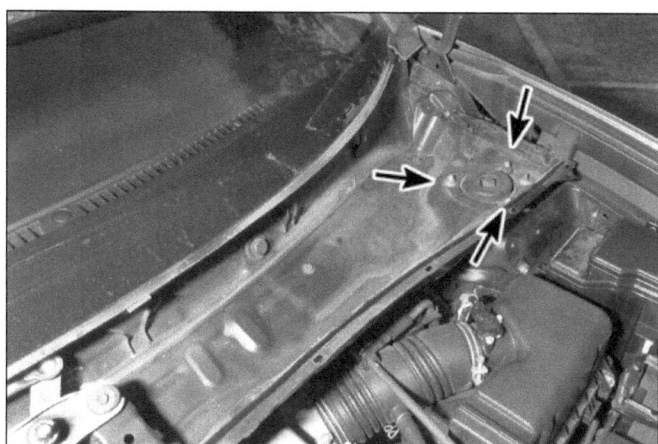

4.6 On GSU40R/GSU45R models, remove the wiper arms, upper cowl cover and lower cowl assembly to access the strut upper mounting

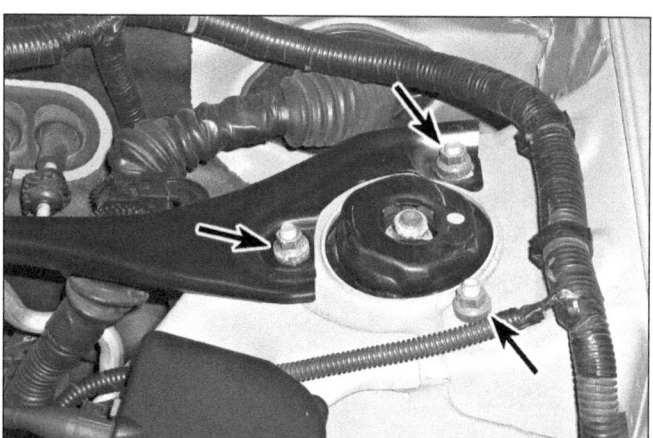

4.8 Mounting fasteners for the upper part of the strut and the strut brace. Warning: Don't remove the large nut in the centre

5.3 Install the spring compressor in accordance with the tool manufacturer's instructions and compress the spring until all pressure is relieved from the upper spring seat

5.4 Remove the damper shaft nut

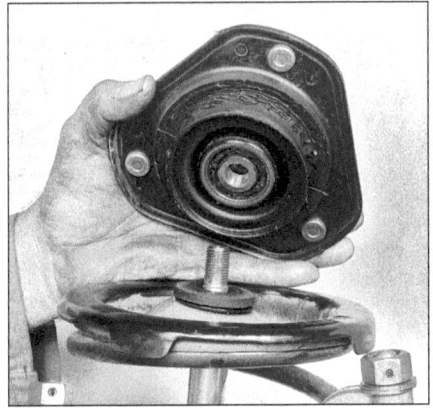

5.5 Lift the suspension support off the damper shaft

Installation

13   Guide the strut assembly up into the inner guard and insert the three upper mounting studs through the holes in the shock tower. Once the three studs protrude from the shock tower, install the nuts so the strut won't fall back through. This is most easily accomplished with the help of an assistant, as the strut is quite heavy and awkward.

Note: *Don't forget to install the strut brace, on MCU28R models.*

14   Slide the steering knuckle into the strut flange and insert the two bolts. Install the nuts, match the position of the strut to the steering knuckle that was previously marked and tighten them to the torque listed in this Chapter's Specifications.

15   Reattach the brake hose bracket to the strut and the wheel speed sensor wiring harness bracket.

16   Install the wheel and wheel nuts, then lower the vehicle and tighten the wheel nuts to the torque listed in the Chapter 1 Specifications.

17   Tighten the three upper mounting nuts to the torque listed in this Chapter's Specifications.

18   If you're working on a model equipped with the electronic modulated air suspension, be sure to attached the air-line to the top of the strut and then install the cap.

5   Strut/coil spring assembly - replacement

Note: *The following procedure applies to strut assemblies that are not used in the electronically modulated air suspension.*

1   If the struts or coil springs exhibit the telltale signs of wear (leaking fluid, loss of damping capability, chipped, sagging or cracked coil springs) explore all options before beginning any work. The strut/shock absorber assemblies are not serviceable and must be replaced if a problem develops. However, strut assemblies complete with springs may be available on an exchange basis, which eliminates much time and work. Whichever route you choose to take, check on the cost and availability of parts before disassembling your vehicle.

Warning: *Disassembling a strut is potentially dangerous and utmost attention must be directed to the job, or serious injury may result. Use only a high-quality spring compressor and carefully follow the manufacturer's instructions furnished with the tool. After removing the coil spring from the strut assembly, set it aside in a safe, isolated area.*

Disassembly

Refer to illustrations 5.3, 5.4, 5.5, 5.6 and 5.7

2   Remove the strut and spring assembly (see Section 4 [front] or Section 11 [rear]). Mount the strut assembly in a vise. Line the vise jaws with wood or rags to prevent damage to the unit and don't tighten the vise excessively.

3   Following the tool manufacturer's instructions, install the spring compressor (which can be obtained at most auto parts stores or equipment yards on a daily rental basis) on the spring and compress it sufficiently to relieve all pressure from the upper spring seat **(see illustration)**. This can be verified by wiggling the spring.

4   Loosen the damper shaft nut **(see illustration)**.

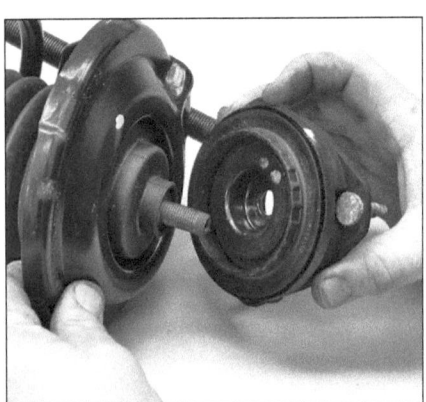

5.6 Remove the spring seat from the damper shaft

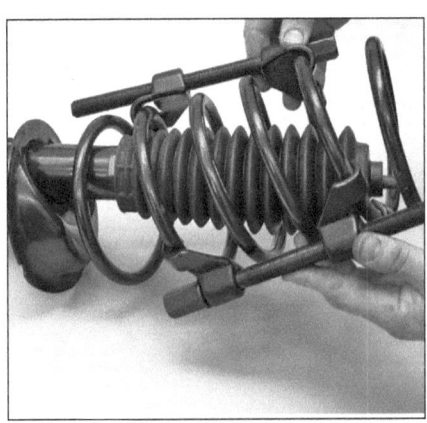

5.7 Remove the compressed spring assembly - keep the ends of the spring pointed away from your body

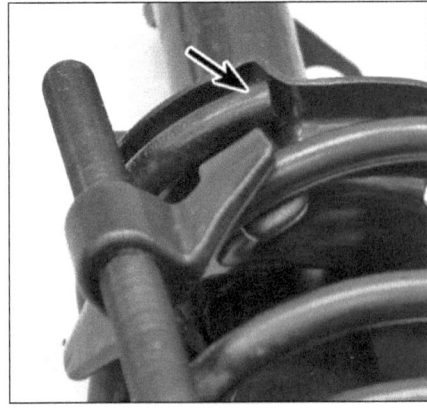

5.11 When installing the spring, make sure the end fits into the recessed portion of the lower seat

5.12 The flats on the damper shaft must match up with the flats in the spring seat

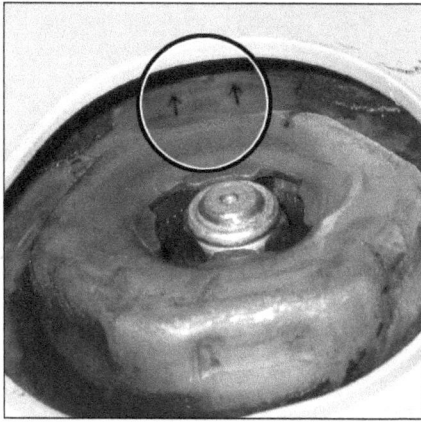

5.14 Make sure the arrows on the upper spring seat face toward the outside of the vehicle

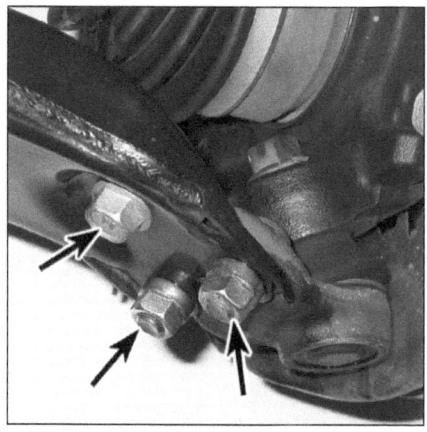

6.3a Remove these nuts and this bolt to disconnect the control arm from the balljoint

5   Remove the nut and suspension support **(see illustration)**. Inspect the bearing in the suspension support for smooth operation. If it doesn't turn smoothly, replace the suspension support. Check the rubber portion of the suspension support for cracking and general deterioration. If there is any separation of the rubber, replace it.

6   Remove the upper spring seat from the damper shaft **(see illustration)**. Check the spring seat for cracking and hardness; replace it if necessary. Remove the upper insulator.

7   Carefully lift the compressed spring from the assembly **(see illustration)** and set it in a safe place.

Warning: *Never place your head near the end of the spring!*

8   Slide the rubber bumper off the damper shaft.

9   Check the lower insulator for wear, cracking and hardness and replace it if necessary.

Reassembly

Refer to illustrations 5.11, 5.12 and 5.14

10   If the lower insulator is being replaced,

set it into position with the dropped portion seated in the lowest part of the seat. Extend the damper rod to its full length and install the rubber bumper.

11   Carefully place the coil spring onto the lower insulator, with the end of the spring resting in the lowest part of the insulator **(see illustration)**.

12   Install the upper insulator on the spring, with the mark on the top of the insulator pointing the same direction as the strut bracket (for the steering knuckle). Install the spring seat, making sure that the flats in the hole in the seat match up with the flats on the damper shaft **(see illustration)**.

13   Align the OUT mark of the spring upper seat with the mark of the upper insulator.

14   If you're working on a front strut, make sure the arrow on the spring seat faces toward the lower bracket, where the steering knuckle fits **(see illustration)**.

15   Install the dust seal and suspension support to the damper shaft.

16   Install the damper nut and tighten it to the torque listed in this Chapter's Specifications. Remove the spring compressor tool.

17   Install the strut/spring assembly (see Section 4 [front] or 11 [rear]).

6   Control arm - removal, inspection and installation

Removal

Refer to illustrations 6.3a, 6.3b, 6.4 and 6.5

1   Loosen the wheel nuts on the side to be dismantled, raise the front of the vehicle, support it securely on jackstands (see Jacking and Towing) and remove the wheel.

2   Remove the transverse engine mount at the subframe that covers the front mounting bolts for the control arms.

Note: *The procedure is difficult and requires the use of an engine lifting hoist or support fixture. Refer to the Engine chapters (see Chapter 2A) or (see Chapter 2B) for engine mount removal/installation.*

3   Remove the balljoint retaining bolt and nuts **(see illustration)**. Use a prybar to disconnect the balljoint from the control arm **(see illustration)**.

4   Remove the two bolts that attach the front of the control arm to the engine cradle **(see illustration)**.

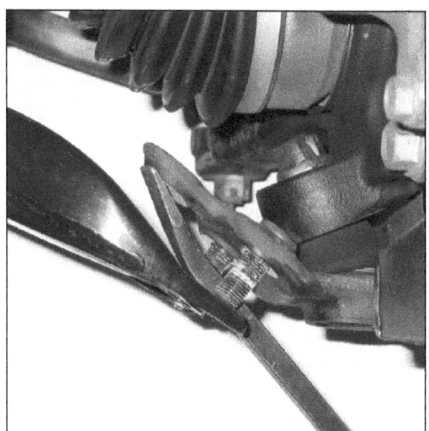

6.3b Separate the control arm from the balljoint with a prybar

6.4 To detach the front end of the control arm from the engine cradle, remove these two bolts

6.5 To detach the rear end of the control arm from the engine cradle, remove this nut and bolt

7.13 To separate the balljoint from the steering knuckle, install a small puller and pop the balljoint stud loose

5   Remove the bolt and nut that attach the rear of the control arm to the engine cradle **(see illustration)**.
6   Remove the control arm.

Inspection

7   Make sure the control arm is straight. If it's bent, replace it. Do not attempt to straighten a bent control arm.
8   Inspect the bushings. If they're cracked, torn or worn out, replace the control arm.

Installation

9   Installation is the reverse of removal. Be sure to tighten all fasteners to the torque listed in this Chapter's Specifications.
10   Install the wheel and wheel nuts, lower the vehicle and tighten the wheel nuts to the torque listed in the Chapter 1 Specifications.
11   It's a good idea to have the front wheel alignment checked, and if necessary, adjusted after this job has been performed.

7   Balljoints - replacement

1   Loosen the wheel nuts, raise the vehicle and support it securely on jackstands (see Jacking and Towing). Remove the wheel.
Note: *If you're going to remove the balljoint using a puller (as described in Steps 9 through 13), loosen the driveshaft/hub nut before raising the vehicle (see Chapter 8).*

Picklefork method

Caution: *The following procedure is the quickest way to detach a balljoint from the steering knuckle, but it will very likely damage the balljoint boot. If you want to save the boot, proceed to Step 9.*
2   Remove the split pin from the balljoint stud and loosen the nut a few turns (but don't remove it yet).
3   Separate the balljoint from the steering knuckle with a picklefork-type balljoint separator. Remove the balljoint stud nut.
4   Remove the bolt and nuts securing the balljoint to the control arm **(see illustration 5.3a)**. Separate the balljoint from the control arm with a prybar **(see illustration 6.3b)**.

5   To install the balljoint, position it on the steering knuckle and install the nut, but don't tighten it yet.
6   Attach the balljoint to the control arm and install the bolt and nuts, tightening them to the torque listed in this Chapter's Specifications.
7   Tighten the balljoint stud nut to the torque listed in this Chapter's Specifications and install a new split pin. If the split pin hole doesn't line up with the slots on the nut, tighten the nut additionally until it does line up - don't loosen the nut to insert the split pin.
8   Install the wheel and wheel nuts. Lower the vehicle and tighten the wheel nuts to the torque listed in the Chapter 1 Specifications.

Puller method

Refer to illustration 7.13

9   Remove the wheel speed sensor (see Chapter 9).
10   Separate the control arm from the balljoint (see Section 6).
11   Pull the outer end of the driveshaft from the steering knuckle (see Chapter 8) and suspend the driveshaft with a piece of wire.
12   Remove the split pin from the balljoint stud and loosen the nut a few turns (but don't remove it yet).
13   Install a small puller **(see illustration)** and pop the balljoint stud from the steering knuckle.
14   Remove the nut and remove the balljoint.
15   Install the new balljoint into the steering knuckle and tighten the nut to the torque listed in this Chapter's Specifications. Install a new split pin. If the split pin hole doesn't line up with the slots on the nut, tighten the nut additionally until it does line up - don't loosen the nut to insert the split pin.
16   Insert the outer end of the driveshaft through the steering knuckle and install the nut. Tighten it securely, but don't attempt to tighten it completely yet.
17   Connect the balljoint to the lower arm and tighten the fasteners to the torque listed in this Chapter's Specifications.
18   Install the wheel speed sensor.
19   Install the wheel and wheel nuts, lower the vehicle and tighten the wheel nuts to the

torque listed in the Chapter 1 Specifications.
20   Tighten the driveshaft/hub nut to the torque listed in the Chapter 8 Specifications, then stake it in place (see Chapter 8).

8   Steering knuckle and hub - removal and installation

Warning: *Dust created by the brake system is harmful to your health. Never blow it out with compressed air and don't inhale any of it. Do not, under any circumstances, use petroleum-based solvents to clean brake parts. Use brake system cleaner only.*

Removal

1   Loosen the driveshaft/hub nut (see Chapter 8). Loosen the wheel nuts, raise the vehicle and support it securely on jackstands (see Jacking and Towing). Remove the wheel.
2   Remove the wheel speed sensor from the knuckle and remove the brake disc from the hub (see Chapter 9).
3   Loosen, but do not remove, the strut-to-steering knuckle bolts **(see illustration 4.3)**.
4   Separate the tie-rod end from the steering knuckle arm (see Section 19).
5   Remove the balljoint-to-lower arm bolt and nuts **(see illustration 6.3a and 5.3b)**. The strut-to-knuckle bolts can now be removed.
6   Push the driveshaft from the hub as described in Chapter 8. Support the end of the driveshaft with a piece of wire.
7   Separate the steering knuckle from the strut. If necessary, detach the balljoint from the steering knuckle.

Installation

8   Guide the knuckle and hub assembly into position, inserting the driveshaft into the hub.
9   Push the knuckle into the strut flange and install the bolts and nuts, but don't tighten them yet.
10   Connect the balljoint to the control arm and install the bolt and nuts (don't tighten them yet).
11   Attach the tie-rod to the steering knuckle arm (see Section 19). Tighten the strut bolt nuts, the balljoint-to-control arm bolt and nuts and the tie-rod nut to the torque values listed in this Chapter's Specifications. Replace all split pins with new ones.
12   Place the brake disc on the hub and install the caliper and wheel speed sensor as outlined in Chapter 9.
13   Install the driveshaft/hub nut and tighten it securely (final tightening will be carried out when the vehicle is lowered).
14   Install the wheel and wheel nuts, lower the vehicle and tighten the wheel nuts to the torque listed in the Chapter 1 Specifications.
15   Install the driveshaft/hub nut and tighten it to the torque listed in the Chapter 8 Specifications, then stake it in place (see Chapter 8).

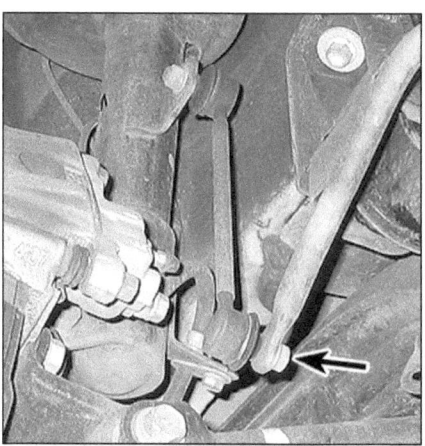

10.3 To detach the stabiliser bar link from the bar, remove the lower nut

9 Hub and bearing assembly (front) - removal and installation

Due to the special tools and expertise required to press the hub and bearing from the steering knuckle, this job should be left to a professional shop. However, the steering knuckle and hub may be removed and the assembly taken to a dealer service department or other qualified repair shop. See Section 8 for the steering knuckle and hub removal procedure.

10 Stabiliser bar and bushings (rear) - removal and installation

Refer to illustration 10.3

1   Loosen the rear wheel nuts. Raise the rear of the vehicle and support it securely on jackstands (see Jacking and Towing). Remove the rear wheels.

2   Remove the heat insulator from the exhaust system.

3   Disconnect the stabiliser bar links from the bar **(see illustration)**. If the ballstud turns with the nut, use an Allen wrench to hold the stud.

4   Unbolt the stabiliser bar bushing retainers. Remove the two retainer brackets from the body, if necessary.

5   The stabiliser bar can now be removed from the vehicle. Remove the bushings from the stabiliser bar, noting their positions.

6   Check the bushings for wear, hardness, distortion, cracking and other signs of deterioration, replacing them if necessary. Check the stabiliser bar links (see Section 2). When installing the bushings, the slit should be positioned towards the top.

7   Using a wire brush, clean the areas of the bar where the bushings ride. Lubricate the inside and outside of the new bushings with vegetable oil (used in cooking).

11.1 Pull the plastic trim cover up to remove it

Caution: *Don't use petroleum or mineral-based lubricants or brake fluid - they will lead to deterioration of the bushings.*

8   Installation is the reverse of removal.

11 Strut assembly (rear) - removal, inspection and installation

Removal

Refer to illustrations 11.1 and 11.4

Note: *When removing/replacing any rear suspension arms, loosely tighten all the bolts, move the suspension to its normal ride-height angle and position, then fully tighten the bolts.*

1   Remove the interior trim covering the upper mounting fasteners for the strut **(see illustration)**.

2   Loosen the rear wheel nuts, raise the rear of the vehicle and support it securely on jackstands (see Jacking and Towing).

3   Remove the wheel.

4   Detach the brake hose and the wheel speed sensor harness from the strut **(see illustration)**.

5   Disconnect the stabiliser bar link from the strut (see Section 10).

6   Support the rear knuckle with a floor jack.

7   Loosen the strut-to-rear knuckle bolt nuts **(see illustration 11.4)**.

8   If the strut is to be disassembled, loosen, but do not remove, the damper shaft nut (in the centre).

9   Remove the three upper strut-to-body mounting nuts.

10   Lower the rear knuckle with the jack, remove the two strut-to-rear knuckle bolts and then remove the strut assembly.

Inspection

11   Follow the inspection procedures for the front strut (see Section 4). If you determine that the strut assembly must be disassembled for replacement of the strut or the coil spring, refer to Section 5.

Installation

12   Have an assistant manoeuvre the assembly up into the inner guard and insert the mounting studs through the holes in the body. Install the nuts, but don't tighten them yet.

13   Push the rear knuckle into the strut lower bracket and install the bolts and nuts, tightening them to the torque listed in this Chapter's Specifications.

14   Connect the stabiliser bar link to the strut bracket.

15   Attach the brake hose bracket and wheel speed sensor harness to the strut.

16   Install the wheel and wheel nuts, lower the vehicle and tighten the wheel nuts to the torque listed in the Chapter 1 Specifications.

17   Tighten the three strut upper mounting nuts to the torque listed in this Chapter's Specifications and replace the interior trim that covers the mounting fasteners.

12 Strut rod - removal and installation

Refer to illustration 12.2

Note: *When removing/replacing any rear suspension arms, loosely tighten all the bolts, move the suspension to its normal ride-height angle and position, then fully tighten the bolts.*

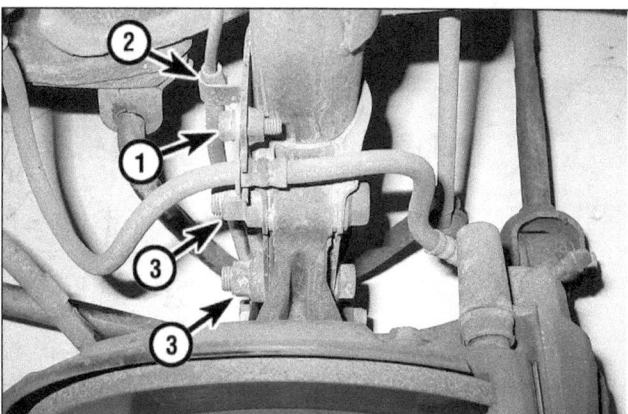

11.4 Strut mounting details at the lower bracket:

1   *Brake hose bracket bolt*
2   *ABS harness bracket*
3   *Strut mounting fasteners*

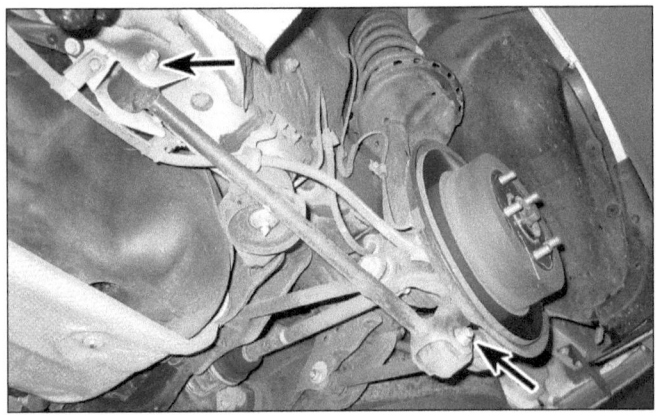

12.2 Strut rod fasteners

13.3 The number 1 suspension arm fasteners on 2WD models

1   Loosen the wheel nuts, raise the vehicle and support it securely on jackstands (see Jacking and Towing). Remove the wheel.

2   Remove the strut rod-to-rear knuckle bolt **(see illustration)**.

3   Remove the strut rod-to-body bracket bolt and detach the rod from the vehicle.

Note: *The parking brake cable bracket may need to be removed to allow removal of the strut bolt.*

4   Installation is the reverse of the removal procedure. Be sure to tighten the bolts to the torque listed in this Chapter's Specifications.

---

13   Suspension arms (rear) - removal and installation

Note: *Note that the paint marks on all of the suspension arms face to the rear of the vehicle. If no paint marks are visible, mark the suspension arms so that they can be installed back to their original positions.*

Removal

1   Loosen the rear wheel nuts, raise the rear of the vehicle and support it securely on jackstands (see Jacking and Towing). Remove the rear wheel.

Number 1 (front) suspension arm (2WD)

Refer to illustration 13.3

2   Remove the rear stabiliser bar (see Section 10).

3   Remove the arm fasteners from the knuckle and the rear suspension crossmember and then remove the arm **(see illustration)**.

Number 1 (front) suspension arm (AWD)

Refer to illustrations 13.10a and 13.10b

4   On AWD models, it is necessary to lower the rear suspension crossmember to access the bolt on the inner end of the number 1 suspension arm.

5   Disconnect the strut rods from the knuckle on both sides of the vehicle (see Section 11).

6   Remove the exhaust centre section and tailpipe (see Chapter 4).

7   Remove the driveshaft and centre bearing assembly (see Chapter 8).

8   Remove both rear driveshafts (see Chapter 8).

9   Detach the suspension arms from both rear knuckles.

10   Position a floor jack under the centre of

the crossmember (beneath the differential), then loosen and remove the crossmember-to-body fasteners **(see illustration)**. Carefully lower the rear suspension crossmember with the jack (do not place any part of your body under the suspension while it is supported only by the jack) until the suspension arm bolts are accessible. Remove the bolts **(see illustration)**.

Caution: *A floor jack with a transmission adapter head is recommended for this procedure in order to securely support the crossmember.*

Number 2 (rear) suspension arm

Refer to illustrations 13.12 and 13.13

11   Remove the rear stabiliser bar (see Section 10).

12   Where fitted, mark the cam bolt (on both sides) to preserve the toe-in alignment angle **(see illustration)**.

13   Remove the arm fasteners from the rear knuckle and the suspension crossmember, then remove the arm **(see illustration)**.

Installation

Note: *When installing any rear suspension arms, loosely tighten all the bolts, move the suspension to its normal ride-height angle and position, then fully tighten the bolts.*

13.10a Rear suspension crossmember mounting fasteners on AWD models

13.10b The number 1 suspension arm fasteners on AWD models.

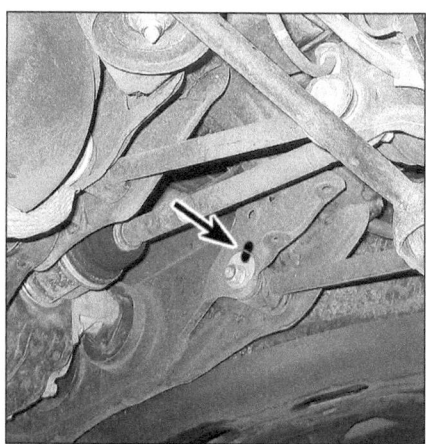

13.12 The cam bolt marked in relation to the rear suspension crossmember

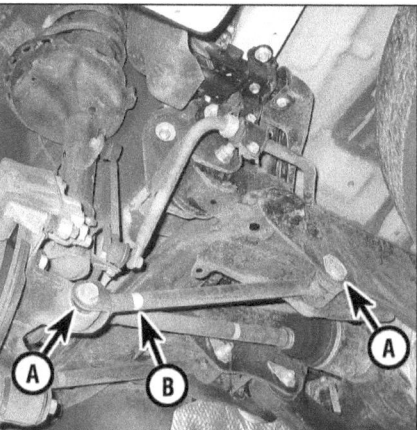

13.13 The number 2 suspension arm fasteners (A) on AWD models. Note the paint mark (B), which faces the rear of the vehicle

14.3 To remove the four bolts that attach the hub and bearing assembly to the rear knuckle, rotate the hub flange and align one of the holes in the flange with each of the bolts

14   Installation is the reverse of removal. Be sure to tighten all fasteners to the torque listed in this Chapter's Specifications.

Note: *When reinstalling the suspension arms, the factory paint marks on the arms should face the rear of the vehicle.*

15   Install the wheel and wheel nuts, then lower the vehicle to the ground. Tighten the wheel nuts to the torque listed in Chapter 1 Specifications. If you're working on an AWD model, tighten the driveshaft/hub nut to the torque listed in Chapter 8 Specifications.

16   Have the rear wheel alignment checked by a dealer service department or an alignment shop.

14   Hub and bearing assembly (rear) - removal and installation

Warning: *Dust created by the brake system is harmful to your health. Never blow it out with compressed air and don't inhale any of it. Do not, under any circumstances, use petroleum-based solvents to clean brake parts. Use brake system cleaner only.*

Note: *The following procedure applies to 2WD models only. On AWD models, special tools and expertise are required to press the hub and bearing from the rear knuckle, so this job should be left to a professional shop. However, the rear knuckle and hub may be removed and the assembly taken to a dealer service department or other repair shop. See Section 15 for the rear knuckle and hub removal procedure.*

Note: *The rear hub and bearing assembly is not serviceable. If found to be defective, it must be replaced as a unit.*

Removal

Refer to illustration 14.3

1   Loosen the wheel nuts, raise the vehicle and support it securely on jackstands (see Jacking and Towing). Remove the wheel.

2   Remove the disc from the hub and dis-

connect the wheel speed sensor electrical connector (see Chapter 9).

3   Remove the four hub-to-rear knuckle bolts, accessible by turning the hub flange so that the large circular cutout exposes each bolt **(see illustration)**.

4   Remove the hub and bearing assembly from its seat, manoeuvring it out through the parking brake assembly.

Installation

5   Position the hub and bearing assembly on the rear knuckle and align the holes in the backing plate. Install the bolts. A magnet is useful in guiding the bolts through the hub flange and into position. After all four bolts have been installed, tighten them to the torque listed in this Chapter's Specifications.

6   Install the disc and caliper, and the wheel. Lower the vehicle and tighten the wheel nuts to the torque listed in the Chapter 1 Specifications.

15   Rear knuckle - removal and installation

Warning: *Dust created by the brake system is harmful to your health. Never blow it out with compressed air and don't inhale any of it. Do not, under any circumstances, use petroleum-based solvents to clean brake parts. Use brake system cleaner only.*

Removal

1   Loosen the wheel nuts. On AWD models, also loosen the driveshaft nut (see Chapter 8). Raise the vehicle and support it on jackstands (see Jacking and Towing). Block the front wheels and remove the rear wheel.

2   Remove the rear brake disc (see Chapter 9).

3   Remove the rear hub and bearing assembly (see Section 14). On AWD models, remove the driveshaft nut in order to remove

the driveshaft from the rear hub (see Chapter 8).

4   Detach the backing plate and parking brake assembly from the rear knuckle. Suspend the backing plate and brake assembly from the coil spring with a piece of wire.

Note: *It isn't necessary to disassemble the parking brake shoes or disconnect the parking brake cable from the backing plate.*

5   Remove the wheel speed sensor or sensor harness from the rear knuckle (see Chapter 9).

6   Loosen (but don't remove) the strut-to-rear knuckle bolts **(see illustration 11.4)**.

7   Detach the strut rod and suspension arms from the rear knuckle (see Sections 12 and 13).

8   Remove the strut-to-rear knuckle bolts while supporting the carrier so it doesn't fall, then detach the rear knuckle from the strut bracket.

Installation

9   Inspect the carrier bushing for cracks, deformation and signs of wear. If it is worn out, take the carrier to a dealer service department or other repair shop to have the old one pressed out and a new one pressed in.

10   Push the rear knuckle into the strut bracket, aligning the two bolt holes. Insert the two strut-to-carrier bolts and tighten them to the torque listed in this Chapter's Specifications. On AWD models, place the driveshaft in the hub before installing the carrier into the strut bracket, then loosely install the driveshaft nut.

11   Connect the suspension arms to the rear knuckle, but don't tighten the nut(s) yet.

12   Connect the strut rod to the rear knuckle, but don't tighten the nut yet.

13   Place a jack under the carrier and raise it to simulate normal ride height.

14   Tighten the suspension arm bolt(s)/ nut(s) and the strut rod bolt/nut to the torque listed in this Chapter's Specifications.

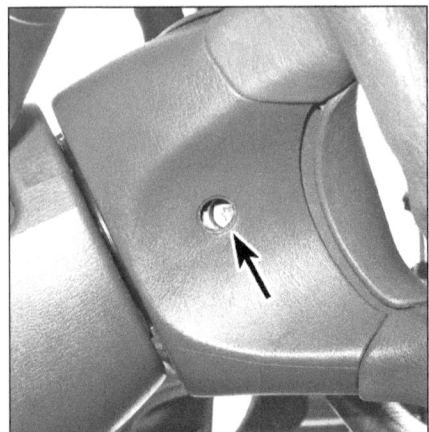

17.3 Pry off the small covers on either side of the steering wheel, then loosen the airbag module Torx screws

17.4 Disconnect the electrical connector for the airbag module

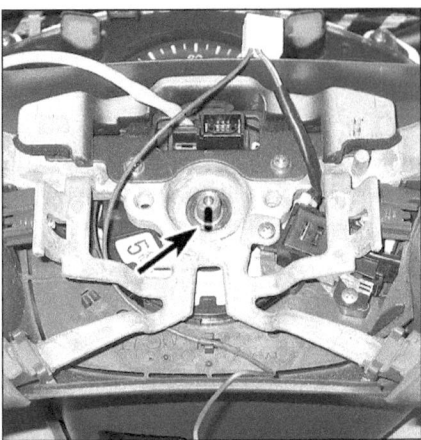

17.5 Mark the steering wheel hub in relation to the steering shaft

15   Reattach the wheel speed sensor or sensor harness to the rear knuckle.

16   Attach the brake backing plate to the rear knuckle, install the hub and tighten the four bolts to the torque listed in this Chapter's Specifications.

17   Install the rear brake disc and caliper and then reattach the wheel speed sensor or sensor harness (see Chapter 9).

18   Install the wheel and wheel nuts.

19   Lower the vehicle and tighten the wheel nuts to the torque listed in the Chapter 1 Specifications. On AWD models, tighten the driveshaft nut to the torque listed in Chapter 8 Specifications.

16   Steering system - general information

All models are equipped with rack-and-pinion steering. The steering gear is bolted to the subframe and operates the steering knuckles via tie-rods. The inner ends of the tie-rods are protected by rubber boots that should be inspected periodically for secure attachment, tears and leaking lubricant.

The power assist system consists of a belt-driven pump and the associated lines and hoses. The fluid level in the power steering pump reservoir should be checked periodically (see Chapter 1).

The steering wheel operates the steering shaft, which actuates the steering gear through universal joints. Looseness in the steering can be caused by wear in the steering shaft universal joints, the steering gear, the tie-rod ends and loose retaining bolts.

17   Steering wheel - removal and installation

Warning: *The models covered by this manual are equipped with Supplemental Restraint Systems (SRS), more commonly known as airbags. Always disable the airbag system before working in the vicinity of any airbag system component to avoid the possibility of accidental deployment of the airbag(s), which could cause personal injury (see Chapter 12).*

Removal

Refer to illustrations 17.3, 17.4 and 17.5

1   Turn the steering wheel so that the wheels are pointing straight ahead. Turn the ignition key to Off

2   Disconnect the negative (-) battery terminal (see Chapter 5).

3   Pry off the small covers on either side of the steering wheel and loosen the Torx screws that attach the airbag module to the steering wheel **(see illustration)**. Loosen each screw until the groove in the circumference of the screw catches on the screw case.

Note: *The screws do not need to be removed completely.*

4   Pull the airbag module off the steering wheel and disconnect the electrical connector for the module **(see illustration)**.

Warning: *Carry the airbag module with the trim side facing away from you and set it down in an isolated area with the trim side facing up.*

5   Mark the relationship of the steering shaft to the hub (if marks don't already exist or don't line up) to simplify installation and ensure steering wheel alignment, then loosen the steering wheel retaining nut **(see illustration)**. Do not remove it at this stage.

6   Grasp the steering wheel with both hands placing them at opposite points around the circumference of the steering wheel. Rock the wheel back and forth while moving both hands around the steering wheel **(see illustration)**. After a short time, the steering wheel will come off the splines retaining it to the steering shaft. Remove the nut and lift the steering wheel from the shaft, guiding the wiring through the holes in the steering wheel.

Note: *If you can't remove the wheel using the previous method, use a commercially available steering wheel puller **(see illustration)**.*

Warning: *Do not hammer on the shaft or the puller in an attempt to loosen the wheel from the shaft. Also, don't allow the steering shaft to turn with the steering wheel removed. If the shaft turns, the airbag clock spring will no*

17.6a Rock the steering wheel back-and-forth to break the connection between the wheel and steering column

17.6b Use a steering wheel puller to remove the steering wheel

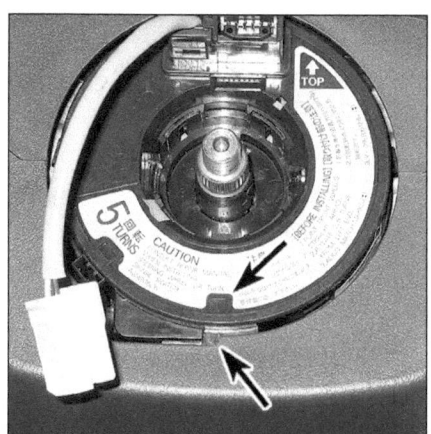

17.7 To centre the spiral cable, turn the cable counterclockwise until it's harder to turn, rotate the cable clockwise two and a half turns and align the two small arrows (the cable should be able to rotate about two and a half turns in either direction when it's properly centred)

longer be centred, which may cause the wire inside to break when the vehicle is returned to service.

Installation

Refer to illustration 17.7

7   Make sure that the front wheels are facing straight ahead. Turn the spiral cable counterclockwise by hand until it becomes harder to turn the cable. Rotate the cable clockwise about two and a half turns and align the two pointers **(see illustration)**.

7   To install the wheel, align the mark on the steering wheel hub with the mark on the shaft and slip the wheel onto the shaft. Install the nut and tighten it to the torque listed in this Chapter's Specifications.

8   Plug in the electrical connectors for the airbag module and any other connectors. Make sure the connector locks are pushed back into position for the module.

9   Install the airbag module and tighten the

18.5a Location of the steering column harness connector - MCU28R models

Torx retaining screws to the torque listed in this Chapter's Specifications.

10   Connect the negative battery terminal (see Chapter 5).

---

18   Steering column - removal and installation

Removal

Refer to illustrations 18.5a, 18.5b, 18.6, 18.7a and 18.7b

1   Park the vehicle with the wheels pointing straight ahead. Disconnect the cable from the negative terminal of the battery.

2   Remove the steering wheel (see Section 16), then turn the ignition key to the LOCK position to prevent the steering shaft from turning.

Caution: *If this is not done, the airbag clockspring could be damaged.*

3   Remove the lower finish panel under the column and the knee bolster behind it (see

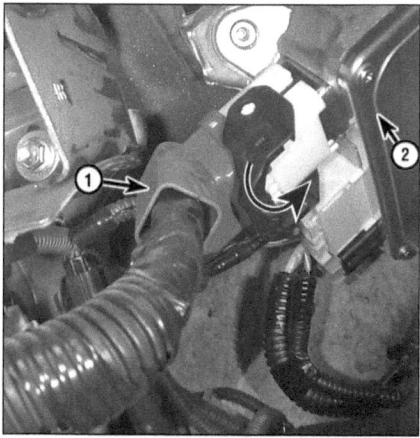

18.5b On GSU40R/GSU45R models, rotate the connector clip in the direction of the arrow to disconnect the wiring harness (1) for the steering column from the power steering control module (2)

Chapter 11).

4   Remove the steering column covers and the lower dash panel (see Chapter 11).

5   Disconnect the electrical connector(s) for the steering column harness **(see illustration)**. On GSU40R/GSU45R models, disconnect the wiring from the steering column control assembly **(see illustration)**.

6   Mark the relationship of the steering shaft U-joint to the intermediate shaft, then remove the pinch bolt **(see illustration)**.

7   Remove the steering column mounting fasteners **(see illustration)**, lower the column and pull it to the rear, making sure nothing is still connected. Separate the intermediate shaft from the steering shaft and remove the column.

Installation

8   Guide the steering column into position, connect the intermediate shaft, then install the mounting fasteners, but don't tighten them yet.

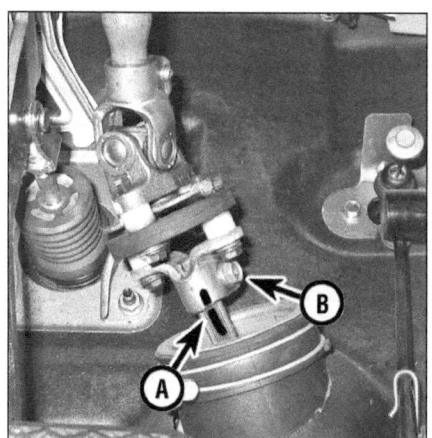

18.6 Mark the relationship of the U-joint to the intermediate shaft (A) and then remove the pinch bolt (B)

18.7a Mounting fasteners for the steering column (one hidden from view - vicinity given) - MCU28R models

18.7b Rear mounting fasteners for the steering column - GSU40R/GSU45R models

18.7c Pinch bolt (1); intermediate shaft (2) and steering column front mounting fastener (3) - GSU40R/GSU45R models

9   Tighten the column mounting fasteners to the torque listed in this Chapter's Specifications.
10   Install the pinch bolt, tightening it to the torque listed in this Chapter's Specifications.
11   The remainder of installation is the reverse of removal.

---

19   Tie-rod ends - removal and installation

Removal

Refer to illustrations 19.2a, 19.2b and 19.4

1   Loosen the wheel nuts. Raise the front of the vehicle, support it securely on jackstands, block the rear wheels and set the parking brake. Remove the front wheel.
2   Hold the tie-rod with a pair of locking pliers or wrench and loosen the jam nut enough to mark the position of the tie-rod end in relation to the threads **(see illustrations)**.
3   Remove the split pin and loosen the nut on the tie-rod end stud.

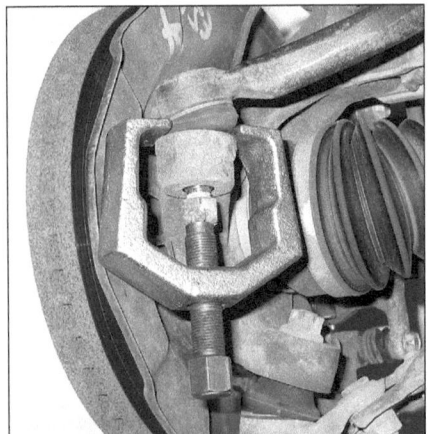

19.4 Install a small puller to separate the tie-rod end from the steering knuckle

19.2a Hold the tie-rod end with a wrench and break the jam nut loose with another wrench

4   Disconnect the tie-rod from the steering knuckle arm with a puller **(see illustration)**. Remove the nut and separate the tie-rod.
5   Unscrew the tie-rod end from the tie-rod.

Installation

6   Thread the tie-rod end on to the marked position and insert the tie-rod stud into the steering knuckle arm. Tighten the jam nut securely.
7   Install the castle nut on the stud and tighten it to the torque listed in this Chapter's Specifications. Install a new split pin.
8   Install the wheel and wheel nuts. Lower the vehicle and tighten the wheel nuts to the torque listed in the Chapter 1 Specifications.
9   Have the alignment checked by a dealer service department or an alignment shop.

---

20   Steering gear boots - replacement

Refer to illustration 20.3

1   Loosen the wheel nuts, raise the vehicle

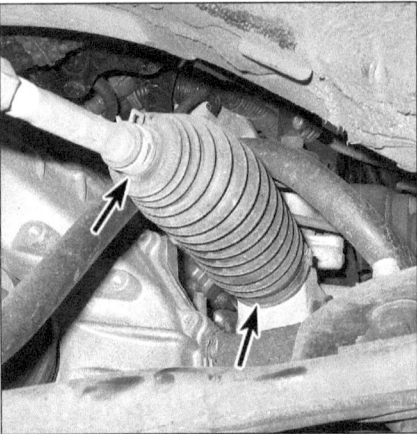

20.3 Remove the outer clamp from the steering gear boot with a pair of pliers; the inner clamp must be cut or pried off

19.2b Back off the jam nut and mark the exposed threads to ensure that the new tie-rod end is threaded on the same number of turns

and support it securely on jackstands (see Jacking and Towing). Remove the wheel.
2   Remove the tie-rod end and jam nut (see Section 18).
3   Remove the steering gear boot clamps **(see illustration)** and slide off the boot.
4   Before installing the new boot, wrap the threads and serrations on the end of the steering rod with a layer of tape so the small end of the new boot isn't damaged.
5   Slide the new boot into position on the steering gear until it seats in the groove in the steering rod and install new clamps.
6   Remove the tape and install the tie-rod end (see Section 19).
7   Install the wheel and wheel nuts. Lower the vehicle and tighten the wheel nuts to the torque listed in the Chapter 1 Specifications.

---

21   Steering gear - removal and installation

Warning: *Make sure the steering shaft is not turned while the steering gear is removed or you could damage the spiral cable for the airbag system. To prevent the shaft from turning, place the ignition key in the lock position or thread the seat belt through the steering wheel and clip it into place.*

Note: *On GSU40R/GSU45R models, remove the engine/transaxle assembly to replace the power steering gear (see Chapter 2C).*

Removal

Refer to illustrations 21.2a, 21.02b, 21.3 and 21.8

1   Park the vehicle with the front wheels pointing straight ahead. Loosen the front wheel nuts, raise the front of the vehicle and support it securely on jackstands (see Jacking and Towing). Apply the parking brake and remove the wheels. Remove the engine under-covers on models so equipped.
2   On MCU28R models, place a drain pan

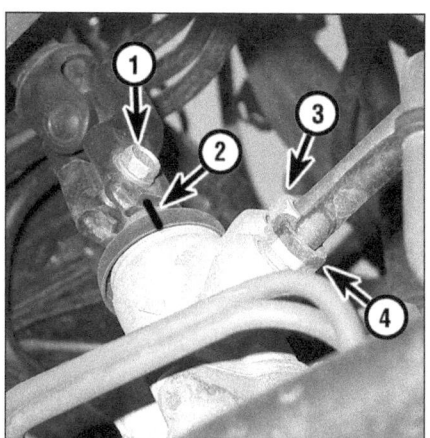

21.2a Steering gear connection details:

1 *Lower intermediate shaft U-joint pinch bolt*
2 *Mark on steering input shaft in relation to U-joint*
3 *Return line fitting*
4 *Pressure line fitting*

21.2b Disconnect the steering gear line fittings using a crow's-foot wrench (designed for line fittings) and a short extension

21.3 Upper intermediate shaft details:

1 *Mark on upper intermediate shaft in relation to steering shaft U-joint*
2 *Shaft cover clamp bolt*
3 *Steering shaft U-joint pinch bolt*

---

under the steering gear. Detach the power steering pressure and return lines **(see illustration)** and cap the ends to prevent excessive fluid loss and contamination. Detach the tube-support bracket from the top of the steering gear assembly.

Caution: *Use a line fitting wrench for detaching the lines from the steering gear or the fittings could be severely damaged* **(see illustration)**.

3   Mark the relationship of the intermediate shaft to the steering shaft U-joint and remove the pinch bolt. Loosen the shaft cover clamp bolt and pull the cover up **(see illustration)**.

4   On models equipped with the electronically modulated air suspension, detach the height control sensor linkage from the left control arm, then remove the sensor.

5   Mark the relationship of the lower intermediate shaft U-joint to the steering gear input shaft and then remove the U-joint pinch bolt **(see illustration 20.2a)**.

6   Separate the tie-rod ends from the steering knuckle arms (see Section 19).

7   Detach the links from the ends of the stabiliser bar and remove the bushing retainer bolts (see Section 2).

Note: *The steering gear mounting bolts cannot be removed until the stabiliser bar is lifted up out of the way.*

8   Remove the steering gear mounting nuts **(see illustration)**, lift up the stabiliser bar and knock out the steering gear mounting bolts.

9   Separate the intermediate shaft U-joint from the steering gear input shaft and then remove the steering gear assembly out the left side of the vehicle.

10   Check the steering gear mounting grommets for excessive wear or deterioration, replacing them if necessary.

Installation

11   Raise the steering gear into position and connect the intermediate shaft U-joint to the steering input shaft, aligning the marks.

12   Install the mounting bolts and nuts and tighten them to the torque listed in this Chapter's Specifications.

13   Connect the tie-rod ends to the steering knuckle arms (see Section 19).

14   Install the steering shaft U-joint pinch bolt (in the passenger cab) and tighten it to the torque listed in this Chapter's Specifications. Make certain that the alignment marks match if the intermediate shaft was separated from the steering shaft U-joint.

15   On MCU28R models, connect the power steering pressure and return hoses to the steering gear and fill the power steering pump reservoir with the recommended fluid (see Chapter 1). Reattach the bracket to the top of the steering gear assembly.

16   Install the remaining suspension components and then tighten them to the torque listed in this Chapter's Specifications.

17   Lower the vehicle.
18   On MCU28R models, bleed the power steering system (see Section 23).

---

22 Power steering pump - removal and installation

Removal

Refer to illustration 22.6

1   Disconnect the negative (-) battery terminal (see Chapter 5).

2   Using a large syringe or suction gun, suck as much fluid out of the power steering fluid reservoir as possible. Place a drain pan under the vehicle to catch any fluid that spills out when the hoses are disconnected.

3   Loosen the right front wheel nuts, raise the vehicle and support it securely on jackstands (see Jacking and Towing). Remove the right front wheel.

4   Remove the right front guard apron seal and liner, if necessary (see Chapter 11).

21.8 Steering gear mounting fasteners

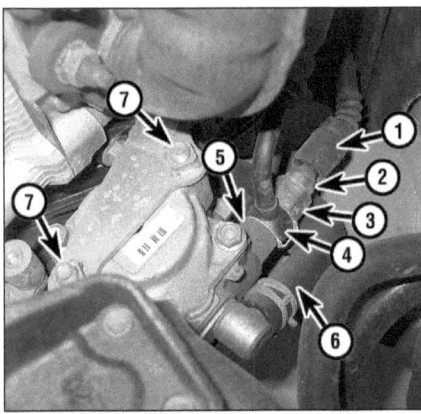

22.6 Installation details of the power steering pump - MCU28R models

1 *Power steering pressure switch electrical connector*
2 *Power steering pressure switch*
3 *Union bolt*
4 *Pressure feed line*
5 *Pressure port fitting*
6 *Fluid feed hose*
7 *Mounting bolts (viewed from behind - access can be made through a hole in the pulley and at the top of the pump)*

5   Remove the drivebelt (see Chapter 1).
6   Detach the fluid feed hose from the pump **(see illustration)**. Disconnect the electrical connector from the power steering pressure switch.
7   Remove the pressure line-to-pump union bolt and separate the line from the pump **(see illustration 22.6)**. Use two wrenches, one to hold the pressure port fitting and one to remove the union bolt. Remove the sealing washers on each side of the fitting - these should be replaced when installing the pump.
8   Remove the mounting bolts, then remove the pump **(see illustration 22.6)**.

Note: *The upper bolt does not come out entirely; loosen it enough to release it from the engine, and the bolt will come out with the pump.*

Installation

9   Installation is the reverse of removal. Tighten the pressure line union bolt and the mounting bolts to the torque listed in this Chapter's Specifications. Adjust the drivebelt tension (see Chapter 1).
10   Top up the fluid level in the reservoir (see Chapter 1) and bleed the system (see Section 23).

23   Power steering system - bleeding

1   Following any operation in which the power steering fluid lines have been disconnected, the power steering system must be

bled to remove all air and obtain proper steering performance.
2   With the front wheels in the straight ahead position, check the power steering fluid level and, if low, add fluid until it reaches the Cold mark on the dipstick.
3   Start the engine and allow it to run at fast idle. Recheck the fluid level and add more if necessary to reach the Cold mark on the dipstick.
4   Bleed the system by turning the wheels from side to side, without hitting the stops. This will work the air out of the system. Keep the reservoir full of fluid as this is done.

Note: *This procedure can be done with the front of the vehicle raised with a jack and supported on jackstands (see Jacking and Towing). This makes it easier to turn the wheels back and forth during the bleeding process.*

5   When the air is worked out of the system, return the wheels to the straight-ahead position and leave the vehicle running for several more minutes before shutting it off.
6   Road test the vehicle to be sure the steering system is functioning normally and noise free.
7   Recheck the fluid level to be sure it is up to the Hot mark on the dipstick while the engine is at normal operating temperature. Add fluid if necessary (see Chapter 1).

24   Subframe - removal and installation

Removal

Front subframe

Refer to illustration 24.11

1   Disconnect the negative (-) battery terminal (see Chapter 5).
2   Loosen the front wheel nuts, raise the front of the vehicle and support it securely on jackstands (see Jacking and Towing). Remove both front wheels.

Note: *The jackstands must be behind the front suspension subframe, not supporting the vehicle by the subframe.*

3   Remove the front bumper cover (see Chapter 11).
4   Disconnect the stabiliser bar bushing retainers from the subframe (see Section 2).
5   Disconnect the control arms from the steering knuckles (see Section 6). Also, detach height sensor linkage, if equipped.
6   Remove the steering gear mounting bolts from the subframe (see Section 21).

Note: *Support the steering gear from above with a rope.*

7   Inspect the subframe for any hose, line or harness brackets that may be attached and detach them.
8   Support the engine from above using an engine hoist or equivalent (see Chapter 2C).

Warning: *DO NOT place any part of your body under the engine when it's supported only by a hoist or other lifting device.*

9   Detach all engine and transaxle mounts from the subframe (see Chapter 2A) or (see Chapter 2B)
10   Using two floor jacks, support the subframe. Position one jack on each side of the subframe, midway between the front and rear mounting points.
11   With the jacks sufficiently supporting the subframe, remove the fasteners securing the subframe brackets and the subframe **(see illustration)**.
12   With the use of an assistant to steady the subframe, carefully lower the jacks until the subframe is sufficiently resting on the ground.

Rear subframe

13   Loosen the rear wheel nuts, raise the rear of the vehicle and support it securely on jackstands (see Jacking and Towing). Remove both rear wheels.

Note: *The jackstands must be positioned on the frame of the vehicle not supporting the vehicle by the subframe.*

2WD models

14   Working inside the cargo area, remove all the deckboards and the spare tyre.
15   Remove the spare tyre lock cover.
16   Remove the rear stabiliser bar (see Section 10).

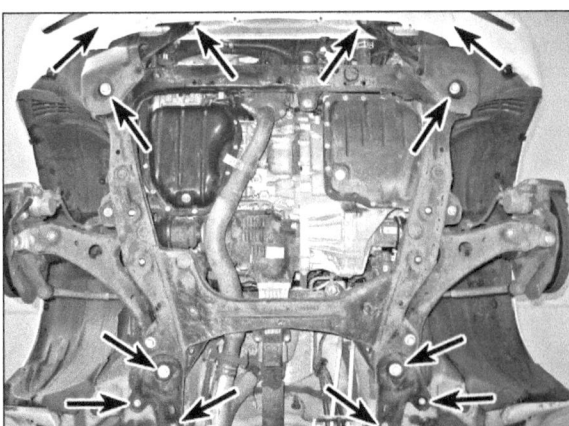

24.11 Subframe and bracket mounting bolts

17 Remove the suspension arms (see Section 13).
18 Remove the exhaust pipe support bracket.
19 Using two floor jacks, support the subframe. Position one jack on each side of the subframe, midway between the front and rear mounting points.
20 With the floor jacks sufficiently supporting the subframe, remove the rear subframe mounting bolts.
21 Carefully lower the subframe assembly from the vehicle.

AWD models

22 Disconnect the rear parking brake cables (see Chapter 9).
23 Remove the rear brake calipers and tie them using wire in a secure position (see Chapter 9).
24 Remove the rear brake discs (see Chapter 9).
25 Remove the exhaust system (see Chapter 4).
26 Remove the driveshaft (see Chapter 8) and the exhaust system (see Chapter 4).
27 Remove the rear driveshafts (see Chapter 8).
28 Remove the strut rods (see Section 12).
29 Remove the suspension arms (see Section 13).
30 Remove the rear knuckle (see Section 15) on each side of the rear suspension.
31 Using two floor jacks, support the subframe. Position one jack on each side of the subframe, midway between the front and rear mounting points.
32 With the floor jacks sufficiently supporting the subframe, remove the rear subframe mounting bolts.
33 Carefully lower the differential and subframe assembly from the vehicle.

Installation

34 Installation is the reverse of removal. Tighten all suspension and subframe fasteners to the torque listed in this Chapter's Specifications. Tighten all other fasteners to the torque listed in the Engine and Body chapters (see Chapter 2A), (see Chapter 2B) and (see Chapter 11).

25 Wheels and tyres - general information

Refer to illustration 25.1

1 All vehicles covered by this manual are equipped with metric-sized fibreglass or steel belted radial tyres **(see illustration)**. Use of other size or type of tyres may affect the ride and handling of the vehicle. Don't mix different types of tyres, such as radials and bias belted, on the same vehicle as handling may be seriously affected. It's recommended that tyres be replaced in pairs on the same axle, but if only one tyre is being replaced, be sure it's the same size, structure and tread design as the other.
2 Because tyre pressure has a substantial effect on handling and wear, the pressure on all tyres should be checked at least once a month or before any extended trips (see Chapter 1).
3 Wheels must be replaced if they are bent, dented, leak air, have elongated bolt holes, are heavily rusted, out of vertical symmetry or if the wheel nuts won't stay tight. Wheel repairs that use welding or peening are not recommended.
4 Tyre and wheel balance is important in the overall handling, braking and performance of the vehicle. Unbalanced wheels can adversely affect handling and ride characteristics as well as tyre life. Whenever a tyre is installed on a wheel, the tyre and wheel should be balanced by a shop with the proper equipment.

26 Wheel alignment - general information

Refer to illustration 26.1

A wheel alignment refers to the adjustments made to the wheels so they are in proper angular relationship to the suspension and the ground. Wheels that are out of proper alignment not only affect vehicle control, but also increase tyre wear. The alignment angles normally measured are camber, caster and toe-in **(see illustration)**.

Getting the proper wheel alignment is a very exacting process, one in which complicated and expensive machines are necessary to perform the job properly. Because of this, you should have a technician with the proper equipment perform these tasks. We will, however, use this space to give you a basic idea of what is involved with a wheel alignment so you can better understand the process and deal intelligently with the shop that does the work.

Toe-in is the turning in of the wheels. The purpose of a toe specification is to ensure

METRIC TYRE SIZES

P 185 / 80 R 13

TYRE TYPE
P-PASSENGER
T-TEMPORARY
C-COMMERCIAL

ASPECT RATIO
(SECTION HEIGHT)
(SECTION WIDTH)
70
75
80

RIM DIAMETER
(INCHES)
13
14
15

SECTION WIDTH
(MILLIMETERS)
185
195
205
ETC

CONSTRUCTION TYPE
R-RADIAL
B-BIAS - BELTED
D-DIAGONAL (BIAS)

SECTION WIDTH

SECTION HEIGHT

25.1 Metric tyre size code

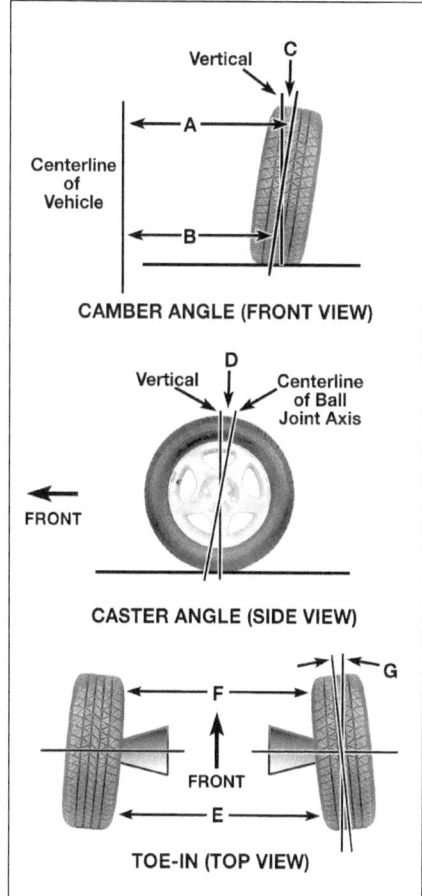

CAMBER ANGLE (FRONT VIEW)

CASTER ANGLE (SIDE VIEW)

TOE-IN (TOP VIEW)

26.1 Camber, caster and toe-in angles

A minus B = C (degrees camber)
D = caster (expressed in degrees)
E minus F = toe-in (measured in mm)
G = toe-in (expressed in degrees)

parallel rolling of the wheels. In a vehicle with zero toe-in, the distance between the front edges of the wheels will be the same as the distance between the rear edges of the wheels. The actual amount of toe-in is normally only very small. On the front end, toe-in is controlled by the tie-rod end position on the tie-rod. On the rear end, it's controlled either by a threaded adjuster on the rear (number two) suspension arm, or a cam at the inner end of the arm, depending on model year.

Incorrect toe-in will cause the tyres to wear improperly by making them scrub against the road surface.

Camber is the tilting of the wheels from vertical when viewed from one end of the vehicle. When the wheels tilt out at the top, the camber is said to be positive (+). When the wheels tilt in at the top the camber is negative (-). The amount of tilt is measured in degrees from vertical and this measurement is called the camber angle. This angle affects the amount of tyre tread which contacts the road and compensates for changes in the suspension geometry when the vehicle is cornering or travelling over an undulating surface.

Caster is the tilting of the front steering axis from the vertical. A tilt toward the rear is positive caster and a tilt toward the front is negative caster. Too little caster will make the front end wander, while too much caster can make the steering effort higher.

Chapter 11
Body

Contents

---

1 General information

These models feature a "unibody" layout, using a floor pan with integral side frame rails which support the body components, front and rear suspension systems and other mechanical components.

Certain components are particularly vulnerable to accident damage and can be unbolted and repaired or replaced. Among these parts are the body mouldings, bumpers, front guards, the bonnet and tailgate, doors and all glass.

Only general body maintenance practices and body panel repair procedures within the scope of the do-it-yourselfer are included in this Chapter.

Warning: *The front seat belts on some models are equipped with pre-tensioners, which are pyrotechnic (explosive) devices designed to retract the seat belts in the event of a collision. On models equipped with pre-tensioners, do not remove the front seat belt retractor assemblies, and do not disconnect the electrical connectors leading to the assemblies. Problems with the pre-tensioners will turn on the SRS (airbag) warning light on the dash. If any pre-tensioner problems are suspected, take the vehicle to a dealer service department.*

2 Repair minor paint scratches

No matter how hard you try to keep your vehicle looking like new, it will inevitably be scratched, chipped or dented at some point. If the metal is actually dented, seek the advice of a professional. But you can fix minor scratches and chips yourself. Buy a touch-up paint kit from a dealer parts department or an auto parts store. To ensure that you get the right colour, you'll need to have the specific make, model and year of your vehicle and, ideally, the paint code, which is located on a special metal plate under the bonnet or in the door jamb.

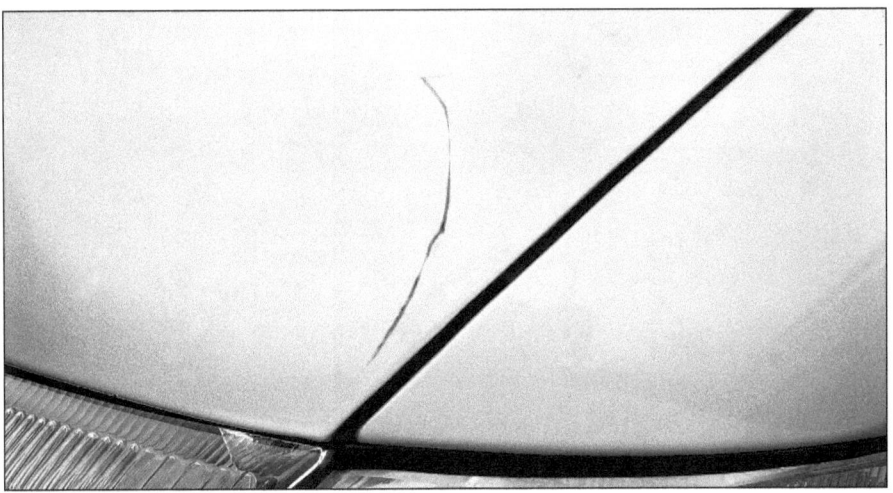

2.1 Make sure the damaged area is perfectly clean and rust free. If the touch-up kit has a wire brush, use it to clean the scratch or chip. Or use fine steel wool wrapped around the end of a pencil. Clean the scratched or chipped surface only, not the good paint surrounding it. Rinse the area with water and allow it to dry thoroughly

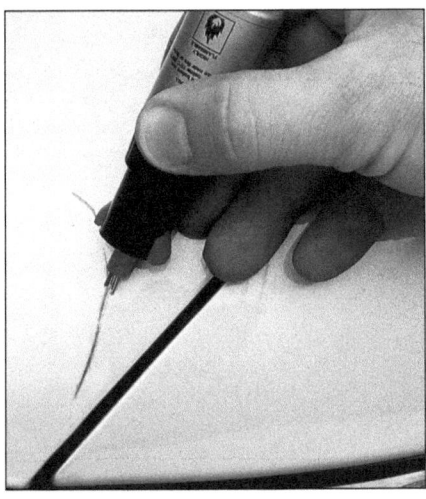

2.2 Thoroughly mix the paint, then apply a small amount with the touch-up kit brush or a very fine artist's brush. Brush in one direction as you fill the scratch area. Do not build up the paint higher than the surrounding paint

3   Body repair - minor damage

Plastic body panels

The following repair procedures are for minor scratches and gouges. Repair of more serious damage should be left to a dealer service department or qualified auto body shop. Below is a list of the equipment and materials necessary to perform the following repair procedures on plastic body panels.

Wax, grease and silicone removing solvent

Cloth-backed body tape
Sanding discs
Drill motor with 75 mm disc holder
Hand sanding block
Rubber squeegees
Sandpaper
Non-porous mixing palette
Wood paddle or putty knife
Curved-tooth body file
Flexible parts repair material

Flexible panels (bumper trim)

1   Remove the damaged panel, if necessary or desirable. In most cases, repairs can be carried out with the panel installed.
2   Clean the area(s) to be repaired with a wax, grease and silicone removing solvent applied with a water-dampened cloth.
3   If the damage is structural, that is, if it extends through the panel, clean the backside of the panel area to be repaired as well. Wipe dry.
4   Sand the rear surface about 40 mm beyond the break.
5   Cut two pieces of fibreglass cloth large enough to overlap the break by about 40 mm. Cut only to the required length.

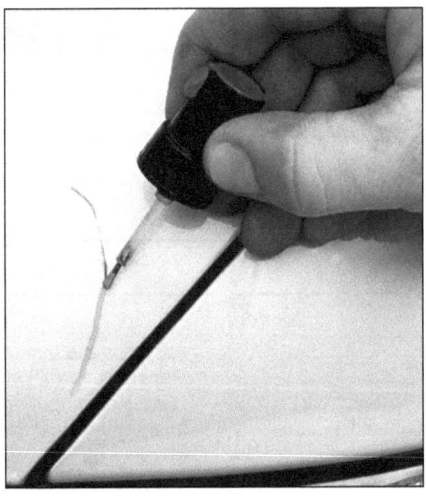

2.3. If the vehicle has a two-coat finish, apply the clear coat after the colour coat has dried

6   Mix the adhesive from the repair kit according to the instructions included with the kit, and apply a layer of the mixture approximately 3 mm thick on the backside of the panel. Overlap the break by at least 40 mm.
7   Apply one piece of fibreglass cloth to the adhesive and cover the cloth with additional adhesive. Apply a second piece of fibreglass cloth to the adhesive and immediately cover the cloth with additional adhesive in sufficient quantity to fill the weave.
8   Allow the repair to cure for 20 to 30 minutes at 15 degrees to 25 degrees C.
9   If necessary, trim the excess repair material at the edge.
10   Remove all of the paint film over and around the area(s) to be repaired. The repair material should not overlap the painted surface.
11   With a drill motor and a sanding disc (or

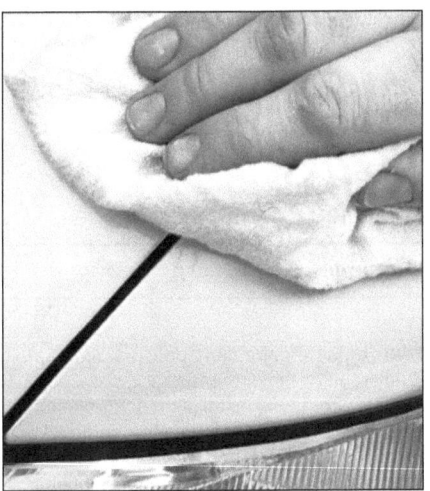

2.4 Wait a few days for the paint to dry thoroughly, then rub out the repainted area with a polishing compound to blend the new paint with the surrounding area. When you're happy with your work, wash and polish the area

a rotary file), cut a "V" along the break line approximately 12 mm wide. Remove all dust and loose particles from the repair area.
12   Mix and apply the repair material. Apply a light coat first over the damaged area; then continue applying material until it reaches a level slightly higher than the surrounding finish.
13   Cure the mixture for 20 to 30 minutes at 15 degrees to 25 degrees C.
14   Roughly establish the contour of the area being repaired with a body file. If low areas or pits remain, mix and apply additional adhesive.
15   Block sand the damaged area with sandpaper to establish the actual contour of the surrounding surface.

These photos illustrate a method of repairing simple dents. They are intended to supplement *Body repair - minor damage* in this Chapter and should not be used as the sole instructions for body repair on these vehicles.

1 If you can't access the backside of the body panel to hammer out the dent, pull it out with a slide-hammer-type dent puller. In the deepest portion of the dent or along the crease line, drill or punch hole(s) at least one inch apart . . .

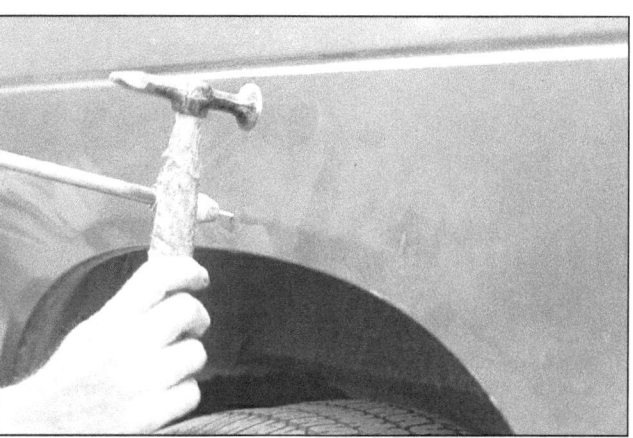

2 . . . then screw the slide-hammer into the hole and operate it. Tap with a hammer near the edge of the dent to help 'pop' the metal back to its original shape. When you're finished, the dent area should be close to its original contour and about 1/8-inch below the surface of the surrounding metal

3 Using coarse-grit sandpaper, remove the paint down to the bare metal. Hand sanding works fine, but the disc sander shown here makes the job faster. Use finer (about 320-grit) sandpaper to feather-edge the paint at least one inch around the dent area

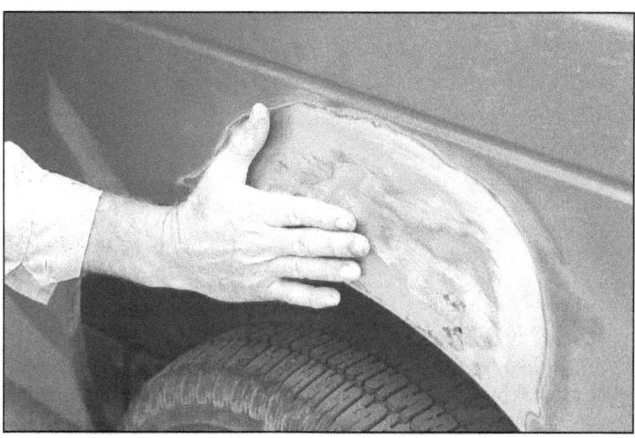

4 When the paint is removed, touch will probably be more helpful than sight for telling if the metal is straight. Hammer down the high spots or raise the low spots as necessary. Clean the repair area with wax/silicone remover

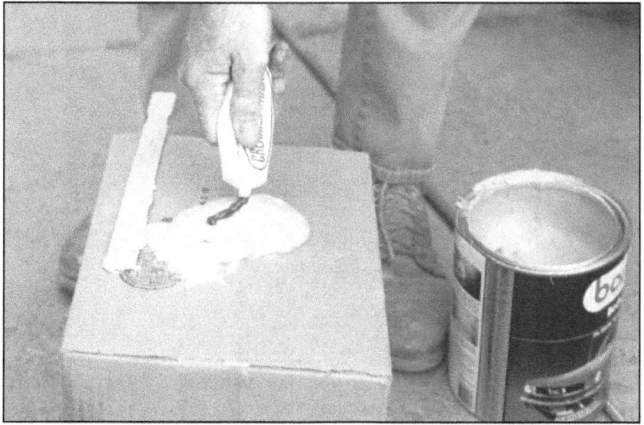

5 Following label instructions, mix up a batch of plastic filler and hardener. The ratio of filler to hardener is critical, and, if you mix it incorrectly, it will either not cure properly or cure too quickly (you won't have time to file and sand it into shape)

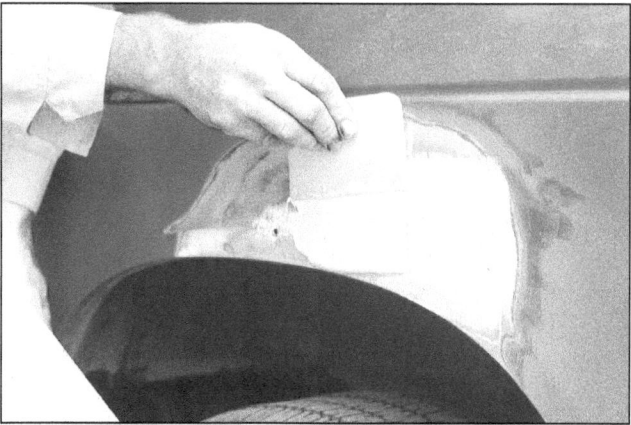

6 Working quickly so the filler doesn't harden, use a plastic applicator to press the body filler firmly into the metal, assuring it bonds completely. Work the filler until it matches the original contour and is slightly above the surrounding metal

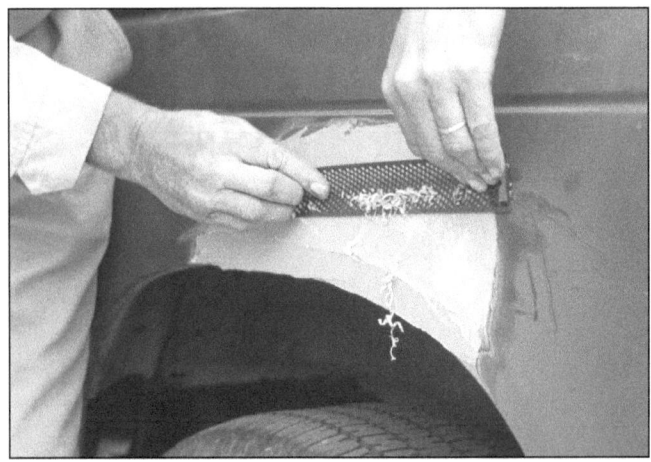

7 Let the filler harden until you can just dent it with your fingernail. Use a body file or Surform tool (shown here) to rough-shape the filler

8 Use coarse-grit sandpaper and a sanding board or block to work the filler down until it's smooth and even. Work down to finer grits of sandpaper - always using a board or block - ending up with 360 or 400 grit

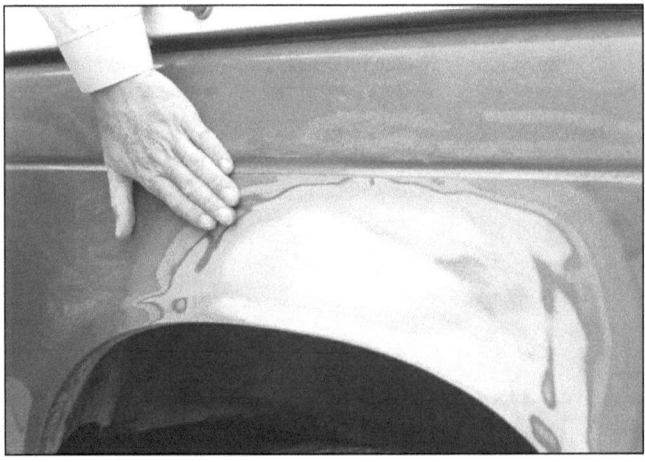

9 You shouldn't be able to feel any ridge at the transition from the filler to the bare metal or from the bare metal to the old paint. As soon as the repair is flat and uniform, remove the dust and mask off the adjacent panels or trim pieces

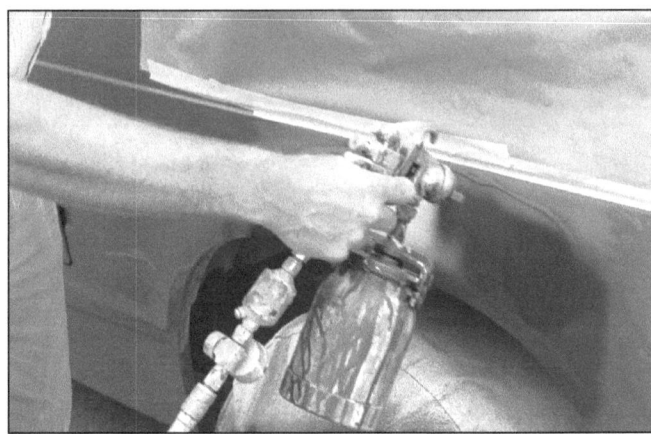

10 Apply several layers of primer to the area. Don't spray the primer on too heavy, so it sags or runs, and make sure each coat is dry before you spray on the next one. A professional-type spray gun is being used here, but aerosol spray primer is available inexpensively from auto parts stores

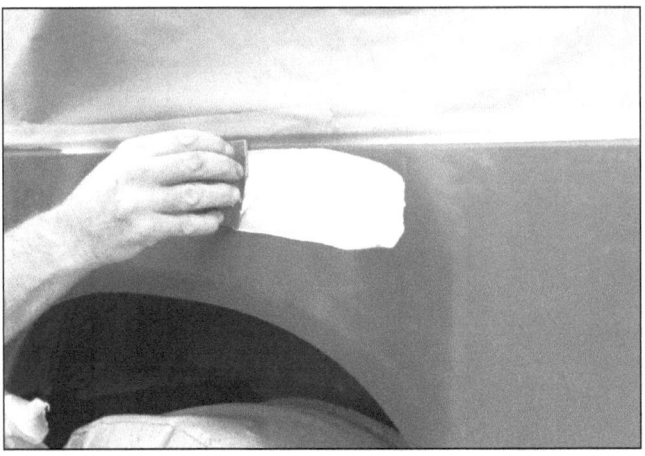

11 The primer will help reveal imperfections or scratches. Fill these with glazing compound. Follow the label instructions and sand it with 360 or 400-grit sandpaper until it's smooth. Repeat the glazing, sanding and respraying until the primer reveals a perfectly smooth surface

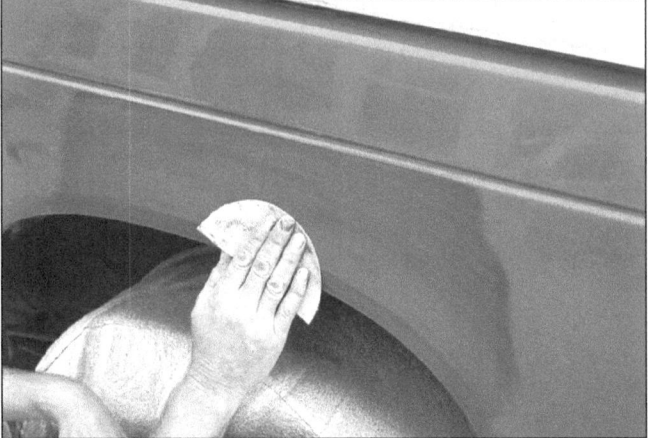

12 Finish sand the primer with very fine sandpaper (400 or 600-grit) to remove the primer overspray. Clean the area with water and allow it to dry. Use a tack rag to remove any dust, then apply the finish coat. Don't attempt to rub out or wax the repair area until the paint has dried completely (at least two weeks)

16   If desired, the repaired area can be temporarily protected with several light coats of primer. Because of the special paints and techniques required for flexible body panels, it is recommended that the vehicle be taken to a paint shop for completion of the body repair.

Steel body panels

See photo sequence

Repair of dents

17   When repairing dents, the first job is to pull the dent out until the affected area is as close as possible to its original shape. There is no point in trying to restore the original shape completely as the metal in the damaged area will have stretched on impact and cannot be restored to its original contours. It is better to bring the level of the dent up to a point that is about 3 mm below the level of the surrounding metal. In cases where the dent is very shallow, it is not worth trying to pull it out at all.

18   If the backside of the dent is accessible, it can be hammered out gently from behind using a soft-face hammer. While doing this, hold a block of wood firmly against the opposite side of the metal to absorb the hammer blows and prevent the metal from being stretched.

19   If the dent is in a section of the body which has double layers, or some other factor makes it inaccessible from behind, a different technique is required. Drill several small holes through the metal inside the damaged area, particularly in the deeper sections. Screw long, self-tapping screws into the holes just enough for them to get a good grip in the metal. Now pulling on the protruding heads of the screws with locking pliers can pull out the dent.

20   The next stage of repair is the removal of paint from the damaged area and from an 25 mm or so of the surrounding metal. This is easily done with a wire brush or sanding disk in a drill motor, although it can be done just as effectively by hand with sandpaper. To complete the preparation for filling, score the surface of the bare metal with a screwdriver or the tang of a file or drill small holes in the affected area. This will provide a good grip for the filler material. To complete the repair, see the Section on filling and painting.

Repair of rust holes or gashes

21   Remove all paint from the affected area and from 25 mm or so of the surrounding metal using a sanding disk or wire brush mounted in a drill motor. If these are not available, a few sheets of sandpaper will do the job just as effectively.

22   With the paint removed, you will be able to determine the severity of the corrosion and decide whether to replace the whole panel, if possible, or repair the affected area. New body panels are not as expensive as most people think and it is often quicker to install a new panel than to repair large areas of rust.

23   Remove all trim pieces from the affected area except those which will act as a guide to the original shape of the damaged body, such as headlight shells, etc. Using metal snips or a hacksaw blade, remove all loose metal and any other metal that is badly affected by rust. Hammer the edges of the hole in to create a slight depression for the filler material.

24   Wire-brush the affected area to remove the powdery rust from the surface of the metal. If the back of the rusted area is accessible, treat it with rust inhibiting paint.

25   Before filling is done, block the hole in some way. This can be done with sheet metal riveted or screwed into place, or by stuffing the hole with wire mesh.

26   Once the hole is blocked off, the affected area can be filled and painted. See the following subsection on filling and painting.

Filling and painting

27   Many types of body fillers are available, but generally speaking, body repair kits which contain filler paste and a tube of resin hardener are best for this type of repair work. A wide, flexible plastic or nylon applicator will be necessary for imparting a smooth and contoured finish to the surface of the filler material. Mix up a small amount of filler on a clean piece of wood or cardboard (use the hardener sparingly). Follow the manufacturer's instructions on the package, otherwise the filler will set incorrectly.

28   Using the applicator, apply the filler paste to the prepared area. Draw the applicator across the surface of the filler to achieve the desired contour and to level the filler surface. As soon as a contour that approximates the original one is achieved, stop working the paste. If you continue, the paste will begin to stick to the applicator. Continue to add thin layers of paste at 20-minute intervals until the level of the filler is just above the surrounding metal.

29   Once the filler has hardened, the excess can be removed with a body file. From then on, progressively finer grades of sandpaper should be used, starting with a 180-grit paper and finishing with 600-grit wet-or-dry paper. Always wrap the sandpaper around a flat rubber or wooden block, otherwise the surface of the filler will not be completely flat. During the sanding of the filler surface, the wet-or-dry paper should be periodically rinsed in water. This will ensure that a very smooth finish is produced in the final stage.

30   At this point, the repair area should be surrounded by a ring of bare metal, which in turn should be encircled by the finely feathered edge of good paint. Rinse the repair area with clean water until all of the dust produced by the sanding operation is gone.

31   Spray the entire area with a light coat of primer. This will reveal any imperfections in the surface of the filler. Repair the imperfections with fresh filler paste or glaze filler and once more smooth the surface with sandpaper. Repeat this spray-and-repair procedure until you are satisfied that the surface of the filler and the feathered edge of the paint are perfect. Rinse the area with clean water and allow it to dry completely.

32   The repair area is now ready for painting. Spray painting must be carried out in a warm, dry, windless and dust free atmosphere. These conditions can be created if you have access to a large indoor work area, but if you are forced to work in the open, you will have to pick the day very carefully. If you are working indoors, dousing the floor in the work area with water will help settle the dust that would otherwise be in the air. If the repair area is confined to one body panel, mask off the surrounding panels. This will help minimise the effects of a slight mismatch in paint colour. Trim pieces such as chrome strips, door handles, etc., will also need to be masked off or removed. Use masking tape and several thickness of newspaper for the masking operations.

33   Before spraying, shake the paint can thoroughly, then spray a test area until the spray painting technique is mastered. Cover the repair area with a thick coat of primer. The thickness should be built up using several thin layers of primer rather than one thick one. Using 600-grit wet-or-dry sandpaper, rub down the surface of the primer until it is very smooth. While doing this, the work area should be thoroughly rinsed with water and the wet-or-dry sandpaper periodically rinsed as well. Allow the primer to dry before spraying additional coats.

34   Spray on the top coat, again building up the thickness by using several thin layers of paint. Begin spraying in the centre of the repair area and then, using a circular motion, work out until the whole repair area and about 50 mm of the surrounding original paint is covered. Remove all masking material 10 to 15 minutes after spraying on the final coat of paint. Allow the new paint at least two weeks to harden, then use a very fine rubbing compound to blend the edges of the new paint into the existing paint. Finally, apply a coat of wax

4   Body repair - major damage

1   Major damage must be repaired by an auto body shop specifically equipped to perform body and frame repairs. These shops have the specialised equipment required to do the job properly.

2   If the damage is extensive, the frame must be checked for proper alignment or the vehicle's handling characteristics may be adversely affected and other components may wear at an accelerated rate.

3   Due to the fact that all of the major body components (bonnet, guards, etc.) are separate and replaceable units, any seriously damaged components should be replaced rather than repaired. Sometimes the components can be found in a wrecking yard that specialises in used vehicle components, often at considerable savings over the cost of new parts.

Fasteners

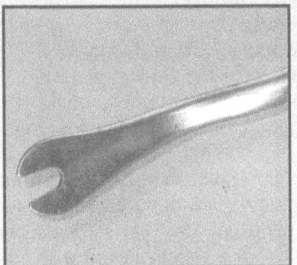

This tool is designed to remove special fasteners. A small pry tool used for removing nails will also work well in place of this tool

A Phillips head screwdriver can be used to release the center portion, but light pressure must be used because the plastic is easily damaged. Once the center is up, the fastener can easily be pried from its hole

Here is a view with the center portion fully released. Install the fastener as shown, then press the center in to set it

This fastener is used for exterior panels and shields. The center portion must be pried up to release the fastener. Install the fastener with the center up, then press the center in to set it

This type of fastener is used commonly for interior panels. Use a small blunt tool to press the small pin at the center in to release it . . .

. . . the pin will stay with the fastener in the released position

Reset the fastener for installation by moving the pin out. Install the fastener, then press the pin flush with the fastener to set it

This fastener is used for exterior and interior panels. It has no moving parts. Simply pry the fastener from its hole like the claw of a hammer removes a nail. Without a tool that can get under the top of the fastener, it can be very difficult to remove

5   Upholstery, carpets and vinyl trim - maintenance

Upholstery and carpets

1   Every three months remove the floormats and clean the interior of the vehicle (more frequently if necessary). Use a stiff whiskbroom to brush the carpeting and loosen dirt and dust, then vacuum the upholstery and carpets thoroughly, especially along seams and crevices.

2   Dirt and stains can be removed from carpeting with basic household or automotive carpet shampoos available in spray cans. Follow the directions and vacuum again, then use a stiff brush to bring back the "nap" of the carpet.

3   Most interiors have cloth or vinyl upholstery, either of which can be cleaned and maintained with a number of material-specific cleaners or shampoos available in auto supply stores. Follow the directions on the product for usage, and always spot-test any upholstery cleaner on an inconspicuous area (bottom edge of a backseat cushion) to ensure that it doesn't cause a colour shift in the material.

4   After cleaning, vinyl upholstery should be treated with a protectant.
Note: Make sure the protectant container indicates the product can be used on seats - some products may make a seat too slippery.
Caution: Do not use protectant on vinyl-covered steering wheels.

5   Leather upholstery requires special care. It should be cleaned regularly with saddlesoap or leather cleaner. Never use alcohol, gasoline, nail polish remover or thinner to clean leather upholstery.

6   After cleaning, regularly treat leather upholstery with a leather conditioner, rubbed in with a soft cotton cloth. Never use car wax on leather upholstery.

7   In areas where the interior of the vehicle is subject to bright sunlight, cover leather seating areas of the seats with a sheet if the vehicle is to be left out for any length of time.

Vinyl trim

8   Don't clean vinyl trim with detergents, caustic soap or petroleum-based cleaners. Plain soap and water works just fine, with a soft brush to clean dirt that may be ingrained. Wash the vinyl as frequently as the rest of the vehicle.

9   After cleaning, application of a high-quality rubber and vinyl protectant will help prevent oxidation and cracks. The protectant can also be applied to weather-stripping, vacuum lines and rubber hoses, which often fail as a result of chemical degradation, and to the tyres.

6   Fastener and trim removal

Refer to illustration 6.4

1   There is a variety of plastic fasteners used to hold trim panels, splash shields and other parts in place in addition to typical screws, nuts and bolts. Once you are familiar with them, they can usually be removed without too much difficulty.

2   The proper tools and approach can prevent added time and expense to a project by minimizing the number of broken fasteners and/or parts.

3   The accompanying illustration shows various types of fasteners that are typically used on most vehicles and how to remove and install them **(see illustration)**. Replacement fasteners are commonly found at most auto parts stores, if necessary.

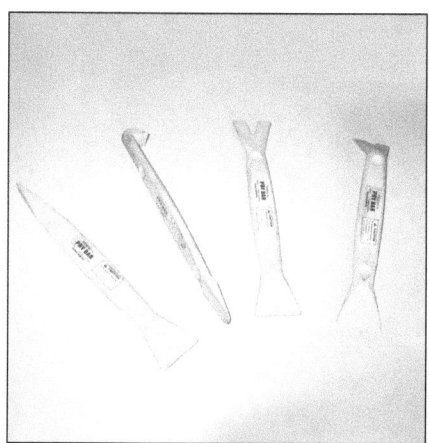

6.4   These small plastic pry tools are ideal for prying off trim panels

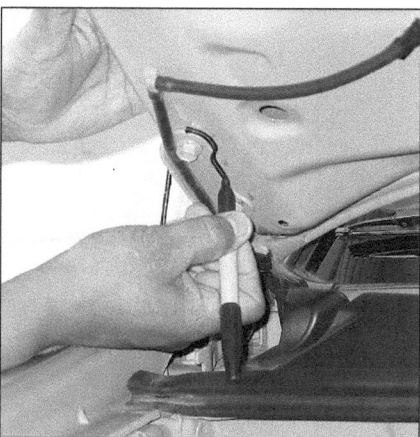

9.3   Draw alignment marks around the bonnet hinges to ensure proper alignment of the bonnet when it's reinstalled

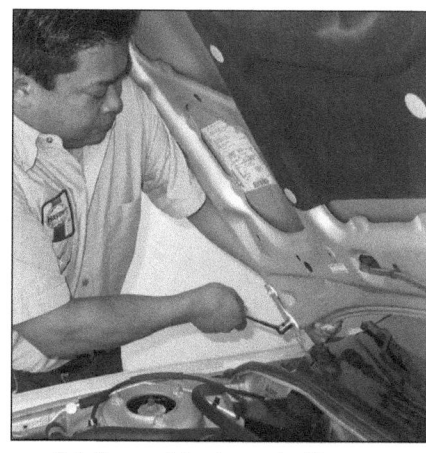

9.4   Support the bonnet with your shoulder while removing the bonnet bolts

4   Trim panels are typically made of plastic and their flexibility can help during removal. The key to their removal is to use a tool **(see illustration)** to pry the panel near its retainers to release it without damaging surrounding areas or breaking-off any retainers. The retainers will usually snap out of their designated slot or hole after force is applied to them. Stiff plastic tools designed for prying on trim panels are available at most auto parts stores **(see illustration)**. Tools that are tapered and wrapped in protective tape, such as a screwdriver or small pry tool, are also very effective when used with care.

7   Hinges and locks - maintenance

Once every 20,000 km, or every twelve months, the hinges and latch assemblies on the doors, bonnet and tailgate should be given a few drops of light oil or lock lubricant. The door latch strikers should also be lubricated with a thin coat of grease to reduce wear and ensure free movement. Lubricate the door and tailgate locks with spray-on graphite lubricant.

8   Windshield and fixed glass - replacement

Replacement of the windshield and fixed glass requires the use of special fast-setting adhesive/caulk materials and some specialised tools and techniques. These operations should be left to a dealer service department or a shop specialising in glass work.

9   Bonnet - removal, installation and adjustment

Note: *The bonnet is somewhat awkward to remove and install, at least two people should perform this procedure.*

Removal and installation
Refer to illustrations 9.3 and 9.4
1   Open the bonnet, then place blankets or pads over the guards and cowl area of the body. This will protect the body and paint as the bonnet is lifted off.
2   Disconnect any cables or wires that will interfere with removal. Disconnect the windshield washer tubing near the right-side hinge.
3   Make marks around the bonnet hinge to ensure proper alignment during installation **(see illustration)**.
4   Have an assistant support one side of the bonnet. Remove the clips from each end of the support, then detach the supports from the bonnet. Take turns removing the hinge-to-bonnet bolts and lift off the bonnet **(see illustration)**.
5   Installation is the reverse of removal. Align the hinge bolts with the marks made in Step 3.

Adjustment
Refer to illustrations 9.9a, 9.9b and 9.10
6   Fore-and-aft and side-to-side adjustment of the bonnet is done by moving the hinge

plate slot after loosening the bolts or nuts.
Note: *The factory bolts are "centreing" type that will not allow adjustment. To adjust the bonnet in relation to the hinges, these bolts must be replaced with standard bolts with flat washers and lock washers.*

7   Mark around the entire hinge plate so you can determine the amount of movement.
8   Loosen the bolts and move the bonnet into correct alignment. Move it only a little at a time. Tighten the hinge bolts and carefully lower the bonnet to check the position.
9   If necessary after installation, the entire bonnet latch assembly can be adjusted up-and-down as well as from side-to-side on the radiator support so the bonnet closes securely and flush with the guards. Scribe a line or mark around the bonnet latch mounting bolts to provide a reference point, then loosen them and reposition the latch assembly, as necessary **(see illustrations)**. Following adjustment, retighten the mounting bolts.
10   Finally, adjust the bonnet bumpers on the radiator support so the bonnet, when closed, is flush with the guards **(see illustration)**.

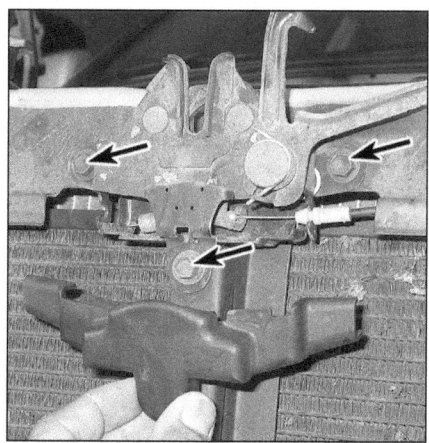

9.9a   To adjust the bonnet latch horizontally or vertically, loosen these bolts

9.9b   On GSU40R/GSU45R models, remove the cap with a screwdriver to access the lower bolt

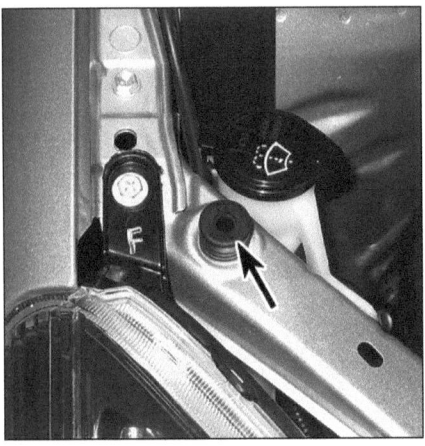

9.10 To adjust the vertical height of the leading edge of the bonnet so that it's flush with the guards, turn each edge cushion (arrow indicates one) clockwise (to lower the bonnet) or counterclockwise (to raise the bonnet)

11   The bonnet latch assembly, as well as the hinges, should be periodically lubricated with white, lithium-base grease to prevent binding and wear.

10 Bonnet latch and release cable - removal and installation

Latch

Refer to illustration 10.2
1   Scribe a line around the latch to aid alignment when installing, then remove the retaining bolts securing the bonnet latch to the radiator support **(see illustration 9.9)**. Remove the latch.
2   Disconnect the bonnet release cable by disengaging the cable from the latch **(see illustration).**
3   Installation is the reverse of removal.

Note: *Adjust the latch so the bonnet engages securely when closed and the bonnet bumpers are slightly compressed.*

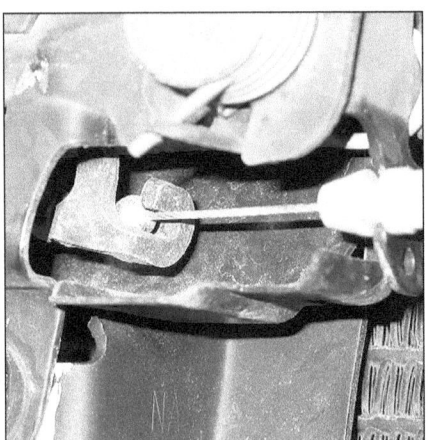

10.2 Pry out the cable retainer from the backside of the bonnet latch assembly, then disengage the cable

Cable

Refer to illustration 10.4
4   Working in the passenger compartment, lift the bonnet release handle lever upward, then pull down on the cable housing end and disengage the cable from the bonnet release lever handle **(see illustration).** If the handle lever needs to be replaced simply pull outward on the handle retaining tab and push downward to release it from the instrument panel.
5   Attach a piece of thin wire or string to the end of the cable.
6   Working in the engine compartment, disconnect the bonnet release cable from the latch as described in Steps 1 and 2. Unclip all the cable retaining clips on the radiator support and the inner guard liner.
7   Pull the cable forward into the engine compartment until you can see the wire or string, then remove the wire or string from the old cable and fasten it to the new cable.
8   With the new cable attached to the wire or string, pull the wire or string back through the firewall until the new cable reaches the inside handle.
9   Working in the passenger compartment, install the new cable into the bonnet release

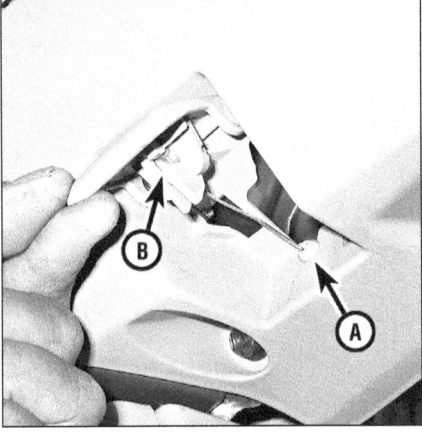

10.4 Lift upward on the handle and pull the cable housing end (A) from the base of the handle, then detach the cable end (B) from the lever

lever, making sure the cable housing fits snugly into the notch in the handle bracket.
Note: *Pull on the cable with your fingers from the passenger compartment until the cable stop seats in the grommet on the firewall.*
10   The remainder of the installation is the reverse of removal.

11 Bumpers - removal and installation

Front bumper

Refer to illustrations 11.3, 11.5a and 11.5b
1   Apply the parking brake, raise the vehicle and support securely on jackstands (see Jacking and Towing).
2   Working below the vehicle, remove the lower splash shields.
3   Remove the inner guard liners **(see illustration).**
4   Detach the fasteners securing the top of the grille **(see illustrations 13.1 and 13.2).**
5   Detach the fasteners securing the sides and bottom of the bumper cover. Pull the cover outward slightly and disconnect the connectors from the fog lights, if equipped. Remove the cover from the vehicle **(see illustrations).**
6   Installation is the reverse of removal. Make sure the tabs (if equipped) on the back of the bumper cover fit into the corresponding clips on the body before attaching the bolts and screws. An assistant would be helpful at this point.

Rear bumper

Refer to illustrations 11.8 and 11.9
7   Working in the rear wheelwell, detach the plastic clips and the upper bolt securing the edge of the bumper cover.
8   Detach the fasteners securing the bottom of the bumper cover **(see illustration).**
9   Open the tailgate and remove the fas-

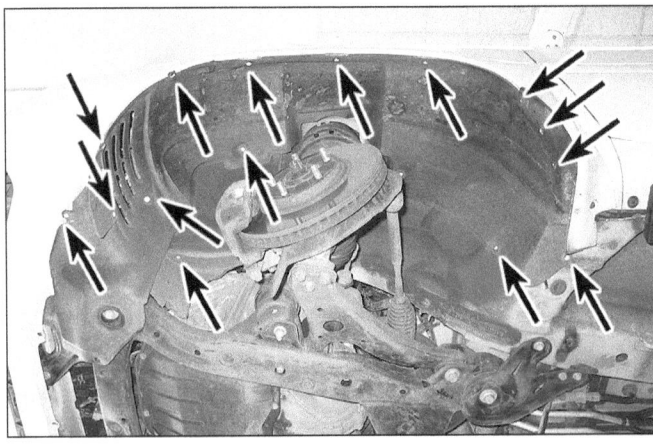

11.3 Detach the main portion of the inner guard liner, secured by bolts, screws and plastic clips

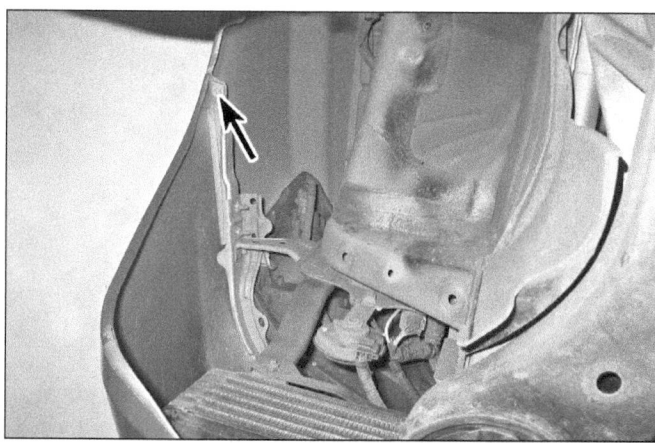

11.5a Inside the inner guard liner, remove the screw securing the bumper cover to the guard

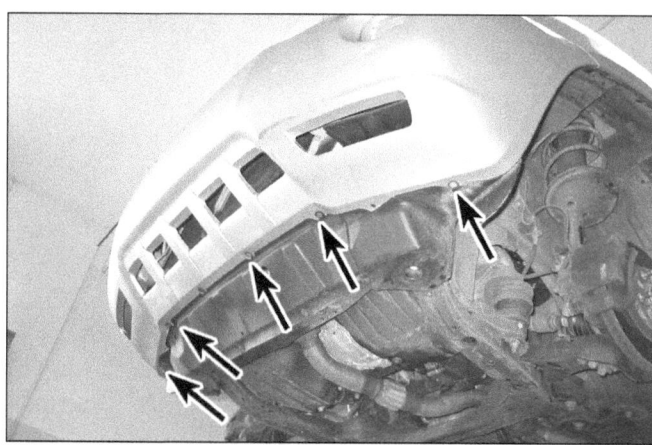

11.5b Remove the fasteners securing the bottom of the bumper cover

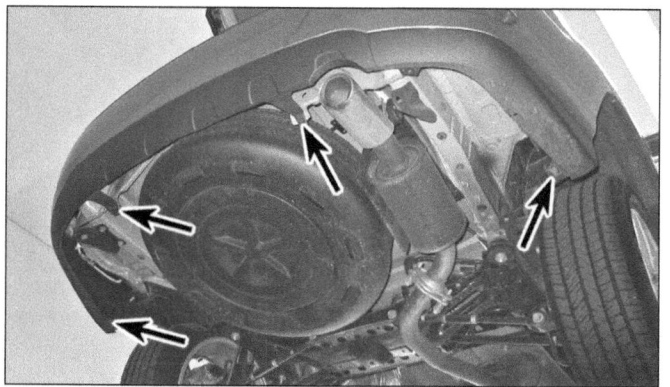

11.8 Remove the fasteners securing the bottom of the bumper cover

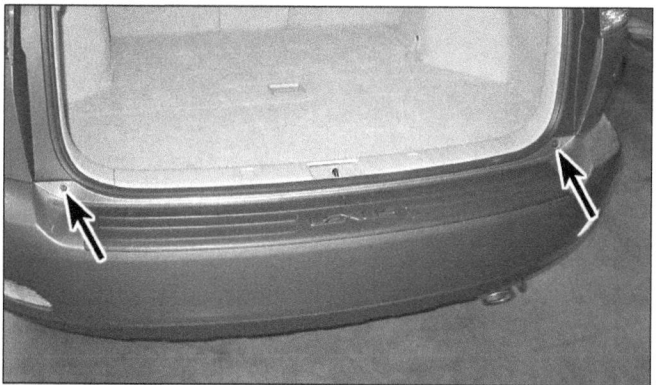

11.9 Open the tailgate and remove the two upper bumper cover fasteners

teners securing the inside edge of the bumper cover **(see illustration)**. Pull the bumper cover out and away from the vehicle.

10   Installation is the reverse of removal.

12 Radiator grille - removal and installation

Refer to illustrations 12.1 and 12.2

1   Open the bonnet. Remove fasteners along the top of the grille **(see illustration)**.

2   Working from the back of the grille, use a pair of pliers and squeeze the plastic retaining clips at the upper corner of both sides of the grille **(see illustration)**.

3   Pull the top of the grille out slightly and disengage the retaining clips at the bottom of the grille with a long screwdriver. The retaining clips can be disengaged by simply pressing downward on the tabs.

4   Once the retaining clips are disengaged, pull the grille out and remove it.

5   Installation is the reverse of removal.

13 Cowl cover and vent tray - removal and installation

Refer to illustrations 13.2a, 13.2b and 13.3

1   Remove the wiper arms (see Chapter 12).

2   Remove the push pin fasteners securing

12.1 Radiator grille upper fasteners

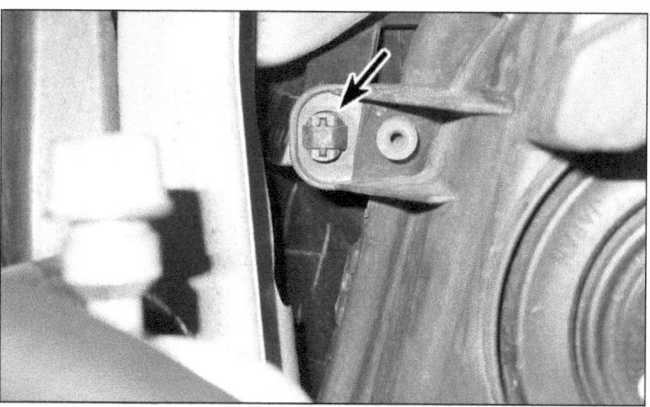

12.2 Disengage the two clips on the back side of the radiator grille

13.2a Remove the cowl fasteners - push down on the centre part with a small screwdriver, then . . .

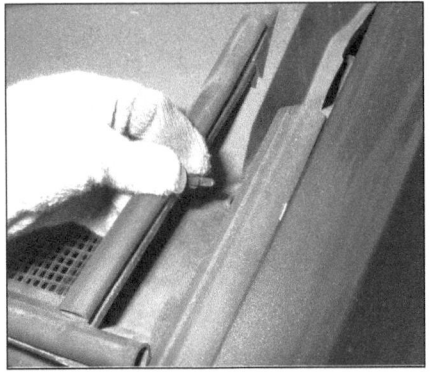

13.2b . . . lift the whole fastener out of the hole

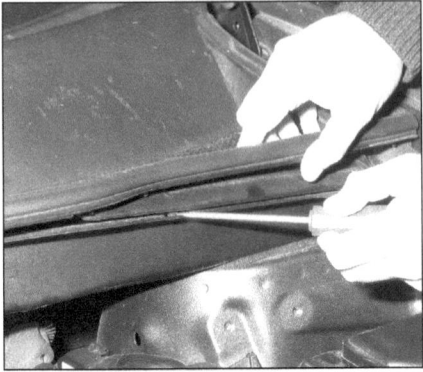

13.3 Remove the clips along the front of the cowl cover using a screwdriver

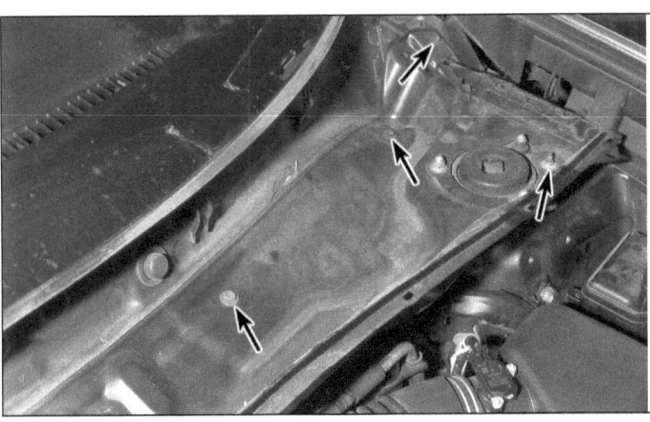

13.4 Some of the vent tray fasteners

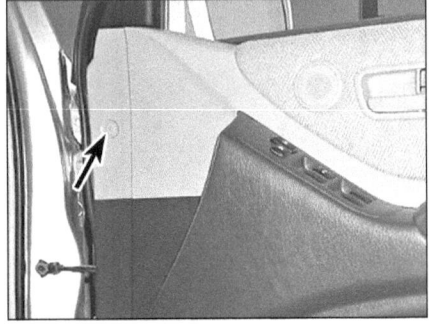

14.2 Remove the push-pin fastener from the door panel

the cowl cover (see illustration).

Note: *Use a small screwdriver to push the centre button down, then lift up the outer part of the fastener and remove* (see illustrations).

3   Disengage the remaining clips along the front of the cowl cover (see illustration).
4   If the vent tray needs to be removed, first remove the wiper motor linkage assembly (see Chapter 12), then remove the vent tray mounting bolts (see illustration).
5   Installation is the reverse of removal.

14 Door trim panels - removal and installation

Warning: *The models covered by this manual are equipped with Supplemental Restraint systems (SRS), more commonly known as airbags. Always disarm the airbag system before working in the vicinity of any airbag system component to avoid the possibility of accidental deployment of the airbag, which could cause personal injury (see Chapter 12).*

Caution: *Wear gloves when working inside the door openings to protect against cuts from sharp metal edges.*

Front and rear doors

MCU28R models
Refer to illustrations 14.2, 14.3a, 14.3b, 14.4, 14.5, 14.6, 14.7 and 14.8
1   Disconnect the negative (-) battery terminal (see Chapter 5).
2   Remove the push-pin fastener (see illustration).
3   Remove the set-screw to remove the bezel around the inside door handle (see illustrations).
4   Using a trim removal tool, pry up the window switch plate and disconnect the electrical connectors (see illustration).

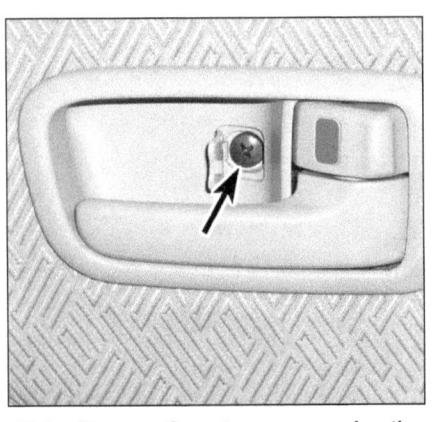

14.3a Remove the set screw securing the inside door handle . . .

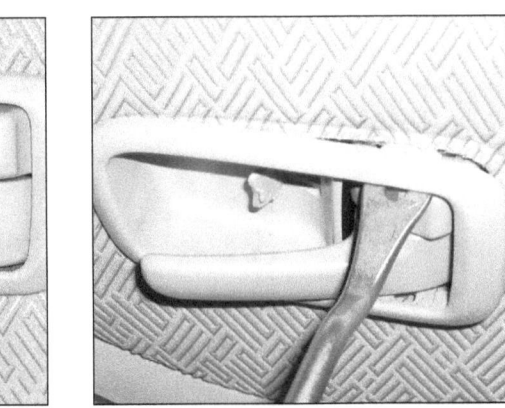

14.3b . . . then using a trim removal tool, carefully pry up the door handle bezel

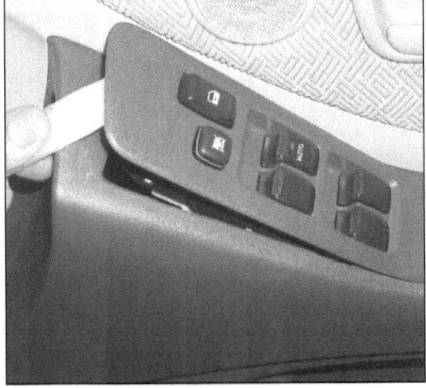

14.4 Pry up the power window switch plate, then disconnect the electrical connectors

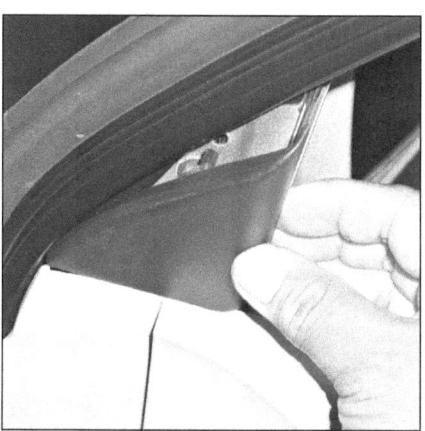

14.5 Pry off the mirror trim cover

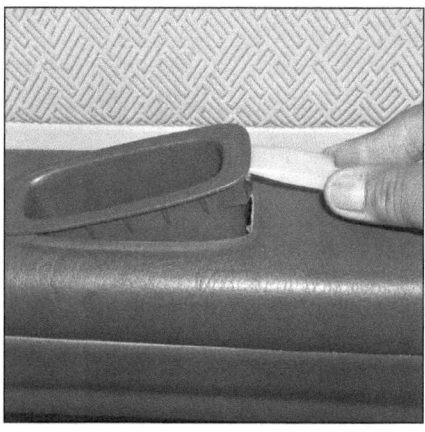

14.6 Pry out the trim cover on the door grip, then remove the door panel mounting screw

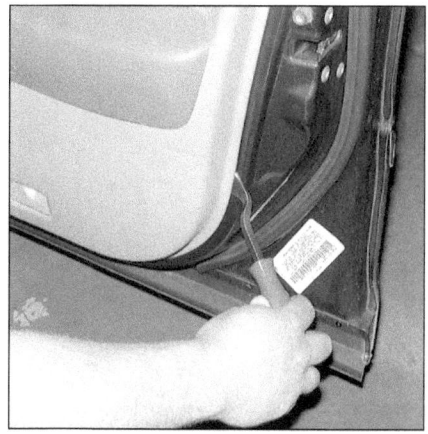

14.7 Carefully pry the clips free so the door trim panel can be removed

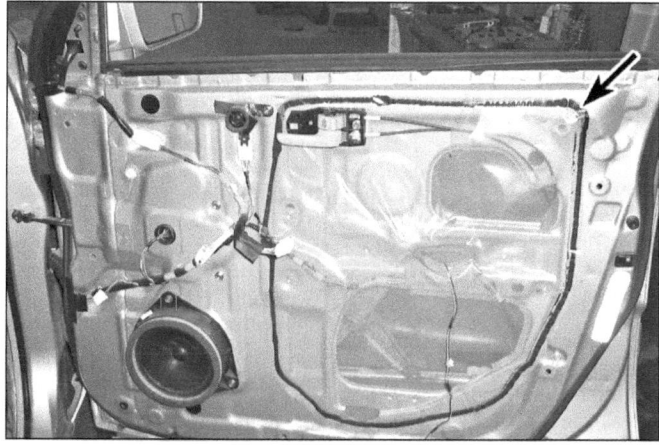

14.8 Starting in the upper corner, carefully peel back the plastic watershield for access to the inner door

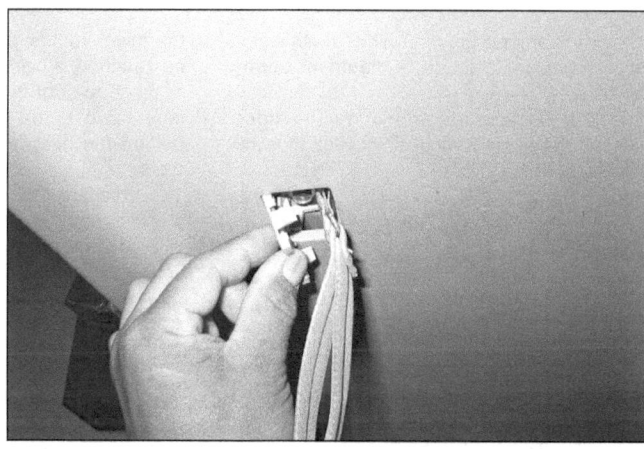

14.10 Remove the mounting fastener securing the door assist strap

5   Using a trim removal tool, pry out the outside mirror trim plate **(see illustration)**.
6   Remove the door pull handle cover, then remove the screw underneath **(see illustration)**.
7   Carefully pry the panel out until the clips disengage **(see illustration)**. Work slowly and carefully around the outer edge of the trim panel until it's free. Unplug any wiring harness connectors and remove the panel.
8   For access to the door outside handle or the door window regulator inside the door, raise the window fully, then carefully peel back the plastic watershield **(see illustration)**.
9   Installation is the reverse of removal.

Tailgate
Refer to illustration 14.10
10   Remove the assist strap mounting bolt **(see illustration)**.
11   Using a screwdriver or trim removal tool pry out the clips and remove the trim panel from the tailgate. Work slowly and carefully around the outer edge of the trim panel until it's free. Unplug any wiring harness connectors and remove the panel.
12   For access to other components inside

the door, carefully peel back the plastic watershield.
13   Installation is the reverse of removal.

---

15   Door - removal, installation and adjustment

Note: *The door is heavy and somewhat awkward to remove and install - at least two people should perform this procedure.*

Removal and installation
Refer to illustrations 15.6 and 15.8
1   Raise the window completely in the door and Disconnect the negative (-) battery terminal (see Chapter 5).
2   Open the door all the way and support it from the ground on jacks or blocks covered with rags to prevent damaging the paint.
3   Remove the door trim panel and watershield (see Section 14).
4   Disconnect all electrical connections, ground wires and harness retaining clips from the door.

Note: *It is a good idea to label all connections to aid the reassembly process.*

5   From the door side, detach the rubber conduit between the body and the door. Then pull the wiring harness through the conduit hole and remove it from the door.
6   Remove the door stop strut bolt **(see illustration)**.

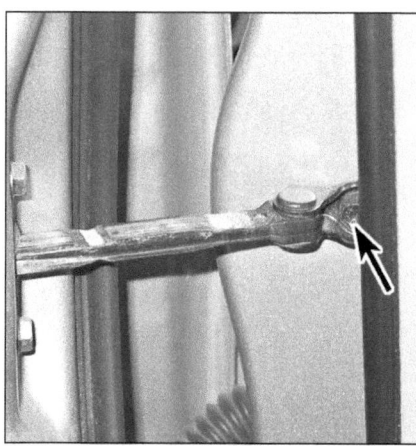

15.6 Remove the bolt retaining the door stop strut

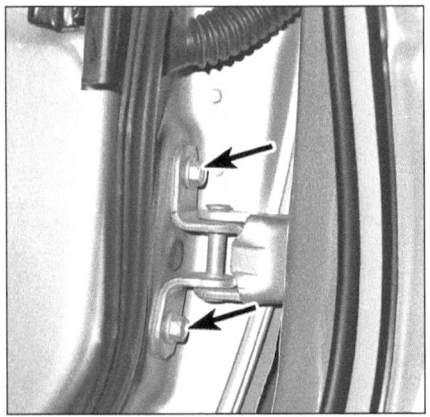

15.8 Remove the door hinge bolts with the door supported (arrows indicate bolts for the bottom hinge, top hinge similar)

15.13 Adjust the door lock striker by loosening the mounting screws and gently tapping the striker in the desired direction

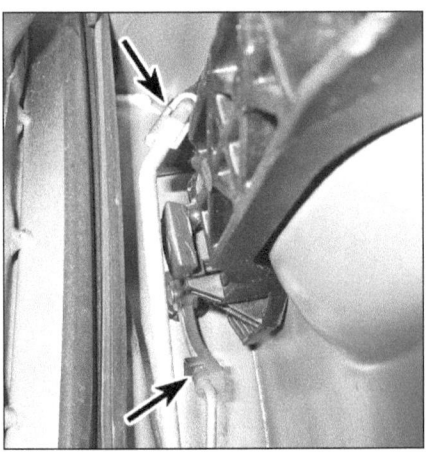

16.2 Disengage the rods from the handle and lock cylinder

7   Mark around the door hinges with a pen or a scribe to facilitate realignment during reassembly.

8   With an assistant holding the door, remove the hinge-to-door bolts **(see illustration)** and lift the door off.

Note: *Draw a reference line around the hinges before removing the bolts.*

9   Installation is the reverse of removal.

Adjustment

Refer to illustration 15.13

10   Having proper door-to-body alignment is a critical part of a well-functioning door assembly. First check the door hinge pins for excessive play. Fully open the door and lift up and down on the door without lifting the body. If a door has 1.5 mm or more excessive play, the hinges should be replaced.

11   Door-to-body alignment adjustments are made by loosening the hinge-to-body bolts or hinge-to-door bolts and moving the door. Proper body alignment is achieved when the top of the doors are parallel with the roof section, the front door is flush with the guard, the rear door is flush with the rear quarter panel and the bottom of the doors are aligned with

the lower rocker panel. If these goals can't be reached by adjusting the hinge-to-body or hinge-to-door bolts, body alignment shims may have to be purchased and inserted behind the hinges to achieve correct alignment.

12   To adjust the door-closed position, scribe a line or mark around the striker plate to provide a reference point, then check that the door latch is contacting the centre of the latch striker. If not, adjust the up and down position first.

13   Finally adjust the latch striker sideways position, so that the door panel is flush with the centre pillar or rear quarter panel and provides positive engagement with the latch mechanism **(see illustration).**

---

16   Door latch, lock cylinder and handles - removal and installation

---

Caution: *Wear gloves when working inside the door openings to protect against cuts from sharp metal edges.*

Door latch

Refer to illustrations 16.2 and 16.4

1   Raise the window, then remove the door trim panel and watershield (see Section 14).

2   Working through the large access hole, disengage the rods from the handle and lock cylinder **(see illustration).** All door lock rods are attached by plastic clips. The plastic clips can be removed by unsnapping the portion engaging the connecting rod and then pulling the rod out of its locating hole.

3   Disconnect the electrical connectors at the latch. Disengage the handle-to-latch cables (see Steps 11 and 12).

4   Remove the screws securing the latch to the door **(see illustration).** Remove the latch assembly through the door opening.

5   Installation is the reverse of removal.

Outside handle and door lock cylinder

Refer to illustrations 16.8a, 16.8b and 16.8c

6   To remove the outside handle and lock cylinder assembly, raise the window and remove the door trim panel and watershield (see Section 14).

Caution: *Take care not to scratch the paint on the outside of the door. Wide masking tape applied around the handle opening before beginning the procedure can help avoid scratches.*

7   Working through the access hole, disengage the plastic clips that secure the outside door lock-to-latch rod and the outside door handle-to-latch rod **(see illustration 16.2).**

8   Remove the plug from the end of the door and remove the lock cylinder retaining screw. Withdraw the lock cylinder from the door and disconnect the electrical connector, if equipped. Unbolt the handle from the inside of the door and remove the handle and the handle frame **(see illustrations).**

9   Installation is the reverse of removal.

Inside door handle

Refer to illustrations 16.11 and 16.12

10   Remove the door trim panel (see Section 14).

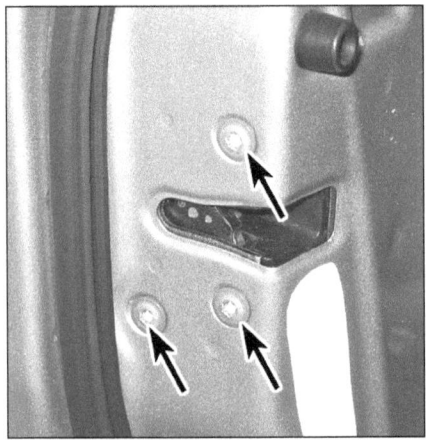

16.4 Remove the door latch mounting fasteners

16.8a Remove the plug from the end of the door to access the door lock cylinder retaining bolt

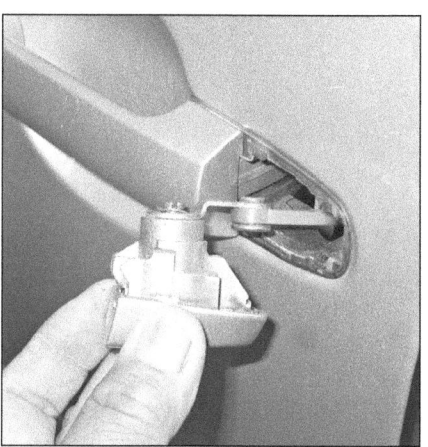

16.8b Slide the lock cylinder out

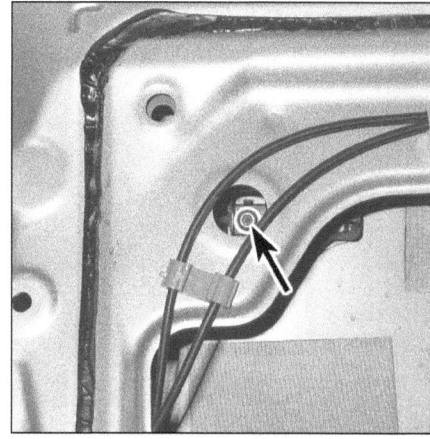

16.8c From inside the door opening, remove the door handle mounting bolt

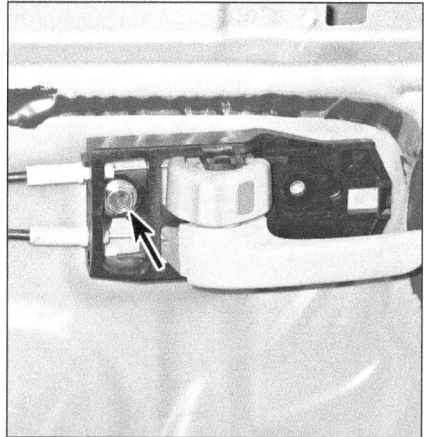

16.11 Remove the inside handle mounting fastener

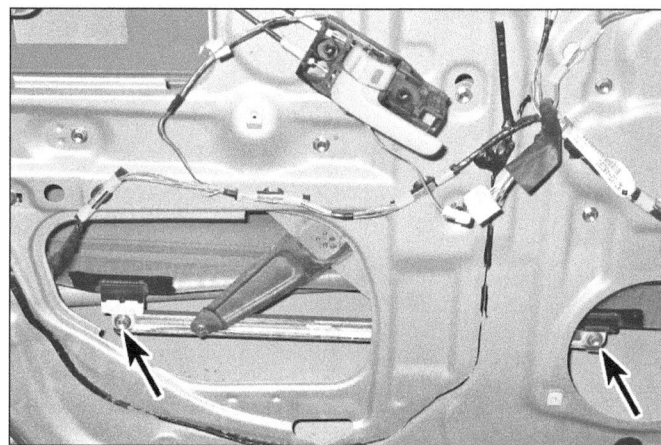

16.12 Detach the cables from the inside handle

11   Remove the handle retaining screw(s) and disengage the handle from the door **(see illustration).**
12   Disengage the handle-to-latch cables and remove the handle from the door **(see illustration).**
13   Installation is the reverse of removal.

17   Door window glass - removal and installation

Caution: *Wear gloves when working inside the door openings to protect against cuts from sharp metal edges.*

Door glass
Refer to illustration 17.4
1   Remove the door trim panel and the plastic watershield (see Section 14).
2   Lower the window glass all the way down into the door.
3   Remove the door speaker (see Chapter 12).
4   Raise the window just enough to access the window retaining bolts through the holes in the door frame **(see illustration).**
5   Place a rag over the glass to help prevent scratching the glass and remove the two glass mounting bolts.
6   Remove the glass by pulling it up and out.
7   Installation is the reverse of removal.

Tailgate glass
8   Replacement of the back door glass requires the use of special fast-setting adhesive/caulk materials and some specialised tools and techniques. These operations should be left to a dealer service department or a shop specialising in glass work.

18   Door window glass regulator - removal and installation

Refer to illustration 18.4
Caution: *Wear gloves when working inside the door openings to protect against cuts from sharp metal edges.*
1   Remove the door trim panel and the plastic watershield (see Section 14).
2   Remove the window glass (see Section 17).
3   Disconnect the electrical connector from the window regulator motor.
4   Loosen the temporary bolt, then remove the regulator/motor mounting bolts **(see illustration).**
5   Remove the regulator/motor assembly. Pull the equaliser arm and regulator assemblies

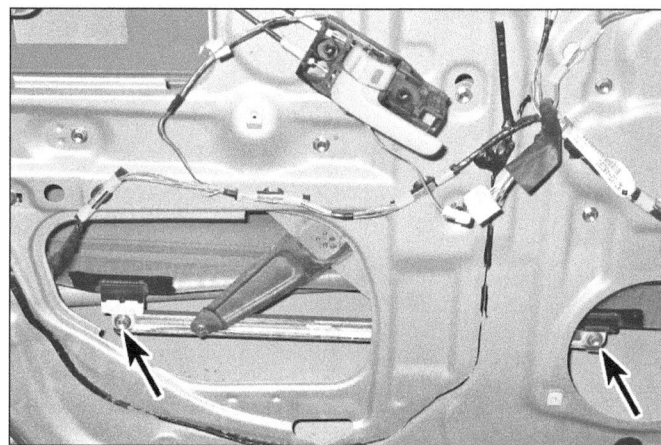

17.4 Raise the window to access the glass retaining bolts through the holes in the door frame

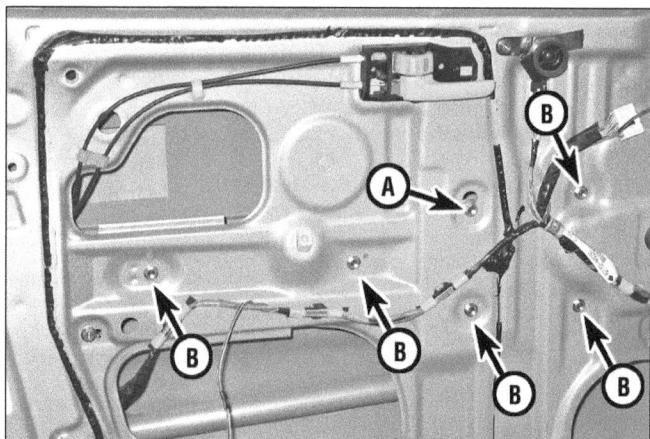

18.4 Loosen the temporary bolt (A), then remove the window regulator mounting bolts (B)

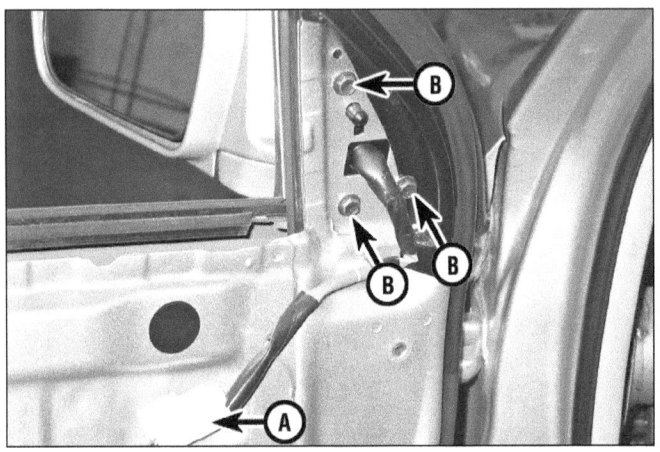

19.2 Disconnect the electrical connector (A), then remove the mirror mounting bolts (B)

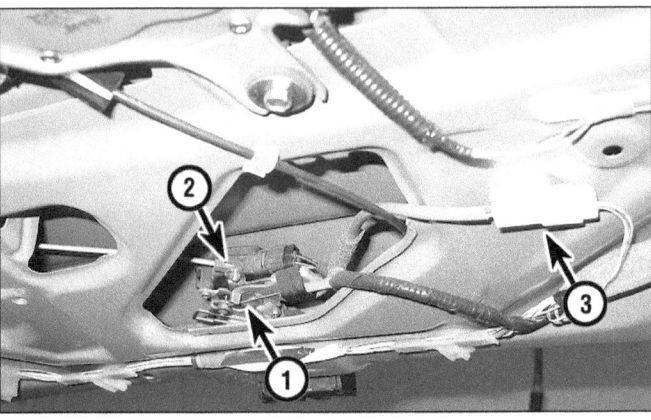

21.3 Tailgate latch details

1 *Handle-to-latch cable*
2 *Tailgate lock-to-latch rod*

3 *Power lock electrical connector*

through the service hole in the door frame to remove it.

6   Installation is the reverse of removal. Lubricate the rollers and wear points on the regulator with white grease before installation.

19   Mirrors - removal and installation

Outside mirrors

Refer to illustration 19.2

1   Remove the door trim panel (see Section 14).

2   Disconnect the electrical connector from the mirror, then remove the three mirror retaining bolts and detach the mirror from the vehicle **(see illustration)**.

3   Installation is the reverse of removal.

Inside mirror

4   Disconnect the electrical connector from the mirror, if equipped.

5   On some models the mirror can be removed by carefully prying between the mirror mount and the notch in the base of the mirror stalk with a screwdriver tip covered with tape. There is a hairpin-type spring holding the mirror stalk in the base. Push the screwdriver in about 18 mm to release the spring. On some other models, the mirror can be removed by removing the set screw located at the base of the mirror stalk.

6   On models without a set screw, to install the mirror, reinsert the spring if it was removed earlier. Insert the mirror stalk's lug into the mount, pushing downward until the mirror is secured.

7   If the mount plate itself has come off the windshield, adhesive kits are available at auto parts stores to re-secure it. Follow the instructions included with the kit.

20   Tailgate - removal, installation and adjustment

Note: *The tailgate is heavy and somewhat awkward to remove and install - at least two people should perform this procedure.*

Removal and installation

1   Disconnect the negative (-) battery terminal (see Chapter 5).

2   Open the tailgate all the way and support it from the ground on jacks or blocks covered with rags to prevent damaging the paint.

3   Remove the tailgate trim panel and watershield (see Section 14).

4   Disconnect all electrical connections, ground wires and harness retaining clips from the tailgate.

Note: *It is a good idea to label all connections to aid the reassembly process.*

5   From the tailgate side, detach the rubber conduit between the body and the tailgate. Then pull the wiring harness through the conduit hole and remove it from the tailgate.

6   Remove the tailgate stop strut bolt(s).

7   Mark around the tailgate hinges with a pen or a scribe to facilitate realignment during reassembly.

8   With an assistant holding the tailgate, remove the hinge-to-tailgate bolts and lift the tailgate off.

Note: *Draw a reference line around the hinges before removing the bolts.*

9   Installation is the reverse of removal.

Adjustment

10   Having proper tailgate-to-body alignment is a critical part of a well-functioning tailgate assembly. First check the tailgate hinge pins for excessive play. Fully open the tailgate and lift up and down on the tailgate without lifting the body. If a tailgate has 1.5 mm or more excessive play, the hinges should be replaced.

11   Tailgate-to-body alignment adjustments are made by loosening the hinge-to-body bolts or hinge-to-tailgate bolts and moving the tailgate. Proper body alignment is achieved when the top of the tailgate is parallel with the roof section and the sides of the tailgate are flush with the rear quarter panels and the bottom of the tailgate is aligned with the lower tailgate sill. If these goals can't be reached by adjusting the hinge-to-body or hinge-to-tailgate bolts, body alignment shims may have to be purchased and inserted behind the hinges to achieve correct alignment.

12   To adjust the tailgate-closed position, scribe a line or mark around the striker plate to provide a reference point, then check that the tailgate latch is contacting the centre of the latch striker. If not, adjust the up and down position first.

13   Finally adjust the latch striker sideways position, so that the tailgate panel is flush with the rear quarter panel and provides positive engagement with the latch mechanism.

21   Tailgate latch, lock cylinder and handle - removal and installation

Tailgate latch

Refer to illustration 21.3

1   Disconnect the negative (-) battery terminal (see Chapter 5).

2   Open the tailgate and remove the door trim panel and watershield (see Section 14).

3   Working through the large access hole, disengage the outside tailgate handle-to-latch cable and the outside tailgate lock-to-latch rod **(see illustration)**. Disconnect the electrical connector for the power lock.

4   All tailgate lock rods are attached by plastic clips. The plastic clips can be removed by unsnapping the portion engaging the connecting rod and then pulling the rod out of its locating hole.

5   Remove the fasteners securing the latch

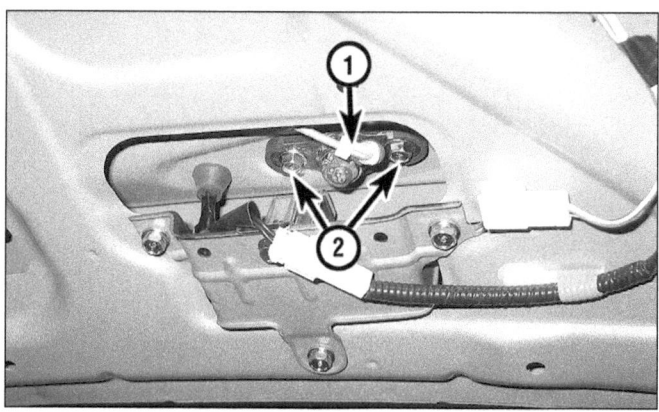

21.8 Tailgate lock cylinder details

1 Tailgate lock-to-latch rod
2 Lock cylinder mounting fasteners

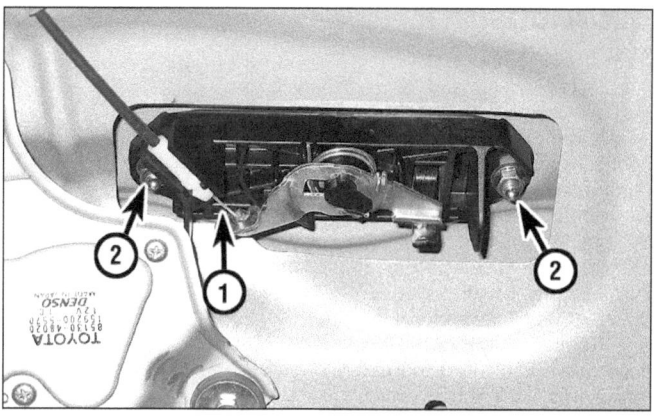

21.13 Tailgate outside handle details

1 Tailgate handle-to-latch cable
2 Tailgate handle retaining fasteners

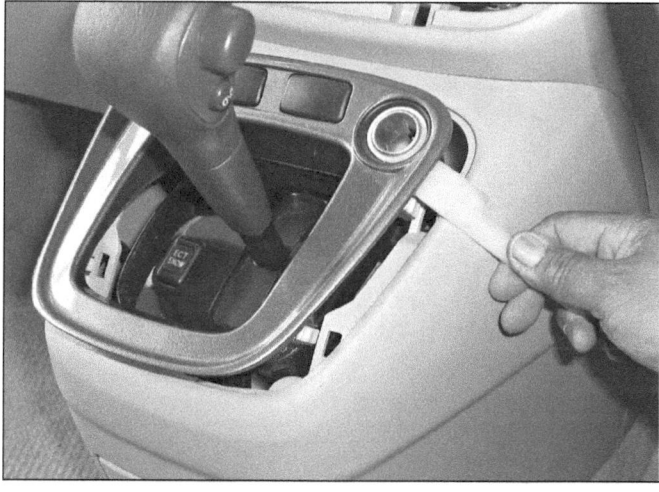

22.2 Using a trim pry tool, carefully disengage the clips securing the shifter bezel

to the tailgate. Remove the latch assembly.
6   Installation is the reverse of removal.

Tailgate lock cylinder

Refer to illustration 21.8
7   Open the tailgate and remove the door trim panel and watershield (see Section 14).
8   Working through the large access hole,

disengage the outside tailgate lock-to-latch rod **(see illustration)**.
9   All tailgate lock rods are attached by plastic clips. The plastic clips can be removed by unsnapping the portion engaging the connecting rod and then pulling the rod out of its locating hole.
10   Remove the lock cylinder retaining fas-

teners. Remove the lock cylinder.
11   Installation is the reverse of removal.

Tailgate outside handle

Refer to illustration 21.13
12   Open the tailgate and remove the door trim panel and watershield (see Section 14).
13   Working through the large access hole, disengage the outside tailgate handle-to-latch cable **(see illustration)**.
14   Remove the handle retaining fasteners through the holes in the door frame and detach the handle from the tailgate.
15   Installation is the reverse of removal.

---

22   Centre console - removal and installation

Refer to illustrations 22.2, 22.3 and 22.4
Warning: *The models covered by this manual are equipped with Supplemental Restraint systems (SRS), more commonly known as airbags. Always disable the airbag system before working in the vicinity of any airbag system component to avoid the possibility of accidental deployment of the airbag, which could cause personal injury (see Chapter 12).*

MCU28R models
1   Disconnect the negative (-) battery terminal (see Chapter 5).
2   Using a trim tool, carefully disengage the clips securing the shifter bezel, then disconnect the electrical connectors from the back of the bezel **(see illustration)**. Remove the shifter bezel.
3   Remove the trim covers at the front of the console **(see illustration)**.
4   Remove the retaining screws and detach the rear half of the console from the vehicle **(see illustration)**.
5   Installation is the reverse of removal.

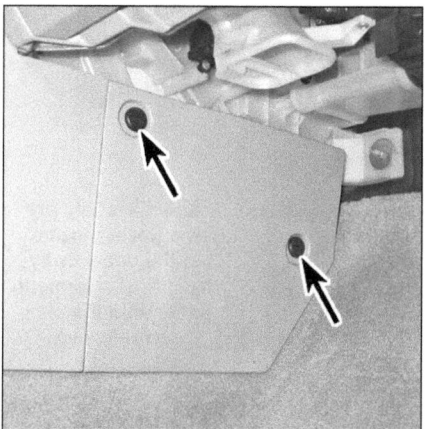

22.3 Remove the fasteners securing the trim covers at the front of the console

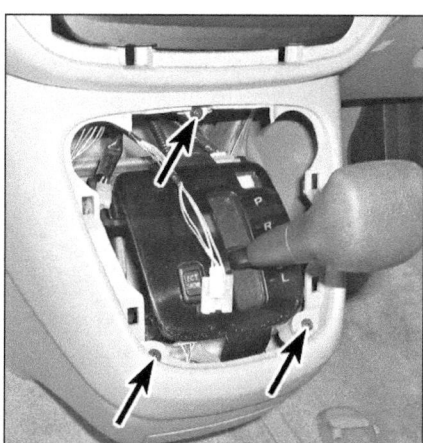

22.4 Remove the fasteners securing the rear half of the console

GSU40R/GSU45R models

Refer to illustration 22.7

6   Disconnect the negative (-) battery terminal (see Chapter 5).

7   Using a trim tool, carefully disengage the centre trim panel from the dashboard **(see illustration)**.

8   Grasp the upper console cover at the two cup holders and lift up, disengaging the retaining clips. Disconnect the wiring from the switches and power outlet before removing the cover from the vehicle.

9   Remove the screws retaining the rear console box to the side console trim panels.

10   Remove the bolts retaining the rear console box to the floor and remove the rear console box.

11   Remove the screws and push pins and remove the side console trim panels.

Note: *Slide each side panel rearward to release the clips retaining them to the dashboard and to the lower brackets.*

12   Installation is the reverse of removal.

---

23   Dashboard trim panels - removal and installation

Warning: *Models covered by this manual are equipped with a Supplemental Restraint System (SRS), more commonly known as airbags. Always disable the airbag system before working in the vicinity of any airbag system component to avoid the possibility of accidental deployment of the airbag, which could cause personal injury (see Chapter 12).*

1   These panels provide access to various instrument panel mounting screws. Some of the covers use fasteners and others are easily pried off with a screwdriver or trim pry tool. If you're going to remove the instrument panel, remove all of the covers.

2   Disconnect the negative (-) battery terminal (see Chapter 5).

MCU28R models

Instrument cluster lower finish panel

Refer to illustration 23.4

3   On models with tilt steering, lower the steering column as far down as it can go.

4   Using a trim pry tool, carefully pry the lower portion of the panel away from the instrument panel until the clips are released. Take care not to scratch the surrounding trim on the instrument panel **(see illustration).** Disconnect the electrical connectors for the switches mounted on the finish panel.

5   Installation is the reverse of the removal procedure. Make sure the clips are engaged properly before pushing the panel firmly into place.

Instrument cluster bezel

Refer to illustration 23.7

6   Remove the instrument cluster lower finish panel (see Steps 3 and 4).

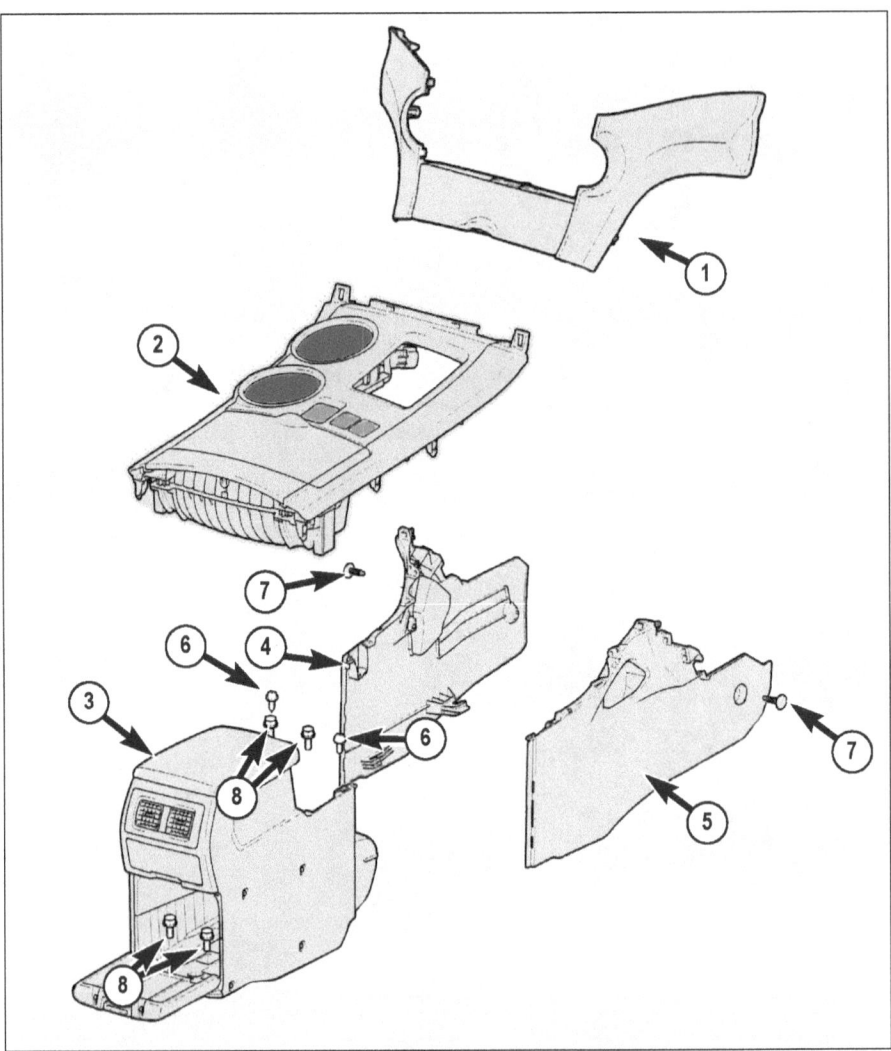

22.7 Centre console components - GSU40R/GSU45R models

1 Centre trim panel
2 Upper console cover
3 Rear console box
4 LH side console trim
5 RH side console trim

6 Rear console box-to-side console trim screws
7 Side console push pins
8 Rear console box-to-floor bolts

23.4 Carefully pry the lower portion of the panel away from the instrument panel until the clips are released

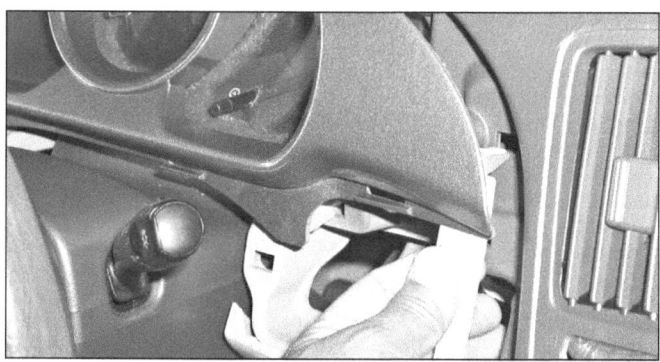

23.7 Carefully pry the bezel to release the clips, then remove the bezel

23.9 Carefully pry the bezel to release the clips, then remove the panel

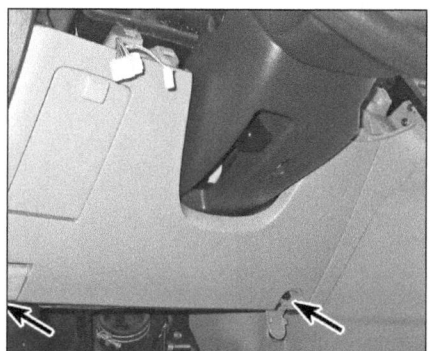

23.12 Remove the two fasteners securing the knee bolster cover

7   Using a trim pry tool, carefully pry the bezel to release the clips, then remove the bezel **(see illustration)**.

8   Installation is the reverse of the removal procedure. Make sure the clips are engaged properly before pushing the bezel firmly into place.

Audio unit and air conditioning control panel centre trim panel

Refer to illustration 23.9

9   Using a trim pry tool, carefully pry the bezel to release the clips, then remove the panel **(see illustration)**. Take care not to

scratch the surrounding trim on the instrument panel.

10   Installation is the reverse of the removal procedure. Make sure the clips are engaged properly before pushing the panel firmly into place.

Knee bolster

Refer to illustrations 23.12 and 23.14

11   Remove the instrument cluster lower finish panel (see Steps 3 and 4).

12   Remove the two fasteners securing the knee bolster cover **(see illustration)**.

13   Pull the knee bolster out to disengage the clips behind it.

14   Remove the retaining bolts securing the knee bolster reinforcement, if needed for access to components under the dashboard **(see illustration)**.

Note: *On models equipped with a driver's knee airbag, refer to Chapter 12 for the removal procedure.*

15   Installation is the reverse of the removal procedure.

Glove box door

Refer to illustration 23.16

16   Remove the two pins at the bottom of the glove box door and remove the door **(see illustration)**.

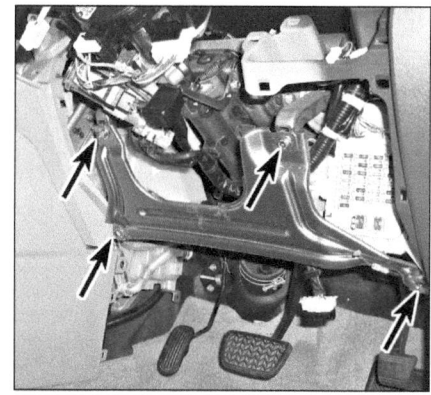

23.14 Remove the retaining bolts securing the knee bolster reinforcement

17   Installation is the reverse of the removal procedure.

Glovebox trim panel

Refer to illustration 23.19

18   Remove the glove box door (see Step 16).

19   Remove the fasteners securing the trim panel, then remove the panel **(see illustration)**.

20   Installation is the reverse of the removal procedure.

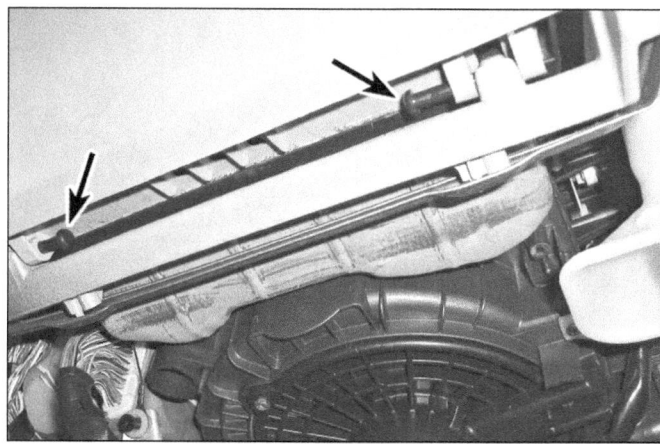

23.16 To remove the glove box door, remove the two pins at the bottom of the door

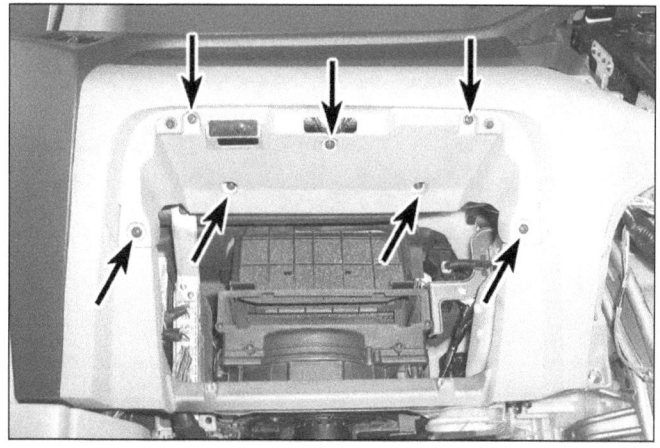

23.19 Remove the fasteners securing the trim panel, then remove the panel

23.22 This plastic nut retains the kick panel - GSU40R/GSU45R models

GSU40R/GSU45R models

Kick panel

Refer to illustration 23.22

21   Place a trim removal tool under the tread in the front door opening and pry the tread up, disengaging the retaining clips.

22   Remove the plastic nut retaining the kick panel **(see illustration)**. Pull the rear of the panel away from the door frame and then back to remove the stud from the hole in the panel.

23   Installation is the reverse of the removal procedure.

Instrument cluster lower finish panel

24   Remove the kick panel as previously described.

25   Remove the two bolts retaining the lower portion of the finish panel.

26   Using a trim pry tool, carefully pry the upper half of the finish panel away from the instrument panel. With it partially removed, disconnect the electrical connectors for the switches mounted on the finish panel.

27   Installation is the reverse of the removal procedure. Make sure the clips are engaged properly before pushing the panel firmly into place.

Instrument cluster bezel

28   Remove the instrument cluster lower finish panel (see Steps 3 and 4).

29   Remove the steering column covers (see Section 24).

30   Using a trim pry tool, carefully pry the bezel to release the clips, then remove the bezel.

31   Installation is the reverse of the removal procedure. Make sure the clips are engaged properly before pushing the bezel firmly into place.

Centre vent assembly and air conditioning control panel centre trim panel

32   Grasp the centre vent assembly and pull from the dashboard.

Note: *The centre vent is retained by four clips.*

33   Using a trim tool, carefully disengage the centre trim panel from the dashboard **(see illustration 23.7)**.

34   Installation is the reverse of the removal procedure. Make sure the clips are engaged properly before pushing the panel firmly into place.

Knee bolster

Refer to illustrations 23.36 and 23.38

Warning: *The knee bolster, on these models contains an airbag. Ensure the battery is disconnected (see Chapter 5) before proceeding.*

35   Remove the instrument cluster lower finish panel.

36   Disconnect the big yellow electrical connector for the driver's knee airbag **(see illustration)**.

37   Unclip the diagnosis connector from the knee bolster/airbag bracket and position clear of the work area.

38   Remove the four driver's knee airbag mounting bolts and remove the airbag module **(see illustration)**.

39   Installation is the reverse of removal.

Glove box door

Refer to illustration 23.16

40   Open the glove compartment and prise in the sides of the glove box to disengage the stops from the glove box opening. Roll the glove box down, unclipping the hinges from the bottom of the glove box and remove it from the vehicle.

41   Installation is the reverse of the removal procedure.

Glovebox trim panel

Refer to illustration 23.19

42   Remove the glove box door.

43   Remove the fasteners securing the trim panel, then remove the panel **(see illustration)**.

44   Installation is the reverse of the removal procedure.

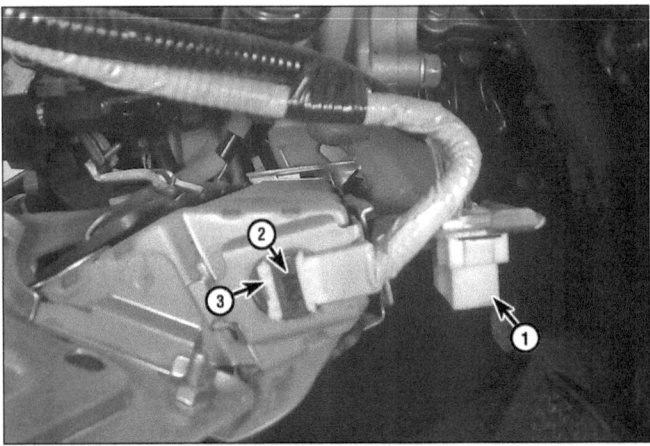

23.36 Airbag connector location

1   Diagnosis connector Note, the connector is clipped into the airbag bracket
2   Lift the tab out to unlock the airbag connector

3   Pull the connector from the airbag

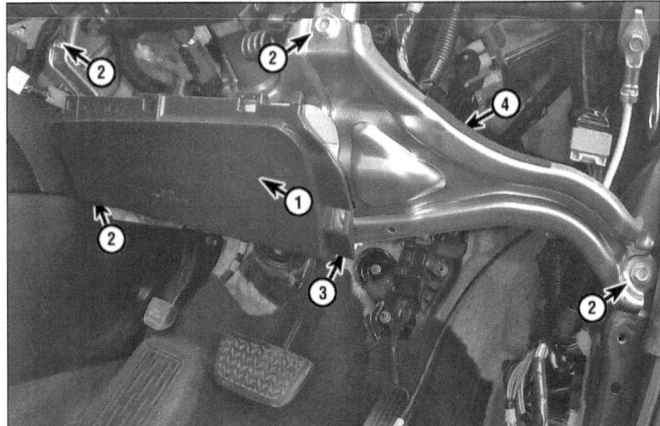

23.38 Knee airbag components

1   Knee airbag
2   Retaining bolts

3   Diagnosis connector location.
4   Airbag connector location

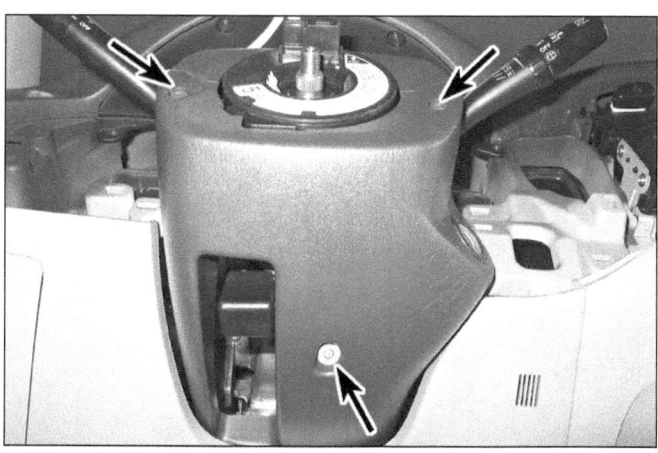

24.3 Remove the screws, then remove upper and lower covers

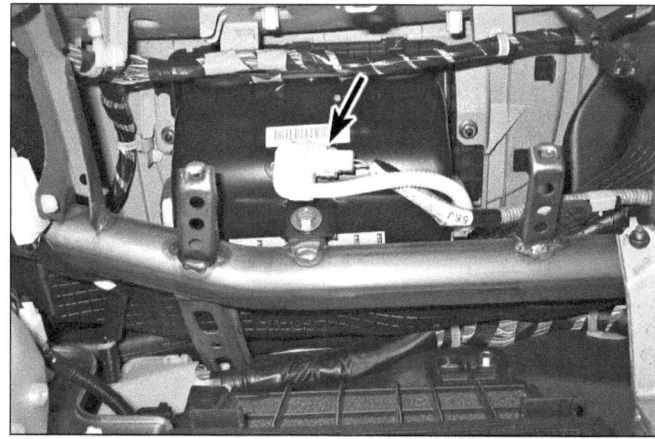

25.5 Disconnect the electrical connector from the passenger's side airbag

24 Steering column covers - removal and installation

Refer to illustration 24.3

Warning: *Models covered by this manual are equipped with a Supplemental Restraint System (SRS), more commonly known as airbags. Always disable the airbag system before working in the vicinity of any airbag system component to avoid the possibility of accidental deployment of the airbag, which could cause personal injury (see Chapter 12).*

1   Disconnect the negative (-) battery terminal (see Chapter 5).
2   On tilt steering columns, move the column to the lowest position and then remove the steering wheel (see Chapter 10).
3   Remove the screws, then separate the halves and remove the upper and lower steering column covers **(see illustration)**. On some models it may be necessary to remove the instrument cluster lower finish panel (see Section 23).
4   Installation is the reverse of the removal procedure.

25 Instrument panel - removal and installation

Refer to illustrations 25.5, 25.9, 25.10a, 25.10b, 25.10c, 25.12a, 25.12b, 25.13a, 25.13b and 25.13c

Warning: *Models covered by this manual are equipped with a Supplemental Restraint System (SRS), more commonly known as airbags. Always disable the airbag system before working in the vicinity of any airbag system component to avoid the possibility of accidental deployment of the airbag, which could cause personal injury (see Chapter 12).*

Note: *This is a difficult procedure for the home mechanic. There are many hidden fasteners, difficult angles to work in and many electrical connectors to tag and disconnect/connect. We recommend that this procedure be done only by an experienced do-it-yourselfer.*

Note: *During removal of the instrument panel, make careful notes of how each piece comes off, where it fits in relation to other pieces and what holds it in place. If you note how each part is installed before removing it, getting the*

instrument panel back together again will be much easier.

Note: *It is not necessary, but it is suggested to remove both front seats to allow additional working space and lessen the chance of damage to the seats during this procedure.*

1   Disconnect the negative (-) battery terminal (see Chapter 5).
2   Remove the dashboard trim panels (see Section 23) and the centre console (see Section 22).
3   Remove the glove box (see Section 24).
4   Remove the instrument cluster (see Chapter 12).
5   Disconnect the electrical connector from the passenger's side airbag **(see illustration)**.
6   Remove the audio unit and air conditioning control panel at the centre of the dashboard (see Chapter 3).
7   Remove the driver's knee bolster and reinforcement panel (see Section 23).
8   Unscrew the bolts securing the steering column and lower it away from the instrument panel (see Chapter 10).
9   Remove the side kick panels **(see illustration) and (see illustration 23.22)**.

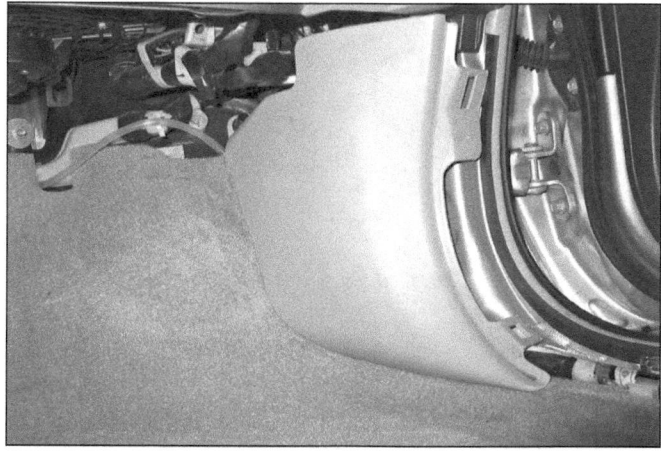

25.9 Carefully detach the kick panels from each side by pulling them out and releasing the clips - MCU28R models

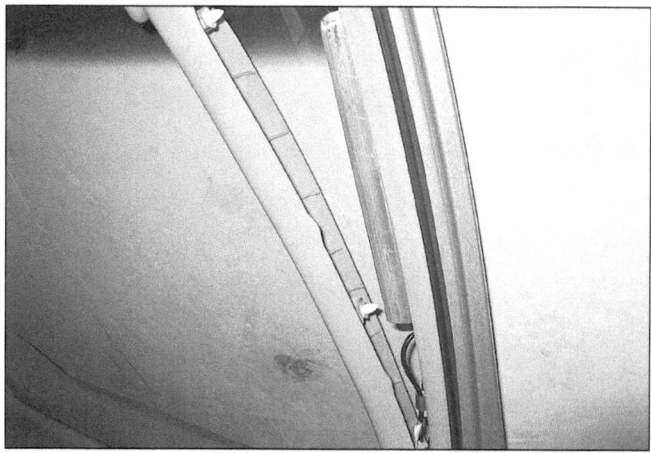

25.10a Remove the front pillar trim by carefully releasing the clips

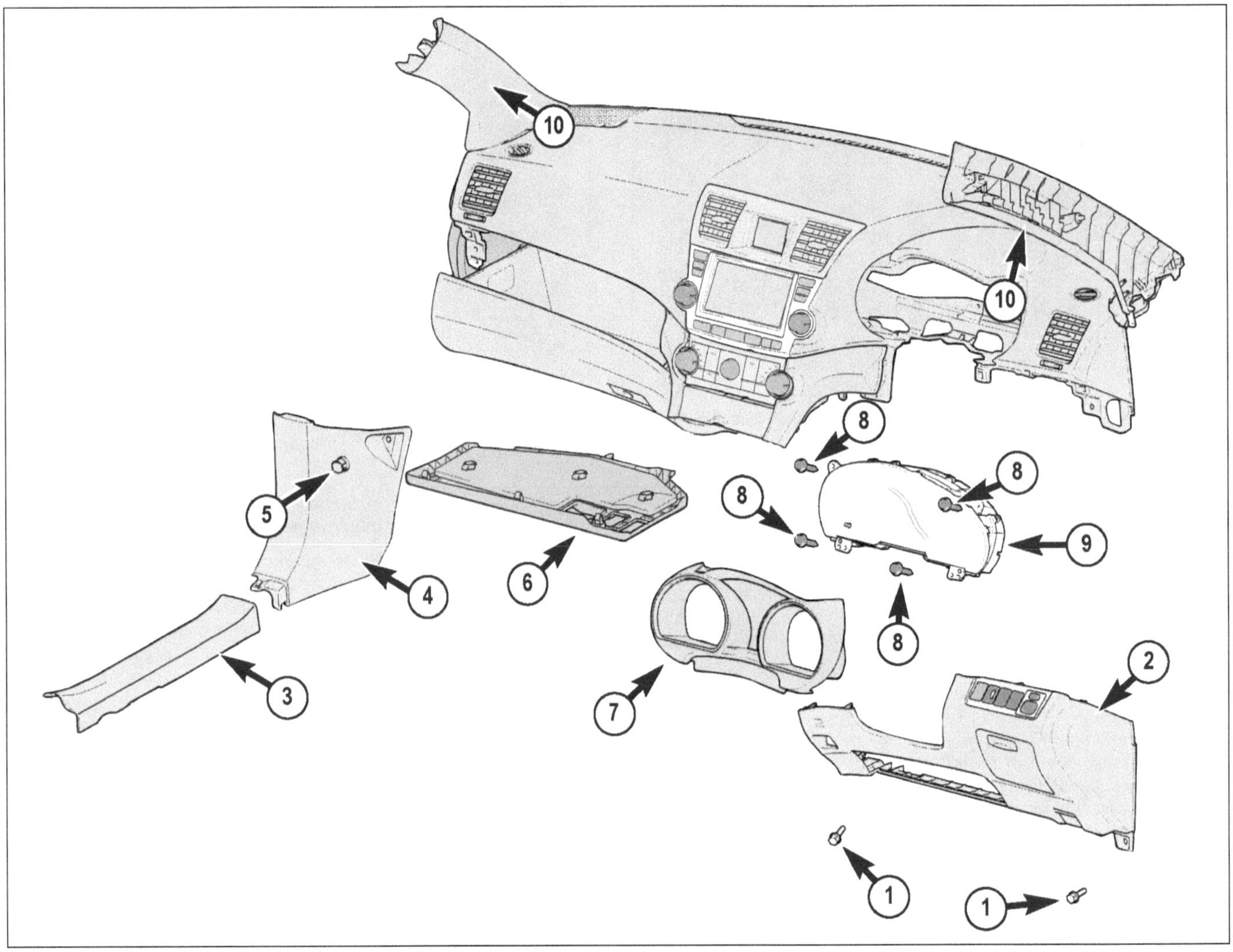

25.10b Dashboard components - GSU40R/GSU45R models

1 Lower dash panel fasteners	5 LH kick panel fastener	9 Instrument cluster
2 Lower dash panel	6 Glove box undertray	10 A-Pillar trim panels
3 LH scuff plate	7 Instrument cluster surround panel	
4 LH kick panel	8 Instrument cluster fasteners	

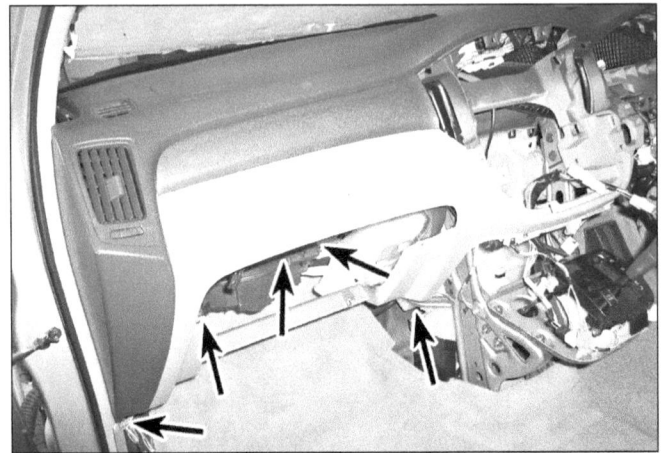

25.12a Remove all of the fasteners (bolts, screws and nuts) on the left . . .

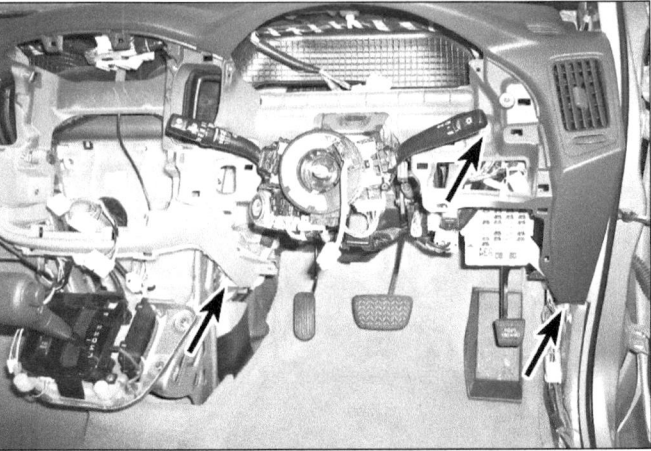

25.12b . . . and the right side of the instrument panel - MCU28R models

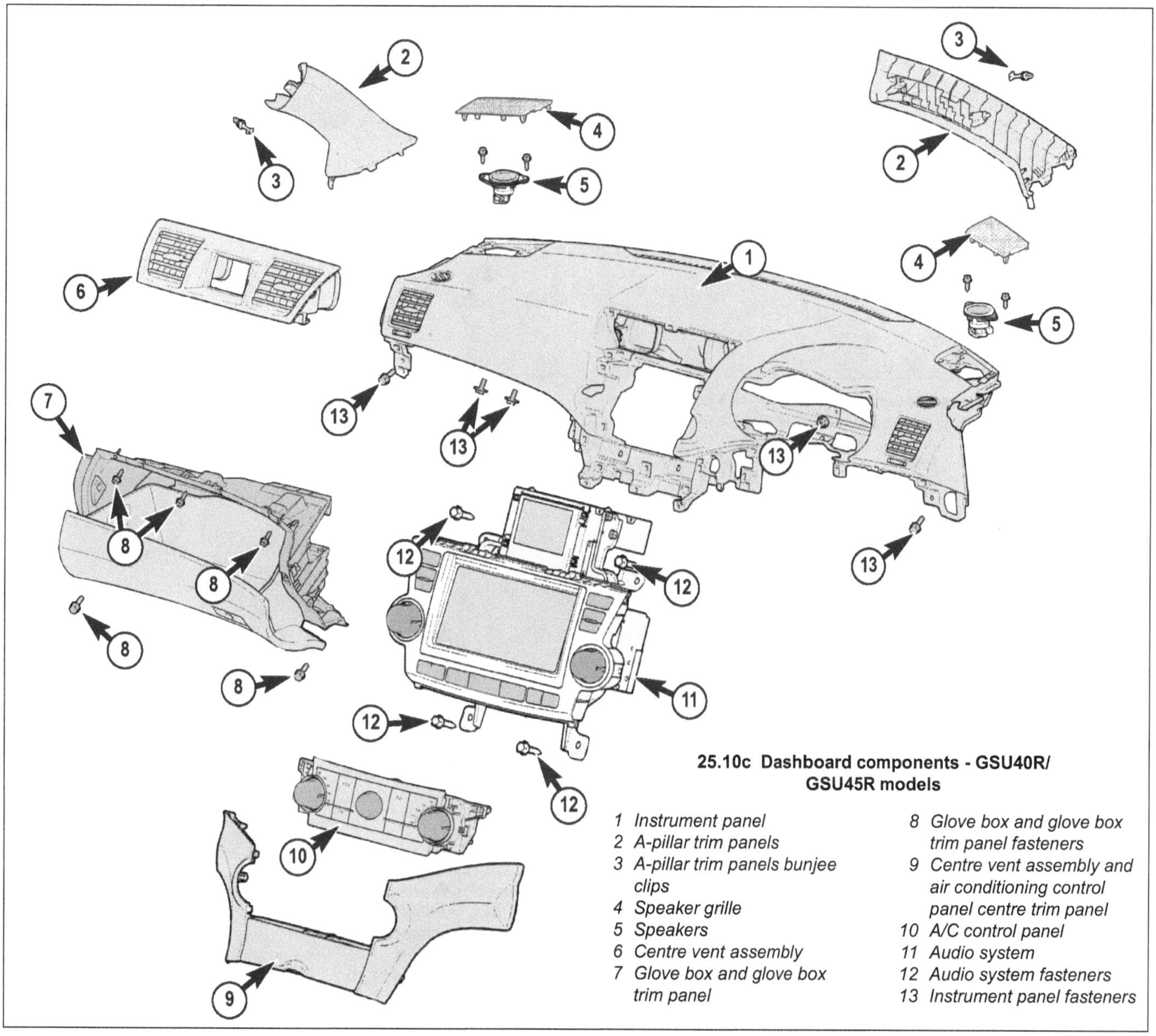

**25.10c Dashboard components - GSU40R/
GSU45R models**

1 Instrument panel
2 A-pillar trim panels
3 A-pillar trim panels bunjee
   clips
4 Speaker grille
5 Speakers
6 Centre vent assembly
7 Glove box and glove box
   trim panel
8 Glove box and glove box
   trim panel fasteners
9 Centre vent assembly and
   air conditioning control
   panel centre trim panel
10 A/C control panel
11 Audio system
12 Audio system fasteners
13 Instrument panel fasteners

25.13a To remove the instrument panel reinforcement tube,
remove the fasteners on the right side . . .

25.13b . . . and the fasteners on the left side . . .

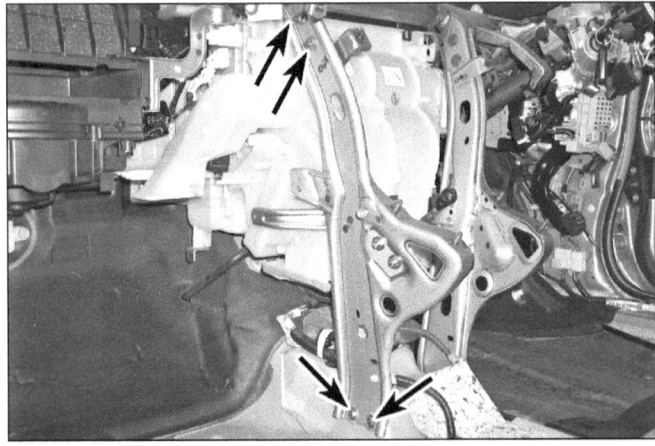

25.13c ... then remove the fasteners securing the centre brace (left side shown, right side similar) - MCU28R models

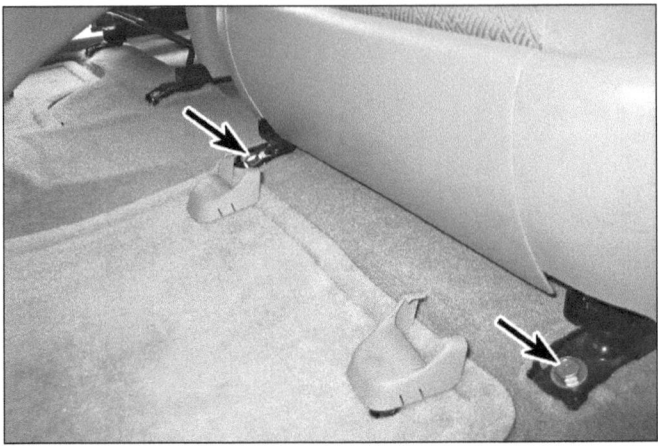

26.2a Remove the front ...

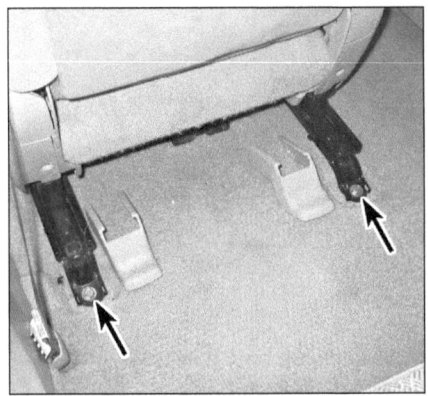

26.2b ... and rear retaining bolts

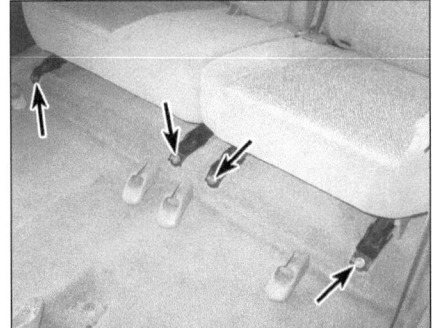

26.5 Remove the retaining bolts at the front of the rear seats

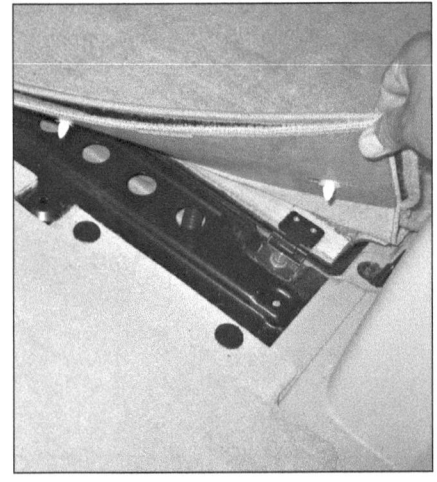

26.6 Unclip the seat track covers

10   Remove the front pillar trim **(see illustrations).**
11   A number of electrical connectors must be disconnected in order to remove the instrument panel. Most are designed so that they will only fit on the matching connector (male or female), but if there is any doubt, mark the connectors with masking tape and a marking pen before disconnecting them.
12   Remove all of the fasteners (bolts, screws and nuts) holding the instrument panel to the body **(see illustrations).** Once all are removed, lift the panel then pull it away from the windshield and take it out through the driver's door opening.

Note: *This is a two-person job.*

13   If you're also removing the instrument panel reinforcement tube, remove the fasteners securing the tube and take it out through the driver's door opening **(see illustrations).**
14   Installation is the reverse of removal.

---

26   Seats - removal and installation

Front seat

Refer to illustrations 26.2a and 26.2b

Warning: *The front seat belts on some models are equipped with pre-tensioners,*
which are pyrotechnic (explosive) devices designed to retract the seat belts in the event of a collision. On models equipped with pre-tensioners, do not remove the front seat belt retractor assemblies, and do not disconnect the electrical connectors leading to the assemblies. Problems with the pre-tensioners will turn on the SRS (airbag) warning light on the dash. If any pre-tensioner problems are suspected, take the vehicle to a dealer service department. Also on these models, be sure to disable the airbag system (see Chapter 12).

Warning: *On models with side-impact airbags, be sure to disarm the airbag system before beginning this procedure (see Chapter 12).*

1   Pry out the plastic covers to access the seat tracks and their mounting bolts.
2   Remove the retaining bolts **(see illustrations).**
3   Tilt the seat upward to access the underside, then disconnect any electrical connectors and lift the seat from the vehicle.
4   Installation is the reverse of removal.

Rear seat

Refer to illustrations 26.5, 26.6 and 26.7

5   Working at the front of the rear seats, remove the retaining bolts **(see illustration).**
6   Flip the seats backs down, then unclip the seat track covers **(see illustration).**

7   Remove the remaining seat retaining bolts **(see illustration).**
8   Installation is the reverse of removal.

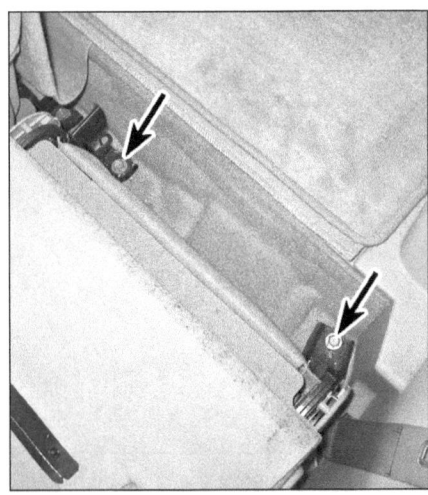

26.7 Remove the retaining bolts at the rear of the seats

Chapter 12
Chassis electrical system

Contents

1 General information

The electrical system is a 12 volt, negative ground type. Power for the lights and all electrical accessories is supplied by a lead/acid-type battery, which is charged by the alternator.

This Chapter covers repair and service procedures for the various electrical components not associated with the engine. Information on the battery, alternator and starter motor can be found in Chapter 5.

It should be noted that when portions of the electrical system are serviced, the cable should be disconnected from the negative battery terminal to prevent electrical shorts and/or fires.

2 Electrical troubleshooting - general information

Refer to illustrations 2.5a and 2.5b

A typical electrical circuit consists of an electrical component, any switches, relays, motors, fuses, fusible links or circuit breakers related to that component and the wiring and connectors that link the component to both the battery and the chassis. To help you pinpoint an electrical circuit problem, wiring diagrams are included at the end of this Chapter.

Before tackling any troublesome electrical circuit, first study the appropriate wiring diagrams to get a complete understanding of what makes up that individual circuit. For

instance, noting whether other components related to the circuit are operating correctly can often narrow down potential causes of trouble. If several components or circuits fail at one time, chances are the problem is in a fuse or ground connection, because several circuits are often routed through the same fuse and ground connections.

Electrical problems usually stem from simple causes, such as loose or corroded connections, a blown fuse, a melted fusible link or a failed relay. Visually inspect the condition of all fuses, wires and connections in a problem circuit before troubleshooting the circuit.

If test equipment and instruments are going to be utilised, use the diagrams to plan ahead of time where you will make the nec-

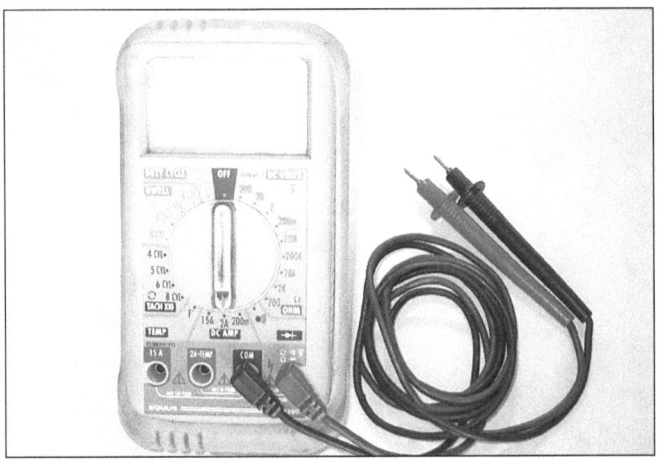 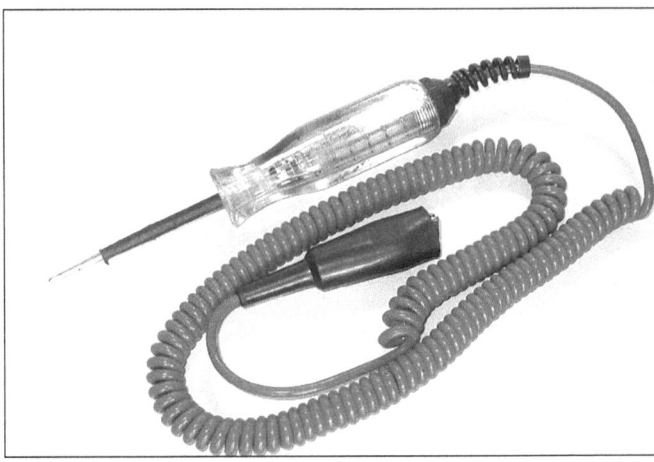

2.5a The most useful tool for electrical troubleshooting is a digital multimeter that can check volts, amps, and test continuity

2.5b A simple test light is a very handy tool for testing voltage

essary connections in order to accurately pin-point the trouble spot.

The basic tools needed for electrical troubleshooting include a circuit tester or voltmeter (a 12 volt bulb with a set of test leads can also be used), a continuity tester, which includes a bulb, battery and set of test leads, and a jumper wire, preferably with a circuit breaker incorporated, which can be used to bypass electrical components **(see illustrations)**. Before attempting to locate a problem with test instruments, use the wiring diagram(s) to decide where to make the connections.

Voltage checks

Refer to illustration 2.6

Voltage checks should be performed if a circuit is not functioning properly. Connect one lead of a circuit tester to either the nega-tive battery terminal or a known good ground. Connect the other lead to a connector in the circuit being tested, preferably nearest to the

battery or fuse **(see illustration)**. If the bulb of the tester lights, voltage is present, which means that the part of the circuit between the connector and the battery is problem free. Continue checking the rest of the circuit in the same fashion. When you reach a point at which no voltage is present, the problem lies between that point and the last test point with voltage. Most of the time the problem can be traced to a loose connection.

Note: *Keep in mind that some circuits receive voltage only when the ignition key is in the Accessory or Run position.*

Finding a short

One method of finding shorts in a live cir-cuit is to remove the fuse and connect a test light in place of the fuse terminals (fabricate two jumper wires with small spade terminals, plug the jumper wires into the fuse box and connect the test light). There should be volt-age present in the circuit. Move the suspected wiring harness from side-to-side while watch-

ing the test light. If the bulb goes off, there is a short to ground somewhere in that area, prob-ably where the insulation has rubbed through.

Ground check

Perform a ground test to check whether a component is properly grounded. Discon-nect the battery and connect one lead of a continuity tester or multimeter (set to the ohm scale), to a known good ground. Connect the other lead to the wire or ground connection being tested. If the resistance is low (less than 5 ohms), the ground is good. If the bulb on a self-powered test light does not go on, the ground is not good.

Continuity check

Refer to illustration 2.9

A continuity check is done to determine if there are any breaks in a circuit - if it is pass-ing electricity properly. With the circuit off (no power in the circuit), a self-powered continuity tester or multimeter can be used to check the

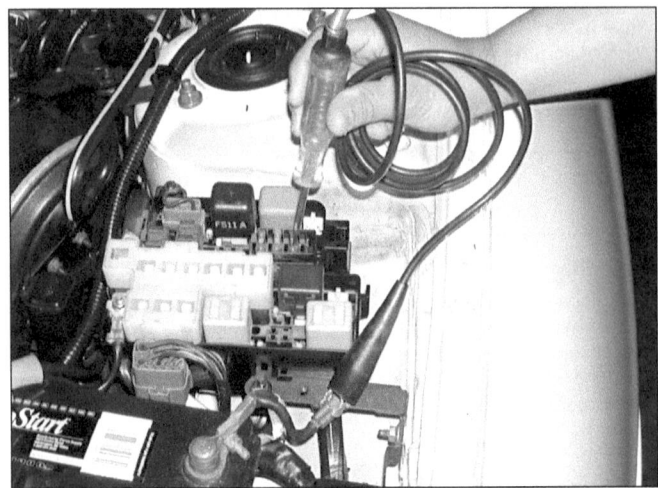 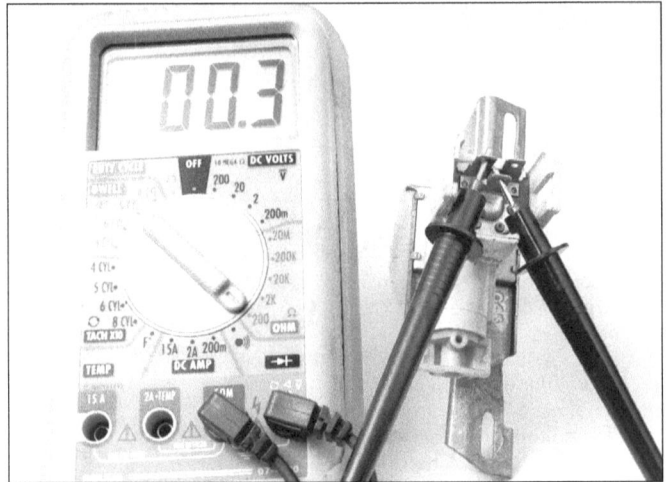

2.6 In use, a basic test light's lead is clipped to a known good ground, then the pointed probe can test connectors, wires or electrical sockets - if the bulb lights, the circuit being tested has battery voltage

2.9 With a multimeter set to the ohm scale, resistance can be checked across two terminals - when checking for continuity, a low reading indicates continuity, a high reading or infinity indicates lack of continuity

3.1a The engine compartment fuse and relay box is located at the left side of the engine compartment. There's a guide on the underside of the cover. The area between the arrows is the fusible link area, where cartridge-style fusible links are located - MCU28R models

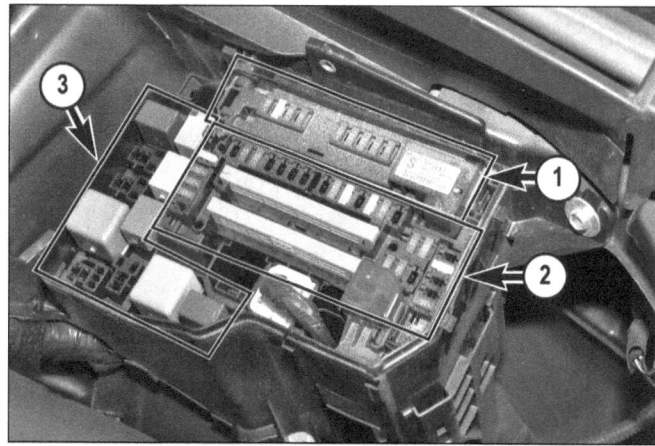

3.1b Engine compartment fuse and relay box - GSU40R/GSU45R models

1 Combined relay unit
2 Fuses and fusible links
3 Relays

circuit. Connect the test leads to both ends of the circuit (or to the "power" end and a good ground), and if the test light comes on the circuit is passing current properly **(see illustration)**. If the resistance is low (less than 5 ohms), there is continuity; if the reading is 10,000 ohms or higher, there is a break somewhere in the circuit. The same procedure can be used to test a switch, by connecting the continuity tester to the switch terminals. With the switch turned On, the test light should come on (or low resistance should be indicated on a meter).

Finding an open circuit

When diagnosing for possible open circuits, it is often difficult to locate them by sight because the connectors hide oxidation or terminal misalignment. Merely wiggling a connector on a sensor or in the wiring harness may correct the open circuit condition.

3.1c On MCU28R models, there's also a fuse box inside the vehicle, at the driver side of the dash, behind a small access door, which has a fuse guide on it

Remember this when an open circuit is indicated when troubleshooting a circuit. Intermittent problems may also be caused by oxidised or loose connections.

Electrical troubleshooting is simple if you keep in mind that all electrical circuits are basically electricity running from the battery, through the wires, switches, relays, fuses and fusible links to each electrical component (light bulb, motor, etc.) and to ground, from which it is passed back to the battery. Any electrical problem is an interruption in the flow of electricity to and from the battery.

Connectors

Most electrical connections on these vehicles are made with multi-wire plastic connectors. The mating halves of many connectors are secured with locking clips moulded into the plastic connector shells. The mating halves of large connectors, such as some of those under the instrument panel, are held together by a bolt through the centre of the connector.

To separate a connector with locking clips, use a small screwdriver to pry the clips apart carefully, then separate the connector halves. Pull only on the shell, never pull on the wiring harness as you may damage the individual wires and terminals inside the connectors. Look at the connector closely before trying to separate the halves. Often the locking clips are engaged in a way that is not immediately clear. Additionally, many connectors have more than one set of clips.

Each pair of connector terminals has a male half and a female half. When you look at the end view of a connector in a diagram, be sure to understand whether the view shows the harness side or the component side of the connector. Connector halves are mirror images of each other, and a terminal shown on the right side end-view of one half will be on the left side end view of the other half.

3 Fuses and fusible links - general information

Fuses

Refer to illustrations 3.1a, 3.1b, 3.1c and 3.3

1   The electrical circuits of the vehicle are protected by a combination of fuses, circuit breakers and fusible links. Fuse blocks are located under the instrument panel and in the engine compartment **(see illustrations)**.

2   Each of the fuses is designed to protect a specific circuit, and the various circuits are identified on the fuse panel cover.

3   Miniaturised fuses are employed in the fuse blocks. These compact fuses, with blade terminal design, allow fingertip removal and replacement. If an electrical component fails, always check the fuse first. The best way to check a fuse is with a test light. Check for power at the exposed terminal tips of each fuse. If power is present on one side of the fuse but not the other, the fuse is blown. A blown fuse can also be confirmed by visually inspecting it **(see illustration)**.

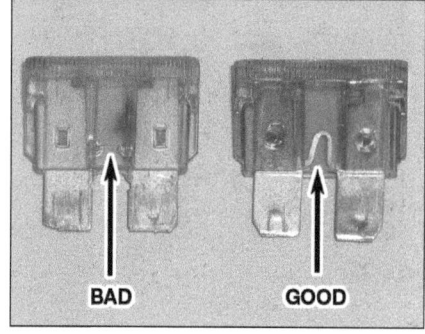

3.3 When a fuse blows, the element between the terminals melts

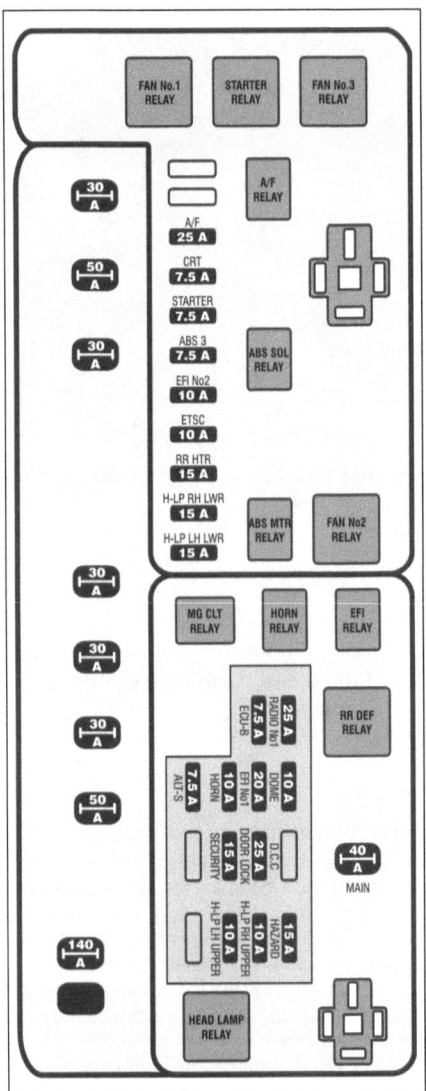

3.6a Engine compartment fuse and relay box - MCU28R models

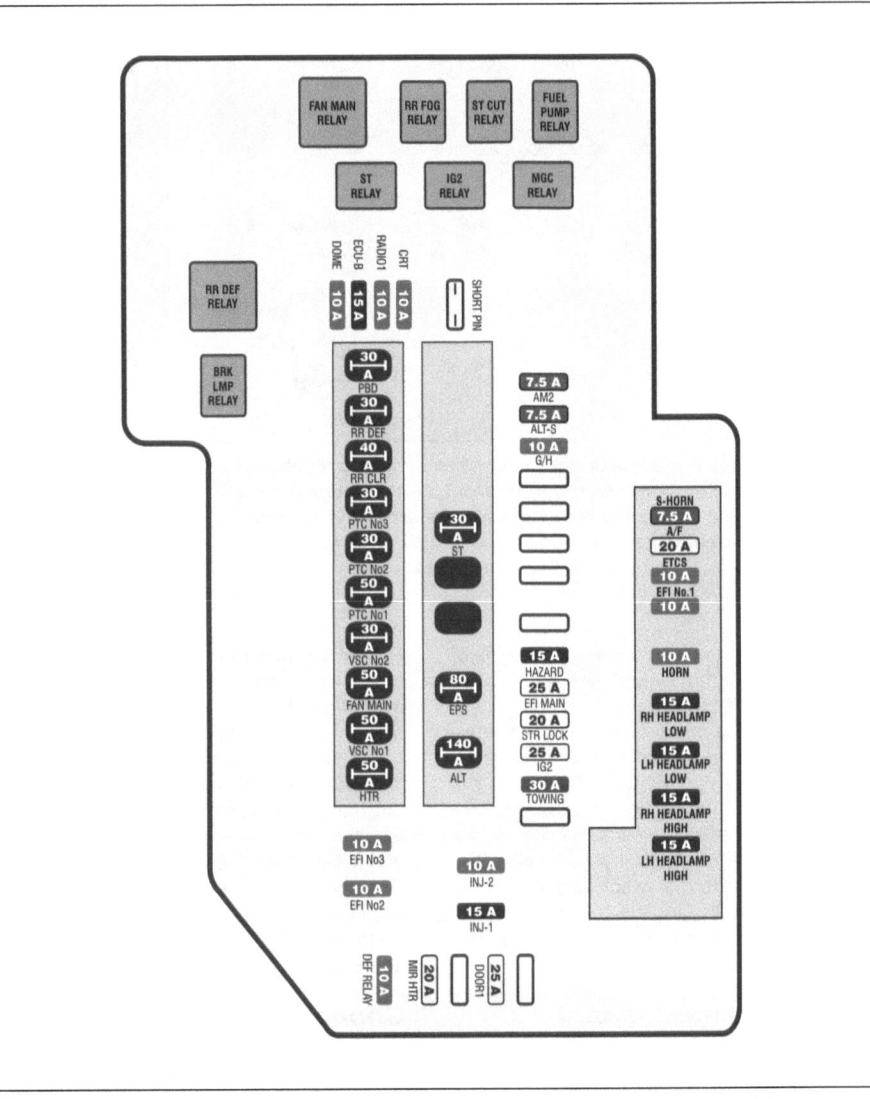

3.6b Engine compartment fuse and relay box - GSU40R/GSU45R models

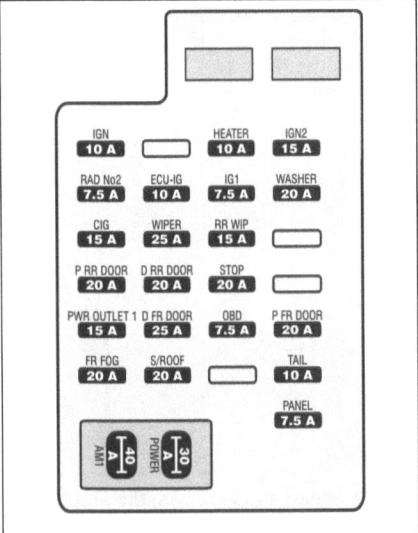

3.6c Interior fuse and relay box - MCU28R models

4   Be sure to replace blown fuses with the correct type. Fuses of different ratings are physically interchangeable, but only fuses of the proper rating should be used. Replacing a fuse with one of a higher or lower value than specified is not recommended. Each electrical circuit needs a specific amount of protection. The amperage value of each fuse is moulded into the fuse body.

5   If the replacement fuse immediately fails, don't replace it again until the cause of the problem is isolated and corrected. In most cases, this will be a short circuit in the wiring caused by a broken or deteriorated wire.

Fusible links

Refer to illustrations 3.6a, 3.6b, 3.6c and 3.6d

6   Some circuits are protected by fusible links. The links are used in circuits that are not ordinarily fused, such as the high-current side of the charging or starting circuits. Conventional inline fusible links **(see illustrations)**, such as those used in the starter cable, are characterised by a bulge in the cable. Newer

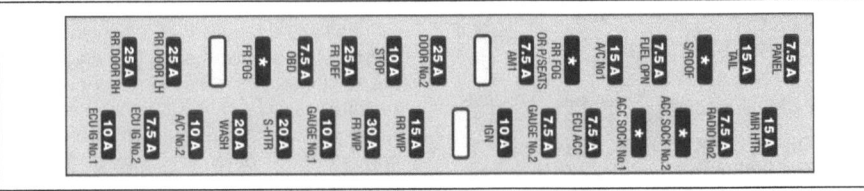

3.6d Interior fuse box layout - GSU40R/GSU45R models

cartridge-type fusible links, which are similar in appearance to a large cartridge-type fuse, are located in their own fusible link block in the engine compartment fuse and relay box **(see illustration 3.1a)**. After disconnecting the negative (-) battery terminal, simply remove the fusible link and replace it with a unit of the same amperage.

4 Circuit breakers - general information

Circuit breakers protect certain circuits, such as the power windows or heated seats. Depending on the vehicle's accessories, there might be circuit breakers in or near either of the fuse and relay boxes.

Because the circuit breakers reset automatically, an electrical overload in a circuit-breaker-protected system will cause the circuit to fail momentarily, then come back on. If the circuit does not come back on, check it immediately.

For a basic check, pull the circuit breaker up out of its socket on the fuse panel, but just far enough to probe with a voltmeter. The breaker should still contact the sockets.

With the voltmeter negative lead on a good chassis ground, touch each end prong of the circuit breaker with the positive meter probe. There should be battery voltage at each end. If there is battery voltage only at one end, the circuit breaker must be replaced.

Some circuit breakers must be reset manually.

5 Relays - general information and testing

General information

1   Several electrical accessories in the vehicle, such as the fuel injection system, horns, starter, and fog lamps use relays to transmit the electrical signal to the component. Relays use a low-current circuit (the control circuit) to open and close a high-current circuit (the power circuit). If the relay is defective, that component will not operate properly. Most relays are mounted in the engine compartment fuse/relay box, with some specialised relays located in the under bonnet box at the right fender. On some models, the ABS relays are located in a separate under bonnet relay box. If a faulty relay is suspected, it can be removed and tested using the procedure below or by a dealer service department or a repair shop. Defective relays must be replaced as a unit. Identification of the circuit the relay controls is often marked on the top of the relay, but the decal or imprint inside the cover of the relay box should also indicate which circuits they control. On GSU40R/GSU45R models, a combined relay assembly in the engine compartment fuse and relay box is used to house several

5.5 Terminal identification is sometimes printed on the side of the relay - the control circuit is what turns On, or energises the relay - the power circuit allows power to flow from the power supply to the component

fuses as well as the A/F sensor relay, the EFI relay and the circuit opening relay. This assembly is replaced as one unit if necessary. A procedure to test the combined relay unit is described in the Fuel and Exhaust Systems chapter (see Chapter 4) under the Fuel Pump/Fuel Pressure - Check heading.

Testing

Refer to illustrations 5.5 and 5.6

2   Refer to the wiring diagrams for the circuit to determine the proper connections for the relay you're testing. If you can't determine the correct connection from the wiring diagrams, however, you may be able to determine the test connections from the information that follows.

3   There are four basic types of relays used on these models. Some are normally open type and some normally closed, while others include a circuit of each type.

4   On most relays, two of the terminals are the relay control circuit (they connect to the relay coil which, when energised, closes the large contacts to complete the circuit). The other terminals are the power circuit (they are connected together within the relay when the control-circuit coil is energised).

5   Some relays may be marked as an aid **(see illustration)** to help you determine which terminals make up the control circuit and which make up the power circuit. If the relay is not marked, refer to the wiring diagrams at the end of this Chapter to determine the proper hook-ups for the relay you're testing.

6   To test a relay, connect an ohmmeter across the two terminals of the power circuit, continuity should not be indicated **(see illustration)**. Now connect a fused jumper wire between one of the two control circuit terminals and the positive battery terminal. Connect another jumper wire between the other control circuit terminal and ground. When the connections are made, the relay should click and continuity should be indicated on the meter. On some relays, polarity may be critical, so, if the relay doesn't click, try swapping the jumper wires on the control circuit terminals.

7   If the relay fails the above test, replace it.

6 Turn signal and hazard flasher relay - check and replacement

Check

Warning: *The models covered by this manual are equipped with Supplemental Restraint Systems (SRS), more commonly known as airbags. Always disable the airbag system before working in the vicinity of any airbag*

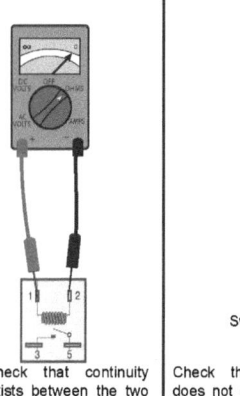
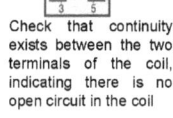
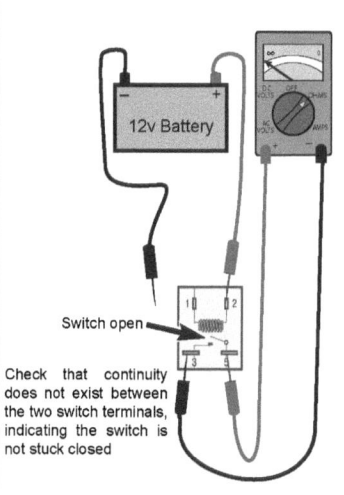
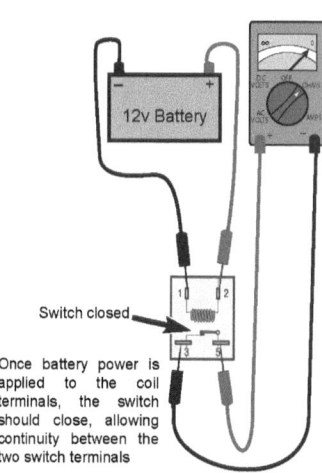

Check that continuity exists between the two terminals of the coil, indicating there is no open circuit in the coil

Check that continuity does not exist between the two switch terminals, indicating the switch is not stuck closed

Once battery power is applied to the coil terminals, the switch should close, allowing continuity between the two switch terminals

5.6 Illustration shows how a typical four-terminal normally open relay operates and is tested using a power supply and an ohmmeter

6.5 The turn signal and hazard flasher relay is located at the left end of the instrument panel junction block - MCU28R models

system component to avoid the possibility of accidental deployment of the airbags, which could cause personal injury (see Section 24).

1   When the turn signal and hazard flasher relay is functioning properly, you can hear an audible click when it's operating.

2   If the turn signals fail on one side or the other and the flasher unit does not make its characteristic clicking sound, or if a bulb on one side of the vehicle flashes much faster than normal but the bulb at the other end of the vehicle (on the same side) doesn't light at all, a turn signal bulb is probably faulty.

3   If both turn signals fail to blink, the problem might be a blown fuse, a faulty flasher unit, a defective switch or a loose or open connection. If a quick check of the fuse box indicates that the turn signal fuse has blown, check the wiring for a short before installing a new fuse.

Replacement

Refer to illustration 6.5

Note: *The turn signal and hazard flasher*

---

relay is located behind the knee bolster, on the left end of the instrument panel junction block, on MCU28R models. On GSU40R/ GSU45R models, it is forward of the instrument cluster, above the brake pedal assembly.

4   Remove the knee bolster (see Chapter 11).

5   Locate the turn signal and hazard flasher relay on the instrument panel junction block assembly **(see illustration)**.

6   Disconnect the electrical connector from the flasher unit.

7   Remove the flasher unit from the instrument panel junction block assembly.

8   Make sure that the replacement unit is identical to the original. Compare the old one to the new one before installing it.

9   Installation is the reverse of removal.

---

7   Ignition switch and key lock cylinder - replacement

Warning: *The models covered by this manual are equipped with Supplemental Restraint Systems (SRS), more commonly known as airbags. Always disable the airbag system before working in the vicinity of any airbag system component to avoid the possibility of accidental deployment of the airbag(s), which could cause personal injury (see Section 24).*

1   Disconnect the negative (-) battery terminal (see Chapter 5).

2   Remove the upper and lower steering column covers (see Chapter 11).

Ignition switch

Refer to illustrations 7.3 and 7.4

3   Disconnect the electrical connector from the ignition switch **(see illustration)**.

4   Remove the ignition switch retaining screws **(see illustration)** and remove the switch from the key lock cylinder housing.

5   Installation is the reverse of the removal.

7.3 To disconnect the electrical connector from the ignition switch, depress this release tab and pull off the connector

Key lock cylinder

Refer to illustrations 7.7, 7.8a and 7.8b

6   Place the ignition key in the ACC position.

7   If the vehicle is equipped with an immobiliser system, disconnect the electrical connector from the immobiliser module, then slide the immobiliser module and the key lock cylinder illumination ring as a single assembly **(see illustration)**.

8   Use an awl or punch to depress the key lock cylinder retaining pin and remove the key lock cylinder from the housing **(see illustrations)**.

9   To install the lock cylinder, depress the retaining pin and guide the lock cylinder into the housing until the retaining pin extends itself back into the locating hole in the housing.

10   The remainder of installation is the reverse of removal.

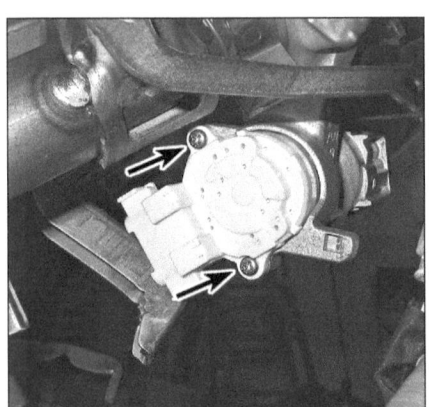

7.4 To detach the ignition switch from the key lock cylinder housing, remove these two screws

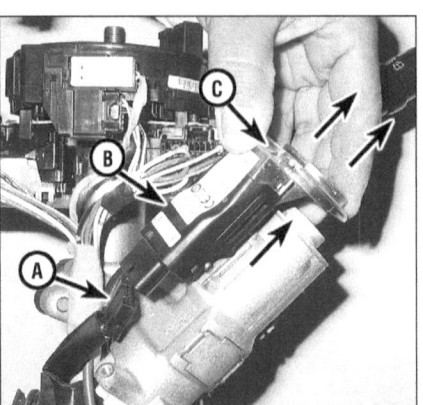

7.7 To remove the immobiliser module and the key lock cylinder illumination ring, disconnect the electrical connector (A), then slide off the immobiliser (B) and the illumination ring (C) from the key lock cylinder housing

7.8a To remove the key lock cylinder from the lock cylinder housing, put the lock cylinder in the ACC position, insert an awl or punch into this small hole in the housing, push it in until it depresses the lock cylinder retaining pin . . .

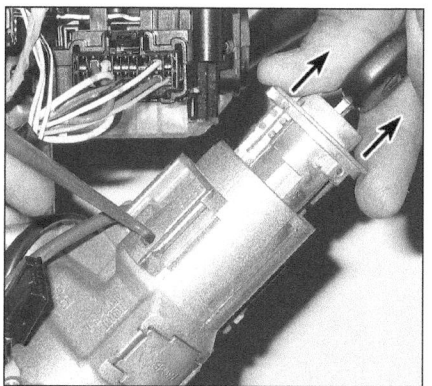

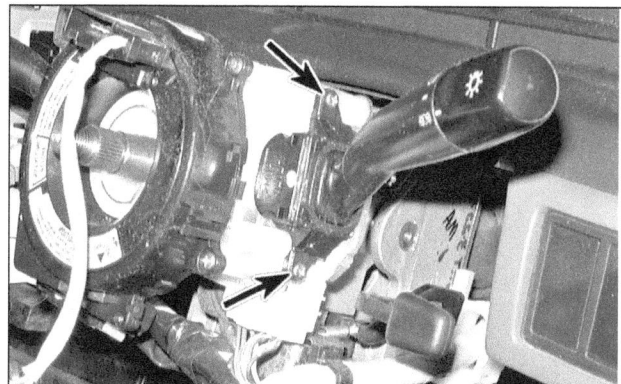

8.3a On some models, the multi-function switch is retained by these two screws

7.8b . . . and pull out the key lock cylinder

8 Multi-function switches - replacement

Refer to illustrations 8.3a and 8.3b

Warning: *The models covered by this manual are equipped with Supplemental Restraint Systems (SRS), more commonly known as airbags. Always disable the airbag system before working in the vicinity of any airbag system components to avoid the possibility of accidental deployment of the airbag(s), which could cause personal injury (see Section 24).*

Note: *The multi-function switches (also referred to as combination switches or steering column switches) are two separate switch units connected to a central plastic housing known as the switch body, which encircles the steering column. The left multi-function switch controls the headlights and the turn signals; the right switch controls the windshield washer/wiper system. Either switch can be replaced separately.*

1 Disconnect the negative (-) battery terminal (see Chapter 5).
2 Remove the upper and lower steering column covers (see Chapter 11).

3 The multi-function switches are secured to the switch body one of two ways, depending on the year and model. The switches are secured to the switch body by retaining clips that must be depressed to disengage the switch **(see illustrations)**.
4 Remove the multi-function switch and disconnect the electrical connectors from the switch.
5 Installation is the reverse of removal.

9 Instrument panel switches - replacement

Warning: *The models covered by this manual are equipped with Supplemental Restraint Systems (SRS), more commonly known as airbags. Always disable the airbag system before working in the vicinity of any airbag system component to avoid the possibility of accidental deployment of the airbag(s), which could cause personal injury (see Section 24).*

Switches located at the lower right end of the instrument panel

Refer to illustrations 9.1, 9.2a, 9.2b, 9.3a and 9.3b

Note: *Various switches are housed in the lower right end of the instrument panel, to the right of the steering column. They include (but are not limited to) the power mirror switch, the theft deterrent system/engine immobiliser system indicator and fog lights - where fitted.*

1 Carefully pry the switch panel out of the instrument panel with a suitable trim panel tool **(see illustration)**.
2 To replace the power mirror switch, disconnect the electrical connector and remove the switch from the switch panel **(see illustrations)**.
3 To replace the theft deterrent/engine immobiliser system indicator, disconnect the electrical connector and remove the switch from the switch panel **(see illustrations)**.
4 The rest of the switches housed in the switch panel are replaced the same way as the two described above. To replace any of the other switches on this panel, refer to illustrations 9.2a, 9.2b, 9.3a and 9.3b.

8.3b To detach either multi-function switch from the switch body on MCU28R models, depress the clip with a screwdriver and slide out the switch

9.1 Use a trim panel tool to pry off the switch panel from the instrument panel - MCU28R models

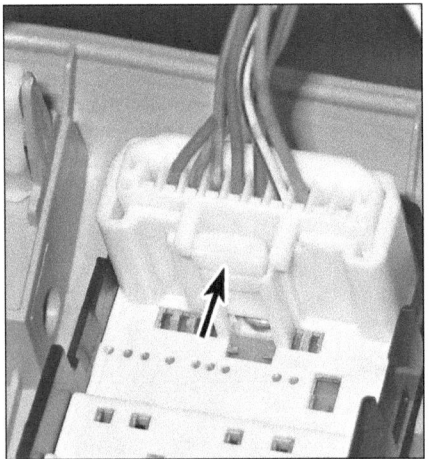

9.2a To disconnect the electrical connector from the power mirror switch, depress this release tab and pull out the connector

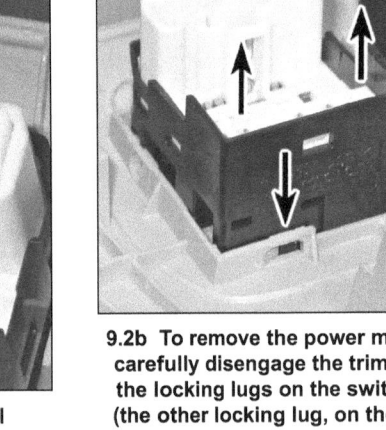

9.2b To remove the power mirror switch, carefully disengage the trim panel from the locking lugs on the switch housing (the other locking lug, on the other side of the switch housing, not visible in this photo) and pull the switch out of the trim panel

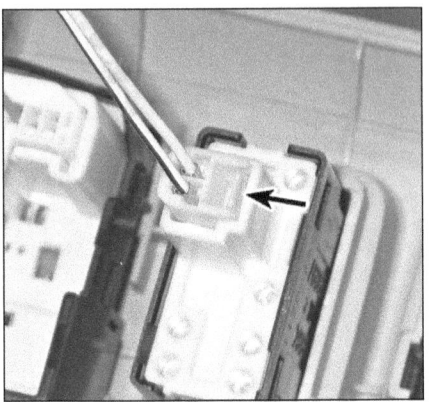

9.3a To disconnect the electrical connector from the theft deterrent/engine immobiliser system switch, depress this release tab and pull off the connector

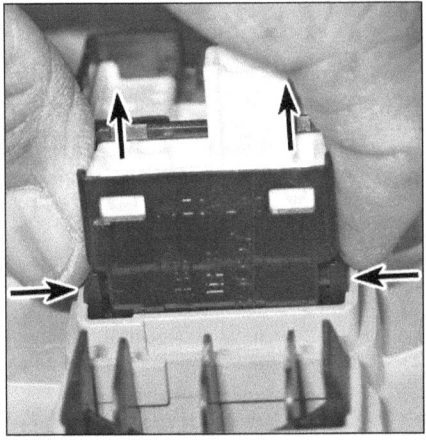

9.3b To remove the theft deterrent/engine immobiliser system switch, depress these release tabs on both sides of the switch and pull the switch out of the trim panel

5   Installation is the reverse of the removal procedure.

Electrical devices on the climate control assembly

Refer to illustration 9.8

Note: *On MCU28R models, electrical devices such as the hazard warning switch, digital clock and passenger seatbelt reminder light protrude through the upper part of the centre trim panel, but they're actually located on the heater and air conditioning control assembly.*

6   Remove the centre trim panel (see Chapter 11).
7   Remove the climate control assembly (see Chapter 3).
8   Remove the cover from the back of the climate control assembly **(see illustration)**.
9   Remove the hazard warning switch, digital clock or passenger seatbelt reminder light from the climate control assembly.
10   Installation is the reverse of removal.

10   Instrument cluster - removal and installation

Refer to illustrations 10.3 and 10.4

Warning: *The models covered by this manual are equipped with Supplemental Restraint Systems (SRS), more commonly known as airbags. Always disable the airbag system before working in the vicinity of any airbag system component to avoid the possibility of accidental deployment of the airbag(s), which could cause personal injury (see Section 24).*
1   Disconnect the negative (-) battery terminal (see Chapter 5).
2   Remove the instrument cluster trim panel (see Chapter 11).
3   Remove the cluster mounting screws **(see illustration)** and pull the instrument cluster towards the steering wheel.
4   Disconnect the electrical connectors from the backside of the cluster **(see illustration)**.
5   Installation is the reverse of removal.

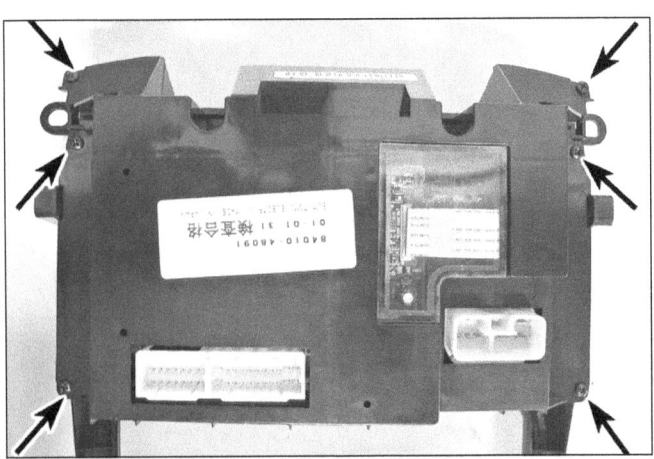

9.8 Remove these screws to detach the cover from the climate control assembly

10.3 To detach the instrument cluster, remove these mounting screws

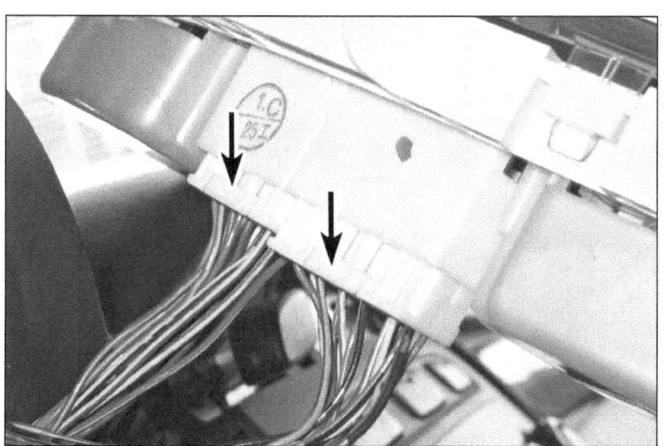

10.4 Pull out the cluster far enough to disconnect the electrical connectors from the backside of the cluster

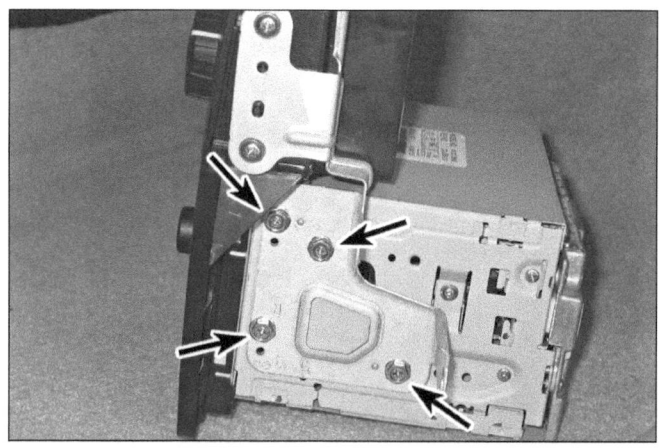

11.4 To detach the radio unit from the radio/heater/air conditioning mounting bracket, remove these bolts from each end (right end shown, left end identical)

11 Radio and speakers - removal and installation

Warning: *The models covered by this manual are equipped with Supplemental Restraint Systems (SRS), more commonly known as airbags. Always disable the airbag system before working in the vicinity of any airbag system component to avoid the possibility of accidental deployment of the airbag(s), which could cause personal injury (see Section 24).*

Radio

Refer to illustration 11.4

1 Remove the centre trim panel (see Chapter 11).
2 Remove the radio and heater/air conditioning control assembly mounting bolts **(see illustration 10.4)** in Chapter 3.
3 Pull out the radio and heater and air conditioning control assembly and disconnect the electrical connectors from the radio and from the heater and air conditioning control assembly **(see illustration 10.5)** in Chapter 3.
4 Detach the radio unit from the radio/

heater/air conditioning control assembly mounting bracket **(see illustration)**.
5 Installation is the reverse of removal.

Speakers

Door speakers

Refer to illustration 11.7

Note: *All models have speakers in both front and rear doors. The photos accompanying this section depict front door speakers, but the procedure applies to rear door speakers as well, which are mounted in a fashion similar to the front door speakers.*

6 Remove the door trim panel (see Chapter 11).
7 Disconnect the electrical connector from the speaker, remove the speaker mounting screws **(see illustration)** and remove the speaker.
8 Installation is the reverse of removal.

Tweeters

Refer to illustration 11.10

Note: *The tweeters are located in the front doors.*

9 Remove the door trim panel (see Chapter 11).
10 Disconnect the electrical connector, remove the mounting bolt **(see illustration)** and remove the tweeter.
11 Installation is the reverse of removal.

12 Antenna - replacement

MCU28R models

Refer to illustration 12.1

1 Unscrew the antenna mast from the mounting base **(see illustration)**.

Antenna mounting base

Refer to illustrations 12.3, 12.4, 12.5, 12.8 and 12.9

2 Remove the antenna mast **(see illustration 12.1)**.
3 Working inside the vehicle, remove the right A-pillar trim panel **(see illustration)** and the right kick panel. (For help with removing either of these trim pieces, refer to Chapter 11.)

11.7 To remove a door speaker, disconnect the electrical connector and remove the speaker mounting screws

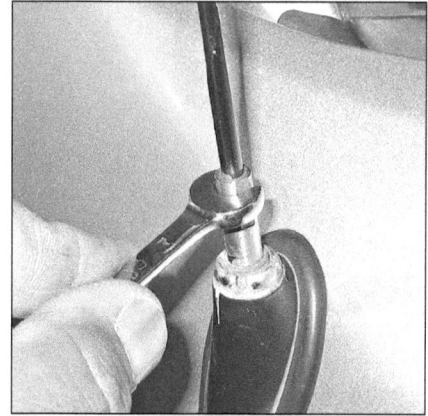

11.10 To remove a tweeter, disconnect the electrical connector and remove the mounting bolt

12.1 To remove the antenna mast from its mounting base, simply unscrew it

12.3 Use a trim removal tool or a slotted screwdriver to pry off the right A-pillar trim panel (if you're going to use a screwdriver, tape the tip to protect the plastic trim)

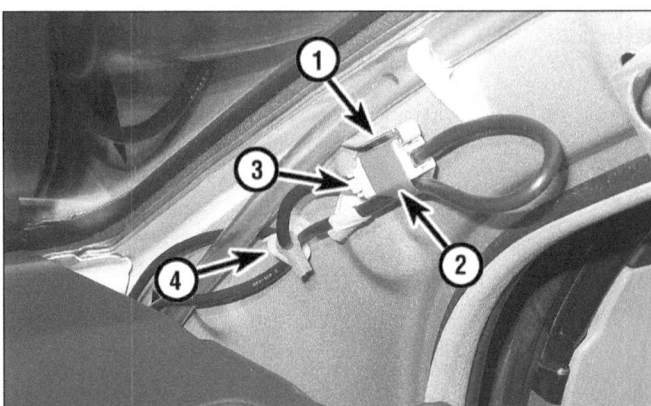

12.4 This electrical connector connects the cable from the antenna mounting base to the antenna cable that's routed through the dash. To disconnect it, detach it from the mounting bracket (1), cut the tape (2) wrapped around it, then depress the release tab (3) and disconnect the connector. Then pull the antenna mounting base cable out of the clip (4)

4   Disconnect the electrical connector that connects the cable from the antenna mounting base to the cable that goes through the dash **(see illustration)**.
5   Remove the castellated nut from the top of the antenna mounting base **(see illustration)**.
6   Loosen the right front wheel nuts, raise the front of the vehicle and place it securely on jackstands, then remove the right front wheel.
Warning: *If the vehicle is equipped with an electronically modulated air suspension, make sure that the height control switch is turned off before raising the vehicle.*
7   Remove the right wheel arch splash shield (see Chapter 11).
8   Locate the lower part of the antenna mounting base assembly **(see illustration)**. Carefully pull the antenna mounting base cable through the grommet.
9   Using a flashlight, insert the antenna mounting base cable into the grommet and

up through the right corner of the passenger compartment, between the end of the instrument panel and the A-pillar **(see illustration)**.
10   Installation is otherwise the reverse of removal.

Antenna cable between the antenna cable and the radio

11   Remove the instrument panel assembly (see Chapter 11).
12   Study the routing of the antenna cable. Make a sketch if necessary.
13   Unclip the antenna cable from the backside of the instrument panel.
14   Installation is the reverse of removal. Make sure that the cable is routed correctly and that all clips are installed.

GSU40R/GSU45R models

15   GSU40R/GSU45R models are equipped with a wire grid-type antenna attached to the rear window glass. If you have this type

of antenna on your vehicle, the only way to repair any antenna faults at the glass is to have the window replaced.

---

13 Wiper motor - check and replacement

Wiper motor circuit check

Note: *Refer to the wiring diagrams for the following checks. When checking for voltage, probe a grounded 12 volt test light to each terminal at a connector until it lights; this verifies voltage (power) at the terminal. If the following checks fail to locate the problem, have the system diagnosed by a dealer service department or other properly equipped repair facility.*

1   If the wipers work slowly, make sure that the battery is in good condition and has

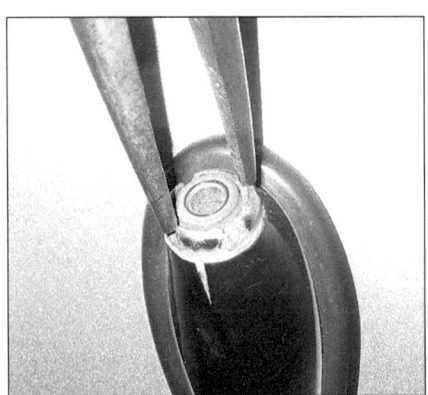

12.5 To detach the antenna mounting base from the fender, unscrew this castellated retaining nut. Special wrenches for this task are available at auto parts stores, but you can also use a pair of needle-nose pliers

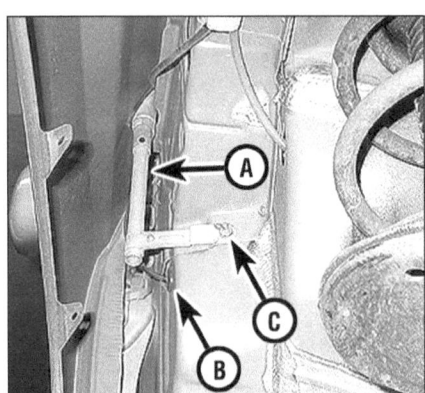

12.8 To remove the antenna mounting base (A), snake out the antenna cable through the grommet (B) and remove mounting bracket nut (C). When installing the mounting base assembly, don't forget to reattach the ground wire at the mounting nut

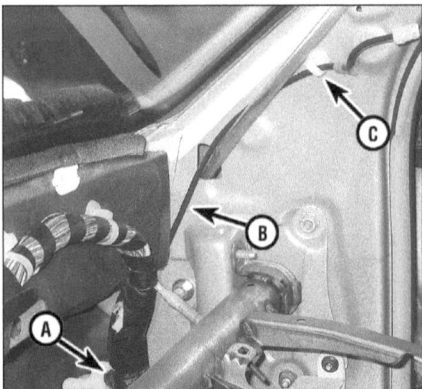

12.9 Using a flashlight, insert the antenna mounting base cable through the grommet (A), up between the end of the dash and the A-pillar (B), then through the clip on the A-pillar (C) (instrument panel removed for clarity)

13.6a   Remove the cap from wiper arm, on MCU28R models to access the nut

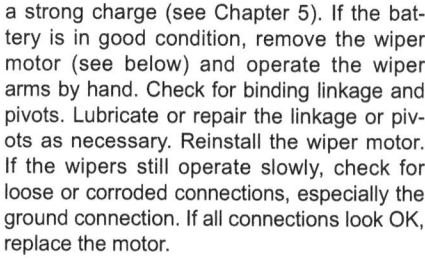

13.6b   Wiper arm retaining nut (1); on some models, the arm is marked with a "D" for driver side (2), or "P" for passenger side

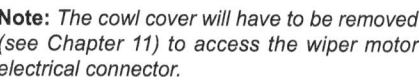

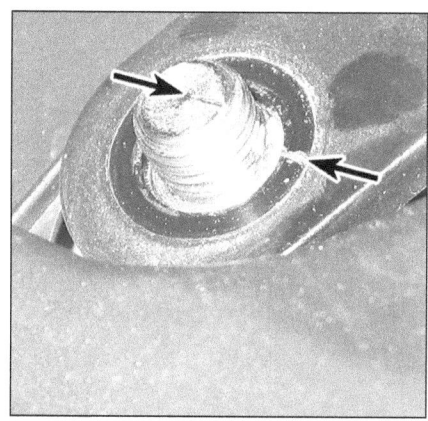

13.6c   Remove the nut and mark the relationship of the arm to the shaft

a strong charge (see Chapter 5). If the battery is in good condition, remove the wiper motor (see below) and operate the wiper arms by hand. Check for binding linkage and pivots. Lubricate or repair the linkage or pivots as necessary. Reinstall the wiper motor. If the wipers still operate slowly, check for loose or corroded connections, especially the ground connection. If all connections look OK, replace the motor.

2   If the wipers fail to operate when activated, check the fuse in the driver's side interior fuse panel. If the fuse is OK, connect a jumper wire between the wiper motor's ground terminal and ground, then retest. If the motor works now, repair the ground connection. If the motor still doesn't work, turn the wiper switch to the HI position and check for voltage at the motor.

Note: *The cowl cover will have to be removed (see Chapter 11) to access the wiper motor electrical connector.*

3   If there's voltage at the connector, remove the motor and check it off the vehicle with fused jumper wires from the battery. If the motor now works, check for binding linkage (see Step 1). If the motor still doesn't work, replace it. If there's no voltage to the motor, check for voltage at the wiper control relays. If there's voltage at the wiper control relays and no voltage at the wiper motor, have the switch tested. If the switch is OK, the wiper control relay is probably bad. See Section 5 for relay testing.

4   If the interval (delay) function is inoperative, check the continuity of all the wiring between the switch and wiper control module.

5   If the wipers stop at the position they're in when the switch is turned off (fail to park), check for voltage at the park feed wire of the wiper motor connector when the wiper switch is OFF but the ignition is ON. If no voltage is present, check for an open circuit between the wiper motor and the fuse panel.

Replacement

Windshield wiper motor

Refer to illustrations 13.6a, 13.6b, 13.6c, 13.8a, 13.8b, 13.10 and 13.11

6   Remove the wiper arm nuts and mark the relationship of the wiper arms to their shafts **(see illustrations)**. Remove both wiper arms.

7   Remove the plastic cowl cover (see Chapter 11).

8   Disconnect the electrical connector from the wiper motor **(see illustrations)**.

9   Remove the windshield wiper motor and link assembly mounting bolts **(see illustrations 13.8a and 13.8b)** and remove the wiper motor and link assembly.

10   Use a screwdriver to pry the linkage rod from the crank arm pivot of the wiper motor **(see illustration)**.

11   Remove the crank arm nut **(see illustration)**, mark the relationship of the crank arm to the motor shaft and remove the crank arm from the shaft.

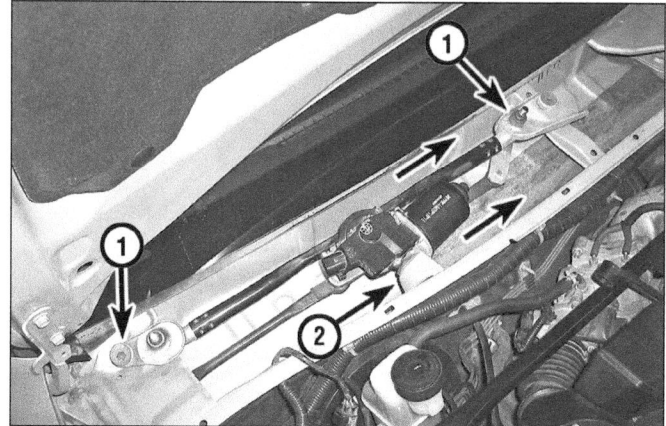

13.8a   Wiper motor and linkage assembly - MCU28R models; remove the retaining bolts (1) and slide the assembly in the direction of the arrows to release the assembly from the retainer (2)

13.8b   Wiper motor and linkage assembly - GSU40R/GSU45R models

1   Mounting nuts   *2   Wiring connector*

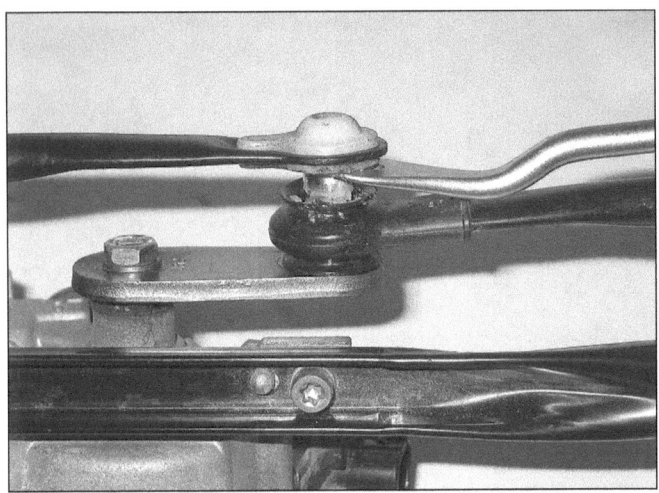

13.10 Use a trim panel tool to separate the link rod from the crank arm pivot

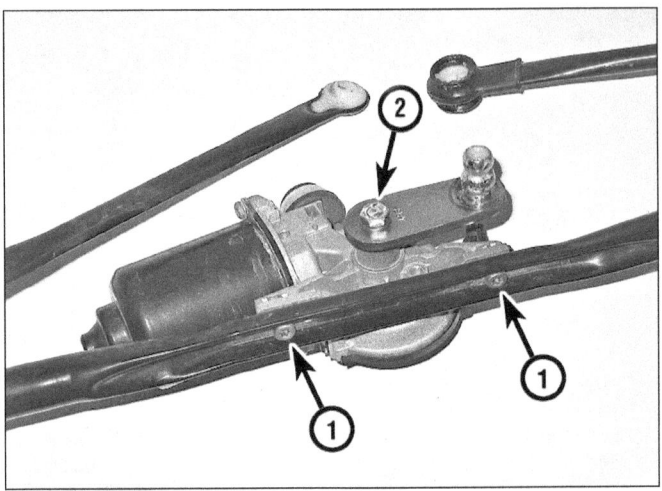

13.11 To detach the wiper motor from the link rod assembly, remove these two bolts (1). If you're replacing the motor, remove the crank arm nut (2)

13.14 To remove the rear wiper arm, flip up the cap covering the retaining nut, remove the nut, mark the relationship of the wiper arm to the motor shaft, then remove the arm and the grommet

12   Remove the wiper motor mounting bolts and separate the motor from the link rod assembly.
13   Installation is the reverse of removal.

Rear wiper motor

Refer to illustrations 13.14, 13.17 and 13.18

14   Flip open the cap covering the rear wiper arm retaining nut **(see illustration)** and remove the nut.

15   Mark the relationship of the rear wiper arm to the motor shaft, then remove the arm.
16   Remove the trim panel from the rear hatch (see Chapter 11).
17   Disconnect the electrical connector from the rear wiper motor **(see illustration)**.
18   Remove the rear wiper motor mounting bolts **(see illustration)** and remove the motor.
19   Installation is the reverse of removal.

***

14   Headlight bulbs - replacement

Warning: *Gas-filled bulbs are under pressure and may shatter if the surface is scratched or the bulb is dropped. Wear eye protection and handle the bulbs carefully, grasping only the base whenever possible. Do not touch the surface of the bulb with your fingers because the oil from your skin could cause it to overheat and fail prematurely. If you do touch the bulb surface, clean it with rubbing alcohol.*

Note: *The inner headlight bulbs are the*

13.17 Disconnect the electrical connector from the rear wiper motor

13.18 To detach the rear wiper motor from the hatch, remove these three bolts

14.1 To disconnect the electrical connector from either headlight bulb holder, depress this release tab and pull off the connector

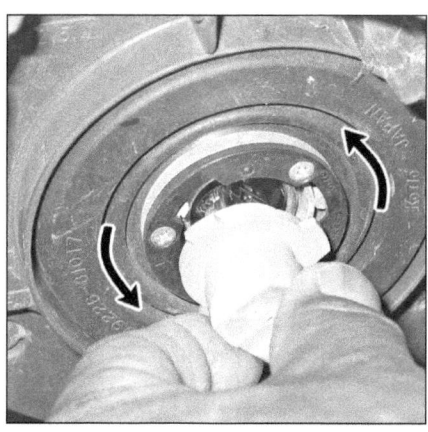

14.2 To remove the headlight bulb holder from the headlight housing, rotate the bulb holder counterclockwise and pull it out (this step also applies to the fog lamp bulb holder)

14.4a Disconnect the electrical connector from the headlight bulb - GSU40R/GSU45R models

14.4b Remove the rubber cover from the headlight housing - GSU40R/GSU45R models

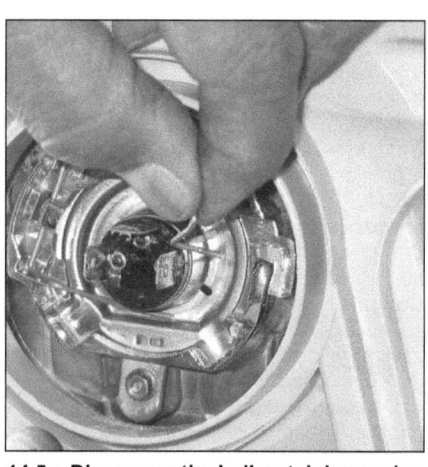

14.5a Disengage the bulb retaining spring and swing it out of the way

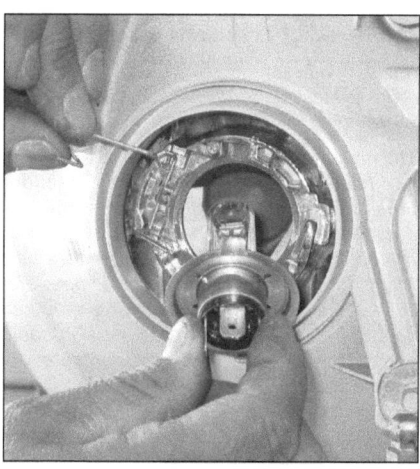

14.5b Remove the bulb from the headlight housing

high-beam bulbs. The outer bulbs are the low-beam bulbs (these bulbs are also illuminated when the high-beam bulbs are turned on).

MCU28R models

Refer to illustrations 14.1 and 14.2

1   Disconnect the electrical connector from the bulb holder assembly **(see illustration)**.
2   Grasp the bulb holder securely and rotate it counterclockwise to remove it from the housing **(see illustration)**.
3   Without touching the bulb glass with your bare fingers, insert the new bulb assembly into the headlight housing. Twist it clockwise to lock it in place, then plug in the electrical connector.

GSU40R/GSU45R models

Refer to illustrations 14.4a, 14.4b, 14.5a, 14.5b and 14.6

4   Disconnect the wiring and remove the rubber weather cover from the back of the headlight housing **(see illustrations)**.
5   Unhook the locking spring from the tab, and remove the bulb from the housing **(see illustrations)**.
6   When installing the bulb, align the top lug on the bulb's flange with their corresponding cutout, insert the bulb into the headlight housing and hook the spring over the tab to lock it into place **(see illustration)**. When installing the new bulb, make sure that you don't touch it with your fingers, because the oil from your hands will cause the bulb to overheat and fail prematurely. If you do touch the bulb, be sure to wipe it off with rubbing alcohol and a clean soft cloth. Installation is otherwise the reverse of removal.

14.6 When installing the new bulb, align the lugs on the bulb mounting flange with the cutouts in the headlight housing

15.2 To detach the upper part of the headlight housing from the upper radiator crossmember, remove these two bolts - MCU28R model shown, GSU40R/GSU45R models similar

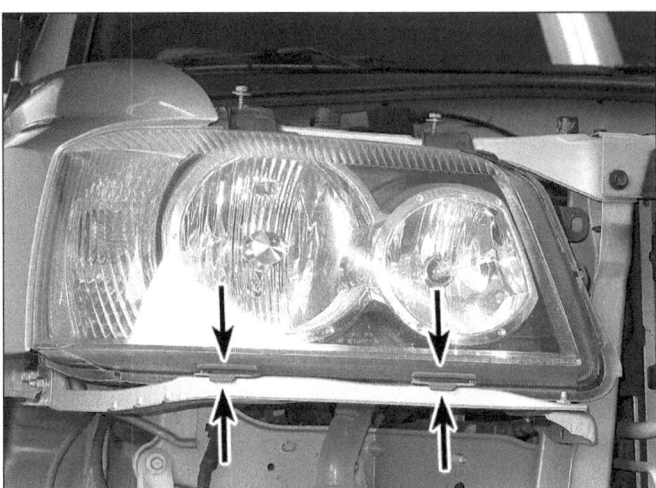

15.6 To disengage these two headlight housing mounting clips, grasp the headlight firmly and carefully pull it out - MCU28R model shown, GSU40R/GSU45R models similar

15   Headlight housing - replacement

Refer to illustrations 15.2, 15.6, 15.7a and 15.7b

Warning: *These vehicles are equipped with gas-filled headlight bulbs that are under pressure and may shatter if the surface is damaged or the bulb is dropped. Wear eye protection and handle the bulbs carefully, grasping only the base whenever possible. Do not touch the surface of the bulb with your fingers because the oil from your skin could cause it to overheat and fail prematurely. If you do touch the bulb surface, clean it with rubbing alcohol.*

1   Disconnect the negative (-) battery terminal (see Chapter 5).

2   Remove the upper headlight mounting bolts **(see illustration)**.

3   Remove the grille and the bumper cover (see Chapter 11).

4   Remove the headlight housing retaining bolt located at the outer lower corner of the housing.

5   On MCU28R models, there is two locator clips along the bottom of the headlamp. On GSU40R/GSU45R models, there is a locater on the bottom of the inside of the headlamp.

6   Disengage the headlight housing clip by pulling the headlamp housing out **(see illustration)** far enough to access the electrical connectors on the backside of the headlight assembly.

7   Disconnect the electrical connectors from the headlight housing **(see illustration)**. There are two headlight connectors, on MCU28R models and one headlight connector on GSU40R/GSU45R models. Both models also have a park lamp and turn signal lamp bulb

holder and connectors **(see illustration)**.

8   Installation is the reverse of removal.

9   Be sure to check headlight adjustment when you're done (see Section 16).

16   Headlights - adjustment

Refer to illustrations 16.4, 16.7a and 16.7b

Warning: *The headlights must be aimed correctly. If adjusted incorrectly, they could temporarily blind the driver of an oncoming vehicle and cause an accident or seriously reduce your ability to see the road. The headlights should be checked for proper aim every 12 months and any time a new headlight is installed or front-end bodywork is performed. The following procedure is only an interim step to provide temporary adjustment*

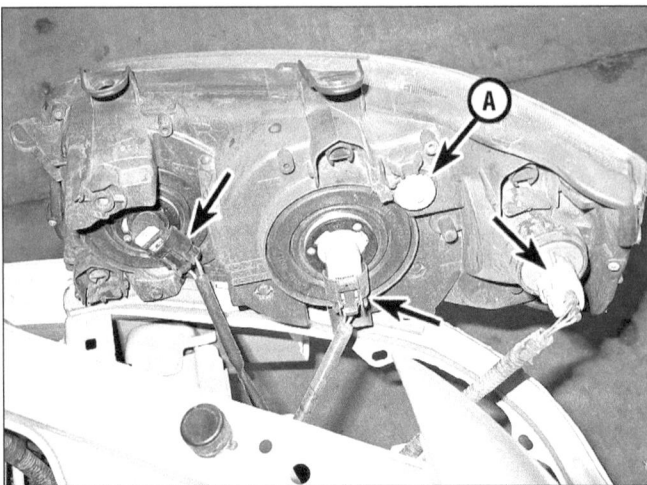

15.7a Pull out the headlight housing and disconnect the electrical connectors from the headlights and from the turn signal/ sidemarker light. After you've installed the headlight housing, use the vertical adjuster (A) to adjust the headlights (see Section 16)

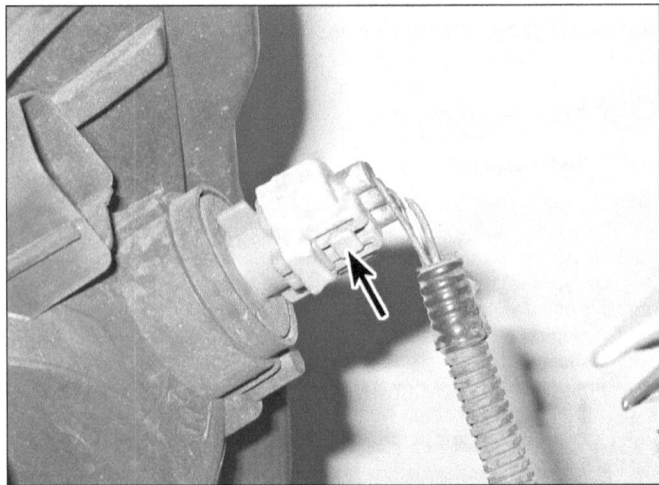

15.7b To disconnect the electrical connector from the front turn signal/parking and sidemarker light, depress this release tab and pull off the connector

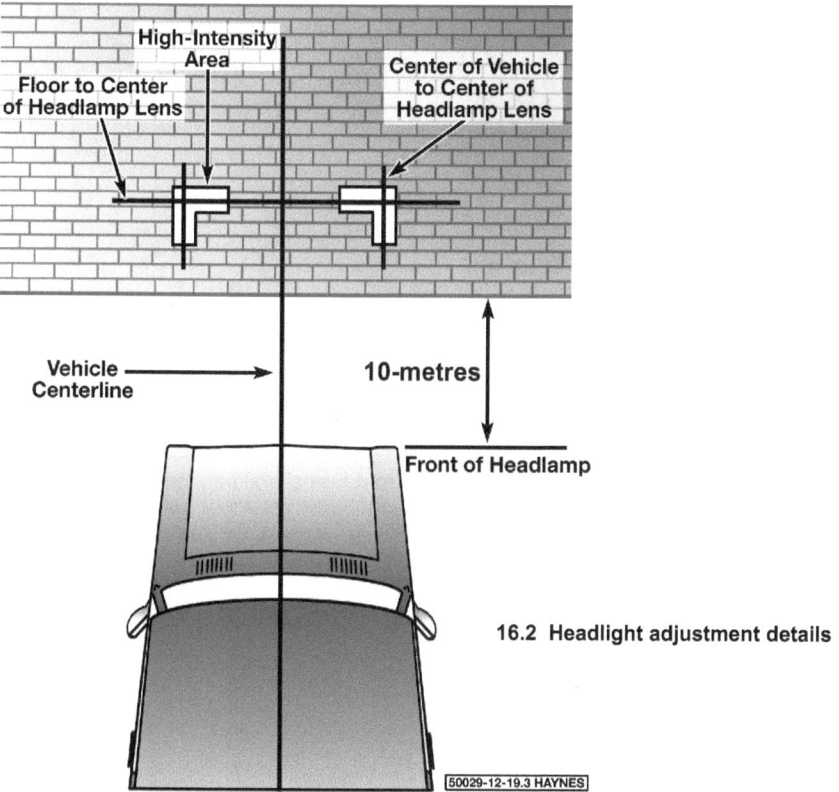

16.2 Headlight adjustment details

system components to avoid the possibility of accidental deployment of the airbag(s), which could cause personal injury (see Section 24).

Check

Note: *Check the fuses before beginning electrical diagnosis.*

1   Disconnect the electrical connector from the horn.
2   To test the horn, connect battery voltage to the horn terminal with a jumper wire. If the horn doesn't sound, replace it.
3   If the horn does sound, check for voltage at the terminal when the horn button is depressed. If there's voltage at the terminal, check for a bad ground at the horn.
4   If there's no voltage at the horn, check the relay (see Section 5).
5   If the relay is OK, check for voltage to the relay power and control circuits. If either of the circuits is not receiving voltage, inspect the wiring between the relay and the fuse panel.
6   If both relay circuits are receiving voltage, depress the horn button and check the circuit from the relay to the horn button for continuity to ground. If there's no continuity, check the circuit for an open. If there's no open circuit, replace the horn button.
7   If there's continuity to ground through the horn button, check for an open or short in the circuit from the relay to the horn.

Replacement

Refer to illustrations 17.8a, 17.8b and 17.8c

Note: *On MCU28R models, there are two horns. One is located in front of the condenser and the other is located below and in front of the engine compartment fuse and relay box. On GSU40R/GSU45R models, the horns are behind the front grille.*

8   Disconnect the electrical connector **(see illustrations)**.
9   Remove the bracket bolt.
10   Installation is the reverse of removal.

---

until the headlights can be adjusted by a properly equipped workshop.

1   Ensure that the tyres are inflated to the correct pressure and that the vehicle is positioned on level ground.
2   Ensure that the vehicle is unladen, except for a normal amount of fuel in the fuel tank and the driver seated in the driver's seat. If the vehicle regularly carries unusual load or tows a caravan, those loads should be in the vehicle while checking/adjusting the headlamp aim.
3   When using headlamp aiming equipment, refer to the manufacturer's instructions for the equipment being used.
4   When using an aiming board, position the vehicle immediately in front of, and square to the board **(see illustration)**.
5   Mark a reference line on the board to correspond with the horizontal and vertical centre lines of the headlamps.
6   Move the vehicle 10 metres from the board, ensuring that it is square to the board and that the centre lines are correctly aligned.
7   To adjust the headlamps, proceed as follows:

  a   *Raise the bonnet. Switch On the headlamps and select low beam.*
  b   *Adjust the headlamps to comply with local regulations. As a guide, adjust the lamps so that the low beam pattern strikes the aiming board with the horizontal cut off point 100 mm below the horizontal centre line and the point where the beam raises from horizontal is on or to the left of the vertical centre line (see illustrations).*

---

17   Horn - check and replacement

Warning: *The models covered by this manual are equipped with Supplemental Restraint Systems (SRS), more commonly known as airbags. Always disable the airbag system before working in the vicinity of any airbag*

16.5 To turn the vertical adjuster wheel, insert a Phillips screwdriver into the gap at the top, engage the head of the screwdriver with the teeth on the adjuster wheel and turn the wheel (if you can't locate the adjuster wheel, refer to illustration 15.7a)

17.8a To remove the horn that's located below and in front of the fuse and relay box, disconnect the electrical connector and remove the mounting bracket bolt - MCU28R models

17.8b To remove the horn that's located in front of the condenser, disconnect the electrical connector and remove the mounting bracket bolt - MCU28R models

17.8c Front grille removed showing the horns - GSU40R/GSU45R models

18.2 To remove the bulb holder for the front turn signal/parking and sidemarker light bulb, rotate it counterclockwise and pull it out of the headlight housing

18   Bulb replacement

Exterior light bulbs

Front turn signal/parking and sidemarker light bulbs

Refer to illustrations 18.2 and 18.3

Note: *The front turn signal/parking and sidemarker light bulbs are located in the headlight housing.*

1   Remove the headlight housing (see Section 15).
2   Remove the bulb holder for the front turn signal/parking and sidemarker light bulb from the headlight housing **(see illustration)**.
3   Remove the bulb from the holder **(see illustration)**.
4   Installation is the reverse of removal.

Fog lamp bulbs

5   Raise the front of the vehicle and support on jackstands (see Jacking and Towing).

6   Disconnect the electrical connector from the fog lamp bulb holder.
7   Turn the fog lamp bulb holder counter-clockwise and pull it out of the fog lamp housing.
8   Installation is the reverse of removal.

Centre high-mounted brake light

Refer to illustrations 18.9, 18.10, 18.11 and 18.12

Note: *The centre high-mounted brake light bulb is located in the upper edge of the rear hatch.*

9   Open the rear hatch and remove the trim piece from the upper inside edge of the hatch, between the two hinges **(see illustration)**.
10   Disconnect the electrical connector from the centre high-mounted brake light bulb holder **(see illustration)**.
11   Remove the centre high-mounted brake light bulb holder from the housing **(see illustration)**.
12   Remove the centre high-mounted brake light bulb from the holder **(see illustration)**.
13   Installation is the reverse of removal.

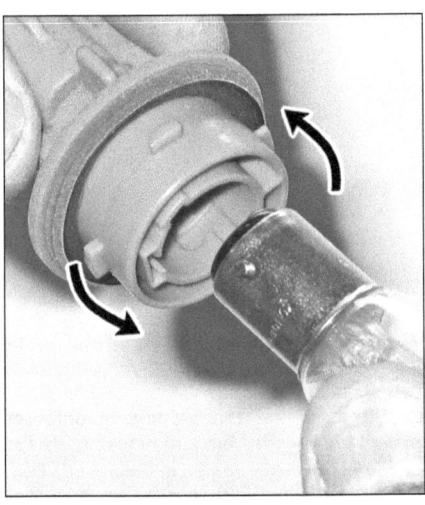

18.3 To remove the front turn signal/ parking and sidemarker light bulb from the bulb holder, push it into the bulb holder, turn it counterclockwise and pull it out

18.9 Remove this trim piece from the upper inside edge of the rear hatch to access the centre high-mounted brake light bulb. To detach the trim piece, simply pull it off

18.10 To disconnect the electrical connector from the centre high-mounted brake light bulb holder, depress this release tab and pull off the connector

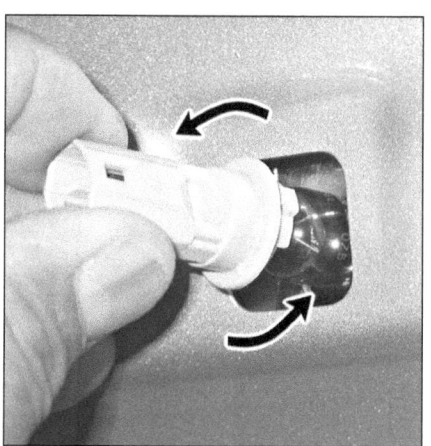

18.11 To remove the bulb holder from the centre high-mounted brake light housing, rotate it counterclockwise and pull it out

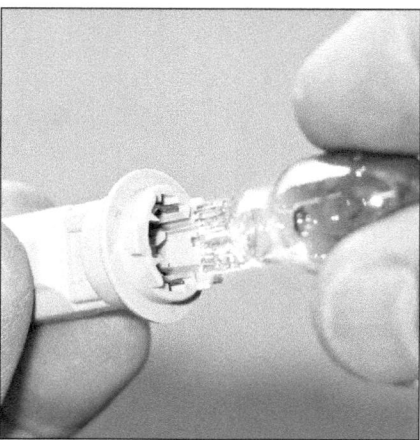

18.12 To remove the centre high-mounted brake light bulb from the bulb holder, pull it straight out of the holder. After installing the new bulb, wipe it off with a clean cloth

18.14 Open this small panel to access the rear brake, turn signal, brake and back-up light bulbs

Rear brake/tail, turn signal, brake and back-up light bulbs

Refer to illustrations 18.14, 18.15, 18.16 and 18.17

14   Open the rear hatch. Remove the rear brake/tail, turn signal, brake and back-up light access panel **(see illustration)**.
15   Locate the bulb that you want to replace **(see illustration)**.
16   Remove the bulb holder from the taillight housing **(see illustration)**.
17   Remove the bulb from its holder **(see illustration)**.
18   Installation is the reverse of removal.

License plate light bulbs

Refer to illustrations 18.19 and 18.20

19   Remove the license plate light housing screws **(see illustration)** and remove the license plate light housing.
20   Remove the bulb from the license plate light housing **(see illustration)**.

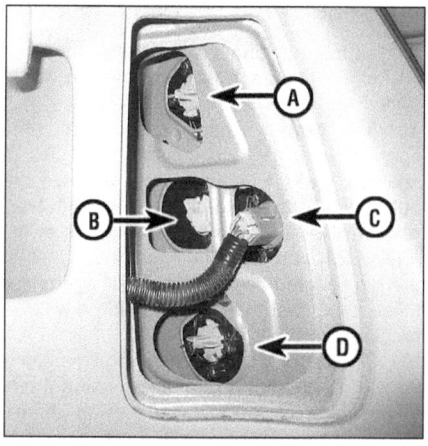

18.15 Typical taillight bulb locations:

A *Rear brake/taillight bulb*
B *Rear turn signal bulb*
C *Brake/taillight bulb*
D *Back-up light bulb*

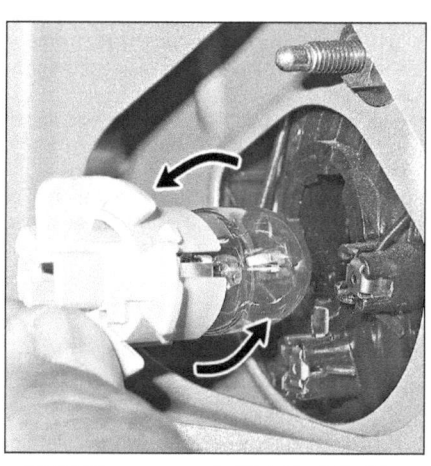

18.16 To remove a taillight bulb holder from the taillight housing, rotate it counterclockwise and pull it out of the taillight housing

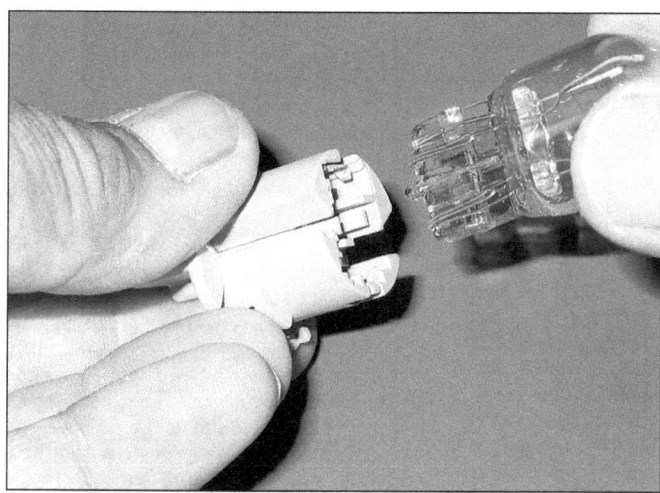

18.17 To remove a taillight bulb from its holder, pull it straight out of the holder. After installing the bulb, wipe it off

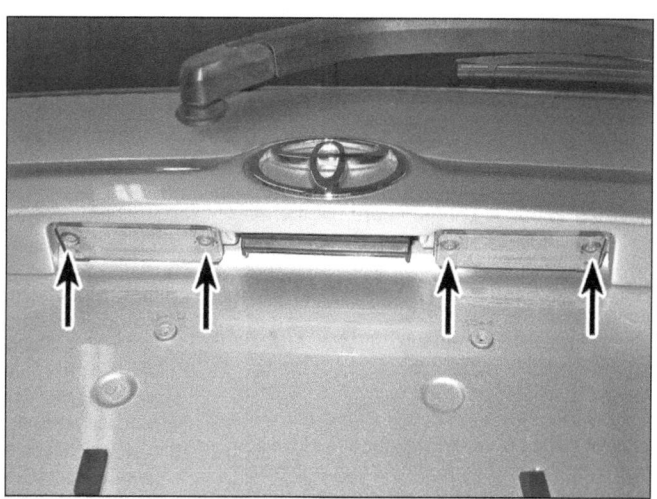

18.19 To remove either license plate light housing, remove the two screws from the lens

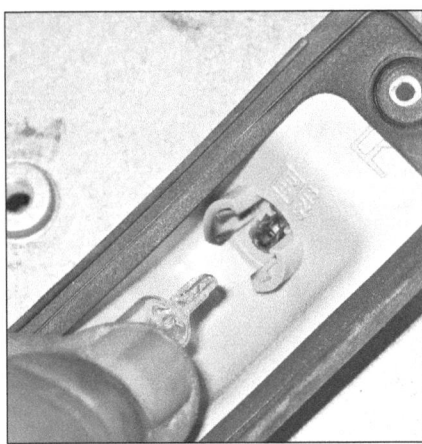

18.20 To remove a bulb from a license plate light housing, pull it straight out

21   Installation is the reverse of removal.

Interior light bulbs

Map reading light and dome light bulbs

Refer to illustrations 18.22 and 18.23

Note: *The photos accompanying this section depict the map reading light, but they apply to the dome light as well.*

22   Remove the lens from the map reading light housing **(see illustration)**.
23   Remove the bulb from the terminals **(see illustration)**.
24   Installation is the reverse of removal.

---

19   Electric side view mirrors - description

---

1   Most electric rear view mirrors use two motors to move the glass; one for up and down adjustments and one for left-right adjustments.
2   The control switch has a selector portion that sends voltage to the left or right side mirror. With the ignition ON but the engine OFF, roll down the windows and operate the mirror control switch through all functions (left-right and up-down) for both the left and right side mirrors.
3   Listen carefully for the sound of the electric motors running in the mirrors.
4   If the motors can be heard but the mirror glass doesn't move, there's a problem with the drive mechanism inside the mirror. Remove and disassemble the mirror to locate the problem.
5   If the mirrors do not operate and no sound comes from the mirrors, check the fuse (see Chapter 1).
6   If the fuse is OK, remove the mirror control switch from the dashboard. Have the switch continuity checked by a dealership service department or other qualified automobile repair facility.
7   Test the ground connections. Refer to

18.22 Using a small screwdriver, carefully pry off the lens from the map reading light housing (this procedure applies to the dome light as well)

the wiring diagrams at the end of this Chapter.
8   If the mirror still doesn't work, remove the mirror and check the wires at the mirror for voltage.
9   If there's not voltage in each switch position, check the circuit between the mirror and control switch for opens and shorts.
10   If there's voltage, remove the mirror and test it off the vehicle with jumper wires. Replace the mirror if it fails this test.

---

20   Cruise control system - description

---

1   These models have an electrically controlled throttle body - there is no accelerator cable. The accelerator pedal communicates with the throttle body through the Powertrain Control Module (PCM) (see Chapter 6). The PCM also controls the cruise control system, which is now an integral function of the electronic throttle control system. If the system malfunctions, take it to a dealer service department or other qualified repair shop for further diagnosis.

---

21   Power window system - description

---

1   The power window system operates electric motors, mounted in the doors, which lower and raise the windows. The system consists of the control switches, relays, the motors, regulators, glass mechanisms and associated wiring.
2   The power windows can be lowered and raised from the master control switch by the driver or by remote switches located at the individual windows. Each window has a separate motor that is reversible. The position of the control switch determines the polarity and therefore the direction of operation.
3   The circuit is protected by a fuse and a circuit breaker. Each motor is also equipped

18.23 To remove a light bulb from the reading light housing, grasp it firmly and pull it straight down from the terminal clips. If necessary, pry only on the metal ends of the bulb, not the glass

with an internal circuit breaker; this prevents one stuck window from disabling the whole system.
4   The power window system will only operate when the ignition switch is ON. In addition, many models have a window lockout switch at the master control switch that, when activated, disables the switches at the rear windows and, sometimes, the switch at the passenger's window also. Always check these items before troubleshooting a window problem.
5   These procedures are general in nature, so if you can't find the problem using them, take the vehicle to a dealer service department or other properly equipped repair facility.
6   If the power windows won't operate, always check the fuse and circuit breaker first.
7   If only the rear windows are inoperative, or if the windows only operate from the master control switch, check the rear window lockout switch for continuity in the unlocked position. Replace it if it doesn't have continuity.
8   Check the wiring between the switches and fuse panel for continuity. Repair the wiring, if necessary.
9   If only one window is inoperative from the master control switch, try the other control switch at the window.

Note: *This doesn't apply to the driver's door window.*

10   If the same window works from one switch, but not the other, check the switch for continuity. Have the switch checked at a dealer service department or other qualified automobile repair facility.
11   If the switch tests OK, check for a short or open in the circuit between the affected switch and the window motor.
12   If one window is inoperative from both switches, remove the trim panel from the affected door and check for voltage at the switch and at the motor while the switch is operated.

13   If voltage is reaching the motor, disconnect the glass from the regulator (see Chapter 11). Move the window up and down by hand while checking for binding and damage. Also check for binding and damage to the regulator. If the regulator is not damaged and the window moves up and down smoothly, replace the motor. If there's binding or damage, lubricate, repair or replace parts, as necessary.

14   If voltage isn't reaching the motor, check the wiring in the circuit for continuity between the switches and motors. You'll need to consult the wiring diagram for the vehicle. If the circuit is equipped with a relay, check that the relay is grounded properly and receiving voltage.

15   Test the windows after you are done to confirm proper repairs.

22   Power door lock system - description

1   A power door lock system operates the door lock actuators mounted in each door. The system consists of the switches, actuators, a control unit and associated wiring. Diagnosis can usually be limited to simple checks of the wiring connections and actuators for minor faults that can be easily repaired.

2   Power door lock systems are operated by bi-directional solenoids located in the doors. The lock switches have two operating positions: Lock and Unlock. When activated, the switch sends a ground signal to the door lock control unit to lock or unlock the doors. Depending on which way the switch is activated, the control unit reverses polarity to the solenoids, allowing the two sides of the circuit to be used alternately as the feed (positive) and ground side.

3   Some vehicles may have an anti-theft system incorporated into the power locks. If you are unable to locate the trouble using the following general Steps, consult a dealer service department or other qualified repair shop.

4   Always check the circuit protection first. Some vehicles use a combination of circuit breakers and fuses.

5   Operate the door lock switches in both directions (Lock and Unlock) with the engine off. Listen for the click of the solenoids operating.

6   Test the switches for continuity. Remove the switches and have them checked by a dealer service department or other qualified automobile repair facility.

7   Check the wiring between the switches, control unit and solenoids for continuity. Repair the wiring if there's no continuity.

8   Check for a bad ground at the switches or the control unit.

9   If all but one lock solenoid operate, remove the trim panel from the affected door (see Chapter 11) and check for voltage at the solenoid while the lock switch is operated. One of the wires should have voltage in the

Lock position; the other should have voltage in the Unlock position.

10   If the inoperative solenoid is receiving voltage, replace the solenoid.

11   If the inoperative solenoid isn't receiving voltage, check the relay for an open or short in the wire between the lock solenoid and the control unit.

Note: *It's common for wires to break in the section of harness that goes between the body and door because opening and closing the door fatigues and eventually breaks the wires.*

23   Daytime Running Lights (DRL) - general information

Some models are fitted with a Daytime Running Lights (DRL) system, which illuminates the headlights whenever the engine is running. The only exception is with the engine running and the parking brake engaged. Once the parking brake is released, the lights will remain on as long as the ignition switch is on, even if the parking brake is later applied.

The DRL system supplies reduced power to the headlights so they won't be too bright for daytime use, while prolonging headlight life.

24   Airbag system - general information

All models are equipped with a Supplemental Restraint System (SRS), more commonly known as the airbag system. The airbag system is designed to protect the driver and the front seat passenger from serious injury in the event of a head-on or frontal collision. It consists of the impact sensors, a driver's airbag module in the centre of the steering wheel, a passenger's airbag module in the glove box area of the instrument panel and a sensing/diagnostic module mounted in the centre of the floorpan, ahead of the centre console. Some models are also equipped with side-impact airbags, side-curtain airbags and a driver's knee airbag.

Airbag modules

Driver's airbag

The airbag inflator module contains a housing incorporating the cushion (airbag) and inflator unit, mounted in the centre of the steering wheel The inflator assembly is mounted on the back of the housing over a hole through which gas is expelled, inflating the bag almost instantaneously when an electrical signal is sent from the system. A spiral cable assembly on the steering column under the steering wheel carries this signal to the module. This spiral cable assembly can transmit an electrical signal regardless of steering wheel position. The igniter in the airbag con-

verts the electrical signal to heat and ignites the powder, which inflates the bag.

Driver's knee airbag

On some models there is a second driver's airbag located under the steering column, just ahead of the knee bolster. Its only purpose is to protect the driver's knees from serious damage in the event of a collision. If you're not sure whether you have a drive's knee airbag, refer to your owner's manual.

Passenger's airbag

The airbag is mounted inside the right end of the instrument panel, in the vicinity of the glove box compartment. It's similar in design to the driver's airbag, except that it's larger than the steering wheel unit. The passenger airbag is mounted between the instrument panel reinforcement bar and the underside of the instrument panel. The trim cover (on the side of the instrument panel that faces toward the passenger) is textured and coloured to match the instrument panel and has a moulded seam that splits open when the bag inflates.

Side impact airbags

Extra protection is provided by side-impact airbags on some models. These are smaller devices, which are located on the outer sides of the seat backs, and deploy in the event of a severe side-impact collision.

Side curtain airbags

In addition to the side-impact airbags, extra side-impact protection is also provided by side-curtain airbags on some models. These are long airbags that, in the event of a side impact, come out of the headliner at each side of the car and come down between the side windows and the seats. They are designed to protect the heads of both front seat and rear seat passengers.

Sensing and diagnostic module

The sensing and diagnostic module supplies the current to the airbag system in the event of the collision, even if battery power is cut off. It checks this system every time the vehicle is started, causing the "AIR BAG" light to go on then off, if the system is operating properly. If there is a fault in the system, the light will go on and stay on, flash, or the dash will make a beeping sound. If this happens, the vehicle should be taken to your dealer immediately for service.

Disarming the system and other precautions

Warning: *Failure to follow these precautions could result in accidental deployment of the airbag and personal injury.*

Whenever working in the vicinity of the steering wheel, steering column or any of the other SRS system components, the system must be disarmed.

To disarm the airbag system:

a   *Point the wheels straight ahead and turn the key to the Lock position.*
b   *Disconnect the negative (-) battery terminal (see Chapter 5).*
c   *Wait at least two minutes for the back-up power supply to be depleted.*

Whenever handling an airbag module:

Always keep the airbag opening (the trim side) pointed away from your body. Never place the airbag module on a bench of other surface with the airbag opening facing the surface. Always place the airbag module in a safe location with the airbag opening facing up.

Never measure the resistance of any SRS component. An ohmmeter has a built-in battery supply that could accidentally deploy the airbag.

Never use electrical welding equipment on a vehicle equipped with an airbag without first disconnecting the electrical connector for each airbag.

Never dispose of a live airbag module. Return it to a dealer service department or other qualified repair shop for safe deployment and disposal.

Component removal and installation

Driver's side airbag module and spiral cable

Refer to Chapter 10, Steering wheel - removal and installation, for the driver's side airbag module and spiral cable removal and installation procedures.

Driver's knee airbag

Refer to illustrations 24.3 and 24.5

1   Disarm the airbag system (see above).
2   Remove the lower dash panel (see Chapter 11).
3   Disconnect the big yellow electrical connector for the driver's knee airbag **(see illustration)**.
4   Unclip the diagnosis connector from the knee bolster/airbag bracket and position clear of the work area.
5   Remove the four driver's knee airbag mounting bolts and remove the airbag module **(see illustration)**.
6   Installation is the reverse of removal.

Other airbag modules

We don't recommend removing any of the other airbag modules. These jobs are best left to a professional. Should you ever have to remove the instrument panel, you'll have to disconnect the electrical connector for the passenger airbag module and remove one nut and bolt that secures the passenger airbag module to the instrument panel reinforcement bracket, but you don't have to remove the passenger airbag module to remove the instrument panel.

---

25   Wiring diagrams - general information

Since it isn't possible to include all wiring diagrams for every year covered by this manual, the following diagrams are those that are typical and most commonly needed.

Prior to troubleshooting any circuits, check the fuse and circuit breakers (if equipped) to make sure they're in good condition. Make sure the battery is properly charged and check the cable connections (see Chapter 1).

When checking a circuit, make sure that all connectors are clean, with no broken or loose terminals. When unplugging a connector, do not pull on the wires - pull only on the connector housings.

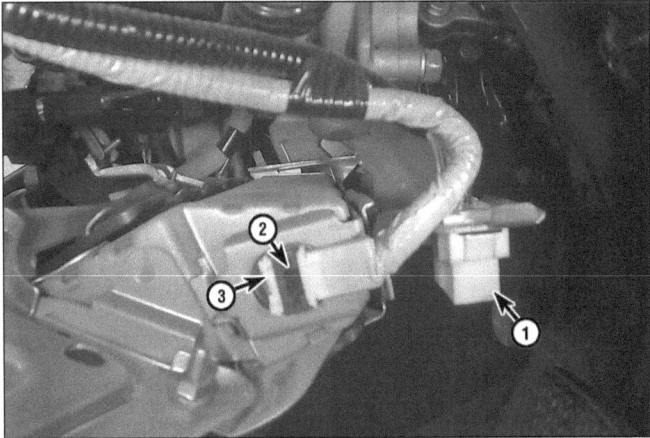

24.3 Airbag connector location

1   *Diagnosis connector Note, the connector is clipped into the airbag bracket*
2   *Lift the tab out to unlock the airbag connector*
3   *Pull the connector from the airbag*

24.5 Knee airbag components

1   *Knee airbag*
2   *Retaining bolts*
3   *Diagnosis connector location.*
4   *Airbag connector location*

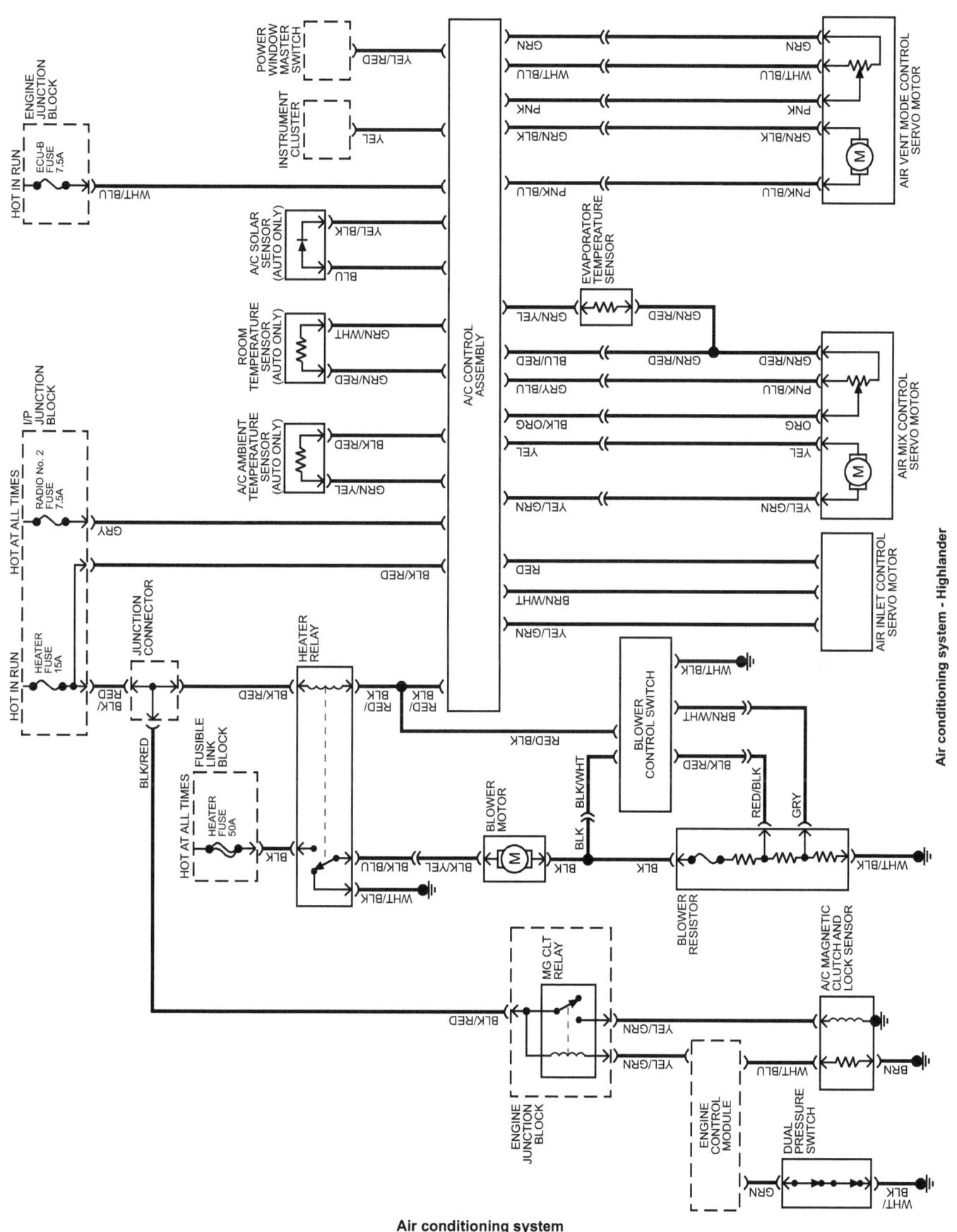

Air conditioning system

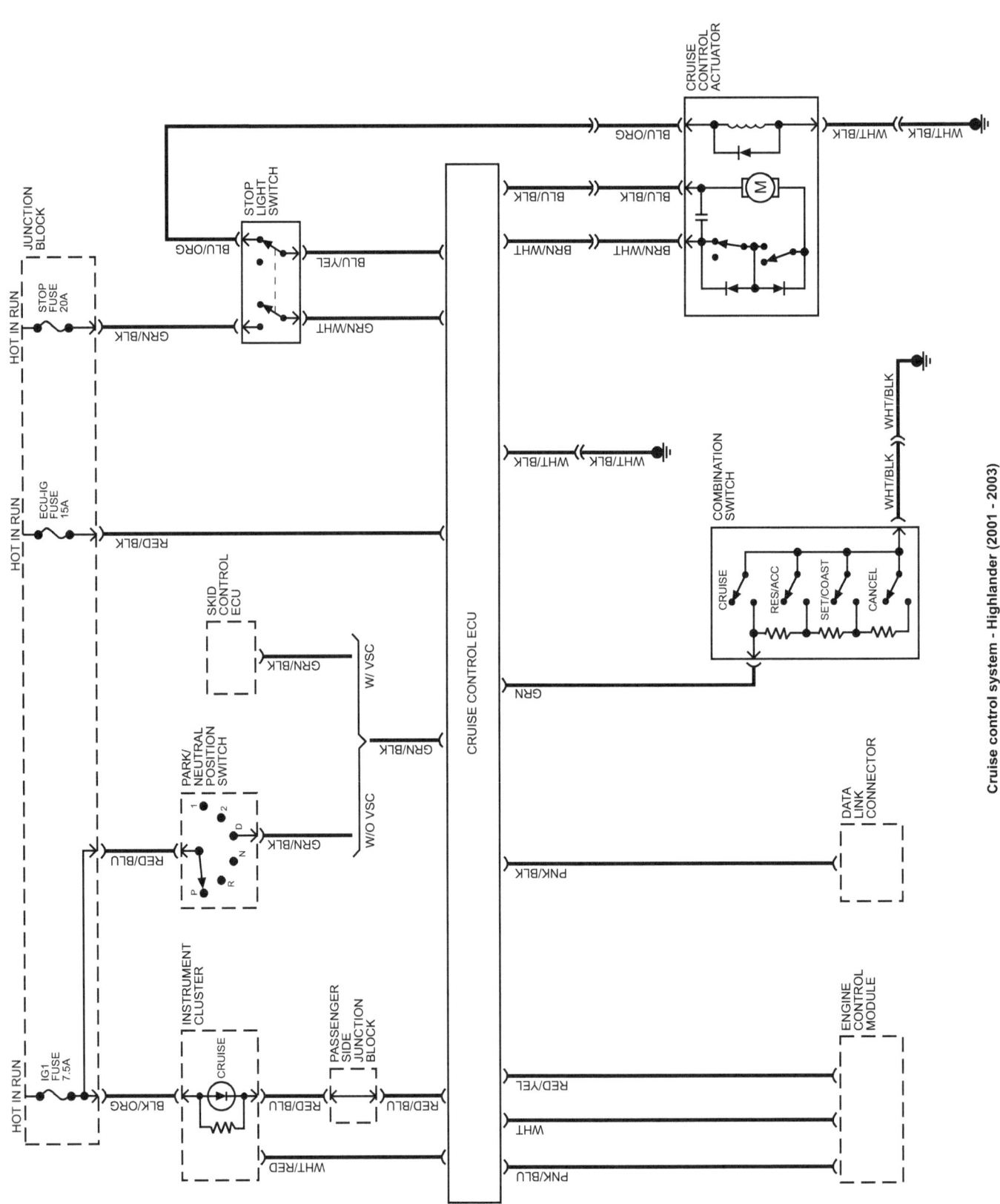

Cruise control system

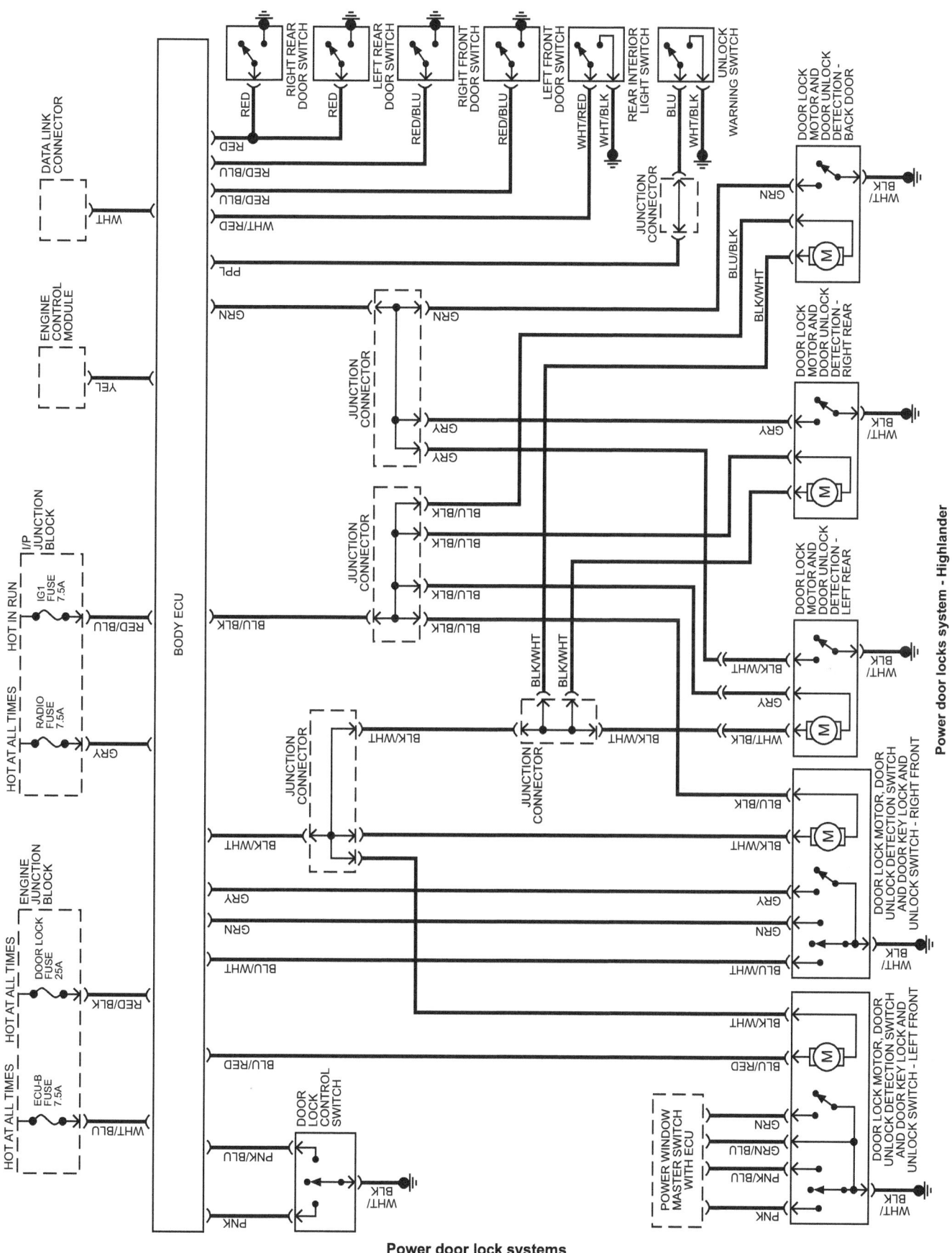

Power door lock systems

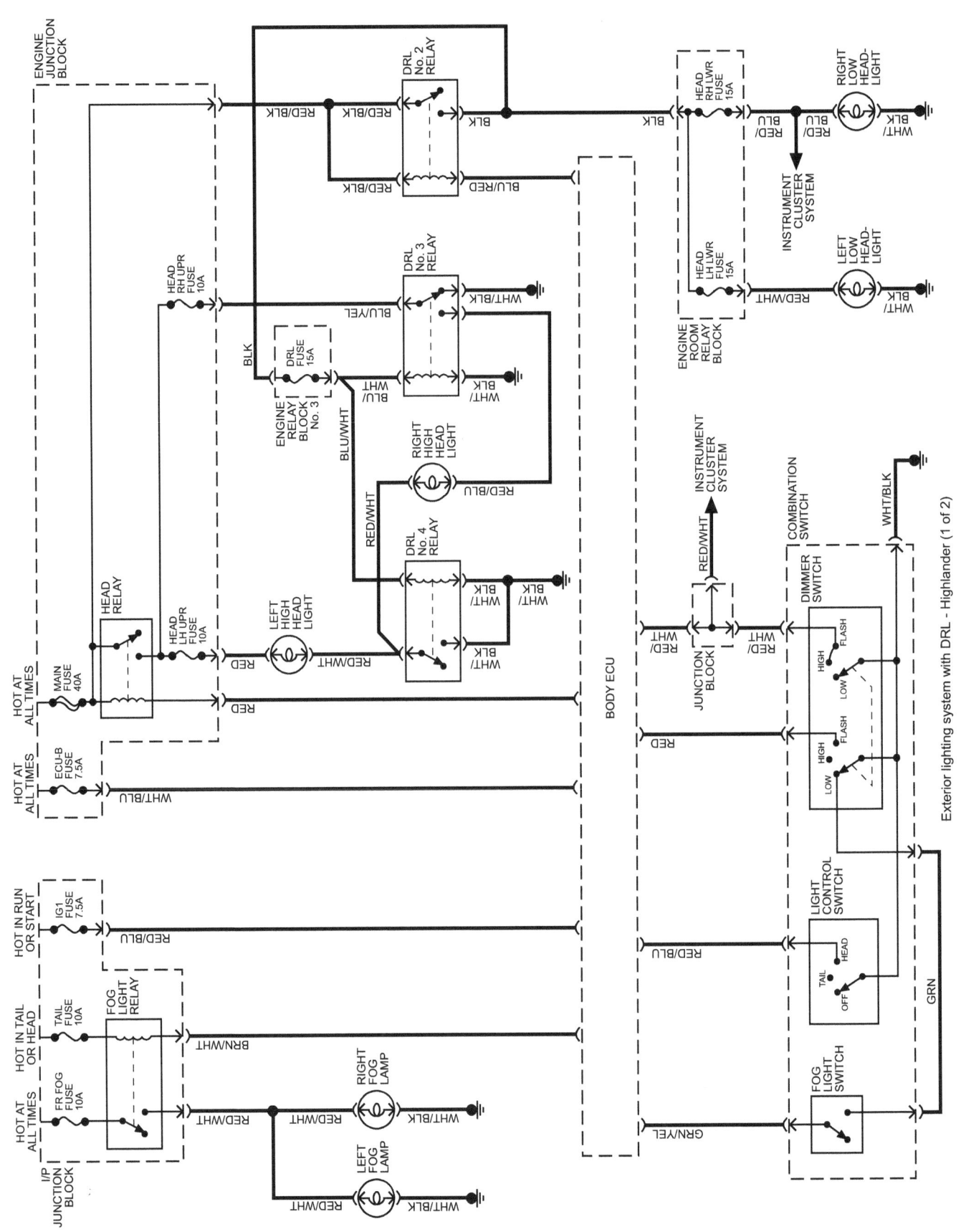

Exterior lighting system with DRL - 1 of 2

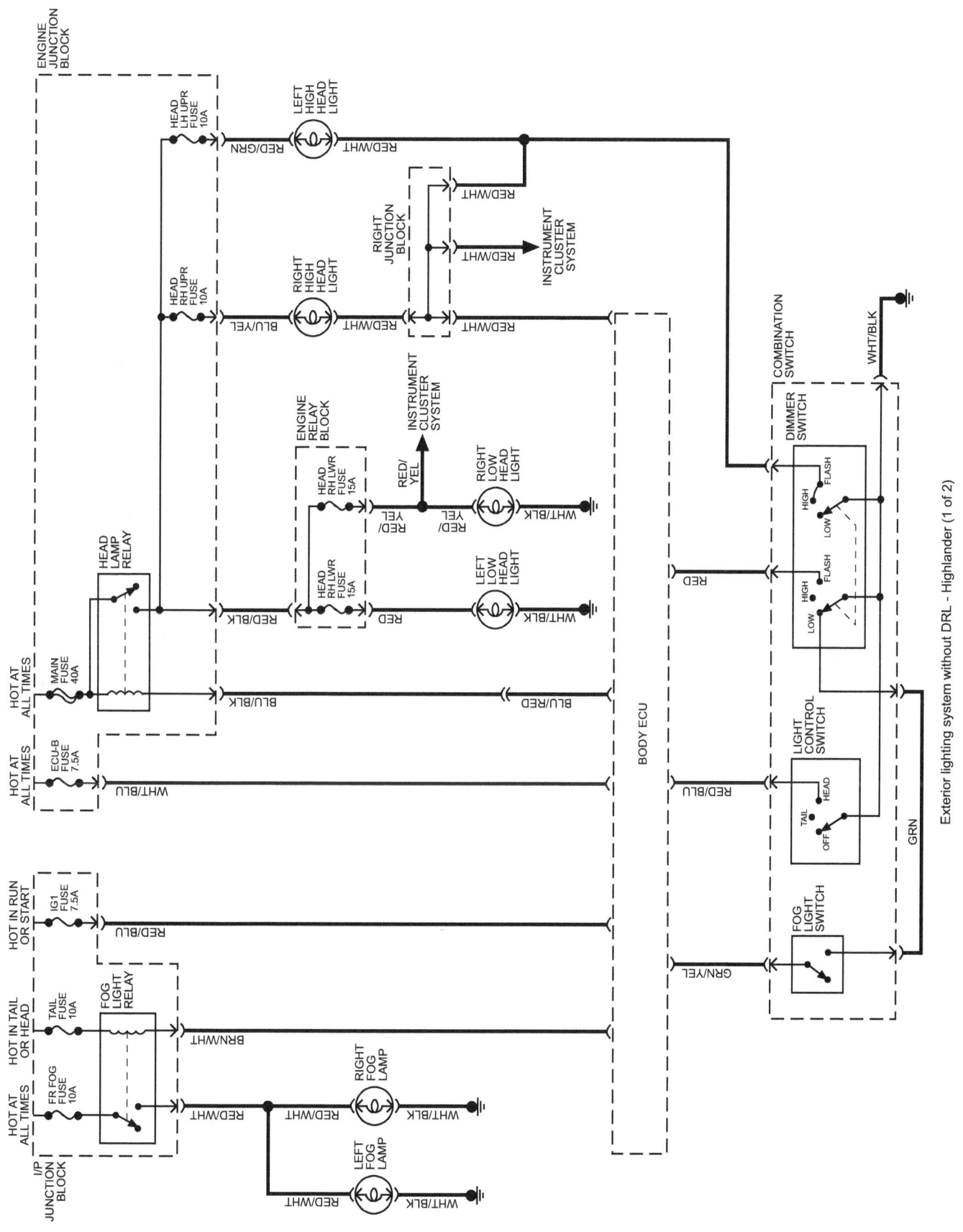

Exterior lighting system without DRL - 1 of 2

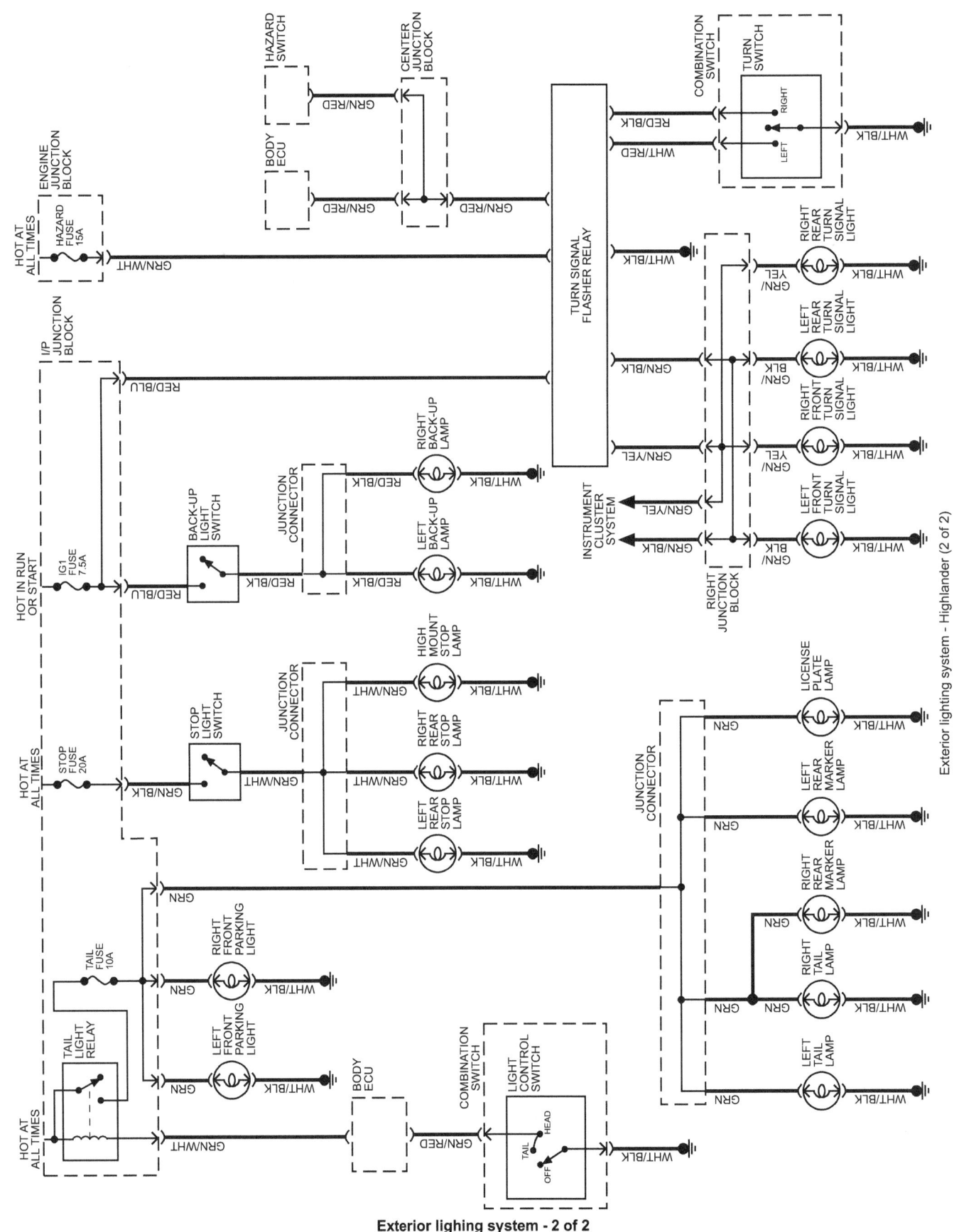

Exterior lighting system - Highlander (2 of 2)

Exterior lighing system - 2 of 2

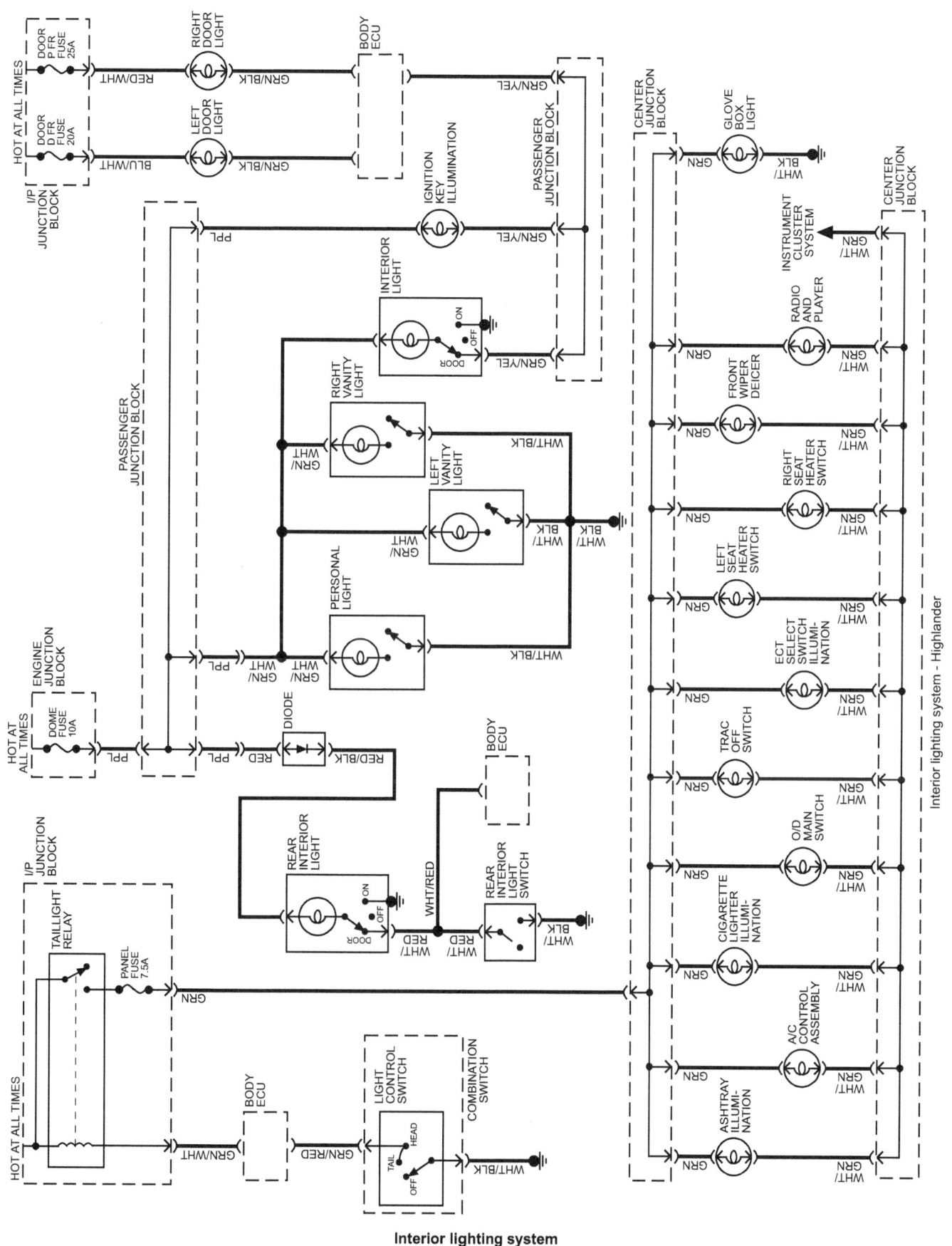

Interior lighting system

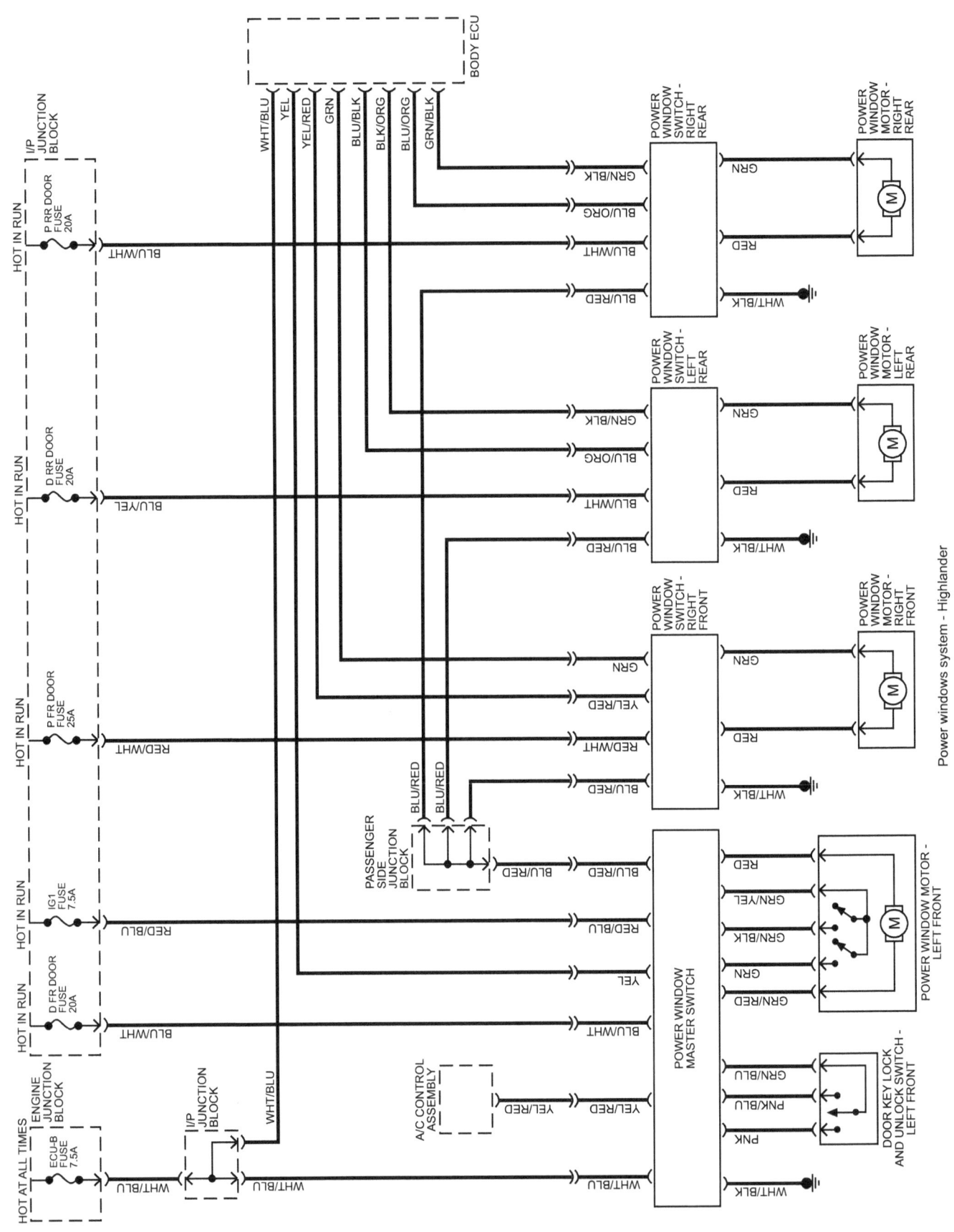

Power window systems

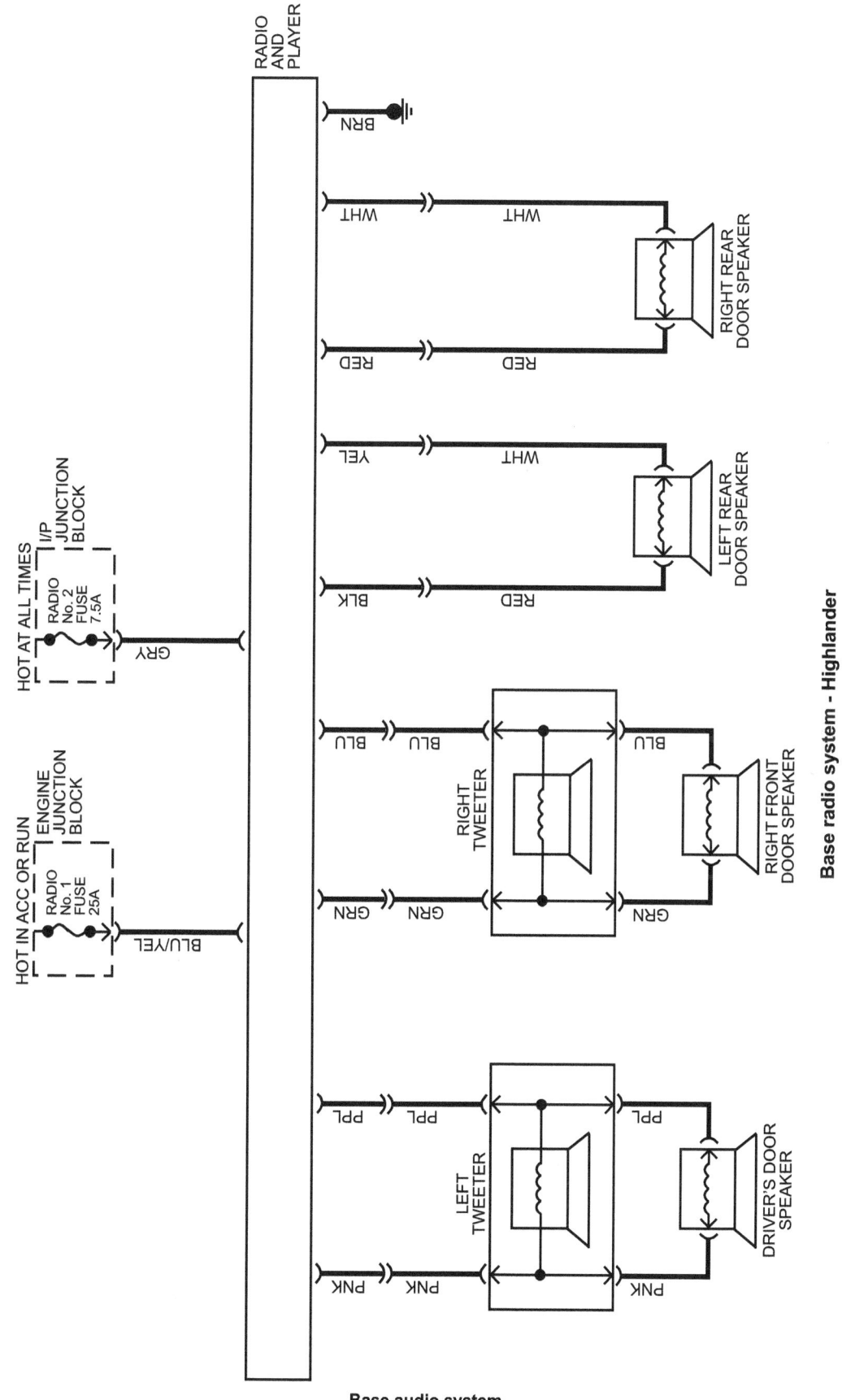

Base radio system - Highlander

Base audio system

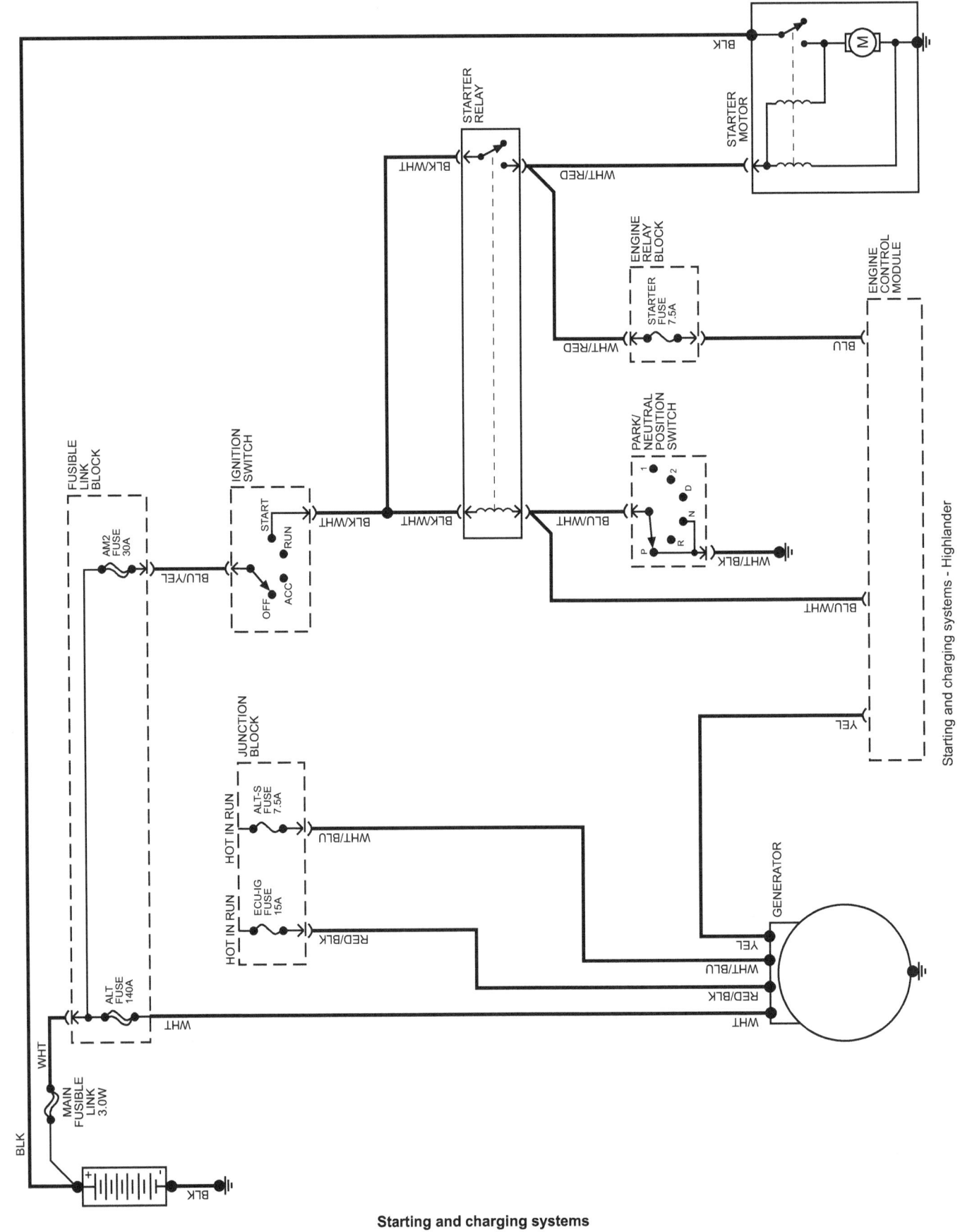

Starting and charging systems

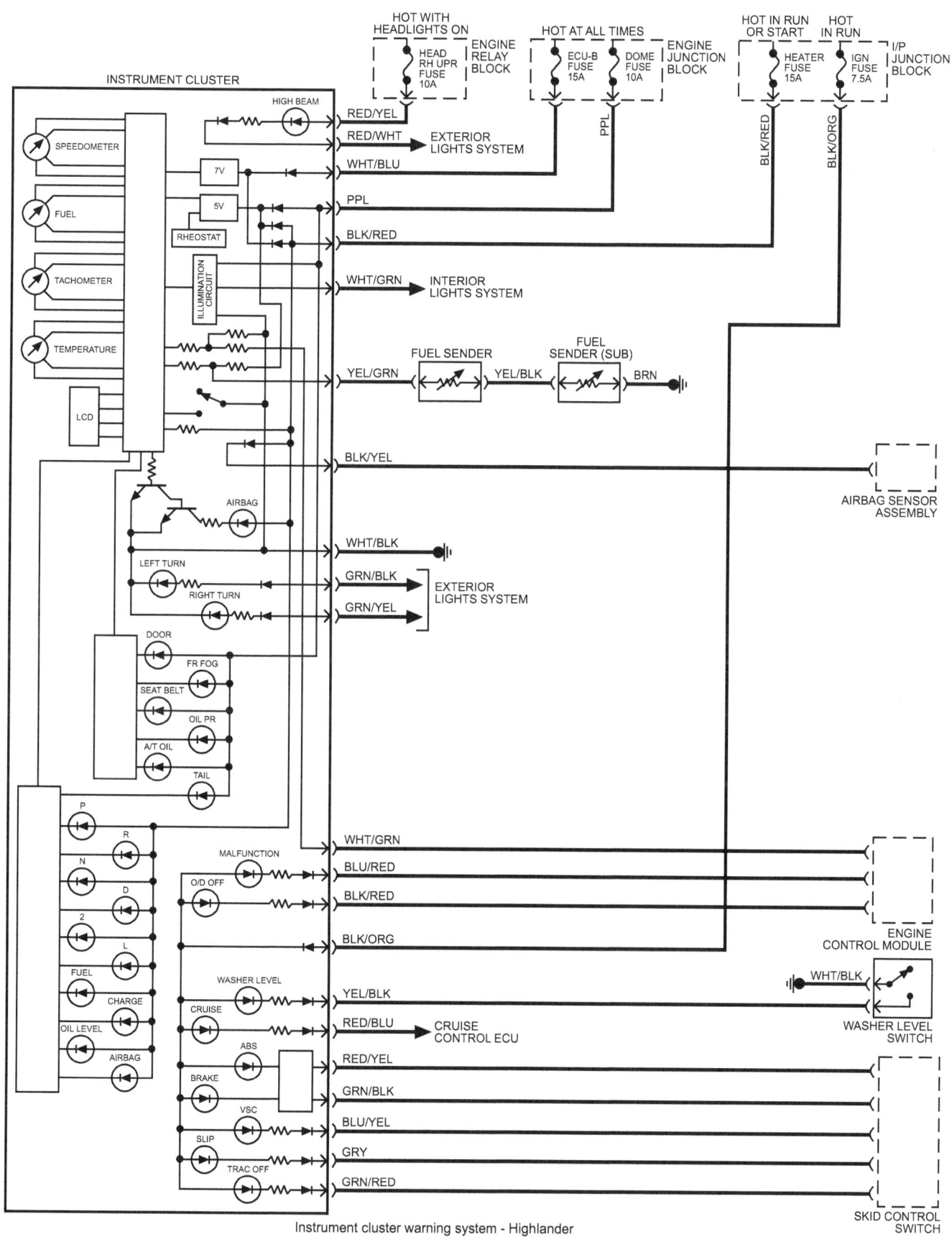

Instrument cluster warning system - Highlander

Instrument cluster warning systems

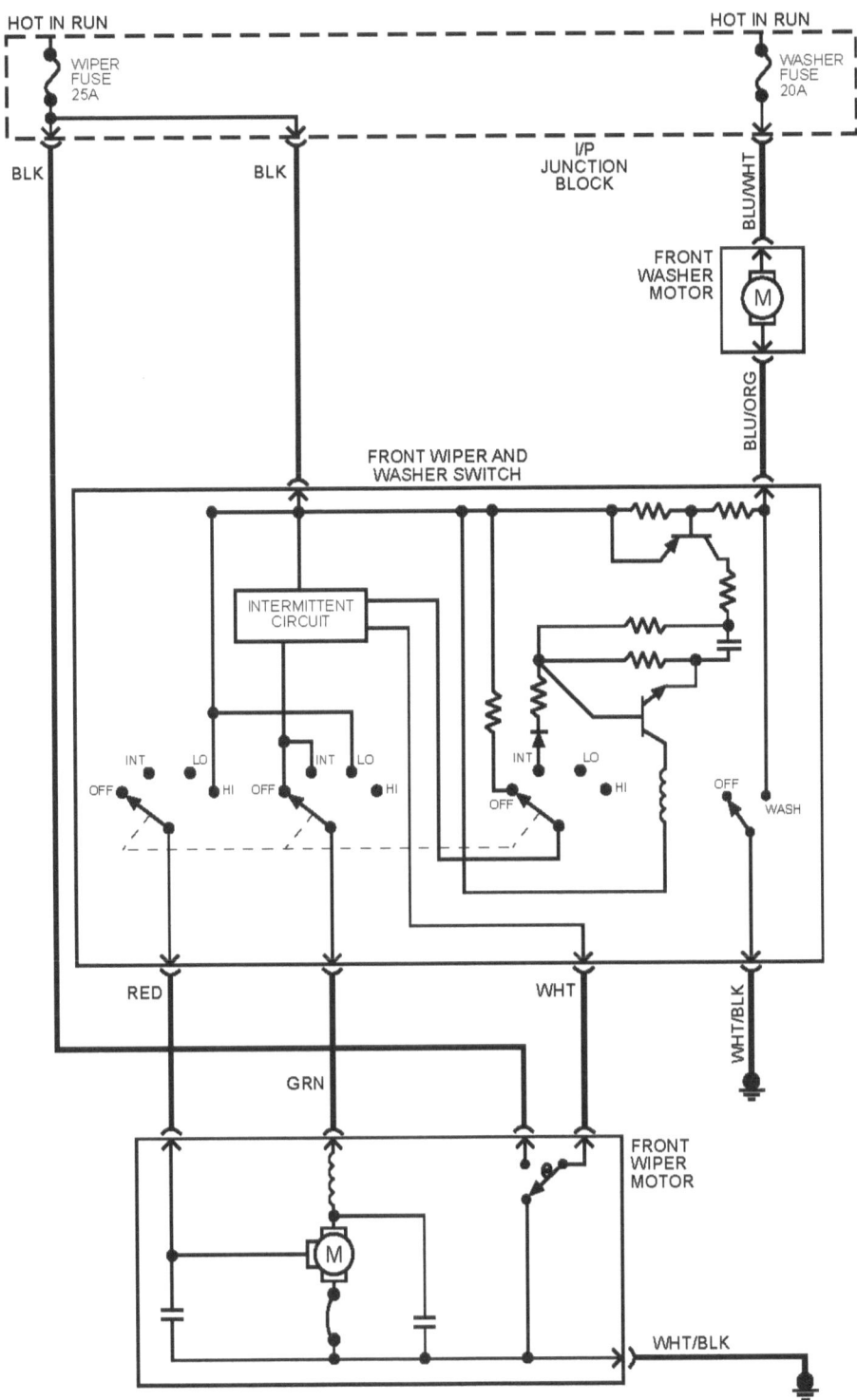

Front wiper and washer system

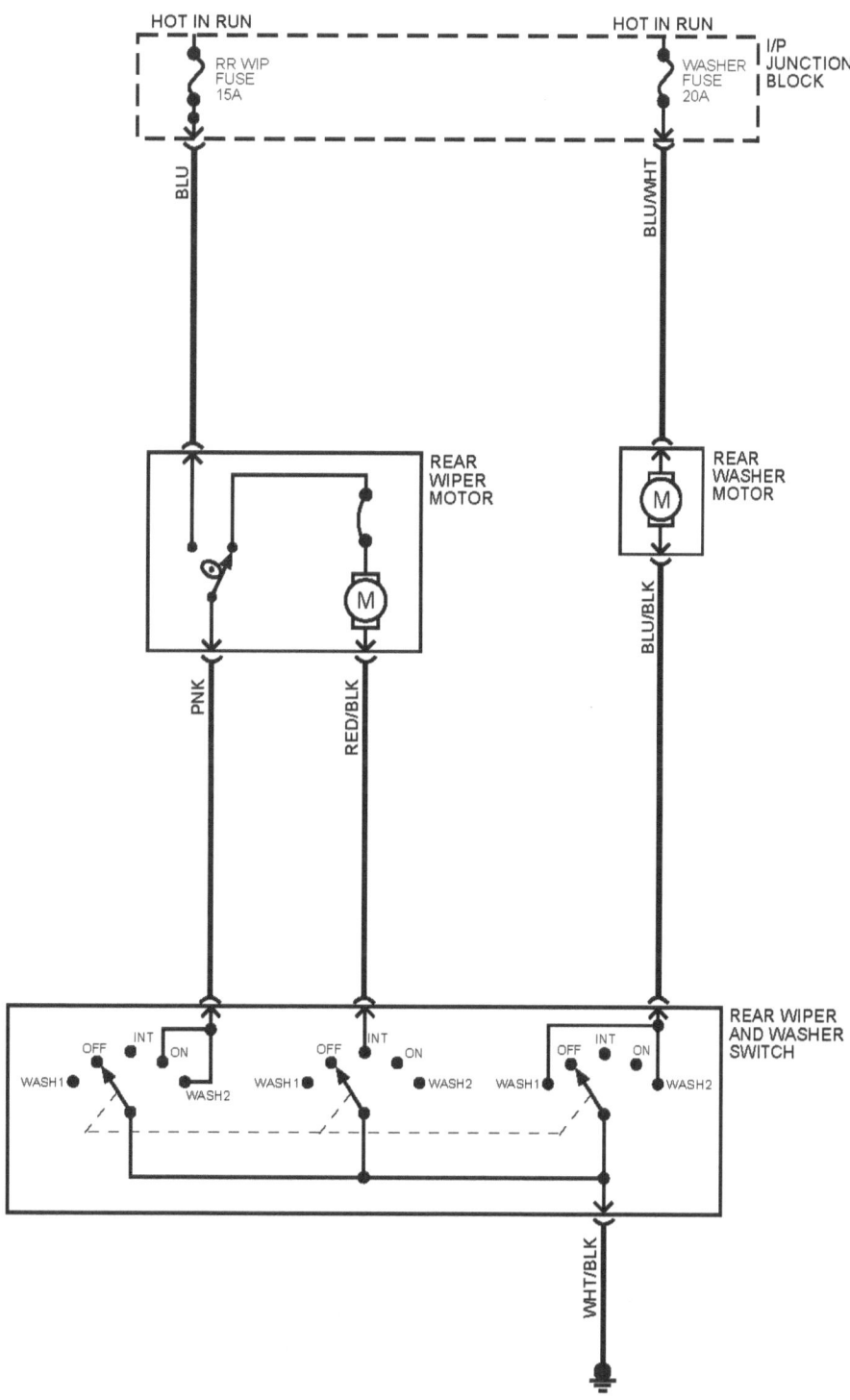

Rear wiper and washer system

Index

A

SERVICE HISTORY

Date Odometer \ Part No.	ENGINE OIL	ENGINE OIL FILTER	FAN BELTS	AIR FILTER	FUEL FILTER	RADIATOR HOSE	COOLANT	FRONT BRAKES	REAR BRAKES	BRAKE FLUID	WHEEL ALIGNMENT	WHEEL BALANCE										

SERVICE HISTORY

Date Odometer \ Part No.	ENGINE OIL	ENGINE OIL FILTER	FAN BELTS	AIR FILTER	FUEL FILTER	RADIATOR HOSE	COOLANT	FRONT BRAKES	REAR BRAKES	BRAKE FLUID	WHEEL ALIGNMENT	WHEEL BALANCE											

FSC

www.fsc.org

MIX

Papier | Fördert
gute Waldnutzung

FSC® C083411

Zeitfracht Medien GmbH
Ferdinand-Jühlke-Straße 7
99095 Erfurt, Deutschland
produktsicherheit@kolibri360.de